QUANTITATIVE BUSINESS ANALYSIS

Text and Cases

THE IRWIN/MCGRAW-HILL SERIES
Operations And Decision Sciences

QUANTITATIVE BUSINESS ANALYSIS

Text and Cases

Samuel E. Bodily
Darden Graduate School of Business Administration
University of Virginia

Robert L. Carraway
Darden Graduate School of Business Administration
University of Virginia

Sherwood C. Frey, Jr.
Darden Graduate School of Business Administration
University of Virginia

Phillip E. Pfeifer
Darden Graduate School of Business Administration
University of Virginia

Boston, Massachusetts   Burr Ridge, Illinois   Dubuque, Iowa
Madison, Wisconsin   New York, New York   San Francisco, California   St. Louis, Missouri

Irwin/McGraw-Hill

*A Division of The **McGraw·Hill** Companies*

QUANTITATIVE BUSINESS ANALYSIS: TEXT AND CASES

 This book is printed on recycled paper containing 10% postconsumer waste.

1 2 3 4 5 6 7 8 9 0 DOC/DOC 9 0 9 8 7

ISBN 0-256-14713-2

Vice president and Editorial director: *Michael W. Junior*
Publisher: *Jeffrey J. Shelstad*
Executive editor: *Richard T. Hercher, Jr.*
Developmental editor: *Wanda J. Zeman*
Senior marketing manager: *Colleen J. Suljic*
Senior project manager: *Jean Lou Hess*
Production supervisor: *Heather D. Burbridge*
Designer: *Larry J. Cope*
Compositor: *Shepard Poorman Communications*
Typeface: *10/12 Times Roman*
Printer: *R. R. Donnelley & Sons Company*

Library of Congress Cataloging-in-Publication Data

Quantitative business analysis : text and cases / Samuel E. Bodily . . . [et al.].
    p.   cm.
  Includes index.
  ISBN 0-256-14713-2
  1. Industrial management—Mathematical models. 2. Decision-making—Mathematical models.   I. Bodily, Samuel E.
  HD30.25.Q348   1998
  658.4′032—dc21   98-24214

http://www.mhhe.com

To our families, for the patience and support they offer our professional lives, for the pleasure and purpose they add to the rest of our lives.

This book contains the text and cases forming the core of what has been and continues to be a highly successful MBA-level course in quantitative business analysis. The course represents an alternative to the traditional technique-driven, compartmentalized, quantitative methods course. Instead, it is a course that is

- decision and action oriented, not technique and numbers driven;
- integrated in both form and pedagogy within a business curriculum, not compartmentalized;
- managerially exciting, not methodologically dull.

It contains all of the usual topics of existing quantitative courses. Students develop the skill and the perspective to use quantitative techniques artfully to gain insight into the resolution of practical business problems. They not only master the specific techniques, but also develop the ability to garner information from commonly available sources and to recognize when a particular technique is appropriate, when additional analysis is called for, and when to end the analysis and make the decision. The most widely applicable methodologies of decision and risk analysis, probability and statistics, competitive analysis, and management science are thus integrated with personal judgment and intuition in a way that is meaningful to MBA and executive learners alike.

Two key components of the course are: (1) field-based (i.e., they actually happened) cases drawn from all functional areas of business, and (2) clearly-written, pragmatically-focused text explaining technical concepts and the strategic frameworks of quantitative analysis. The cases feature realistic, un-structured business settings wherein the methodologies of the course can be usefully and creatively applied to the decisions of the practicing manager. They thus provide vivid answers to the questions, Why is this stuff useful?

The text, which has its origin in "technical notes" used for years in the course, gives the background theory and technical details necessary to perform solid, insightful quantitative analysis of business issues. It thus provides answers to the questions, What do I do now?, which are triggered by the complex issues raised in the cases.

The Cases

Just what is a case? The answer must recognize that cases play a variety of roles in a course. They may be focused on understanding core tools and concepts, on applying methodology appropriately, on defining the limits of good practice, or on inventing new methods and adapting existing ones for the problem at hand.

Some cases in this book are highly structured, focused on a single issue, with needed data laid out. These cases can be used to develop methodology; the cases are not intended merely to present institutional information and provide practical enrichment. Such a case is more than a problem or exercise; it requires some initial assumptions, which may lead to alternative answers, and the analysis must be explained by the student in the case context.

Some of the cases are appraisal cases, where the analysis is partly or wholly done. The student will evaluate the work, applying what has been learned about good practice, and perhaps push the analysis further.

Finally, and more commonly in this book, many cases are unstructured, with multiple issues and data challenges (missing or incomplete data, choices among data, or data preparation needed). In these cases, the student must diagnose the situation, perform the analysis, and explain the use of the analysis and its limits. The intent here is not to produce apprehension, but to show that skills can be confidently applied to realistic situations. Some of the student's fear that may arise when using cases comes from concern that there is a single right answer and that the student will be unable to find it. If students can see that many reasonable assumptions may be made (some more reasonable than others, to be sure) and that they can do a variety of analyses (some more insightful than others), they will find their own way and complement their efforts with ideas that emerge in class.

A common theme cutting across all cases, and indeed across the entire course, is the need to make real *decisions*. The cases thus avoid being academic exercises, but assume the vitality of business itself. Thus, *decision analysis* becomes an accurate descriptor of all the cases in this book and is a critical framework from which this new type of quantitative methods course hangs.

What makes a strong case? A leading characteristic is the aforementioned *decision orientation*. *Relevance* is key; students recognize that the resolution of the situation matters to them. A strong case demonstrates *a need to know* something not currently known. It involves the *practice of skills*, including new and recently acquired skills. And it requires some *internaliza-*

tion of concepts and the *articulation* of the reasoning process. Students will see that they are involved in situations that can be key to their careers.

In addition to these characteristics, these cases provide integration with other courses. Issues come up from other disciplines that provide bridges to other courses. If these issues are not immediately put aside in class and built upon, the course is not pigeon holed: "That's *quant*, not management, and therefore not for me." These cases provide many opportunities for joint class sessions, where the regular instructor can be joined by a professor of accounting, ethics, economics, finance, marketing, operations, or human resources to bring together two streams of concepts and to solidify the role of quantitative analysis in each of the business functions.

The Text

The course's dedication to student-centered learning places both responsibility and ownership of the learning process squarely on the shoulders of the student. The cases force the student to confront tricky issues and complex situations. The text provides a readily-available source of guidance on how to structure and resolve the issues and situations. The general flow of learning embraced by the course and supported by this book is then: analyze a case and draw on the text as the need arises. The cases challenge; the text prescribes how to address those challenges.

The text is organized as follows: Chapter 1 is an overview of the process of quantitative business analysis, using a simple but realistic example. The four major components of good analysis are introduced: *alternatives, assumptions, assessment,* and *performance.* Each of these components is the topic of one of the following four chapters, which together with Chapter 1 comprise Part 1, the core of the text.

The remaining chapters build on the four basic components of analysis, each representing a more advanced treatment of one (or more) of the components. Chapter 6 addresses the issue of how to restructure *assumptions* in a way that helps mitigate risk. Chapters 7–10 address complications arising from how to evaluate *performance.* Chapters 11–14 address issues of how to calibrate *assessments* of uncertainty in key assumptions. Chapters 15–17 address complications associated with having a large number of *alternatives* to consider (Chapter 15 also addresses complications associated with how performance is assessed, when assumptions are difficult to structure).

Concluding remarks

The cases are organized alphabetically, not according to particular methodological approach. This organization allows flexibility in the use of the cases and preserves student responsibility to determine what should be done with each case. Of course, the cases are not to be taught in alphabetical order. The *Instructor's Manual* describes the typical use of each case, refers to the appropriate text for each case, and provides sample course outlines. (Many of the cases have also been used in executive education in short, non-degree programs. They would fit nicely in courses more narrowly focused in decision analysis, management science, or forecasting and regression. For short courses, any subset of these cases can be selected for custom publishing by Irwin/McGraw-Hill.)

The course based on this book assumes virtually no prerequisites. Although calculus is not needed, some algebra is assumed, but rarely getting as far, for example, as solving two equations in two unknowns. Although no prior probability or statistics is presumed, some familiarity can help the student. The principal requirements are clear thinking, the ability to conceptualize, and the ability to cut to the core of an issue.

Even though this book of texts and cases is software neutral, the electronic spreadsheet is assumed to be a fundamental tool available to the student. The spreadsheet is a very helpful way for instructors to provide the right amount of help to students. Spreadsheets containing data from case exhibits and, sometimes, the setup for analysis are available with the *Instructor's Manual.* They may also be downloaded from the QBA home page accessible through the Darden School's home page (http://www.darden.virginia.edu/) on the Internet. It will be necessary to use @Risk or Crystal Ball, and the Solver within Excel or What'sBest! to do some of the cases. Other software tools, such as TreePlan Precision Tree, or DPL, may be useful to students in the course but are not necessary.

A complete instructor's manual, with sample course outlines and an extensive teaching note for each case, is available from Irwin/McGraw-Hill. To the instructor's advantage the authors have put as much effort and time into teaching notes as the cases. Each note is the product of many teaching meetings and discussions of pedagogy.

The production of this book reaffirms our commitment to what we have been doing in our quantitative analysis course for many years. We are glad to see that others in our discipline are also interested in this approach, as evidenced by many sessions on the topic at the meetings of such professional societies as the Institute for Operations Research and Management Sciences, and the Decision Sciences Institute. We welcome the interest and hope that our experience may be found useful elsewhere.

Please provide feedback (especially about successes and failures with these cases), new case ideas, and innovative ways of teaching. Write to any of the authors at Darden Graduate Business School, University of Virginia, Box 6550, Charlottesville, VA 22906-6550, or send e-mail.

Samuel E. Bodily (bodilys@virginia.edu)
Robert L. Carraway (carrawayr@virginia.edu)
Sherwood C. Frey, Jr. (scf@virginia.edu)
Phillip E. Pfeifer (pep8s@virginia.edu)

ACKNOWLEDGMENTS

We thank the students at the Darden School for their comments and contributions during the development and refinement of these cases. We gratefully acknowledge the resources of the Darden School for case writing support in the form of research assistants, travel expenses, and summer salaries. Debbie A. Quarles provided able assistance in keeping track of various versions of the manuscript and proof pages. Many individuals contributed to specific cases including the following:

Edward R. Case	*T. Rowe Price*
Dana Clyman	*Athens Glass Works, Harimann International*
John L. Colley, Jr.	*Oakland A's (A)*
Glenn A. Ferguson	*Edgcomb Metals (A)*
James V. Gelly	*Lesser Antilles Lines*
Lonnie Gorban	*Lightweight Aluminum Company*
C. William Hosler	*Foulke Consumer Products, Inc.; Sleepmore Mattress Manufacturing: Plant Consolidation*
James C. McLean	*American Lawbook Corporation*
Donna M. Packard	*Jade Shampoo (A) and (B)*
Michel Schlosser	*Dhahran Roads (A) and (B)*
Douglas L. Schwartz	*Roadway Construction Company*
Steven R. Scorgie	*The Waldorf Property*
George R. Stearns	*Piedmont Airlines (A)*
Ann C. Stephans	*Oakland A's (A)*
William T. Stewart	*Edgcomb Metals (A)*
Hasmeeth S. Uppal	*Harimann International*
Larry Weatherford	*CyberLab (A), (B), and Supplement; Shumway, Horch, and Sager (A); Sprigg Lane (A), Wachovia Bank and Trust Company N.A. (B): Supplement*

We acknowledge Harvard Business School Publishing for their permission to use the following cases: C. K. Coolidge, Inc. (A), Freemark Abbey Winery, Maxco, Inc., and the Gambit Company.

We thank the many companies and individuals who willingly cooperated with the field research needed for the cases. We are pleased to note that there are many managers who recognize the educational value of field-based course materials and, as a result, who generously contributed their time and experience. Some of the companies are named in the cases; others for a variety of reasons chose to have their material disguised. Although the cases in this book are written as fact, almost all of them have some facts disguised. In some, individual names have been changed; in others, some of the numbers are changed. Some are written from general experience, without a specific sponsoring company. We are pleased if the cases appear to be totally realistic, but the reader should be aware that names, numbers and situations are not all real.

We benefited (as will the users) from the efforts of Darden editors Bette Collins, Stephen Smith, and Elaine Moran.

We appreciate very much the comments and evaluations of Sergios Koreisha, University of Oregon; Frederick Davidson, Mary Washington College; Terry P. Harrison, Penn State University; Peter M. Ellis, Utah State University; and James G. Morris, University of Wisconsin.

Finally, we thank the Irwin/McGraw-Hill editors Dick Hercher, for approving this project, and Wanda Zeman, for shepherding it along.

C O N T E N T S

Cases

1   PROACTIVE DECISION MAKING

A couple of weeks ago a real estate broker with whom you had previously worked approached you, inquiring of your interest in a 1,100-acre tract of gently rolling woodlands on the perimeter of the Washington, D.C., metropolitan area. The site was ideal for the development of a mid- to upscale residential community, and the timing of the query was ideal. Your firm, which specializes in residential land development, was just completing a moderately sized project and was seeking a new venture to take its place, particularly a project that would enhance the firm's reputation.

Preliminary investigations of Potomac Manors, as the site had become known within the firm, were encouraging. The site was zoned R3 for low-density residential housing. The zoning stipulated a minimum lot size of three acres and spelled out, among other things, specific requirements for lot dimensions, roads, septic systems, and public spaces. Your design team had arrived at a preliminary plan that carved out 300 three-acre lots, each with at least one very attractive marketing feature. The 200 acres that were not being used for lots were devoted to roads and public space. It was estimated that the lots would sell for an average price of $150,000. It was also estimated that the development and selling costs would be $8,000 per acre and miscellaneous expenses, such as permits and legal fees, would total $400,000.

The property was being offered at $23,000 per acre. The broker had allowed you two weeks to explore the opportunity and was expecting a response within the next few days. Is Potomac Manors a profitable project? Should you put forward the required $250,000 in earnest money to secure the property or let it go back on the open market?

The Potomac Manors decision is stereotypical of the decisions managers must make. There are alternatives (to buy the property or not); there is a performance measure (profits); and there are assumptions (the linkages among the selling price, the costs, and profits; the estimation of the average selling price and the costs). In addition, the decision must be made in a timely fashion and cannot be procrastinated, for as the maxim says, "Not to decide is to decide." This chapter will explore the various aspects of situations that make proactive decision making challenging and that make analysis valuable.

Routine Decisions

Many decisions in our lives are routine—which route to take from home to the office, where to invest excess money in the short term, what foods to buy at the supermarket. In each of these instances, we may quickly consider several alternatives, evaluate a measure of performance for each alternative, and make a choice. All of this is done in our head in a split second without an explicit consideration of our assumptions. Even more simply, we may apply a well-established rule of thumb or just do what we have always done, without even thinking about alternatives. Generally we are comfortable with such simplified decision processes because the consequences of the decisions are often not very significant and because over time we have implicitly considered (or experienced) the linkages between the alternatives and the performance measure and we do not feel the need to explicitly acknowledge them.

Sometimes, however, even routine decisions need more careful consideration. Changes in the situation can invalidate the tried-and-true decision rules. A new stoplight may be installed or a construction project begun on the route from home to office; the bank may impose minimum balance requirements for checking accounts; the supermarket may buy its fresh produce from a different supplier. These changes in the environment disrupt the assumptions that we have made regarding the relationship between alternative and performance. The change may be manifest in the structure of the linkages (the presence of delays due to the stoplight) and in the assessment of a key parameter (the distance from home to office because of the construction detour). As a result of such changes in assumptions, a new alternative may become more attractive and the old alternative may result in a surprise, if it were implemented. **Even in routine situations, there is a need to be aware of the assumptions that are being made and the degree of congruity between those assumptions and reality.** Small amounts of dissonance can require a review of the routine decision-making process.

Even though it is unlikely that anyone would treat the Potomac Manors project as if it were a routine decision, a simple appraisal of the profit of the project, using the estimates provided by the design team, might form the basis of the project's financial evaluation. A relevant calculation might simply be

Revenues	$45,000,000
Land cost	25,300,000
Development and selling costs	8,800,000
Miscellaneous expenses	400,000
Profits before tax	$10,500,000

The project's substantial profit would certainly contribute to its favorable assessment and might drive the decision to undertake it.

The Challenges of Proactive Decision Making

A proactive decision maker looks beyond the routine by (1) seeking a richer set of **alternatives** than those that are initially presented or traditionally considered, (2) questioning assumptions that are made regarding the **structure** of the relationships between alternatives and performance, (3) questioning assumptions regarding the **assessment** of important parameters that can potentially drive the decision, and (4) considering diverse measures of **performance** that incorporate the perspectives of the various stakeholders in the decision.

Alternatives

In the Potomac Manors project, the design team proposed a preliminary plan that carved out 300 three-acre lots that were expected to sell at an average price of $150,000 per lot. This preliminary design may be anchored by the minimum lot size demanded of the property's R3 zoning and may be driven by a desire to maximize the number of the lots that could be developed. Anchors are a common phenomenon that can severely limit the development of alternatives because they constrain the decision maker's scope. Although the notion of maximizing the number of lots may seem to be a reasonable rule of thumb, it also may limit the consideration of alternatives that could result in greater profits.

A more proactive consideration of alternatives could lead to the possibility of dividing the property into larger lots that might command a substantially greater price per acre. One possibility would be a plan with a standard lot size of four acres. A better alternative might be a mixture of three-, four-, and five-acre lots. A mixture of lot sizes not only might make more efficient use of the property, but also might increase the market value of all the lots because the larger lots could create the impression of an upscale development and the effect could trickle down to the smaller lots. The variety of lot sizes might also take advantage of a heterogeneous market allowing Potomac Manors to serve simultaneously several types of customers.

Although the consideration of a richer set of alternatives makes the decision more complex and more challenging, it also offers the possibility of achieving greater profits.

Assumptions—Structure

An assumption implicit in the design team's plan for the Potomac Manors project was that all lots would satisfy the septic percolation requirements of the R3 zoning. Often the enthusiasm for an exciting project or the inherent momentum of decision-making processes lead to a superficial examination of assumptions or, even worse, to a climate in which the questioning of assumptions is interpreted as disruptive. Such behavior prevents the consideration of different assumptions when the decision is being made and from the development of contingency plans for those occasions when reality deviates from assumption. As a result, the decision makers may be constantly reacting to changes and "putting out fires" or, in extreme situations, may face catastrophic surprises from which recovery is impossible. A proactive decision maker would seek out and query assumptions regarding the fundamental linkages between alternative and performance.

Suppose the assumption that all lots would meet the septic percolation requirements were queried and it was acknowledged that there was some possibility that a substantial portion of the Potomac Manors property might not meet the requirements. Now the calculation of the profits from the project would have to be made on the basis of the number of lots that would meet the requirements. This is a structural change in the linkage between the alternative of developing the property and the performance measure of profits. If there were the possibility that the local board of supervisors would allow the affected portion of the development to be connected to the municipal sewer system (even though this violated the R3 zoning code), there would be an additional structural change in the linkage between alternative and performance. Several possible profit calculations would be

Number of lots passing percolation	300	200	200
Board of supervisors' approval	N/A	No	Yes
Number of lots developed	300	200	300
Revenues	$45,000,000	$30,000,000	$45,000,000
Land cost	25,300,000	25,300,000	25,300,000
Development and selling costs	8,800,000	8,800,000	8,800,000
Miscellaneous expenses	400,000	400,000	400,000
Sewer connection costs			1,700,000
Profits before tax	$10,500,000	($ 4,500,000)	$ 8,800,000

This is certainly a more complete evaluation of the project and one that might even lead to the rejection of the proposed project because of the substantial loss associated with being able to develop just 200 lots.

Not only does the acknowledgment of the possibility of percolation problems result in a more accurate assessment of the value of the Potomac Manors project, but it might also result in the recognition of a new alternative. The approval of the board of supervisors could take several months, so rather than buying the property now, it might be possible to pay a fee to the seller for the option to buy the property in three months (after the board of supervisors meeting). Although a cost would be involved, this alternative would avoid losing $4,500,000 if the property were to be bought now and only 200 lots could have septic systems and the board of supervisors denied the request to connect to the municipal sewer. The benefit of eliminating the risk may outweigh the cost of the option. As a result, this could be a very attractive alternative that would have gone unnoticed without considering the assumptions underlying the initial assessment.

Assumptions—Assessments

The Potomac Manors design team estimated the average selling price of the lots would be $150,000. Even if this best estimate were based on a careful examination of comparable properties, the ultimate average selling price may be substantially different. Many factors contribute to the marketability of a residential development—some specific to the development itself and some related to prevailing macroeconomic conditions. Each makes forecasting difficult and can result in considerable uncertainty in whatever estimate is made.

It is natural, however, to forecast in terms of best estimates. The culture of forecasting encourages being right, and best estimates offer the best chances of being right. In addition, best estimates are single numbers and it is easy to think and to calculate in terms of single numbers. Single numbers, however, can be misleading in the complex world in which decisions are made today. By ignoring the spectrum of potential possibilities, alternatives can be misevaluated and the potential risks of the alternatives overlooked. For example, two alternatives may result in the same best estimate of profits, but when the spectrum of possibilities is considered, one alternative can have a substantial upside potential with little downside exposure and the other can be just the opposite. These are hardly the equally attractive alternatives that a best-estimate evaluation would suggest. As in the previous section, ignoring the spectrum of possibilities can also inhibit development of new alternatives that reduce risk because the need for such alternatives is never recognized.

For the Potomac Manors project, the average selling price per lot might be as low as $120,000 (if economic conditions slump and if other developments of a similar nature come on the market at the same time) or as high as $160,000 (if the economy is strong and Potomac Manors becomes a trendy location). The effects of this spectrum of potential average selling prices can be evaluated as follows for the scenario "percolation-problems-and-supervisors-approve-sewer-connection."

Number of lots passing percolation	200	200	200
Board of supervisors' approval	Yes	Yes	Yes
Number of lots developed	300	300	300
Average selling price	$ 120,000	$ 150,000	$ 160,000
Revenues	36,000,000	45,000,000	48,000,000
Land cost	25,300,000	25,300,000	25,300,000
Development and selling costs	8,800,000	8,800,000	8,800,000
Miscellaneous expenses	400,000	400,000	400,000
Sewer connection costs	1,700,000	1,700,000	1,700,000
Profits before tax	($ 200,000)	$ 8,800,000	$11,800,000

The spectrum of potential average selling prices can swing the project from profitable to unprofitable. In an effort to proactively manage the project by attenuating the downside exposure of a low average selling price, special marketing efforts might enhance the fashionableness of the development, especially if the economy appears to be weakening.

When considering a spectrum of possibilities, there is a need not only to consider the possibilities, but also to acknowledge the likelihood of those possibilities occurring. In the absence of some recognition of likelihoods, an evaluation of an alternative may be overly influenced by the abysmally poor performance of the absolutely worst possibilities or by the extraordinarily positive performance of the absolutely best possibilities. As a result, the vocabulary with which forecasts are made will have to be enlarged to include the probability of potential outcomes. For the Potomac Manors project, assessments will have to be made of the probability that the lots will not satisfy the percolation requirements, that the board of supervisors will approve the request for the sewer connection, and that the average selling price will be a specific value (or more precisely that the price will be within various ranges of potential prices).

Although assessing probabilities is more challenging than assessing best estimates, worst cases, and best cases, the evaluation of an alternative's performance will be more complete and will not be driven by the myopia of the best estimate nor the extremes of the best and the worst cases. In addition, considering both the possibilities and the probabilities will permit the proactive decision maker to direct attention to the most significant (in terms of both impact on performance and chances of occurring) dimensions of the decision and to develop alternatives that either accentuate the positives or ameliorate the negatives (or both).

Performance

The Potomac Manors project has been evaluated on the basis of its profitability. Although this is certainly a key performance measure, it is not the only important one. Other significant considerations might include the strategic benefits of bringing an upscale development to the market and the implementation concern regarding the timing and the extent of the cash required to conduct the project. An evaluation of the project on the basis of profits as the single measure of performance might result in rejecting a project that could result in small losses but that has significant long-term strategic benefits that far outweigh the short-term loss. Alternatively, the project might be undertaken but require massive amounts of cash to which the firm does not have access or for which high, profit-consuming interest rates must be paid. A proactive decision maker would recognize the multidimensional aspects of a decision and take actions that would ensure the positives (the strategic benefits) and minimize the negatives (the cash demands).

In addition to the breadth of the performance measures that are considered in an evaluation, the form in which those measures are presented is important. In the previous section, it was observed that a single number does not adequately capture the inherent uncertainty of the assessments used in an evaluation. Similarly, an average or best-estimate figure for a performance measure does not adequately portray the uncertainty in the resulting evaluation of the performance measure. As a result, probabilities that are consistent with the probabilities of the assessments should also be associated with performance measures. This combination of performance measure and probability presents a total profile of the risks associated with an alternative.

Relevant performance measures may not be limited to those directly related to the decision maker. In an earlier section, the alternative of offering a fee to the seller for the option to buy the property in several months emerged as a result of the acknowledgment of potential problems with percolation. An appropriate amount for that fee depends not only on the economics of the Potomac Manors project, but also on the economics of the seller. As a result, an offer to the seller should depend on what would be acceptable to the seller as well as what can be afforded by the project. Consequently, a proactive decision maker expands the scope of the performance measures beyond those that are directly related to the evaluation to include those that are relevant to others who have (or could have) a stake in the decision.

Summary

Many decisions can be addressed in a routine fashion. For those decision situations, rules of thumb emerge over time that very effectively address the needs of the situations and substantially streamline the decision process. There are, however, many important decisions that, because of the uniqueness of the situation or because of the magnitude of the potential consequences, cannot be appropriately dispatched on a routine basis with rules of thumb. Such decisions need to be addressed in a proactive manner. Many alternatives need to be explored; assumptions need to be reviewed from the perspective of the structure of the relationships between alternatives and performance as well as from the perspective of the assessments of important parameters; performance measures need to be considered that span the full spectrum of issues on which the decision will be made, as well as the perspectives of the stakeholders in the decision.

This book offers perspectives, languages, and tools that will facilitate one's development as a proactive decision maker—a decision maker who steps beyond the routine and addresses situations in a comprehensive but timely fashion using formal analytical tools that are guided by judgment and intuition.

2   ALTERNATIVES

Chapter 1 introduced the three basic elements of decision making: alternatives, performance measure, and assumptions. The alternatives are the set of possible actions the decision maker can take, the performance measure is the yardstick by which the decision maker will judge results, and assumptions are the simplifications of reality the decision maker uses to evaluate the performance of each alternative. All three of these elements can contribute to the difficulty of a decision and the need for proactive decision making. In subsequent chapters we will deal with assumptions and performance measures as the primary source of difficulty. In this chapter we consider alternatives. In this discussion of alternatives as the source of decision-making difficulty, we will assume the decision maker can evaluate the performance of every alternative.

Small Number of Alternatives

Choosing among a small number of alternatives is simply a matter of picking the one with the best performance measure. If the alternatives in Potomac Manors are "buy" or "not buy" and the performance measure is profit, the decision maker should simply choose the alternative with the higher profit.

Potomac Manors

Alternatives	Profit
Buy	$10,500,000
Not buy	$0

In general, the choice among a small number of alternatives simply involves evaluating the performance of each possible alternative and then selecting the one that performs best. In Potomac Manors, select "buy" because it brings a higher profit than "not buy."

If the estimation of the performance of each alternative is carried out in an electronic spreadsheet, the evaluation of each alternative may occur in separate columns of the spreadsheet.

		Alternative		
		A	B	C
Input Assumptions				
Common assumption 1	xxx			
Common assumption 2	xxx			
Assumption 3		xxx	xxx	xxx
Assumption 4		xxx	xxx	xxx
Intermediate Calculations				
Intermediate variable 1		xxx	xxx	xxx
Intermediate variable 2		xxx	xxx	xxx
Intermediate variable 3		xxx	xxx	xxx
Performance Measure				
Performance measure		xxx	xxx	xxx

Notice that this spreadsheet template separates the three elements of decision making: alternatives (specified in the spreadsheet as A, B, and C— each occupying a column), performance measure (the bottom-line calculation in this spreadsheet), and assumptions (the linkages between alternatives and performance measure). The assumptions are further divided into input assumptions (or assessments), which contain numerical inputs, and intermediate calculations, which contain the relationships between variables in the spreadsheet. In this spreadsheet template, input assumptions are further divided into assessments that are common to all alternatives and assessments that differ across the alternatives. The term *structure* refers not only to which variables the decision maker decided to use in the model, but also the relationships (linkages) among those variables the decision maker decided to include. Because the relationships among variables are found in the formulas entered in the spreadsheet, the entirety of the decision maker's structural assumptions is not apparent from the numerical results displayed in the foreground of the spreadsheet.

Although choosing among a small number of alternatives is not difficult (given the decision maker's estimated performance measures, simply choose the best-performing alternative), specifying the alternatives sometimes is. As mentioned in Chapter 1, extra thought should go into expanding the set of alternatives beyond the initial, obvious ones. At every stage of analysis, the decision maker should look for ways to improve on the set of alternatives under consideration. Insights from early stages of the analysis can often help uncover even better alternatives.

For example, acknowledging the possibility of percolation problems with the Potomac Manors property led not only to a more accurate assessment of the risk inherent in the "buy" alternative but also to the identification of a new alternative. Understanding why the "buy" alternative was risky helped the proactive decision maker create this new alternative: seek a three-month purchase option on the property. Because the three-month option would be exercised only if the board of supervisors approved the request to connect to the municipal sewer, this new alternative avoids the large losses associated with purchasing the property and developing only 200 lots if the sewer connection is not approved.

Sequential Decisions

Alternatives can complicate decision making when the decision maker faces an entire sequence of decisions. For example, suppose the decision maker must choose immediately among A_1, A_2, A_3. Later, after observing some key events, the decision maker must choose among B_1, B_2, B_3. After receiving still more information, the decision maker may have to choose among C_1, C_2, C_3, C_4. The overall realized performance may depend not only on the sequence of choices made but also on the results of the intermediate events.

For example, in relationships with prospects and customers, a catalog marketer faces a sequence of decisions. How should I contact potential customers (prospects) and try to encourage them to try our merchandise (A_1—aggressively, A_2—mildly, or A_3—not at all)? Based on the results of the prospecting effort (did they order? how much did they order? what did they order?), how should I attempt to remarket them (with catalog version B_1, with catalog version B_2, or B_3—not at all)? Based on the customer's response to the remarketing efforts, how should I respond (C_1—aggressively, C_2—normally, C_3—with a last-chance offer, or C_4—not at all)?

At first glance, we might think of the sequence of possible choices at each stage (for example, $A_1B_2C_4$, $A_3B_1C_1$, etc.) as comprising 36 ($3 \times 3 \times 4$) alternatives. If this were the case, we could make the decision the same way we did when there were but a few alternatives—simply choosing the alternative with the best performance among the 36. Although evaluating the performance of 36 alternatives would involve some work, it could be done.

But the presence of the intermediate events complicates things. There really are far more than 36 alternatives when we realize that downstream choices can and should be contingent on the information received in each prior stage. For example, one alternative might be:

Select A_1, then select B_1 if more than $29.95 was spent on clothing in the initial purchase or if the initial purchase was paid with a credit card, B_2 if less than $29.95 was spent on clothing in the initial purchase and payment was made by means other than credit card, and B_3 otherwise. If we selected B_1 or B_2, respond with C_1 if the customer purchases more than $200 in the next year, C_2 if he purchases less than $200, C_3 if he purchases nothing, and C_4 if he purchased nothing and returned the initial purchase. If we selected B_3, then select C_4.

This lengthy description defines but one alternative. This alternative might be better called a decision strategy because it is a description of exactly how our future choices will be made contingent on the outcomes of earlier choices.

The number of possible decision strategies is limited only by the richness of the information received at each stage and the imagination and creativity of the decision maker. Since each decision strategy is an alternative and the number of possible alternatives is essentially unlimited, it will be impossible to evaluate all possible alternatives. Since we cannot simply evaluate all alternatives, the challenge becomes one of using our judgment and insights from earlier analyses to chose which alternatives deserve to be evaluated and which can be safely ignored.[1] Later in this chapter we will offer decision rules as one approach for simplifying the set of alternatives in a sequential decision problem. In Chapter 3 we present decision trees as another tool for dealing with the complexities associated with sequential decision problems.

A Single Decision Quantity

Sometimes the alternatives are defined by a single decision quantity. The decision maker must pick a single number (a price, an order quantity, the number of lots to develop on Potomac Manors, etc.). This situation is really no different from the ones above except that each alternative corresponds to a numerical value of the decision quantity. The decision problem is again one of finding the alternative with the best estimated performance. But now rather than a column for alternative A and a column for alternative B, the decision maker's spreadsheet might have a single column headed by a cell

---

[1]More sophisticated techniques (such as dynamic programming) are available for dealing with problems of this type but are beyond the scope of this book. If the decision situation has these characteristics and the economics warrant it, the proactive decision maker would do well to seek the advice of an expert.

containing the decision quantity. Once the spreadsheet is built that calculates the performance for any decision quantity value, the table and graph features of the electronic spreadsheet can be used to quickly evaluate the alternatives and find the one with the best performance.

For example, consider the following business situation:

The XYZ Company assembles a product for which an important component, subassembly A, is purchased from an outside vendor. Annual demand for the component is 10,000 units and is distributed evenly throughout the year (i.e., there is no significant seasonality). Each subassembly A unit costs $325, delivered. There is a fixed cost of approximately $500 to place an order for subassembly A, irrespective of how many units are included in the order. The company estimates a cost of 12 percent of the unit cost per year to carry a unit in inventory (this includes the cost of capital). To minimize production costs, how many units of subassembly A should be ordered at a time, and how many orders should be placed per year?

The decision in this case is a single decision quantity: how many units of subassembly A should be ordered at a time. The performance measure will be total annual cost, which will consist of three components: purchase cost,[2] ordering costs, and inventory carrying costs. The input assumptions (assessments) consist of the 10,000 units annual demand, the $325 unit cost, the $500 cost per order, and the 12 percent inventory carrying cost. Important structural assumptions include the fact that demand is known and constant throughout the year and costs of carrying inventory are proportional to the dollar purchase value of the units in inventory.

A spreadsheet that calculates total annual cost (the performance measure) for a given order quantity is shown on the next page. The order quantity of 1,000 in the spreadsheet is arbitrary. Number of orders per year is calculated as the annual demand divided by the order quantity. Average inventory is calculated as order quantity divided by two under the assumptions that the amount in inventory varies between the order quantity (right after delivery of an order) and zero (right before the delivery of an order). Annual purchase cost is calculated as purchase cost per unit times annual demand. Annual ordering cost is calculated as the cost of ordering times the number of orders per year. Annual carrying cost is calculated as annual inventory carrying cost times purchase cost per unit times average inventory. Finally, the total annual cost (the performance measure) is calculated as the sum of the three annual

---

[2]In this example, annual purchase cost is a constant $3,250,000 and is not affected by the order quantity. Therefore, we would not need to include annual purchase costs as one of the components in the total cost performance measure in this example. We chose to do so in anticipation of situations (such as quantity discounts offered by the supplier) in which the purchase cost will be affected by the order quantity.

Alternative	
Order quantity	1,000
Input Assumptions	
Annual demand	10,000
Purchase cost per unit	$325
Cost per order	$500
Annual inventory carrying cost	12%
Intermediate Calculations	
Number of orders per year	10
Average inventory	500
Annual purchase cost	$3,250,000
Annual ordering cost	$5,000
Annual carrying cost	$19,500
Performance Measure	
Total annual cost	$3,274,500

cost components. For an order quantity of 1,000, the performance measure is $3,274,500.

Once the spreadsheet is built that calculates the performance for any decision quantity value, the table and graph features of the electronic spreadsheet can be used to quickly evaluate the alternatives and find the one with the best performance. For the XYZ Company example, the resulting table and graph of total annual cost versus order quantity suggests that a quantity of approximately 500 is best (see Table 2–1 and Figure 2–1).

The decision quantity with the best performance measure is called the optimal decision quantity. Best and optimal can be either the maximum value or minimum value, depending on the nature of the performance measure. In the XYZ example, the performance measure was total annual cost and the best or optimal decision quantity is the one that minimizes the performance measure. If the performance measure is profit, the best or optimal decision quantity is the one that maximizes the performance measure.

Using the resulting table and associated graph, it should be easy to find the optimal decision quantity. If additional accuracy is necessary, the decision maker can use smaller increments for the input values to the table. When we return to this example in Chapter 16, we will see that 506 is the exact value.

Care should be taken to explore a wide range of possible decision quantities. Sometimes (but rarely) the best decision quantity over a limited range

TABLE 2–1

Order Quantity	Total Annual Cost
100	$3,301,950
150	$3,286,258
200	$3,278,900
250	$3,274,875
300	$3,272,517
350	$3,271,111
400	$3,270,300
450	$3,269,886
500	$3,269,750
550	$3,269,816
600	$3,270,033
650	$3,270,367
700	$3,270,793
750	$3,271,292
800	$3,271,850
850	$3,272,457
900	$3,273,106
950	$3,273,788
1,000	$3,274,500
1,050	$3,275,237
1,100	$3,275,995
1,150	$3,276,773
1,200	$3,277,567
1,250	$3,278,375

FIGURE 2–1

Graph of Total Annual Cost versus Order Quantity

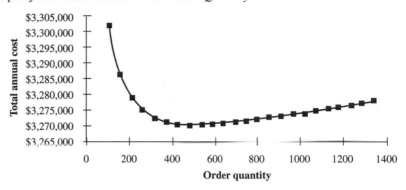

is not the best overall. A decision quantity that is best over a limited range but not best overall is called a **local optimum.** The decision quantity that is best over all possible quantities is called the **global optimum.**

To illustrate, consider the following modification to the XYZ Company example:

Suppose the vendor that supplies subassembly A offers the XYZ Company the following discounts based on size of order:

Order Quantity	Per Unit Price
Less than 750	$325
From 750 to less than 1,000	$320
1,000 or more	$315

After the appropriate modifications to our spreadsheet, the graph of total annual cost versus order quantity changes to reflect this new volume-discount pricing scheme (see Figure 2–2). Notice that a quantity of approximately 500 is a local optimum. The performance measure is better (lower) at 500 than it is at either 400 or 600. If the decision maker had tabled and graphed decision quantities in the limited range of 100 to 700, the even better decision quantity of 1,000 would never have been discovered. Can we be certain that 1,000 is the global optimum, or must we explore quantities above 1,250 (the highest of those tabled and graphed)? Because we know that 1,000 is the order quantity at which we receive the last volume discount, we can be confident that total annual costs will only continue to increase (due to rising carrying costs) for quantities above those in the graph. The quantity 1,000 is the global optimum.

FIGURE 2–2

Graph of Total Annual Cost versus Order Quantity Reflecting Volume Discounts

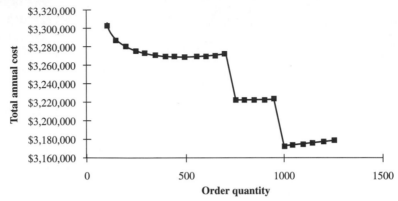

This example was designed to clarify the difference between a local and global optimum. Because the benefits of ordering at least 750 or 1,000 units are so obvious, it is difficult to imagine a decision maker ignoring order quantities of 750 and 1,000 and thereby incorrectly concluding that 500 is the best order quantity. Incorrectly concluding that 500 is the best order quantity when better ones exist is called getting "stuck" at a local optimum. To avoid getting stuck at a local optimum, the proactive decision maker must understand the importance of evaluating a wide range of decision quantities. When obvious discontinuities exist (like the volume discounts available at 750 and 1,000), the proactive decision maker will explore both sides of the discontinuities so as to avoid getting stuck at a local optimum.

Rather than table and graph the relationship between performance and decision quantity, the decision maker might also use the mechanized search tool available with most spreadsheets. In Excel, that tool is called Solver. The decision maker fills in the Solver menu to ask the tool to find the maximum value of the performance measure (target cell) by changing the decision quantity cell. At the push of a button, the tool will attempt to find the decision quantity value that maximizes the performance measure. The tool is flexible in that it can maximize, minimize, or find a specified value of the performance measure. It can search over one decision quantity or many. It can also restrict its search to decision quantities that satisfy certain conditions or constraints. Its biggest limitation is that it gets stuck easily at local optima. If there is but a single decision quantity, it is often worthwhile to table and graph the relationship between performance and decision quantity rather than rely solely on Solver. Not only is this more pedestrian approach less likely to get fooled by a local optimum, but also the table and graph offer insights into the decision problem that might be missed if only Solver is used.

Two or More Decision Quantities

With two decision quantities, the table and graph approach is doable. Electronic spreadsheet tabling features can fill in a two-way table. One decision variable will be the row entries, the other decision variable will be the column entries, and the body of the table (the values calculated by the spreadsheet tabling feature) will be the performance measure. The body of the table can be scanned to find the best performance value. The table can be redone using finer increments for more accuracy. It may even be helpful to graph the performance measure versus one of the decision quantities for various values of the other decision quantity.

For more than two decision quantities, it will take some creativity to use tables and graphs. Constraints often complicate the search for the optimal decision quantities, and care must be taken to limit the search to those combinations of decision quantities that are feasible (i.e., those combinations of decision quantities that satisfy all the constraints). Tools such as Solver will become a much more attractive option in these situations. Chapters 15 through 17 deal with the general topic of optimization, the process by which the best or optimal value of the performance measure can be found given the complexities of many decision quantities and the presence of constraints.

Decision Rules

One way to attack problems complicated by sequential decisions with intervening events is to simplify the set of alternatives using decision rules. Rather than consider all possible decision strategies, we might restrict our attention to a decision rule and then treat the parameters of that decision rule as decision quantities.

For example, the catalog marketer mentioned earlier prospects for new customers knowing that information collected from each newly acquired customer will be used to help make decisions about how to remarket to these customers. Because the information collected from the prospecting effort is extensive (number of purchases, amount purchased, products purchased, method of payment, etc.), the number of possible decision strategies about how to react to that information is staggering. Rather than consider all possible decision strategies, the proactive decision maker must make some simplifications. In the same way that decision maker's assumptions linking alternatives to performance represent a necessary simplification of reality, decision rules represent a necessary narrowing of the set of possible decision strategies.

For example, the catalog marketer may adopt a decision rule such as: first prospect aggressively (A_1), then remarket with catalog B_1 if purchase amount is greater than Q, remarket with catalog B_2 if purchase amount is less than Q, and do not remarket (B_3) if purchase amount is zero. This decision rule has narrowed the set of possible prospecting/remarketing decision strategies. The decision maker has exercised judgment in the formulation of the decision rule. The rule is based only on total purchase amount and not the number or kinds of products purchased. There is a single cutoff value, Q, rather than several. The unmanageable set of decision strategies has been simplified, and the decision task is now one of finding the best decision quantity Q. A one-way table of the performance measure versus Q can be used to find the best decision quantity.

Although decision rules facilitate the selection of the "best" alternative, they do so at a "cost." That cost is the possibility that some other decision strategy is better than those captured by the chosen decision rule. In the same way that proactive decision makers question the assumptions that link alternatives to the performance measure, they should also question the form of the chosen decision rule.

Summary

This chapter examined alternatives, one of the three basic elements of decision making. We described several decision situations in which alternatives are the primary source of decision-making difficulty and discussed methods for dealing with those difficulties. The next two chapters examine the structuring and the assessment of assumptions, and are followed by a chapter on performance measurement.

3   STRUCTURING ASSUMPTIONS IN DECISION MAKING

Decision making involves knowing your *alternatives* and having a way to measure their *performance*. In only the simplest situations can we directly determine the performance level of all alternatives. Generally, we make *assumptions* about the linkage between a specific alternative and its level of performance.

This chapter is designed to help one get started in structuring assumptions about how alternatives connect to performance. This involves thinking about what quantities are useful in establishing this linkage and envisioning what relationships should exist among these quantities.

The chapter will describe the use of an *influence diagram*, which shows what quantities are involved, how they are related to each other, how they are affected by *alternatives,* and, in turn, how they affect *performance*. The influence diagram is helpful for framing assumptions and can ensure that a messy situation has been brought under control. It can provide the structure for building a spreadsheet model and for assessing the quantities that go into it. Presenting the influence diagram can be more effective than displaying the mathematics of a decision model or the background of a spreadsheet. New software tools use this diagram as a graphical interface for creating, manipulating, and presenting the assumptions underlying a decision model.

A related diagram, the *decision tree,* can help us structure a decision model when a tricky chronological sequence of decisions interrelates with uncertain quantities or events. Relating to a decision tree may sometimes be easier than an influence diagram, because the tree includes more detail about distinct paths we may follow, or along which events may take us in the future. We will begin our discussion with influence diagrams for situations of certainty, where we expect to know the quantities that are important. Then we introduce the decision tree, which leads us into considering uncertain quantities and events. Finally, we return to the influence diagram, this time including quantities that may be uncertain along with those that are known with certainty.

19

Structuring Relationships Using an Influence Diagram

An influence diagram graphically displays the elements of a decision model and their relationships. It consists of *decision* nodes (denoted by rectangles), *intermediate* quantities (ovals), a single (usually) *value* or *performance* node (a rounded square), and *directed arcs* (influences) between quantities. An influence arrow pointing to a performance node or intermediate quantity means that the influencing quantity is used in determining the performance node or intermediate quantity. In cases where quantities become known at different times, an influence arrow indicates that the influencing quantity is known before the influenced quantity.

Figure 3–1 shows the simplest of influence diagrams. In this example, price is a decision that influences profit, the measure of performance or the value node, that is, the quantity we wish to use in making a decision. The influence diagram reflects the assumption that for any level of price, the profit level can be determined directly.

It may be easier to come up with the numbers for profit through a richer structure. Figure 3–2, for example, illustrates the probable first useful step in expanding the linkage between the price decision and the performance measure. In this influence diagram, revenue and total cost are separate quantities about which some assumptions can be made. It is reasonable to expect that decomposing the assessment of quantities in this way would help provide better overall assessments of profit. It is still true that price affects profit, except that now the influence is through an intermediate quantity revenue.

FIGURE 3–1
The Simplest Influence Diagram

FIGURE 3–2
Separating Revenue and Total Cost

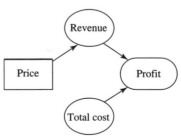

The diagram indicates that price must be known to calculate revenue; however, we don't need it directly to calculate profit provided we have revenue and total cost. The diagram doesn't tell us how to calculate profit (which we could easily establish to be revenue − total cost), yet it does indicate what quantities are needed to calculate profit; it tells us the structure of the relationships we have assumed.

At first glance, the structure in Figure 3–2 seems reasonable, and it certainly is a good first step. If you look at it closely, however, you may wonder if it is reasonable to have total cost hanging out there by itself, unaffected by price. There are, of course, multiple sources of cost that might be separately calculated. If one worked to improve the structure of assumptions, the thinking might run like this:

> Let me break out fixed cost from variable cost, because variable cost will change if the volume of product sold changes, while fixed cost will not change, and to be fair, I ought to reflect that in my assumptions. Then I had better be explicit about the volume of product sold. I'll add the quantity "units sold," and the quantity "variable cost per unit," which together will influence variable cost. Oh, of course units sold will also be used in calculating revenue, I'll also draw an arrow there. (The resulting structure is shown in Figure 3–3.)

With this structure, the quantities units sold, variable cost per unit, and fixed cost must be assessed, which will then (through some multiplication and addition) provide a number for total cost. Expanding the structure of the assumptions by moving from Figure 3–1 to Figure 3–3, will likely give better assessments of total cost.

There is a difference in Figure 3–3 between quantities like revenue and total cost, which have arrows both coming and going out, and a quantity like fixed cost, which has no arrow coming into it. The quantity fixed cost is an

---

FIGURE 3–3

Breaking Out Fixed and Variable Cost and Units Sold

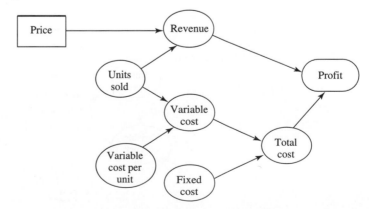

example of what might be called an *exogenous* quantity, one unaffected by any decision or other intermediate quantities. At the assessment stage, an *exogenous* quantity requires a number to be estimated, while *intermediate* quantities, such as total cost, require a logical or algebraic relationship (and possibly estimates for parameters of that relationship). In the case of total cost, for example, the relationship is simply the sum of variable cost and fixed cost.

Perhaps the best way to create an influence diagram is to start by defining the decision quantity(ies) and the performance measure and then work from the left and right ends of the diagram to fill out the middle. Usually, there will be several stages of progression from one diagram to successively better diagrams. At this stage, the creator may wish to get someone else's opinion of the direction the diagram is heading; assume that the creator shows it to his or her boss. What do you think the boss would say after perusing the influence diagram in Figure 3–3? The boss might ask: "Why doesn't price affect units sold? If units sold is constant as we raise price, then it would follow that to improve profit, we should raise the price, and then raise it some more, and why not keep raising it, if it will only give more profit?" The answer may be, "Well, I guess I left that linkage out, and I'll put it in, now that you mention it." Interestingly with an influence diagram, missing arrows often communicate more significant information about assumptions than included arrows. Like the hound of the Baskervilles, whose failure to bark was its strongest statement, an absent arrow may be the pivotal disclosure of an influence diagram.

If an arrow were added from price to units sold (see Figure 3–4), the influence diagram would declare that sales is affected by price or, in other words, that there is price elasticity. If units sold goes down as price increases,

---

FIGURE 3–4

Adding Influences Suggesting Price Affects Units Sold
which Affects Variable Cost Per Unit

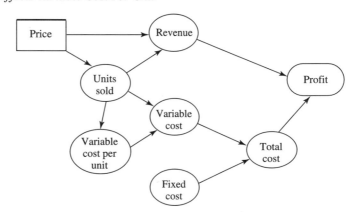

then we could not assume that it would still be best to increase price indefinitely. Interestingly the influence diagram shows two separate effects of price on profit: one effect through revenue that would give higher profit with rising price, and another through the quantity units sold that presumably would give lower profits.

The influence diagram in Figure 3–4 also includes an arrow from units sold to variable cost per unit. Think for a minute about what this implies and why it might be included. Why would variable cost per unit change as units sold changes? Perhaps there are economies of scale in production.

Of course, it is possible to continue to expand the structure of assumptions beyond that in Figure 3–4. And yet, as we add quantities and relationships, we increase our assessment burden, and at some point we should conclude that we have captured the core of the situation in enough detail. It is apparent that Figure 3–1 does not include enough detail, and for some purposes Figure 3–4 may include too much. Experience with decision modeling will help develop judgment as to the appropriate amount of detail; decision modeling is art as well as science.

The choice of structure does matter beyond its effects on the amount of assessment effort that it imposes. The structure of Figure 3–4, for example, would lead to a different choice of price level than would Figure 3–3, the best price level using the structure in Figure 3–3 would differ from that of Figure 3–2, and so on. We always seek the most reasonable structure without going overboard with complexity.

Suppose we adopt Figure 3–4 as our structure of assumptions and think about what we might do with it. It would be straightforward to create a spreadsheet model to flesh out the relationships. The spreadsheet would have a cell for each node in the diagram. For any node that has arrows coming into it, the corresponding cell in the spreadsheet must have a formula that references each influencing quantity. For example, the formula for the profit cell must use the cells for revenue and total cost, and the formula for revenue must use price and units sold.

A spreadsheet model can be made to correspond to the structure in *any* influence diagram, but what about the opposite? In fact, *any* spreadsheet model must have a corresponding, unique influence diagram showing all nodes and influence arrows. Otherwise, the computer would not know the order in which to calculate the cells of the spreadsheet. It may not be obvious from the spreadsheet, however, whether a particular quantity node is a decision quantity or a value node. These interpretations have to do with how the model will be used and the context of the problem. Nonetheless, a unique structure of quantities and influences exists for each spreadsheet model.

Although the types of quantities of the influence diagram may appear in virtually any order, the meaning of certain structures should be clarified:

- Having an arrow emanating from a value node would be pointless (although permissible). Students sometimes place an arrow from a value node to a decision node, reflecting their thinking that because the value node is the ultimate basis for a decision, it should influence the decision. This action reflects a misunderstanding of what the decision model does. The influence diagram reflects the world as it is and will ultimately be used as an aid in making decisions. In the structuring stage, we do not know what the decision will be. For example, in Figure 3–4, we have linked price to profit, because price affects profit and we have not yet set the level of price. When a model is complete, we'll try a few different prices and pick one that gives us a high profit. If someone stated a profit level, however, we couldn't respond right now with an appropriate price. Thus, we can't express a relationship wherein profit influences price. The fact that price must be set before profit is known is a tipoff of the appropriate direction of the arrow.

- An arrow into a decision quantity suggests that we have in mind how we would make that decision based on the influencing quantities. For example, the influence diagram in Figure 3–5 shows an additional decision node, subcontract, which is influenced by units sold. This node allows for subcontracting the manufacture of some of the product out to another party. The existence of the added arrow into this node suggests that we know how the number of units sold will affect our decision about subcontracting. For example, we might create a model such that if the units sold exceeds our existing capacity, we would subcontract the excess—we might call this a *decision rule*. We could easily write the decision rule into a spreadsheet. In fact, if you cannot write a decision rule about the relationship between a decision quantity and some influencing quantity, then it is best not to

---

FIGURE 3–5

Revised to Show Arrow into Decision Node

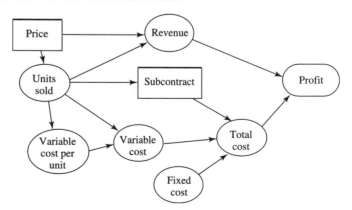

show an arrow into the decision quantity. The fact that we have specified that subcontract is a decision quantity (inside a rectangle) and not just another intermediate quantity suggests that as part of our analysis we will test alternative decision rules. One such decision rule, for example, might be, "If units sold is greater than 10,000 (our capacity), then Subcontract = Units sold − 10,000."

- It is best to have a single *value* or *performance* node, even when there are multiple objectives. If there are separate objectives relating to maximizing profit and minimizing environmental damage, then each of these could be intermediate quantities with arrows from them leading into a single *value* node (denoted by a rounded square), that could be given a name such as "overall desirability."

- It is best to avoid two-way influences or loops in the influence diagram (see Figure 3–6). A cycle is technically possible, but like a circular reference in a spreadsheet, it would have to be resolved by iteration. A cycle may be avoided by defining separate quantities for each time period and using a quantity in one time period to influence a quantity in another time period. Thus, we could modify the first example of Figure 3–6 so that the previous period's debt level would influence interest expense for the current period, as shown in the top of Figure 3–7.

Many influence diagrams contain separate quantities representing the same item in different time periods. A shorthand way to avoid a large, cluttered influence diagram is to indicate in a quantity's name that it is associated with a particular time period. We can indicate that a quantity is influenced by the previous value of another quantity by writing "previous" beside the arrow. In Figure 3–7, for example, the bottom diagram shows the shorthand

---

FIGURE 3–6

Two-Way Influence and Loop

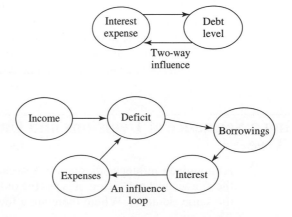

FIGURE 3–7
Elimination of Loops

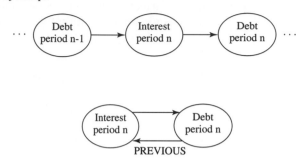

equivalent of the top diagram. Because the arrow is labeled "previous," the diagram has no loop.

The influence diagram appears to be a tool of value and simplicity. Nevertheless, first-time users may misconstrue what influence diagrams represent. The following tips and caveats may provide clarity and prevent misuse:

- The influence diagram is *not:*
  - —A flowchart (that is, an arrow does not indicate things such as "units shipped from A to B").
  - —A precedence chart, such as those used in project planning (an arrow does not mean "must be preceded by").
  - —A representation of hierarchical structure, such as in an organization chart (an arrow does not mean "is an element of").
- Quantities may be levels of some continuous quantity or a set of discrete alternatives. Unless what constitutes higher or lower levels of the quantity is clear, the name of the quantity may not be meaningful. For example, a quantity such as cost or revenue is more meaningful than a quantity called economic performance.
- If an influence arrow is ambiguous, inserting another quantity may be helpful. If the influence of price on sales is not clear, for example, perhaps it would be clearer to expand the diagram so that price influences demand, which along with supply, influences sales.

Structuring a Sequence of Decisions and Uncertainties Using a Decision Tree

Although an influence diagram is a wonderful way to capture and structure the elements of a decision, it is not the only way; a decision tree can represent the same elements. Where there are a few distinct alternatives for decisions

FIGURE 3–8

Decision Tree for Figure 3–2 Influence Diagram

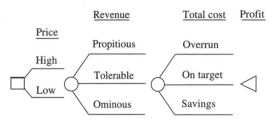

and a few distinct outcomes for other quantities (or uncertain events), a tree may be better because it can show more detail about possible paths the decision situation may take.

For example, Figure 3–8 shows a decision tree that might have been drawn for the decision situation of Figure 3–2. As with influence diagrams, squares represent decisions and circles represent quantities. Circles in both decision trees and influence diagrams may also represent categorical outcomes rather than quantitites that range over some continuous interval. Often these categorical outcomes relate to uncertain events. The typical use for circles in decision trees has been to represent such uncertain events.

The third component of a decision tree is a consequence, which is analogous to a *value* node in an influence diagram. In this example, a profit level is the consequence of a particular combination of price, revenue, and total cost, and a column heading is provided for profit numbers to be written at the ends of branches of the tree. Specific alternatives for a decision are represented by branches coming from a decision node, for example, high and low price. Branches are drawn for specific outcomes for revenue (the labels "Propitious," "Tolerable," and "Ominous" designate outcomes that would not appear in an influence diagram but might be identified as part of using an influence diagram) and for cost (with labels "Overrun," "On target," and "Savings"). Figure 3–8 has been drawn as a generic schematic of a more detailed tree that would show every possible path: three revenue branches would spring from each of the two decision branches for price and three cost branches would spring from each revenue branch, showing a total of 18 complete paths through the tree ($2 \times 3 \times 3$).

In this example, the chances for various cost outcomes may be the same regardless of the revenue outcome. There is no way to represent this in a generic decision tree. The lack of an arrow from revenue to cost in the influence diagram, however, suggests that revenue does not affect the cost outcome. Thus, the influence diagram may show more information about the structure of dependence among quantities.

It is usually appropriate to think of the nodes in a decision tree as occurring in a time sequence. In this example, the chronological order of revenue and cost is not apparent, so we arbitrarily put one ahead of the other. The influence diagram is more flexible and free form in that no order is necessary.

A decision tree may have an advantage over an influence diagram when there is a tricky sequence of decisions and uncertainties through time. Because it shows the detail of specific possibilities for decisions and uncertainties, it may convey dynamics more clearly than an influence diagram. For these reasons, we describe here the most important points when constructing or using such a diagram.

Let us consider how to construct a decision tree, using as an example a company's decision about litigating a business claim. The company believes that another company legitimately owes it money; no criminal claim is involved; and the case has no relation to any other court, business claim, or arrangement.

Figure 3–9 shows where one might start in structuring the components of this decision situation. It contains a single decision node, with two branches emanating from it, representing the possibilities "Sue" or "Don't Sue."

The branches from any node in a decision tree should be both *collectively exhaustive* and *mutually exclusive.* The term *collectively exhaustive* means simply that all possibilities are included. For example, had we used the branches "Sue" or "Settle Out of Court" we would not have included every possibility; adding a "Do Nothing" branch could exhaust the possibilities.

The term *mutually exclusive* means the branches do not overlap. For example, the branches "Sue" and "Sue in Federal Court" overlap, leading to possible ambiguity about which path is chosen. Ideally the branches are constructed in such a way that exactly one may be chosen without ambiguity.

To develop the decision tree further, we could think about what is next in the time sequence. The next node could be a decision or an uncertain event. In the litigation decision, we would naturally consider next whether we win or lose the case. This outcome would bear directly on performance and be affected by our choice of whether we sue. The possibilities are shown in Figure 3–10, where, in order to have *collectively exhaustive* possibilities, we have included a branch for the suit being thrown out of court. We have drawn Figure 3–10 with every possible path explicit (rather than using a generic schematic). Notice that there is a single branch if we "Don't Sue" on the

---

FIGURE 3–9

A Start on a Decision Tree for a Litigation Decision

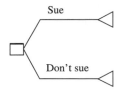

initial decision, and three branches otherwise. A decision tree can show that the set of possible paths through a decision–outcome sequence is not always symmetric.

Knowing the court's judgment outcome may not be the end of the story in litigation. Of course, an appeal is possible, as shown by the further extension of the decision tree in Figure 3–11. If we win, the other side may appeal; we do not know whether that side will appeal, so even though it is a decision from that side's perspective, it is an uncertainty from ours, represented by a circular node (not a square). If we lose, then it is our decision, represented by a square node, whether to appeal or not. Their decision about whether to appeal would not necessarily match our own.

If the case is thrown out of court, then there is no possibility for an appeal. Here again, the decision tree with its detailed paths can show asymmetries explicitly.

The complete decision tree will include the outcomes of the appeal, as shown in Figure 3–12. In the decision tree, the chances for any event are conditional on the path that leads to that event. For example, the chances that we "win appeal" may depend on whether we won or lost the original court case. If we win the original case, the chances of winning the appeal could be higher, for example, than if we lost the original court case.

We have now completed our brief discussion of creating decision trees. Decision trees may be helpful as a complement to influence diagrams when the time sequence of actions and events is tricky to capture. Branches on a decision tree represent specific paths into the future, whereas arcs of an

FIGURE 3–10

Decision Tree with Court Outcome Uncertainty

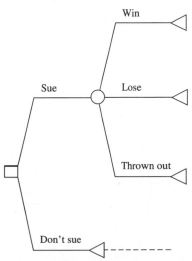

FIGURE 3–11
Decision Tree with Appeal Decisions

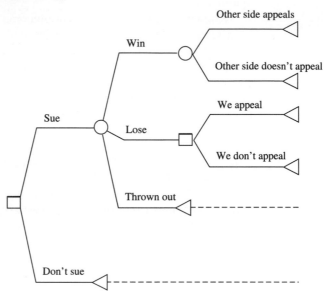

FIGURE 3–12
Complete Decision Tree for Litigation Decision

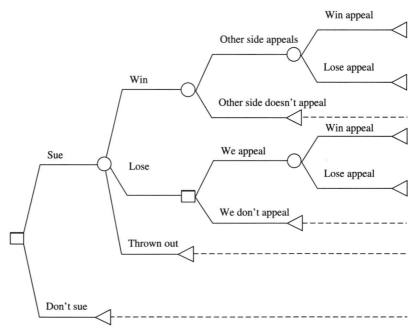

FIGURE 3–13
Influence Diagram for Litigation Decision

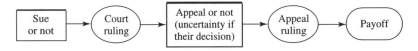

influence diagram show what influences what. For a small number of such paths, a decision tree may be easier to understand because it shows the distinct possibilities for each decision and each uncertain event or quantity. On the other hand, the influence diagram tells us more about dependencies among variables and may be better when decision quantities and intermediate quantities are continuously ranging.

For any decision tree, a corresponding influence diagram can always be drawn, and vice versa. Thus, it is useful to be conversant with both diagrams. For example, Figure 3–13 is an influence diagram for the decision tree in Figure 3–12. The appeal node is placed in a square, as though it were a decision, even though when we win it is really the other party's decision and an uncertainty to us. We don't really know whether to denote this node as a decision square or an uncertainty circle, so we make a parenthetical note on the influence diagram. As mentioned above, the decision tree portrays more effectively such an asymmetry. As we discuss the use of influence diagrams for situations where uncertainty exists, we will come back to the respective merits of each diagram.

Influence Diagrams with Uncertain Quantities

Although it is easy enough to make any node in an influence diagram uncertain (that is, a chance node), doing so has an effect on the meaning of arrows into or out of that node. In this section we will clarify the definitions of nodes and arrows in conditions of uncertainty and provide some illustrative examples.

Let us indicate a quantity that is to be treated as uncertain with a tilde ($\sim$) above the label.[1] The types of influences possible are shown in Figure 3–14. In the upper diagrams of Figure 3–14, the influencing arc affects uncertain quantities, while in the lower diagrams decision quantities are affected. The diagrams in the left column have uncertain quantities as influencing quantities, while in the right column, decision quantities provide influence.

An arrow pointing into a chance node designates *relevance,* which means the influencing node is relevant to the assessment of the chances for the

---

[1]We assume that quantities are deterministic unless indicated by the $\sim$. An alternative convention commonly used is to assume that all quantities are uncertain unless indicated by a double oval.

uncertain quantity. In Figure 3–14, for example, when assessing the chances that an individual uses computers, the individual's educational level is relevant. Stated another way, the probability distribution for use of computer is dependent on educational level. Note that the arrow could just as well be drawn the opposite way (from use of computer to educational level) because if B is not probabilistically independent of A, then A is not probabilistically independent of B. The direction of the arrow is, rather, like a statement of the structure of the available information; we can more easily assess probability distributions for use of computer conditional on education level, than vice versa. For example, we may have data on the extent of use for people with various degrees, but not information about the education level of various classes of computer use.

When the arrow runs from a decision quantity to an uncertain quantity, we are indicating that the level of the decision quantity is *relevant* to an assessment of the uncertain quantity. For example, in Figure 3–14, we may need to assess different demand probability distributions for alternative levels of price.

The definition of an arrow is not really different when quantities are uncertain. As for deterministic quantities, an arrow means the outcome for the influenced quantity is affected by the influencing quantity. It is simply a tougher task to structure probabilistic dependencies than deterministic ones since the distribution for an uncertain quantity depends on all the quantities along any influencing path. It is a good idea to limit the quantities that are treated as uncertain to a small number.

Figure 3–14 also illustrates the use of arrows into decision quantities. For example, we would know the diagnosis when we select the medical procedure, and we can therefore make our decision conditional on the diag-

---

FIGURE 3–14   *Types of Influence Arrows*

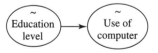

The education level is relevant for assessing the chances associated with use of computer.

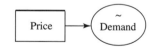

The price level is relevant for assessing the chances associated with demand.

Conditioning arrows into uncertain quantities

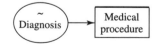

The diagnosis outcome is known at the time the decision on the medical procedure is made.

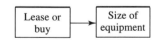

The lease or buy decision is made before the size of equipment choice.

Conditioning arrows into decision quantities

nosis. When an arrow runs from a decision node to a decision node, it means that we know what choice was made in the first decision before we make the influenced decision: We will know whether it is lease or buy when we make the decision about the size of equipment. This signifies that we wish the decision to be conditional on whether we are leasing or buying. When we have an arrow coming into a decision quantity, then rather than simply setting the level for that decision quantity, we want to know a decision rule that states what to do for each possible outcome of the conditioning quantity.

Figure 3–15 shows an example influence diagram involving a decision about which computer should be the standard for a department. There are characteristics of the employee population that will affect the use of the computer and the benefit derived. The characteristics chosen to be included—ones for which information is available—are job and educational level.

Figure 3–16 shows a corresponding decision tree for this same situation. The tree has three quantities: job (with two possible outcomes), educational level (with three possibilities), and use of computer (high and low). These quantities describe an individual randomly selected from a given population. The arrows in that diagram suggest that educational level is dependent on job and use of computer is dependent on both job and educational level. The

FIGURE 3–15

Influence Diagram for Computer Decision

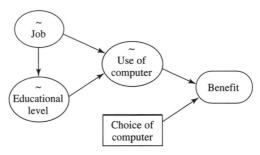

FIGURE 3–16

Decision Tree for Computer Decision

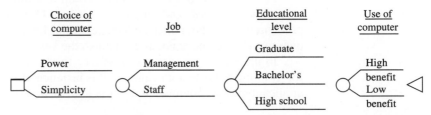

arrow from one quantity to another—job to educational level—does not imply causality. Job does not determine whether a degree has been attained; however, it may be relevant in assessing the chances that a degree has been obtained. Again, a more significant statement would be the absence of an arrow, which suggests probabilistic independence. The order of job and educational level could just as well be reversed in the decision tree, or equivalently, the arrow between them reversed in the influence diagram. The only consequence of such a reversal would be that the assessment of conditional probabilities would be conducted in a different order.

Once again we see differences between what the influence diagram communicates compared to the decision tree. In the tree, we must know the actual probabilities on the tree to know whether use of computer depends on job, but in the structure of the influence diagram it is already evident. In the decision tree, you must put a quantity either in front of or behind another quantity even when they are independent, but in the influence diagram you can show that no influence relationship exists between two quantities. For example, job and educational level could be placed ahead of choice of computer in Figure 3–16, given that the probabilities do not change with the decision. The influence diagram also makes apparent that the decision about the computer does not affect any of the uncertain quantities (such as job or educational level). Again, we could not make that determination using the decision tree without knowing the conditional probabilities on the tree.

Nevertheless, the decision tree does explicitly show timing. It also shows asymmetric structures; for example, for persons with a degree, another quantity may affect use of computer but not for persons without a degree. The decision tree can easily display such an asymmetry, whereas with the influence diagram it would be necessary to look at background relationship formulas.

Final Examples of How to Develop an Influence Diagram

The influence diagram can be a boon to modeling because it lets you design a model quickly and allows you to alter that design as you check its efficacy. It is easily expandable. A quantity can be broken down into fine-grained quantities, and additional influencing or influenced quantities can be added to provide detail or completeness.

The best way to use this tool to structure a model is to start simply and expand it *as needed* (and only as necessary). One starts on both ends of the problem (worry about intermediate quantities later). Try to identify a decision quantity, on the one hand, and establish the value or performance quantity.

To illustrate, consider a loan officer thinking about the approval system for granting loans to applicants. In this instance, the decision about a specific applicant may be obvious—make the loan or do not make it. The measure of performance applicable may also be apparent—the payoff at the end of the loan period. Figure 3–17 shows a first step in putting these elements into the influence diagram. As expected, the loan decision does affect the payoff.

The question the loan officer should ask herself at this point is, "What other quantities can affect my payoff?" Of course, a key consideration would be whether the loan is repaid, which is an uncertain quantity. Figure 3–18 shows the influence diagram after adding this quantity.

So far so good, but the loan officer should now consider whether other quantities relate to the decision. She thinks for a minute and suggests to herself that a credit rating is generally used in making the loan decision. Would a credit rating influence the payoff? This relationship is a little harder to think about. She realizes, however, that if she knew the answer to whether the loan candidate would repay (this quantity is already in the diagram), then the credit rating would not provide additional help. Should she put the credit rating in the diagram? Yes, if she will use it in the loan approval process to make a better decision, which would suggest that she should put it in with an arrow into the decision, as shown in Figure 3–19.

Now she asks herself if anything is missing. She can come up with no other quantities to add. But what about additional arrows? Thinking for a moment, she rejects an arrow from repay to make loan as unrealistic, because she would not know whether the loan has been repaid until long after the decision on the loan had been made. What about an arrow between repay and credit rating? This arrow seems necessary, because it would be hard to argue that the rating is independent of the ultimate result (this argument would make getting the credit rating a waste of time). She considers now which direction

FIGURE 3–17
Starting an Influence Diagram

FIGURE 3–18
Expanding the Influence Diagram

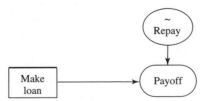

FIGURE 3–19
Further Development of Diagram

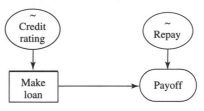

FIGURE 3–20
Final Influence Diagram

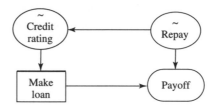

to draw the arrow. She could draw it either way, since if A affects the probability distribution for B, then it is also true that B affects the probability distribution for A. However, her approach to assessing this relationship will be to find cases in which it is known whether or not the candidates have repaid and to get the probability distribution for the credit rating that these candidates received. Thus, she draws the arrow from repay to credit rating. After a little more thinking, she considers the structure sufficient for now; her final influence diagram is shown in Figure 3–20.

The structure in Figure 3–20 suggests that her next steps would be to assess the probability that a candidate will repay, to estimate the probability distribution for the credit rating, conditional on the repayment quantity, and quantify the payoffs, conditional on the repayment quantity. Her analysis would then consist of comparing various decision rules for the loan decision, conditional on the credit rating.

For comparison, Figure 3–21 shows a decision tree for this same scenario. Note that credit rating is put ahead of the make loan decision, since we will have that information when we make the decision. However, we don't know the repay outcome of the loan until later, as shown in the decision tree. Because there is an arrow between repay and credit rating in the influence diagram, the chances that the loan is paid would depend on whether the credit

FIGURE 3–21
Decision Tree Loan Decision

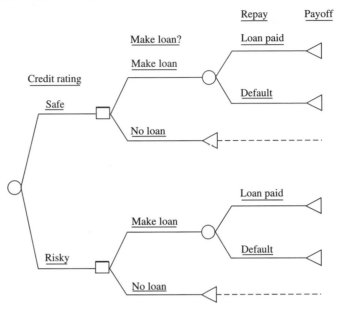

rating were "Safe" or "Risky." Once again we see how the information about structure in the influence diagram is complementary to that in the decision tree.

The Use of Influence Diagrams and Decision Trees

The conventional approach to decision modeling has been separate, sequential activities: structuring, mathematical formulation, data collection, creation of computer program, analysis, and presentation of results. Each of these steps typically requires its unique representation of the problem. The influence diagram, in combination with software and the desktop computer, may provide the opportunity to change the need for several representations: It offers promise as a single representation of a model that is useful for many or all of the stages in the modeling process. Software, such as DPL™ and Precision Tree™, allows the user to draw the decision model with a mouse as an influence diagram and then incorporate data for each node and arrow. Using the mouse and the diagram, the user can conduct an analysis of the best decision, including sensitivity analysis. This software will also create the corresponding decision tree structure.

Once the analysis is complete, the task of preparing a presentation begins. In addition to the results of the analysis and recommendations, the structure and concept of the model is presented. It is key that the representation of the model be understood quickly by the nonspecialist. Unfortunately, many common representations of models in management science are of limited use with general audiences.

A nice feature of influence diagrams and decision trees is that the very tool used to structure the problem and guide the analysis may be the most effective way of presenting it to others, particularly if the audience includes generalists not acquainted with algebraic or other mathematical representations of problems and if new software is available to aid the real-time projection or preparation of high-quality graphics.

In a live presentation, it is usually most effective to introduce an influence diagram or decision tree in stages with, say, three nodes added on each screen until the structure is complete. With some experience, one can understand a great deal about a decision situation with just the stand-alone influence diagram or decision tree. For example, a study of Figure 3–22 would give substantial insight into the structure of assumptions for the Potomac Manors real estate development decisions. The key issues, the uncertainties to consider, and how they interrelate are included. The stage is set for assessing specific quantities and perhaps for further discussions about the structure of assumptions.

FIGURE 3–22

Potomac Manors Influence Diagram

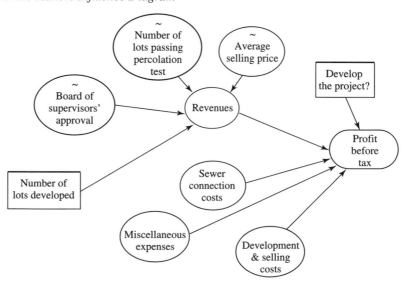

End-of-Chapter Case

DESTINY CONSULTING GROUP

Destiny Consulting Group (DCG) hibernated from September to April, then came alive like a hungry bear in the summer months, when its principals, rising second-year MBA students, worked on projects for small companies. DCG's mission was to provide experience and much-needed compensation for its principals and to give high value-added advice to its loyal clients. Carol Smith had started with DCG two weeks earlier and had two live projects, which she had named the Downsize Debate—on which she had already given an interim report—and the Futures Position, which was a brand new project.

The Downsize Debate

On her first day on the job, a company presented the question of whether it should downsize a subsidiary by reducing its headquarters expenditures. In her interim report, Smith suggested reducing this expense by $1 million, which would increase aftertax profit by $610,000. She included a printout of a pared-down spreadsheet in her report to the company's president. To her surprise, the president asked for the electronic file for the spreadsheet upon receipt of the report. He said he was intrigued by her recommendation and wanted to try out some other downsizing possibilities. Even though Smith had used the spreadsheet simply for some rough-cut numbers, it had led to a distressing memo from the president (Exhibit 1).

After reflecting on the memo, Smith knew that, in her exuberance to provide a quick response on her initial project, she had acted hastily. Of course, she did not think that the headquarters of the SQZ subsidiary should be wiped out entirely. "What kind of ruthless maniac does he think I am, anyway?" she said out loud to herself. That thinking applied to the company as a whole would take out even President Lewis, to say nothing about fees for consultants. She had to admit, though, that the spreadsheet really supported cutting them out. She pulled the spreadsheet up on her screen to see what was going on.

As she worked, Smith thumbed through the notes of her conversations with Mr. Lewis and others. SQZ was a price taker, which was why she had simplified matters by using margin in her spreadsheet, instead of having an explicit price and variable cost, which would net out to give margin. This still seemed fine to her.

She checked her estimates of various numbers as well. Market share, for example, had been at various levels historically, but was always very close to SQZ's advertising share (SQZ's portion of total industry advertising expenditures). Her notes indicated that the rest of the industry was spending $1.5 million on advertising. Using this number, she calculated SQZ's advertising share to be 45.3 percent, which was, in fact, the number she had in the spreadsheet. This apparently checked out, so she went on to consider the other source of headquarters (HQ) spending for personnel.

HQ head count worked on quality control and cost containment. Quality control was necessary to retain product competitiveness. It had been done every year for at least the last 10 years, because quality standards were continuously moving up. Lewis had declared that if it were not done, the company would need to discount price in order to compete.

Similarly, cost containment had been done by HQ people in recent years, through both supervision of the assembly process and cost-reducing projects, which generally had led to price cuts in the industry. If the people who worked on cost containment were gone, variable costs might creep up.

Smith had no idea what the combined effects of reducing head count would be. She might try, say, $6 per unit if head count were eliminated and a proportionate amount if head count were partially reduced, just to see what would happen. She would not show this to Lewis; in fact at this stage she saw her task as one of preparing to ask Lewis the right questions, not give answers. She would complete her understanding of the quantities and relationships in her spreadsheet, then note where the gaps in her understanding were.

The Futures Position

Smith's work was interrupted when she was handed a short note from the client in her new project. The note described the client's problem as he saw it. At planting time, the client (in agribusiness) was considering a futures contract on his corn crop. More specifically, he would choose the number of bushels of corn (which might be 0) to sell for future delivery at harvest time for a set price of $3.10, which would be received at harvest time. If his crop exceeded the amount he had sold forward for future delivery, the excess would be sold at the prevailing price when the harvest came in. Conversely, if he produced less than he sold forward, he would buy the shortfall at the prevailing price at harvest. Although he had decided to plant acreage that would produce 100,000 bushels of corn in an average year, the exact number of bushels produced was highly uncertain. His objective was to maximize profit before tax, and his particular concern was to manage the risk.

Smith knew that this analysis would also be based on a spreadsheet that she would construct. "This seems like a relatively simple problem—how much analysis could it take?" she commented under her breath. This time, however, she would be careful; she would present the basic assumptions of her spreadsheet to the client, then collect some data, build the spreadsheet, and then do the analysis. The place to start was to think about the decision quantity, a performance measure for comparing alternatives, and intermediate quantities necessary to tie the two together.

EXHIBIT 1   The Critical Memo

To: Carol Smith
From: John Lewis, President
Subject: Downsizing Study

Thanks for your prompt report about downsizing our SQZ subsidiary. The sober question we're all pondering is the level of headquarters expenditures for SQZ. Your preliminary recommendation was to cut HQ expenditures by $1 million, based on your analysis, which was supported by the spreadsheet. I used your spreadsheet to test some other levels of spending. To my surprise, the profit got better and better as HQ expenditures were reduced, as you can see in my data table shown along with the spreadsheet below. This indicates we should reduce these expenditures to zero! This analysis seems naive. The spreadsheet apparently ignores several important considerations. Please tell me what is missing and how you would improve the spreadsheet.

Headquarters expenditures go for three different activities. Forty percent is spent directly on advertising. The other sixty percent pays the salaries and support expenses of people that carry out two activities: quality control and cost containment. I see that you preserved the 60–40 split between head count and advertising; this is still our planned allocation.

Won't reductions in these activities hurt us? Our analysis has to consider the consequence of cutbacks. I'm more than willing to articulate more on these consequences in our next meeting.

The Questionable Spreadsheet with Data Table

Downsize Debate (all units in thousands unless otherwise indicated)

		HQ Expenditures	Profit before Taxes	Profit after Taxes
Headquarters expenditures (000)	$3,100			
Market size (in thousand units)	300	3,100	$ 977	$ 596
Market share	45%	0	4,077	2,487
Margin (per unit)	$ 30	500	3,577	2,182
		1,000	3,077	1,877
Headquarters head-count expense	$1,860	1,500	2,577	1,572
Advertising expenditures	$1,240	2,000	2,077	1,267
Unit volume	136	2,500	1,577	962
		3,000	1,077	657
Contribution	$4,077	3,500	577	352
Fixed cost	$3,100	4,000	77	47
Profit before tax	$ 977	4,500	−423	−258
Taxes	$ 381	5,000	−923	−563
		5,500	−1,423	−868
Profit after tax	$ 596			

4 ASSESSMENT

Chapter 1 noted that the proactive decision maker does not limit the evaluation of an alternative to a single estimate of its potential performance, but acknowledges explicitly the uncertainties that affect that performance. The consideration of the spectrum of possibilities to which an alternative's performance may be subjected can lead to a better understanding of the risks involved in pursuing the alternative. This in turn can motivate the search for new alternatives that reduce those risks. In addition to acknowledging the range of potential possibilities, Chapter 1 also observed that there is a need to acknowledge the likelihood of the possibilities within that range. By considering the likelihoods, an overreaction to the extremes of an optimistic/ pessimistic analysis can be avoided and new alternatives can be developed that respond to the likely outcomes as well as to the extremes.

This chapter will develop a language for describing and communicating the spectrum of potential possibilities and tools for analyzing the impact of those possibilities on performance. The first section will present approaches for exploring and presenting the sensitivity of performance to changes in assessments. These methods will assist in identifying the key drivers of performance so that future analysis can be focused on them and attention directed to reducing their effects. In the second section, a language for describing uncertainty will be presented. This language will be the language of probability and will apply both to uncertainties for which there are a few possible outcomes and to uncertainties for which outcomes may be anywhere within a continuous range. The final section presents a tool to derive a probabilistic assessment of the performance of an alternative as a result of the probabilistic assessments of the underlying drivers of that performance.

The following example will be used to develop and illustrate the language, tools, and techniques of the chapter:

Suppose you are the product manager for a children's breakfast cereal. A special holiday trinket was recently developed, and you are considering including the trinket in your product's 28-ounce box during the two months preceding the holiday season. The trinket has performed extraordinarily well in a full battery of children's preference panels and is expected to result in a 12 percent increase in volume. Children's test panels are notoriously unreliable, however, and the increase could be anywhere between 8 and 14 percent. Without the trinket, sales of the 28-ounce box during the two-month period are forecast to be 6.5 million boxes, plus or minus 2 percent. The production process and the distribution system are sufficiently flexible to permit production to match demand. The trinket will cost $0.10 per unit, if the supplier who has worked on its development can resume production in a timely fashion after a recent fire. Fortunately, alternative sources have been found, but at a premium of either $0.010 or $0.015 per unit, depending on the final selection of the alternative vendor. The trinket will be featured on the front and back of the box and the alteration to the box's artwork is anticipated to cost $125,000. Neither the art layout nor the production modifications have been finalized, and it is believed the final cost could be 20 percent higher to 5 percent lower than the initial estimate. The 28-ounce box has a unit contribution of $1.48 per box. Would you include the trinket in the boxes for the holiday season?

Sensitivity Analysis

On the basis of best estimates of the assessments underlying the trinket's performance and assuming that total production equals total sales, the trinket will increase gross margin by $301,400 as shown in Table 4–1. Note that the increase in contribution depends only on the increase in sales due to the trinket (780,000 boxes[1]) and that the total trinket cost depends on the total volume (7,280,000 boxes). This analysis would certainly suggest that the trinket should be introduced during the holiday season. This best-estimate analysis ignores, however, the spectrum of possibilities that might occur and the impact that those possibilities might have on performance.

A common way to determine the **aggregate** impact of the potential possibilities is to specify and evaluate an **optimistic scenario** (all uncertainties result in favorable outcomes) and a **pessimistic scenario** (all uncertainties result in unfavorable outcomes). Table 4–2 presents the results of such an analysis. Note that these scenarios must be carefully composed because an

---

[1]In this case, there is no error in the base volume forecast. More generally, the volume increase will be the base volume (adjusted for forecast error) times the volume increase percentage due to the trinket.

TABLE 4–1   Increase in Contribution: Best-Estimate Scenario

Forecast error in base volume	0%
Volume increase percentage	12%
Unit cost per trinket	$0.10
Artwork cost variance	0%
Base volume (boxes)	6,500,000
Volume increase (boxes)	780,000
Increase in contribution	$1,154,400
Trinket cost	728,000
Artwork cost	125,000
Incremental gross margin	$301,400

TABLE 4–2   Increase in Contribution: Optimistic and Pessimistic Scenarios

	Optimistic	*Pessimistic*
Forecast error in base volume	2%	−2%
Volume increase percentage	14%	8%
Unit cost per trinket	$0.10	$0.115
Artwork cost variance	−5%	20%
Base volume (boxes)	6,630,000	6,370,000
Volume increase (boxes)	928,200	509,600
Increase in contribution	$1,373,736	$754,208
Trinket cost	755,820	791,154
Artwork cost	118,750	150,000
Incremental gross margin	$499,166	−$186,946

optimistic scenario does not necessarily have all the underlying uncertainties at the high-end of their possible ranges. In the trinket example, an artwork cost variance of minus 5 percent is part of the specification of the optimistic scenario, even though it is the low end of the possible range for the artwork cost. Whether or not a variable is at its high end or its low end for a particular extreme scenario depends on the direction of the variable's effect on the performance measure. If a variable has a positive effect on performance (i.e., when the variable increases, performance increases), then the variable should be at its low end in a pessimistic scenario and at its high end in an optimistic scenario. If the variable has a negative effect on performance, then it should be at its high end in a pessimistic scenario and at its low end in an optimistic scenario. Intuition is often, but not always, a reliable guide in assessing the direction of effect.[2]

_____

[2]The one-at-a-time analysis that will be developed later in this section can serve as a check of one's intuition on the directional effect of a variable.

TABLE 4–3   One-at-a-Time Sensitivity Analysis: Volume Increase Percentage

	Lowest Value	*Highest Value*
Forecast error in base volume	0%	0%
Volume increase percentage	8%	14%
Unit cost per trinket	$0.10	$0.10
Artwork cost variance	0%	0%
Base volume (boxes)	6,500,000	6,500,000
Volume increase (boxes)	520,000	910,000
Increase in contribution	$1,346,800	$769,600
Trinket cost	741,000	702,000
Artwork cost	125,000	125,000
Incremental gross margin	$480,800	−$57,400

These two extreme scenarios suggest that the uncertainty in the assessments has a significant impact on performance—enough to swing the decision from a substantial gain (nearly a half a million dollars) to a substantial loss (nearly two hundred thousand dollars). If this aggregate risk is to be proactively managed, the key drivers of the risk need to be identified. This leads to the question, which of the several sources of uncertainty are the principal sources of the risk?

One way to determine the key drivers of performance is to conduct a **one-at-a-time** sensitivity analysis. Such an analysis begins with the base case, that is, the best-estimate scenario. It then evaluates each potential source of uncertainty at its extreme values, while holding all the other uncertainties at their best-estimate values. Note that the one-at-a-time analysis is conducted on the basis of the decision maker's extreme values for the uncertainties, not on the basis of plus and minus some percentage from the base case. By focusing on the extreme values, the analysis will show the total potential impact of the uncertainty over its relevant range, not just the incremental effect of changing the value of the uncertainty by some arbitrary amount. For the uncertainty in the volume percentage increase attributed to the trinket, the incremental gross margin would be evaluated with the percentage at 8 percent and with the percentage at 14 percent. These results are shown in Table 4–3. For the best-estimate scenario, the incremental gross margin is $301,400. Changes in the volume increase percentage can by itself swing the evaluation from an even more positive outcome to a disappointingly negative outcome. Performance is sensitive to changes in this estimate.

The results of similar analyses for each of the uncertainties are reported in Table 4–4. The volume increase percentage has by far the most significant effect. It has the largest difference in performance between its extreme values ($538,200); it results in the greatest upside potential ($480,800) and the

TABLE 4–4   One-at-a-Time Sensitivity Analysis: All Uncertainties

	Lowest Value		Highest Value	
Uncertainty	*Value*	*Performance*	*Value*	*Performance*
Forecast error	−2%	$292,872	2%	$309,928
Volume increase percentage	8%	−$57,400	14%	$480,800
Unit cost per trinket	$0.10	$301,400	$0.115	$192,200
Artwork cost variance	−5%	$307,650	20%	$276,400

greatest downside exposure (−$57,400). The volume increase percentage is clearly a key driver of performance. On the other hand, the least significant uncertainty is the forecast error—the range in performance between its extreme values is only $17,056. Note that the results in Table 4–4 confirm the earlier observation that the artwork cost variance has a negative effect on performance (as does unit cost per trinket).

The impacts of the one-at-a-time variations in the uncertainties can be graphically presented as in Figure 4–1. There are several features of this chart worth noting. The uncertainties are ordered according to the swing in performance between their extreme values. The largest swing in performance is at the top of the chart; the smallest is at the bottom. The base case is presented as a reference point. The values for the uncertainties that gave rise to the results are shown near their performance results. Because of the ordering of the uncertainties, the chart will always have the appearance of a funnel. This distinctive shape is the source of the chart's name, **tornado diagram.**

The one-at-a-time sensitivity analysis shows that when the volume increase percentage is at its lowest potential value (8 percent) and all the other uncertainties are at their best estimates, the incremental gross margin is negative (−$57,400) and the trinket should not be introduced. How low could the volume increase percentage go before the incremental gross margin turns negative? Equivalently, at what volume increase percentage does the incremental gross margin equal zero or what's the threshold at which the volume increase percentage drives the incremental gross margin to negative? A **threshold analysis**[3] can be conducted by trial and error. If the volume increase percentage is 8 percent, the incremental gross margin is negative, so the threshold is above 8 percent. What if the volume increase percentage is 9 percent? Using the same spreadsheet as Table 4–1 but with volume increase percentage at 9 percent results in an incremental gross margin of $32,300. The threshold must be between 8 and 9 percent. What if the volume increase

---

[3]Analyses of this nature are often called break-even analyses. The term *threshold analysis* is chosen here because the marketing discipline widely uses the term break-even analyses to refer to a special case of threshold analyses (the volume at which contribution equals fixed cost).

FIGURE 4–1
Tornado Diagram

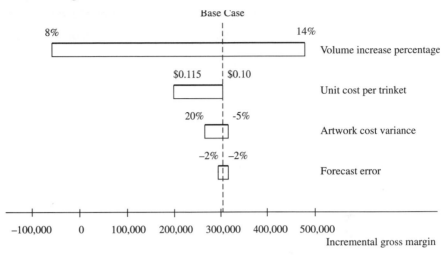

percentage is 8.5 percent? The incremental gross margin is now −$12,550, so the threshold must be between 8.5 and 9 percent. What if the volume increase percentage is 8.75 percent? The incremental gross margin is now $9,875, so the threshold is between 8.5 and 8.75 percent. This trial and error search can be continued until the incremental gross margin gets as close to zero as desired. The actual threshold is 8.64 percent.[4] This threshold is interpreted as follows: If the volume increase percentage is below 8.64 percent and all other uncertainties are at their best-estimate values, the incremental gross margin will be negative; if above 8.64 percent, the incremental gross margin will be positive.

The threshold can also be found algebraically. Let the volume increase percentage be called X and let us find the value of X for which the incremental gross margin is zero. The incremental gross margin involves three terms: the increase in contribution, the trinket cost, and the artwork cost. The first two of these change when the volume increase percentage changes. The increase in contribution is $1.48 times the volume increase. The trinket cost is $0.10 times the total volume. The artwork cost is constant at $125,000. The following algebraic expression for incremental gross margin captures these relationships:

---

[4]With an Excel spreadsheet, the Table command from the Data menu can be used to create a one-way table in which the performance measure is evaluated at several input values of the volume increase percentage. Furthermore, the search can be automated with the Goal Seek command from the Options menu by instructing the software to set the incremental gross margin cell to the value zero by changing the volume increase percentage cell.

$$\{1.48 \times 6{,}500{,}000 \times X\} - \{.10 \times (6{,}500{,}000 + 6{,}500{,}000 \times X)\}$$
$$- 125{,}000.$$

Simplifying this expression and setting it equal to zero results in the equation

$$\{9{,}620{,}000 \times X\} - \{650{,}000 + 650{,}000 \times X\} - 125{,}000 = 0.$$

The solution of this equation is

$$X = 775{,}000/8{,}970{,}000 = .0864,$$

the same threshold that was discovered by trial and error. In summary, the process for an algebraic solution is to let the value of the variable in question be X, develop an algebraic expression for the performance measure as a function of X, set the expression equal to zero, and solve the equation for X.

This section explored various means for understanding the impact of uncertainty on the performance of an alternative. First, the aggregate impact of the potential possibilities was determined by evaluating an optimistic scenario and a pessimistic scenario. Second, the key drivers of performance were determined by conducting one-at-a-time sensitivity analyses for each of the uncertainties. The results of these analyses were then summarized in a tornado diagram. For those uncertainties whose impacts were sufficiently large to change the performance of an alternative from positive to negative (or vice versa), the one-at-a-time analysis was refined by finding threshold values, either by trial and error or by algebra.

The Language of Probability

A full understanding of the potential impact of uncertainty on the performance of an alternative includes an assessment of the likelihood with which the potential outcomes might occur. If likelihoods are ignored, the proactive decision maker may overreact to the possibility of an extreme outcome even though its likelihood may be minimal. By assessing the likelihoods, the proactive decision maker can be guided by those likelihoods in interpreting appropriately the impact of uncertainty on an alternative and can also productively focus attention in directions that may lead to new alternatives with improved performance and reduced risks. This section will introduce the language of probability as a means to express judgments about likelihoods. Chapter 11 will further develop the vocabulary of probability and suggest various means to augment the probability assessment process.

Uncertainties with a Few Potential Outcomes

The language of probability, as it applies to uncertainties with a few potential outcomes, is very much part of everyone's day-to-day speaking. There are overt probability statements such as "the probability is more than 90 percent." In addition, there are statements that use a variety of synonyms for probability: "the chances of that happening are 20 percent," "that wouldn't happen more than one out of five times," and "the odds are four to one against that happening."[5] Such statements are often off the cuff and are made without deliberately considering the probability assessment that is being offered.

In the trinket example, it might be stated that "there is a 75 percent chance that our original supplier will resume production in time to meet our schedule." What does this mean? It is easy and common to think of probability in terms of relative frequency. A 75 percent chance of occurrence is interpreted to mean that, if the situation in question were to present itself many times, the event would occur in three out of four of the occasions. Although this is the most easily communicated interpretation, it does not apply in the case of the trinket vendor. There will be only one occasion; it is impossible for there to be the multiple occurrences required by the relative frequency interpretation. In these one-shot situations, probability must be interpreted as an **intensity of belief.** A 75 percent chance means the assessor believes the chances of the event occurring are three times as likely as it not occurring. If the assessor's belief in the event occurring were more intense, say nine times, the probability would be 90 percent.

The degree-of-belief interpretation moves probability from the objective world of relative frequency in which everyone can agree on the appropriate calculation of a probability, to a world of subjectivity where personal judgment is the determinant of probabilities and where individual judgments may legitimately differ. How can such judgmental probabilities be assessed?

As suggested by the degree-of-belief interpretation, the assessment of judgmental probabilities boils down to the assessment of the relative likelihood of an event occurring as compared to the event not occurring. These judgments are often difficult to make and can be constructively assisted (or checked) by engaging the assessor in a process that involves choosing between two hypothetical options. In the first option, a desirable prize will be won if the event being assessed occurs. If the event does not occur, the assessor receives neither a reward nor a penalty. Such an option is certainly attractive because there is no downside, only upside opportunity. In the second option, the assessor will hold a specified number of tickets in a lottery for which there are 100 tickets. The same desirable prize as in the first option will be won if one of the assessor's tickets is drawn and the same neutral outcome will occur if one of the assessor's tickets is not drawn.

The assessment process begins by indicating that the assessor has a certain number of tickets, say 20, and asking which option is the more desirable. Because the two options have the same prizes, the assessor's choice will implicitly communicate which option has the more likely mechanism for

---

[5]All three of these statements imply a 20 percent probability of occurrence.

winning the desirable prize. Suppose that in the case of the trinket supplier, the answer is the first option. From this choice, it can be concluded that the assessor believes the chances of the original vendor being able to supply the trinket are at least 20 percent. Note that this assessment process is using an objective probability to help assess a subjective probability. The process continues by indicating that the assessor has a different number of tickets, say 90, and asking for a choice. Suppose the answer is the second option. Now it can be concluded that the chances of the original vendor being able to supply the trinket are less than 90 percent. On the basis of these two statements, the probability is somewhere between 20 and 90 percent. The process continues by offering a different number of tickets in a fashion such that the bounds are gradually shrunk and the assessor ultimately becomes indifferent between the two options. Suppose that in the trinket vendor example, the process ends with the assessor being indifferent when 70 tickets are offered. On the basis of this process, the probability of the original vendor supplying the trinket is 70 percent, different from the original statement of 75 percent.

If the original assessment was based on the judgment that the relative likelihood was three to one, it is not surprising that the two assessments are slightly different. By their nature, relative likelihood assessments are rather lumpy—one to one (50 percent), two to one (66 percent), three to one (75 percent), four to one (80 percent), and so on. The lottery comparison offers slightly more specificity because the number of tickets can be finely adjusted.[6]

To finish the probability assessment of the cost of the trinket, assume it is equally likely that the cost will be $0.110 and $0.115 if the original vendor does not supply the trinket. This assessment of a one-to-one relative likelihood could be checked by employing the process just described. Because there is a 30 percent chance that the original vendor will not supply the trinket (probabilities must sum to one), the probabilities of each of these two possibilities is 15 percent. The complete probability assessment of the cost of the trinket is then:

Cost	Probability
$0.100	.70
$0.110	.15
$0.115	.15

---

[6]In theory, the lottery approach can be adjusted to within a probability of 0.01. There are, however, practical limits to which an assessor's judgment can comfortably be expressed. Experience suggests that these limits are plus or minus 0.10 for most assessors.

FIGURE 4–2
Probability Distribution for Unit Cost per Trinket

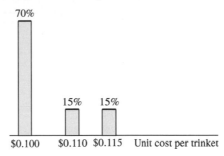

The graph of this assessment is shown in Figure 4–2. This full assessment is called a **probability distribution**—an assignment of a probability to each of the possible outcomes of an uncertainty.

Uncertainties with Many Potential Outcomes

In the trinket example, there are several uncertainties (the volume forecast error, the volume increase percentage, and the artwork cost variance) that cannot be legitimately characterized as having a few possible outcomes. The outcomes of these uncertainties can be any value within a range and, as a result, there are an extremely large number of possible outcomes. It would be impossible to assess the probability of each one of them using the process described above. Even so, the notion of relative likelihood still applies—some outcomes within the range may be relatively more likely than others.

Let us consider two possibilities. First, suppose there is no reason to assume that any one outcome within the range is more likely than any other outcome. In this case, the relative likelihoods would be constant for all values within the range. This probability distribution is called the **uniform distribution** and is defined by two numbers, the minimum and the maximum possible outcomes for the uncertainty. Suppose the volume forecast error was judged to be equally likely for any possible outcome within its potential range of −2 percent to +2 percent. The graph of its probabilities is shown in Figure 4–3. Note that the relative likelihood abruptly drops to zero at the limits of the range of possibilities.

An assessor's judgment regarding the relative likelihoods within the range of possibilities can be more focused than being equally likely everywhere within that range. This focus is often expressed in terms of a most likely value, away from which the likelihoods steadily decline until they reach zero at the extremes of the range. This probability distribution is called a **triangular distribution** and is defined by three numbers, the minimum, the

FIGURE 4–3
Probability Distribution for Volume Forecast Error

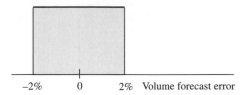

FIGURE 4–4
*Probability Distributions for Volume Increase Percentage
and for Artwork Cost Variance*

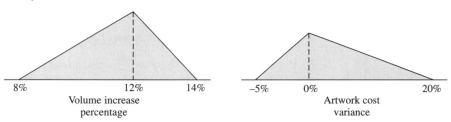

most likely (ML), and the maximum possible outcomes for the uncertainty. Suppose the volume increase percentage and the artwork cost variance were judged to have a triangular distribution. The graphs of these probability distributions are shown in Figure 4–4.

Summary Measures of Probability Distributions

The probability distribution is a complete and detailed description of the probability assessment of an uncertain quantity. It is sometimes useful, however, to refer to certain characteristics of a distribution that partially summarize its properties. There are two major categories of such summary measures—those that provide measures of the "center" of the distribution and those that provide measures of the "dispersion" of the distribution.

The most commonly quoted summary of the center of the distribution is the **mean.** The mean is the sum (over all possible outcomes) of each outcome multiplied by its probability. For the probability distribution of the unit cost per trinket, the mean is

$$(\$0.100 \times .70) + (\$0.110 \times .15) + (\$0.115 \times .15) = \$0.10375$$

Note that the mean is not one of the possible outcomes of the distribution, nor does it have to be. It is simply the weighted average of the outcomes with the probabilities used as the weights. In a physical analogy, the mean is the balancing point of a bar that has the weight of each probability placed along it at points corresponding to the potential outcome with which that probability is associated. It is the "center" of the distribution, in the sense of the weighted average. With this analogy in mind, the mean of the uniform distribution will simply be the midpoint of its range, (Minimum + Maximum)/2, because all outcomes are equally weighted (equally likely). As a result, the mean of the distribution of the volume forecast error is zero. The mean of a triangular distribution cannot be so easily discerned, but its formula is equally simple, (Minimum + ML + Maximum)/3. For the probability distribution of the volume increase percentage, the mean is an 11.33 percent increase; for the artwork cost variance, the mean is a 5 percent cost variance.

A second summary measure of the center of a probability distribution is the **mode,** the most likely outcome of the uncertain quantity. For the probability distribution of the unit cost per trinket, the mode is $0.100, the most probable outcome. A distribution can have more than one mode. This is the case for the uniform distribution where all the possible outcomes are modes of the distribution because they are all equally likely. The mode of the triangular distribution is the most likely outcome (one of the defining parameters). The mode is a 12 percent increase in volume in the case of the volume increase percentage and a zero percent cost variance in the case of the artwork cost variance.

A third measure of centrality is the **median.** Loosely speaking, the median is that outcome that divides the range of possible outcomes in half, probabilistically. Due to the lumpiness of distributions of uncertainties with a few possible outcomes, formal definitions of the median tend to be rather awkward. One such definition is the following: The median of a probability distribution is the value for which it is true that (1) there is at least a .50 probability of that value or smaller, and (2) there is at least a .50 probability of that value or greater. For the distribution of unit cost per trinket, the median is $0.100—the probability of being $0.100 or less is .70 (more than .50) and the probability of being $0.100 or more is 1.00 (more than .50). Because all outcomes are equally likely, the median of the uniform distribution is the midpoint of the range, (Minimum + Maximum)/2. The formula for the median of a triangular distribution is more complex and depends on the position of the most likely outcome relative to the midpoint of the range,

$$\text{if ML} \leq (\text{Minimum} + \text{Maximum})/2, \text{ median}$$
$$= \text{Maximum} - \sqrt{(\text{Maximum} - \text{Minimum})(\text{Maximum} - \text{ML})/2},$$

$$\text{if ML} \geq (\text{Minimum} + \text{Maximum})/2, \text{ median}$$
$$= \text{Minimum} + \sqrt{(\text{Maximum} - \text{Minimum})(\text{ML} - \text{Minimum})/2}.$$

The median for the distribution of the volume increase percentage is 11.46 percent; the median for the distribution of the artwork cost variance is 4.19 percent. Thus, there is a 50 percent chance that the volume increase percentage will be less than 11.46 percent. Similarly, there is a 50 percent chance that the artwork cost variance will be less than 4.19 percent.

Notice that the mean, the mode, and the median of a probability distribution are not necessarily the same values, nor are they necessarily different. Each of these summary measures takes a different perspective on the notion of centrality—the mean is a weighted average, the mode is the most likely, and the median is the 50 percent point. There is no reason for these different perspectives to yield identical results, nor are they necessarily different. For the distribution of the volume increase percentage, the mean, the mode, and the median are different values. For the distribution of the forecast error, a zero percentage error is the mean, the median and one of the modes.

An often-used measure of the dispersion of a probability distribution is the **range,** the difference between the largest and smallest possible outcome. For each of the distributions considered in the trinket evaluation, the range is well defined. There are, however, probability distributions for which it is impossible to quote the range because there is no clearly defined smallest or largest outcome.[7] This difficulty is avoided by quoting the range between the **.10 fractile** and the **.90 fractile**. A fractile is a generalization of the concept of the median; in fact, the median is the .50 fractile. The informal definition of the k-fractile is that it is the outcome for which the probability of being below that value is k (the more precise definition has the same cumbersome structure as the definition of the median and will not be stated here).

Another frequently quoted measure of dispersion is the **standard deviation.** Loosely speaking, the standard deviation can be interpreted as the average amount by which individual outcomes differ from the mean of the distribution. More precisely, the standard deviation is the square root of the weighted average of the individual outcome's squared deviations from the mean. For the probability distributions of uncertainties with a few possible outcomes, this calculation is relatively straightforward: find the deviations of each outcome from the mean, square each deviation, multiply each squared deviation by its respective probability, sum these weighted squared deviations, and finally take the square root of the sum. This method is illustrated in Table 4–5 for the probability distribution of the unit cost per trinket. The larger the standard deviation, the more dispersed is the distribution. Although it is popular to interpret the standard deviation in terms of the chances that the outcome will be within one or two standard deviations of the mean, this interpretation only applies to the normal distribution (a topic for Chapter 11) and not to distributions in general.

---

[7]Several distributions with this property will be considered in Chapter 11, in particular, the normal, the Poisson, and the exponential distributions.

TABLE 4–5   Calculating the Standard Deviation of the Unit Cost per Trinket

Cost	Probability	Deviation from the Mean of $0.10375	Squared Deviation	Probability × Squared Deviation
$0.100	.70	−0.00375	0.00001406	0.000009842
0.110	.15	0.00625	0.00003906	0.000005859
0.115	.15	0.01125	0.00012656	0.000018984
				0.000034685

Standard deviation = $\sqrt{.000034685}$ = .00589

A summary measure that is very closely related to the standard deviation is the **variance.** The variance is the standard deviation squared and thus can be interpreted as the averaged squared amount by which individual outcomes differ from the mean. Note that this figure was calculated in the next to last step of computing the standard deviation. As with the standard deviation, the larger the variance, the larger the dispersion of the probability distribution.

Although these summary measures are sometimes useful in characterizing the center and the dispersion of uncertain quantities, it is emphasized that they are *not* a substitute for the complete description provided by the probability distribution function.

Deriving the Probability Distribution for Performance

As was noted earlier in this chapter, a preliminary analysis would suggest that the trinket should be introduced because it will result in an incremental gross margin of $301,400. This appraisal was based on best estimates of the assessments underlying the trinket's performance. When the impact of the uncertainty in those estimates was quantified, the decision was not quite so clear. Optimistically, the trinket could increase the gross margin by as much as $499,166. On the other hand, the trinket could reduce gross margin by $186,946, if the pessimistic scenario were to materialize. The actual outcome will be somewhere between these extremes, and the decision must depend on the probability distribution of the incremental gross margin. If that distribution is heavily weighted to the high end of the range, the decision may be to introduce the trinket; if it is heavily weighted to the low end, the decision may be the opposite.

Because the incremental gross margin is a consequence of the outcomes of the underlying uncertainties, its probability distribution will be determined by the probability distributions of the underlying uncertainties. Recall that the extreme values for the incremental gross margin were calculated on the basis of scenarios composed of extreme values for each of the underlying uncertainties. Similarly, the distribution of the incremental gross margin could be based on a collection of scenarios composed of representative values from the probability distributions of each of the underlying uncertainties. What would be the properties of a collection of representative scenarios? First, if the probability of an outcome occurring is 70 percent, that outcome should be present in 70 percent of the scenarios. Second, if the scenarios are viewed in sequence, the outcomes of a particular uncertainty should "jump around" among its potential outcomes. A collection of scenarios with these two properties is called a **random sample.** Random in the sense of unpredictable, but not in the sense of freewheeling, because the frequency of occurrence is dictated by the underlying probability distributions.

Within a large random sample,[8] the vast array of possible outcomes would have an opportunity to occur in their various combinations. As a result, the relative frequency of the incremental gross margin within the random sample can be used as an estimate of its probability distribution.

The creation of a sufficiently large random sample is greatly facilitated by several commercially available electronic spreadsheet add-ins.[9] Starting with an electronic spreadsheet that calculates the relevant performance measures, these add-ins permit the cells containing the values for the underlying uncertainties to be replaced by special functions representing the probability distributions of those uncertainties. The software then creates a random sample and reports the results for selected output cells.

For the trinket example, the electronic spreadsheet that was used to assess the aggregate risk of the decision and to conduct the one-at-a-time sensitivity analysis of the tornado diagram is the starting point. The cells for the four uncertainties (forecast error in base volume, volume increase percentage, unit cost per trinket, and artwork cost variance) would be replaced by special functions representing their probability distributions, as shown in Figures 4–2, 4–3, and 4–4. The software would then create a random sample and report the resulting distribution of incremental gross margin. The results of a random sample of 1,000 scenarios are reported in Figure 4–5. The interpretation of these results is the topic of the next chapter.

Summary

This chapter developed processes, languages, and tools for assessing and describing the impact of uncertainty on the performance of alternatives. The assessment process began with sensitivity analysis. The aggregate impact of

---

[8]Techniques for understanding how large the random sample must be will be developed in Chapter 12.

[9]@RISK and Crystal Ball are the two most widely used tools of this nature.

FIGURE 4–5
Probability Distribution for Incremental Gross Margin

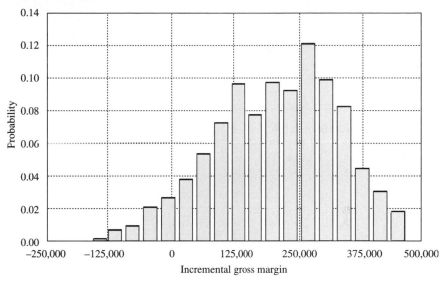

the uncertainties was assessed through the evaluation of an optimistic scenario and a pessimistic scenario. The key drivers of performance were identified through a one-at-a-time sensitivity analysis in which each uncertainty is evaluated at its extreme values while holding all other uncertainties at their best-estimate values. The results of the one-at-a-time sensitivity analysis were summarized in a tornado diagram. For those uncertainties whose impact was sufficient to swing performance from positive to negative (or vice versa), the threshold at which the transition took place was computed. Each of these sensitivity analyses addresses the possibility of uncertainties making a difference in the evaluation of an alternative.

The assessment process continued by adding to the overall appraisal, the probability with which the potential outcomes of an uncertainty might occur. The language of probability was used to express judgments about the assessor's intensity of belief regarding the potential outcomes of uncertainties. These judgments were collected into a probability distribution which assigned to each potential outcome a probability. The probability distribution is a full description of an uncertainty. Several measures of centrality (mean, mode, and median) and of dispersion (range, fractile, and standard deviation) were introduced as means to partially summarize and communicate key properties of the full distribution.

The assessment process ended by deriving the probability distribution of an alternative's performance from the probability distributions of the individual uncertainties influencing that performance. Potential scenarios were created by randomly defining an outcome for each of the underlying uncertainties in accordance with that uncertainty's probability distribution. A large collection of these scenarios (a large random sample of potential scenarios) would be representative of the potential performance of an alternative and, as a result, would closely estimate the probability distribution of performance. The interpretation of that probability distribution is the topic of the next chapter.

5   PERFORMANCE

In prior chapters we have discussed alternatives, and the structuring and assessment of assumptions, all of which leads us toward the measurement of performance and the comparison of alternatives. This discussion starts by considering which monetary measures are relevant for comparing alternatives and moves to the comparison of alternatives under uncertainty.

Relevant Monetary Flows

Relevant monetary flows are those that depend on which alternative is selected. Those monetary flows that are not relevant are constant with respect to the decision being made and can be ignored.[1] The following example will help illustrate the concept of relevant cash flows.

> Jonathon is an apple grower who purchased his orchard 10 years ago for $20,000. Normal cultivating and maintenance costs are $1,000 per year, and picking costs are another $1,500. The average yield from the orchard is 5,000 bushels. Jonathon has been thinking about using a new fertilizer that he expects to increase yields by 10 percent. He wonders whether it might be worth the $500 cost. Jonathon expects to sell his apples at the market price of $1.35 per bushel.

Which of the monetary flows mentioned in this example are relevant to Jonathon's decision concerning the new fertilizer?

---

[1]There may be exceptional instances where a constant monetary quantity is part of the context for decision making and should not be ignored in evaluating performance. For example, to adequately judge how much risk we might be willing to take on, we would benefit from knowing the value of all other assets we own even though they are not affected by the decision at hand.

First, the $20,000 cost of the orchard is not relevant. This flow occurred in the past and nothing that Jonathon does now can change this, including anything he does about a new fertilizer. A cost or cash flow that occurred in the past is sometimes called a **sunk cost**. Decisions should be forward-looking and reflect the comparative or incremental effects of the choices we make. If we include past flows in our analysis, we might burden good alternatives with past sins or credit bad alternatives with unrelated successes. We really want to credit every alternative with exactly what it deserves.

The cultivation and maintenance costs of the orchard are not relevant to this decision. We expect that Jonathon will continue to cultivate and maintain his orchard as he has in the past. His decision to use the new fertilizer will not affect this $1,000 annual operating expense. This is one example of a **fixed cost**, one that does not change with volume, in this instance the amount of apples produced. Because this cost is fixed, it is not relevant to the decision at hand. For many decisions, such as common pricing decisions, the relevant monetary value is contribution margin, or contribution to fixed costs, which accounts for revenue and variable costs, but not fixed costs. Be careful, however, not to think that a fixed cost is never a relevant flow; there are some decisions that will affect fixed costs, for example the decision not to produce apples for a season.

So far the flows considered have been easy to judge as either relevant or irrelevant to the decision. What about the $1,500 picking cost? This one is a little more difficult. If the picking cost is related to the number of bushels produced and if the number of bushels produced is affected by the decision about the fertilizer, then this cost is relevant. At first glance you might think it is obvious that the picking cost is relevant. However, even if the new fertilizer results in extra picking time but the picking is done by salaried year-round employees, there may be no increase in costs. The extra time spent picking may simply mean less time spent on other activities with negligible effects on Jonathon. This example illustrates that sometimes it can require some thought and maybe some investigation to identify relevant monetary flows. Let's proceed with the assumption that picking costs vary directly with number of bushels.

The $500 cost of the new fertilizer is definitely a relevant flow as it is incurred only if Jonathon chooses to use the new fertilizer. Finally, the revenue received from the apples is also a relevant flow because the number of bushels produced will be affected by Jonathon's decision.

Using just the relevant monetary flows in this instance, we can calculate the effects of using the new fertilizer in this way:

Revenue from increased yield − *Additional picking cost*

− *Cost of fertilizer* =

$[(10\%) \times (5,000 \text{ bushels}) \times \$1.35] - [(10\%) \times (5,000 \text{ bushels}) \times \$0.30]$

$- \$500 = \$675 - \$150 - \$500 = \$25$

On this basis, Jonathon should use the new fertilizer.

This seems easy, and you are wondering perhaps, how anyone could foul this up. Consider several common relevant flow mistakes:

1. *Allocating fixed costs.* Accountants may wish to answer other important questions unrelated to the decision at hand. For instance, they may wish to know what it is costing us to produce a bushel of apples, so they take the fixed cultivation and maintenance cost, divide by 5,000, getting $.20 which they might include with the $.30 of picking cost to get a total cost per unit of $.50. If we used this number in our calculation, we would have as the incremental profit (loss) due to the new fertilizer,

$$.1*5,000*(1.35 - .5) - 500 = -\$75.$$

   The resulting loss would suggest that we shouldn't use the new fertilizer. And what have we assumed in doing this? We've assumed that an increase in volume due to the new fertilizer will increase cultivation and maintenance cost, which we have already claimed is constant. Our decisions should, again, always look forward and should capture the true economic effects. Accountants, on the other hand, are generally looking backward to report how well the firm did, which means they sometimes must allocate fixed costs to activities. To the accountant, all costs are relevant and cannot be ignored. Making a decision is different—if irrelevant costs are included, we can make the wrong decision. Be suspicious of items labeled as an "allocation" or a "charge."

2. *Ignoring effects elsewhere in the company.* Suppose that by switching to the new fertilizer, Jonathon loses a $40 rebate from the cooperative that sold him his former fertilizer. Considering this effect would suggest that the new fertilizer should not be used. In looking at opportunities within firms, it is necessary to consider the effect of a decision throughout the firm: erosion of sales elsewhere in the firm, increasing costs to other projects/divisions, for example. Many times abandonment costs are ignored; for example, use of the new fertilizer may require some environmental cleanup sometime in the future.

3. *Including flows of unrelated activities.* Alternatives may be grouped into packages in such a way that a particular package looks undesirable or less desirable than another. However, if the alternatives are unbundled into the smallest separable components, a particular component from the less desirable package may turn out to be the most desirable. There is no value in confounding alternatives that are separable; separate the wheat from the chaff.

Identifying the appropriate relevant monetary flows for your decision will require thought and judgment. The influence diagram from Chapter 3 will undoubtedly aid the consideration of which monetary flows are and are not affected by decision quantities. And consideration of relevant monetary flows may be useful in building the influence diagram.

This process may uncover some related issues that will be taken up in later chapters. One important concern is that monetary flows do not all occur at the same time, and hence would not be valued the same and should not be lumped together. Methods for dealing with multi-period consequences will be addressed in Chapter 7. Another issue is that there may be many attributes affected by the decision, only some of which are monetary. Chapter 8 describes how to combine multiple attributes to make decisions, even when those attributes may affect different stakeholders.

Evaluating Alternatives under Uncertainty

Comparison of the performance of alternatives is simple when there is a single monetary value and there is no uncertainty. Presumably, it is clear whether we want to increase or decrease the monetary value; we want to maximize contribution or maximize profit, but minimize costs. In conditions of uncertainty, however, there is more than one possible outcome that we must somehow weigh to compare alternatives. In considering how to evaluate the performance of alternatives under uncertainty, we will first consider situations in which there are but a few potential outcomes.

Few Potential Outcomes

To illustrate consider the litigation decision of Chapter 3. Let us complete the decision tree in Figure 3–12 to include probabilities and monetary outcomes, as shown in Figure 5–1. The numbers at the right end of the branches represent the relevant payoff from the litigation, the damage payment less any costs of conducting the litigation. The numbers above branches emanating from event nodes (the circles) are probabilities assessed using the methods described in Chapter 4. Without delineating the thinking behind these numbers, let's accept them as including all of the relevant monetary flows and turn our attention to how the performance of the alternatives could be compared and the decisions made.

If we start at the left side of the tree to consider whether or not to sue, we face an immediate complication. Performance of the "sue" alternative depends on whether we win, lose, or the case is thrown out. We'll need to consider all the possible outcomes as we make the choice. In addition, we must anticipate how the alternatives will play out. For example, to evaluate the "lose" branch, we must anticipate whether we will appeal or not. Let's consider this choice first, and then return to the decision of whether to sue or not.

FIGURE 5–1   *Decision Tree for Litigation with Probabilities and Relevant Monetary Outcomes*

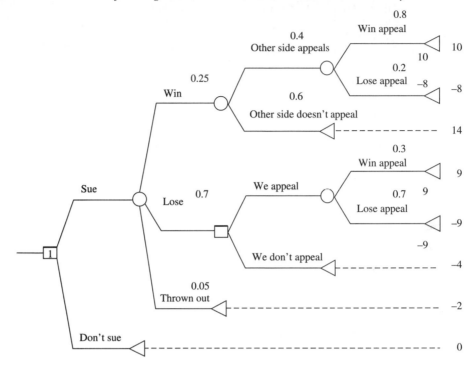

In the scenario in which we decide to sue and then lose, we face the decision subtree shown in Figure 5–2. The most favorable outcome would be to win the appeal. However, if we appeal and lose, we will lose $9 million; in fact, it is more likely that we will lose (probability equals .7) than win the appeal. If we don't appeal, our outcome is to lose $4 million, due to our legal and court costs.

To decide whether or not to appeal if we lose, we should consider all possible outcomes associated with such an appeal and their likelihood of occurrence. These are shown as a probability distribution in Figure 5–3. Because this probability distribution describes everything there is to know about the risks we face if we lose and then appeal, it is called the **risk profile** of this option. The risk profile shows what we are betting on if we should choose to appeal. We need to weigh the outcomes and their associated probabilities as summarized in the risk profile in deciding whether or not the appeal is preferable to not appealing.

As we mull over the implications of the risk profile, it might help our thinking to consider the summary measures of probability distributions described in Chapter 4. Of particular interest is the mean of the distribution, the weighted average of the outcomes where the weights are the associated

FIGURE 5–2

Our Decision whether to Appeal if We Sue and Lose

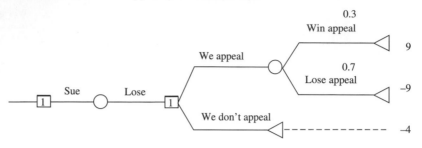

probabilities. When computed for a probability distribution where the outcomes are the potential monetary consequences of an action, the mean is known as the **expected monetary value** (EMV). The mean of the probability distribution depicted in Figure 5–3 is

$$.3*9 + .7*(-9) = -3.6$$

which indicates that the EMV of appealing our loss is a negative $3.6 million. In general, the formula for calculating the EMV of a course of action having a few possible outcomes is

$$\text{EMV} = \Sigma_i \text{ Probability}_i * \text{Monetary value}_i,$$

where the subscript *i* refers to the ith outcome and Σ_i is read as the summation for all *i*.

Clearly, in the event we lose and appeal, the EMV number of −3.6 is not an outcome that ever occurs. The advantage it has, however, is that it combines both the consequences of action and their likelihoods into a single number. If one were to look for one number that represents the "center" of the risk profile, this number would come to mind. If we faced 1,000 situations in which the risk profile of Figure 5–3 accurately described the consequences and their likelihoods in each individual situation, then the *average* of our realizations over all 1,000 replications would be very close to the EMV of −3.6.[2]

The EMV for the "we appeal" alternative exceeds the consequence associated with the "we don't appeal" branch (−4). This in itself does not mean we must take that choice. Indeed, the alternatives are close, and given that the negative $4 million is an outcome with certainty, a judgment taking risk aversion into account could be made that it is the preferable alternative.

---

[2]In other words, sum up the monetary consequence of all 1,000 replications and divide by 1,000; this number will be very close to −3.6. The more replications we do, the closer this average will likely be to −3.6.

FIGURE 5–3
Risk Profile if Appeal

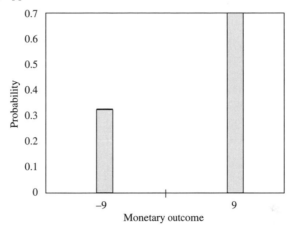

Let's assume, however, that the decision is made that if we lose the case, we will appeal on the basis of a slightly better EMV.

Given we have anticipated and evaluated the appeal decision, we now can think about the original decision whether to sue or not. If we consider every possible outcome of that choice and the associated probability, we face the risk profile shown in Figure 5–4. The probabilities in the risk profile were calculated by multiplying the probabilities along the path to that outcome. For example, the probability of $10 million is .08, the product of the probabilities that we win, .25, that the other party then appeals, .4, and that we win that appeal, .8. Because the outcomes are mutually exclusive and collectively exhaustive, the sum of the probabilities on the risk profile is 1.0. Note that the −$4 million outcome from not appealing if we lose the suit is not on the diagram; instead the outcomes after appealing, if we lose, namely + $9 million and −$9 million, are. This is consistent with our earlier decision that we would appeal if we lose.

There are a number of intriguing aspects of this risk profile, which at first look a little odd. There is more upward potential (+$14 million) than downward exposure (−$9 million), which is attractive. On the other hand, the most likely outcome is the worst outcome, −$9 million, with a probability of .49. A negative outcome (probability .56) happens more often than a positive one. These characteristics of a risk profile—the high value, the low value, where probability is concentrated, the probability of losing monetary value— are all important in evaluating the risk profile. Also important would be the EMV, which we calculate as

$$EMV = .49*-9 + .02*-8 + .05*-2 + .21*9 + .08*10 + .15*14 = .12.$$

FIGURE 5–4

Risk Profile for Sue Alternative

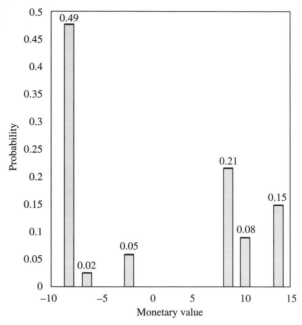

Since this is positive, we would choose to sue on the basis of EMV alone. Of course, on the basis of the risk characteristics we have just described, we might decide it is best not to sue.

Whether or not to accept the risk displayed by a risk profile or take an alternative value (in this case 0) for certain is a judgment call that may involve many contextual considerations relating to the firm, its asset value, the impact on stockholders, and the impact on short-term and long-term opportunities. It may not be easy to make these kinds of choices consistently, and it is even harder when one is comparing more than one alternative risk profile. In Chapter 9, we discuss additional methodologies that can aid in these choices.

If one is not much concerned about risk, either because the stakes are small or the assets of the firm are huge in comparison, then it would be fine to make the decision on the basis of EMV. If we were willing to go strictly with EMV, then we could make all our calculations directly on the decision tree. There is a well-established procedure known as "folding back the tree" that includes:

1. Starting at the right side of the decision tree with the monetary outcomes, and working back to the initial node.

FIGURE 5–5   *Folded-Back Decision Tree with Intermediate EMVs*

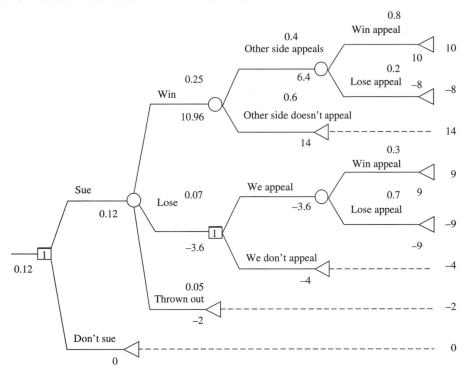

2. At a decision node, choosing the branch with the highest (lowest) EMV if the monetary value is one for which more (less) is better.

3. At an event node, calculating the EMV of the branches emanating from it (which corresponds to finding the EMV of the risk profile associated with finding yourself at that point on the tree).

Figure 5–5 shows the results of using the fold-back procedure on the litigation decision tree. The number near each node represents the EMV of the **remainder** of the tree, assuming that any decisions taken subsequently will optimize EMV.

Having completed the fold-back procedure in Figure 5–5, the EMV at the beginning of the tree is .12, the same number we computed from the risk profile in Figure 5–4. This number represents the expected value of this entire opportunity. If someone offered that amount, $.12 million, to take over the rights and obligations represented by the tree, we would be willing to sell. We might even take less than that if we consider the effects of risk and therefore don't strictly optimize EMV.

Many Potential Outcomes

To illustrate the situation with many possible outcomes, consider again the trinket promotion example discussed in Chapter 4. Our analysis of that example generated the graph contained in Figure 4–5, duplicated here as Figure 5–6. This histogram summarizes the results of 1,000 randomly generated scenarios. Thus, for example, in slightly more than 2 percent of the scenarios, the incremental gross margin was around $0, while in slightly more than 12 percent of the scenarios, the incremental gross margin was slightly more than $250,000 (eyeballing the graph might suggest between $250,000 and $280,000, approximately). We concluded that these relative frequencies were good approximations of the probability of what the actual incremental gross margin level would be if we proceeded with the trinket promotion, and hence we were willing to accept this graph as our probability distribution of incremental gross margin from the trinket promotion. As such, using the language of this chapter, it becomes the risk profile of the trinket promotion option.

Compare this risk profile to the one of our previous example (Figure 5–4). At first glance, they look similar: each appears to be a histogram, the height of the bars representing the probability of achieving that monetary outcome. However, in Figure 5–4, there are only six possible outcomes, and each bar represents the probability of achieving that individual outcome, while in Figure 5–6, there are as many possible outcomes as there are dollars in the relevant range, and the bars represent *ranges*, not individual outcomes.

The first potential problem this creates is that it is impossible to precisely calculate the EMV from the risk profile[3] the way we did it with a few outcomes. In fact, the whole notion of EMV as the weighted average of individual outcomes using their probabilities as weights is now hard to make operational. First, there are many possible outcomes, so the number of terms to be added can be prohibitively large. Even more significantly, however, is that the probability of achieving any one individual outcome (such as $210,346.72) is very small; in fact, many would argue that it is for all practical purposes zero. (Play the lottery game introduced in Chapter 4: Would you rather have your chance of winning the desirable prize depend on incremental gross margin being exactly $210,346.72—or any other individual monetary amount—or on the lottery where you have 1 out of 100 tickets? You have a much greater chance of having your single ticket drawn than having any previously selected individual incremental gross margin level eventuate.)

However, the concept of EMV is equally as appropriate for alternatives with many potential outcomes as it is for those with a few outcomes; in fact,

---

[3]Remember, the EMV of the risk profile is the same as the mean of the probability distribution of possible outcomes.

FIGURE 5–6

Probability Distribution for Incremental Gross Margin for Trinket Promotion Example

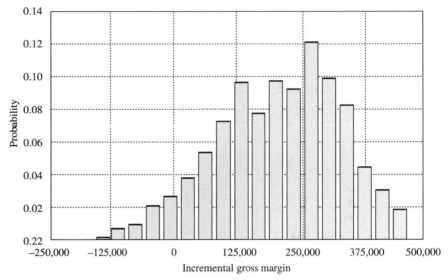

in some respects, it is even more intuitive. Remember that the EMV is nothing more than the mean of the probability distribution of potential outcomes. Recall also the interpretation we provided earlier in this chapter of EMV as the *average* of all the outcomes we would receive if we faced the situation described by the risk profile many times. Hence, one way to approximate the EMV is to simply repeat the situation a large number of times (scenarios), keeping track of the incremental gross margin we receive each time; the average of these would then approximate the EMV.

Repeating the situation a large number of times is precisely what we did in generating the risk profile reported in Figure 5–6; in this case, we repeated it 1,000 times. With a computer, it is easy to track the average incremental gross margin for these 1,000 scenarios; it turned out to be $235,330 for the 1,000 scenarios summarized in Figure 5–6. Hence, this number is a good approximation of the EMV of going with the trinket promotion. Just as in the case of the EMV for alternatives with few potential outcomes, this number considers the entire range of potential outcomes (the 1,000 outcomes span the range of possible outcomes) and the relative likelihood of the different outcomes (if, for example, there was a 12 percent likelihood of an outcome in the range \$250,000–\$280,000, then in approximately 12 percent of 1,000 = 120 of the scenarios we generated, the outcome would have been somewhere in this range).

It is possible to approximate the EMV directly from the risk profile in Figure 5–6. For example, you could select the midpoint of each bar (along the horizontal axis) and arbitrarily let that point be weighted by the probability assigned to the range associated with that particular bar. Thus, the profile in Figure 5–6 would be replaced by one with precisely 18 individual outcomes, one for each bar. The EMV could then be calculated in the same fashion as we used for alternatives with few outcomes. If 18 is still considered too many, we could define larger "bars"—wider ranges with more probability associated with each range—and repeat this procedure. These approaches are called **bracket-median approximation techniques**, where bracket refers to the range represented by the bar, and median refers to the midpoint that is used to represent that range. Yet another option is to use an even simpler technique, called the **Pearson-Tukey approximation technique**, which selects the .05, .5 (median), and .95 fractiles (see Chapter 4 for an explanation of fractiles) of the distribution and weights them with probabilities of .185, .63, and .185, respectively. This simple technique works surprisingly well, given it uses only three points of the probability distribution.

Once we have the EMV, we can examine the risk profile in much the same manner as we did alternatives with few outcomes, making allowances for the fact that to think about probability in any kind of meaningful fashion, we need to think in terms of ranges rather than individual outcomes. Thus, for example, consider the worst possible outcome. It appears that the minimum incremental gross margin we might get is a loss of slightly more than \$125,000. However, the chance of actually losing \$125,000 appears to be very small. It would perhaps be more meaningful with respect to the downside risk to consider the overall chance of losing money. We can estimate this probability by adding together the height of the bars corresponding to ranges less than \$0 in Figure 5–6; a rough eyeballing of the graph might suggest a number of around 5 percent.[4] Thus, a more meaningful estimate of the downside risk involved in the project might be that there is a 5 percent chance of losing money, with an even smaller chance of the loss exceeding \$50,000, and a cap of around \$125,000. Determining if this is an acceptable risk involves considering all the factors identified in the earlier discussion of alternatives with few outcomes.

The decision of whether or not to go with the trinket promotion thus revolves around its attractive EMV of \$235,330 versus the amount of risk involved—a 5 percent chance of losing money, capped by \$125,000. We have structured our decision so as to compare this rich risk profile of outcomes for the trinket promotion to the alternative of *not* going with the promotion, in

---

[4]Most simulation software tracks this information directly, so it is not necessary to eyeball the graph.

which the incremental gross margin is by definition $0 (i.e., if we do not go with the trinket promotion, we *know* we are going to get no incremental gross margin from the use of the trinket promotion). Hence, we are comparing an alternative with a distribution of many possible outcomes to an alternative with a single known outcome.

Alternatively, we could have approached this decision from a slightly different perspective, namely that there are *two* uncertain alternatives: going with the trinket promotion, whose risk profile we have already explored, and *not* going with the trinket promotion, where the outcome is still exposed to the volume forecast error. Rather than track the *incremental* gross margin— from going with the trinket promotion—as before, we now track the *total* gross margin associated with (1) going with the trinket promotion and (2) not going with the promotion. The resulting risk profiles of total gross margin for each alternative (from conducting a simulation of 1,000 scenarios) are contained in Figure 5–7.

The task of deciding whether or not to go with the promotion now involves comparing two risk profiles, rather than a risk profile to a single value.[5] In comparing two risk profiles, we probably again want to start with the EMV of the two; for the trinket promotion, it is $9,855,309, while for no promotion, it is $9,620,000. Thus, the trinket promotion has a higher EMV, and therefore an apparent advantage. We next consider the riskiness of the two options. Notice first how different the two risk profiles appear. The risk profile for the trinket promotion alternative resembles a triangle distribution with a most likely value closer to the maximum than the minimum value. The risk profile for not going with the trinket promotion more closely resembles a uniform distribution, which should not be surprising since the sole uncertainty driving this distribution is the forecast error in base volume, which is itself uniformly distributed. The distribution for the trinket promotion option is more spread out than the other; that is, there is a greater dispersion between the minimum and the maximum. This is further supported by the fact that the standard deviation for the trinket promotion alternative is higher, $157,959 as compared to $111,080. Thus, one is tempted to conclude that the trinket promotion alternative is riskier than its alternative, since we have more uncertainty as to its outcome.

However, further inspection of the risk profiles indicates the minimum outcomes associated with the two alternatives are roughly the same. Hence, if risk is concerned primarily with negative outcomes, it is not clear that going with the trinket promotion is riskier. The graph in Figure 5–8 provides additional insight into the two alternatives: at almost every level of total gross margin, the cumulative probability for the trinket promotion option is less than that of the no-promotion alternative. This means that for virtually any specified level of total gross margin, the chance of exceeding that level is

---

[5]Technically, an alternative with a single, known outcome can also be thought of as having a risk profile, with a probability 1 associated with the single known outcome.

FIGURE 5–7

Risk Profile of Total Gross Margin for Trinket Promotion Alternative

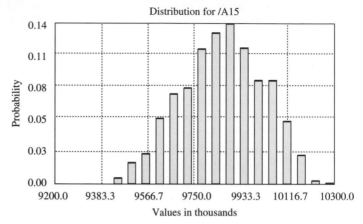

Risk Profile of Total Gross Margin for Not Going with the Trinket Promotion

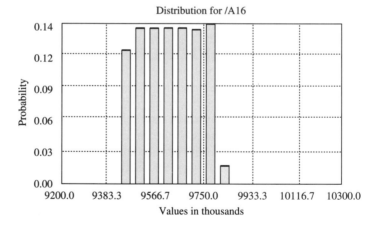

greater with the trinket promotion than without. If this condition were to hold for all levels, we would say that the trinket promotion option *stochastically dominates* the no-promotion option, where the term *stochastic* is used because the domination is based on the probability of it producing a better outcome. Since it does not hold for a few low values, we are reduced to concluding that the trinket promotion option *almost* stochastically dominates the no-promotion option.

It would thus appear that the trinket promotion alternative has a higher EMV and is not much riskier than the no-promotion alternative, despite the fact that its actual outcome is less predictable. Is this consistent with our

FIGURE 5–8 *Cumulative Probability for Trinket Promotion and No Trinket Promotion*

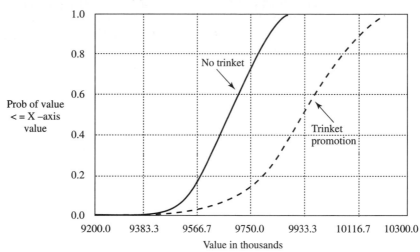

earlier analysis that focused on the incremental gross margin? Basically, yes, in that the trinket promotion appears to be strongly supported as the preferred alternative. However, there are two dimensions of the analyses that might give you pause:

1. In the incremental analysis, we determined that there was a 5 percent chance we would make a lower gross margin with the trinket promotion than without. However, this possibility did not seem to surface when we conducted our separate analyses of the total margin associated with each alternative. The reason for this is that the outcomes of the two alternatives are *positively correlated* to one another in the sense that scenarios in which the no-promotion alternative has a higher gross margin—for example, when there is a forecast error of plus 1 percent in the base volume—will also tend to lead to higher gross margins for the trinket promotion alternative. This is because the higher base volume benefits both alternatives; the relationship is not exact because, in a given scenario, a higher base volume may be associated with a low volume increase percentage and/or high unit cost per trinket and/or a high artwork cost variance. Nonetheless, the general relationship holds.

   In situations such as this, the individual risk profiles fail to capture the implications of this kind of relationship. In these situations, it is useful to consider the *difference* between the outcomes associated with the two alternatives under each scenario. This is precisely what our incremental analysis did. By focusing on differences, we filter out the impact of scenario characteristics that affect both alternatives in the same way (such as higher base sales in our example). Thus, while the individual risk profiles are not incorrect, they may fail to provide potentially valuable information when the two alternatives are correlated with one another.

2. In the incremental analysis, we calculated an EMV of $235,330 for the trinket promotion alternative; in the total analysis, we compared EMVs of $9,855,309 and $9,620,000. In both cases, the trinket promotion option is approximately $235,300 better than the no-promotion alternative.[6] However, one is tempted to call the difference slight when considering the totals, while the incremental figure, when considered by itself, seems more significant.

The issue is how our perspective on risk changes as the context changes, particularly our level of wealth (or, in this case, the general magnitude of the total gross margin we expect to receive). Thus, one might say that the expected benefit to be derived from the trinket promotion is overstated when the incremental rather than the total gross margin number is considered, and use this as an argument for doing the total analysis.

While this concern is certainly valid, it probably does not outweigh the desirability of including the correlation between the two alternatives. If this issue is considered particularly important, the interested reader is referred to Chapter 9, which contains more rigorous approaches to problems of this type.

Summary

In measuring the financial performance of alternatives, we must first identify the relevant monetary flows. *Relevant* is defined as those flows that depend on which alternative is selected. Identifying the appropriate flows for your decision requires careful thought and judgment. Common mistakes include allocating fixed costs, ignoring effects elsewhere in the company, and including flows of unrelated activities.

Once the relevant monetary flows are identified, evaluating the performance of an alternative involves analyzing this set of flows. If all the flows are known with certainty, then this is typically just a matter of calculating the desired measure—such as profit, contribution, or cost, incremental or total—from the flows. The alternative that maximizes (or minimizes) the desired measure is then selected. If there is uncertainty associated with some of the

[6]The difference between the $235,330 and $9,855,309 − $9,620,000 = $235,309 is due to the fact that two different sets of 1,000 scenarios were used for the two analyses. For more on this aspect of interpreting simulation results, see Chapter 15.

flows, then we must consider the set of all possible outcomes of the desired measure and the likelihood of each.

If the uncertain flows can assume only a few possible values, then the number of possible outcomes of the desired measure will also be few. Alternatively, if the uncertain flows can assume many possible values, then the number of possible outcomes will also be many. In either case, our primary descriptive tool is the *risk profile*, which details all possible outcomes and their associated probabilities. The risk profile contains everything we need to know about the alternative to make a decision. In the case of many possible outcomes, where the likelihood of receiving any individual outcome is small, the risk profile expresses the probability of receiving outcomes in specified ranges. Selecting from among several alternatives, each with its own risk profile, is a matter of individual preference.

In either case—few or many possible outcomes—the *expected monetary value (EMV)* is a useful summary measure of the risk profile of an alternative. The EMV of the desired measure is the "average" value we would receive if we selected this alternative a large number of times, each time being exposed to the possible outcomes and associated probabilities described by its risk profile. Mechanically, for alternatives with but a few possible outcomes, this value can be calculated directly as the weighted average of the possible outcomes, with each outcome's associated probability serving as its weight. For alternatives with many possible outcomes, this value can be approximated by simulating the act of taking the alternative a large number of times and calculating the average value received. In either case, the EMV is often a valuable starting point for the evaluation of alternatives. Once EMVs are calculated and compared, the decision maker can then move to the risk profiles to determine how much impact the riskiness of the alternative should have on the eventual decision.

6   RISK MANAGEMENT

Understanding the risk associated with particular alternatives helps us appraise which of the alternatives we may wish to take. Simply by making these choices well, we can add a lot of monetary value to a firm, even if we accept the world as it is. Even greater value can be achieved by improving upon the alternatives the world offers us. We discuss in this chapter ways to create value and reduce risk, by obtaining better information on which to base decisions and by controlling factors that contribute to increased monetary value. Our discussion will cover how to identify the significant uncertainties and factors and how to calculate a monetary value for information about them and the ability to control their outcome. We end by describing some management practices and business arrangements that can be used to subdue risk and bring it under control.

Value of Information

In many decision situations, we can turn information into value by using the information to select a better alternative with a higher monetary value. Here we show how to infer the expected monetary value of the information, based on the improvement due to the better decision.

We start by considering the very best information possible about an uncertainty, namely perfect information, as if coming from a clairvoyant. We then show how to place a monetary value on imperfect information, where the clairvoyant was unavailable and we must settle for information that is good, yet not perfect. An example will help illustrate these concepts.

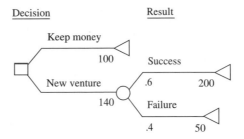

Vicky's old college friends are planning to start a new venture and they would like her to come in as an investor. Vicky has family money that would provide her $100,000 guaranteed upon maturity in its current investment. If she put this money into her friends' venture, the value of the venture, which would mature at the same time as her current investment, depends on whether her friends can obtain approval and a license from the city to operate a new cable company. Vicky believes she will receive the equivalent of $200,000 from the venture if they get approval. Otherwise, she'll get back the equivalent of half of her guaranteed investment. Based on her decision tree, shown here, she plans to invest in the new venture.

Perfect Information

Vicky believes she should explore some sources of information that are available to her. She has an infallible source of perfect information (yes, it's legal) on whether the approval from the city will be forthcoming. However, the information could be expensive. Before approaching the source, she will calculate what it is worth to her. This we call EVPI or

---

Expected Value of Perfect Information =
EMV with perfect information − EMV without perfect information

---

It amounts to what she would pay a clairvoyant to tell her the outcome of some uncertain event, in this case whether the venture will be a success or a failure. It is sometimes called the value of **clairvoyance**.

To calculate the EMV with perfect information, Vicki must first consider what decision she would make if she had the information. And she needs to think about both possible cases—either the clairvoyant says "approval-success" or "disapproval-failure." She can look at this analysis with a decision tree, but the key is to recognize that the uncertainty is resolved before the decision is made, as shown in the new decision tree.

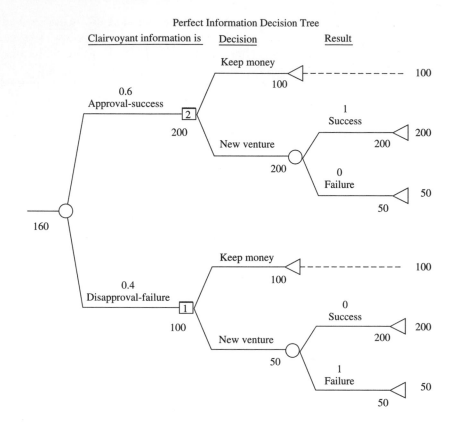

Perfect Information Decision Tree

The clairvoyant is perfect, so whenever the prediction is "approval-success," success does result. Likewise, for a "disapproval-failure" prediction, failure follows. As a result, Vicky's assessment of the chances that the clairvoyant will say "approval-success" must be the same as her assessment that success will occur, namely 0.6.

The EMV is $160,000 from the perfect information decision tree. This is higher than before; it should never be lower unless there is an arithmetic mistake, since she should always do at least as well with perfect information if she makes the best decisions with the information. Now she can calculate the expected value of perfect information:

EMV with perfect information	160
− EMV without perfect information	− 140
EVPI	20

So if she paid less than $20,000 for perfect information, she would come out ahead on average. Vicky may use this number to rule out some information-gathering opportunities that are more costly than this and/or not perfect. The $20,000 is also a measure of how important this uncertainty is to Vicki's decision. There is up to $20,000 in value to be gained by resolving the uncertainty.

Notice that the perfect information tree starts with the outcome for the clairvoyant's information, followed by the original tree (with the probabilities modified to reflect the perfect information) at the end of each of the potential statements of the clairvoyant. If we had represented the decision with an influence diagram, the perfect information case would also have the uncertainty ahead of the decision in an influence path. Both the decision tree and the influence diagram show, as part of the structure of assumptions, the state of information for any decision. All uncertainties earlier in the tree or predecessors in the influence diagram are known when the decisions are made, and those that follow the decision remain uncertain. It is possible with software for decision trees or influence diagrams to easily reorder decisions and uncertainties and calculate EVPI.

Imperfect Information

Of course, not all sources of information provide perfect predictions, even though they may still reduce uncertainty. In reality, market research, diagnostic tests, and other information-gaining activities move us to improved states of knowledge about the potential success of a prospect, but short of a probability of success of 1.0 (or, on the other hand, 0.0). After gaining the information, the probability of success has either increased, for example when a test is positive, or has decreased, if the test is negative. This makes it clearer which alternative to take, which leads to improved monetary value. For such opportunities to gain information, we can calculate EVII:

Expected Value of Imperfect Information =
EMV with imperfect information − EMV without information

To calculate the EMV with imperfect information, we'll need a decision tree. This tree (shown on the next page) would include the possibilities for the imperfect information available, followed by the decision, and then the actual result, in that order. In this example, we would like to know the value of information provided by an expert who makes categorical judgments about the chances that the city will approve a license for Vicky's cable company. To extend our example, the expert may say one of three things: approval is "likely," the chances are "less than even," or approval is "doubtful." Discussion with the expert has determined that if the expert says "likely," then

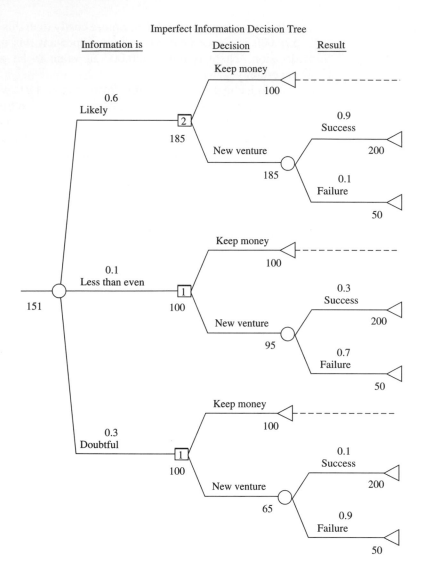

Imperfect Information Decision Tree

Information is   Decision   Result

Keep money
100

0.6
Likely
2
185

New venture
185

0.9
Success
200

0.1
Failure
50

151

0.1
Less than even
1
100

Keep money
100

New venture
95

0.3
Success
200

0.7
Failure
50

0.3
Doubtful
1
100

Keep money
100

New venture
65

0.1
Success
200

0.9
Failure
50

the probability of approval moves up to 0.9, "less than even" is associated
with a probability of 0.3, and "doubtful" implies a probability of 0.1. To
complete the tree, we need the chances that the expert will issue each of these
three statements. We need these probabilities now, in advance of hiring the
expert; otherwise we have no way of placing a value on the information.
From previous experience with this expert in similar situations, the probabil-

ities were assessed[1] to be 0.6, 0.1, and 0.3, respectively, which are shown on the tree. It is a good idea to check that the expert's overall assessment of the chance of success is consistent with the probability we used in the initial tree and in the perfect information tree. Note that the overall probability of success, calculated

$$.6*.9 + .1*.3 + .3*.1 = .6$$

is the same probability as in the original decision analysis.

We can see in the decision tree that if the imperfect information is "doubtful," it is best not to invest in the venture. Folding back the tree (see the EMVs near the nodes of the tree), we find the EMV to be 151 and we can calculate the EVII:

EMV with imperfect information	151
− EMV without imperfect information	− 140
EVII	11

The information quality is such that she should pay no more than $11,000 for it.

Of course, there may be many sources of imperfect information, each having their own EVII. Those sources that are more discriminating, that is, that divide more effectively into high success probability and low success probability situations, will have greater value. For none of them will their EVII exceed the EVPI, however. We would always seek to find a way to obtain the information for a cost that is less than its EVII.

Value of Control

If we were able to *choose* the outcome we want for an uncertainty, rather than simply *learn* what it will be, the possibilities for monetary reward would be even greater. While it is conceivable that we might throw efforts toward

---

[1]It is worth noting that obtaining the probabilities on the decision tree for imperfect information may not be as simple as it appears here. Take the case of an imperfect diagnostic test for a cancer, for example. Suppose the test outcomes are "positive" and "negative" for the cancer; these outcomes would come first in the decision tree for imperfect information. Later in the tree would come probabilities for outcomes such as "healthy" and "cancer." How would one get these probabilities? They would probably come from calibrating the test on patients that are known to be healthy or cancerous. These are called calibration probabilities and are commonly referred to as false positive and false negative rates for the tester. They are not the probabilities needed for the tree. On the tree would go the probability of cancer for a patient that has tested positive, for example, not the probability of testing positive if we are known to have cancer. The probabilities needed could be calculated from the calibration probabilities based on Bayes theorem using a procedure known as Bayesian revision which is discussed in many textbooks.

ensuring a particular outcome, such as the successful engineering of a particular product function, such an effort will cost money. We would like to know what it would be worth to us to control specific uncertain outcomes.

Perfect Control

Vicky may wish to go beyond simply getting a prediction about whether her license will be approved. She might have opportunities available to her to control her destiny. For example, a guarantee to share revenue with the city may ensure approval. How much would she be willing to spend to have this perfect control? This is sometimes called the value of **wizardry**, that is, to be able to wave a magic wand to obtain the desired outcome. The calculation for EVPC is:

Expected Value of Perfect Control =
EMV with perfect control − EMV without control

With perfect control, we would choose to have the city's approval and therefore a successful venture, which would give Vicky $200,000. Thus

$$
\begin{array}{lr}
\text{EMV with perfect control} & 200 \\
-\ \text{EMV without perfect control} & -\,140 \\
\hline
\text{Expected value of perfect control} & 60
\end{array}
$$

There is $60,000 to be gained by controlling the uncertainty. This number is larger than that for EVPI above, which should be the case. It makes sense to pay more to control what will happen than simply to predict the outcome. We should always expect EVPC ≥ EVPI ≥ EVII.

One note of caution about EVPC or EVPI. These are really approximations of the maximum we would pay for information and control, since we used only the change in EMV to calculate them, not the entire risk profiles. Because of the reduction in risk associated with perfect information and/or control, one may be willing to pay more than EVPC or EVPI.

Control of Continuously Ranging Quantities

When we consider discrete uncertain events, we know what perfect control means; it is the ability to choose the outcome that is best. If the uncertainty is a continuously ranging quantity, however, perfect control is not so well defined. For example, suppose we have as an uncertainty the market size for a new product. If asked what we would choose for market size, given we could control it, we may face no upper limit. Regardless of the number we pick, a higher number is better; in other words, the probability distribution for market size has a tail that goes out forever.

When dealing with control of continuous uncertain quantities, it is useful to be very clear about the degree of control we have in mind. Are we allowing an uncertainty to be set to either its 5th or 95th percentile (.05 or .95 fractile), or alternatively to its 1st or 99th percentile (.01 or .99 fractile), or instead to some other range? The value of control may be greatly affected by this choice; the choice itself is arbitrary, but it is important to be clear what definition is being used and to be consistent across various uncertainties.

A tornado diagram can be used to display the value of control for continuously ranging uncertainties. For example, Figure 4–1 shows the relative effects of controlling four uncertainties related to the introduction of a trinket promotion for a breakfast cereal. Notice that the favored choice for some uncertainties (the costs) would be on the low side, not on the high side, as in, say, the volume increase percentage. The tornado diagram is not symmetrical—some quantities have more significant upside possibilities than downside threats. For use as an indication of the value of control, the bars in the tornado diagram might be placed in order of upside potential, rather than in order of the swing from upside to downside, which is indicated by the length of the bar.

The tornado diagram can be augmented by including decision quantities in it. In this way the value of control for variables we know we can control can be compared to that for variables we would like to control if we could. We might find that there is little value in being able to choose some decision quantities and we could give up control of them, particularly if it might provide the ability to control other, more significant, uncertainties.

Adding Value and Reducing Risk

Knowing the value of information and control provides great insight that can be used to manage a risky opportunity so as to add value and reduce risk. The risk profile for a given alternative indicates the world as it is. An example is shown in Figure 6–1a. Rather than accept the world that way, we may improve it, in at least three ways.

We may take actions that shift the risk profile to the right, thereby adding value for all possible outcomes. The effect on the risk profile is shown in Figure 6–1b. Such an effect might be brought about, for example, by eliminating an operating cost in a project.

Alternatively, we may find ways to cut off the downside and move those outcomes to some guaranteed level, thereby shifting the mean up and, importantly, removing the most disastrous possibilities. This is shown in Figure 6–1c. A guarantee for a minimum purchase quantity in a contract with a customer might provide such a shift. Insurance is another example of how to cut off the downside; however, insurance costs money, and so its expense would generate in addition a downward shift in the whole risk profile. Assuming that insurance markets are efficient in pricing the risk and that insurance

FIGURE 6–1

Actions to Add Value and Reduce Risk

- internal management
  of the firm
  - cost controls
    — setting milestones
    — monitoring outflows
    — quick response
  - productivity increases
    — incentive systems
    — labor coordination
  - technological innovation
    — design engineering
    — product improvements
- external arrangements
  - controls
    — reduce accounts
      receivable
    — increase accounts payable
    — delivery times
    — supplier cooperation
  - contract arrangements
    — take or pay clauses
    — penalty clause warranty
    — incentive clause
    — performance-based
      contingent claim
    — match exposure to
      interests
      (ours and theirs)
      · length of contract
        commitment
      · reliability requirements
      · termination option
      · variable usage option

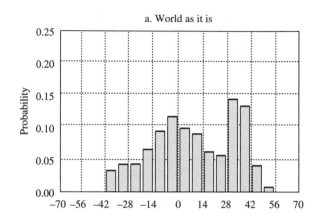

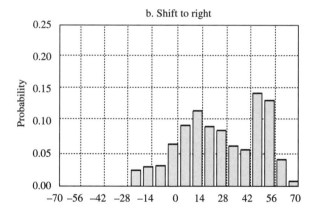

FIGURE 6–1
Continued

◦ financial markets
— hedges
— options
— derivatives
— shared ownership
  ▪ risk sharing
  ▪ alliance
  ▪ joint venture
◦ insurance against
— property damage
— international political instability
— catastrophic events

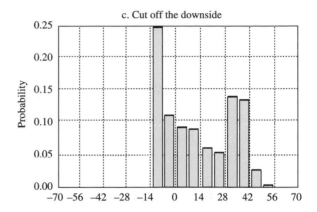

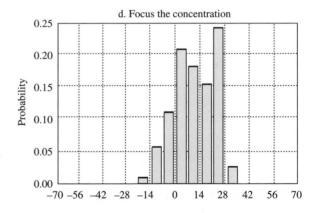

companies make a profit, the overall effect of an insurance policy would be a downward shift in the mean combined with cutting off the downside.

Lastly, we may be able to focus the concentration of uncertainty in the risk profile, thereby reducing the risk, even though the mean performance does not change. Figure 6–1d shows a risk profile for such a risk-reducing activity. In fact, this risk profile was created in a way that reflects risk sharing. It is the risk profile that results from taking one-half of the monetary value from the risk profile for the "World as it is" and adding to it one-half of the EMV for the "World as it is." Thus, if we could sell half of our risky opportunity for a price equal to half of its EMV, and keep the rest of the risky opportunity, we would have the focused concentration shown in Figure 6–1d.

Some management actions may produce more than one of these desirable effects, and yet virtually all management attempts to improve a risky opportunity do so by one of these effects, or some combination of them. The specific actions that can be taken will depend greatly on the risky opportunity being considered, and characteristics of the firm evaluating it, as well as the circumstances in which it finds itself. Even so, it is worthwhile to catalog some management activities that may result in these improvements. For this reason, we have provided with Figure 6–1 an outline of possible management activities for adding value and reducing risk in the risk profile. This will provide both a framework and checklist for brainstorming ideas in a specific context.

Summary

Analysis of risk is often initiated to evaluate alternatives. Yet a large portion of the value of creating a decision model is its use in generating insight into how to improve opportunities that are available to us. The process of adding value and reducing risk is both a creative one and an analytic one; it will employ both sides of the brain. One part of the task is to generate creative possibilities, starting from an outline like the one we have provided. EVII, EVPI, EVPC, and the tornado diagram can all contribute to sorting through the comparative significance of ideas that relate to specific uncertainties. Another part of the task is to modify the decision model to incorporate the management ideas. By doing so we can then place monetary value on specific management plans. The rewards of analyzing the risk will then be realizable.

7   EVALUATING MULTIPERIOD PERFORMANCE

A tract of land is developed for the resale value of the lots into which it will be subdivided. A promising new product is nationally introduced on the basis of its future sales and subsequent profits. A piece of equipment is ordered for the improved operating efficiency and increased capacity that it will provide relative to the piece it replaces. A corporate bond is purchased for its coupons and the ultimate repayment of its par value.

These decisions are similar in that each requires the investment of money in anticipation of benefits whose realization will be spread out over time. The value of such an investment depends on many factors including the magnitude of the benefits, the timing of those benefits, and the degree of uncertainty in actually receiving the anticipated benefits. Although the prediction of future benefits is perhaps the most significant challenge in appraising investments, the careful and consistent consideration of the effects of time are necessary, even when those benefits are known. Suppose the monetary return of an investment far exceeds the initial investment, but the return is delayed into the distant future. Does the magnitude of the return justify the wait? Suppose one investment yields greater monetary returns than another, but the returns of the first are received over a longer period than the second. Which is better? Are either desirable?

A systematic approach to answering these questions is the topic of this chapter. The focus will be on the measurement of the monetary returns of an investment (cash flow) and on the evaluation of the effects of timing on the value of those returns (discounted cash flows). It will be assumed that the returns are known with certainty. The concepts and techniques for explicitly addressing uncertainty are discussed in other chapters.

Cash Flow

Why is real estate developed, a new product introduced, equipment replaced, or a bond purchased? In each decision there are a host of reasons, ranging from the strategic goals of the firm to the personal desires of the manager. Common to almost all investment decisions, however, is the objective of earning financial returns from the invested money. This section concentrates on the identification and measurement of these financial returns and ignores the other, more subjective, considerations that significantly influence investment decisions.

Rather simply stated, the returns from an investment can either be reinvested in the firm or distributed to the shareholders. As a result, the returns from an investment should be viewed as "usable" funds generated by the investment and the outlays for an investment should be viewed as the money withdrawn from the pool of "usable funds." Usable funds are cash and thus investments should be evaluated in terms of **cash flow**—the inflow and outflow of usable funds—and not in terms of the profits that are reported by the firm's accounting system. Profits and cash flow are not the same. As an illustration of this difference, suppose a manager were offered the choice between prepaying the entire premium of $15,000 for a three-year insurance program or paying the premium in three annual installments of $5,000 each. Almost certainly, the manager would select the installment option. But why? For each payment option, the firm's income statement would report the same annual insurance cost of $5,000 (accrual accounting methods require that the prepayment be spread evenly over the three-year life of the policy) and hence the same profits would be reported for both plans. The difference between the two options lies in their differing schedules of demand for cash, that is, their differing cash flows. The installment plan is preferred because it actually spreads the payments over the next three years, which is observed by focusing on the cash flow and is obscured by considering profits.

The common practice in calculating cash flows for an investment is to calculate the **incremental cash flows** of the investment—the difference between the cash flows from the investment and the cash flows of a "do-nothing" alternative. If there are several alternative investments, several cash flow calculations are required, one for each investment relative to the same do-nothing alternative. In addition to calculating the cash flows on an incremental basis, care must be taken in distinguishing between items that are really cash flows and those noncash items masquerading as cash flows that are the result of accounting conventions. A simple rule is that if you write a check for it, it's a cash outflow; if you can deposit it in the bank, it's a cash inflow. In the above insurance example, the prepayment option has a cash outflow of $15,000 now and no cash outflows in the subsequent years, regardless of how the payment may be expensed over the life of the policy.

Making an exhaustive list of the sources of cash flows is impossible, but the cash flows that are most commonly encountered in practice can be grouped into several comprehensive categories. When calculating the initial outlay of an investment, look first for the obvious initial purchase or construction cost, and then note any changes in working capital (the holding of cash, inventories, the net of accounts receivable and accounts payable) required to support the project, the salvage value of any equipment that is being replaced or discarded, and any investment incentives offered by the tax authorities. For cash flows subsequent to the initial outlay, look for revenues (sales, dividends, or interest payments if it is a purely financial investment) resulting from the investment, for cost of goods sold (materials, manufacturing costs), for changes in selling and administrative expenses, for any subsequent investment costs, and for taxes; avoid expenses that do not change if the investment is not done but are allocated to the investment as if they were incremental; do not credit the investment with sales that are cannibalized from existing sales. At the end of the life of the investment, be sure to include the recovery of working capital, any shutdown costs, and the salvage value of any equipment.

Note that neither depreciation nor financing expense is included as a cash flow. Depreciation is simply an accounting provision whose effects are reflected in the calculation of taxes. Depreciation is not itself a cash flow. The financing costs of an investment are excluded because of the widely accepted practice of separating the evaluation of the investment itself from the financing of the investment. There are several reasons for keeping these two considerations separate. A firm's portfolio of investments is generally funded from capital that is raised through a combination of debt, equity, and retained earnings. Without the perspective of the entire demand for capital within the firm, it would be inappropriate to assume the cost on any one of these sources (or any mix) in evaluating a specific project. Even if an investment were clearly to be financed out of either debt or equity but not both, the cost of either means would not reflect the real cost of financing, because the funding of the investment would affect the firm's ability to acquire future capital by either means.[1] Thus, the financing decision is a corporatewide decision and should not be implicitly made (or assumed) at the individual investment decision level.

An Example

As an illustration of these concepts, consider a proposed investment of $128,000 that will expand production operations for three years and allow

---

[1]An exception to this statement would occur when the financing of an investment is specific to the investment itself and the firm is fully insulated from any risks associated with the investment. Some real estate projects may be financed in this fashion. When these conditions apply, the investment is de facto a separate entity and the terms of the financing are integral to the project. As a result, neither the investment nor the financing of the investment can be isolated from the other and the two must be treated together.

TABLE 7–1   Cash Flows

	Now	Year 1	Year 2	Year 3
Cost of project	$(128,000)			
Sales		$108,000	$108,000	$108,000
Cost of goods sold		(48,000)	(48,000)	(48,000)
Taxes*		(7,600)	(7,600)	(7,600)
Changes in working capital	(32,000)			32,000
Salvage of equipment				8,000
Taxes on salvage[†]				0
Total cash flow	$(160,000)	$ 52,400	$ 52,400	$ 92,400

*Tax computation
Sales	$108,000
Cost of goods sold	(48,000)
Depreciation	(40,000)
Profits before taxes	20,000
Taxes (38% of profit)	$7,600

[†]Taxes are zero because the equipment is sold at book value; that is, there is no capital gain or loss on the sale.

the firm to satisfy demand that is currently being lost. It is anticipated that the revenue from the incremental sales will be $108,000 with a cost of goods sold of $48,000. Although the company allocates its selling and general administrative expenses as 12 percent of revenue, there would be no increase in the actual selling and administrative expenses. To support the increased sales volume, $32,000 must be set aside at the time of the investment to cover increases in inventories and accounts receivable, all of which will be recoverable at the end of the third year. Also at the end of the third year, there will be usable equipment with a salvage value of $8,000. The initial investment will be straight-line depreciated so that the book value is $8,000 at the end of the third year. The marginal tax rate (federal as well as state and local) is assumed to be 38 percent.

The cash flows for this investment are shown in Table 7–1. Note that the flows during each year have been aggregated to give an annual total even though most of them will actually occur continuously during the year. In addition, revenues are just from the incremental sales, and the increased allocation of selling and administrative expenses are not included because the actual selling and administrative expenses do not increase because of the investment. The format of Table 7–1 highlights the actual cash flows by never including *directly* in the calculations any noncash items such as depreciation. As a result, taxes are computed as a side calculation. An alternative format that many find useful follows the layout of an income statement. This format will yield the same results as long as the noncash items that have been included in the calculation of profits before tax are "added back" to convert

TABLE 7–2   Cash Flows: Income Statement Format

	Now	Year 1	Year 2	Year 3
Cash flow of initial investment	$(128,000)			
Sales		$108,000	$108,000	$108,000
Cost of goods sold		48,000	48,000	48,000
Depreciation		40,000	40,000	40,000
Total cost		$ 88,000	$ 88,000	$ 88,000
Pretax profits from sales		20,000	20,000	20,000
Taxes (38% of profits)		7,600	7,600	7,600
Aftertax profits from sales		12,400	12,400	12,400
Plus: noncash charges to sales*		40,000	40,000	40,000
Cash flow from sales		$ 52,400	$ 52,400	$ 52,400
Salvage of equipment				$ 8,000
Book value of equipment				8,000
Pretax profits from equipment salvage . . .				0
Capital gains tax				0
Aftertax profits from equipment salvage				0
Plus: noncash charges to equipment				
salvage				8,000
Cash flow from equipment salvage				$ 8,000
Cash flow from working capital	(32,000)			32,000
Total cash flow	$(160,000)	$ 52,400	$ 52,400	$ 92,400

*Because noncash items (depreciation and book value of equipment) are subtracted in calculating aftertax profits, these items must be added back to convert profits into cash flow.

profits after tax into cash flows. Table 7–2 presents the calculation of the cash flows for the example using the income statement format.

Time Value of Money

Once the cash flows for a proposed investment have been calculated, it still must be determined whether the proposal is a sound investment. In addition, if a choice must be made between mutually exclusive alternatives or if there are several attractive alternatives but limited available capital, the alternatives must be evaluated to determine which ones make the most effective use of the invested funds. A systematic way to make these evaluations is the topic of this section.

Suppose a manager is faced with a choice between two investment opportunities, A and B, each of which requires an initial investment of $50,000. Investment A produces cash flows of $22,000 at the end of each of the next three years. The cash flows of investment B are $12,000 at the end of the next two years and $46,000 at the end of the third year. Which investment, if any, should the manager select?

Accumulated Value

Over their lifetimes each alternative will return more than the initial investment of $50,000: $66,000 for investment A, $70,000 for investment B. At first blush, it would appear that both investments are attractive and that investment B is better because it returns more for the same initial investment.

Such an initial reaction should be tempered, however, by the realization that in the early years the cash flows from investment A exceed those from investment B. Because the manager would certainly not leave the cash flows idle from either of the investments, the larger earnings from the reinvestment of the larger flows from investment A in years 1 and 2 could offset investment B's larger cash flow in year 3. The extent to which the larger reinvestment earnings will benefit investment A depends on the attractiveness of the reinvestment opportunities. Assume the manager will aggressively manage any cash returns so they would earn 15 percent after taxes. With this reinvestment environment, what would be the total value (including reinvestment) of each of the alternatives at the end of their lifetimes?

This question can be answered with a calculation that is identical to the calculation of the balances in a savings account. For a savings account, the interest rate is applied to the average balance in the account, and the ending balance for a time period is the total of the opening balance, the interest earned, and any deposits or withdrawals made during the time period. In the investment example, the returns from the investments are the "deposits" to the savings account and the earnings from reinvesting the returns are the "interest payments." More specifically, for investment A, there are zero dollars on deposit during year 1, so no interest is earned, but a deposit of $22,000 is made at the end of the year. For year 2, the opening balance of $22,000 is carried throughout the year. That balance will earn $3,300 in interest at a 15 percent rate. At the end of year 2, the balance will be $47,300—the sum of the opening balance of $22,000, the interest of $3,300, and year-end deposit of $22,000. Similarly, the balance at the end of year 3 will be $76,395— the sum of the opening balance of $47,300, the interest earned during the year of $7,095 ($47,300 × .15), and the year-end deposit of $22,000. Table 7–3 presents these calculations for investment A and for investment B.

When the two investments are evaluated in light of the 15 percent reinvestment opportunities for their returns, investment A is preferred because it accumulates $76,395 by the end of year 3, as compared to the $75,670 accumulated by investment B. Even though investment A offers a smaller total return, those returns come earlier and permit greater earnings from reinvestment. The figures in Table 7–3 show that the earlier cash flows of investment A earn $10,395 in reinvestment income compared to the $5,670

TABLE 7–3 **Comparing Investment A and Investment B**
(Reinvestment at 15 Percent)

Investment A			
	Year 1	*Year 2*	*Year 3*
Cash balance at beginning of year	$ 0	$22,000	$47,300
Earnings from reinvestment of balance at 15%	0	3,300	7,095
Cash inflow at end of year from investment A	22,000	22,000	22,000
Total cash available at end of year for			
reinvestment next year	$22,000	$47,300	$76,395
Investment B			
	Year 1	*Year 2*	*Year 3*
Cash balance at beginning of year	$ 0	$12,000	$25,800
Earnings from reinvestment of balance at 15%	0	1,800	3,870
Cash inflow at end of year from investment B	12,000	12,000	46,000
Total cash available at end of year for			
reinvestment next year	$12,000	$25,800	$75,670

for investment B. The added reinvestment earnings of investment A are sufficient to offset the $4,000 difference in total return.

If the manager's reinvestment opportunities were less attractive, investment A might not be the more attractive choice. Suppose the reinvestment opportunities were 10 percent instead of 15 percent, which investment would be the better? Table 7–4 presents the same calculation as Table 7–3 but with a reinvestment rate of 10 percent. Now investment B has the greater accumulated value at the end of year 3 and is the more attractive investment. At this lower reinvestment rate, the accelerated cash flows of investment A do not earn sufficient reinvestment income to offset the $4,000 difference in total return.

The above examples show that the evaluation of investments whose payoffs extend into the future depends not only on the magnitude of the cash flows but also on the timing of the flows and the subsequent use to which those flows can be put. To appropriately evaluate alternative cash flow streams, all three aspects—**magnitude, timing**, and **reinvestment rate**—must be considered.

Thus far, the analysis of the two investments has compared only the two alternatives but has not determined if either of them is an attractive use of the $50,000 initial investment. Would it be better to put the $50,000 into the 15 percent investment opportunities rather than either of the two alternatives? One way to answer this question is to calculate the accumulated value of $50,000 after three years and compare it to the accumulated values of the two investment alternatives. At a 15 percent rate with the earnings from one

TABLE 7–4   Comparing Investment A and Investment B
(Reinvestment at 10 Percent)

Investment A

	Year 1	Year 2	Year 3
Cash balance at beginning of year	$ 0	$22,000	$46,200
Earnings from reinvestment of balance at 10%	0	2,200	4,620
Cash inflow at end of year from investment A	22,000	22,000	22,000
Total cash available at end of year for reinvestment next year	$22,000	$46,200	$72,820

Investment B

	Year 1	Year 2	Year 3
Cash balance at beginning of year	$ 0	$12,000	$25,200
Earnings from reinvestment of balance at 10%	0	1,200	2,520
Cash inflow at end of year from investment B	12,000	12,000	46,000
Total cash available at end of year for reinvestment next year	$12,000	$25,200	$73,720

year reinvested for the next, the $50,000 will compound to $57,500 at the end of the first year, $66,125 at the end of the second year, and $76,044[2] at the end of the third year. Comparing this final figure to the accumulated value of investment A ($76,395) shows that investment A is a slightly better use of the $50,000 than simply investing in the available 15 percent opportunities. On the other hand, investment B ($75,670) is not a sound investment when 15 percent opportunities exist. What do you expect to happen if the investment opportunity rate were 10 percent? Check your intuition with a numerical calculation similar to the one just performed.

Present Value and Net Present Value

In the above discussion, the evaluation of a stream of cash flows was based on the accumulated value (including reinvestment income) of the cash flows to the end of the stream's lifetime. This is a very natural way to approach the evaluation because it so closely parallels the compounding calculations of a savings account. There are, however, several drawbacks to this "future value" approach. First, the value of an investment is associated with a future point in time. For short-lived investments, like the examples, this is not a problem. For investments with long lifetimes, say 20 or 40 years, it is very difficult to internalize the significance of their accumulated values. The num-

---

[2]The exact number is $76,043.75, but to simplify the presentation, figures will be rounded to whole dollars.

bers will be extraordinarily large and very distant in time. Even if the investments under consideration have moderate lifetimes, they may be of different lengths. As a result, their evaluations will be associated with different points in time, making comparison difficult. Finally, the financial attractiveness of each investment would require the calculation of two accumulated values—one for initial investment and one for the future cash flows.

If the perspective of the evaluation were changed from "future dollars" to "today dollars," these difficulties would be eliminated. The frame of reference would be today, not some distant time; all investments would be evaluated at a common point in time, today, not potentially different points; the attractiveness of an investment could be based on the simple comparison of the initial investment and the "today value" of the future cash flows.

From the "future dollars" perspective, $50,000 today is worth $76,044 in three years in an environment of 15 percent reinvestment opportunities. (This figure was calculated in the previous section.) If we shift our perspective to today, it could be said that $50,000 is the present value of $76,044 received three years from now when 15 percent opportunities exist. The $50,000 is the present value in the sense that if it were invested today at 15 percent it would grow to $76,044 three years in the future. As a result, $50,000 today and $76,044 in three years are financially equivalent when 15 percent investments are available. This leads to the definition that *the present value of a future payment is the amount today for which the investor is indifferent between receiving the present value or waiting for the future payment.*

This concept can be applied to a stream of future cash flows, for example, the three annual payments of $22,000 that make up the returns from investment A. The present value of these flows at a reinvestment rate of 15 percent would be the amount of money required today to generate the future stream of cash flows. Each of the individual cash flows in the stream has a present value (the amount required today to generate it). The sum of these individual present values would be the amount required to generate the entire stream. Because the accumulation over time of a reinvested dollar is the underlying concept of present value, the following table of the accumulated value of a reinvested dollar at 15 percent will help in calculating the present values of each of the cash flows resulting from investment A.

	Year 1	Year 2	Year 3
Beginning amount	1.0000	1.1500	1.3225
Interest at 15 percent	.1500	.1725	.1984
Ending amount	1.1500	1.3225	1.5209

The first component of investment A stream is $22,000 one year from now. A dollar that is invested at 15 percent will accrue to $1.15 one year from now. Thus, $22,000 equals 115 percent of the amount that would be necessary to invest today to have $22,000 at year's end. The present value of $22,000 is therefore $19,130 ($22,000/1.15). Similarly, the cash flows of years 2 and 3 of investment A would require $16,635 (or $22,000/1.3225) and $14,465 (or $22,000/1.5209), respectively. The entire cash flow stream would require an investment at 15 percent of the sum of these individual investments, $50,230 ($19,130 + $16,635 + $14,465). This sum is the present value of the stream of future cash flows of investment A.

Because it would take $50,230 to generate the stream of future cash flows of investment A with 15 percent investments and investment A requires an initial investment of only $50,000, investment A is an attractive investment when 15 percent alternatives are available. Not surprisingly, because present value and accumulated value are so tightly related, this is the same conclusion that was reached when the accumulated value of the cash flow stream of investment A was compared to the accumulated value of $50,000 after three years. If investment A were made, it would add today $230 ($50,230 − $50,000) in value above the use of the $50,000 in the manager's usual 15 percent investments. *The difference between the present value of the future cash flow stream and the initial investment is called the net present value.* The net present value (or NPV) is a measure of the attractiveness of an investment. If the NPV is positive, an investment is attractive, because it would require more money to generate the investment's future cash flows through the manager's reinvestment opportunities than is required by the investment itself. Value is being added by positive NPV investments and the more positive the NPV, the more attractive the investment. If the NPV is negative, the investment is unattractive and value is depleted. If the NPV is zero, the investment is equivalent to earning the reinvestment rate and the investment neither adds nor depletes value. As such, a zero NPV investment is an indifferent opportunity.

Note that in the above calculations, the present value of a future cash flow is less than the cash flow itself. The future flows have been discounted to account for the time value of money. At a 15 percent reinvestment rate, $22,000 received one year from now has a present value of $19,130 or .8696 of its future value. To account for the time value of money, the flow one year from now must be multiplied by the factor, .8696, to bring the flow to its present value. This factor is the one year discount factor at 15 percent. Similarly, the discount factors at 15 percent are .7561 for two years and .6575 for three years. Each of these can be easily calculated as the reciprocal of the accumulated values of a dollar—.8696 = 1/1.15, .7561 = 1/1.3225, and .6575 = 1/1.5209. Discount factors can be interpreted as the present values of future $1 payments and can be used to calculate the present value of future streams of cash flows. For investment A, the calculation is:

($22,000 × .8696) + ($22,000 × .7561) + ($22,000 × .6575) = $50,230

Formulas for Accumulated and Present Value Calculations

Underlying the calculations of accumulated value and present value are several straightforward equations. The accumulated value (A) at reinvestment rate (r), of a single payment (P), after one year is $P \times (1 + r)$, the payment P plus the interest $r \times P$. After two years, the accumulated value is $[P \times (1 + r)] \times (1 + r)$, the amount after one year multiplied by $1 + r$. The accumulated values in subsequent years would be calculated by the successive multiplications of the ending value by $1 + r$. This would yield the general formula for the accumulated value after n years, A_n, of a payment, P, at a reinvestment rate, r,

$$A_n = P \times (1 + r)^n.$$

This formula can then be used to express the present value (P) of an amount A_n that is available n years in the future with a reinvestment rate (r) as

$$P = A_n/(1 + r)^n.$$

Although these formulas were developed on the basis of the cash flows occurring at the end of their respective years, they apply just as well to flows that occur within years. For example, the calculation of the present value of a cash flow that occurs after 2 years and 3 months would use the above formula with $n = 2.25$.

Streams in Perpetuity

There is one cash flow stream worthy of special consideration—a stream of equal year-end cash flows continuing forever. Such a stream is called a **perpetuity**. At a reinvestment rate of 15 percent, $20,000 will produce a cash flow stream of $3,000 per year forever. The $20,000 will not accumulate because the annual interest of $3,000 is taken out as a cash flow. By definition, the present value of this perpetuity of $3,000 per year is the amount required today to generate that never-ending stream. With a 15 percent rate, the stream can be generated with an initial amount of $20,000, so the stream's present value is $20,000. Note that the present value is the annual payment divided by the rate ($3,000/.15). In general, a stream of equal annual cash flows has a present value equal to the annual payment, C, divided by the reinvestment rate, this is C/r. If investment A were a perpetuity with an annual payment of $22,000, it would have a present value at a reinvestment rate of 15 percent of $146,667 ($22,000/.15). The exponential effects of discounting can be seen from this figure because the present value of the first three years of the perpetuity ($50,340) accounts for more than one-third of the present value of the entire perpetuity.

Pretax versus Aftertax Analyses

On some occasions, calculations can be simplified by working with pretax monetary flows and avoiding tax calculations. Pretax analyses are appropriate when the pretax monetary flows are proportional to their cash flows, which are always aftertax. This proportionality will not be the case when the investments under consideration involve differences in depreciation, investment tax incentives, or working capital. When these conditions exist, a doubling of the pretax monetary flow will not result in a doubling of the cash flow.

When a pretax analysis is appropriate, at what reinvestment rate should the monetary flows be discounted? It is tempting to think that a pretax reinvestment rate would be consistent with the pretax nature of the flows, but this would be incorrect. Because a full cash flow analysis will always be appropriate, it is necessary to have any pretax (shortcut) analysis be consistent with it. Tax considerations will affect the numerator of the present value calculation in a proportional fashion (remember this was the condition necessary for a pretax analysis to be appropriate), but an adjustment to the reinvestment rate will not affect the denominator in the same fashion. The denominator of the present value calculation involves one plus the reinvestment rate and, as a result, increasing the reinvestment rate proportional to the tax rate will not increase the denominator proportionally. The nonproportional changes to the denominator will lead to an inconsistency between the always correct cash flow analysis and the pretax analysis with a pretax reinvestment rate. As an illustration, suppose the tax rate is 50 percent, the reinvestment rate is 10 percent, and a pretax monetary flow in year 1 is $100. The present value of the cash flow associated with the monetary flow would be $45.45 ($100 × .50/1.10). The correct pretax analysis would result in a present value of $90.90 ($100/1.10), which has the pretax and the cash flow analyses in proportion to the tax rate. An incorrect pretax analysis would be $83.33 ($100/1.20), which does not preserve the proportionality of the results. The only meaningful reinvestment rate is the aftertax reinvestment rate and it should be used under all circumstances.

The Reinvestment Rate

Present value calculations require a reinvestment rate. Throughout this chapter, the rate has been assumed to be known, but the methodology suggests the fundamental principle upon which such a rate should be based. Cash that becomes available does not lie idle but is recommitted to other activities throughout the firm. Strictly speaking, the appropriate rate is the amount that must be earned on a dollar so the investor/manager is indifferent between receiving the dollar now and receiving the dollar plus its earnings a year from now. Because the estimation of this rate is difficult, the objective of this section is to provide a flavor (not a complete exposition) of approaches to the issue.

Hurdle Rate

One approach to the estimation of the reinvestment rate is to estimate the "opportunity rate," that is, the marginal rate of return of the pool of investment opportunities that the firm might undertake with its available cash spin-offs. It was in this context that the 15 percent rate was established for the assessment of investment A and investment B. In practice, where the profile of potential investment opportunities is complex, the opportunity rate is a difficult number to estimate.

An alternative approach is to seek the rate from the perspective of the company's cost of capital. The prices that investors are willing to pay for a firm's securities and the yields that they demand from those securities determine a market cost of capital raised through debt and equity. The cost of debt is simply the interest that must be paid, but because interest expenses are tax deductible, the effective cost of debt is the aftertax interest rate. There is a corresponding cost for shareholder's equity because investors want to earn a satisfactory rate of return as compensation for the use of their money and for the risks that they take by investing in the firm. This cost applies both to the new investments made in the firm through the purchases of stock and to the earnings that are retained in the firm rather than paid out in dividends. These costs combined with the capital structure of the firm result in a weighted average cost of capital (WACC). Because the WACC is the average rate demanded by the capital markets for investment funds, the firm should consider only those investments whose cash flows will yield at least that rate. Thus, the value of the investment, from the perspective of the capital markets, is the present value of the cash flows using the WACC.

In a perfect environment, where both the firm and the investors have complete information, the WACC and the opportunity rate will be identical because the firm will invest in all projects with a positive net present value at the weighted average cost of capital. As a result, the marginal project will have a net present value equal to zero so its rate of return will be the WACC. Even though the capital markets are not perfect, the WACC is commonly used as the reinvestment rate. It is often referred to as the **hurdle rate** because investments with a positive net present value at this rate are judged to be financially attractive, that is, they passed the hurdle. Similarly, investments with negative net present values fail the hurdle.

Internal Rate of Return

Frequently the "accept/reject" decision is not particularly sensitive to the exact value of the hurdle rate and there may be a comfortable leeway for error in its specification. To find out how much leeway there may be, the hurdle rate could be compared to the reinvestment rate for which the NPV of the investment is zero. At this break-even reinvestment rate, the decision will change from accept to reject or from reject to accept. This break-even reinvestment rate is called the **internal rate of return (IRR).**[3]

There is no formula for computing the internal rate of return; it must be found by trial and error. For example, consider investment A. At a 15 percent reinvestment rate, the net present value is $230. If the reinvestment rate were 10 percent, the investment would be even more attractive and would have a net present value of $4,711. On the other hand, if the reinvestment rate were increased to 17 percent, the net present value would be $-1,389. As the reinvestment rate changes from 10 percent to 17 percent, the net present value changes from being very positive to very negative. Figure 7–1 is a graph of the relationship and shows that the net present value is zero somewhere between 15 and 16 percent. Thus, the internal rate of return is between 15 and 16 percent. By continuing a trial and error process, values in this range can be tested until the reinvestment rate that results in a zero net present value is found. For investment A, the internal rate of return is approximately 15.3 percent. If the reinvestment rate is less than 15.3 percent, the net present value will be positive and the investment will be judged to be attractive. If the reinvestment rate is greater than 15.3 percent, the net present value will be negative. There is little leeway between the reinvestment rate of 15 percent and the point where the investment changes from attractive to unattractive, so a careful consideration of the appropriate reinvestment rate is necessary.

In the "accept/reject" decision for an investment, the internal rate of return and the net present value are equivalent. If an investment's net present value at the reinvestment rate is positive, the investment's internal rate of return must be greater than the reinvestment rate. Refer to Figure 7–1 for a visual confirmation of this statement. Similarly, if the internal rate of return is greater than the reinvestment rate, the investment's net present value at the reinvestment rate must be positive. Regardless of the perspective, the investment is attractive, so the two figures can be used interchangeably in this case.

Although net present value and internal rate of return are equivalent in the accept/reject decision, internal rate of return should not be used to rank alternative, mutually exclusive investments. The internal rate of return for an investment is calculated on the basis of the investment's stream of cash flows and is divorced from the actual reinvestment opportunities in which the cash flows of the investment could be put. As its name states, the internal rate of return is "internal" to the investment and does not reflect the reality of the reinvestment environment facing the investor. As a result, internal rate of return does not apply a common standard of comparison to each of the investments under consideration. Consequently, the selection of a project with

---

[3]In certain circumstances there may be more than one reinvestment rate that results in a zero net present value for an investment. Such cases may arise when the cash flow stream has more than one change in sign between successive cash flows (that is, more than one time when successive cash flows change from negative to positive or positive to negative). For these cases, the internal rate of return is not a useful concept.

FIGURE 7–1

NPV of Investment A for Different Reinvestment Rates

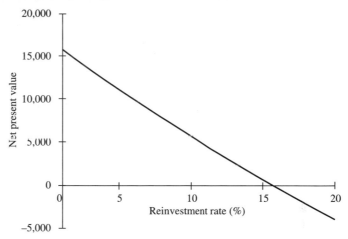

a larger internal rate of return does not guarantee that it will have the larger net present value at the appropriate reinvestment rate (rather than its own internal rate). To illustrate this point, consider the two investments whose net present values are graphed in Figure 7–2. If a choice between these two alternatives is made on the basis of the larger internal rate of return, investment 1 would be selected. If the reinvestment rate is 15 percent, however, investment 2 is the better choice because it has the larger net present value at the actual reinvestment rates available to the investor. Because of its inward-looking nature, the internal rate of return can be a misleading criterion for selecting among mutually exclusive investments.

Nominal versus Effective Rates of Return

Suppose an annual reinvestment rate is quoted as 12 percent. Does this mean each dollar invested will earn one cent at the end of the first month? It all depends on whether the annual rate is being quoted as an effective annual rate or a nominal annual rate and on how frequently earnings are compounded. There is considerable room for confusion unless terms and assumptions are carefully specified.

Let us suppose that a 12 percent annual rate results in a 1 percent payment each month. Because of the compounding of the monthly payments ("interest being earned on interest"), the year-end value of an investment will be more than 112 percent of the initial investment. A $1,000 investment would have a year-end value of

$$\$1{,}127 = \$1{,}000 \times 1.01 \times 1.01 \times 1.01 \times \cdots \times 1.01 = \$1{,}000 \times (1.01)^{12}.$$

FIGURE 7–2
NPV and IRR

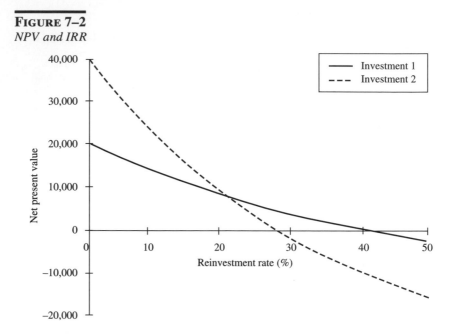

This is equivalent to a 12.7 percent annual rate, even though a 12 percent annual rate was quoted. A vocabulary that would clarify the situation is to state that the nominal annual rate is 12 percent compounded monthly and the effective annual rate is 12.7 percent. Reinvestment rates are quoted as effective annual rates.

Not only is it important to distinguish between nominal and effective annual rates, but also care must be taken when stating equivalent rates for periods less than a year. For a 12 percent nominal annual rate that is compounded monthly, the equivalent monthly rate is 1 percent (the annual rate divided by 12). For an effective annual rate of 12 percent, the monthly rate must be calculated taking into account the compounding during the year. If the effective annual rate is 12 percent, the value of a dollar at the end of the year is $1.12. If returns are made on a monthly basis, the monthly rate must satisfy the following equation,

$$\$1.12 = \$1.00 \times (1 + \text{monthly rate})^{12}.$$

The solution to this equation is a monthly rate of .95 percent (.0095). Note that because of the compounding that is inherent in effective rates, the equivalent monthly rate for an effective annual rate is less than the equivalent monthly rate for a nominal annual rate. In general, the equivalent periodic rate of an effective annual rate is

$$(1 + \text{Effective annual rate})^{1/\text{Number of periods}} - 1.$$

8   MULTIOBJECTIVE AND MULTISTAKEHOLDER CHOICE

Important decisions—what job to take, where to locate a production facility, which product to develop—usually involve more than one objective. A number of significant choices generally affect many stakeholders who will take part in the decision-making process. We may muddle through a decision with many objectives or stakeholders. Yet we recognize that some aids and a conceptual foundation for our decisions would be welcome, even in some of the more straightforward situations. In cases that have many objectives, stakeholders, or alternatives, our intellects are overloaded and we need help.

This chapter describes how you can evaluate alternatives based on multiple objectives by using your own personal preferences or by assessing the preferences of others. First, methods are given that don't require trade-offs among objectives. These methods are simple and may lead to a unanimous decision without requiring that parties state opposing preferences. This is useful when the justification for decisions will be made public.

In many instances, however, trade-offs between objectives are necessary and should be based on personal judgments and preferences. The second part of this chapter presents procedures for assessing personal trade-offs among attributes and using these preferences to compare alternatives. As we proceed, several examples will show how simple spreadsheet analysis may aid this process.

The Generic Choice Problem

This chapter deals with choices among alternatives that have consequences that can be characterized by a list of quantities. Each quantity represents an attribute score for a specific objective. An attribute may relate to the impact on a single individual or on a class of stakeholders.

TABLE 8–1   Example Sets of Attributes

Choosing a Home	Promoting a Product	Treating a Minor Ailment
Price	Cost	Days of discomfort
Suitability of location	Increase in market share	Time until relapse
Size	Customer goodwill	Pain index score
Desirability of architecture		Cost
Condition		
Quality of neighborhood		

Problems with multiple objectives may involve many different types of attributes. Table 8–1 shows three choice problems with their own sets of attributes. Some of these attributes are objectively measured scores, such as the *price* or *size* of a home. Other attributes are scored in a totally subjective way by direct preference assessment; one such attribute is the *desirability of architecture*.

These two types of attributes represent opposite ends of the objective–subjective spectrum. Many other types of attributes are in the middle of the spectrum. For example, the *pain index score* may be based on a medically agreed on scoring system for pain. A given medical condition rates a given score, and medical professionals would argue about what score to apply to a given condition. This is an example of a subjective index. It is scored once the composition of the index has been determined based on subjective professional judgment.

Other indices that could be used as attributes may be even closer to the objective end of the spectrum, so close that they may seem completely objective. The Consumer Price Index (CPI) is one example of a pseudo-objective attribute. Since it has become so familiar to us, some may wonder why this isn't a totally objective attribute. The composition of goods and services that are tracked in calculating the CPI are selected in a manner that is not totally objective.

Example

To enliven our discussion of how one may progress through the various stages of analysis of a multiobjective choice, let's use an example of a familiar problem: selecting a home. For simplicity, we shall assume the home buyer has settled on three objectives to be used in making the decision: to minimize the cost of the purchase, to maximize the size of the home, and to maximize the quality of the neighborhood. The relevant attributes of any prospective home may then be *price* (P), *size* (S), and *quality of neighborhood* (Q). Natural objective measures (dollars and square feet of interior space) will be used for the first two attributes, while the last (Q) is a direct preference

TABLE 8–2   Prospective Homes for Purchase

	Price	Size (Square Feet)	Quality of Neighborhood
Antrim Street (A)	$176,000	2,800	75
Brookmere Road (B)	$164,000	3,600	85
Canterbury Lane (C)	$140,000	2,600	85
Downfield Avenue (D)	$190,000	3,650	60

assessment. Thus, Q is scored from 0 (worst possible neighborhood in the city) to 100 (best possible) for each alternative. In this oversimplified example, knowing the attribute scores for the three attributes would be all that would be needed to evaluate which home would be the most attractive to the buyer.

Table 8–2 shows the attribute scores for four homes now being considered by the home buyer. This set of alternatives is the result of a process that many of us use to pare down the initial list of possibilities, what we may call elimination by aspects. In this process, alternatives are excluded because of some unacceptable aspects. For example, the home buyer may drop a prospective home from consideration because of its adobe construction or because it just doesn't look right on the lot. It usually makes sense to carry out this elimination process before scoring alternatives on the attributes.

First-Round Eliminations

There are simple ways of reducing the number of attractive alternatives, which we explore first. If we reduce enough of the alternatives, we may produce a unanimous choice. Where this does not prove conclusive, the decision maker's trade-offs among attributes will be needed.

Dominance

After alternatives are scored on all attributes, we might see that one (or several) alternatives are inferior to some other alternative with respect to every attribute. Then the alternative may be dropped from consideration.

> *Dominance:* If alternative I is at least as desirable as alternative J on all attributes and more desirable on at least one attribute, then alternative J is dominated by I.

The home on Antrim Street (A), for example, has a higher price tag, a smaller size, and a less appealing neighborhood than the Brookmere Road home (B). Thus, A is dominated by B and can be dismissed. The home on Canterbury Lane (C), on the other hand, has a better price than (B) and (A), but it is

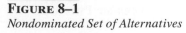

FIGURE 8–1

Nondominated Set of Alternatives

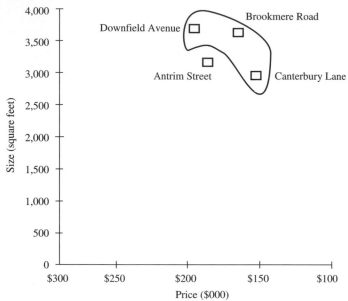

smaller than the others. Therefore, C is not dominated. Neither is the home on Downfield Avenue.

The nondominated alternatives then are B, C, and D. Nondominated alternatives are often referred to as the *efficient* set or the *admissible* set of alternatives. A scatter plot of all four alternatives for *price* and *size* (Figure 8–1) shows that the efficient alternatives are the upper right-hand frontier. Note that the scale for *price* on the horizontal axis decreases from left to right, since lower values of *price* are preferred. Again, B dominates A because it is both above and to the right of A (and has a higher Q, even though Q is not shown).

It may be tedious to identify the nondominated set of alternatives when there are many alternatives and/or attributes. A useful trick for identifying dominance with any number of attributes or alternatives is to generate a so-called radar chart, as is done in Figure 8–2. Each spoke represents a dimension. Distance from the center represents attribute values. This chart can be produced by most spreadsheet programs. Note that the *price* attribute is inverted (smaller is better) and that each attribute is rescaled over a 0 to 100 range, so that each can be plotted on axes with similar scaling.[1] Since the

---

[1]The *size score* is calculated (*Size* − 2,000)/20 and *price score* is (200 − *Price* in thousands).

FIGURE 8–2

Radar Chart for Viewing Dominance

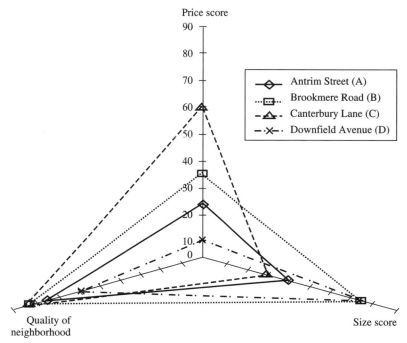

line for the Brookmere residence is always at least as high as that for the Antrim residence, and above it for *price*, the graph in Figure 8–2 indicates that the Brookmere home dominates the Antrim home.

Figure 8–2 also shows how easy it is to discern when an alternative comes close to dominating another alternative. Simply observe the area below the radar line for that alternative that is above the line for another alternative and compare it mentally to the opposite area where that alternative is below the other alternative. For example, home B comes close to dominating home D. Be aware, however, that eliminating home D from consideration based on this observation is dangerous. It makes an implicit judgment about the relative importance of attributes, which is exactly what dominance seeks to avoid.

Decision Rules without Trade-off Judgments

Ordinarily, the efficient set of alternatives cannot be pared further without making value judgments concerning the relative importance of the attributes. Sometimes, however, it is appropriate to employ easy-to-use decision rules that do not require apparent trade-offs. Let's consider several of these decision rules.

The Lexicographic Rule

The lexicographic rule works in an alphabetizing manner that is appropriate for its name (a *lexicon* is a dictionary). First, alternatives are ranked according to their scores on a most-important attribute. If alternatives score the same on this attribute, they are ranked using a second attribute, then a third, and so on, until all ties are broken.

The decision maker specifies in advance the order in which attributes are used to rank the alternatives. For example, assume the home buyer first uses *quality of neighborhood*, then *price*, then *size* to order homes lexicographically. Using Q, there is a tie between B and C. This tie is broken using price in favor of C. Thus, the lexicographic ranking would be $C>B>A>D$, where $>$ is read "is preferred to."

The lexicographic procedure is easy to use because the decision maker specifies only the order in which the attributes are to be considered. Unfortunately, the rule is often inadequate because it doesn't fully consider every attribute. Only one attribute is used unless there is a tie.

Satisficing

Herbert Simon, Nobel laureate in economics, has suggested that a "satisficing" rule is often used by decision makers. The decision maker searches until finding an alternative that exceeds some aspiration level on each attribute. Like the efficient set, there may be more than one satisficing alternative, but unlike the efficient set, there may be none.

Simon asserts that decision makers seldom exhibit optimizing behavior rather than this satisficing behavior. Even though perhaps everyone satisfices in routine decisions, it may not be the best approach for important choices, or for those based on formal analysis. The aspiration levels may not be easy to set explicitly. Conceptually, they may not hold up under scrutiny because an infinitesimal decline in some attribute level may change an alternative from acceptable to unacceptable.

The satisficing approach may be used in conjunction with the lexicographic procedure when the decision maker has an aspiration level in mind for the most important attribute. For any alternatives that exceed this aspiration level, the next most important attribute is considered. For any alternatives that are at or above the aspiration level for the second most important attribute, another attribute will be called into consideration, and so on.

Suppose the home buyer considers *quality of neighborhood* most important and has an aspiration level of 70. *Price* is next most important with an aspiration level of $170,000 (remember lower prices are better). Finally, the aspiration level on *size* is 3,000 square feet. The lexicographic procedure with aspiration levels would, on the basis of *quality of neighborhood*, give three satisficing alternatives: A, B, and C. A would have an unsatisfactory *price*, leaving B and C. Only B would satisfice on *size*. Thus, B would be the favored home.

Neither the lexicographic nor satisficing approaches allow consideration of the compensating effects of attributes. In other words, a superior performance on one attribute (e.g., *size*) may not compensate for a poor performance on another attribute (e.g., *price*).

The lexicographic rule, satisficing, and a combination of the two avoid trade-offs among the attributes. Nonetheless, in setting the order of importance of the attributes in the lexicographic rule, or the aspiration levels in the satisficing rule, it is necessary to make very strong preference statements. Because these rules are simple to use, they have their place in practice. Yet more robust **compensatory** methods are needed to capture explicit trade-offs among attributes and to value an alternative with a number.

Rate and Weight: Linear Additive Scoring Rules

The simplest decision rule that allows high scores on one attribute to compensate for lower scores on other attributes uses ratings and weightings and combines attributes in a linear and additive fashion. Ratings are scores for alternatives for the separate attributes; weightings are desirability scores for the attributes themselves. The process is outlined as follows:

Rate and Weight

Step 1. Rate the alternatives on each attribute:

r_{ij} = Rating of alternative i on attribute j.

Step 2. Weight the relative importance of each attribute:

w_j = Weighting of attribute j.

Step 3. Score the alternatives using the sum of the weights multiplied by the rates:

$$V_i = w_1 r_{i1} + w_2 r_{i2} + \cdots + w_m r_{im} \qquad (8\text{--}1)$$

where alternatives are ranked according to:

V_i = value assigned to alternative i.

Rating Alternatives

The method used to rate alternatives depends on what type of attribute is being used. One major type of attribute includes those that can be **objectively** measured, such as *price* and *size* in the home buyer's choice. With these quantities, the units are unambiguous (e.g., dollars and square feet). Indices, such as the Consumer Price Index, also usually have unambiguous scales.

Subjective measures generally have their own specific scale. For example, an air quality index might be measured on a scale from 1 to 10; a student may be graded on a scale of A, B, C, D, F; an individual's cardiopulmonary capability might be scored on a scale of I, II, III, IV. When subjective attributes such as these are used, it is necessary to convert ratings into numerical scores. In the rate and weight process, these ratings will be used eventually as measures of desirability; thus, the numerical scores should reflect value. If a student grade of A is given a rating of 4.00, B is given a rating of 3.00, and C a rating of 2.00, then the difference between the desirability of A versus B is the same as the difference between the desirability of B over C. The definition of a unit for the attribute scale and the zero rating is arbitrary. Thus, grades F, D, C, B, A may be converted into the numerical ratings 0, 1.0, 2.0, 3.0, 4.0 or into the numerical ratings 20, 40, 60, 80, 100 or into some other scale with a different zero level and definition of a unit. However, the definition of the unit is a key determinant in assigning weightings to attributes.

Sometimes there is neither an objective measure nor an appropriate scale for a subjective measure. In such cases it is appropriate to rate alternatives by **direct preference measurement**. Then the attribute is scored on a scale of 0 to 100, as was done for *quality of neighborhood* in the home buyer example. There are two common ways in which the decision maker may define 0 and 100.

1. Predefined range: Set upper and lower limits for the attribute such that no alternative would ever be considered that had an attribute rating outside these limits. Assign the rating 0 to the least desirable end of the interval, which may be the upper limit when more of the attribute is less preferred. The most desirable end of the interval is given the rating 100.

2. Range defined by alternatives: If the set of alternatives to be considered is complete (no new alternatives remain to be identified), find the worst and best alternative with respect to the attribute and give them ratings of 0 and 100, respectively.

In the home buyer example, the first approach was used to define the scale for *quality of neighborhood*, since new homes will be considered as they come on the market. The 0 and 100 levels are defined by the worst and best *quality of neighborhood* imaginable in the region in which the home buyer was looking for a home.

Weighting Attributes

The weights associated with the attributes indicate their importance in the decision. Only relative weights matter; weights of 1, 2, 3 assigned to the attributes *price, size,* and *quality of neighborhood* would give the same rankings of alternatives as the weights 10, 20, 30 or the weights .2, .4, .6. It is usually convenient, but not necessary, to have the weights sum to 1.0.

When there are two or more objectively measured attributes, it may be possible to combine them with objective weights. For example, suppose there are two cost attributes—one is an annual operating cost and the other a onetime capital cost. An appropriate hurdle rate might be used to convert an annual cost to an equivalent capital cost. For instance, if the hurdle rate is 12.5 percent and the annual cost will continue forever (over an infinite time horizon), then the weight on a dollar of annual cost would be 8 times that of a dollar of capital cost ($8 or 1/.125 is the net present value of an infinite stream of annual $1 costs at a hurdle rate of 12.5 percent). Using objective weights where possible saves effort and potential controversy in the subjective assessment of weights.

Subjective weights are often obtained in practice simply by asking the decision maker to compare the relative importance of attributes. For example, "Which is more important to you, *price* or *quality*?" Suppose the off-the-cuff response is that "*quality of neighborhood* is twice as important as *price*." This statement really means very little without knowing how the attributes are measured. For example, suppose we rate *quality of neighborhood* over a range from 0 to 100 and measure *price* in dollars over a range from $100,000 to $200,000. Then the statement "The weight placed on *quality of neighborhood* points is twice that placed on dollars of *price*" is equivalent to requiring $2 to compensate for a loss of 1 quality point. This implies it would take only $200 to compensate for the entire range of quality from 0 to 100, which hardly suggests that *quality of neighborhood* is very important.

A meaningful statement of the relative importance of attributes cannot be made except in the context of some definition of the units of measure for each attribute. One couldn't be clear about the value of improving temperature one degree without specifying whether it is measured in Fahrenheit or Celsius. Likewise, the value of an automobile means little unless we specify whether the amount is denominated in dollars or yen!

The weights multiply the rates when an alternative is scored. If the weights have a consistent meaning, they must depend on the units used for each attribute. See the appendix to this chapter for an example of how the overall ranking of alternatives can be altered by a simple linear rescaling of attributes. That example shows that even a statement like "40 percent of your grade is based on an exam and 30 percent on written work" may mean different things depending on how the exam and the written work are scaled.

Pricing Out   The assignment of relative weights is based on trade-offs. Suppose, for example, the weight on *quality of neighborhood* is 1.0 and the weight on *price* is −.001 (this weight is negative because we like lower prices). This would imply that the home buyer would trade a price increase of $1,000 to achieve an increase of 1 point in *quality of neighborhood* (since −.001*1,000 = 1).

A process called *pricing out* may be used to obtain these weights. The decision maker is asked to determine what change in one attribute would compensate for a given change in another attribute. The decision maker may have stated, "I would give up $1,000 in *price* to improve *quality of neighborhood* by one point." Then using weight times rate gives the following relationship

$$\text{Change in value} = w_p \, \Delta_p + w_q \, \Delta_q = 0$$

where Δ_p and Δ_q are the changes in attributes *price* and *quality of neighborhood*, respectively, that compensate for one another. Substituting for these changes, we have

$$w_p \, 1{,}000 + w_q \, 1 = 0, \text{ or}$$

$$w_p = -.001 \, w_q.$$

The reader can verify that we could have gotten the same result if the decision maker had said, "I would allow a reduction of only .001 points of *quality of neighborhood* for $1 reduction in *price*." Obviously, it is best to allow the decision maker to express trade-offs in the most convenient terms and then translate them to weights on attributes.

When there are several attributes, it is generally best to choose one attribute, say *price*, to price out relative to the others. Thus, we may ask the decision maker, "What increase in *price* would compensate for an additional square foot of *size?*" Suppose the answer is $60. Using similar logic to that above would give

$$w_s 1 = -60 \, w_p$$

We may substitute $w_p = -.001$ into this expression to obtain

$$w_s = .06 \, w_q.$$

If we arbitrarily choose w_q to be 1.0, then we have the following weights for attributes:

$w_p = -.001$ for *price* in $
$w_s = .06$ for *size* in square feet
$w_q = 1.0$ for *quality of neighborhood* in direct preference units ranging from 0 to 100.

Again, we must be careful to change the weights if the definition of the units changes. Thus, if we change the measurement of *price* to use units of thousands of dollars, then we would change the weight on *price* from $-.001$ to -1.0. Under the old system, an increase in *price* of $1,000 would be valued at (using Weight $\times$ Rate)

$$(-.001)*1000 = -1$$

and under the new definition, Weight $\times$ Rate would also give a change in score of -1:

$$(-1.0)*1 = -1.$$

To test that the decision maker really believes the weights that have been assigned, ask a number of trade-off questions, starting at different levels for the attributes. Thus, the above weights might be checked by assuring that the home buyer would trade a house with a *price* of $160,000 and *quality of neighborhood* of 70 for one that had a *price* of $170,000 and a *quality of neighborhood* of 80, given they were the same size. If the answer is no, then the weights must be adjusted. If the decision maker insists on different weights for different starting values, then the weight-times-rate model doesn't apply.

Swing Weights   Instead of pricing out, we might use another method to define what are called *swing weights*. These weights require each attribute to be scaled the same way. Suppose we arbitrarily scale each attribute with a score ranging from 0 to 100. Assume that predefined ranges are used to define how attribute ratings map to the [0–100] scores. The following table shows the mapping that has been assumed.

	Worst (0)	*Best (100)*
Price	$200,000	$100,000
Size	2,000 sq. ft.	4,000 sq. ft.
Quality.	0 points	100 points

The best house imaginable would be one that would cost $100,000, have 4,000 square feet, and be in a neighborhood of quality 100. The fact that such a house doesn't exist doesn't really hamper us in using this house as a reference point for thinking about trade-offs. The "worst of the worst" house with a *price* of $200,000, 2,000 square feet of *space*, and a *quality of neighborhood* score of 0, also doesn't exist (luckily enough, because we wouldn't want it if it did!).

We can use these ranges to develop proportional rating scores for each attribute, which are always between 0 and 100. Thus, the proportional score for *price* is

Proportional price score $= (\text{Rating} - 200{,}000)*100/(100{,}000 - 200{,}000)$

and in general the proportional score is (Rating $-$ Worst) $\times$ 100/(Best $-$ Worst). Table 8–3 shows the proportional scores for the alternatives.

TABLE 8–3   Proportional Scores for Prospective Homes

	Price	*Size*	*Quality of Neighborhood*
Antrim Street (A)	24	40	75
Brookmere Road (B)	36	80	85
Canterbury Lane (C)	60	30	85
Downfield Avenue (D)	10	82.5	60

Now we can use these extremes to compare the significance of attributes. The first question is: Which attribute contributes the most to overall value? If we swing from the worst level to the best level on an attribute, which swing gives the most value? Suppose the answer is *size*. This means our proportional score weight would be highest for the *size* attribute.

We will then compare swings of the other attributes to that of *size*. For *quality of neighborhood*, we would ask the decision maker "A swing in *quality of neighborhood* from its worst (0 points) to its best (100 points) would be as valuable as a swing in *size* from its worst to what proportional score?" Suppose the decision maker responds that a swing in *quality of neighborhood* is equivalent to a change of *size* about 5/6 of the way across its range. Then

$$w_q = 5/6 \; w_s,$$

where we use italics to distinguish these weights from the weights obtained by pricing out. If a similar question asked about *price* elicits a response of 5/6 also, then

$$w_p = 5/6 \; w_s.$$

Now that we have the relative weights for the other attributes in terms of the weight for *size*, we can set all the weights. It is useful to set the weights so that they sum to 1.0. Thus, we have

$w_p + w_s + w_q = 1.0$ or

$5/6 \; w_s + w_s + 5/6 \; w_s = 1$ or

$2 \; 2/3 \; w_s = 1$ or

$w_s = .375$, which implies that $w_p = .3125$ and $w_q = .3125$.

These weights happen to be consistent with the weights obtained by pricing out, if one accounts for the scaling. That is:

$$\frac{\dfrac{w_p}{range_p}}{\dfrac{w_q}{range_q}} = \frac{w_p}{w_q}$$

For example, replacing these terms with their numerical values we have:

$$\frac{\dfrac{.3125}{100,000 - 200,000}}{\dfrac{.3125}{100}} = \frac{-.001}{1}$$

Similar consistencies would be found for w_p and w_s, and for w_p and w_q.

Combining Rates and Weights   The comparison of the home buyer's alternatives by rate and weight can now be completed. The value score for each house could be calculated using

$$V = -.001 * \text{Price} + .06 * \text{Size} + 1.0 * \text{Quality},$$

which conforms to expression (8–1) above using the weights assessed by pricing out.

The results of using this expression to evaluate each home (Table 8–4) indicate the ranking would be B>C>D>A. In Table 8–3, separate weight-times-rate scores are evaluated for each attribute for each alternative. In a spreadsheet the weight-times-rate calculations can be done for all alternatives with one keystroke using the matrix multiply capabilities.

Alternatively, a value score

$$V = .3125 * \text{Proportional price score} \\ + .375 * \text{Proportional size score} \\ + .3125 * \text{Proportional quality score}$$

would give a completely consistent ranking of alternatives, although not identical scores.

Assumptions of Rate and Weight

There are two strong assumptions implicit in the rate and weight procedure as it has been described:

1. Linear value in each attribute. The desirability of an additional unit of any attribute is constant for any level of that attribute. Thus, an additional 100 square feet in a home is worth the same regardless of whether it is added to a home of 1,000 square feet or one of 5,000 square feet.

2. Additive attributes. There is no interaction between attributes. An interaction might occur, for example, if the value of an additional 100 square feet of home size were higher for a home in a higher quality neighborhood than for a home in a lower quality neighborhood.

TABLE 8–4   Rate and Weight Results for Possible Homes

| | Price ($000) | | Size (sq. ft.) | | Quality | | Total |
	Amount	w*r	Amount	w*r	Amount	w*r	V Score
Home A	$176,000	−176	2,800	168	75	75	67
Home B	164,000	−164	3,600	216	85	85	137
Home C	140,000	−140	2,600	156	85	85	101
Home D	190,000	−190	3,650	219	60	60	89

There are many situations where these two assumptions do not apply. What do you do then? Suppose we didn't accept linearity in an attribute. Then it would be appropriate to convert the attribute into a value score that is linear in desirability. If additivity doesn't apply, then it may be necessary to add terms that are the products of value scores for individual attributes. Both of these extensions of rate and weight go beyond the scope of this chapter.

Where applicable, the rate and weight procedure is a particularly simple and handy way of treating choices with multiple objectives. It may be used to make *go/no go* decisions or to rank a finite set of alternatives. We simply compute the value score for each alternative, then compare alternatives on the basis of that score.

Multiple Stakeholder Problems

The home buying problem has been treated as a multiobjective choice situation where the attributes have an impact on an individual. The ideas extend nicely, however, to situations where there are impacts on various stakeholders. We could add attributes that primarily affect other stakeholders in addition to the decision maker. For instance, *quality of schools* may be an attribute that affects the children of the decision maker. *Availability of children's playmates* may be another attribute. The procedures we have described here for multiobjective problems could then be applied to multistakeholder decisions, at least as viewed from the perspective of a single decision maker. Dominance would be especially valuable in the multistakeholder context, because it avoids trading off one stakeholder's interests against those of another.

In cases where trade-offs are necessary and where the choice is not in the hands of a single individual, the methods that have been described are still useful as a decision-making aid. The weights and rates may be established by group consensus or by some agreed-on group process. Experts may be called on to do the rating of alternatives. Even where group consensus is difficult, interested parties may use the rate and weight procedure to establish their own positions.

APPENDIX 1
COMMENTS ON THE DEPENDENCE OF WEIGHTS ON THE SCALING OF ATTRIBUTES

It may not be apparent how important it is for the weights to reflect the scaling of the attributes. Many believe that the importance of an attribute is given by the weight, and that the weight is absolute—the scaling of the attributes has nothing to do with its interpretation.

Consider, for example, weights used by a professor to calculate grades of students. Suppose the professor announces at the beginning of the course that three attributes will be used in grading: participation in class (Part), a final examination (Exam), and other written work (Writn). The professor announces that the weights will be .30, .40, and .30, respectively. How can the students know what these weights mean without knowing the scaling of each individual element? While an assumption may be implicitly made that the weights suggest literally that total performance is based 30 percent on participation, 40 percent on the final examination, and 30 percent on the other written work, such an outcome would only be assured if the range of scores for each element were identical. This outcome is rarely the case, for scores depend on several factors: how hard the exam is; how well the students do; and what rescaling may be made of the data.

Table 8–5 has scores on the three parts of the grade for 10 students. Each part is rated on a 0-to-100 basis. Consider three approaches to using the attribute weightings. The first approach simply uses the value score

$$\text{Total} = .3 * \text{Part} + .4 * \text{Exam} + .3 * \text{Writn}.$$

The other two approaches transform the scores according to how the scores turn out for the class.

The first transformation is to standardize scores based on the mean and the standard deviation of the scores. Each score is transformed into a so-called z-score, which is the number of standard deviations (SD) that the score differs from the mean. Thus, a student's z-score for participation would be

$$z_{\text{Part}} = (\text{Part} - \text{Mean}_{\text{Part}})/\text{SD}_{\text{Part}}.$$

This approach is appropriate if you suspect that scores will be normally distributed and you intend to grade on the bell-shaped curve. Once the z-scores for the attributes have been calculated, the value score would be

$$z_{\text{Total}} = .3 * z_{\text{Part}} + .4 * z_{\text{Exam}} + .3 * z_{\text{Writn}}.$$

TABLE 8–5   Attribute Scores for Grading Example

Student	Part	Exam	Writn
1	34	69	83
2	39	73	82
3	59	73	86
4	68	59	86
5	45	59	84
6	50	73	83
7	53	61	87
8	58	80	85
9	47	75	75
10	70	82	80

The second way to transform the attributes would be to normalize so that the best student on each attribute received a score of 100 and the worst student a score of 0. Thus, the normalized score for participation would be

PartN = [Part − Minimum(Part)]/[Maximum(Part) − Minimum(Part)].

After Exam and Writn were also normalized in this way, a third value score would be

TotalN = .3 * PartN + .4 * ExamN + .3 * WritnN.

The question is: Would these three ways of using the same weights give the same ranking of the students in the class? It would simplify life if they did. They do **not!** For the data in Table 8–4, the scores and rankings of students would be those given in Table 8–6. The rankings of the students (10 is the highest, 1 is the lowest) are given by Rank, ZRank, and RankN for the three scoring expressions, respectively. Notice the difference in rankings.

The moral of the story is to be sure what the units of the attributes are in assessing and interpreting attribute weights. In this example there were three different definitions for the units of the attributes—one was the raw scores, one was in terms of the standardized z-score, and one was a transformation to a 0 to 100 relative scale based on the lowest and highest scores.

TABLE 8–6   Scores and Rankings by Three Methods of Using the Same Weights

Student	Zpart	Zexam	Zwritn	PartN	ExamN	WritnN
1	−1.57	−0.17	−0.03	0.00	43.48	66.67
2	−1.14	0.32	−0.31	13.89	60.87	58.33
3	0.57	0.32	0.82	69.44	60.87	91.67
4	1.35	−1.38	0.82	94.44	0.00	91.67
5	−0.63	−1.38	0.26	30.56	0.00	75.00
6	−0.20	0.32	−0.03	44.44	60.87	66.67
7	0.06	−1.14	1.11	52.78	8.70	100.00
8	0.49	1.16	0.54	66.67	91.30	83.33
9	−0.45	0.56	−2.30	36.11	69.57	0.00
10	1.52	1.41	−0.88	100.00	100.00	41.67

Student	Total	Ztotal	TotalN	Rank	Zrank	RankN
1	62.70	−0.55	37.39	2.00	3.00	2.00
2	65.50	−0.31	46.01	3.00	4.00	4.00
3	72.70	0.55	72.68	8.00	8.00	8.00
4	69.80	0.10	55.83	7.00	7.00	6.00
5	62.30	−0.66	31.67	1.00	1.00	1.00
6	69.10	0.06	57.68	6.00	6.00	7.00
7	66.40	−0.11	49.31	4.00	5.00	5.00
8	74.90	0.77	81.52	9.00	10.00	9.00
9	66.60	−0.60	38.66	5.00	2.00	3.00
10	77.80	0.75	82.50	10.00	9.00	10.00

Exercises

1. The Pismo Beach Consulting Group (PBCG) was completing a study
    comparing three microcomputer systems for a not-for-profit client. The
    ratings of the three systems and the weights on attributes are given below.
    Complete the rate and weight analysis for PBCG.

		Computer		
Attribute	*HAL*	*MSO*	*HNS*	*Weight*
1. Dollar cost of system	.7	1.0	.7	1.0
2. Manufacturer's commitment	1.0	.1	.6	1.0
3. Number of units sold	1.0	.1	.3	.9
4. On-site maintenance	1.0	1.0	.0	.875
5. Ease in understanding manuals . . .	.5	.4	.4	.75
6. Password protected	.1	1.0	.1	.75
7. Link to national data	1.0	.8	.8	.7
8. Training	.6	1.0	.8	.7
9. Vendor commitment	.5	.7	.1	.7
10. Ease of use	.5	.7	.7	.6
11. Software available now	.6	1.0	.8	.45
12. Software in future	1.0	.5	.3	.4
13. Ease of expansion	1.0	.0	.3	.3

2. Take a problem of importance to you, such as the choice of an
    automobile, house, vacation, position of employment, etc. and work
    through the multiobjective choice:
    a. Identify the objectives and develop measures of performance
        (attributes) for each objective.
    b. Determine the alternatives available and score each alternative with
        respect to each attribute.
    c. Weight the attributes.
    d. Compute the total score for each alternative using the sum of "rate
        times weight." Which is the best alternative?

9 RISK PREFERENCE AND UTILITY

Many risky opportunities are evaluated solely by the average of the possible financial outcomes, that is, by the EMV or expected monetary value. The EMV is a convenient single number to help compare alternatives that have complicated risk profiles, but very few people in reality are willing to play the averages when making decisions of any importance. For example, most people would sell for less than $500 a lottery ticket that gave them a 50 percent chance at winning $1,000.

In this chapter, methods are presented for explicitly factoring risk into decision making in a consistent, systematic way. The approach is to assess the decision maker's degree of risk tolerance and to identify an appropriate model of his or her risk preferences. This is done using a so-called utility function, which scores the "utility" of various outcomes. The best action is the one with the highest probability-weighted or "expected" utility. The power of the utility method is that we can represent a rich variety of risk tolerances within a single unifying concept and set of procedures. With this approach we can determine how much below the $500 average value is acceptable for the above-mentioned lottery ticket. And we can similarly put a price on a complicated risk profile that is consistent with the price placed on the lottery ticket.

The Utility of Monetary Consequences

Consider a risky opportunity (call it a lottery for simplicity) that has equally likely possible outcomes of $2,500 and $10,000. The expected monetary value is .5(10,000) + .5(2,500) or $6,250. Would you pay $6,250 to purchase this lottery? Most people would not. Not even close. We all use something besides monetary value and probability to evaluate uncertain prospects. Our evaluation usually involves a third factor: our willingness to face risk.

Suppose a friend decides that if she owned the lottery and were offered $5,000 for it, she'd be indifferent about selling it or keeping it. The $5,000 is termed the *certainty equivalent* (CE) of the gamble. The difference between the EMV of the gamble ($6,250) and the CE ($5,000) is called the *risk premium* (RP). The risk premium is the amount of money you're willing to give up to avoid the risk of loss. By definition,

$$RP = EMV - CE$$

and in this instance,

$$RP = \$6,250 - \$5,000 = \$1,250.$$

Individuals who have positive risk premiums are called *risk-averse* individuals. The utility function can help us understand what it means to be risk-averse. Consider the utility function drawn in Figure 9–1. It represents a way to score dollar amounts in terms of their utility to the individual, using the individual's own subjective risk preference. For example, look up 10,000 on the horizontal scale and read the U(10,000) to be about .87. This happens to be more than halfway between the utility of 5,000, which is .63 and the utility of 15,000, which is .95. One implication of this utility curve is that it would be better to keep $10,000, with a .87 utility, than to trade it for a 50-50 chance at $5,000 and $15,000, which has an average utility of (.63 + .95)/2 = .79.

FIGURE 9–1

A Risk-Averse Utility Function

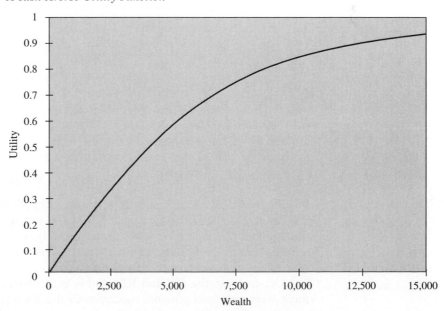

Note that the utility function is bent and opens downward (in technical terms, this is called *concave*). Any *risk-averse* utility function would display this concave shape. An interesting property of this shape is that the utility increment for a given increase in wealth declines as wealth increases. This is shown in the accompanying table for $2,500 increments of wealth. In other words, the utility of $5,000 is more than halfway between U(2,500) and U(7,500), so the individual would prefer $5,000 to a 50-50 lottery with outcomes $2,500 and $7,500. Similarly $6,250 is more desirable than a 50-50 lottery with outcomes $2,500 and $10,000.

Wealth	Utility
0	0.00
2,500	0.39
5,000	0.63
7,500	0.78
10,000	0.87
12,500	0.92
15,000	0.95

The arithmetic of utility is straightforward once one accepts the idea of scoring the **utility** of outcomes rather than their monetary value. Suppose you wished to evaluate the lottery just described—a 50-50 chance of making $2,500 or making $10,000. If the utility of $2,500 is labeled U(2,500) and the utility of $10,000 is labeled U(10,000), then the utility of the lottery is expressed as follows:

$$\text{Expected utility} = .5 \, U(2{,}500) + .5 \, U(10{,}000).$$

The value of the lottery is the same as that of the certainty equivalent. Thus,

$$U(\text{Certainty equivalent}) = \text{Expected utility of the lottery, or}$$
$$U(5{,}000) = .5 \, U(2{,}500) + .5 \, U(10{,}000)$$
$$= .5 \,(.39) + .5 \,(.87)$$
$$= .63.$$

Searching for the CE that has a .63 utility, we find that the CE is 5,000. Then

$$RP = 6{,}250 - 5{,}000 = 1{,}250.$$

Figure 9–2 shows graphically how the concepts of certainty equivalent, EMV, and risk premium tie together. Note that the utility curve at 5,000 is at the same level as the expected (or average) utility of the lottery. The expected utility of the lottery is halfway along the straight line that connects the utility values of the two outcomes of the lottery.

Determining the CE and RP in this example was fairly simple, since there were only two possible outcomes in the lottery and the decision tree was not complex. For problems that have many possible outcomes, the ap-

FIGURE 9–2

Graphical Representation of Utility Arithmetic

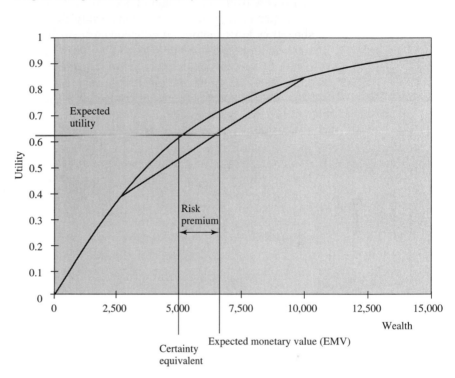

proach to using utility is the same. Once monetary values are placed on the end of a decision tree, then the utility value is scored for each endpoint. The tree is evaluated by folding back the expected utility score rather than the expected monetary value. Alternatives are compared directly on the basis of expected utility. Or the CE and RP of an alternative can be evaluated as follows:

1. Calculate the expected utility for a gamble.
2. Find the certainty equivalent wealth having the same utility level.
3. The risk premium is the difference between the EMV and the CE.

Risk Aversion

The larger the risk premium for a given gamble, the greater the person's risk aversion. On the other hand, if the CE exceeds the EMV (and the risk premium is therefore negative) the individual is "risk seeking." If the CE always equals the EMV, then the person is "risk neutral." For a risk-neutral individual, it is unnecessary to assess a utility curve, since an EMV evaluation will always rank alternatives the same as expected utility. The utility function in this case would be a straight line.

A person may be risk-averse in one region and risk-seeking or risk-prone in another. For example, an s-shaped curve would indicate risk-proneness for low outcomes (i.e., a willingness to gamble when things are bad) and risk-aversion when outcomes are high. Most individuals, however, tend to be risk-averse for all significant monetary levels. Managers in firms are even more likely to be risk-averse regarding company money. There is a good reason for this. If a firm consistently pays more than the EMV for risky opportunities, then statistical laws predict economic ruin in the long run.

There are many different utility functions that display risk aversion for all monetary values. However, there are two specific types of utility function that are widely applicable and very convenient to use. The first such type exhibits a characteristic called constant risk aversion.

Constant Risk Aversion: Negative Exponential Utility

A decision maker shows *constant risk aversion* if he or she has the same positive risk premium for any two risky opportunities that have respective outcomes that differ only by a constant amount. The series of risky opportunities and their associated risk premiums shown in Table 9–1 illustrate constant risk aversion. Note that each successive gamble in Table 9–1 has outcomes that are a constant $2,500 higher than the gamble listed just above it. Their certainty equivalents are each $2,500 higher than the one in the row above it also, which means that, given that their EMVs also increase with the same $2,500 increment, the risk premiums are all the same. These 50-50 gambles and their certainty equivalents exhibit what is called the *delta property*: Add a delta constant to each outcome, and the new certainty equivalent can be found by adding the same delta constant to the former certainty equivalent.

This assumption of constant risk aversion may be appropriate for many individuals and firms. Even if it doesn't apply strictly, it may serve as a reasonable model of risk attitude, especially if the range of monetary outcomes is not wide. Care must be taken about what this assumption does and

TABLE 9–1   Example of Constant Risk Aversion

50-50 Gamble		Expected Monetary Value	Certainty Equivalent	Risk Premium
$−2,500,	5,000	$1,250	$ 0	$1,250
0,	7,500	3,750	2,500	1,250
2,500,	10,000	6,250	5,000	1,250
5,000,	12,500	8,750	7,500	1,250

does not imply. It implies that as wealth level increases, the degree of aversion to risk does not change. It does not imply that (1) the utility for wealth is constant (in fact, utility will be higher for higher amounts of wealth) nor that (2) the risk premium for every risky opportunity is the same (only the set of opportunities exhibiting the *delta property* will have the same risk premiums).

When an individual is constantly risk-averse, we don't need to draw a utility curve nor read utilities off the curve. Rather we can express the curve mathematically and use this equation to compute certainty equivalents. When constant risk aversion applies, the utility of any outcome is given by a negative exponential expression:

$$U(x) = 1 - e^{-x/R} \tag{9–1}$$

where R = a constant expressing the degree of risk tolerance and e = 2.718 (a constant, like pi). (Note that $e^{-x/R}$ is the constant e taken to the power $-x/R$, which is equivalent to $1/e^{x/R}$.)

To determine the risk tolerance for a decision maker who is constantly risk-averse, it is necessary to ask only a single question, which sets R. Offer the decision maker the 50-50 gamble with outcomes Y and $-Y/2$, increasing the value of Y in the gamble until the decision maker is indifferent about the gamble and zero. The risk tolerance, R, is *approximately* the Y that gives indifference. Thus, if one were indifferent between the status quo and a 50-50 gamble with outcomes $5,000 and $-2,500, then R = 5,000. The utility function in Figures 9–1 and 9–2 is the constant utility function for R = 5,000.

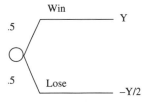

The risk tolerance for an individual is a matter of personal judgment. We would expect that individuals would generally have less tolerance for risk than firms, unless the particular individual has more financial strength than the particular firm. What are reasonable values of R for a firm? Again, there is no rule on how much risk is acceptable for a firm; risk tolerance depends on the strategy of the firm, its financial stability, the businesses it is in, and many other factors. One consultant's wide experience with corporations led him to suggest rough guidelines for reasonable values of R to be 6 percent of sales, 1 to 1.5 times net income, and 1/6th of equity.[1] Such guidelines are based on observations across many industries and many types of companies

[1]Ronald A. Howard, "Decision Analysis: Practice and Promise," *Management Science* 34 (1988), pp. 679–95.

and are not meant to dictate risk tolerance for a specific company. Often the behavior of a firm in other situations will suggest a level of R appropriate for that firm.

With the utility curve written mathematically as in expression (9–1) above, we can compute the CE of any lottery directly without drawing the curve and then reading values from it. Any lottery having outcomes $x_1, x_2, \ldots, x_n$ with respective probabilities $p_1, p_2, \ldots, p_n$ has a CE given by the following:

$$CE = -R \left[\ln(p_1 e^{-x_1/R} + p_2 e^{-x_2/R} + \cdots + p_n e^{-x_n/R}) \right] \qquad (9–2)$$

where ln is the natural logarithm (ln x is the number that when taken as the power of e gives x). If we were finding the CE for a 50-50 lottery with outcomes 0 and $10,000 for R = 5,000, then the calculations would be

$$CE = -5{,}000 \ln(.5 \, e^{-0/5{,}000} + .5 \, e^{-10{,}000/5{,}000})$$
$$= -5{,}000 \ln(.5(1) + .5 \, (.1353))$$
$$= -5{,}000 \ln(.5677) = -5{,}000(-.5662) = 2{,}831.$$

Many software programs for decision analysis will compute automatically an expected utility or a certainty equivalent for a constant risk-averse individual. Only the risk tolerance parameter R is needed. Another way to calculate the expected utility or certainty equivalent is with risk analysis simulation. We will describe this approach after we have introduced another significant model of utility.

Decreasing Risk Aversion: Logarithmic Utility

Most of us become more tolerant to risk as we become wealthier. For example, in our poorer student days we choose to have no deductible on our auto insurance. At that time it may have seemed impossible to cover a deductible in the event of an accident. As our asset positions improve, the deductible looks more attractive, until eventually we look for the highest deductible available. What has happened? The probability of an accident may not have changed. But in evaluating the alternative losses, we are willing to pay less to avoid risk, or in other words, our risk premium for a given risky opportunity has decreased. When the risk premium drops sufficiently, we self-insure, partially (with a deductible) or wholly (by choosing to have no collision or theft coverage, for example). If our asset position were to increase enough to the point where it was comparable to that of, say, Traveler's Insurance, then we would probably be willing to sell insurance to others!

Decreasing risk premiums explain why large companies with huge assets may self-insure the same risks that smaller companies would insure against. In fact, if risk aversion did not decrease over a very wide increase in wealth, the insurance industry might not exist. Why else would one company willingly seek to take on the risks of a smaller company?

TABLE 9–2   **Example of Decreasing Risk Aversion**

50-50 Gamble		Expected Monetary Value	Certainty Equivalent	Risk Premium
$-10,000,	0	$-5,000	$-6,339	$1,339
0,	10,000	5,000	4,365	635
10,000,	20,000	15,000	14,580	420
20,000,	30,000	25,000	24,686	314

If the risk premium decreases for gambles that are identical (except for adding the same constant to each possible payoff), then the decision maker has *decreasing risk aversion*. Table 9–2 shows the risk premiums of such a person. Note that these examples of risky opportunities satisfy the *delta property*, but the certainty equivalents do not. The risk premiums decrease because each successive gamble has a larger expected value, meaning that the wealth base of the decision maker is getting larger. With a larger wealth base, the individual can reasonably take more risk (and would pay or give up less to avoid risk).

Given the prevalence of decreasing risk-averse behavior, it is fortunate that there are easy-to-use utility curves that exhibit this property. In fact, there are many utility curves consistent with decreasing risk aversion. A particularly simple one is the generalized logarithmic utility model. This model has been labeled the "premier model of financial markets," because of its superior ability to model investor behavior.[2] This model may be written

$$U(x) = \ln(x + A) \qquad \text{for } x > -A$$

where ln( ) is the natural logarithm, x is a monetary outcome of a risky opportunity, and A sets the degree of risk tolerance (larger A is lower risk aversion). Typically, x is an incremental aftertax cash flow and A is the decision maker's (or institution's) net worth before realizing benefit due to the decision at hand. Then x + A is ending net worth after realizing benefit from the current decision.

A larger A means more risk tolerance. That is, the richer you are, the less likely you would be to worry about solvency; thus, you would be less averse to uncertainty. Figure 9–3 shows an example of a logarithmic utility function. Note that as x approaches −A (that is, you lose an amount approaching your net worth), utility approaches negative infinity. Thus, A may be interpreted as your distance from economic ruin. Using this interpretation, you may wish to set A to some other number than your current net worth. For example, making A greater than your net worth simply means that you

[2]Mark Rubenstein, "The Strong Case for the Generalized Logarithmic Utility Model as the Premier Model of Financial Markets," *Journal of Finance*, May 1976, pp. 551–71.

FIGURE 9–3

Decreasingly Risk-Averse Logarithmic Utility Curve

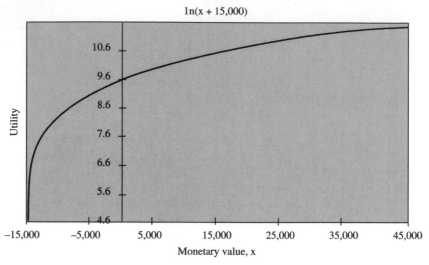

allow yourself to go to a negative net worth before your utility goes to negative infinity. Or conversely, A may be less than your net worth if there is some positive level of reserve for future consumption below which you will not let your wealth drop. Note that as x becomes large, risk aversion approaches zero. Thus, the utility curve approaches a straight line for large x.

A useful property of the logarithmic utility model (like the constant risk-aversion model) is that CEs can be calculated directly. For the log utility model they are computed using

$$CE = [(x_1 + A)^{p_1} * (x_2 + A)^{p_2} * \cdots * (x_n + A)^{p_n}] - A.$$

Again, p_i represents the probability of outcome x_i.

For instance, let us calculate one of the CEs of Table 9–2. They were obtained from a utility function with A = 15,000 as shown in Figure 9–3. To find the CE for the 50-50 lottery between 0 and $10,000, the calculations are the following:

$$CE = [(0 + 15,000)^{.5} * (10,000 + 15,000)^{.5}] - 15,000$$
$$= 19,365 - 15,000 = 4,365.$$

The logarithmic utility model is easy to use, requiring just a calculator. The only judgment necessary is the parameter A, which may be set to be the existing level of net worth (or alternatively, the point of economic ruin). The model may be generalized somewhat by adjusting A to reflect a desired degree of risk aversion based on an individual's preferences, rather than a measure of wealth.

There are other forms of utility curves that display decreasing risk aversion. The logarithmic utility model is the only one, however, that is consistent with the following condition: the decision maker is indifferent between receiving an incremental amount x (ending with net worth x + A) and the following lottery for any x > −A and m > 0.

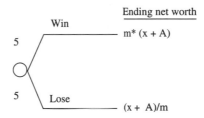

If m is set to 2, x is $25,000, and A is $15,000 for example, the decision maker would be indifferent between staying put at a certain ending net worth x + A, $40,000, and a coin flip to determine whether ending net worth is doubled, to $80,000, or halved, to $20,000. The model implies also that the decision maker would find a coin flip that determines whether ending net worth is tripled, to $120,000, or reduced to a third, to $13,333, equally desirable to $40,000, using m = 3. Similar preferences would hold also for coin flips involving other multiples (other values of m). The logarithmic utility curve exhibits a type of constant *proportional* risk aversion that is illustrated by these equally desirable risky opportunities with different multiples of ending net worth. This contrasts with the constant risk aversion (constant in an absolute, not a proportional sense) of the negative exponential curve.

Using a Utility Curve for Risk Analysis

Once identified, a utility function can be used for any number of decision analyses. The function is in effect until it is changed; it can be adjusted at any time. Using this function, even in the face of uncertainty we can make decisions consistently and efficiently.

So far we have described how to use the utility curve with discrete outcomes in a decision tree. To deal with continuous probability distributions, it is convenient to use a utility curve in a Monte Carlo simulation. To do this, one simply adds a cell to a risk analysis model (using @RISK or Crystal Ball, for example) to express the utility function. An expression for utility might be written directly using the negative exponential or logarithmic forms (or some other curve, for example, a piecewise-linear curve). Table 9–3 is an @RISK model for choosing between self-insurance, a deductible insurance policy, and an insurance policy with no deductible. The amount of loss that

TABLE 9–3   Insurance Model with Annotated Formulas

	A	B	C	D	E
1		\multicolumn{3}{c}{Insurance model}		
2	Loss distribution	7,120			
3	Net worth: A	15,000			
4		*Base fee*	*Loss*	*Total cost*	*Utility*
5	Self-insurance	$ 0	$7,120	$7,120	8.9721
6	$3,000 deductible	4,800	3,000	7,800	8.8818
7	Full insurance	7,350	0	7,350	8.9425

	A	B	C	D	E
1		\multicolumn{3}{c}{Insurance Model Formulas}		
2	Loss distribution	\multicolumn{2}{l}{= RiskCumul(0,14800,{1000,2000,3000,4700,7500,9100,10500,12000, 14000}, {0.1,0.2,0.3,0.4,0.5,0.6,0.7,0.8,0.9})}		
3	Net worth: A	\multicolumn{2}{l}{= RiskSimtable({15000,30000,90000,3})}		
4		*Base fee*	*Loss*	*Total cost*	*Utility*
5	Self-insurance	$ 0	= +B2	= +B5+C5	= LN(−D5+$B$3)
6	$3,000 deductible	4,800	= IF(B2<3000,+B2,3000)	= +B6+C6	= LN(−D6+$B$3)
7	Full insurance	7,350	0	= +B7+C7	= LN(−D7+$B$3)

may be incurred is expressed by the cumulative probability distribution (the numbers in parentheses are deciles). The deductible amount is $3,000 and deductible insurance costs $4,800. Without the deductible, the insurance costs $7,350. The logarithmic utility curve is used to evaluate the three options.

The three insurance alternatives may be compared by running a Monte Carlo simulation of the model, then ranking alternatives according to the expected (or mean) utility. Although the simulation will give a distribution for utility, only the mean utility is relevant for decision purposes. This stems from the definition of utility, which uses only the expected utility to compare risky opportunities.

To establish how risk aversion affects the choice, the simulation may be run for several levels of the effective net worth parameter, A. Example results are shown in Table 9–4, which indicate that it is best to buy full insurance at A = 15,000 and at A = 30,000, and to self-insure for A = 90,000.

We need not go beyond the comparison of expected utility in order to choose the best alternative. However, if we were interested in calculating the

---

TABLE 9–4   Insurance Model Simulation Results

Alternative	Mean utility for A = 15,000	Mean utility for A = 30,000	Mean utility for A = 90,000
Self-insurance	8.638	10.0156	11.3235
$3,000 deductible	8.937	10.0273	11.3223
Full insurance	8.942	10.0279	11.3224

CE for an alternative (say for the self insurance alternative with A = 90,000) we could do it in two ways:

1. By trial and error or goal-seek in a spreadsheet, find a total cost that gives the expected utility 11.3235, which results in a certainty equivalent of 7,256.

2. Write the expression for the utility of the CE and solve it algebraically for the CE, as follows:

$$U(CE) = \text{Expected utility of the risky opportunity}$$
$$\ln(CE + 90,000) = 11.3235$$
$$CE + 90,000 = e^{11.3235}$$
$$CE = 7,256.$$

This might be compared to the CE for the full insurance case, which we know to be 7,350. Note that the expected utility numbers seem very close, particularly for the case where A = 90,000. For example, even though the CEs differ by over $100, the expected utility numbers differ only by .0011 in these two cases. This will happen when using the logarithmic utility model for large numbers. In situations with large numbers, it would be better to do all calculations in thousands of dollars (or in other cases, millions) to produce results in which alternatives have expected utilities that are more clearly separated. We would need to run the simulation long enough so that the uncertainty in our estimate of the mean utility is small enough to be sure that there really is a difference between alternatives.

The approach we have just described would allow us to build adjustments for risk into any simulation model. All that is needed is to add a utility curve and then to apply the expected utility to evaluate alternatives.

Separation of Risk–Return and Mean–Variance Analysis

A simplified way to value risky opportunities is to base the risk premium strictly on a measure of risk and to combine it with a measure of return. The most common approach is to use the variance (standard deviation squared) as the statistical measure of risk and the EMV as a measure of return. Thus, the

CE is computed using only the EMV, or the mean, and the variance. Such an approach is based on the approximation

$$RP \approx \text{Variance}/(2*R)$$

where R measures the degree of risk aversion. This approximation, while often assumed, holds exactly only in certain circumstances, the most important of which are as follows:

1. Utility is negative exponential (constant risk aversion).
2. The risky quantity being evaluated is normally distributed.

When these conditions apply, the CE is easily computed as

$$CE = \text{Mean} - \text{Variance}/(2R)$$

where R is the risk tolerance coefficient defined in a previous section.

There is a catch to using the approximation at any other time. The only other condition for which the approximation is exact is a quadratic utility function of the form

$$a + bx - cx^2, \text{ with a,b,c positive}$$

Unfortunately, the quadratic utility function has the undesirable property that its risk aversion *increases*. The value of R would not be a constant, but instead increase with the mean of the gamble. In a previous section, it was argued that as wealth increases, risk-aversion behavior tends to decrease, not increase! Thus, use of mean-variance analysis, except in the conditions above, usually leads to an undesirable increase in risk aversion.

If one desires a utility curve that is built on separate notions of risk and return, consider using

$$U(x) = x - be^{-x/R}$$

where b and R are positive constants. The parameter R sets the level of risk tolerance used to identify the degree of riskiness of an opportunity, and the parameter b weights concern for risk versus return.[3]

Corporate Risk Policy

A person's attitude toward risk for money depends on whose money it is—the person's own money or the firm's money for which the person is responsible. Because a firm can generally absorb a higher loss than an individual, a manager usually is less risk-averse with the company's money than with personal money. The manager is not being profligate; if risk premiums are

---

[3]See David E. Bell, "Risk, Return, and Utility," *Management Science* 41 (1995), pp. 23–30, for properties of this utility curve.

set as high for the firm as they are for the individual, the firm might reject profitable, though risky, projects, losing them to other firms or even to other individuals. Thus, it would be desirable for the manager to consistently adopt a treatment of risk that fits the firm rather than the individual.

In addition, managers in separate parts of a firm ought to be consistent in their treatment of risk. It is inefficient, for example, for one department to readily accept investments that would be avoided by another department. The company would be better served if both departments took opportunities with riskiness halfway between two such projects. Using a utility function would provide for such consistency; it would also help assure that risk judgments are in the firm's best interests rather than merely meeting a manager's private level of risk aversion.

Realistically, few companies will go through the formality of using a utility function for every risky decision. Nonetheless, it would be to the company's advantage at least on occasion to test decision behavior in the firm against a utility model. It would identify (1) inconsistencies in the use of probabilistic information, (2) overly timid behavior toward risk, and (3) more efficient uses of resources in selecting among risky opportunities in various parts of the firm. At the very least it would enhance communication in the firm about corporate policies toward risk. Using a risk-preference model will prove more beneficial in those cases where the decision is especially difficult or involves large amounts of money or sets policy for many routine decisions.

Exercises

1. A friend of yours confidentially asks for your help in choosing between some risky investment opportunities. Trying to impress her with your recently developed skills, you ask her a few questions about her risk preferences. You determine that she is constantly risk-averse in personal wealth. You also find that she is indifferent between a 50-50 lottery with outcomes +$4,166 and −$2,083 and the status quo. You learn that she owns an investment that will leave her with personal wealth of either $21,000 or $11,000 in today's dollars with equal probabilities. She can sell out of the investment for $14,000. She has asked you for advice. Should she sell out?

2. Your friend in question 1 suggests that she could, if she wished, keep half of her investment and sell the other half for $7,000. Is this a better idea for her than what you suggested? Why?

10   COMPETITOR ANALYSIS

Significant sources of uncertainty in many decisions are the actions that others may take in response to or in preemption of the actions that we take. The language of probability that was introduced in Chapter 4 and that will be expanded on in Chapter 11 applies to these uncertain behaviors just as well as it does to the uncertainties arising from imperfect knowledge of the physical or economic environments around us. But, because the actions of others are driven by their interests and by their economics, the probability assessment process should be informed by a careful consideration of the forces that motivate those actions. It would be myopic and naive to pretend that the actions of others are simply random and not the result of mindful thought and analysis. In addition to making an informed assessment about the actions of others, the proactive decision maker should explicitly consider the options and motivations of the other parties in an effort to create new alternatives that might guide the behaviors of others and/or that might be more attractive to all parties involved. This chapter provides a framework for explicitly considering the interactions between our actions and the actions of others who may be directly or indirectly involved in the situation.

Throughout the discussion that follows, the other parties will be referred to as "competitors" and the situation will be described as "competitive." Although this is the common context in which the interactions addressed in this chapter arise, the broader perspective of *interested party* should be kept in mind. An interested party may be a competitor, but might also be a colleague, a partner, a government agency, or a special interest group. The critical characteristic of these competitive situations is that the performance of our alternatives is impacted by the actions of the competitors. This does not necessarily mean that our interests will be in conflict with those of others, as the word *competitor* might suggest, but just that our performance is linked to their actions.

This chapter begins by presenting a variety of characteristics that can be used to frame different competitive situations and to better understand the potential implications of the competitive interaction. In the second section, the format of matrix games is introduced as a means to succinctly present the alternatives available to the parties involved and the mutual consequences of all the potential combinations of actions. The chapter ends with a description of three classical competitive situations (no conflict, prisoner's dilemma, and preemption) and the managerial messages associated with each.

Characterizing Competitive Situations

Although all competitive situations share the common property that the performance of the interested parties is determined in part by the actions of other parties, there are several important dimensions along which competitive situations can be differentiated—the number of competitors, the potential for repeated engagements, the norms of conduct governing interactions among the competitors, and the degree of conflict among the competitors. These differences can significantly influence the behaviors of the interested parties and the options available to the proactive decision maker for influencing those behaviors. As a result, it is important that these aspects of the competitive situation and their implications be considered before assessing the probabilities that a competitor will adopt any particular action or attempting to influence that choice.

One of the fundamental ways to characterize competitive situations is the **number of competitors**. Situations involving two competitors[1] present the simplest competitive form and are by far the easiest situation to understand and analyze. For a situation to be conceptualized as two-competitor, a competitor does not necessarily have to be an individual, but could be a group of individuals with shared interests who act as if they were one. This would be the case when a vendor is structuring a subassembly supply contract for a multidivisional firm and the divisions might be considered to be monolithic, or when a company is considering alternative labor contracts with a union and the union presents a common front. Multi-competitor situations are far more complex than two-competitor situations. Not only is there more information to assimilate (each competitor's alternatives and interests for example), but also the competitors might bond together in various combinations to form coalitions. The presence of coalitions makes it much more difficult to anticipate behaviors. Which parties will form a coalition? How stable will the

---

[1]Situations involving two competitors have received considerable attention in the game theory literature and are customarily referred to as two-person games. *Person* is the game theoretic terminology for competitor or interested party. When the number of competitors, n, is greater than 2, the situations are called n-person games.

coalition be? What might trigger the dissolution of the coalition or prompt a realignment of its membership? These issues compound the complexity so that it is often tempting, in the name of simplicity, to characterize a situation as two-competitor. Such a simplification must be done with caution. By treating competitors in the aggregate, differences among them might be overlooked and alternatives more satisfying to all parties missed. For example, if in the sale of a small business venture the two partners are treated as one (even though one is seeking retirement and the other is eager to continue in the business), alternatives that are tailored to the interests of the partners and less expensive for the buyer may be missed. Similar issues may also be present in the two illustrations presented earlier in this paragraph.

A second dimension that significantly influences the nature of a competitive situation is the opportunity for **repeated interactions**. In one-shot situations, competitors often take a short-term view and try to get all that they can from the immediate situation. The potential for repeated interactions, however, will often temper behaviors and induce more cooperative activity. The presence of a long-term relationship offers the threat of retaliation if actions are extreme, as well as the opportunity to create a climate of cooperation. A supplier may resist demanding an aggressive price when a customer is in dire need of product because the customer could retaliate by developing other suppliers for future needs. The price premium may also be bypassed because the supplier anticipates a possible future need to move product and the customer may be inclined to take a larger delivery than was ordered. The potential for repeated interactions can significantly influence behavior and present opportunities for cooperation.

Most competitive situations arise within a context in which there are well understood **norms of conduct**. There are a host of potential norms, but two commonly encountered categories are those that limit the alternatives available to the competitors and those that govern the form of the interaction among the competitors. Norms that limit alternatives may arise from explicit laws and regulations or may result from implicit industry practice. The Sherman Antitrust Act defines "fair practices" on a national basis and forbids collaboration among competitors in setting prices or allocating market share. The public utility industry is regulated so that price changes must be approved by local rate commissions. As a result, utilities must find means other than price to compete with private electricity generation alternatives. The auto industry introduces its new models during the late summer preceding the model year. As a result, the timing of new products is generally not one of the dimensions on which industry members compete.

Norms that limit the form of interaction among competitors range from those that allow full communication among the competitors (the bargaining situation) to those that prohibit any communication (the sealed-bid auction). Commonly, competitive situations are somewhere between these extremes. Limited communications, such as public pronouncements, are permitted, but direct communication is prohibited. Such communications, whether they be threat, bluff, or promise, are attempts to influence behaviors and potentially limit them. When a department store announces it will match the prices of any competitor, it is not only communicating to its customers that it is the low-price alternative, but it is also communicating to its competitors that price wars will be fruitless.

Competitive situations can also be distinguished by the **degree of conflict** that exists among the competitors. In some situations, the competitors are strictly opposed to each other—what one competitor receives, the other loses. The purchase of a used car from its previous owner may be of this nature, if the only performance measure for both parties is the selling price. These are just exchanges of assets from one competitor to another and represent one end of the conflict spectrum, pure conflict. Because gains are just balanced by losses, pure conflict situations are called *zero-sum*. At the other extreme are situations in which there is pure cooperation. In these situations, all competitors gain and lose together and each prefers the same outcome. A business partnership may be of this nature, if the interests of all partners are exactly congruent.

In reality, few competitive situations are at the extremes of this spectrum from pure conflict to pure cooperation. Most involve a mixture of common interest and competition. In the purchase of a used car, the seller may have an immediate need to get rid of the car (it's an extra vehicle and cash is short) and the buyer may need a car immediately (new to town and needs transportation). Now the situation has a blend of cooperation (make the transaction happen) and of competition (achieve a favorable price). Similarly a business partnership is rarely a purely cooperative relationship because each partner has a multitude of interests, many of them shared with the other partner, but some of them in conflict. Competitive situations that are not pure conflict are called *non-zero-sum* because gains to one competitor are not necessarily offset completely by losses to the others—there are opportunities for mutual gain for all competitors.

Matrix Format

The interactions between any two competitors in a competitive situation can be summarized in a matrix. The alternatives of one competitor form the rows of the matrix; the alternatives of the other competitor form the columns. Each cell of the matrix is a possible outcome—a combination of actions by both parties—with performance values for each competitor. When there are only two competitors, this matrix compactly and completely defines the structural interactions of the situation.[2] An example of such a matrix is shown

---

[2]It does not capture the behavioral aspects of the situation and leaves unanswered the question of whether or not both competitors will act rationally and in accordance with their performance measures.

FIGURE 10–1

An Illustration of the Matrix Format

	C1	C2	C3	C4
R1	6,5	5,9	4,7	8,4
R2	7,8	4,7	7,6	6,5
R3	5,6	3,3	6,5	9,4

in Figure 10–1. Note that the row competitor has three alternatives and the column competitor has four. There is no need for both competitors to have the same number of alternatives. In each cell of the matrix, there are performance outcomes for both competitors, the row competitor's outcome first and the column competitor's outcome second. If the row competitor were to adopt alternative R2 and the column competitor adopt C3, the result for the row competitor (using its performance measure), would be 7 and the result for the column competitor (using its performance measure) would be 6. In the terminology of the previous section, this is a non-zero-sum situation.[3] The gains of one competitor are not the losses of the other—moving from the outcome of R3 and C2 to the outcome of R2 and C3 is substantially better for both competitors.

The matrix format highlights the importance of carefully considering the **alternatives** available to each of the competitors and the **performance measures** driving their actions. It is critical not to assume that all competitors will have the same alternatives and the same performance measure, but rather to consider the specific circumstances of each competitor. As was observed in the previous section, partners in the sale of a small business may have very different sets of alternatives and may be motivated by different objectives. The misspecification of either the alternatives or the performance measure of a competitor can lead to faulty assessments of behavior and to overlooked opportunities for creating new alternatives. As a result, it is important to validate one's assumptions about a competitor's alternatives and/or performance measures. In repeated competitive situations, moderate (rather than dramatic) changes in one's behavior can permit a test of whether or not a competitor's reactions are consistent with the predictions from one's matrix model.

The compactness of the matrix format is often an aid in analyzing the potential behaviors of the competitors. In the situation depicted in Figure 10–1, it could be anticipated that the column competitor would not choose C4

---

[3]If this were a zero-sum situation, there would be no need to note the performance values of both competitors, because by knowing the values for one you know that the impact on the other is the opposite. Traditionally, the performance values of the row competitor are the only values presented in the matrix of a zero-sum situation. There is no harm, however, in presenting the performance measures of both competitors.

because, regardless of the choice that the row competitor makes, the outcomes of C3 are always better than the outcomes of C4 (7 versus 4, 6 versus 5, and 5 versus 4). C4 is dominated by C3 and, as a result, C4 should be eliminated from further consideration. This **analysis by domination** assumes the competitor will act rationally and make informed choices consistent with the performance measure. For either the row competitor or the column competitor, no other alternative dominates another. If, however, the row competitor is willing to assume that the column competitor will not choose the dominated alternative, C4, the outcomes of R2 are always better than the outcomes of R3 (7 versus 5, 4 versus 3, and 7 versus 6). It is said that R2 **iteratively dominates** R3—it does not strictly dominate, but dominates only after potential alternatives for the opposing competitor have been eliminated by prior domination arguments. The analysis can be carried one step further. If the column competitor is willing to assume that the row competitor will recognize the iterative domination of R3, then C2 iteratively dominates C3 (9 versus 7 and 7 versus 6). The more iterations through which an analysis by domination goes, the greater its reliance on the validity of the assumptions underlying the construction of the matrix, in particular the selection and evaluation of the performance measure, and on the assumption of rational and informed behavior on the part of the competitors. Nonetheless, analysis by domination is a powerful tool for simplifying competitive situations. If those alternatives that are dominated either directly or iteratively are eliminated from consideration, the three-by-four matrix of Figure 10–1 can be reduced to the two-by-two matrix of Figure 10–2.

Within the simplified context of Figure 10–2, consider the outcome in which the row competitor chooses R1 and the column competitor chooses C1. This is clearly an inferior outcome. Both competitors would be better off if their respective choices were R2 and C1 (7 versus 6 for the row competitor and 8 versus 5 for the column competitor). On the other hand, no such mutually beneficial change can be made with the selection of R2 and C1, that is, movement to any of the other three possibilities would result in at least one (if not both) of the competitors being worse off.[4] The outcome of R2 and C1 is said to be a **Pareto-optimal outcome**. For a Pareto-optimal outcome, neither competitor can do better except at the expense of the other competitor. Note that the outcome of R1 and C2 is also a Pareto-optimal outcome.

In addition to resulting in a Pareto-optimal outcome, the choices R2 and C1 are in **equilibrium**. In Figure 10–2, once R2 and C1 have been selected, the row competitor is not tempted to switch to R1 (6 versus 7) nor is the

---

[4]The choices of R2 and C1 by the row and the column competitor result in outcomes of 7 and 8, respectively. Any other pair of choices is worse off for at least one competitor: with R1 and C1, both are worse off (6 versus 7 and 5 versus 8); with R1 and C2, the row competitor is worse off (5 versus 7); with R2 and C2, both competitors are worse off (4 versus 7 and 7 versus 8).

FIGURE 10–2

The Effects of Analysis by Domination

	C1	C2
R1	6,5	5,9
R2	7,8	4,7

FIGURE 10–3

Pareto-optimal Outcome, not Equilibrium Choices

	C1	C2
R1	6,5	5,9
R2	7,8	4,9

FIGURE 10–4

Equilibrium Choices, not Pareto-optimal Outcome

	C1	C2
R1	6,5	9,9
R2	7,8	4,7

column competitor tempted to switch to C2 (7 versus 8). The choices of R2 and C1 are stable—neither competitor is tempted to alter its choice. This leads to the definition that a pair of choices is in equilibrium if neither competitor can gain by unilaterally changing its choice. The choices R1 and C2 are also in equilibrium.

Even though the concepts of Pareto-optimal outcomes and equilibrium choices have definitions that sound rather similar, they are not equivalent to each other. On the one hand, a pair of choices can result in a Pareto-optimal outcome, but not be in equilibrium. Figure 10–3 is a slight modification of Figure 10–2 in which the column competitor's outcome of R2 and C2 has been changed to 9. Despite this change, the choices of R2 and C1 still result in a Pareto-optimal outcome, but they are not in equilibrium because the column competitor can now unilaterally improve its result by choosing C2. On the other hand, a pair of choices can be in equilibrium, but not result in a Pareto-optimal outcome. Figure 10–4 is another slight modification of Figure 10–2. This time the row competitor's result for the choices of R1 and C2 has been changed to 9. The choices of R2 and C1 are in equilibrium, but they do not result in a Pareto-optimal outcome because both competitors would be better off if they adopted R1 and C2.

Returning to the competitive situation depicted in Figure 10–2, one of the Pareto-optimal outcomes is better for the row competitor (R2 and C1, 7 is better than any other possible outcome for the row competitor) and the other is better for the column player (R1 and C2, 9 is better than any other possible outcome for the column competitor). Both of these choices are in equilibrium, so they could become "traps" once they are adopted. Depending on the norms of conduct to which these two competitors are bound, they might seek ways to recognize these two Pareto-optimal outcomes and means to share the value they offer. Alternatively, they might attempt to preempt the other by quickly and convincingly announcing the choice that results in their more favorable equilibrium. Neither of these actions might have been identified if the competitive situation were not explicitly modeled and the resulting matrix analyzed.

Classical Structures

In this section, three classical competitive structures will be discussed. Although they are very simple and abstract in their construct, they are manifest with uncanny regularity in the managerial world. The proactive decision maker is well advised to develop the ability to recognize the presence of these structures amid the complexity of reality and to understand how to address their challenges.

No (or Little) Conflict

The situation depicted in Figure 10–5(a) is an interesting competitive situation because it does not involve any competition. R2 dominates R1 and C2 dominates C1. In addition, the outcome of R2 and C2 is the best of all possible worlds for both competitors. If both competitors were to maximize personal performance, their respective choices would be R2 and C2 and for each there is no better outcome than that of R2 and C2. There is no conflict in the situation of Figure 10–5(a). The situation in Figure 10–5(b) is a weaker form of this same phenomenon. Note that R2 and C2 are still dominant alternatives and, as a result, the outcome of R2 and C2 is still the rational outcome. This outcome, however, is no longer the best of all worlds for each competitor. The row competitor would prefer the outcome of R2 and C1; the column competitor would prefer the outcome of R1 and C2. Neither of these preferences should change either competitor's behavior (R2 and C2 are the

---

FIGURE 10–5
No Conflict or Little Conflict

	C1	C2
R1	4,2	3,3
R2	5,4	8,6

(a)

	C1	C2
R1	4,2	3,7
R2	9,4	8,6

(b)

dominant alternatives), but a slight sense of conflict is present because one competitor could hope that the other would magnanimously grant the best possible outcome.

When faced with a no-conflict situation, the proactive decision maker should focus on actions that will ensure that the other competitors will recognize the noncompetitive nature of the situation. It is important that the competitors do indeed have the performance measure that is being assumed. If it is assumed they are attempting to maximize profits, but in fact they actually are maximizing market share, their behaviors may not be consistent with the analysis. Depending on the permissible norms of conduct, a meeting to discuss perspectives would certainly clarify matters. In the final analysis, the assessment of the chances that a competitor will adopt the noncompetitive posture depends on the assessor's degree of belief that the competitor is motivated by the assumed performance measure, that the competitor has the assumed alternatives available, and that the competitor will act in accordance with the performance measure.

Prisoner's Dilemma

Despite its rather fanciful name, the competitive situation that is widely known as prisoner's dilemma occurs rather frequently in managerial situations. It is a situation in which the best outcome for all competitors results when each competitor refrains from maximizing personal gain. Each competitor in the prisoner's dilemma situation has two alternatives. The two-competitor form of the structure will be described here, but the multi-competitor form is analogous.[5] If both adopt the first alternative, they both benefit. Each competitor has a second alternative that offers the temptation to do better, assuming the other chooses the first. If both succumb to the temptation and choose the second alternative, both are worse off than if both had refrained from the temptation.

This structure occurs in many fights for market share. When enticements are offered by one competitor in an effort to lure customers away from others, the other competitors are faced with a difficult choice: either they respond with similar offerings in an effort to protect market share or they let market share erode. If they respond, market shares will stabilize at their initial levels and all competitors will be worse off, because the total market will not increase appreciably and the cost of the enticements will reduce profitability. If they do not respond, their market shares will decline (to the benefit of the initiator) and their profits will be reduced. The choice is often to respond, because the cost of the enticements is less than the lost contribution from the reduction in market share. The final result of the initiator's action is a reduction in the profitability of every firm in the industry, including the initiator.

---

[5] In the multi-competitor form, the gains and losses are shared by each competitor adopting a particular alternative.

We will analyze this competitive situation in the context from which it derives its name. Two suspects, Robin and Chris, are taken into custody and separated. The sheriff is certain they are guilty of a particular felony but does not have sufficient evidence to convict them. The suspects know they are guilty. Each prisoner has two alternatives, to confess to the felony or not to confess. If neither confesses, the sheriff will convict them of a lesser offense and both will receive minor sentences. If both confess, the sheriff will recommend less than the most severe sentence for the felony. If one confesses and the other doesn't, the confessor will receive lenient treatment for turning state's evidence and the other will receive the maximum sentence. In terms of months in jail, the situation can be represented by the matrix in Figure 10–6. Each prisoner must decide whether or not to confess. Because they are in separate cells, they cannot communicate before choosing their action.

Let's look at the situation from Robin's point of view. If Chris can be relied on not to confess, then Robin might not confess because both of them will serve relatively short sentences. On the other hand, it is tempting for Robin to confess and have to spend only one month in jail instead of two. In fact, regardless of what choice Chris makes, Robin will always be better off confessing (remember each is trying to minimize their months in jail). For Robin, the alternative of confessing dominates the alternative of not confessing. The difficulty is that Chris may reason the same way. As a result, both may choose their dominant strategy (confess) and end up with nine months in jail. Both would have been better off if neither had confessed. Although the outcome of neither confessing is a Pareto-optimal outcome, it does not result from equilibrium choices and, as a result, is unstable. The instability is particularly acute in this situation, because both suspects are tempted to change their choice. The result of this acute instability is that the suspects may ironically end up at the only non-Pareto outcome, both confessing.

If the suspects were allowed to communicate, they might be able to agree that neither of them should confess. Such an agreement, however, might only make the situation worse. The assurances that the other suspect will not confess can increase the temptation to confess, thus adding to the instability of the situation. The agreement is not enforceable.

Proactive decision makers who confront competitive situations with the structure of the prisoner's dilemma must either find a way to make cooperative agreements enforceable or find a way to restructure the situation so that it no longer has the structure of the prisoner's dilemma. A common way to

---

FIGURE 10–6

Prisoner's Dilemma

		Chris	
		Not confess	**Confess**
Robin	**Not confess**	2,2	12,1
	Confess	1,12	9,9

FIGURE 10–7
Preemption

| | Column competitor | |
	Do not introduce	Introduce
Row competitor — Do not introduce	0,0	0,3
Introduce	3,0	−5,−5

foster cooperation is to create opportunities for repeated interactions. With the possibility of future encounters comes the possibility of retaliation. As a result, the temptation to act in one's pure self-interest may be reduced, depending upon the relative magnitude of the retaliatory action. Alternatively, the proactive decision maker may create a new alternative that eliminates the prisoner's dilemma structure. A penalty clause might be added to a contract so that the benefit of being noncooperative is less than the benefit of cooperation. As in the no-conflict situation, the assessment of the chances that a competitor will act cooperatively is enhanced by explicitly analyzing the forces at play.

Preemption

The final classical competitive situation that we will discuss is one that is often characteristic of new product introductions in industries where there is considerable product turnover. An example is the children's breakfast cereal industry in which there is a constant churning of new products. Suppose there are two firms, each of which must decide whether or not to introduce its newly developed product. Due to the high fixed costs associated with production setup and new product roll out, each product will be profitable only if the other is not introduced. If both are introduced, both will show considerable losses. The economic situation might be represented by the matrix in Figure 10–7 in which the payoffs are expected net present values. Note that for each competitor, neither alternative is dominated by the other.

If this is the only time that the two competitors anticipate confronting each other in a situation like this, it is in the interest of each competitor to preempt the action of the other.[6] If the row competitor announces its intention to introduce its product and the column competitor believes the announcement, then the column competitor, acting in its own best interest, will not

---

[6]Traditionally, this competitive situation has been known as the *Battle of the Sexes*, because it has often been described by the following scenario (please excuse its gender stereotyping). A husband and wife have two choices for an evening's entertainment, to go to a boxing match or to a ballet. The man prefers the fight and the woman the ballet; however, to both it is more important that they be together than to attend their preferred entertainment. These preferences give rise to a matrix with the same structure as Figure 10–7.

introduce its new product. The key to the success of this power tactic is the credibility of the announcement. If the product announcement is accompanied by the signing of a million-dollar contract for facility modifications, the credibility of the announcement will certainly be enhanced. If the row player has the reputation for being stubborn and for never wavering from intentions regardless of the counter arguments that are made, the announcement may take on the aura of a foregone conclusion. If the announcement is not believed, both parties run the risk of considerable losses if they simultaneously introduce their products. As a result, they both may decide to forgo introduction, leaving considerable value behind. When considering the possibility of exercising the preemptive strategy, the proactive decision maker should assess the chances that the other party will be intimidated by the announcement. This assessment would be influenced by the strength of the announcement, the reputation for stubbornness, and the magnitude of the losses if both competitors were to introduce their products.

If, on the other hand, the competitors expect to be repeatedly in this type of situation with various new products, they would do well to cooperate by carefully timing the introduction of their new products so that they would alternately approach the market with their new products. In this way, they could share in the benefits of the Pareto-optimal outcomes and not run the risk of simultaneous introduction. The norms of conduct within the industry may prohibit explicit agreements, but the natural course of events may implicitly give rise to the alternating introduction of new products. The heavy cash outflows often associated with new product introductions may necessitate a gap between the introduction of new products. During this period of cash recovery, the other competitor has a natural window during which to introduce its new product. Research and development constraints may also result in a sequential pattern of new product development and, as a result, gaps between introductions as new products are developed. The proactive decision maker should be looking to means to create gaps and have those gaps recognized by industry competitors.

Summary

This chapter has been devoted to the analysis of competitive situations. All competitive situations share the property that the performance of the interested parties is determined in part by the actions of the other parties. Competitor's actions may be significantly influenced by the number of competitors, by the opportunity for repeated interactions, by the norms of conduct that govern behaviors, and by the degree of conflict among the competitors. The matrix format was introduced as a means to concisely display the interactions among competitors and as a discipline to consider carefully the alternatives available to the competitors and the performance measures driving their choices. If one is confident about the completeness of the matrix model and the motivations of the competitor, the matrix may be simplified through analysis by domination and iterative domination. The concepts of Pareto-optimality and equilibrium were introduced as means to describe certain attractive combinations of choices. The chapter concluded with a discussion of three classical competitive situations (no conflict, prisoner's dilemma, and preemption) and the challenges facing the proactive decision maker when addressing competitive situations with these structures.

11 PROBABILITY DISTRIBUTIONS

Chapter 4 introduced the language of probability as a means to communicate uncertainty in assessing those factors that significantly influence the evaluation of an alternative's performance. This additional vocabulary permitted the choice among alternatives to be made not only on the basis of the range of possible outcomes for an alternative, but also on the probability of those possible outcomes occurring. As a result, decisions would not be inordinately driven by extreme possibilities or a best-guess estimate, but by a balance between possibility and probability.

This chapter focuses on enlarging the vocabulary of probability and on addressing the assessment of probability distributions. The enlarged vocabulary will include probability mass function (pmf), cumulative distribution function (cdf), and probability density function (pdf). The assessment of probability distributions will employ means that capture personal judgment, use historical data as a guide to judgment, and appeal to the underlying structure of the uncertainty. The chapter will conclude with a discussion of the biases commonly encountered in making probability assessments.

The Language of Probability Distributions

The **probability distribution** of an uncertain quantity (an uncertainty whose outcomes are numerical) is an assignment of a probability to each of the possible outcomes of the uncertainty. The assigned probability should reflect the assessor's personal judgments about the relative likelihoods of the outcomes. More specifically, if one outcome is judged to be twice as likely as another, the probability assigned to the first outcome should be twice the probability assigned to the second. When all the possibilities are taken collectively, the sum of their probabilities must be one because they represent the totality of possibilities. These two features—nonnegative weights for all possible outcomes and a total weighting that sums to one—are the essential characteristics of all probability distributions.

There are two common ways of presenting a probability distribution: the probability mass function and the cumulative distribution function.

The Probability Mass Function

For uncertain quantities in which there are just a few possible outcomes, it makes sense to consider the probability that the outcome is precisely a particular value. In these circumstances, not only is the task manageable, but also the probabilities are usually of sufficient magnitude to permit meaningful assessments. A **probability mass function** (pmf) assigns to each possible outcome the probability of having exactly that outcome occur. For example, consider a financial analyst who during unusually turbulent economic times is making a forecast of what the prime interest rate will be a month in the future. By convention, the prime rate is quoted in increments of one-eighth of a percent. The analyst, after careful thought, believes the rate will not be below 9 1/8 percent or above 9 5/8 percent and makes the following judgments about the relative likelihoods of the various possibilities:

> 9 1/8 is half as likely as 9 1/4 (the current rate).
>
> 9 3/8 is twice as likely as 9 1/4.
>
> 9 1/2 is as likely as 9 1/4.
>
> 9 5/8 is as likely as 9 1/8.

On the basis of these assessments, the analyst assigns[1] the probabilities given in Table 11–1. Note that each of the probabilities are between zero and one, that they are consistent with the relative likelihood statements, and that they sum to one.

Probability mass functions are sometimes presented in graphical form. The pmf for the prime rate next month, given in Table 11–1, is also shown in Figure 11–1. By custom, a probability function is graphed with probabilities on the vertical axis and possible outcome values on the horizontal axis. A probability mass function is zero for the values of the uncertainty that the assessor considers impossible. Thus, for example, the graph in Figure 11–1 is zero at 9 3/16 percent (not a multiple of an 1/8 of a percent) and 9 3/4 percent (outside the assessor's range of possibility). In fact, the pmf is zero every-

---

[1]The probabilities can be calculated algebraically from the analyst's statements by letting the probability of 9 1/4 be P and by noting that the assessed relative likelihoods require that the probabilities of 9 1/8, 9 3/8, 9 1/2, and 9 5/8 be P/2, 2P, P, and P/2, respectively. The probabilities of the five possible outcomes must sum to one. Thus, P/2 + P + 2P + P + P/2 = 5P = 1 and P (the probability of 9 1/4) is .20. The remaining probabilities can be calculated from the assessed relative likelihoods.

TABLE 11–1   Probability Mass Function (Tabular Format) for the Prime Rate

Prime Rate (%)	Probability
9 1/8	.10
9 1/4	.20
9 3/8	.40
9 1/2	.20
9 5/8	.10

FIGURE 11–1

Probability Mass Function (Graphical Format) for the Prime Rate

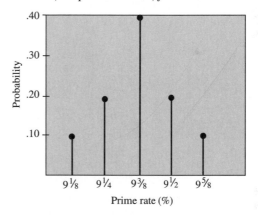

where except at increments of 1/8 percent between 9 1/8 and 9 5/8 percent. The result is a graph with vertical spikes at 1/8 percent increments. The height of each spike represents the probability assigned to that particular interest rate.

The Cumulative Distribution Function

Instead of considering the probability that the outcome of an uncertain quantity will be *exactly* a particular value, it is possible to consider the probability that the outcome will be *less than or equal to* a specific value (or equivalently, not exceed a specific value). In the above example, the financial analyst could have said there is a 30 percent probability that the prime will be 9 1/4 percent or less because there is a 20 percent chance the prime will be exactly 9 1/4, a 10 percent chance the prime will be exactly 9 1/8, and no other outcomes of 9 1/4 percent or less are believed to be possible.

TABLE 11–2   Cumulative Distribution Function for the Prime Rate

Prime Rate (%)	Cumulative Probability
9	0
9 1/8	.10
9 1/4	.30
9 3/8	.70
9 1/2	.90
9 5/8	1.00

The **cumulative distribution function** assigns to each value the probability that the outcome will be less than or equal to that value.[2] It can be easily constructed from the probability mass function by simply summing the probabilities assigned by the probability mass function for all values not exceeding the specific value. The cumulative distribution function corresponding to the probability mass function of Table 11–1 is shown in Table 11–2. Notice, for example, that the cumulative probability associated with a prime rate of 9 3/8 percent is .70, the sum of the individual probability mass values for 9 1/8 percent, 9 1/4 percent, and 9 3/8 percent (.10 + .20 + .40 = .70).

Cumulative distribution functions are often presented in graphical form. By convention, such graphs have the cumulative probability values on the vertical axis and the possible values of the uncertain quantity on the horizontal axis. Such a graph for the distribution in Table 11–2 is shown in Figure 11–2. Notice that, in contrast to the probability mass function, which is positive for only a limited number of values, the cumulative distribution function is positive for every number above the smallest possible outcome. Even for a value that is impossible (such as 9 3/16 percent), it still makes sense to ask for the probability that that number will not be exceeded. For example, 9 3/16 percent will not be exceeded if the rate is 9 1/8 percent or 9 1/4 percent, and the probability of one or the other of these occurring is .30. Similarly, even though it is believed that a prime rate of 9 3/4 percent is impossible, the probability is 1.0 (certainty) that the rate will not exceed that value. If there is an interval containing only impossible values (for example, slightly more than 9 1/4 percent to slightly less than 9 3/8 percent), the cumulative distribution function will be flat over that interval. This accounts for the stair-step appearance of Figure 11–2.

These calculations show that the probability mass function can be used to obtain the cumulative distribution function. It is also possible to reverse

---

[2]Alternatively, the cumulative distribution function could be defined in terms of the probabilities that an uncertainty will be *greater than or equal to* specific values. The most common convention, however, is to define the cumulative distribution function in terms of *less than or equal to*.

FIGURE 11–2

Cumulative Distribution Function for the Prime Rate

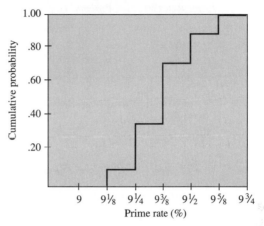

TABLE 11–3   Cumulative Distribution Function for the Prime Rate

Prime Rate (%)	Cumulative Probability
9 3/8	0
9 1/2	.30
9 5/8	.70
9 3/4	1.00

the order and to use a stair-stepped cumulative distribution function to find the corresponding probability mass function. For example, suppose a different analyst has assessed the cumulative distribution function in Table 11–3 for the prime rate one month in the future. Note that, because the second analyst views the economic climate differently from the first, this is a different distribution function than Table 11–2. (Recall that these are judgmental assessments and there is no requirement for them to be identical.) The cumulative distribution function of Table 11–3 gives the probability that the prime rate will be 9 5/8 percent or less as .70 and the probability that the rate will be 9 1/2 percent or less as .30. The only interest rate that is not common to both of these ranges is an interest rate of exactly 9 5/8 percent (remember the interest rates must be quoted in increments of 1/8). The prime rate of 9 5/8 percent must then account for the .40 difference in cumulative probabilities. Consequently, the probability of the prime rate being exactly 9 5/8 must be .40. Because cumulative probabilities are the result of adding mass probabilities, it is reasonable that the mass probabilities should be recovered by subtracting cumulative probabilities. Thus, the probability mass function

TABLE 11–4   Probability Mass Function for the Prime Rate

Prime Rate (%)	Probability
9 1/2	.30
9 5/8	.40
9 3/4	.30

corresponding to the cumulative distribution function of Table 11–3 can be calculated as shown in Table 11–4.

Continuous and Many-Valued Uncertain Quantities

Suppose a meteorologist is forecasting the likely amounts of rain that will fall in a particular area over the next three months. A great many outcomes are possible. For example, the rainfall might be 1.00347528 inches. In fact, there are infinitely many possibilities. Even if we recognize that there are limits to the accuracy of measurement and limit our discussion to numbers with no more than two or three decimal places, there are still many possible outcomes. As a result, the meteorologist will find it virtually impossible to assign probability mass values to individual values in an intelligent way. Not only is it an overwhelming task because of the large number of outcomes, but also the individual probabilities would be infinitesimally small and too difficult to assess.

   Although it is difficult (if not impossible) to think in terms of the probability of a specific outcome when the uncertainty is continuous or many-valued, it is possible to consider the probability that the outcome will be within a range. For example, the meteorologist might be able to think comfortably about the probability that the rainfall will be in the range between 4 and 5 inches or that it will be in the range between 8 and 9 inches. These ranges of outcomes will have a substantial amount of probability associated with them and this facilitates the assessment. Similarly, it may be possible for the meteorologist to think in terms of ranges of outcomes defined as being less than or equal to a specific value; such as the probability of the rainfall being less than or equal to 5 inches. Probabilities of this form are cumulative probabilities and they will be used to describe meaningfully an assessor's belief about the possible outcomes of continuous or many-valued uncertain quantities.

   The meteorologist might, for example, give the cumulative probability function in Figure 11–3. Methods for making such an assessment will be discussed later in this chapter. Figure 11–3 shows that the probability the rainfall will be 11 inches or less is .91, while the probability that it will be 9 inches or less is .75. Thus, the probability that the rainfall will be between these two values can be calculated (using the same logic that we used earlier

FIGURE 11–3

Cumulative Distribution Function for Rainfall

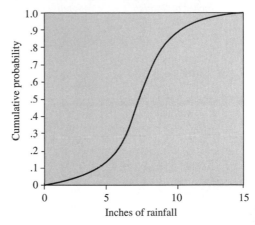

when going from a cumulative function to a probability mass function) as .91 minus .75, or .16. It is a property of cumulative distribution functions that their graphs rise more steeply above ranges of values that are more likely to occur than above ranges that are less likely. For example, notice that the curve in Figure 11–3 rises more steeply over the range between 7 and 9 inches (which has a .25 probability) than it does over the range from 9 to 11 inches (which has a .16 probability).

It is also possible to construct and graph an analog of a probability mass function for a continuous uncertain quantity. Such a function is called a **probability density function**. Although these functions will not be considered in detail, it is worthwhile to note their relationship to cumulative distribution functions. The probability mass function represents the probability that the uncertainty will result in a specific outcome. Such a probability is infinitesimal for continuous uncertainties, but its analog would be the probability that the outcome is an interval. In particular, we might take these intervals to be the interval from 0 to 1 inch, from 1 to 2 inches, from 2 to 3 inches, up to the interval from 14 to 15 inches. The probability that the rainfall in the next three months will be in these ranges can be found by subtracting pairs of values from the cumulative distribution function. For example, the probability that the rainfall will be 9 to 10 inches is .84 − .75 = .09 (the difference between the probability of 10 inches or less and 9 inches or less.) These interval probabilities are shown in Table 11–5.

The probabilities of Table 11–5 are graphed in Figure 11–4 with the height of the bar indicating the probability for that particular interval. An interval whose bar is twice as high as another interval has twice the likelihood of occurring. Now, suppose that a table like Table 11–5, but with intervals half as wide (from 0 to 1/2, etc.), is constructed. The corresponding

TABLE 11–5 Rainfall Probabilities Corresponding to One-Inch Ranges

Inches of Rainfall	Probability
0 and under 1	0.01
1 and under 2	0.02
2 and under 3	0.04
3 and under 4	0.05
4 and under 5	0.09
5 and under 6	0.13
6 and under 7	0.16
7 and under 8	0.14
8 and under 9	0.11
9 and under 10	0.09
10 and under 11	0.07
11 and under 12	0.04
12 and under 13	0.03
13 and under 14	0.01
14 and under 15	0.01

FIGURE 11–4

Probabilities Corresponding to One-Inch Ranges of Rainfall

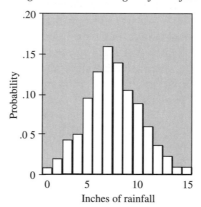

graph would have twice as many bars, but they would be much shorter. It would still be true, however, that the relative heights of the bars would be proportional to the relative likelihoods of the ranges. A probability density function can be thought of as the curve that would represent the relative likelihoods for a very large number of intervals. The probability density function for the cumulative distribution function of Figure 11–3 is given in Figure 11–5.

It was observed earlier that a cumulative distribution curve rises more steeply for regions with a greater likelihood of occurrence and less steeply

FIGURE 11–5
Probability Density Function for Inches of Rainfall

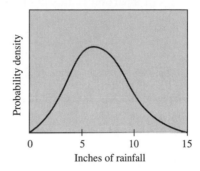

FIGURE 11–6

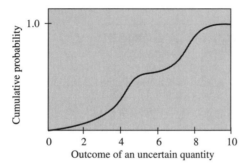

(a) Cumulative Distribution Function

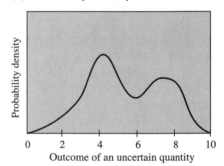

(b) Probability Density Function

for less likely ranges. For the probability density function, the graph is higher for more likely values, lower for less likely values. As an example of the relationship between the shapes of the cumulative distribution function and the shape of the corresponding probability density function, consider Figure 11–6.[3] Figure 11–6(a) is the graph of a cumulative distribution function. Notice that the curve has two particularly steep sections, two modes—one around 4 and one around 8. These two modes signal that the uncertainty has two particularly likely ranges of values.[4] The same fact is shown in the graph of the probability density function in Figure 11–6(b). The curve has two humps, one around 4 and one around 8, corresponding to the two steep sections in Figure 11–6(a).

In the preceding discussion, we have been addressing continuous uncertainties. In practice, such uncertainties are rather unusual. It is much more

---

[3]Readers familiar with calculus will recognize that the pdf is the slope or the first derivative of the cdf.

[4]Such distributions are said to be bimodal.

common to encounter uncertainties that have a very large number of possible outcomes but are not strictly continuous. For example, consider the monthly sales of a particular model of automobile. Surely the sales will be an integer number (not 3276.5, for example, even though there may be buyers who feel that they received only half a car) and thus, strictly speaking, the uncertainty is not continuous. On the other hand, there are so many possible outcomes that the assessor cannot think sensibly about the mass probabilities. It is much more natural to make judgments about cumulative probabilities and to treat the cumulative distribution function as being smooth (as in Figure 11–3) rather than stair-stepped (as in Figure 11–2). Because the probability of a particular outcome is very small, little specific information is lost with such a fabrication, but the probability description of the uncertainty is greatly simplified. For these reasons, many-valued uncertain quantities are treated as if they were continuous.

Assessment: Capturing Personal Judgment

The discussions of the previous section assumed that the probability distribution for many-valued or continuous uncertain quantities was simply "available." This section presents an assessment process that can be used for situations in which an assessor must rely on accumulated experience and judgment. The assessment of a probability distribution for the demand of a new product is often an example of such a circumstance. Although tangentially relevant data, such as the performance of similar products or trends in consumer preferences, may be available, these do not give direct insight into the market acceptance of the new product. As a first step in the product evaluation, the product manager could make an assessment of demand that would be tempered by the indirect data but would be predominantly personal judgment.

The prime rate assessment that was discussed earlier in this chapter provided an example of how an assessment can be made on the basis of relative likelihoods when there are a small number of possible outcomes. In many situations, however, there are many possible outcomes of an uncertainty. An assessor might be concerned with this year's demand for a product, where the demand could conceivably be any value between 1,000 and 10,000. As argued in the previous section, it would be extremely difficult for the assessor to assign a probability to each possible outcome, for example, the probability of exactly 4,127 units of demand. Instead, it is more natural to consider the probabilities that the uncertainty falls within specified ranges. The assessment procedure described in this section is a systematic way of eliciting and using such judgments. The result will be a cumulative distribution function.

The essence of the procedure is to have the assessor concentrate on a few fractiles[5] of the distribution of the uncertain quantity. The first value the assessor selects is the median (the .5 fractile). In specifying the median, the assessor indicates a value that divides the range of possible outcomes into two equally likely ranges. In the assessor's opinion, the outcome is just as likely to be below the specified median as above it. Note that the median is not necessarily the single most likely outcome (that's the mode), rather the median divides the range into two equally likely portions. One way to select the median is to propose to the assessor a choice between two gambles. In the first gamble the assessor will receive $50 if, and only if, the uncertain quantity turns out to be less than or equal to some specified value. In the second gamble the assessor will receive $50 if, and only if, the uncertain quantity turns out to be greater than the specified value. If the first gamble is believed to be more attractive, the specified value is above the median, because there is better than a 50/50 chance of being below the specified value. Alternatively, if the second gamble is believed to be the more attractive, the specified value is less than the median. If the assessor is truly indifferent between the first and the second gamble, the specified value is the median of the distribution. It is this point of indifference that the assessor is asked to assess. When the median is assessed, one point (the .50 fractile) on the cumulative distribution function has been assessed.

The next step in the procedure is to divide the range below the median into the equally likely portions and then to do the same to the range above the median. The values selected to make these divisions will be the .25 and .75 fractiles, respectively. To specify the .25 fractile, it may again be useful to think in terms of a choice between gambles. Assume that it is known for certain that the outcome of the uncertainty will be below the median (or that the bets are off if the outcome is above the median). Now propose a gamble in which the assessor will receive $50 if, and only if, the uncertain quantity turns out to be less than or equal to a specified value. In the alternative gamble, the assessor will win $50 if, and only if, the uncertain quantity has a value between the specified value and the median. If the assessor is indifferent between these two gambles, then the specified value is the .25 fractile of the assessed probability distribution. If the first gamble is preferred, the assessor must believe that the chances are greater than 1 in 4 that the uncertainty will be less than or equal to the specified value, and so the .25 fractile is smaller than the specified value. Similarly, if the second gamble is preferred, the .25 fractile is larger than the specified value. The .75 fractile can be assessed in the same fashion, but the gambles will now be predicated on the assumption that the outcome will be above the median. With the

---

[5]Recall from Chapter 4, the probability of an outcome being at or below the k fractile of a probability distribution is k, where k is a number between zero and one. The .25 fractile of the rainfall distribution of Figure 11–3 is 6.1 inches.

.75 fractile, the assessor should be indifferent between a gamble in which the assessor wins if the outcome of the uncertainty is between the median and the .75 fractile and a second gamble in which the assessor wins if, and only if, the outcome is greater than the .75 fractile.

The final step in this preliminary assessment is to assess the extreme fractiles—the .01 fractile and the .99 fractile. Most people believe it is not difficult to make judgments about the extreme values of a distribution; however, experience indicates the opposite. Experiments with large numbers of people have shown that many assessors give distributions that are too tight, that is, the range between the .01 and .99 fractiles is not wide enough. The phenomenon can be thought of as follows. When the .01 fractile for an uncertainty is being assessed, the assessor is stating the belief that the chances are 1 in 100 that the outcome will be below the value being stated. Thus, if the assessor assesses distributions for many uncertainties, it would be anticipated that only 1/100 of the actual outcomes fall below the respective .01 fractiles. Most beginning assessors find, however, that the outcomes fall below their assessed .01 fractiles considerably more often than once in a hundred times. The experience is not altered by changes in terminology. Even if the extreme fractiles are referred to as "the .001 (.999) fractile," "the smallest (largest) possible outcome," or "an extraordinarily low (high) outcome," the distributions remain too tight. Most assessors find that they must concentrate on spreading out their assessed distributions.

Some people feel comfortable with the sequence of assessments presented above; others prefer to start with the median, proceed to the extremes, and then concentrate on the .25 and .75 fractiles. Still others might want to select the extreme fractiles first and then select the .25, .5, and .75 fractiles. No one procedure dominates the others. Whichever sequence is found to be most comfortable for the assessor should be the one that is used—but remember the warning about distributions that are too tight. If, for example, selecting the extremes first makes the assessor select narrow ranges for the distributions, then that sequence should be avoided.

Once a preliminary list of fractiles (the .01, .25, .5, .75, and .99 fractiles) has been assessed, the assessments should be reviewed, checking that they truly represent the assessor's judgments. There are at least two checks that can be performed. First, because the chance is 1 in 4 that the uncertainty will be below the .25 fractile and 1 in 4 that it will exceed your .75 fractile, the assessor should believe that it is just as likely the value will be inside the interval between these two fractiles (called the interquartile range) as outside it. If that is not the case, then the assessments should be adjusted. A second check is to plot the cumulative distribution implied by the assessments. Generally, but not always, the curve would be expected to be smooth and S-shaped (the most likely values would be concentrated in one area and the remaining likelihood would gradually taper off in the extremes). If there are irregularities or wiggles in the shape of the distribution, the assessments should be reviewed with the objective of being confident that the implications of the irregularities are understood and that they match the assessor's intuition about the uncertainty. This is especially true if the distribution is bimodal.

This procedure of assessing distributions may feel somewhat uncomfortable because it relies so heavily on personal judgment. Remember that the procedure is predicated on uncertainty. It is not the objective of these assessments to eliminate uncertainty, but rather to provide a systematic way to express explicitly an assessor's personal judgments about uncertainty.

An Example of Assessing a Probability Distribution

A person who has to meet a plane on a Friday afternoon might have the following thoughts in assessing a probability distribution for the time of the plane's arrival.

> Rather than think about the time of arrival, it's a whole lot easier for me to think about the number of minutes late. Let's see, that means that early arrivals will be negative numbers. Now, the plane is scheduled to come in at 4:00 and it is coming from New York. The airport will probably be terribly crowded at that time of day, especially on Fridays . . . people who travel on business are trying to get home for the weekend . . . so my best guess is that the plane will be late. It could conceivably be early, but I think that's less likely. Also, because it's coming from New York and it wouldn't have taken off early, there's a limit as to how early it could be. I suppose that the plane is as likely to be 5 minutes or less late as not. If I had to gamble on whether or not the plane would be 5 minutes or more late, I don't know which to choose . . . so I'll call 5 minutes the median of my distribution. I really don't think it's too likely that the plane will be early, but if the plane makes good time, they might want to get it out of the way before the real crunch . . . maybe 1 chance in 4 that it wouldn't be late, I'd say . . . so that would make 0 my .25 fractile . . . and I really couldn't believe a New York flight would be more than 10 minutes early . . . well, maybe once in a blue moon . . . call it 15 minutes to be conservative and I'll call that my .01 fractile. Now about the .75 fractile, I really don't know . . . they do try to get the planes in, at least . . . 10 minutes? . . . that's probably too generous an assessment of their ability to make things work. I'll try 13 . . . and I suppose 20 minutes might be the .99 fractile.

These values give the cumulative distribution function shown in Figure 11–7.

> What's that wiggle in the graph? It says that the outcome is most likely to be between 0 and 5 minutes late or 10 to 15 minutes late. What's that called? . . . bimodal? I'm not sure I believe that . . . there's no reason for it. In fact, I think I've been too generous on the high end . . . airline performance is probably worse than that. I'd bet that at this time of day 1 flight in 100 is at least 25 minutes late . . . or maybe 30. And my .75 fractile should probably be 12 rather than 13. (I seem to think in round numbers like 0 and 5 and 25 . . . I wonder how much of a difference that makes.)

Figure 11–8 presents the revised cumulative distribution function.

FIGURE 11–7

Preliminary Distribution for Number of Minutes Late

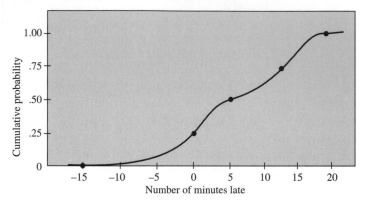

FIGURE 11–8

Revised Distribution for the Number of Minutes Late

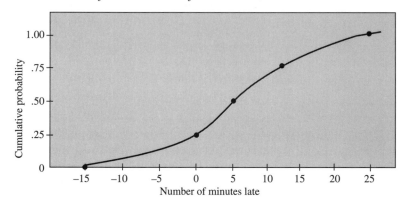

Assessment: Using Historical Data as a Guide

In the previous section, methods were described for capturing in a probability distribution an assessor's judgment about the future outcome of an uncertain quantity. The procedures presume that all the information about the situation (the past and the future) has been incorporated in the assessor's knowledge and judgment and is thus brought to bear in the assessment. This process, however, often leaves the assessor searching for a more concrete and less judgmental method to make the probability assessment.

Frequently it is possible to formally use historical data in assessing probability distributions. For example, suppose a manager has quarterly orders information for a product for the past several years. The methods of the previous section would force the manager to digest all of these data and incorporate them implicitly into a judgmental assessment. In this section, systematic ways for using the available data as a guide in the probability assessment process will be presented. The discussion will begin with a consideration of the conditions under which data from the past can be used in preparing probabilistic forecasts. Not all available data may be relevant (or usable). Methods will then be introduced for explicitly using those data that are appropriate as guidance to the assessment process.

Identifying Suitable Data

The presence of data in the probability assessment process does not absolve the assessor from the application of judgment. Assessors must determine which data are useful and which are reliable, and in doing so, they use their judgment and knowledge about the decision situations and the origins of the data.

What data from the past can be used in planning for the future? Suppose an assessor who is concerned with a future uncertain event has data available from similar situations in the past. If these past situations were such that the outcome from any one of them could also be an outcome for the future event, then the past data are said to have arisen from **indistinguishable situations**. Data from indistinguishable situations can be appropriately and directly used to make statements about the future. The challenge is in deciding when a particular set of data has arisen from indistinguishable situations.

In identifying indistinguishable situations, the concern is with the assessor's beliefs about the potential outcomes before the event occurs, not after the result becomes known. Thus, the assessor is asked to judge whether there was any reason to differentiate, a priori, one *situation* from another before the results are known. If not, the situations are indistinguishable for the assessor. Note that this question does not ask whether the assessor can explain the differences in the actual results after the outcomes of the uncertainties are known. It focuses on the assessor's beliefs and knowledge before the event. If the situations are indistinguishable, the assessor would have given the same forecast in each of the situations.

In some cases, it is relatively easy to feel comfortable with the judgment that the data arose from indistinguishable situations. For an automated production process in which the raw materials are of constant specification and the machinery does not stray from its calibrations, there may be variations in the exact physical characteristics of the output and it may be important to forecast these characteristics for future output. It would certainly seem reasonable in this case to assume that past output arose from situations indistinguishable from what will be faced in the future. As a result, data on past output could then be used for forecasting the physical characteristics of future output. The data would certainly be distinguishable (i.e., not identical), but all would have come from indistinguishable situations.

It is often easy to identify circumstances that will distinguish any two situations. For example, the proprietor of a variety store in a shopping mall is interested in forecasting weekly birthday card sales. If the proprietor has weekly sales figures for birthday cards from the past year, they are candidates for use in predicting next week's sales. On reflection, the proprietor would probably not want to be guided by the sales data from each of the several weeks preceding major holidays. It might be argued that not only would the increased traffic for the specialty cards increase sales for birthday cards, but also there might be an increase in sales per person as customers, once they are in the store, stock up on birthday cards. Now the owner is left with the non-holiday data. Even this might be considered to arise from distinguishable situations. In some weeks, the major stores in the mall conducted special promotions that increased traffic in the mall. This could be viewed as a distinguishable situation. So the argument goes, until each week of each year is viewed as a distinguishable situation.

When first confronted with the challenge of deciding which data can be used, most people tend to one extreme or the other. Many try to use all conceivable data, looking for strength in numbers, and include data from situations that are clearly distinguishable. Others become so concerned with the differences in the situations (it is always possible for creative people to find distinguishing influences) that they despair of finding any useful historical results. Identifying useful data demands balance. The key is to exclude only those data that come from clearly distinguished situations. The screening process is a delicate one for the mesh should be neither too coarse nor too fine. It is a matter of judgment.

Using the Suitable Data as a Guide

Once an assessor has selected the appropriate set of data (the results of indistinguishable situations), how can that data be used as an explicit guide to the assessment process? The data's role and impact on the assessment will generally differ depending on the amount of data available. If there is an overwhelming amount, the data will serve as a very precise guide in the probability assessment, requiring little input from the assessor. On the other hand, if there is a scant amount, the data will generally not play such a dominant role and the assessment will be based on the assessor's experience and judgment augmented by the loose guidance of the data. Although it is certainly preferable to be confronted with plentiful amounts of data, the more common condition will be the opposite. As a result, the technique that we employ must be flexible. It must apply to situations when there are either large or small amounts of data. It must also allow the infusion of the assessor's judgment.

Consider the example of a newspaper dealer who has recorded the demand for the morning paper for the past five weeks and is interested in forecasting the demand for tomorrow's edition. The available data are shown in Table 11–6.

TABLE 11–6   Newspaper Demand Data

Date	Day	Demand	Date	Day	Demand
24	Wednesday	70	11	Sunday	41
25	Thursday	73	12	Monday	59
26	Friday	68	13	Tuesday	43
27	Saturday	56	14	Wednesday	46
28	Sunday	58	15	Thursday	49
29	Monday	71	16	Friday	52
30	Tuesday	65	17	Saturday	39
31	Wednesday	55	18	Sunday	40
1	Thursday	47	19	Monday	44
2	Friday	54	20	Tuesday	59
3	Saturday	42	21	Wednesday	52
4	Sunday	44	22	Thursday	41
5	Monday	61	23	Friday	56
6	Tuesday	51	24	Saturday	44
7	Wednesday	48	25	Sunday	40
8	Thursday	50	26	Monday	54
9	Friday	54	27	Tuesday	46
10	Saturday	45			

The first step in using these data as a guide in assessing a probability distribution for tomorrow's demand is to decide if these data have come from situations that are indistinguishable from tomorrow. Two questions come to mind. From the perspective of this newspaper dealer, is demand on weekends different from weekdays? Have there been any environmental changes that might affect demand? Because the newsstand is located in the business district of the community, it would be reasonable to expect that demand would be lower on the weekends than on the weekdays due to reduced activity in the area. The weekends would thus be distinguishable situations relative to the weekdays. Our forecast is for a weekday and thus the weekend data should be excluded from consideration. This argument might be carried to the extreme of considering each day of the week as distinguishable. It seems reasonable, however, to assume that a business day is a business day, regardless of the day of the week. With regard to changes in the environment, there was a price increase for the newspaper at the beginning of the month and the increase was not matched by the other local papers. As a result, it would be expected then that only this month's data would be relevant to our assessment—last month is clearly distinguishable from this month. On the basis of these two considerations, the data that appear to have arisen from indistinguishable situations are the observations on the weekdays of this month. The data are shown in Table 11–7.

These indistinguishable data can now be used as a guide for forecasting tomorrow's demand for newspapers. One way to proceed is to employ the

TABLE 11–7   Newspaper Demand Data from Indistinguishable Situations

Date	Day	Demand	Date	Day	Demand
1	Thursday	47	15	Thursday	49
2	Friday	54	16	Friday	52
5	Monday	61	19	Monday	44
6	Tuesday	51	20	Tuesday	59
7	Wednesday	48	21	Wednesday	52
8	Thursday	50	22	Thursday	41
9	Friday	54	23	Friday	56
12	Monday	59	26	Monday	54
13	Tuesday	43	27	Tuesday	46
14	Wednesday	46			

fractile assessment procedures of the previous section with the data helping us specify the fractiles. The data can be arrayed in the format of Figure 11–9 by simply sorting it in ascending order. Because the observations have come from indistinguishable situations, each observation should be of equal importance in guiding the assessment. As a result, the median (.50 fractile) of the probability distribution for tomorrow's demand would be reasonably represented by the observation that is in the middle of rank ordering.[6] With 19 observations, this would be the 10th observation; there are 9 observations below and 9 above. It can be seen from Figure 11–9 that this would be 51 papers. In a similar fashion, the .25 fractile would be in the middle of the lower half of the rank-ordered data. With 19 observations, this would be the fifth observation (46 papers) because there are 9 observations in the lower half. The .75 fractile would be the 15th observation (54 papers). The extremes of the .01 and .99 fractiles should extend well beyond the observed data. With just 19 observations we would not expect to have witnessed either the smallest or the largest possible outcome that could ever occur. How far they should be positioned beyond the data is a matter of judgment. Let us place the .01 fractile at 38 and the .99 fractile at 64. We have now assessed the five standard fractiles of the assessment procedure discussed earlier in this chapter. From these fractiles the cumulative probability distribution of Figure 11–10 can be drawn.

In the above procedure, the data were used to provide guidance in assessing the several standard fractiles (.01, .25, .50, .75, .99) of the probability distribution. The procedure did not, however, make explicit use of the specific fashion in which the data were spread out (or clustered) between the standard

---

[6]Not only is it intuitively appealing that the median is best estimated by the "middle" value in the data set, but it also is supported by statistical theory.

FIGURE 11–9
Historical Frequencies of Weekday Newspaper Demand

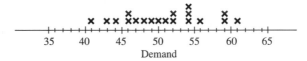

FIGURE 11–10
Cumulative Probability Distribution of Weekday Newspaper Demand
(Based on Fractile Assessment with Data as a Guide)

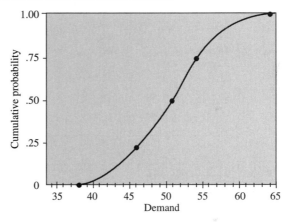

fractiles. Much of that is left to judgment and/or to the flair of a pencil as a curve is drawn through the fractiles.

By assessing more fractiles, it is possible to make the "interpolation" between the fractiles more stringently guided by the specific values in the data set and, as a result, the curve fitting more mechanical. Recall that in the newspaper example, there were 19 observations and the 10th observation was the estimate of the .50 fractile and the 5th observation was the estimate of the .25 fractile. More generally, the k-th observation would be the estimate of the

k/(n + 1) fractile,

where n is the total number of observations. Table 11–8 presents the fractile estimates that can be made using the entire data set. Note that all the data are included (even those that represent "duplicate" observations of the same outcome), the data are presented in rank order, and each observation is associated with a fractile that is a multiple of .05 (1/20). The probability distribution that results from this procedure is shown in Figure 11–11.

With the above procedure, only the data play a role in the assessment. This has its pluses and its minuses. When the data set is rather small, judgment should play a significant role. If the data are exactly followed, the

TABLE 11–8   **Fractile Assessments of Weekday Newspaper Demand**

41 papers	.05 fractile
43 papers	.10 fractile
44 papers	.15 fractile
46 papers	.20 fractile
46 papers	.25 fractile
47 papers	.30 fractile
48 papers	.35 fractile
49 papers	.40 fractile
50 papers	.45 fractile
51 papers	.50 fractile
52 papers	.55 fractile
52 papers	.60 fractile
54 papers	.65 fractile
54 papers	.70 fractile
54 papers	.75 fractile
56 papers	.80 fractile
59 papers	.85 fractile
59 papers	.90 fractile
61 papers	.95 fractile

FIGURE 11–11

Cumulative Probability Distribution of Weekday Newspaper Demand
(Based on Fractiles for Each Observation)

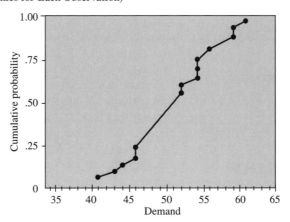

assessment could be influenced significantly by the potential vagaries of just a few outcomes and, as a result, may not be representative of more considered judgment. With just a few data points, the graph of the resulting cumulative distribution could be jagged and not a smooth S-shaped curve that would usually be associated with a cumulative distribution function. If the mechanically drawn graph were not appropriately shaped, it would be reasonable to draw a smooth curve that does not necessarily pass through all the points but use them to help define the shape. Figure 11–11 is a candidate for such smoothing. Finally when there are just a few observations, the extremes of the distribution are not defined by the data and, if required by an analysis, would have to be assessed judgmentally. On the other hand when there are large amounts of data, there is no problem in letting the data take the lead. This assessment can become almost mechanical and the above procedure permits that.[7]

Adjusting Data for One Distinguishing Factor

A simple extension of the methods that have just been discussed can sometimes be useful when data cannot be considered to have come from indistinguishable situations, but the situations would have been indistinguishable if it were not for the effects of a single factor.

For example, consider a chain of five retail stores operating in a no-growth market. The stores are of different sizes and have significantly different levels of monthly sales volume for a particular product but have experienced no growth. The different stores are clearly distinguishable situations, so the data cannot be directly used in aggregate. If there were a long track record, the data could be segmented by store and separate volume distributions could be assessed for each store. With only a short history, it would be helpful if the data could be kept as one set, transforming it in some way so it could be viewed as having arisen from indistinguishable situations. It might be reasonable to hypothesize that although the stores have different average volume levels, the volume of one store relative to its average level would be indistinguishable from the volume of the second store relative to the second store's average. In other words, the first store was just as likely to experience a volume of 110 percent or less of its average as the second store was to experience volume of 110 percent or less of its average. If the data supported this conjecture, the entire data set could be used to assess a cumulative probability distribution of "volume relative to store average." The available data from each of the stores could be combined in making this one assessment because the distinguishing factor of size has been eliminated. To forecast volume for a particular store, the horizontal axis of the distribution of "volume relative to store average" would have to be rescaled to reflect the average volume of the particular store under consideration.

This method of adjusting for a distinguishing characteristic occurs most often when there is a surrogate that is a simple rescaling of the quantity to be forecast. In the above example, it was volume relative to average volume, rather than simply volume. Other examples are sales per foot of shelf space

---

[7]The $k/(n + 1)$ method can be easily implemented with electronic spreadsheet software using the sorting and graphing capabilities.

rather than store sales (to adjust for different exposures of a consumer product in different stores), sales in constant dollars rather than current dollars (to adjust for inflation), and deseasonalized sales rather than sales (to adjust for seasonalities).

Assessment: Appealing to Underlying Structure

Suppose a manufacturer of electrical components has recently experienced difficulty with the reliability of a particular machine. Suppose further that a sales contract with a demanding customer for the output of that machine includes the stipulation that deliveries will be taken in batches of 10 components and the entire batch must be free of defects for the batch to be accepted. If, on average, 5 percent of all the components produced by that machine are defective, what is the probability that the continued use of this machine will produce defect-free batches of 10 components? Because the reliability problem has been recently encountered, an assessor would have little experience with batches of 10 under the present conditions on which to base a purely judgmental assessment. Similarly, there would be little indistinguishable data for batches of 10 that could serve as a guide in the assessment. An alternative approach is to reflect on the underlying process by which the number of defects will be determined. When the underlying process that generates the uncertain quantity is well understood, the probability distribution can often be determined from basic principles.

Consider a regular tetrahedron. What are the chances that it will land on any particular face when fairly tossed? Once it is determined that a regular tetrahedron has four faces of equal area, most people will confidently answer 25 percent without hesitation. Because few people have much experience tossing tetrahedrons, how could such an assessment be made with confidence? Some may appeal by analogy to prior experiences in tossing coins and dice. Others may argue that, because a tetrahedron is perfectly symmetrical, one side cannot fall face down more frequently than any other. *In either case, an understanding of the fundamental characteristics of the underlying process was brought to bear and, through that understanding, the assessment was made.*

Similar opportunities to take advantage of the fundamental characteristics of an underlying process arise in the assessment of many probability distributions. When a reasonable model of the underlying process can be built, the model can be used to derive the probability distribution theoretically. Then, if the model is a reasonable representation of the actual process, the derived theoretical probability distribution will be a "good approximation" of the actual probability distribution of the uncertainty. When the underlying process is well understood and easily modeled, as it is for the tetrahedron, we can derive the probability distribution from fundamental principles and forgo the chore of subjectively estimating it by assessing fractiles or any other means.

This section introduces four common underlying processes and the analytical[8] probability distributions associated with them and presents means to obtain a particular probability from the resulting probability distributions. The four underlying processes and their associated probability distributions are: (1) a simple counting process with a finite number of repetitions, the **binomial distribution**; (2) an accumulation process with a finite number of repetitions, the **normal distribution**; (3) a second counting process, this time with an indefinite number of repetitions, the **Poisson distribution**; and (4) a waiting-time process that ignores history (the time already waited), the **exponential distribution**.

It is very important to emphasize that while these probability distributions have many legitimate applications, they are applicable *only* when the specific assumptions about the underlying processes are satisfied—that is, when the uncertain quantity is obtained from a process similar to the one used to derive the probability distribution in the first place. *When that is not the case, these analytical distributions cannot be used;* instead, the probability distribution must be assessed by the methods presented earlier in the chapter.

The Binomial Distribution

The first underlying process is a simple counting process in which the number of occurrences of an event are counted. In this case, the only concern is whether or not the event occurs, so only two possible outcomes are considered, either the event occurs or it doesn't occur. Traditionally, one of these outcomes is called a "success" and the other a "failure,"[9] and the outcome labeled a success occurs with probability p and the outcome labeled a failure occurs with probability $(1 - p)$. Inspecting a part for defects (defective, not defective) and counting the number of defects, polling voters (for, against) and counting the number who are for, or simply tossing a coin (heads, tails) and counting the number of tails can potentially be examples of such a process.

For a process to have the binomial distribution, however, two conditions must also be satisfied by the underlying counting process. First, the number of opportunities for a success (failure) to occur must be fixed and finite. These opportunities, or repetitions of the process, are generally referred to as trials. Second, the repetitions (trials) must be identical and independent—that is, the probability of a success (failure) must remain the same from one trial to the next.

---

[8]The word *analytical* means the probability distribution can be derived theoretically by analyzing the underlying process and that its resulting form can be expressed mathematically.

[9]The words *success* and *failure* are simply labels used by convention to distinguish the two outcomes. They are not intended to imply that one outcome is preferred to the other, and they may be interchanged at will.

Each repetition of the underlying process is called a Bernoulli trial. When there are a fixed number (n) of identical and independent Bernoulli trials, the resulting probability distribution of the *number of successes in n trials* is the binomial distribution.

To see how the binomial distribution can be derived from this underlying counting process, suppose that an incumbent president of the United States (no matter who) has a 60 percent chance of winning reelection. Because each reelection has only two possibilities (win or lose), each reelection is a Bernoulli trial. The labels *success* and *failure* can now be assigned, and the label *success* is arbitrarily assigned to a win and *failure* to a loss. Because it is assumed that each incumbent has the same probability of winning reelection (the probability of a success is the same from trial to trial), it is assumed that the Bernoulli trials are identical and independent. Therefore, these reelection campaigns represent a series of identical and independent Bernoulli trials.

If attention is limited to the three elections between 1980 and 1992 in which an incumbent ran for reelection, the incumbent won once and lost twice. If the 60 percent chance of a "successful" reelection campaign is correct, what is the probability of the observed result (one success in three trials) occurring?

To calculate this probability, note that there are three ways in which the desired number of successes (*S*) and failures (*F*) can occur to produce one success in three trials, namely, *SFF, FSF*, and *FFS*. Because the probability of each success is 0.60 and the probability of each failure is 0.40, the probability of each of these particular sequences occurring is as follows:

$$\text{Prob } (SFF) = (.6)(.4)(.4) = (.6)^1(.4)^2 = .096,$$
$$\text{Prob } (FSF) = (.4)(.6)(.4) = (.6)^1(.4)^2 = .096,$$
$$\text{Prob } (FFS) = (.4)(.4)(.6) = (.6)^1(.4)^2 = .096.$$

The probability of exactly one success in three trials is equal to the sum of these probabilities, or $(3)(.6)^1(.4)^2 = .288$.

Note that the probabilities of each sequence occurring are the same because of the assumption that the probability of success and failure is the same from one repetition to the next. Two different sequences with the same numbers of successes and failures will always have the same chance of occurring.

This reasoning can now be generalized and the rest of the probability distribution quickly calculated. The probability of no successful reelection campaigns in three trials is $1(.4^3) = .064$, because only one sequence produces this result (namely, *FFF*), and the probability of each failure is .40. Similarly, the probability of two successful reelection campaigns in three trials is $(3)(.6^2)(.4^1) = .432$, and the probability of three successful campaigns in three trials is $(1)(.6^3)(.4^0) = .216$.

These four outcomes (zero, one, two, or three successes) constitute all the possible outcomes for three trials from a Bernoulli process. Because one of them must occur, the sum of their probabilities must equal one, as it does:

Number of Successes	Probability
0	$(1)(.6^0)(.4^3) = .064$
1	$(3)(.6^1)(.4^2) = .288$
2	$(3)(.6^2)(.4^1) = .432$
3	$(1)(.6^3)(.4^0) = .216$

The reelection example, therefore, is an example of one particular binomial distribution—the one for n = 3 trials with a probability p = .60 of success. It is presented graphically in Figure 11–12.

In general, the binomial distribution refers to a family of probability distributions that are defined by two parameters: the number of trials (n) and the probability of success in each trial (p). For any values of these parameters, the probability of r successes in n trials with success probability p can be computed, just as was done for the reelection example. Rather than go through those steps, however, there is a formula that describes this entire family of probability distributions.[10] With this formula, the probability of r successes in n trials, when p is the probability of success, can be computed for any combination of r, n, and p.

Alternatively, the built-in functions of electronic spreadsheets can be used. In Excel™, the function is

$$= \text{BINOMDIST(r,n,p,flag)}$$

When the word *true* is typed in for the parameter *flag*, the function returns the value of the cumulative distribution function—the probability of r or less successes in n trials when the success probability of each trial is p. When the word *false* is typed in for the parameter *flag*, the function returns the value of the probability mass function—the probability of exactly r successes in n trials when the success probability of each trial is p.

With the entire probability distribution defined, the mean of the distribution (the expected number of wins in three trials when the probability of winning in any one trial is .60) can be calculated as

$0 \times \text{Prob[0 Wins]} + 1 \times \text{Prob[1 Win)]} + 2 \times \text{Prob[2 Wins]} + 3$
$\times \text{Prob[3 Wins]} = (0)(.064) + (1)(.288) + (2)(.432) + (3)(.216) = 1.8.$

---

[10]The probability of r successes in n trials with a success probability in each trial of p is

$$\frac{n!}{r!\,(n-r)!}\,p^r(1-p)^{n-r}.$$

The symbol "n!" is read "n factorial" and denotes the product $(n \times (n-1) \times \ldots \times 2 \times 1)$. By convention, $0! = 1$. For the reelection example, the calculation is

$$\frac{3!}{1!2!}(.6)^1\,(.4)^2 = \frac{(3)\,(2)\,(1)}{1\,(2)\,(1)}\,(.6)^1\,(.4)^2 = .288.$$

FIGURE 11–12
Binomial Distribution (n = 3, p = .60)

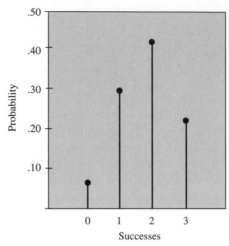

Note that this is n times p (3 × .60). In general, the mean of the binomial distribution with parameters n and p is equal to np. This makes intuitive sense because the average number of successes should be the number of opportunities times the chance of success on any one of them.

The variance of a binomial distribution with parameters n and p is equal to np(1 − p). As always, the standard deviation is equal to the square root of the variance. The formula for the variance can be verified by directly calculating the variance for the reelection example and comparing the result with np(1 − p), 3(.6)(.4) = .72. The direct calculation,

$$(0 − 1.8)^2(.064) + (1 − 1.8)^2(.288) + (2 − 1.8)^2(.432) + (3 − 1.8)^2(.216),$$

also yields .72.

The Normal Distribution

The previous section focused on an underlying uncertain process that counted the number of successes. That counting process is a special case of an accumulation process. If, instead of counting each success, we added one for each success and zero for each failure, the underlying process would have been an accumulation process (adding or accumulating the number of ones).

This section looks at a general accumulation process that is more general than the simple accumulation process just described for two reasons. First, the value of the uncertain quantity generated in each trial is not restricted to zero or one. In fact, the uncertain quantity can take on any value whatsoever. Second, each repetition of the process is not required to be identical to all the others. However, the number of repetitions of the process (or trials) must still be fixed and finite, and each repetition of the process must be independent of all the others.[11]

Under these circumstances, if the number (n) of repetitions of the process is large enough, the resulting probability distribution *of the sum of the uncertain quantities* generated during the n trials is approximately equal to the normal distribution, the bell-shaped curve. Furthermore, if the fixed number of trials is equal to n, because the average of the trials is simply the sum divided by n, when n is large enough, the probability distribution *of the average of the uncertain quantities* is also approximately normal.

These results follow from one of the most famous theorems in statistics, the Central Limit Theorem. This theorem states that, as the number of trials increases, the probability distribution of the sum of the uncertain quantities generated during the trials becomes increasingly normal about the sum of the means of the uncertain quantities.[12] In other words, the Central Limit Theorem tells us that, as the number of trials gets large, the actual distribution of the sum or average of the results of the trials tends toward the normal distribution. Unfortunately, the Central Limit Theorem has nothing to say about how large a number of trials is needed for the approximation to be a good one.

As an example, consider a machine that fills cereal boxes. The actual number of ounces in any one box is an uncertain quantity with some probability distribution. Regardless of what this distribution might be, if a case consists of 48 boxes, if the average cereal box (the mean of the uncertain quantity) is 14.7 ounces, if 48 is a sufficient number of repetitions, and if the weights of the boxes are independent, then the distribution of the weight of a case will be approximately normal about the sum of the mean values of each box, or (48)(14.7) = 705.6 ounces.

The normal distribution has another special property that results in it appearing regularly in business and nature: If an uncertain quantity that is normally distributed is added to a second uncertain quantity that is normally distributed, the sum will also be normally distributed. In other words, if the underlying processes are already normal, then the sum of any number of them (even as few as two) will also be normally distributed.

The normal distribution actually refers to an entire family of distributions. Specific normal distributions depend on two parameters: (1) the center or mean of the distribution and (2) the dispersion or standard deviation. A

---

[11]Actually, there is one other technical restriction—that the variance of each uncertain quantity (from each trial) be finite. This requirement is not restrictive, however, because it is hard to imagine any process in business (or nature, for that matter) having infinite variance.

[12]An equivalent statement can be made about averages: As the number of trials increases, the probability distribution of the average of uncertain quantities generated during the trials becomes increasingly normal about the average of the means of the uncertain quantities.

FIGURE 11–13
Normal Distributions with Different Standard Deviations

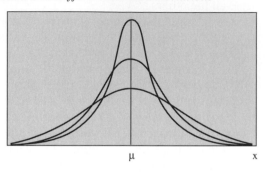

single normal distribution is determined by specifying both parameters.[13] If only the mean is specified, there are many specific normal distributions, all of which have the same mean but *different amounts of dispersion*, as shown in Figure 11–13. On the other hand, if only the standard deviation is specified, there are many specific normal distributions, all with comparable dispersion but with *dissimilar means*, as shown in Figure 11–14.

Despite all this variety, the normal distribution fortunately has yet another property that greatly simplifies its use. *When measured in standard-deviation units, the probability of being any particular number of standard deviations away from the mean is the same for all normal distributions.* More specifically, for all normal distributions, the probability of being plus or minus one standard deviation from the mean is equal to .6826, plus or minus two standard deviations from the mean is equal to .9544, and plus or minus three standard deviations from the mean is equal to .9974. This "standardization" of the normal distribution permits the construction of one table that can be used for all normal distributions. Most statistical texts offer these tables. They are not presented here because electronic spreadsheets permit the easy calculation of probabilities for the normal distribution. In Excel™, the function is

$$= \text{NORMDIST}(x, \mu, \sigma, \text{flag})$$

where x is the outcome whose probability is being calculated, μ is the mean of the distribution, and σ is the standard deviation of the distribution. When the word *true* is typed in place of *flag*, the function returns the value of the

---

[13]The formula for the probability density function of the normal distribution is

$$\frac{1}{\sqrt{2\pi\sigma^2}} e^{-\frac{1}{2}\left(\frac{x-\mu}{\sigma}\right)^2}.$$

As is clear from the formula, the specific distribution depends on the choice of two parameters, μ, the mean, and σ, the standard deviation, as $\pi = 3.14159\ldots$ and $e = 2.71828\ldots$ are mathematical constants.

FIGURE 11–14

Normal Distributions with Different Means

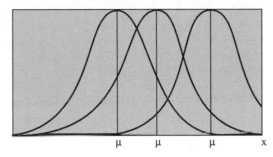

$$\mu \qquad \mu \qquad \mu \qquad x$$

cumulative distribution function (the probability of x or less). When the word *false* is typed in place of *flag*, the function returns the value of the probability density function at the value x.

Now let's revisit the binomial distribution from the previous section. Recall that this section began by pointing out that the accumulation process that gives rise to the normal distribution is simply a generalization of the counting process that gave rise to the binomial distribution. That is, if we assign a value of one to a success and zero to a failure, then the probability of r successes in n trials is just the probability of the sum of the outcomes in n trials. This leads to an apparent contradiction. This section is claiming that, as long as n is big enough, the probability distribution of the sum is normal, whereas the last section claimed that the probability distribution of the sum is binomial. How can this be?

The key to the question lies in the statement *as long as n is big enough.* In each of the examples in the last section, the number of trials was relatively small. Let's look at what happens to the shape of the binomial distribution when we increase the number of trials. Figure 11–15 shows the binomial distribution for p equal to .30 and four values of n (5, 15, 30, and 45). As the number of trials increases, the shape of the distribution progressively approaches that of a bell-shaped curve. This behavior is observed not only when the success probability is 0.30, but also for any success probability. Thus for large enough n, the binomial distribution always approaches the normal distribution,[14] and we have no contradiction.[15]

---

[14]The key to deciding how large is large enough is that the probabilities of success and failure in each trial, when combined with the number of trials, are sufficiently large to make the probability of having either no successes or no failures negligible. A conservative estimate of how large these values need to be is as follows. If both np—the expected number of successes—and n(1 − p)—the expected number of failures—are greater than or equal to 5, then the normal distribution will be a fair approximation of the actual binomial distribution.

[15]The exact distribution is *binomial*; it is only approximately normal.

FIGURE 11–15 *Binomial Distributions for Different Numbers of Trials*

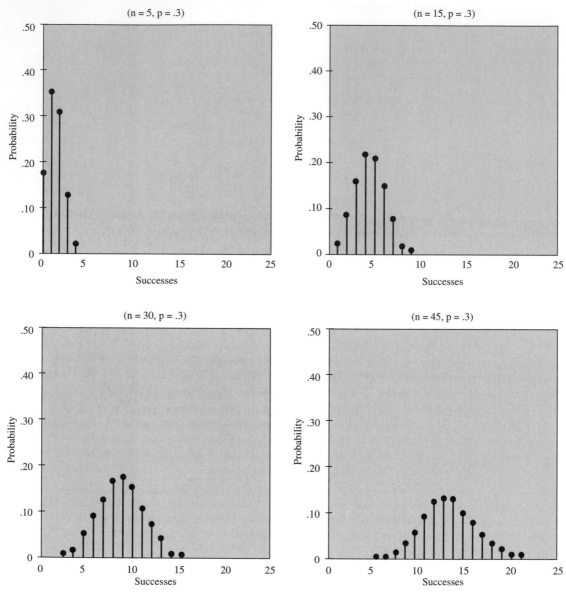

The Poisson Distribution

The underlying process that will be addressed in this section is a counting process with an indefinite number of opportunities for the event to occur. Examples of such counting processes include the number of refrigerators sold in a department store in a week, the number of computer failures at the Pentagon during a year, the number of bond issues on the first of December 1992, the number of errors of fact published in the *Washington Post* during the presidential election campaign of 1992, and so forth. In each case, the number of opportunities for the event to occur is unspecified and potentially limitless.

Because the process is the counting of a number of events and the number of opportunities for the event to occur is unspecified, the resulting probability distribution *of the number of events* will be a distribution whose potential outcomes are all nonnegative whole numbers (0, 1, 2, . . .). In this sense, the distribution is like the binomial distribution, which is defined on the whole numbers from zero to n. However, because there is an unspecified number of opportunities for the event to occur, there is no concept of repeated trials for this underlying process as there is for the underlying processes that give rise to the binomial and normal distributions. Instead, we have four restrictions on the occurrence of an event.

First, the probability of an event occurring over any small unit of measure (short period of time, for example) must be proportional to the length of the unit of measure. While thinking of the unit of measure as a period of time such as a day or week is often convenient, other units of measure such as a page in a newspaper (typographical errors per page) or a roll of sheet metal (blemishes per roll) work as well. Using the time metaphor for unit of measure, another way to state the first restriction is that the probability of an event occurring per unit of time must be constant.

The second restriction states that, over any unit of measure during which occurrences are counted, the number of opportunities for the event to occur must be large. A computer failure or refrigerator sale could occur *at any minute*, for example. Similarly, a blemish on a roll of sheet metal could occur *at any point*.

Third, even though the probability of an event occurring per unit of measure is constant, the likelihood of two or more events occurring during any particular very small unit of measure must be close to nonexistent (infinitesimal or, essentially, zero).

Finally, the probability of an event occurring during any particular unit of measure must be *independent* of what occurs during all other particular units of measure. Using the time metaphor, the probability of an event occurring over the next minute must be independent of whether events occurred in any of the prior minutes, hours, or days. In other words, the history of what has already occurred will not affect the probability distribution of the number of future events.

Any process generating the occurrence of events that satisfies these four conditions is known as a Poisson process. When the number of events generated by a Poisson process are counted, the resulting distribution *of the number of events* during some interval is the Poisson distribution.

The Poisson distribution, like all the others we have discussed in this section, refers to an entire family of distributions. The specific distribution is determined by the single parameter m, the mean number of occurrences per unit of measure. The parameter m is also known as the rate of the Poisson process. For a Poisson process, the probability of r events occurring during the unit of measure is equal to

$$\frac{e^{-m}m^r}{r!},$$

where the parameter m is the expected (or mean) number of occurrences per unit of measure. It so happens that the variance of the Poisson distribution is also equal to m. The Poisson distribution is also available as a special function in electronic spreadsheets in both the probability mass function format and the cumulative probability distribution format. In Excel™, the function is

$$= \text{POISSON}(x,m,\text{flag})$$

where x is the number of occurrences and m is the mean number of occurrences per unit of measure. When the word *true* replaces *flag*, the function returns the cumulative probability (the probability of x occurrences or less); the word *false* returns the probability mass function (the probability of exactly x occurrences).

Figure 11–16 provides four examples of the Poisson distribution for four different values of m. The figure demonstrates that, as the mean number of occurrences per unit of measure increases, the Poisson distribution approaches the normal distribution[16] —for the same reason that the binomial distribution approaches the normal distribution—the Central Limit Theorem.

The Exponential Distribution

The final analytical probability distribution that will be addressed begins once again with an underlying process that generates the occurrence of an event. This time the concern will be the time until the next event occurs, and, therefore, the resulting probability distribution *of the time until the next event,* or *waiting time*, will be over the entire continuum of positive numbers.

The only condition imposed on the event-generating process is that the probability of how much longer it will take until an event occurs cannot depend on how long it has already been since the last event occurred. This condition is known as the *memoryless property*, because the underlying pro-

---

[16]When the mean number of occurrences per unit of measure (m) exceeds 20, the Poisson distribution is approximately a normal distribution with a mean of m and a standard deviation of $\sqrt{m}$.

FIGURE 11–16   *Poisson Distributions for Different Mean Occurrence Rates*

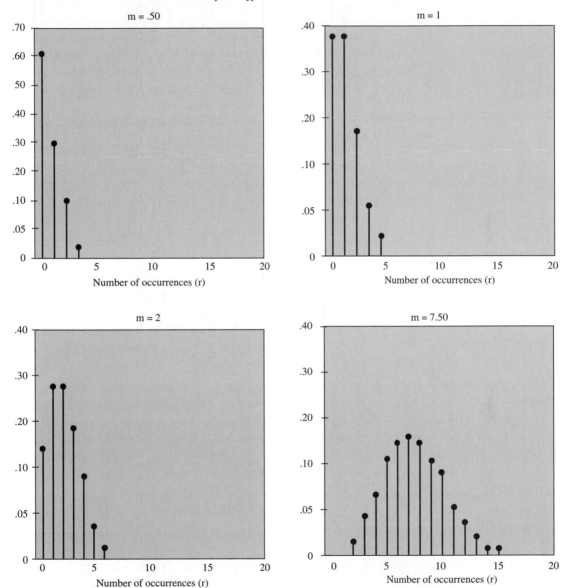

cess *does not remember* when the last event occurred. Whenever this condition is satisfied, the resulting probability distribution *of the time until the next
event* is the exponential distribution.

The memoryless property is not as restrictive as it may at first appear.
Examples of situations for which the memoryless property, and hence the
exponential distribution, have been found to be appropriate include the time

to failure of most electronic components (light bulbs, stereo components, computers, and so forth), the time between arrivals of new people in a line, and the time between arrivals at a service counter (a teller window in a bank or a checkout counter in a supermarket).

Furthermore, all Poisson processes have the memoryless property. It is guaranteed by the fourth condition that all Poisson processes must satisfy, namely, that the probability of an event occurring during any particular interval is independent of what occurred during all prior intervals. Therefore, if we start with a Poisson process, the distribution of the number of events is Poisson; the distributions of the time until the next event and of the time between events (which is often called the interarrival time) are exponential.

The probability density function for the exponential distribution is given by

$$me^{-mx}$$

and the cumulative distribution function is

$$1 - e^{-mx}$$

where m is the rate of the Poisson process. The parameter m, however, is not the mean of the exponential distribution. The mean of the distribution is equal to 1/m, or alternatively, m is the inverse of the mean. To see that this is so, note that a value of m = 2 implies that, on average, there are two arrivals per unit of time, or equivalently, on average, one-half a unit of time will pass before the next arrival. The standard deviation of the exponential distribution is also equal to 1/m.

As is evident from the preceding equations, this distribution, like all the others, refers to an entire family of probability distributions. This time, as with the Poisson distribution, it is dependent on the single parameter m. Even though the distribution has convenient equations with which to compute the probability density function and the cumulative distribution function, electronic spreadsheets provide special functions for computing exponential distribution probabilities. In Excel™, the special function is

$$= \text{EXPONDIST(x,m,flag)}$$

where x is the time until the next occurrence and m is the average rate of arrival of occurrences. When the word *true* replaces *flag*, the function returns the cumulative probability that the next occurrence will be x or less in the future. When *false* replaces *flag*, the function returns the probability density function.

Subjective Biases and Assessment

It was observed in an earlier section of this chapter that assessors tend to make the extreme fractiles of their assessed probability distributions too narrow. They are overconfident of their perspectives. Overconfidence may find its origins in a variety of cognitive influences that can affect the effectiveness of the probability assessment process. Among the sources of these cognitive influences are *a limited information base, anchors, confirmation, implicit conditions,* and *motivations.*

Overconfidence may find its origins in the assessor's failure to consider all the possible outcomes because of limits to the availability of knowledge and experience. Such limits might result from the failure to remember a representative collection of past experiences (it is much easier to remember when one was caught without an umbrella, than to remember the results of all the weather forecasts one has heard), the failure to exhaustively search for a wide range of past experiences, and the failure to imagine the possibilities freely and broadly. These failures might be remedied by increasing the variety of the sources from which information is taken, by hypothesizing extreme scenarios, by seeking explanatory scenarios and then pushing the limits of them, and by imagining the situation retrospectively from the future.

Anchoring is often the result of first forecasting a single "best estimate" and implicitly, if not explicitly, arguing for the reasonableness of that forecast. Those arguments then constrain one's ability to "see" beyond the initial forecast. The resulting distributions will be too narrow. This might suggest that the extreme fractiles should be assessed before assessing any middle fractiles. In addition, if data are being used as a guide, the natural temptation to be anchored by the limited set of observations must be avoided.

Related to anchoring is the phenomenon of confirmation. In an effort to deal with relentless bombardment of information in today's world, many people build mental maps and store information within those frames. These maps are often theories and simplifications of how the complex world works. The theories become sources of comfort and disconfirming information is ignored. As a result, perspectives are narrowed. One way to address this bias is to ask what it would take to change one's perspective on the possibilities and then to determine if these conditions are reasonable.

The range of possibilities is sometimes limited by implicit conditioning. When views are initially developed, the assumptions underlying them are often quite explicit. As time passes, the "ifs" are forgotten and the views take on greater certainty than they deserve. It is helpful to examine the enabling events or conditions of a particular point of view.

On occasions, the narrowness of distributions may occur because of the motivations and incentives that are often present when a forecast is made. Salespeople are rewarded by "making or exceeding" their own forecasts and may be motivated to under-assess the possibilities. The reward structure does not have to be imposed by external sources. Individuals may make themselves "feel good" by exceeding their announced expectations.

Many of these biases might be addressed by conducting the assessment within the context of a group, particularly a diverse group. Within a group there may be a wider information base, a broader set of mental maps, and a greater range of predispositions than any one person. The result could be a broadening of perspective and a questioning of assumptions and opinions.

There is no guarantee of this, however, because group dynamics may be dominated by an articulate individual whose perspectives are narrow. Experiments indicate that group forecasts are more reliable than individual forecasts, especially when the group forecast is preceded by individual forecasts.

Summary

This chapter added several new words to our vocabulary of probability: the probability mass function, the probability density function, and the cumulative distribution function. The probability mass function assigns to each possible outcome of a few-valued uncertain quantity the probability of having exactly that outcome occur. The probability density function is the analogue for continuous uncertain quantities of the probability mass function. The cumulative distribution function assigns to a value (whether it is a possible outcome or not) the probability that the outcome of an uncertain quantity will be less than or equal to that value. The probability mass function (or the probability density function) and the cumulative distribution function are equivalent to each other because either one can be derived from the other.

This chapter also added several approaches for the assessment of probability distributions. A process for eliciting an assessor's knowledge and judgment regarding the potential outcomes of a continuous uncertain quantity was proposed and illustrated. The method focused on the assessment of several fractiles of the probability distribution and used those fractiles to describe the entire distribution. The process presumed that all the information about the uncertain situation (the past and the future) was incorporated in the assessor's knowledge and judgment. On some occasions, however, historical data may be available which could directly guide the assessment. An assessment approach which takes advantage of this opportunity and complements the purely judgmental approach was presented. Although data provide comfort because of their concrete nature, they must be used with caution. The situations from which they come must be indistinguishable from the situation of the future to which they are providing guidance. The final assessment approach was one which appealed to the underlying structure of the uncertain situation and took advantage of fundamental characteristics of that structure. Several classical distributions were presented: the binomial distribution (a counting process with a finite number of repetitions), the normal distribution (an accumulation process with a finite number of repetitions), the Poisson distribution (a counting process with an indefinite number of repetitions), and the exponential distribution (a waiting process). These distributions are convenient to use because they are defined by at most a couple of parameters and are included among spreadsheet software functions, but they must be used with caution and only after the underlying assumptions have been confirmed.

12   SAMPLING

The word *sampling* probably brings to mind a large collection of items from which a small number of items will be selected and measured. We inspect units from yesterday's production and grade their quality. We poll potential voters in an upcoming election and find out how they plan to vote. We capture fish from a lake and measure their length. We study a subset of companies in an industry and summarize their financial performance. We survey customers from our universe of customers and monitor their satisfaction. In the language of sampling, the large collection of items is called the **population** and the smaller number of items actually selected and measured is called the **sample**. Because the number of items in the population can be very large and the costs of sampling nontrivial, a complete sampling of the population (a census) is usually not economical. The challenges become how to select a useful sample and how to interpret and use the information contained in the sample, recognizing that it provides an imperfect picture of the population.

This chapter explains how samples behave so that we can accurately interpret the results of a sample. Our interpretation of a sample begins with an understanding of the method used to collect the sample. For the sample to reflect the population from which it was drawn, the sample must be chosen in a certain way. The most common method for collecting a sample that will accurately reflect the population is random sampling. A **random sample** is one in which each item in the population has an equal chance of being included in the sample. For yesterday's production, randomness requires that we take our sample at randomly chosen times throughout the day. For the fish in the lake example, it will be very difficult to collect a random sample unless every size of fish is equally likely to be caught (a highly unlikely assumption). If the sampling is not done randomly, it is difficult if not impossible to interpret the sample results. If large fish are wiser fish and less likely to be caught, the fish we catch will not be a random sample of the population of fish. The lengths of the fish in our sample will thus be **biased**. The average length of the fish in the sample will tend to understate the average length of the fish in the lake. In situations where the sample was not collected randomly, it is very difficult to interpret the results.

In addition to samples that were collected randomly, this chapter will consider samples collected from very large or **infinite populations**. As long as the size of the sample is small relative to the size of the population, the size of the population is irrelevant to interpreting the sample results. Only if the sampling is accomplished without replacement and the sample size accounts for a noticeable portion of the population will the size of the population affect the interpretation of the sample results.[1]

In summary, this chapter will provide guidance in interpreting and using the results of samples selected randomly from a very large population. You can think of a very large vessel containing millions and millions of items from which we will select some small number at random. For each of the items in the sample, we will measure some characteristic of interest and record the result. We use n to refer to the size of the sample and $x_1, x_2, \ldots x_n$ to refer to the n numerical sample outcomes. We will use x_i to refer to the ith sample outcome, where i can be any number from 1 to n. Very often we will sum the $x_1, x_2, \ldots x_n$ and divide by n to calculate $\bar{x}_n$, the sample average.

$$\bar{x}_n = \frac{(x_1 + x_2 + \cdots x_n)}{n}$$

And finally, we sometimes calculate s, the sample standard deviation of the n observed xs as

$$s = \sqrt{\frac{(x_1 - \bar{x}_n)^2 + (x_2 - \bar{x}_n)^2 + \cdots (x_n - \bar{x}_n)^2}{(n - 1)}}$$

The sample standard deviation is a measure of the scatter among the n observed x's.

The proactive decision maker faces several challenges and questions when dealing with samples. Prior to conducting the sample, how do we forecast x_i, the outcome of the ith sample? If we have a forecast of x_i, how should we forecast $\bar{x}_n$? Once the sample has been taken and we have observed $\bar{x}_n$ and s, how do we use that information to forecast the next x_i or a new $\bar{x}_n$? This chapter will address these challenges.

Forecasting Sample Results

Prior to conducting a sample, the outcomes of the soon-to-be-conducted sample, $x_1, x_2, \ldots x_n$, are uncertain. Proactive decisions made in anticipation of sample results will require forecasts of the uncertain sample outcomes.

---

[1]A description of the special considerations involved in interpreting samples taken without replacement from finite populations can be found in most introductory marketing research texts.

This question of how to forecast an uncertain quantity has been thoroughly addressed in Chapters 4 and 11. There we introduced the concept of a probability distribution as an assignment of probability to each of the possible outcomes of an uncertain quantity. And although many summary measures of a probability distribution (mean, median, mode, standard deviation) are useful in describing features of a probability distribution, they are not a substitute for a complete description provided by the probability distribution. Thus, a complete forecast of x_i, the ith sample outcome, requires a probability distribution. (Here the subscript i simply refers to one of the n sampled items. We start our quest to forecast all the n sample outcomes by focusing on forecasting one.) All the assessment methods of Chapter 11 (personal judgment, historical data, underlying structure) are available to construct such a probability distribution for x_i. This chapter on sampling has little to add with respect to forecasting x_i.

Once you have a probability distribution forecast for x_i, however, the assumptions of random sampling from a large population do have something very important to say about how you should forecast the outcomes of the other $n-1$ samples; namely, you should use the identical probability distribution. Whatever probability distribution you used to forecast x_i, you must also use to forecast the remaining $n-1$ xs. Because the items are drawn randomly from a large population, the n outcomes are indistinguishable ex ante. Thus, our forecast of $x_1, x_2, \ldots x_n$ requires not n different probability distributions, but rather the same probability distribution applied n separate and independent times.

Let us call the probability distribution for x_i the **underlying probability distribution**. The first implication of random sampling from a large population is that this underlying probability distribution applies to each of the n sample outcomes. Our forecast of x_2 is identical to our forecast of x_1. Furthermore our forecast of x_2 will not be affected by the outcome of x_1. If the decision problem requires a forecast of each of the n xs, we will use n independent and identical probability distributions.

It may seem rather obvious that a single underlying probability distribution should be used to forecast each of the individual outcomes of a random sample from a large population. What might not be so obvious is that there are many other situations where a single underlying probability distribution might be used repeatedly and independently to forecast a sequence of outcomes. For example, the weight of containers filled by an automatic filling machine might be one such candidate if we assume the weights in a sequence of containers to be independent and identically distributed. As another example, the demand faced by the news vendor in Chapter 11 was considered indistinguishable from weekday to weekday. In both of these situations, we would use a single underlying distribution repeatedly and independently to forecast the next few observations.

Here is the important point. The ideas of sampling presented in this chapter apply just as well to the filling machine and the news vendor demand as they do to situations where we physically select n items at random from a large population of items. The fill amounts coming off the filling machine are not actually a random sample of some large population of filled containers, but we can look at them as if they are (if we are willing to assume the machine fills containers independently with identical fill distributions). Similarly, demand for the news vendor over the next n weekdays is not actually a random sample from some large vessel containing lots of possible demand amounts. But the ideas associated with random sampling still apply if we assume that future weekday demands come from indistinguishable situations. Here, "indistinguishable situations" is another way of saying we would use a single underlying probability distribution repeatedly and independently to forecast each of the n successive future weekday demand amounts.

To summarize, the ideas of this chapter were introduced as applying to random sampling from a large population. They do apply to that situation. And they apply to other situations as well. They apply to any situation where we would use a single underlying probability distribution repeatedly and independently to forecast $x_1, x_2, \ldots x_n$. This underlying probability distribution, then, is the probability distribution that applies to each x_i. Continuing with the large vessel analogy, the underlying probability distribution is also the distribution of the millions and millions of x values in the large vessel. If we dumped out all the x values in the vessel and put them in a histogram, that histogram would trace exactly the underlying probability distribution. For this reason, the underlying probability distribution is sometimes called the population distribution.

Forecasting a Sample Average

We turn now to the question of forecasting $\bar{x}_n$, the average of our sample of size n. One approach for forecasting $\bar{x}_n$ would be to incorporate n separate and independent forecasts of the xs into our evaluation model and simply average the results to calculate $\bar{x}_n$. If carried out in an electronic spreadsheet with a simulation add-in, this would involve n cells containing the input underlying probability distribution and an n+1st cell containing the calculation of the average of the first n cells. Such a spreadsheet simulation model represents one (long) way to forecast $\bar{x}_n$ as the cell containing the calculated average would follow the probability distribution appropriate for $\bar{x}_n$.

In many decision situations, the performance measure depends only on $\bar{x}_n$ and not on the n individual outcomes. In such situations we need not explicitly forecast each of the n xs and instead can make do with a shortcut single forecast of $\bar{x}_n$. We offer two useful shortcuts for forecasting the sample average directly. These results are useful not so much for the spreadsheet cells and computer time they will save as they are for the insights into sampling and uncertainty that they deliver. What follows are two situations in which a shortcut forecast of $\bar{x}_n$ is available, a description of the appropriate shortcut, and a brief interpretation of the result.

If the underlying probability distribution is normal with known mean μ and standard deviation σ, the forecast of $\bar{x}_n$ will be normal with mean μ and standard deviation $\sigma/\sqrt{n}$.

It should make sense that the forecast of $\bar{x}_n$ should have a mean of μ. (In fact, it is always the case that the mean of the forecast of $\bar{x}_n$ will equal the mean of the underlying probability distribution.) It might also make sense that the probability distribution for $\bar{x}_n$ will be normal if the underlying probability distribution is normal. What may require a little explanation is the fact that the forecast of $\bar{x}_n$ will have a standard deviation equal to $\sigma/\sqrt{n}$.

Remember that the standard deviation of a probability distribution is a measure of dispersion. This $\sigma/\sqrt{n}$ result tells us that the dispersion in our forecast of $\bar{x}_n$ is a function of two things: σ, the dispersion in the underlying probability distribution, and n, the size of the sample. The dispersion in the sample average is directly proportionate to the dispersion in the underlying probability distribution. (This makes sense since the uncertainty in the sample average is a direct result of the uncertainty in the underlying distribution. If the filling machine fills containers exactly with no uncertainty, there will be no uncertainty in the average of the next n containers. If there is a lot of uncertainty in the fill amounts, there will be lots of uncertainty in the sample average of n fill amounts.) And the dispersion in the sample average is inversely proportional to the square root of the sample size. This too should make sense. As the sample size increases, the effects of dispersion in the underlying probability distribution will tend to cancel out as more and more samples are included in the calculation of the sample average. The end result is that the larger the sample size, the less dispersion we expect in the sample average. In other words, the larger the sample, the closer the sample average will be to the mean of the underlying probability distribution. This concept is sometimes called the **law of averages**. If the sample size is large enough, the sample average will always turn out to be about the same number—the mean of the underlying probability distribution or the population mean. In fact, this is one way to define the mean—as the average of an infinitely large sample from the underlying probability distribution.

One other implication of the $\sigma/\sqrt{n}$ result is that increases in sample size decrease the standard deviation of the sample average at a decreasing rate. To illustrate, assume that $\sigma = 100$. Table 12–1 gives the standard deviation of the sample average for various values of n, the sample size.

Notice that at $n = 1$, $\bar{x}_n$ is really the same as x_i, a single observation. It makes sense then that our formula should tell us the standard deviation of a sample average of size 1 is identical to σ, the standard deviation of the underlying probability distribution. Notice also that the standard deviation of the sample average decreases rather dramatically down to 10 for a sample size of 100. But further increases in the sample size result in smaller and smaller decreases in the standard deviation of the sample average. The first 100 in the sample do more to reduce the uncertainty in $\bar{x}_n$ than the second 100, which

TABLE 12–1   Standard Deviation of $\bar{x}_n$ as a Function of n ($\sigma = 100$)

Sample Size	Standard Deviation of $\bar{x}_n$
1	100.00
100	10.00
200	7.07
300	5.77

in turn do more than the third 100. Thus, the benefit for your sampling dollar decreases (rather rapidly) with the sample size. A random sample of size 300 is not that much better than a random sample of size 200.

We turn now to the second sampling result:

> If the underlying probability distribution is *not* normal with known mean μ and standard deviation σ, the forecast of $\bar{x}_n$ will be normal with mean μ and standard deviation $\sigma/\sqrt{n}$ if n is large.

This result is sometimes called the **central limit theorem**. It states that even if the underlying probability distribution is not normal, the forecast of the sample average will be normal if n is large enough. In short, averages tend to follow the normal distribution even if the underlying distribution does not. How large n needs to be in order for the normal to be used to forecast $\bar{x}_n$ depends on how "nonnormal" the underlying probability distribution is. However, an oft-quoted rule suggests that if $n > 30$, the normal is a safe assumption for the forecast of $\bar{x}_n$.

A short demonstration of the central limit theorem is in order. Suppose the underlying probability distribution is triangular with "minimum" equal to 0, "most likely" equal to 100, and "maximum" equal to 500. This distribution is not normal. In particular it is decidedly not symmetric. The mean is 200, the median is 183.8, and the most likely is 100. Figure 12–1 shows the results of several simulations to evaluate the probability distribution of the sample average of n samples from this triangular distribution. Notice that when $n = 1$ the sample average is simply equivalent to x_i and the distribution of the sample average is equivalent to the underlying probability distribution. As n increases, notice two phenomenon. The dispersion of the distribution of the sample average decreases (in exact accordance with the $\sigma/\sqrt{n}$ formula) and the distribution approaches the familiar normal bell-curve shape.

Forecasting a Sample Proportion

In the previous section we talked about forecasting a sample average, $\bar{x}_n$, taken from a known underlying probability distribution. The outcome of each sample, x_i, was a number (the measured quality of a unit of production, the length of a fish, the financial performance of a firm, or the news vendor's weekday demand). In this section we address a somewhat simpler sampling situation. Each sample will not result in a number, but rather the presence or absence of a certain characteristic. The result of our sample of n will be the

FIGURE 12–1   *Forecasts of Xbar$_n$ for Various Values of n. Triangular (0,100,500) Underlying Probability Distribution*

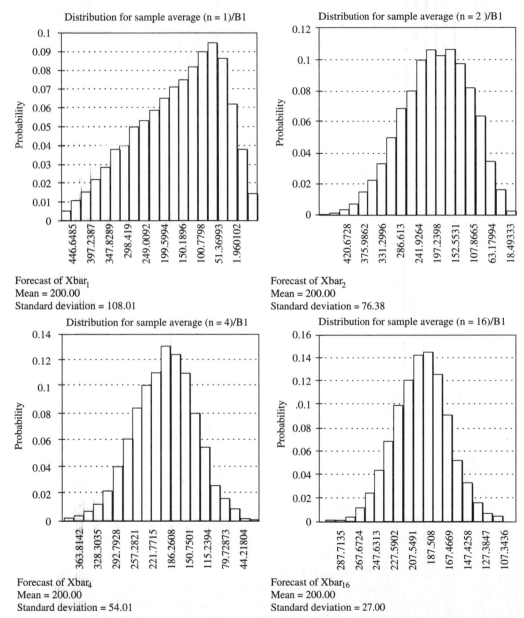

number or proportion of the n that possessed the characteristic of interest. If we sample n balls from an urn, what proportion will be black? If we poll n potential voters, what proportion will state a preference for the Republican candidate? If we survey our customers, what proportion will say they are satisfied?

TABLE 12–2 Forecast of p̂ when n = 8 and p = 0.6

Number of Successes (r)	Associated Sample Proportion (p̂)	Probability Forecast
0	0.000	0.0007
1	0.125	0.0079
2	0.250	0.0413
3	0.375	0.1239
4	0.500	0.2322
5	0.625	0.2787
6	0.750	0.2090
7	0.875	0.0896
8	1.000	0.0168

So rather than trying to forecast $\bar{x}_n$, a sample average, we will be trying to forecast $\hat{p}$, a sample proportion. And instead of using an underlying probability distribution to forecast the outcome of each individual sample, now we only require p, the underlying probability a sampled outcome will have the desired outcome. Again, you can think of the samples as being selected randomly from a very large vessel of items. In this way of thinking, p is the fraction of the items in the vessel that have the characteristic of interest. Or, more generally, you can think of n independent trials where at each trial there is a probability p of achieving the designated outcome.

The situation is exactly the one for which the binomial distribution applies (see Chapter 11). The number of successes in n trials follows the binomial distribution if the outcomes of the trials are independent and the probability of success, p, remains constant from one trial to the next.

> If the underlying probability is p, to forecast $\hat{p}$ (the sample proportion of successes in n trials) first use the binomial distribution to forecast the number of successes and then divide by n to convert number of successes to a sample proportion.

For example, if we randomly sample eight balls from a large urn in which 60 percent of the balls are black, what proportion of the sampled balls will be black? Table 12–2 uses the binomial distribution with n = 8 and p = 0.6 to forecast r, the number of successes. A simple division by 8 converts the forecast of r into a forecast of $\hat{p}$.

In summary, for small values of n, the binomial distribution is used to forecast a sample proportion if we know the underlying probability. In the ball example, the binomial tells us there is a 21 percent probability that $\hat{p}$ will be 0.75, a 9 percent probability that $\hat{p}$ will be .875, and a 2 percent probability that $\hat{p}$ will be 1.00—even though p is only 0.6.

If n is large, the binomial still applies (in theory) when forecasting $\hat{p}$. In practice, however, the precision of the binomial is unwarranted and the normal distribution is used instead.

FIGURE 12–2
Forecast of p̂ Normal with Mean 0.05 and Standard Deviation 0.00975

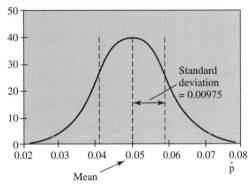

If the underlying probability is p, to forecast p̂ (the sample proportion of successes in n trials) use the normal distribution with mean equal to p and standard deviation equal to $\sqrt{p(1-p)/n}$ if n is large.

Suppose we know from experience that exactly 5 percent of our production is "off spec." What proportion of a batch of 500 items will be off spec? If we assume that a batch of items is a random sample of all items produced (or equivalently that each item in the batch has a 5 percent probability of being off spec) then our forecast of p̂ will be normal with mean 0.05 and standard deviation equal to 0.00975. Figure 12–2 graphs this forecast.

Notice the similarity between this forecasting result and the result given early for forecasting $\bar{x}_n$ when n is large. In both cases we should use the normal and in both cases the formula for the standard deviation contains the square root of n in the denominator. This similarity is not a coincidence. Forecasting a sample proportion is simply a special case of forecasting a sample average. When n is large, the only real difference is in what we use as the standard deviation of the underlying probability distribution. If forecasting a sample average, we need to know and use σ as the standard deviation of the underlying probability distribution. When forecasting a sample proportion, we only need to know p and theory tells us to use $\sqrt{p(1-p)}$ as the standard deviation of the underlying probability distribution. In both cases the law of averages and the central limit theorem apply.

Using Sample Results to Draw Inferences about the Underlying Probability Distribution

In the previous section we considered a situation where we knew the underlying probability distribution and wanted to forecast a sample average. Here we tackle just the reverse situation. What if we have observed a sample and wish to use that sample (and only that sample) to say something about the underlying probability distribution? In particular, how do we use our sample to say something about the mean of the underlying probability distribution? Questions of secondary importance not addressed in this text include questions about the standard deviation of the underlying probability distribution and the form of the underlying probability distribution.[2]

Inferences about the Mean of the Underlying Probability Distribution

After taking a sample and observing $x_1, x_2, \ldots x_n$ we usually calculate $\bar{x}_n$, the sample average, and s, the sample standard deviation. Using only these sample results, what can we say about the mean of the underlying probability distribution? If we have sampled n fill amounts from our filling machine, what can we say about the mean of the underlying probability distribution of fill amounts? If the news vendor observed n recent weekday demand amounts, what can the news vendor say about the mean weekday demand?

We have talked about using a sample to *draw inferences* about the population mean. We have intentionally avoided saying we will use the sample to *forecast* the mean of the underlying probability distribution. We will continue to make this distinction—reserving the word *forecast* for situations where we look forward and predict the results of future samples. When we look backward, we will talk about using the sample to draw inferences about the mean of the underlying probability distribution. One intent of making this distinction is to make things clearer. A second intent is to recognize the subtle differences between the two situations.[3] But for all practical purposes, there is really no difference between forecasting future sample averages and drawing inferences about the mean of the underlying probability distribution.

In using our sample to draw inferences about the mean of the underlying probability distribution, we might first determine our best estimate. It should come as no surprise that $\bar{x}_n$ is our best estimate for the mean of the underlying probability distribution. Remember, we are using only the information in the sample to draw inferences about the population mean. If the sample is all we have to go on, $\bar{x}_n$ is our best estimate.

The more challenging question is how good an estimate is $\bar{x}_n$ for the mean? An even more challenging question is what probability distribution should we use when talking about the mean? When n is large, we know how to answer all these questions:

---

[2]Most introductory statistical texts address these questions under headings such as "inferences concerning population variances" and "chi-squared goodness-of-fit test."

[3]Because $\bar{x}_n$ is the result of a soon-to-be conducted experiment, it is uncertain and the word *forecasting* clearly applies. Some scholars have argued, however, that the mean of the underlying probability distribution is not the result of a soon-to-be conducted experiment. They argue the mean is not uncertain in the same sense that $\bar{x}_n$ is uncertain. These scholars prefer to think of the mean as a number we do not know and object to the idea of "forecasting" the mean.

Inferences about μ should be drawn using the normal distribution with mean $\bar{x}_n$ and standard deviation $s/\sqrt{n}$ if n is large (regardless of the form of the underlying probability distribution).

The symmetry between this result and the previous results for forecasting $\bar{x}_n$ should be striking. If you know μ and want to forecast $\bar{x}_n$, the relevant distribution is the normal (if n is large) with a standard deviation of $\sigma/\sqrt{n}$. If you know $\bar{x}_n$ and want to draw inferences about μ, the relevant distribution is the normal (if n is large) with standard deviation $s/\sqrt{n}$. This symmetry is not a coincidence. The quantity $\sigma/\sqrt{n}$ measures the dispersion of $\bar{x}_n$ around μ. It is this same dispersion that is relevant if we take a known $\bar{x}_n$ and ask about μ. The distance from a future $\bar{x}_n$ to the known μ is the same distance an unknown μ is from the known $\bar{x}_n$. When using only sample information, we must substitute s for σ in the $\sigma/\sqrt{n}$ formula, but when n is large this substitution is of no practical consequence.

Returning to the news vendor example of Chapter 11, recall that the 19 most recent weekday demands were judged to have arisen from indistinguishable situations. In the language of sampling, these 19 observations (see Table 12–3) will be looked at as independent outcomes from a single underlying probability distribution.

Based only on the information in this sample, what can we say about the mean of the underlying probability distribution? Applying the above results, we find out that our understanding of the population mean should be normally distributed with mean 50.84 and standard deviation of 1.30 (calculated as $5.65/\sqrt{19}$). The news vendor can be 95 percent confident that the mean weekday demand is somewhere between 48.3 and 53.4 (50.84 plus or minus 1.96 standard deviations). The width of this confidence interval is a function of two things: the standard deviation of the underlying probability distribution (which we estimate to be 5.65) and the size of our sample (19).

TABLE 12–3   News Vendor Demand Sample

Sample	Demand	Sample	Demand
1	47	11	49
2	54	12	52
3	61	13	44
4	51	14	59
5	48	15	52
6	50	16	41
7	54	17	56
8	59	18	54
9	43	19	46
10	46		
	Sample average	50.84	
	Sample standard deviation	5.65	

This confidence interval is based on the assumption that the 19 observed demand amounts are a random sample from a single underlying probability distribution.[4]

Inferences about the Underlying Probability

If the outcomes of our sample are success/failure rather than numbers, a sample of size n will produce $\hat{p}$, the sample proportion of the n trials that were successes. Given $\hat{p}$, what can we say about p, the underlying probability of success?

Inferences about p should be drawn using the normal distribution with mean $\hat{p}$ and standard deviation $\sqrt{\hat{p}(1 - \hat{p})/n}$ if n is large.

This result follows directly from the previous result recognizing the simplifications afforded by the fact that our sample results in success/failure rather than numbers. This result also follows directly from what we know about how to use p to forecast $\hat{p}$. The relevant standard deviation when forecasting $\hat{p}$ was $\sqrt{p(1 - p)/n}$. This same standard deviation is relevant when using $\hat{p}$ to draw inferences about p, only now we must substitute $\hat{p}$ for p in the formula. When n is large, substituting $\hat{p}$ for p is of no practical consequence.

For example, consider a telephone survey in which a large firm found that 123 of 200 surveyed customers reported being either very satisfied or extremely satisfied with the firm's services. Based on this sample of 200 customers, what can the company say about its overall level of customer satisfaction? If we assume the survey uncovered a random sample of the firm's many customers, then this becomes a question of using a sample proportion,

---

[4]Astute readers will notice that this confidence interval is also based on an assumption that "n is large." Is n = 19 large enough? There are two reasons we require n to be large: (1) so sample averages of size n are normally distributed even if the underlying probability distribution is not, and (2) so s can be substituted for σ with no harmful consequences. In the news vendor example, the second reason gives us more cause for concern than the first. We are not concerned about the first reason because the underlying probability distribution for weekday demand may itself be fairly close to normal. If so, n = 19 will be large enough to produce normal sample averages. Turning now to the concern about the second reason, we know how to correct for the fact that s will be substituted for σ. The correction is called the t-distribution. When s is substituted for σ and n is small, the t-distribution is the correct distribution to use. The sole purpose of the t-distribution is to account for the fact that s is used in place of σ. Most introductory statistical texts cover the t-distribution. In the news vendor example, using the t-distribution tells us that the correct 95 percent confidence interval is 48.1 to 53.6. The difference between this correct confidence interval and the approximate interval based on the normal is a measure of the consequences of assuming n = 19 is large enough to use the normal. Using the normal rather than the correct t-distribution resulted in a confidence interval that was 0.4 units too narrow. As n increases, the difference between the approximate confidence interval based on the normal and the correct confidence interval based on the t-distribution will become even more negligible.

$\hat{p} = 0.615$, to draw inferences about an underlying probability, p. Here p represents the proportion of the entire population of customers who would report being either very or extremely satisfied. We have interpreted p to be the firm's overall level of customer satisfaction.

The question above is fairly typical. Everyone knows that survey results are subject to uncertainty. If we conducted two identical surveys, for example, we would undoubtedly get different results. Thus, we should exercise care in interpreting the results of any survey. The amount of credence we should give to survey results depends on many things—one of which is the size of the sample.[5] Everything we have learned so far about sampling suggests that the larger the sample, the better the sample results will reflect the population. The above result tells us exactly how much credence to give a sample given its limited size.

Since $n = 200$ and $\hat{p} = 0.615$, the result tells us that inferences about the population percentage should be drawn using the normal distribution with mean 0.615 and standard deviation equal to 0.034. The number 0.034 is sometimes called the **standard error**. Roughly speaking, we can be 68 percent confident the true population p is somewhere between 0.581 (0.615 − 0.034) and 0.649 (0.615 + 0.034).

Using Sample Results to Forecast Future Sample Results

In the first section of this chapter, we considered how to use an underlying probability distribution to forecast the results of a sample. In the second section, we addressed the opposite question: how to use the results of a sample to say something about the underlying probability distribution. In this section, we put the two questions together and ask how to use the results of an initial sample to forecast the results of a second sample. Notice that this question skips over the underlying probability distribution. This question attempts to use one set of data (the initial sample) to forecast a second set of data (the second sample) without really pausing to address the underlying probability distribution. This final section addresses the very practical problem of how to use one set of data to forecast the future, and in this sense the results of this final section may be the most useful.

---

[5]Our calculation accounts for only one of many reasons survey results may misrepresent the population. Our calculation addresses sampling error—the uncertainty resulting from the fact that a small, random sample is being used to say something about the entire population. There are many other kinds of errors that affect survey results. These other errors can often be larger than the sampling error. For example, in survey research it is nearly impossible to collect a truly random sample because not everyone responds to the survey. If the opinions of the subjects who responded are different from those who chose not to respond, then $\hat{p}$ will be a biased estimate of p. This introduces a nonresponse error—an error not accounted for in the $\sqrt{\hat{p}(1 - \hat{p})/n}$ formula.

As always we will assume that both the initial sample and the second sample will be random. We will use n to represent the size of the first sample and m to represent the size of the second sample. The size of the second sample, m, need not equal the size of the initial sample. First we consider the situation in which the sampled quantity is a number. After that we consider the success/failure situation wherein the results of the samples are summarized by sample proportions.

Using Sample Results to Forecast a Future Sample Average

Suppose an initial sample of size n produced $\bar{x}_n$ and s. In the preceding section we showed how to use these two numbers (and only these numbers) to say something about the underlying probability distribution. Now suppose we are not interested in the underlying probability distribution, per se. Suppose we are interested only in forecasting the results of a second sample—where that second sample is of size m. In short, how do we use $\bar{x}_n$ and s to forecast $\bar{x}_m$?

> The forecast of $\bar{x}_m$ will be normal with mean $\bar{x}_n$ and standard deviation $\sqrt{(s/\sqrt{n})^2 + (s/\sqrt{m})^2}$ if n is large and either m is large or the underlying probability distribution is normal.

A brief explanation of this result may be helpful. Since $\bar{x}_n$ is our best estimate for the population mean, it makes sense to use $\bar{x}_n$ as the mean of our forecast of $\bar{x}_m$. When n is large, our inferences about the population mean are normal and we may substitute s for σ with no practical consequences as we proceed with the forecasting task. Thus, our resulting forecast of $\bar{x}_m$ will be normal if either m is large (in which case the central limit theorem applies to the second average) or the underlying probability distribution is normal (in which case even a sample average of size 1 will be normal).

The final piece of this result that requires explanation is the somewhat complicated formula for the standard deviation appropriate when using an initial sample of size n to forecast the average of a second sample of size m. The total uncertainty involved in such a task can be broken into two pieces. The first involves the fact that our forecast is based on an initial sample and not the entire population. We must use $\bar{x}_n$ in place of μ. The appropriate measure of this first component of uncertainty is $s/\sqrt{n}$. The second component of our total forecasting uncertainty involves the fact that we must forecast an uncertain m. Even if we knew μ, $\bar{x}_m$ would be uncertain. The appropriate measure of this second component of uncertainty is $s/\sqrt{m}$. Since our forecasting task involves both of these two components of uncertainty, the standard deviation appropriate to our forecasting task must be a combination of the two component standard deviations. Our result tells us to square the two component standard deviations, add them, and then take the square root of the resulting sum.

For example, suppose the news vendor wanted to use the initial 19 data points to forecast average weekday demand for the coming month (m = 20),

---

TABLE 12–4   News Vendor Forecasts of Future Sample Averages

The forecast of $\bar{x}_{20}$ is normal with mean   50.84   and standard deviation   1.81.

The forecast of $\bar{x}_5$ is normal with mean   50.84   and standard deviation   2.84.

The forecast of $\bar{x}_1$ is normal with mean   50.84   and standard deviation   5.80.

---

for the coming week (m = 5), and for tomorrow (m = 1). To apply the above result we must assume that news vendor demand came from and will continue to come from indistinguishable situations and that n = 19 is large.[6] In addition, since we will forecast sample averages for very small values of m, we must assume that the underlying probability distribution is normal.[7] Given all these assumptions, Table 12–4 provides the relevant forecasts.

Notice first that the standard deviations used in these forecasts decrease with m. The larger the new sample, the less uncertainty in the resulting sample average (due to the law of averages). As m gets very, very large, the standard deviation approaches 1.30, the standard deviation used earlier when drawing inferences about the population mean. Forecasting $\bar{x}_m$ when m equals infinity is equivalent to forecasting the population mean. At the other extreme, notice that the standard deviation of 5.80 used to forecast a new x is higher than s = 5.64, the estimate of the standard deviation of the underlying probability distribution. Even though the underlying probability distribution is exactly what we would use to forecast x, we should not use our estimate of the standard deviation of the underlying probability distribution when we attempt to forecast x in this situation. Why? Because in this situation we do not know μ, the mean of the underlying probability distribution. The higher standard deviation of 5.80 accounts for the fact that 50.84, the basis of the forecast, is an uncertain estimate of the population mean. The difference between the standard deviation used to forecast x (5.80) and s (5.64) is a function of the size of the initial sample. The larger the n, the closer the standard deviation for forecasting a new x will be to s.

Using Sample Results to Forecast a Future Sample Proportion

By now the similarity between results for success/failure sampling and the sampling of numbers should be well understood. If so, the results of this section will be unsurprising if not predictable.

Suppose an initial sample of size n produced the sample proportion $\hat{p}$. How can we use only this information to predict $\hat{p}_m$, the proportion of

---

[6]This issue was addressed in footnote 4.

[7]The cumulative probability distribution of the 19 data points drawn in Figure 11–11 appears to have the familiar, symmetric S-shape characteristic of the normal distribution.

successes in a new sample of size m?[8] The following result applies if both the initial and second sample are conducted randomly.

The forecast of $\hat{p}_m$ will be normal with mean $\hat{p}$ and standard deviation $\sqrt{\hat{p}(1-\hat{p})/n + \hat{p}(1-\hat{p})/m}$ if both n and m are large.

For example, suppose the response rate to a 500-piece direct-mail solicitation was 8.4 percent (42 responses). What response rate will the firm get if it remails the same piece to 1,000 new people? For the above result to apply, both the initial 500 people and the new 1,000 people must be random samples from a single population. This means the initial 500 people and the new 1,000 people must be indistinguishable. It also means that nothing has occurred in the interval between the two mailings to change the performance of the solicitation. Given these assumptions, the forecast of $\hat{p}_{1,000}$ will be normal with mean 0.084 (84 responses) and standard deviation 0.0152 (15.2 responses).

Summary

This chapter has explored the basic ideas of sampling. We have explained how to use knowledge of the underlying probability distribution to forecast the results of a sample. Next we considered how to use the results of a sample to draw inferences about the underlying probability distribution. And finally, we have shown how the results of an initial sample can be used to forecast the results of a second sample.

Throughout the chapter we first considered situations in which the sampled quantity was a number and the sample results in a sample average $\bar{x}_n$ and sample standard deviation s. We followed with the simpler success/failure sampling situation in which the sample results in a sample proportion $\hat{p}$.

The ideas of this chapter apply to random sampling from an infinite population or to indistinguishable situations—situations in which a single underlying probability distribution applies repeatedly and independently. The next two chapters build on these sampling ideas to consider forecasting in situations that are *not* indistinguishable.

---

[8]For simplicity, we continue to use $\hat{p}$ to refer to the sample proportion from the initial sample. We could just have easily used $\hat{p}_n$.

13 TIME-SERIES FORECASTING

Chapter 11 (pp. 163–166) used news vendor daily demand to show how historical data from indistinguishable situations may be used to create a probability distribution forecast. In Chapter 12, the same data were used along with an assumption of normality to illustrate sampling with independence. In this chapter we describe what to do when data are not from independent, indistinguishable situations. Specifically, we discuss forecasting where the time an observation is made is related to the magnitude of the observation.

Often the task in business situations is to forecast the next number in a series of periodic observations, for example, demand for a product. These observations form a *time series*. Relying solely on past observations of that quantity and the time of the forecast to predict future occurrences is called *time-series forecasting*. Time-series forecasting does not assume future results will duplicate those of the past, but rather that past **patterns** will be similar in the future.

There are two other general approaches to forecasting distinguishable situations: qualitative and causal. Qualitative techniques are most useful when historical data are nonexistent or if they do exist are not representative or are too expensive to gather and analyze. The objective of these techniques is to bring together, in a logical, unbiased, and systematic way, all relevant information, including the opinions of experts. Some typical techniques are sales force composites, historical analogies, and Delphi methods. The methods discussed in Chapter 3 for structuring assumptions and in Chapter 4 for expressing judgmental probability will be helpful if this approach is taken.

Causal procedures use knowledge about one or more factors (independent variables) to predict the value of another factor (the dependent variable). For example, the demand for a product might be related to its price, the amount of advertising, the amount of promotion, the expanse of its distribution, and so on. Causal techniques often rely on statistical regression methods, which typically require significant amounts of data. They are useful for investigating policy questions (such as what happens to demand when promotion increases) because, in addition to providing a forecast, they explore relationships between dependent and independent variables. These procedures will be taken up in the next chapter.

Forecasts are useful for planning and decision making in the operations, marketing, financial, and human resources functions of business. The time horizon of a forecast indicates how far into the future the forecast predicts. The required time horizon is one factor that determines which forecasting approach to use. In this chapter we address short-term forecasts, that is, forecasts of from one to a few periods into the future. Time-series methods are relatively simple to use and can be quite accurate for short-range forecasting. These simple methods are extremely useful where hundreds or thousands of items must be forecast.

Basic Approaches for One-Period Forecasts

We begin with the simplest case, namely, to forecast an occurrence one period into the future and with the simplest methods. We will then move on to more complex methods. The example used in this section is a sales manager's forecast of sales in the coming month of a particular type of car. It is the first day of October, and we have the prior nine months of sales, through September, which are as follows:

Month	Jan.	Feb.	March	April	May	June	July	Aug.	Sept.	Oct.
Car Sales	21	23	21	20	21	19	28	32	26	?

In time-series forecasting, it will appear that we expend a lot of our effort to come up with a good point forecast, that is a single number, for the next period, which is October in this instance. Keep in mind, however, that we will not stop with a best-guess forecast, rather we will push, as elsewhere in this book, to obtain a complete probability distribution forecast. Later in this chapter we will describe how to get the probability distribution.

Simple Approaches

One straightforward approach to determining the October forecast is to average the sales figures for all prior periods. The average of the sales figures through September is 23.4. This forecast, the **all-period average**, is based on an assumption that the October sales will behave like the composite of sales in prior months, and that no month is given more importance than another. This is exactly what we did in Chapter 12, where we called it $\bar{x}_n$, the sample average. However, the assumption of independent sampling from that chapter will not apply here, where the time of observation matters.

An alternative approach is to base the October forecast on the September sales figure, since it is the most recent information. Therefore, the **prior period** forecast for October would be 26 cars. In this approach, 100 percent of the weight is given to the prior month's sales.

To determine the best technique, we can calculate the forecast for each month before October, except for January (since we have no prior information) and see how close forecasts are to actuals. For February, the all-period average forecast would have been 21 (the average of only January), and the prior period forecast would have also been 21. Since the actual sales total for February was 23, either forecast would have been under by 2. We can calculate forecasts for each of the months, as shown in lines 5–8 of the spreadsheet labeled Sheet 1.

As can be seen from Sheet 1, the all-period average forecast is unresponsive to abrupt fluctuations in sales, whereas the prior period forecast is extremely responsive to sales fluctuations. We next consider forecasting techniques that are somewhere between these two extremes.

Moving Average

A logical compromise between the two extreme approaches just discussed is to use an approach that bases the forecast on the average of a certain number of most recent periods. This is called a **moving average** forecast. For our example, the three-month moving average October forecast would be 28.7, that is the average of July, August, and September sales figures. With this forecast approach, the prior three months are each given equal weight, and all other months are given no weight. We can select the number of months in the moving average according to how far back the data is relevant to future

SHEET 1   Calculation of Historical Forecasts

	A	B	C	D	E	F	G	H	I	J	K	L	M	N	O
1															
2	Month	Jan	Feb	Mar	Apr	May	Jun	Jul	Aug	Sep	Oct		Equations copied across rows		
3	Actual Car Sales	21	23	21	20	21	19	28	32	26	?		Equation in boxed cells:		
4															
5	All-period average	21.0	22.0	21.7	21.3	21.2	20.8	21.9	23.1	23.4		←	@AVG($B$3..J3)		
6	used as forecast		21.0	22.0	21.7	21.3	21.2	20.8	21.9	23.1	23.4	←	+J5		
7															
8	Prior period as forecast		21	23	21	20	21	19	28	32	26	←	+J3		
9															
10	3-Month moving average as forecast				21.7	21.3	20.7	20.0	22.7	26.3	28.7	←	@AVG(H3..J3)		
11															
12			+B3	+$B$15*C3+(1-$B$15)*C14											
13	Exponential smoothing		↓	↓											
14	as forecast		21.0	21.6	21.4	21.0	21.0	20.4	22.7	25.5	25.6	←	+$B$15*J3+(1-$B$15)*J14		
15	alpha=	0.3													
16															

observations. Of course, this approach assumes that the data is relevant n periods back, but the n + 1 period is not relevant. Next we will look at an approach that gives each prior month a weight that declines with the distance in time from the month being forecast.

Smoothed Average

We may believe that the level of sales for the month prior to the forecast month is most relevant, with the month prior to that being somewhat less relevant. Each prior month may be accorded comparatively less relevance. Figure 1 shows the weight for each month's sales being a fixed percentage of the weight of the month preceding. This decline in significance is mathematically represented by an exponential function. Therefore, we refer to a forecasting technique which uses such a weighting scheme as **exponential smoothing**.

FIGURE 13–1
Declining Weight

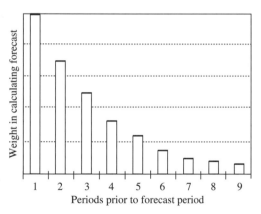

Forecasting by exponential smoothing is actually quite simple to implement. If we have both a forecast and an actual figure for the prior period, then the new forecast can be calculated using the following equation:

$$\text{new forecast} = \text{alpha}' \times (\text{most recent actual}) + (1\text{-alpha})' \times (\text{most recent forecast})$$

Alpha (denoted by the Greek symbol α), represents a value that is greater than zero and we assume to be less than one. For example, if $\alpha = 0.2$, then 20 percent of the forecast weight will go to the prior period sales, and 80 percent will go to the prior forecast.

This is like a moving average, however, in exponential smoothing, the weights are not constant, and some weight is placed on every prior observation.[1] Furthermore, the information requirement is simpler, which may be important if tens of thousands of separate items are being forecasted, such as the inventory of parts. For an n-period moving average, we need to preserve all sales data for the past n periods. If n = 10, then we need to have 10 data items for each product being forecast. However, for exponential smoothing, we need only two items of information (besides the constant alpha): the prior forecast and the current actual observation.

To use exponential smoothing, we need to determine the appropriate alpha factor to use. Alpha determines how responsive the forecast will be to jumps in the prior month's sales figures. A low alpha means the forecast is unresponsive to sudden jumps. An alpha larger than 0.5 means the forecast will be extremely responsive to jumps, and in the extreme case alpha = 1.0 is the same as the naive prior-period forecast. Later in this chapter, we will discuss how to use measures of forecast accuracy to choose an appropriate alpha value.

Sheet 2 shows the calculation of historical forecasts with the two techniques just presented. Note that the October forecasts differ somewhat. The decision maker needs a way to compare the quality of the various forecasts and forecasting techniques.

SHEET 2   Calculation of Forecasts

	A	B	C	D	E	F	G	H	I	J	K	L	M	N	O
1															
2	Month	Jan	Feb	Mar	Apr	May	Jun	Jul	Aug	Sep	Oct		Equations copied across rows		
3	Actual Car Sales	21	23	21	20	21	19	28	32	26	?		Equation in boxed cells:		
4															
5	3-Month moving average as forecast				21.7	21.3	20.7	20.0	22.7	26.3	28.7	←— @AVG(H3..J3)			
6															
7		+B3	+$B$10*C3+(1-$B$10)*C9												
8	Exponential smoothing	↓	↓												
9	as forecast	21.0	21.6	21.4	21.0	21.0	20.4	22.7	25.5	25.6	←— +$B$10*J3+(1-$B$10)*J9				
10	alpha=	0.3													

---

[1]The basic exponential smoothing equation uses only the prior forecast directly, giving it a weight $1 - \alpha$. However, this prior forecast is itself dependent on the forecast before it, and so on. Thus, every prior observation receives some weight in the calculation of the new forecast, with the weight declining exponentially for observations more distant in the past. If the weight on the current actual, α, is small, then it turns out the forecast has more weight on the past, or in other words, a longer memory. An n-period moving average forecast is most similar (but not identical) to an exponential smoothing forecast with alpha set at $2/(n + 1)$.

Note that exponential smoothing begins in March, which arbitrarily uses the January actual for the February forecast.

Comparison of Forecasts

To evaluate the forecasting approaches, we calculate the forecasts that each method would have given in past periods and compare how closely they match actuals. Graphs showing the results of applying the four approaches to our sample data are shown in Figure 13–2. Although based on the same actual data, the four forecast patterns are quite different, particularly in the later months of increased sales.

Each of the forecasting methods results in some amount of error. The **error** of a forecast is the degree the forecast is off from the actual amount:

$$\text{Error} = \text{Actual} - \text{Forecast}$$

Relative error is the percentage the forecast differs from the actual:

$$\text{Relative error} = \frac{\text{Actual} - \text{Forecast}}{\text{Actual}}$$

How might we determine whether error or relative error is the best method to compare forecasts? It is a matter of whether the pattern of error magnitude tends to be constant (error is then best) or instead a constant percentage of actual (which is consistent with relative error).

To compare the forecasting approaches, one can look at the entire distribution of forecast errors an approach generates, plotting them as a histogram, for example. However, it is desirable to have summary measures of the errors over all periods. Then we look for approaches that have the smallest measures of error. Specifically, we want a forecast that is precise; we may also be interested in whether it is unbiased as well.

Precision

Precision measures summarize the *distance* from the actuals to the forecasts. For example, a particular forecasting technique that overestimates by 10 one-half of the time and underestimates by 10 one-half of the time has an average that is right on, or using a term from Chapter 12, it is unbiased. However, the forecast technique is *imprecise*, since it is always off by 10.

There are several simple ways of measuring precision from errors. The first is to calculate the average of the *absolute value* of all the error terms, which is called mean absolute deviation, or MAD. Second, we can calculate the average of the square of each of the error terms, which average is called mean standard error or MSE. Associated with this measure is a common measure of precision, the standard deviation of the error terms (denoted σ_e). The σ_e is a pure measure of precision because it is based on deviations from

FIGURE 13–2   *Comparison of Historical Forecasts*

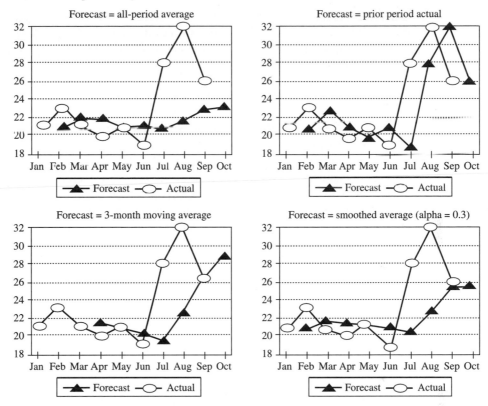

the mean error and therefore is unaffected by bias. Providing we are correcting for bias when we use our forecast (as we shall in a later section), this may be the preferred measure. If errors are normal and have a mean equal to 0, then MSE is an appropriate measure to use.[2]

A simple measure of precision related to the relative error is the average of the absolute value of each relative error (expressed as a percentage), which is called mean absolute percentage error, or MAPE. The MAPE value indicates the average percentage the forecast is off from the actual.

Usually if a forecasting technique produces a better MSE, it will also produce a better MAD and MAPE, but not necessarily. Consider the measure that makes the most sense for your application and then go with that measure to compare methods. Except in unusual circumstances, the various measures will not give significantly conflicting signals.

---

[2]Note that for normally distributed errors, the standard deviation of errors is approximately equal to 1.25 times MAD.

Bias

Bias refers to the expected value of A − F (Actual − Forecast), or the degree to which the forecast tends to overshoot (negative bias) or undershoot (positive bias) the actual amount. An estimate of bias is generated by averaging the errors for all periods and is called average error, or AE. The closer AE is to zero, the less bias exists. If the average is greater than zero, then the forecasts have a positive bias, and if less than zero, a negative bias.

We can also measure relative bias, which is likewise the average of all the relative errors, and is called mean percentage error, or **MPE**. Again, the closer MPE is to zero, the lower the bias.

If a particular forecasting method has a known amount of bias, then we can simply adjust each future forecast for the bias. For example, if a forecast technique tends to underestimate sales by two cars, then we can just add two to all future forecasts to eliminate the bias. For this reason, bias is usually not a significant concern. When we discuss combining a point forecast with a probability distribution of errors to get a probabilistic forecast later in this chapter, we will see that such an approach corrects automatically for bias. It is much worse for forecasts to be imprecise.

Sheet 3 shows the calculation of five error-summary measures for the all-period average forecasting method and reviews the interpretation of each. We repeated these calculations for each of the four forecasting approaches and also for exponential smoothing with $\alpha = .2$, to see if it outperformed $\alpha = .3$. These results are shown in Sheet 4. Which of these forecasting techniques would you use? That depends on which error measure you favor. At first glance we might be tempted to use the prior period approach, which has the lowest absolute and relative bias (AE and MPE). More important is the precision of the forecasting approach. For many approaches, estimated

---

SHEET 3　　Calculation of Error Summary Measures

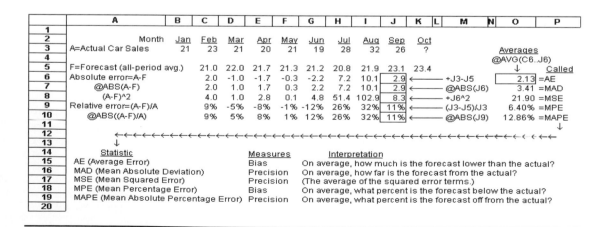

SHEET 4   Comparison of Forecasting Techniques

Statistic (what it measures)	Forecasting Technique				
	All- Period Average	Prior Period	3-Month Moving Average	Exponential Smoothing Alpha=0.3	Exponential Smoothing Alpha=0.2
AE (absolute bias)	2.13	0.63	2.22	1.93	2.17
MAD (absolute precision)	3.41	3.38	3.56	2.93	3.12
MSE (absolute precision squared)	21.90	18.38	26.15	19.42	20.73
MPE (relative bias)	6.40%	1.25%	6.29%	5.82%	6.72%
MAPE (relative precision)	12.86%	13.28%	12.95%	10.94%	11.60%
October forecast	23.4	26	28.7	25.6	24.5

bias may tend to be small over time, and if not, we can always adjust forecasts for bias. Lack of precision cannot be corrected. We note that the prior period technique had the *worst* measure of relative precision (MAPE). Exponential smoothing with alpha = 0.3 had the best absolute precision (MAD) and relative precision (MAPE) and looks good as an approach here. Note that the forecasts with alpha = 0.2 were not quite as good as those with alpha = 0.3. The error-summary measures can be used to select the alpha in exponential smoothing.

Decide which forecasting approach you would use. Having selected it, the forecast for October is available from our calculations shown earlier. You might be interested in comparing your forecast with the actual result for October, which is given at the end of this chapter. Be careful not to be too smug if your forecast was very close to the actual October number; we would want to look at more than one instance to be sure the approach holds up in practice. And we may want to change our method in the future if another approach begins to look better.

It is important to remember that there is no one best forecasting technique for all types of data. A technique may do very well on one type of data, but very poorly on another. In the next section we will discuss characteristics of the data that may influence our choice of forecasting technique.

Exploiting Multiperiod Patterns

When making forecasts from a time series, one can often take advantage of repeating patterns in the data that may have carried over many periods in the past, and plausibly may continue into the future. We will consider two classes of such patterns, which we will label **seasonality** and **trend**.

Seasonality comprises movements up and down in a repeating pattern of constant length. For example, if you were looking at monthly data on sales of ice cream, you would expect to see higher sales in the warmer months (June to August in the northern hemisphere) than in the winter, year after year. The seasonal pattern would be 12 months long. If we used weekly data, the seasonal pattern would repeat every 52 periods. The number of time periods in a seasonal pattern depends on how often the observations are collected.

In another example, we may be looking at daily data on the number of guests staying at a downtown hotel. Our intuition might tell us that we expect high numbers on Monday, Tuesday, and Wednesday nights; low numbers on Friday and Saturday; and medium numbers on Thursday and Sunday. So our pattern would be as follows, starting with Sunday: medium, high, high, high, medium, low, low. The pattern would repeat itself every seven days.

Trend is a long-lasting (through at least several seasons) and consistent period-to-period change. For example, quantities that exhibit consistent growth, such as population, GDP, and income, would have a trend pattern in their time series.

Treating Seasonality

It is easy to capitalize on either trend or seasonality by simply extrapolating the respective pattern into the future and incorporating it into the forecast. The procedure for treating seasonal patterns is illustrated in Figures 13–3 to 13–6. Figure 13–3 shows the original data, which exhibit a seasonal pattern. From examining the data and from our own judgment, we hypothesize an m-period seasonal pattern. Next, using the numerical approach of the next section, we deseasonalize the data, obtaining Figure 13–4. Then, using the best forecasting method available, we make a forecast in deseasonalized terms. Figure 13–5 shows deseasonalized forecasts for the next two periods. Finally, we reseasonalize the forecast to account for the seasonal pattern, as in Figure 13–6. Let us step through this process using some example data, after which we will return to a discussion of how to account for trend.

Deseasonalizing a Time Series

The procedure to deseasonalize data is to average out all variations that occur within one season. Thus, for quarterly data, an average of four periods is used to eliminate within-year seasonality. To deseasonalize a whole time series, the first step is to calculate a series of m-period moving averages, where m is the length of the seasonal pattern.

We will illustrate these concepts with data on U.S. coal receipts by the commercial and residential sectors over the period 1980 to 1988[3] (measured

---

[3]*Quarterly Coal Report,* published by the Department of Energy's Energy Information Administration, January–March 1982 and January–March 1989.

FIGURE 13–3 *Coal Receipts by Commercial/Residential*   **FIGURE 13–4** *Coal Receipts (Deseasonalized)*

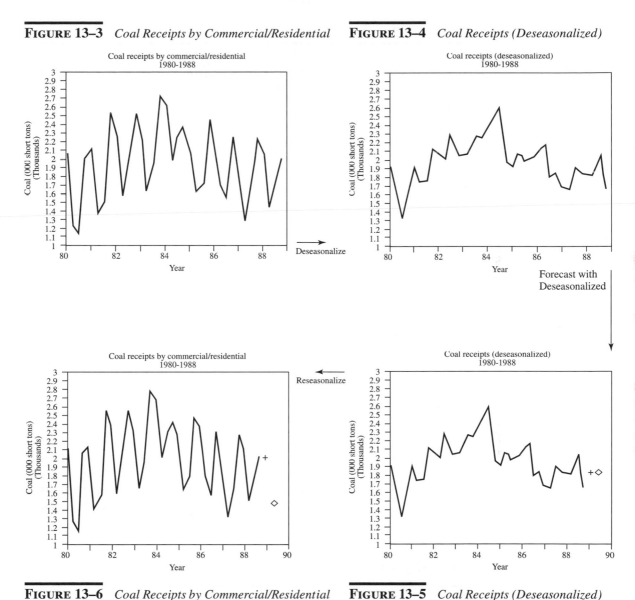

FIGURE 13–6 *Coal Receipts by Commercial/Residential*   **FIGURE 13–5** *Coal Receipts (Deseasonalized)*

in thousands of short tons). The data are given in the third column of Table 13–1 and were graphed in Figure 13–3. Intuition tells us to expect higher than average coal receipts in the first and fourth quarters (winter effects) and lower than average in the second and third quarters (spring/summer effects). The fourth column of Table 13–1 shows a four-period moving average of the data in column three. The first number is the average of the first four periods,

$$(2,159 + 1,203 + 1,094 + 1,996)/4 = 1,613$$

TABLE 13–1

Year	Qtr	Coal Receipts	4 Period Moving Average	Centered Moving Average	Ratio of Coal Receipts to Centered Moving Average
80	1st	2,159	—	—	—
80	2nd	1,203	—	—	—
80	3rd	1,094	1,613	1,603	0.682
80	4th	1,996	1,594	1,610	1.240
81	1st	2,081	1,626	1,674	1.244
81	2nd	1,332	1,721	1,788	0.745
81	3rd	1,476	1,856	1,877	0.787
81	4th	2,533	1,898	1,923	1.317
82	1st	2,249	1,948	2,005	1.122
82	2nd	1,533	2,063	2,061	0.744
82	3rd	1,935	2,060	2,055	0.942
82	4th	2,523	2,050	2,058	1.226
83	1st	2,208	2,066	2,064	1.070
83	2nd	1,597	2,061	2,087	0.765
83	3rd	1,917	2,112	2,163	0.886
83	4th	2,726	2,213	2,255	1.209
84	1st	2,612	2,297	2,335	1.119
84	2nd	1,931	2,373	2,328	0.830
84	3rd	2,223	2,282	2,215	1.004
84	4th	2,363	2,148	2,105	1.123
85	1st	2,074	2,062	1,994	1.040
85	2nd	1,589	1,925	1,935	0.821
85	3rd	1,673	1,945	1,964	0.852
85	4th	2,443	1,984	1,995	1.225
86	1st	2,231	2,006	1,984	1.124
86	2nd	1,675	1,963	1,940	0.863
86	3rd	1,503	1,917	1,864	0.806
86	4th	2,259	1,812	1,759	1.284
87	1st	1,809	1,706	1,720	1.052
87	2nd	1,254	1,734	1,731	0.724
87	3rd	1,613	1,729	1,753	0.920
87	4th	2,238	1,777	1,796	1.246
88	1st	2,004	1,815	1,829	1.096
88	2nd	1,406	1,843	1,813	0.776
88	3rd	1,725	1,782	—	—
88	4th	1,994	—	—	—

The second number is the average of the next four periods, and so on. Notice that the moving average has much less volatility than the original series; again, the averaging process eliminates the quarter-to-quarter movement.

In Table 13–1, the moving average column is offset, with the numbers beginning in the third row. We really would like to center the moving average in the middle of the data from which it was calculated. *If m is odd*, the first moving average (average of points 1 to m) is easily centered on the $(m + 1)/2$ point (e.g., suppose you have daily data where m = 7, the first 7-period moving average is centered on the $(7 + 1)/2$ or 4th point). This process rolls

FIGURE 13–7

Coal Receipts by Commercial/Residential

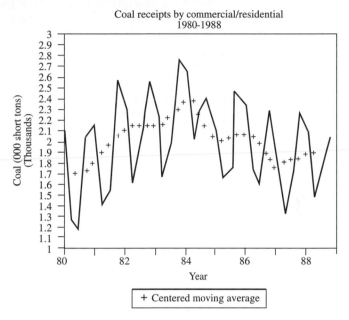

forward to find the average of the 2nd through (m + 1)st point, which is centered on the (m + 3)/2 point and so forth.

If m is even, the task is a little more complicated, requiring an additional step to get the moving averages centered. Since the average of the first four points should really be centered at the midpoint between the second and third data point, and the average of periods two through five should be centered halfway between periods three and four, the value to be centered at period three can be approximated by taking the average of the first two averages. Thus, the first number in the **centered moving average** column is

$$(1,613 + 1,594)/2 = 1,603.$$

A graph of the data along with their centered moving averages is shown in Figure 13–7. Notice that, as we expected, coal receipts are highest in the fourth quarter, above average in the first quarter, and below average in the second and third quarters.

The third step is to divide the actual data at a given point in the series by the **centered** moving average corresponding to the same point. This calculation cannot be done for all possible points, since at the beginning and end of the series we are unable to compute a centered moving average. These ratios represent the degree to which a particular observation is below (as in the .682 for period 3) or above (as in the 1.24 for period 4) the typical level. Note that these ratios for the third quarter tend to be below 1.0 and the ratios for the fourth quarter tend to be above 1.0. These ratios form the basis for developing a seasonal index.

To develop the seasonal index, we first group the ratios by quarter, as shown in Table 13–2. We then average all the ratios quarter by quarter. For example, all the ratios for the first quarter average 1.108. This is a seasonal index for the first quarter, and we conclude that the first quarter produces coal receipts that are on average about 110.8 percent of the average of all quarters.

These seasonal indices represent what that particular season's data look like on average compared to the average of the entire series. A seasonal index greater than 1 means that season is higher than the average for the year, likewise an index less than 1 means that season is lower than the average for the year.

The last step of deseasonalization is to take the actual data and divide it by the appropriate seasonal index. This is shown for the coal data in Table 13–3. The data in the "Deseasonalized Coal Receipts" columns are graphed in Figure 13–4.

Forecasting the Deseasonalized Series

Once the data have been deseasonalized, a deseasonalized forecast can be made. In our example, it might be appropriate to forecast the first quarter 1989 coal receipts by exponential smoothing. It turns out that a good smoothing constant is $\alpha^* = .60$, which yields an MSE of 42,828. Using this forecasting method, one could determine that the deseasonalized forecast would be 1,733 thousand short tons for January–March 1989. If we were to use this method to forecast two or more periods out, we would use the same deseasonalized forecast. Figure 13–5 showed this forecast for both January– March 1989 and April–June 1989.

Reseasonalizing the Forecast

The last step in the process is to reseasonalize our forecast of 1,733. The way to do this is to multiply 1,733 by the seasonal index for the first quarter (1.108) to obtain a value of 1,920. A seasonalized forecast for the second quarter would be 1,733 times the seasonal index (0.784), giving a value of 1,358. These values are shown in Figure 13–6 and would represent our point forecasts for the coming two quarters.

Generating the Probability Distribution Forecast

A single number is only part of a forecast; we need the entire probability distribution in order to reflect the uncertainty that we face. We can use methods in earlier chapters to complete the task. In Chapter 11 we saw how to use data independently observed from indistinguishable situations to construct a probability distribution. Here, however, the observations of the quantity we

TABLE 13–2   Ratios of Actuals to Moving Averages: Seasonal Factors

	Quarter			
Year	*1st*	*2nd*	*3rd*	*4th*
1980	—	—	0.682	1.240
1981	1.244	0.745	0.787	1.317
1982	1.122	0.744	0.942	1.226
1983	1.070	0.765	0.886	1.209
1984	1.119	0.830	1.004	1.123
1985	1.040	0.821	0.852	1.225
1986	1.124	0.863	0.806	1.284
1987	1.052	0.724	0.920	1.246
1988	1.096	0.776	—	—
Average	1.108	0.784	0.860	1.234

TABLE 13–3

Year	Actual Coal Receipts	Seasonal Index	Deseasonalized Coal Receipts	Year	Actual Coal Receipts	Seasonal Index	Deseasonalized Coal Receipts
1980	2,159	1.108	1,941	1985	2,074	1.108	1,865
	1,203	0.784	1,530		1,589	0.784	2,021
	1,094	0.860	1,268		1,673	0.860	1,939
	1,996	1.234	1,612		2,443	1.234	1,973
1981	2,081	1.108	1,871	1986	2,231	1.108	2,006
	1,332	0.784	1,694		1,675	0.784	2,130
	1,476	0.860	1,710		1,503	0.860	1,742
	2,533	1.234	2,046		2,259	1.234	1,824
1982	2,249	1.108	2,022	1987	1,809	1.108	1,626
	1,533	0.784	1,949		1,254	0.784	1,595
	1,935	0.860	2,242		1,613	0.860	1,869
	2,523	1.234	2,037		2,238	1.234	1,807
1983	2,208	1.108	1,985	1988	2,004	1.108	1,802
	1,597	0.784	2,031		1,406	0.784	1,788
	1,917	0.860	2,221		1,725	0.860	1,999
	2,726	1.234	2,201		1,994	1.234	1,610
1984	2,612	1.108	2,348				
	1,931	0.784	2,456				
	2,223	0.860	2,576				

are forecasting are not independent and from indistinguishable situations; in fact, the reason for time-series methods is that observations differ according to the time when they were taken. We have built models in this chapter to account for these time patterns. Having successfully accounted for the time patterns, the **errors** (actuals − forecasts or, alternatively, relative errors) will be independent observations from indistinguishable situations. We can create a cumulative distribution function (CDF) of the forecast errors by sorting the n errors and giving the kth observation in the sorted list a cumulative probability of k/n + 1 as we did in Chapter 11.[4] To obtain a probability distribution forecast, we would add the point forecast of 1,733 to a probability distribution of past forecast errors. Where zero would appear in the CDF of forecast errors, we would place 1,733, our point forecast. If the forecast is biased, in other words if this CDF of errors were not centered on zero, this procedure would automatically adjust for the bias.

Decomposition of Time Series into Seasonality and Trend Components

In the example with the coal data, we took advantage of the obvious seasonal pattern to improve our forecasts. We may do even better if we can make use of more than one kind of temporal pattern in the data. In this section we make combined use of a seasonal component and a trend component in our forecasts. This can give greater accuracy for one-period-ahead forecasts and could provide even greater accuracy improvements in the forecasts that go two months out, three months out, or more.

Digging into the archives for car sales from our earlier example, we found sales figures for two additional prior years; all of the data are shown in Figure 13–8. It is reasonable to assume that automotive sales are **seasonal**, with increases and decreases occurring at about the same time each year.[5] This seasonality can be observed by graphing the three years of sales figures with the months aligned, as shown in Figure 13–9. The correspondence of the two recent years is most pronounced, with a slight sales decline from January through May, then a sharp increase until about October followed by a decline until the end of the year. For any future year, it is reasonable to expect that August sales will be higher than April sales—the actual amount can be quantified by calculating seasonality indices.

It also appears that there is some downward trend in the data, although the seasonality pattern clouds this effect. Let us assume that components combine to give us the time series using a model

$$\text{Actual} = \text{Trend} \times \text{Cycle} \times \text{Seasonality} \times \text{Irregular.}[6]$$

To use this model we will need to separate out trend, cycle, and seasonality factors and project them forward. The irregular component is what is not accounted for by the other components; we cannot extrapolate it.

---

[4]Because we are sampling the errors, the true uncertainty in the forecast is somewhat larger than this CDF, recalling the sampling ideas presented in Chapter 12. We generally don't worry about this because we usually have a large sample size in time-series forecasting, which makes the uncertainty only slightly understated.

[5]These sales data are real, but the industry is disguised as the automotive industry. There is every reason to expect a seasonal pattern in the actual industry.

[6]We use a multiplicative model here. We might have chosen an additive model, instead. We would then subtract out, not divide, a seasonal component to deseasonalize, and so on.

FIGURE 13–8
Car Sales

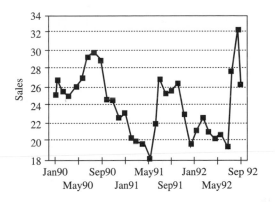

FIGURE 13–9
Three Years of Sales Aligned by Month

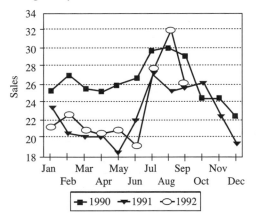

Separating out Seasonality

First, we obtain seasonality factors using the same method shown in the earlier section with the coal data. Here we have monthly, not quarterly data, so there will be a seasonality factor for each month. Column E of Sheet 5 shows seasonality factors for each observation, excepting the first five months and the last six months, for which we do not have a complete year surrounding the observation. Now we can average all seasonality factors available for a particular month to obtain a seasonal index for that month. For example, we average the seasonality factor for March 1991 with that for March 1992 to come up with a factor for March forecasting. This is done for March and all other months in column J of Sheet 5 to identify 12 seasonality factors or seasonal indices for forecasting.

SHEET 5　Considering Seasonality

	A	B	C	D	E	F	G	H	I	J	K	L	M	N
		STEPS:		Calculate seasonality factors---						Deseasonalize-------		Forecast--	Reseas.-
										Seasonality			0.2	
					Season-	Line up seasonality fac-				Factors		Deseas-	Exp.	Reseas-
			Actual	Centered	ality	tors for similar months:	1990	1991	1992	for	Season'y	onalized	Smooth	onalized
5	Month	Year	Sales	Average	Factors		1990	1991	1992	Forecast	Factors	Sales	Forecast	Sales
6			NA											
7	Jan	90	25.5	NA	NA	Jan	NA	0.980	0.934	0.957	0.957	26.64	26.64	25.50
8	Feb	90	27.1	NA	NA	Feb	NA	0.878	0.987	0.932	0.932	29.07	26.64	24.84
9	Mar	90	25.6	NA	NA	Mar	NA	0.878	0.897	0.887	0.887	28.85	27.13	24.07
10	Apr	90	25.2	NA	NA	Apr	NA	0.872	NA	0.872	0.872	28.91	27.47	23.95
11	May	90	26.0	NA	NA	May	NA	0.807	NA	0.807	0.807	32.23	27.76	22.39
12	Jun	90	26.9	NA	NA	Jun	NA	0.964	NA	0.964	0.964	27.91	28.65	27.62
13	Jul	90	29.8	26.3	1.131	Jul	1.131	1.204	NA	1.168	1.168	25.52	28.50	33.28
14	Aug	90	30.0	26.0	1.155	Aug	1.155	1.124	NA	1.139	1.139	26.33	27.91	31.80
15	Sep	90	29.2	25.5	1.146	Sep	1.146	1.135	NA	1.141	1.141	25.60	27.59	31.48
16	Oct	90	24.6	25.0	0.983	Oct	0.983	1.164		1.073	1.073	22.92	27.19	29.19
17	Nov	90	24.7	24.5	1.008	Nov	1.008	0.996		1.002	1.002	24.66	26.34	26.39
18	Dec	90	22.7	24.0	0.946	Dec	0.946	0.860		0.903	0.903	25.13	26.00	23.49
19	Jan	91	23.2	23.7	0.980					0.957		24.24	25.83	24.72
20	Feb	91	20.5	23.4	0.878					0.932		21.99	25.51	23.78
21	Mar	91	20.2	23.0	0.878					0.887		22.77	24.81	22.01
22	Apr	91	20.0	22.9	0.872					0.872		22.94	24.40	21.27
23	May	91	18.5	22.9	0.807					0.807		22.93	24.11	19.45
24	Jun	91	21.9	22.7	0.964					0.964		22.72	23.87	23.01
25	Jul	91	27.1	22.5	1.204					1.168		23.21	23.64	27.60
26	Aug	91	25.3	22.5	1.124					1.139		22.21	23.56	26.84
27	Sep	91	25.7	22.6	1.135					1.141		22.53	23.29	26.56
28	Oct	91	26.4	22.7	1.164					1.073		24.60	23.13	24.83
29	Nov	91	22.7	22.8	0.996					1.002		22.66	23.43	23.47
30	Dec	91	19.6	22.8	0.860					0.903		21.70	23.27	21.02
31	Jan	92	21.2	22.7	0.934					0.957		22.15	22.96	21.97
32	Feb	92	22.7	23.0	0.987					0.932		24.35	22.80	21.25
33	Mar	92	20.9	23.3	0.897					0.887		23.55	23.11	20.50
34	Apr	92	20.4	NA	NA					0.872		23.40	23.20	20.22
35	May	92	20.9	NA	NA					0.807		25.91	23.24	18.75
36	Jun	92	19.3	NA	NA					0.964		20.02	23.77	22.91
37	Jul	92	27.6	NA	NA					1.168		23.64	23.02	26.88
38	Aug	92	32.1	NA	NA					1.139		28.18	23.15	26.37
39	Sep	92	26.0	NA	NA					1.141		22.79	24.15	27.55
40	Oct	92	NA							1.073		forecast:	23.88	25.63
41	Nov	92	NA							1.002		forecast:	23.88	23.92
42	Dec	92	NA							0.903		forecast:	23.88	21.57
43	Jan	93	NA							0.957		forecast:	23.88	22.86
44	Feb	93	NA							0.932		forecast:	23.88	22.26

The following formulae (except C7) are copied down the respective columns.

Cell	Formula
C6:	@NA
C7:	{actual sales}
D7:	@avg(c1..c12,c2..c13)
E7:	+C7/D7
G7:	+E7
H7:	+E19
I7:	+E31
J7:	@AVG(H7..I7)
J10:	+H10
J13:	@AVG(G13..H13)
K7:	+J7
K19:	+K7
L7:	+C7/K7
M7:	+L7
M8:	+L7*$M$2+ M7*(1-$M$2)
M41:	+M40
N7:	+M7*K7

When we have a seasonal index for each month, we can then deseasonalize the prior sales figures by dividing the actual sales figures by the corresponding seasonal index—this will remove the variation we attribute to seasonality. What's left is the trend, cycle, and the irregular. One alternative for forecasting what's left is to simply use exponential smoothing to forecast the deseasonalized data, then to reseasonalize it. Sheet 5 illustrates this process in columns M and N.

Extrapolating Trend and Cycle Components

It was necessary to use the same deseasonalized forecast in column M of Sheet 5 for October 1992 and for forecasts of two months ahead, three months ahead, up to five months ahead. The exponential smoothing approach gives only one forecast, and if we need to forecast more than one period ahead, a flat extrapolation into the future is necessary (which is one downside of exponential smoothing). We may believe, however, that over time the deseasonalized sales figures are generally increasing or decreasing. We would then wish to exploit the trend, which is a consistent, long-term movement. Usually we assume the trend is a straight-line pattern up or down; however, exponentially increasing or other curved trends are also possible.

The deseasonalized data are the combination of trend and cycle patterns, along with irregular variations. Cycle is an up and down movement with an irregular period that is very hard to predict associated with general business conditions. In many industries the business cycle typically ranges from 2 to 10 years, although shorter or longer cycles are certainly possible. We won't provide much assistance here on predicting a cycle, however, we do want to separate out the Trend from the Cycle.

One simple way to estimate Trend is to calculate a linear regression of the deseasonalized (or Trend-Cycle-Irregular) data. The independent variable will be the period number (e.g., January 1990 equals 1, February 1990 equals 2, etc.), and the dependent variable will be the deseasonalized sales figures. Results are shown below.

Regression output:

Constant	27.24783
Standard error of Y estimate	2.23829
R squared	0.33506
Number of observations	33
Degrees of freedom	31
X coefficient(s)	−0.16173
Standard error of coefficient	0.04092

The X coefficient of −0.16 indicates that the deseasonalized sales figures tend to decrease by about −0.16 cars per month. Figure 13–10 compares the

FIGURE 13–10

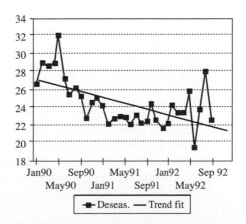

deseasonalized sales figures to the regression trend line. The wandering of the data around the trend line reflects the cycle that is part of the data and the unpredictable irregular occurrences (note, for example, the observation for June 1992, which for one month falls below the trend line).

We might improve the exponential smoothing of Sheet 5 using the Trend estimate by assuming that the October forecast is 0.16 lower than the 23.75 forecast, and that the November forecast is 0.16×2 lower than the 23.75 forecast, and so on. The Trend can enhance the forecasts for the next three months as shown in the table below.

	Forecast from September 1992	Trend from Regression	Number of Periods Out	Forecast with Trend	Seasonality Factor for Month	Reseasonalized Forecast
	A	B	C	D = A + (B × C)	E	D × E
October 1992	23.75	−0.16	1	23.59	1.077	25.406
November 1992	23.75	−0.16	2	23.43	1.006	23.571
December 1992	23.75	−0.16	3	23.27	0.909	21.152

Holt's Model: Exponential Smoothing with Trend

One weakness of the linear regression approach is that it assumes the trend is a straight line with a constant one-period change over time. In actuality, the trend may be down for a few years, then up for a few years. If we have good reason to believe that the trend is not a constant amount, we would prefer an approach that will continuously change the trend estimate over time. Holt's model meets this requirement.

Regular exponential smoothing attempts to estimate the *level* of sales in the future. Holt's model improves on this by forecasting both the level of sales and a trend amount. The Trend forecast reflects the current expected period-to-period change in sales level for the future. Given the Level and Trend estimates made in a particular month, we can produce a k month-ahead forecast that would be the current estimate of Level plus k*Trend.

All we need then is to be clear about how the estimates of Level and Trend are updated each period; Holt's idea was to smooth each estimate with exponential smoothing. For example, the September actual sales can be used to update the Level forecast according to the following equation:

$$\text{Level}_{\text{Sept}} = \text{alpha*Sales}_{\text{Sept}} + (1 - \text{alpha})*(\text{Level}_{\text{Aug}} + \text{Trend}_{\text{Aug}}),$$

where alpha is the smoothing constant, as in exponential smoothing.

Now that we have updated the Level forecast, we can use it to update the Trend forecast as follows. We aren't actually given Trend actuals, so we calculate a Trend for September using the new September Level by taking the difference $\text{Level}_{\text{Sept}} - \text{Level}_{\text{Aug}}$. The smoothing equation for the Trend estimate is thus:

$$\text{Trend}_{\text{Sept}} = \text{beta}*(\text{Level}_{\text{Sept}} - \text{Level}_{\text{Aug}}) + (1 - \text{beta})*\text{Trend}_{\text{Aug}},$$

where beta is another smoothing constant that determines the sensitivity of the Trend estimate to changes in Trend. Generally, the beta is small (for example 0.2) because, recall, trend is a long-term effect that shouldn't change rapidly.

We can use the September Level and Trend estimates to forecast future sales as follows:

$$\text{Forecast}_{\text{Oct}} = \text{Level}_{\text{Sept}} + 1*\text{Trend}_{\text{Sept}},$$

$$\text{Forecast}_{\text{Nov}} = \text{Level}_{\text{Sept}} + 2*\text{Trend}_{\text{Sept}},$$

$$\text{Forecast}_{\text{Dec}} = \text{Level}_{\text{Sept}} + 3*\text{Trend}_{\text{Sept}},$$

and so on. This approach is illustrated in Sheet 6, which has been truncated in the middle to save space. The initial Level and Trend can usually be chosen arbitrarily. For example, the prior period's sales can be used for the starting Level, and the initial Trend can be zero. It will take a few periods of updating for the two estimates to stabilize for good forecasting.

Observe that Holt's model does not consider seasonality. If we believe that the actual sales data contain both trend and seasonality, it would be easier to have one model that considers both, which is embodied in Winter's model.

Winter's Model: Exponential Smoothing with Trend and Seasonality

Winter's model is similar to Holt's model in that it contains updating estimates of Level and Trend. In addition, Winter's model updates estimates of the seasonality factors each period, again using exponential smoothing.

As with the Holt's model example, assume that we have Level and Trend estimates from August. Further, assume that we have a seasonality factor that was updated from September of the prior year (the seasonality factors will be denoted Season). Observe that the deseasonalized September sales equals $\text{Sales}_{\text{Sept}}/\text{Season}_{\text{priorSept}}$. The September sales can be used to update the Level forecast (done in Sheet 7) with the following equation:

$$\text{Level}_{\text{Sept}} = \text{alpha}*(\text{Sales}_{\text{Sept}}/\text{Season}_{\text{priorSept}})$$
$$+ (1 - \text{alpha})*(\text{Level}_{\text{Aug}} + \text{Trend}_{\text{Aug}}).$$

The Trend estimate can also be updated the same as with Holt's model, namely:

$$\text{Trend}_{\text{Sept}} = \text{beta}*(\text{Level}_{\text{Sept}} - \text{Level}_{\text{Aug}}) + (1 - \text{beta})*\text{Trend}_{\text{Aug}}.$$

Finally, we need to update the September seasonality estimate. Note that $\text{Level}_{\text{Sept}}$ represents an updated deseasonalized forecast for September

SHEET 6   Holt's Model

	A	B	C	D	E
1				alpha:	beta:
2			**Actual**	0.20	0.20
3	**Month**	**Year**	**Sales**	**Level**	**Trend**
4	-------------	-------------	NA	25.00	0.00
5	Jan	90	25.5	25.10	0.02
6	Feb	90	27.1	25.52	0.10
7	Mar	90	25.6	25.61	0.10
8	Apr	90	25.2	25.61	0.08
9	May	90	26.0	25.75	0.09
10	Jun	90	26.9	26.05	0.13
11	Jul	90	29.8	26.91	0.28
12	Aug	90	30.0	27.75	0.39
13	Sep	~~	~~.~	~~.~~	~ ~~
	...~y	~~	~~.~	~~.~~	-0.20
34	Jun	92	19.3	20.61	-0.27
35	Jul	92	27.6	21.79	0.02
36	Aug	92	32.1	23.87	0.43
37	Sep	92	26.0	24.65	0.50
38				**Forecast**	
39	Oct	92	1	25.15	
40	Nov	92	2	25.65	
41	Dec	92	3	26.15	
42	Jan	93	4	26.65	
43	Feb	93	5	27.15	
44					
45		D5:	+$D$2*C5+(1-$D$2)*(D4+E4)		
46		E5:	+$E$2*(D5-D4)+(1-$E$2)*E4		
47		D39:	+$D$37+$E$37*C39		

sales, so $\text{Sales}_{\text{Sept}}/\text{Level}_{\text{Sept}}$ represents the implied seasonality factor. Therefore, we can update the September seasonality factor with the following equation:

$$\text{Season}_{\text{Sept}} = \text{gamma}*(\text{Sales}_{\text{Sept}}/\text{Level}_{\text{Sept}})$$
$$+ (1 - \text{gamma})*(\text{Season}_{\text{priorSept}}),$$

where gamma, like alpha and beta, is a smoothing constant between 0 and 1 (perhaps 0.3).[7]

---

[7]Gamma is typically higher than alpha and beta since each seasonality estimate is only updated once per year.

SHEET 7   Winter's Model

5	*Initial trend used is 0:*					1.00	Feb
6	E16: 0					1.00	Mar
7	*Trend updates by:*					1.00	Apr
8	E17: +$E$14*(D17-D16)+(1-$E$14)*E16					1.00	May
9	*Initial seasonality indices used are 1.0:*					1.00	Jun
10	F4: 1.0					1.00	Jul
11	*Seasonality indices update by:*					1.00	Aug
12	F16: +$F$2*(C16/D16)+(1-$F$2)*F4					1.00	Sep
13				alpha	beta	1.00	Oct
14				0.10	0.10	1.00	Nov
15	**Month**	**Year**	**Actual**	**Level**	**Trend**	1.00	Dec
16	Jan	90	25.5	25.50	0.00	1.00	
17	Feb	90	27.1	25.66	0.02	1.01	
18	Mar	90	25.6	25.67	0.02	1.00	
19	Apr	90	25.2	25.64	0.01	1.00	
20	May	90	26.0	25.68	0.01	1.00	
46	Jul	92	27.0	21.8	3.13		
47	Aug	92	32.1	22.57	-0.06	1.11	
48	Sep	92	26.0	22.78	-0.03	1.05	
49			months in				
50			future:	**Forecast**			
51	Oct	92	1	23.0	(D$48+C51*E$48)*F37		

The forecasts for subsequent periods can be calculated as with Holt's model, except that they will be reseasonalized with the most recently available seasonality estimates for the corresponding months, i.e.:

$$\text{Forecast}_{Oct} = (\text{Level}_{Sept} + 1*\text{Trend}_{Sept})*\text{Season}_{priorOct},$$
$$\text{Forecast}_{Nov} = (\text{Level}_{Sept} + 2*\text{Trend}_{Sept})*\text{Season}_{priorNov},$$
$$\text{Forecast}_{Dec} = (\text{Level}_{Sept} + 3*\text{Trend}_{Sept})*\text{Season}_{priorDec},$$

and so on. Winter's model (also called Winter's three-factor model) is presented in Sheet 7.

Other Advanced Techniques

Winter's model is a general method that will work quite well in a variety of settings and should be more than adequate in most situations. Nevertheless, other variations of models exist:

- In the models described in this chapter, we assumed that the trend is linear. Other models consider trend to be exponential, quadratic, etc.
- The models described here assume that the trend is additive (i.e., the Trend estimate is added to the Level estimate). Other models assume a multiplicative trend.

- Other models also consider the possibility of a dramatic jump in the actual sales data, such as from a competitor suddenly going out of business. Such models may have alpha, beta, and gamma parameters that will adjust automatically.
- The forecasting approaches described here assume a given period (12 months in the example above) for seasonality. More complex methods, such as Box-Jenkins, can superimpose combinations of seasonal patterns with different lengths of seasonality (e.g., three months, six months) and separate out the estimates of their effects.

All forecasting approaches will be wrong to some extent, and the good forecaster remembers that simplicity is essential. Add complexity only when you understand what it is doing and it's superiority is convincing. A highly complex model, like a jet fighter designed for high performance, can create a spectacular disaster when it fails.

Considerations in Preparing and Using a Forecast

We have presented a number of methods for time-series forecasting. In implementing these techniques, several tasks must be performed, which may raise a number of issues.

Choose a Technique and Monitor It.   Not only should one evaluate accuracy in choosing a forecasting technique, but one also should consider the reasonableness of the assumptions of the model. For example, if seasonality exists, it would be better to use Winter's model than Holt's model.

Decide on Aggregation.   An important consideration in forecasting is the level of aggregation in which to forecast. For example, a car sales company may sell three types of vehicles (cars, trucks, and vans), with a half-dozen models of each. Further, a particular model can come with various options and colors. We may attempt to forecast sales of blue model XYZ sports cars with the luxury options, which is at a **detailed level**. However, sales of such a specific item may be so low that the forecasts are likely to have a relatively high error. We could more accurately forecast sales of cars in general (an **aggregate level**). Of course, we then face the added problem of disaggregating the forecast to decide how many of the specific models to order. Thus, we see the trade-off between accuracy and usefulness.

Determine Initial Model Parameters.   Although advanced techniques can be used to calculate initial Level, Trend, and so on, research has shown that models such as Holt's and Winter's tend to have low sensitivity to the initial parameters. After a few periods of updating, the parameters tend to stabilize to appropriate values. Therefore, it is usually all right to use almost any reasonable values to start the forecasting process.

Use the Forecasts in Decision Making.   It is essential to remember in using any forecast that error exists. Earlier in this chapter methods were shown for estimating forecast error. The probability distribution of the errors can be used to develop a probabilistic forecast, which is the basis for decisions by a proactive decision maker. Basing the decision only on a point forecast (and not the uncertainty) can cause serious problems—particularly if the cost of the actual outcome exceeding the forecast is quite different from the cost of it being lower than the forecast. Consideration of risk can occur only if the uncertainty is known.

Include Qualitative Judgments.   Sometimes the decision maker believes the future will be somewhat different from that forecasted because his or her beliefs are not fully represented in the numerical data. For this reason, the forecast values may be adjusted to consider these subjective judgments.

Monitor Forecast Accuracy.   The forecaster needs to be aware that even though the chosen forecasting technique is appropriate given past history, future conditions may change, causing the forecast error to rise dramatically. A simple way to watch for this is by the use of a **tracking signal**. A chart could easily be made to track the actual forecast error realized after each period. The so-called tracking signal could be any of the error calculations described in this chapter. The forecaster may choose a threshold value of error that is considered unacceptable. If the tracking signal goes beyond the threshold value for more than one period, the appropriateness of the forecasting technique may be reevaluated; it may be time to consider a change of forecasting method.

Actual October sales for the examples used in this chapter was 25 cars.

C H A P T E R

14 REGRESSION: FORECASTING USING EXPLANATORY FACTORS

We begin this chapter with a simple example concerning Lawrence Construction, the new-home construction arm of Lawrence Properties. Jerry Baugher, sales manager for Lawrence Construction, had just finished gathering data on the company's 30 most recent single-family homes (see Table 14–1). Early in conversations with prospective customers, Baugher was often asked about the company's typical cost per square foot. Baugher always responded with a list of factors affecting the final cost of a new house and a caution against relying too heavily on square footage as the sole determinant of cost. Having said all that, however, he knew he would be pressed to provide some numbers.

A scatter plot of cost versus square feet (Figure 14–1) shows that there was indeed a strong relationship between these two variables. The bigger the home, the more it cost. In keeping with Baugher's understanding of the components of cost, however, the plot suggested to him that smaller homes cost more per square foot than larger homes. This reflected the fact that many components of a home's construction costs had nothing to do with the size of the home. Consequently, a single average cost per square foot such as $84.86 (calculated as $218,900, the average cost of the 30 homes, divided by 2,579.5, the average square feet per home) would understate the cost of a small home and overstate the cost of a large home.

The Simple Linear Model

The situation at Lawrence Construction is typical of many business forecasting problems. A variable of interest, call it Y, is known to be related to a second variable, X. The decision maker knows the history of observed X and Y pairs and wishes to use the known value of X in the current situation to forecast the uncertain quantity Y. Because the forecast of Y will depend on

TABLE 14–1   Lawrence Construction Cost Data

Square Foot	Cost	Square Foot	Cost
2,885	$231,000	2,323	$219,000
2,230	170,000	3,279	267,000
2,377	217,000	3,308	297,000
2,551	209,000	2,140	192,000
2,592	218,000	2,029	217,000
3,341	218,000	2,879	234,000
2,632	310,000	2,408	177,000
3,034	248,000	3,228	234,000
2,052	186,000	2,560	249,000
2,066	204,000	2,500	206,000
2,193	185,000	2,248	112,000
2,392	216,000	2,696	283,000
2,060	146,000	2,400	153,000
3,457	293,000	2,196	251,000
2,450	234,000	2,880	191,000
Average		2,579.5	$218,900
Standard deviation		429.56	$ 45,256

FIGURE 14–1
Scatter Plot of Cost versus Area in Square Feet

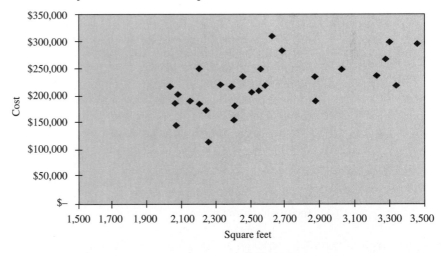

X, Y is called the **dependent variable** and X is called the **independent variable**.

The first step in solving the forecasting problem is to hypothesize the form of the relationship between Y and X. We need a simple, logical equation that describes how Y is related to X. Such an equation is called a model.

One simple and often-used model assumes that the underlying relationship between X and Y is linear. In other words, the equation that shows the relationship of Y to X is the equation for graphing a straight line. Furthermore, the model should recognize that this relationship is not perfect. The scatter plot of Y versus X is almost never a perfectly straight line with all points falling on the line. The scatter plot is typically like that in Figure 14–1, with points scattered about some imaginary straight line.

The model we have just described is called the **simple linear model**. In equation form we write it as

$$Y = a + bX + \text{Error}. \qquad (14\text{–}1)$$

Notice that this equation says that Y is equal to a, a constant amount, plus the product of b times X, plus an error. This equation says that Y is linearly related to X but that the relationship is not perfect.[1] The error term in the model reminds us that in our uncertain world, Y will not exactly equal a + bX. Our scatter plots of Y versus X will not trace out a perfectly straight line.

Let us focus, for a moment, on the a + bX component of our model. This a + bX component is the equation for the imaginary line that we hypothesize describes the underlying relationship between Y and X. Besides "imaginary line" and "underlying relationship," is there some other way to label just what a + bX represents? Yes. The a + bX component represents the mean of Y for a given X:

$$\text{Mean of } Y|X = a + bX. \qquad (14\text{–}2)$$

Recall from sampling theory that the mean is the long-run average of some population. In sampling, we usually talked about a single population and a single mean. Now in equation (14–2) we shift to a situation where, rather than a single mean, the mean changes depending on the value of X.[2] The imaginary line that describes the underlying relationship between Y and X is a line of means.

Equations (14–1) and (14–2) are two ways to say the same thing. Equation (14–1) is a model for Y. Equation (14–2) is a model for the mean of Y given X. Both equations assume that Y is related to X. Equation (14–2) says the mean of Y is linearly related to X and equation (14–1) simply goes one step further and says that Y (like all uncertain quantities) is equal to its mean plus some error.

---

[1] We chose to use $Y = a + bY$ as the equation of a line. This is the convention used by most statistical texts and statistical software packages. From algebra, you may remember the equation of a line as $Y = mX + b$. Both are correct. In fact, they are equivalent. We use a as the intercept and b as the slope. In the $Y = mX + b$ expression, b is the intercept and m is the slope.

[2] For those of you who like to think in terms of urns, in sampling we had one urn and one mean. Now we have a whole series of urns, one for each possible value of X. The mean of each urn in this series of urns is given by equation (14–2).

FIGURE 14–2
Mean of Y|X = 2 + 1.2X

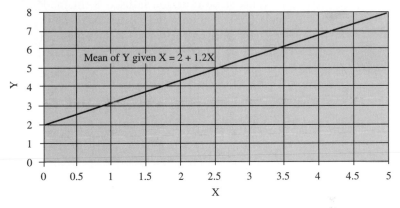

The constants a and b are called **coefficients**. They determine just exactly what the linear relationship between Y and X looks like. For example, if a = 2 and b = 1.2, the graph of the mean of Y versus X is as shown in Figure 14–2. The "a" coefficient is called the **intercept**, because it is the value at which the line intercepts the Y axis. It is the value of the mean of Y when X = 0. The "b" coefficient is called the **slope** because it measures the pitch or slope of the line. That is, b is the amount by which the mean of Y changes if X increases one unit. If b is positive, the mean of Y increases as X increases and the line goes from the lower left of the graph to the upper right. Conversely, if b is negative, the mean of Y decreases as X increases and the line goes from upper left to lower right. If b equals zero, then the line is horizontal and the mean of Y does not change as X increases. In this case, X is of no use in forecasting Y.

Fitting the Model Using "Least Squares"

After the model form has been chosen, the next step is to determine the particular coefficient values, a and b, that seem best suited for the current situation. A past history of relevant X, Y pairs is used to guide this selection, which is called fitting the model to a set of data. Fitting the straight-line model means determining exactly how to draw a straight line through the scatter of Y versus X points (Figure 14–1, for example). The process of using data to "fit the line" or "estimate the coefficients of the model" is sometimes referred to as "regressing Y on X."

Since the ultimate objective of this modeling is to forecast Y, a good way to fit the model is to pick coefficients that would have done the best job of forecasting past actuals. An accepted measure of forecasting accuracy is **mean squared error**, the average squared difference between actuals and forecasts. The averaging is done on squared differences so that positive and negative errors do not cancel each other out and so that the relative severity of large errors is emphasized.[3]

This same criterion is used to fit models to past data. The procedure known as **least squares** chooses coefficient values that minimize the sum (or average) squared differences between actuals and fitted values. Graphically, least squares chooses the fitted line that minimizes the sum of the squared vertical distances between each point (actual) and the line (fitted value). These differences between actuals and fitted values are called **residuals**. The resulting line that minimizes the sum of squared residuals is called the **least-squares regression line**.[4]

The computations necessary to compete least-squares coefficient estimates are very straightforward. Most electronic spreadsheet software packages can carry out the necessary calculations to determine the least-squares regression line.

Table 14–2 shows the results from using Excel's regression feature with the data in Table 14–1. Amid the wealth of numbers in this report (many of which, believe it or not, you will come to appreciate) are the two we want. The estimated intercept, $\hat{a}$, is \$56,104. The estimated slope, $\hat{b}$, is 63.11.[5] Thus, the least-squares regression line relating Lawrence new-home construction cost to home size measured in square feet is

$$\hat{Y} = \$56,104 + 63.11(X) \tag{14–3}$$

where $\hat{Y}$ is the proposed forecast of cost and X is the area of the house in square feet.

Figure 14–3 shows this line superimposed on the scatter plot from Figure 14–1. This particular line is the "best" line we can draw through the 30 points—best in the sense that the 30 points are "closer" to this line than any other possible line. Our measure of closeness is the sum (average) of squared distances of the points from the line.

Table 14–3 presents the regression results in table form. The first two columns contain the original data. The third column contains the fitted values, $\hat{Y}$, found by substituting each X into the regression equation. The last column contains the residuals—the difference between Y and $\hat{Y}$. These residuals are the "distances" of the points from the line. They measure how

---

[3]Statistical theory also dictates mean squared error as the best measure of forecasting accuracy if the forecast errors are unbiased and normally distributed.

[4]The term *regression* comes from the pioneering work of Sir Francis Galton (1822–1911) who studied the strength of the resemblance between parents and their offspring. The best-fitting line through a scatter plot of heights of sons versus heights of their fathers revealed that sons' heights "regressed" toward the overall mean height. Tall fathers tended to have shorter sons and short fathers tended to have taller sons. Because of this phenomenon, the best-fitting line was labeled the regression line. The name stuck despite the fact that the regression-to-the-mean phenomenon was a characteristic of the situation being studied rather than the technique used for finding the best-fitting line.

[5]The terms $\hat{a}$ and $\hat{b}$ are used to refer to specific estimates of a and b in model (14–1).

TABLE 14–2   Excel Summary Regression Output

Regression Statistics				
Multiple R	0.599			
R square	0.359			
Adjusted R square	0.336			
Standard error	36879			
Observations	30			
		ANOVA		
	df	*SS*	*MS*	*F*
Regression	1	21313807694.5	2.131e + 10	15.67
Residual	28	38080892305.5	1.360e + 09	
Total	29	59394700000		
	Coefficients	*Standard Error*	*t Stat*	*P-value*
Intercept	56103.661	41670.92	1.35	0.1890
Square Feet	63.111	15.94	3.96	0.0005

close the fitted values (the $\hat{Y}$) came to the actual values (the Ys). Remember that the sum of squares of these residuals was the criterion we used to select â and b̂.

Now that we have the least-squares regression line, we can use it to provide a point forecast for construction cost of any new home. For example, to estimate the cost of a new home with an area of 2,500 square feet, we substitute X = 2,500 into the least-squares regression equation (14–3) to obtain $\hat{Y}$ = \$213,879. Thus, our best guess for construction cost for this new home is \$213,879. Additionally, the regression results suggest to Baugher that a simple cost-per-square-foot forecast will not be as accurate as the new forecasting rule suggested by equation (14–3). A better rule would use \$56,000 (rounding off) plus \$63 per square foot to estimate the cost of a Lawrence Construction new home. Now Baugher must decide whether and how to use this new forecast in conversations with prospective buyers.

Important Properties of the Least-Squares Regression Line

In Table 14–3 we see that the average of the residuals is zero. Stop and think about what that means. Since residuals measure the differences between the past actuals and fitted values, an average of zero for the residuals means that the fitted values were, on average, neither too high nor too low. On average,

FIGURE 14–3

Graph of Regression Line

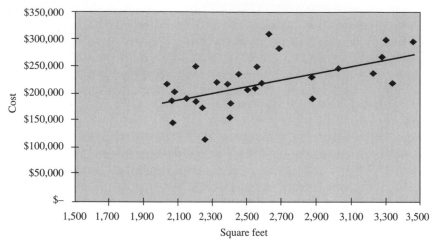

the fitted values were "right on." Because the average of the residuals is zero, we don't have to worry about correcting the fitted values (and future forecasts) for bias.

Were we just lucky, or will this happen all the time? This desirable property is shared by all least-squares regression lines. Residuals from a least-squares regression line sum (average) to zero. To minimize the sum of squared residuals, the least-squares technique naturally selects â to ensure that the residuals sum to zero.

A related property of the least-squares regression line is that it always goes through the point $\overline{X}$, $\overline{Y}$.[6] Another way to say the same thing is the least-squares forecast of Y for $X = \overline{X}$ is $\overline{Y}$. Verify for yourself that substituting $\overline{X} = 2{,}579.53$ into equation (14–3) produces a forecast equal to $218,900, the average construction cost. Some people use this property to say "the regression line goes through the center of the data." It is not a coincidence then, that the average of the fitted values in Table 14–3 ($218,900) is equal to the average construction cost of the 30 homes.

Summary Regression Statistics

Put yourself back in the shoes of Jerry Baugher. You carefully compiled the data in Table 14–1 in an attempt to understand how Lawrence's construction cost varies with home size. The graph in Figure 14–1 confirmed your belief that construction costs were highly dependent on home size. The graph also

---

[6]The terms $\overline{X}$ and $\overline{Y}$ are used to refer to the sample averages of X and Y, respectively.

TABLE 14–3   Fitted and Residual Values

	Square Feet	Cost	Fitted $\hat{Y}$	Residual $Y - \hat{Y}$
	2,885	$231,000	238,178.2	−7,178.2
	2,230	170,000	196,840.7	−26,840.7
	2,377	217,000	206,118.0	10,882.0
	2,551	209,000	217,099.2	−8,099.2
	2,592	218,000	219,686.8	−1,686.8
	3,341	218,000	266,956.7	−48,956.7
	2,632	310,000	222,211.2	87,788.8
	3,034	248,000	247,581.7	418.3
	2,052	186,000	185,607.0	393.0
	2,066	204,000	186,490.5	17,509.5
	2,193	185,000	194,505.6	−9,505.6
	2,392	216,000	207,064.6	8,935.4
	2,060	146,000	186,111.9	−40,111.9
	3,457	293,000	274,277.6	18,722.4
	2,450	234,000	210,725.1	23,274.9
	2,323	219,000	202,710.0	16,290.0
	3,279	267,000	263,043.9	3,956.1
	3,308	297,000	264,874.1	32,125.9
	2,140	192,000	191,160.7	839.3
	2,029	217,000	184,155.4	32,844.6
	2,879	234,000	237,799.6	−3,799.6
	2,408	177,000	208,074.4	−31,074.4
	3,228	234,000	259,825.2	−25,825.2
	2,560	249,000	217,667.2	31,332.8
	2,500	206,000	213,880.6	−7,880.6
	2,248	112,000	197,976.7	−85,976.7
	2,696	283,000	226,250.3	56,749.7
	2,400	153,000	207,569.5	−54,569.5
	2,196	251,000	194,694.9	56,305.1
	2,880	191,000	237,862.7	−46,862.7
Average	2,579.53	$218,900	218,900.0	0.0
Standard deviation	429.56	$ 45,256		

helped you judge that the underlying relationship was linear and led you to fit the model summarized by equation (14–1). You scanned the output in Table 14–2 for the numbers you needed to forecast cost (â = $56,104 and b̂ = 63.11). The large positive constant term confirmed your belief that many cost components of a new home were constant and did not increase with size of the home. For good measure, you examined the regression line both in graphical (Figure 14–3) and tabular (Table 14–3) form.

Now what? Are we done? How well did we do? How "good" is this model? Have we made any mistakes? What are all those extra numbers in Table 14–2 for? Do we have to know what they all mean?

First, much of the information in Table 14–2 is redundant. You really don't have to look at all of it. Second, this chapter will attempt to explain the more important summary statistics you find in Table 14–2.

Standard Error of Estimate

After reading the values of the estimated coefficients, we suggest you next look at the standard error of estimate.[7] In the Lawrence Construction example, the standard error of estimate is 36,879. Just what does this number tell us?

Recall from equation (14–1) that we recognized that the Ys would not fall exactly on the imaginary line. The differences between Y and the imaginary line are called errors. The standard error of estimate is our estimate, based on these data, of the standard deviation of the errors. The standard error of estimate is a measure of how close the points are to the imaginary line. If the errors are normally distributed, we would say that 68 percent of the errors would be within plus or minus 36,879 of the imaginary line.

Because the standard error of estimate measures how close the points are to the imaginary line, it is a measure of how well the model fit the data. The lower the standard error of estimate, the closer the points are to the imaginary line, and the better the fit.

The standard error of estimate is an *absolute* measure. We should interpret the 36,879 as 36,879 *dollars*. The standard error of estimate is always measured in the same units as Y. To judge how big this standard error of estimate is, you should compare it to the magnitude of Lawrence construction costs, which ran from \$112,000 to \$310,000.

One final interpretation of the standard error of estimate has to do with forecasting. Suppose in addition to the point forecast, Baugher required a probabilistic forecast. How much uncertainty is there in the construction cost of a new home? What standard deviation should we use when we forecast construction cost? The simple answer is: use the standard error of estimate, \$36,879.[8] Thus, the standard error of estimate is a measure of how much uncertainty we face when we use the model to forecast Y.

---

[7]This statistics has a variety of names. It is sometimes called the standard error of the y-estimate, the standard deviation of residuals, or simply the standard error.

[8]This is the simple answer, but not the totally correct answer. Since the standard error measures the standard deviation of the errors in model (14–1), we can use it as the standard deviation when we forecast only if we know the true imaginary line. If our sample size was huge (and a sample size of 20 is not huge) we could safely assume that $\hat{a}$ and $\hat{b}$ were essentially identical to the true a and b. With a huge sample size, we would "know" the true line and would use the standard error as the standard deviation when we forecast. When the sample size is not huge, the standard error of estimate (although still our best guess for the standard deviation of the errors in the model) understates the standard deviation when we use $\hat{Y}$ to forecast the next Y. Why? Because $\hat{Y}$ is not the same as the mean of Y|X. Why? Because $\hat{a}$ and $\hat{b}$ are not the same as a and b. We use an estimated line when we forecast. And the standard error of estimate applies to errors about the true imaginary line.

Adjusted R Square

Whereas the standard error of estimate is an *absolute* measure of how well the model fit the data, adjusted R square is a *relative* measure. To judge whether the standard error of estimate of $36,879 is big or small, you need to know something about the Y variable and the surrounding context.

To put the $36,879 in context we need a benchmark. If $36,879 measures how well the model did, we need to measure how well we would do without the model. If we did not use the model to forecast, what would we do? Without the model, we might resort to using $\overline{Y}$ = $218,900 as the forecast of cost. Remember that the model is how we incorporated information on home size. If we are not to use this information, we have no choice but to treat all homes the same. Our forecast would be $218,900, and it would not change based on the size of the home. If $\overline{Y}$ is our forecast, the standard deviation of the Ys is the uncertainty relevant to our forecast. In Lawrence Construction this number is $45,256 (reported in Table 14–1).

We are now in a position to compare the $36,879 (a measure of how well the model does) to the $45,256 (a measure of how well we can do without the model). Adjusted R square is the accepted way to compare these two numbers:

$$\text{Adjusted R square} = 1 - \frac{(\text{Standard error of estimate})^2}{(\text{Sample standard deviation of Y})^2}$$

For the Lawrence Construction example, the adjusted R square is $1 - 36,879^2/45,256^2$, or 0.336.

To explain just what the adjusted R square tells us, we consider two extreme examples. First, consider the case where all the points fall exactly on the line (a perfect fit). In that case, the standard error of estimate will be zero and adjusted R square will be one. So an adjusted R square of one signifies a perfect fit. At the other extreme, suppose the model is of no help in predicting Y. In that case the line will be perfectly flat, $\hat{Y}$ will equal $\overline{Y}$ no matter what the value of X, the standard error of estimate will approximately equal the standard deviation of Y, and the adjusted R square will be approximately zero. So an adjusted R square of zero signifies the model is of no help in predicting Y (see Figure 14–4).

FIGURE 14–4

Adjusted R Square Scatter Plots

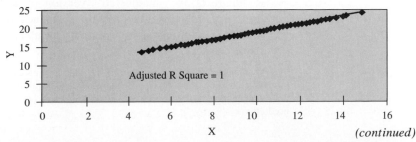

(continued)

FIGURE 14–4
(concluded)

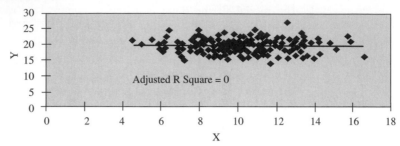

Of course most situations are somewhere between these two extremes, and the adjusted R square will fall somewhere between zero and one. The higher the adjusted R square, the smaller the standard error of estimate *relative* to the standard deviation of Y. Whereas the standard error of estimate is an *absolute* measure, adjusted R square is a *relative* measure. Whereas the standard error of estimate carries the same units as the Y variable, the adjusted R square is scaled to be between zero and one.

Finally, we offer one more way to interpret adjusted R square—as the percentage of variation explained by the model. You may remember that the square of any standard deviation carries the name variance. With this in mind, adjusted R squared is equal to one minus the ratio of the variance of the errors to the variance of the Ys. Since the variance of the Ys is what we face without the model and the variance of the errors is what we face if we use the model, the ratio of the two is the percentage of the variance in Y that is unexplained by the model. Since adjusted R square is one minus this ratio, adjusted R square is the percentage of variance (or variation) explained by the model.[9] The model in Lawrence Construction explains 33.6 percent of the variation in new-home construction cost. The variance in construction cost is \$45,256^2, 33.6 percent is explained by the model, and 66.4 percent (\$36,879^2) remains unexplained.

Two measures very similar to the adjusted R square are the **R square** and the **multiple R**. These latter two measures are clearly redundant in that the multiple R is the square root of R square. Because of this redundancy, we restrict our attention to R square.

R square is an "unadjusted" version of adjusted R square. Without getting into the details, adjusted R square "adjusts" R square downward to account for the number of independent variables used in the model. Adding

---

[9]Please be careful not to misinterpret adjusted R square as the percentage of time the model's predictions were correct. Because the model produces numerical forecasts of uncertain quantities, it makes no sense to talk in terms of correct versus incorrect predictions.

variables to the model will always decrease the sum of squared residuals and thereby increase the (unadjusted) R square. But the adjustments built into the calculation the standard error of estimate and the adjusted R square correctly account for the number of variables used. Adding variables to a model will not necessarily increase the adjusted R square. The difference between R square and adjusted R square is a function of the number of independent variables in the model relative to the number of data points. If there are lots of independent variables in the model and few data points, the adjusted R square will be much lower than the unadjusted. If there are a small number of independent variables and a huge number of data points, adjusted and unadjusted R square will be almost identical.

Standard Error of the Coefficients

We turn next to questions about the coefficients. Recall that we were careful to make a distinction between $\hat{b}$, the estimated coefficient, and b, the coefficient in equation (14–1). It should be clear that $\hat{b}$ is the slope of the fitted line (shown in Figure 14–3). It should also be clear that in the Lawrence Construction example, $\hat{b}$ equals 63.11. It might not be as clear what b is.

One way to think about b is as the slope of the imaginary line. The number b is the slope of the true underlying relationship between the mean of Y and X. Only with an infinite number of data points would we be able to know b.

Our fitted line is an estimate of the imaginary line (which has slope b). Although $\hat{b}$ is our best estimate of b, it is not perfect. Luckily we have some information about how close $\hat{b}$ is likely to be to the true b. The measure of how close $\hat{b}$ is to b (and b is to $\hat{b}$) is the standard error of the coefficient. In the Lawrence Construction example, the standard error of the $\hat{b}$ coefficient is 15.94. Our best estimate of b is 63.11 and the uncertainty surrounding that estimate has a standard deviation equal to 15.94. Our estimate of b is 63.11 plus or minus 15.94. Figure 14–5 shows this distribution.[10]

The standard error of the coefficient allows us to draw inferences about b and answer almost any question we have concerning b. Most regression software packages anticipate questions about whether b is different from zero. We are often interested in whether b is different from zero because a b of zero means there is no relationship between X and Y. The t-statistic (which is simply the estimated coefficient divided by its standard error) measures the distance between zero and $\hat{b}$ in units of standard error. The higher the magnitude of the t-statistics, the further zero is from $\hat{b}$ and the more confident we are that X and Y are actually related. The P-value goes one step further and tells you the probability of seeing t-values greater

---

[10]Forecasts of model coefficient are normally distributed if the number of data points is large.

FIGURE 14–5
Probability Distribution for b

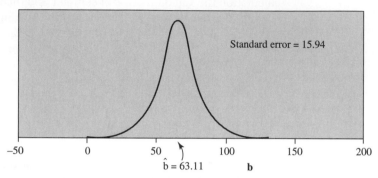

Standard error = 15.94

$\hat{b} = 63.11$ **b**

in magnitude than the t-statistic if b is actually equal to zero. In Lawrence Construction, if b is actually zero there is a 0.0005 probability of seeing a t-statistic with magnitude greater than 3.96. Because the t-statistic is so large in Lawrence Construction and the P-value so small, we are very confident that b is greater than zero. Based on the data alone, we are very confident that construction cost is related to the size of the home. Put even more simply, the relationship between the cost of a new home and its size is statistically significant.

Assumptions behind the Linear Regression Model

Earlier in this chapter we have seen how least squares can be used to fit the simple linear model to historical data. The resulting model can then be used to forecast the next occurrence of Y, the dependent variable, for a given value of X, the independent variable. This use of least squares to fit a forecasting model requires no assumptions. It can be applied to almost any situation, and a reasonable forecast results. At this level of analysis, least-squares modeling is equivalent simply to fitting a straight line through a cloud of points and interpolating or extrapolating for a new value of Y for a given X using the fitted line.

Although we need not make any assumptions to use this procedure, we leave an important question unanswered: How close can we expect the new Y to be to our forecast? Without some additional assumptions, we have no way of making a probability statement about the new Y. In many practical business situations, such a probability statement is an essential element in the decision-making process.

There is a procedure for measuring the uncertainty associated with a least-squares forecast that will produce a complete probability distribution for a new Y. This procedure brings real value and legitimacy to the regression modeling and forecasting process, changing it from a simple process—one step above graph paper and a ruler—to one that intelligently combines managerial judgment and statistical theory to produce believable point and interval forecasts.

That's the good news. The inevitable bad news is that to make probability statements about a new Y using a least-squares regression model, a variety of assumptions must be made. In other words, probability statements made using linear regression theory are true only if certain assumptions hold. You can thus see the importance of (1) understanding these assumptions, (2) knowing how to check their validity, (3) understanding the consequences of an incorrect assumption, and (4) knowing what can be done if the assumptions do not hold. This note addresses each of these four points for the four general assumptions behind linear regression. The model must be checked for (1) linearity, (2) independence, (3) homoscedasticity, and (4) normality.

For simplicity and convenience, most of this note will refer to the simple linear regression model. The material presented, however, can be applied as well to the general linear multivariate regression model.[11]

Linearity

The first and most fundamental assumption behind simple linear regression is that the model does indeed fit the situation at hand. The expectations for the Y variable, therefore, are linearly related to the value of the X variable. The equation expressing this relationship was given earlier as equation (14–2)

$$\text{Mean of } Y|X = a + bX,$$

which tells us that the mean value of Y changes in a linear manner with X.

As a further explanation of this assumption, recall that the mean of an uncertain quantity is the long-run average value expected from an infinite number of trials. Thus, if we held X constant, observed Y many times, and then calculated the average of the Ys, we would get a value pretty close to the mean of Y. Equation (14–2) states that if we did the same thing for a variety of different X values, a plot of the means of Y versus X would be a straight line with slope b and intercept a.

This suggests a very simple way to check to determine if the simple linear model fits the situation at hand. A scatter plot of Y versus X values should show a pattern that looks linear. Figure 14–6 shows a situation for which this assumption definitely does not hold. In this case, we say that the linear model exhibits **lack of fit**.

---

[11]The multivariate linear regression model expresses Y as a linear function of more than one independent variable.

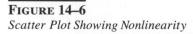

FIGURE 14–6

Scatter Plot Showing Nonlinearity

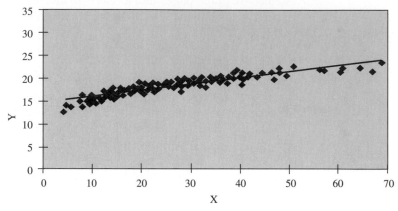

A second way to check for linearity is to examine a scatter plot of residuals versus fitted values for the least-squares regression line. This method is particularly useful when the fitted model contains several X-variables. If the model fits the data, the residuals should appear to have a mean of zero for all values of X. Figure 14–7 is a scatter plot of residuals versus fitted values for the data in Figure 14–6. Notice that these residuals tend to be negative at the ends of the plot and positive in the middle—indicating an inadequacy in the form of the fitted model.

In addition to these simple checks for lack of fit, there are statistical tests designed to measure the degree to which the proposed model fits the observed data.[12]

Using the least-squares model for forecasting requires considerable judgment on the part of the model builder, who must be willing to assume that equation (14–2) is reasonable over the relevant range of interest. In any case, the modeler should proceed only with the understanding that the accuracy of his or her forecasts is predicated on the assumption that the model is indeed correct.

What are the consequences of employing a model that does not fit the situation? Quite simply, the model gives inaccurate forecasts. Looking again at Figure 14–6 or 14–7, we see that the forecasts would be too high when X is either very low or very high and would be too low if X is close to the average.

What can be done if a prospective model exhibits a significant degree of lack of fit? Find a better model, probably one with a different functional

[12]For an explanation of one such test, see Terry E. Dielman, *Applied Regression Analysis for Business Economics* (Boston: PWS-Kent, 1991), pp. 196–97.

FIGURE 14–7
Scatter Plot of Residuals versus Fitted Showing Nonlinearity

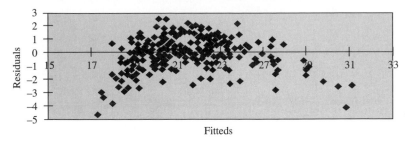

form. After studying Figure 14–6, for example, the model builder might assume that the mean value of Y is linearly related to the square root of X rather than to X itself. The resulting model

$$\text{Mean of } Y|X = a + bX^{1/2}$$

would still be a simple linear regression model (the new independent variable is now the square root of X) that could fit the situation better than the old model.

The remaining three assumptions all deal directly with the errors in the model. Recall that the complete specification of the simple linear model given earlier as equation (14–1),

$$Y = a + bX + \text{error},$$

includes an error term representing the uncertainty inherent in the situation. We assume that the mean of Y varies linearly with X and, furthermore, that each Y will vary consistently and randomly about its mean. The remaining three assumptions specify what we mean by consistently and randomly.

Independence

This second assumption is especially important in those situations where there is a definite time ordering of the X and Y observations. It states that error_i and error_j, the uncertain portions of Y for any two trials, must be uncorrelated—that is, the outcomes from different trials must be independent.

Figures 14–8 and 14–9 show a situation in which the assumption is violated. From the scatter plot of Y versus X in Figure 14–8, we see that the simple linear model fits the data quite well. Judging from this figure, everything looks fine. If, however, we plot the errors from the model in their correct order (Figure 14–9), we see a definite pattern: a run of nine consecutive negative residuals followed by a run of many positive residuals and another run of nine negative residuals. These long runs indicate the errors are

FIGURE 14–8

Scatter Plot of Y versus X Not in Time Order

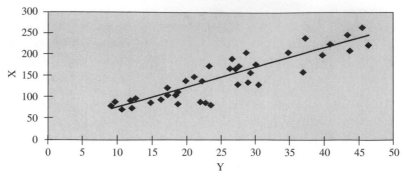

FIGURE 14–9

Time Series Plot of Residuals

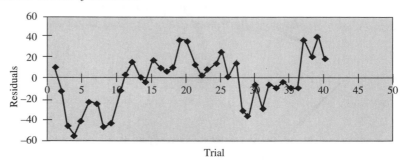

not random across time. This pattern indicates these errors do not satisfy the second assumption, independence. Because these errors are correlated with each other, we say they are **autocorrelated**.

What are the consequences of using the model when there is temporal dependence or autocorrelation within the errors? Again, the model will give poor forecasts. Looking carefully at Figure 14–9, we see that the time pattern of the residuals strongly suggests that the residual for the next trial, trial 41, will be positive. If we used the model to forecast observation 41, the forecast would likely be too low. Ignoring the autocorrelation, therefore, would lead to forecasts that are not as accurate as they could be. A secondary consequence of autocorrelation is that the least-squares estimates of the model coefficients are not as accurate as they could be.

Perhaps the easiest way to check temporal independence is to plot the least-squares residuals from the fitted model in time sequence (as in Figure

FIGURE 14–10

Scatter Plot of Residuals versus Fitted Showing Heteroscedasticity

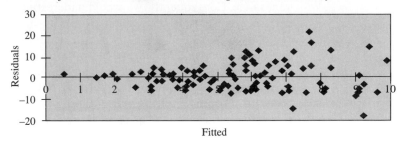

14–9). A visual inspection can often reveal significant patterns that suggest the independence assumption is violated. If the plot appears to represent a completely random sequence, however, the model builder should accept the assumption of temporal independence. Because this visual inspection can sometimes be misleading, however, a variety of tests are available that specifically address the hypothesis of independence across time.[13]

What can be done when significant autocorrelation presents itself? Again, we can only suggest that the model be improved to explain the cause of the autocorrelation. Often the model builder must find a new independent variable or use lagged versions of current variables.

Homoscedasticity

Homoscedasticity is a big word with a simple definition: constant variance. The homoscedasticity assumption in a model means that the variance or scatter of the errors does not change from trial to trial. By implication, there is a constant amount of uncertainty surrounding each Y, regardless of the value of X.

Figure 14–10 depicts a situation where **heteroscedasticity**, nonconstant variance, is present. Note that the variance or scatter of the Ys about the line increases with X. This situation is common. Uncertainty often increases with the size of the dependent variable. A second (less likely) way for heteroscedasticity to occur is across time—that is, when the variance of the errors increases or decreases with time (as shown by a time-series plot of the residuals).

How does heteroscedasticity affect our forecasts? Although the point forecasts themselves are not necessarily directly affected, heteroscedasticity does lead to a misspecification of the uncertainty surrounding a forecast. For

---

[13]For a description of statistical tests for temporal independence, see Terry E. Dielman, *Applied Regression Analysis for Business Economics,* pp. 271–77.

the example in Figure 14–10, linear regression theory would use an average measure of uncertainty (the standard error of estimate) over the entire relevant range. Consequently, we would underestimate the amount of actual uncertainty present in high-valued forecasts and overestimate the amount present in low-valued forecasts. Thus, heteroscedasticity can be critical in making decisions that require both a point and an interval forecast.

The presence of heteroscedasticity also indicates that least-squares coefficient estimates are not quite as good as they could be. Better estimates are obtained if more weight is put on those observations that are more certain (have lower variance) relative to those observations that are less certain. Because least-squares weights each observation equally (it minimizes the total sum of squared residuals), the high-variance observations exert too much influence on coefficient estimates.

We offer a pair of alternatives for dealing with heteroscedasticity. One approach is to transform the Y-variable, changing both its units and its interpretation. Instead of using the original Y-variable as the dependent variable, a model builder might try either the square root of Y, the logarithm of Y, or the reciprocal of Y as a new dependent variable. The hope is that this new dependent variable will not exhibit heteroscedasticity but will still be relevant to the decision at hand. The second alternative requires using a more sophisticated estimation procedure called weighted least squares.[14] Essentially, the model builder replaces the assumption of homoscedasticity with one that explains exactly how the variance of the errors changes with X.

Normality

The final assumption required to use the model to produce probability forecasts is that errors are normally distributed. Because these errors are the net effect of a very large number of unmeasurable or unexplainable factors that exert influence on the dependent variable, it is often reasonable to assume that the sum of a large number of small uncertain quantities follows the normal distribution.

Consequently, if the error is normally distributed, then Y for a given X will also be normal. This assumption is important because, knowing the probability distribution of the dependent variable, we can easily make probability statements. All we need in order to use the normal distribution is the mean value and the standard deviation.

One easy way to check this assumption is to plot a histogram of the residuals from the model. If the plot approximates the well-known bell-shaped normal curve, the assumption of normality is probably reasonable. Figure 14–11 shows a histogram of residuals that suggests nonnormality.

---

[14]Details of weighted least squares can be found in most texts on regression analysis or econometrics (e.g., Norman Draper and Harry Smith, *Applied Regression Analysis,* 2nd ed. [New York: John Wiley & Sons, 1981], pp. 108–16).

FIGURE 14–11

Histogram of Residuals Showing Nonnormality

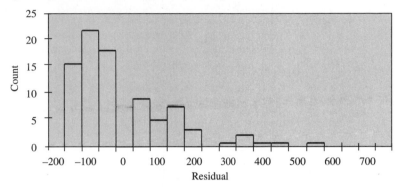

More sophisticated ways to test normality include the normal probability plot[15] and the chi-squared goodness-of-fit test.[16]

The consequences of an incorrect assumption of normality are not that severe. For example, if we used the normal distribution to make a probability statement for the example in Figure 14–11, our biggest mistake would be in underestimating the probability of a very large error. This inaccuracy would occur because the distribution of errors is skewed, but the normal is symmetric.

One possible solution to a problem of severe nonnormality is to take the logarithm of the original dependent variable. Doing so will change the nature of the Y-variable but may produce a new dependent variable that satisfies the normality assumption. Another solution is to abandon the normality assumption in favor of a more appropriate probability distribution for the errors. Unfortunately, this latter solution is difficult to implement.

Summary of Regression Assumptions

We have seen that to make intelligent use of the simple linear regression model in decision making, we must realize what assumptions we are making. Most of these assumptions can be stated using the error term in the model

$$Y = a + bX + error.$$

---

[15]Sort the residuals, assign sample cumulative probability $k/(n + 1)$ to the kth ranked residual, calculate the standard normal values for each of these probabilities (use = NORMSINV in Excel), scatter plot these standard normal values versus the sorted residuals. If the residuals are normal, the plot should be a straight line.

[16]Details of the chi-squared goodness-of-fit test can be found in most statistics texts. The test compares the observed cell frequencies of a histogram such as in Figure 14–11 with the frequencies expected if the observations came from a normal distribution.

TABLE 14–4   Diagnostic Checking of Regression Assumptions

Assumption	Diagnostic Checking	Possible Remedy
Linearity	Examine scatter plot of residuals versus fitted ($\hat{Y}$) for evidence of nonlinearity.	Try transforming X-variables or including new X-variables that explain/eliminate the nonlinearity.
Independence	Plot residuals in time order and look for patterns.	Include lagged variables in the model.
Homoscedasticity	Examine scatter plots of residuals versus fitted ($\hat{Y}$) and residuals versus time and look for changing scatter.	Transform the Y-variable.
Normality	Examine histogram of residuals. Look for departures from normal bell-curve shape.	Transform the Y-variable.

These assumptions are

- Linearity (the mean of Y must be a linear function of X).
- Independence (the errors must be uncorrelated with each other).
- Homoscedasticity (the errors must have constant variance).
- Normality (the errors must be normally distributed).

To check these assumptions we usually begin by examining the residuals from the least-squares regression model. Table 14–4 summarizes how to use residuals and residual plots to check each assumption. If the assumptions hold, the residuals should appear completely random and without pattern, no matter how they are viewed. Two very important ways to look at these residuals are to plot them in time sequence (checking for autocorrelation and, perhaps, heteroscedasticity) and scatter plot them against the fitted values (checking for lack of fit and heteroscedasticity). If inadequacies are found, this chapter has suggested alternatives for correcting—or at least improving—the situation. Table 14–4 summarizes these proposed remedies. We have also outlined the consequences of employing the model when these assumptions are violated.

Model-Building Philosophy

Linear (regression) models are used in a variety of business situations for a variety of purposes. One reason for their popularity is that they can be easily understood and implemented. All that is needed are data on two or more variables and a computer or calculator. With a minimal amount of effort, a manager obtains (1) an equation for the relationship between the dependent variable (Y) and one or more independent variables (the Xs), (2) a forecast of Y for any given set of X-values, and (3) a host of statistics to complement the analysis. Because so much is obtained so easily, the potential for misuse is great if the model builder is not careful about how the model is built and applied.

This section provides guidelines for the effective construction and application of linear models. We begin with a discussion and categorization of the various **uses of the linear model** (description, forecasting, and control). Whether a given model is appropriate for a particular use depends on the **nature of the relationship among the variables** (chance, correlation, or causal). We give particular attention to illustrating **the importance of the underlying relationship to the use of the model**.

Even when a manager understands what kind of relationship is necessary for the particular way the model will be used, there still remains the question of how best to combine this manager's knowledge of the situation with available data to build an effective model. We propose a **model-building procedure** for building a linear model when there is only limited prior knowledge about the underlying relationships among the variables. The procedure suggested attempts to maximize the use of the managers' prior knowledge and judgments, yet allows for the constructive and intelligent use of the available data. The objective is to guard against overreacting to peculiarities of the data and to build a sound and effective model that is consistent with both the modeler's prior knowledge and the information found in the data. In contrast to this advice on how to go about building a good model, we end this section with a list of things not to do, explaining some common mistakes associated with the building and using of linear models.

Uses of the Linear Model

Description is perhaps the least ambitious of the three uses. The purpose of the model is merely to describe and measure the historical relationship among two or more variables. Although the resulting model often has no direct or immediate impact on a decision, the knowledge gained implicitly affects future decisions. For example, if a regression model were used to describe the relationship between salaries and work experience of a group of employees, the only reason for constructing such a model would be to better understand the relative importance the company has placed on longevity or seniority in its salary practices.

A second use of the linear model is for **forecasting** the variable of interest (the dependent or Y-variable) for a given set of known, independent X-variables. The resulting forecast can be a valuable aid to decision making. For example, an office-cleaning company employs a linear model relating the time to clean an office building to the physical characteristics of the building (size, number of windows, number of offices, etc.). A forecast of how long it will take to clean a new office building is then used to decide how much to charge for cleaning services.

The most ambitious use of a linear model is **control**. Once the relationship between X and Y is established through a linear model, the decision maker then might use the model to decide how best to change the value of X to induce a desired change in Y. An example is a marketing-mix model relating the sales of a product to its price, advertising expenditures, and levels of distribution. The model is used for control if its purpose is to determine the optimum level of advertising. Here the manager changes X (advertising expenditures) to induce a change in Y (sales). Control is more ambitious than forecasting because of the requirements it places on the nature of the underlying relationship between the dependent and independent variables.

Nature of the Relationship among Variables

The strongest relationship between two variables is **causal**. If the value taken by the dependent Y-variable actually depends directly on the value of the independent X-variable, we say that X causes Y. For example, X, the level of advertising, causes Y, the level of sales. If we changed X, we would expect to see a change in Y.

Variables X and Y are positively **correlated** if high values of X tend to occur with high values of Y and vice versa. Negative correlation between two variables implies that high values of X occur with low values of Y. Obviously, if X causes Y, then X and Y are correlated,[17] but the opposite is not always true. Variables X and Y could be correlated because they both are caused by a third lurking variable, Z.

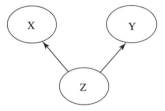

For example, X and Y, a student's scores on two separate tests of intelligence, would be correlated because both are caused by a lurking third variable, actual intelligence. Clearly, however, the student's score on one test does not cause the score on the second test.

---

[17]There are, however, pathological examples of variables that are causal but not linearly correlated.

We use a third category to refer to those situations in which no actual underlying relationship exists between X and Y even though the available data strongly suggest otherwise. **Chance** relationships are sure to be found if the model builder blindly dredges through a large number of independent variables in an attempt to find one that shows a strong historical relationship with the dependent variable of interest. If enough different X variables are considered, one or more will always be found that appear to be significantly related to Y.

A well-known example is that a relationship has been found to exist between the league that produced the World Series winner and the political party of the person elected president of the United States. Perhaps one can never be absolutely certain that there is not some underlying relationship between baseball and politics, but the much more plausible explanation for this observed relationship is that many people looked at many possible ways to predict winning candidates and this relationship was found and reported. Most likely it occurred by chance alone.

The Importance of the Underlying Relationship to the Use of the Model

If the eventual purpose of the model-building effort is to control, to change X in order to induce a desired change in Y, then it should be clear that the underlying relationship must be causal. If advertising causes sales, a change in advertising expenditures will change sales. In contrast, if the underlying relationship is only correlative, changing X does not change Y. In the example of the two IQ tests, if we increase a student's score on the first test (by giving the student the questions beforehand or simply adding 10 bonus points to the score), we do not expect to produce a change in the score the student will get on the second test.

The only way to prove and measure causality is by experimentation. To see if a change in X will change Y, we actually have to change X and observe what happens to Y. If we rely only on available data (sometimes referred to as happenstance or unplanned data), it is very difficult to distinguish causation from mere correlation.

For example, the observed correlation coefficient of $+0.90$ between the number of stork nests counted in the city of Stockholm, Sweden, and the number of babies born over several years in the 1930s and 1940s, did not prove, as some might suggest, that storks were responsible for babies. One explanation is that the racket made by the storks in the early-morning hours as they left their nests caused the inhabitants of the houses below to wake up, having trouble getting back to sleep, and . . . (you can figure out the rest). An alternate and more plausible explanation is the 30s and 40s were a period of affluence in Stockholm—with considerable home construction providing new nesting places for storks as well as living space for the expanding population. The point is that a strong correlation between X and Y does not necessarily imply that X causes Y. Thus, to use a linear model for control, the modeler must either experiment with X and observe the change in Y or rely on some prior knowledge or theoretical considerations as a basis to assume that X causes Y. Otherwise, we might find ourselves shooting storks to slow down the population growth of Stockholm.[18]

If the purpose of the model-building effort is forecasting, causation is not necessarily required and correlation can suffice. The student's score on the first IQ test can certainly be used to forecast the score on the second. Similarly, it might even be possible to use the number of stork nests to forecast the number of babies. One note on using X to forecast Y: X must be known in order to use it in the model to provide a forecast of Y. Thus, to be of direct use in forecasting, the stork/baby model would have to relate the number of babies born during a period to the number of stork nests at the beginning of the period.

Finally, if the purpose of the linear model is only to describe the observed historical relationship among two or more variables, its use is always appropriate. Even if there is no underlying relationship between X and Y, it is correct to use the linear model to make a statement about what was observed in the data.

The accompanying table summarizes the nature of the underlying relationship necessary for each of the three uses of the linear model.

Model Purpose	Relationship Required
Control	Causal
Forecasting	Causal or correlative
Descriptive	Causal or correlative or chance

We can look at the three uses of the linear model as three kinds of statements we wish to make about X and Y.

The weakest statement is simply a description of an observed relationship. For example, if the variables of interest are yearly sales and advertising expenditures, then the following is an example of a purely descriptive statement about their relationship:

The best (least-squares) linear relationship between sales and advertising expenditures was

$$\text{Sales} = \$400{,}000 + 2 \times \text{Advertising}$$

based on the previous 20 years of annual data.

---

[18]This and other examples of faulty inferences can be found in Robert E. Fuerst, "Inference Peddling," *Psychology Today,* March 1979, pp. 92–95.

Note that this statement requires no assumption about the underlying relationship; it is merely a statement about what happened.

A slightly stronger statement is

> Since advertising expenditures for next year will be $100,000, we expect sales to be $600,000.

This forecasting statement is appropriate only if we assume that the historical relationship is representative of some underlying relationship that will continue unchanged next year. We must assume that advertising and sales are correlated.

The strongest statement to bc made is

> If we increase our advertising $1, we expect an increase of $2 in salcs.

To make this statement, we must assume that advertising causes sales, and that the causal relationship continues unchanged next year.

Model-Building Procedure

Figure 14–12 outlines a six-step iterative procedure for building a linear model. The purpose of this procedure is to combine intelligently and carefully the modeler's knowledge of the situation with the information available in the data to produce a useful model.

The important thing to keep in mind is that modeling is not an exact science. When drawing conclusions from the data, the model builder must be careful to use sound judgment and to rely heavily on prior knowledge of the situation. It is quite acceptable to study the available data and learn from it, but the model builder must be stingy with its use to avoid being misled into believing in a relationship that happened in the past but that will probably not happen in the future.[19]

1. Determine the Dependent Variable (Y)   The purpose of the modeling effort usually dictates what quantity is of interest. Exactly how to define the dependent variable, however, is not. Suppose we wish to forecast sales. Should it be sales in units or in dollars? Should we use constant dollars or current dollars? Should it be total sales or our share of the total market? Should it be our sales or industry sales? Should it be sales for a month,

---

[19]This admonition to be stingy with the use of data assumes we are working with a small data set. With a large data set, the model builder has the luxury of setting aside or holding out a subset of the data for later use in validating a candidate model. Using this split-sample technique, the model builder can be more aggressive in exploring the data in the modeling set knowing that the candidate model will be tested on the holdout sample. For additional details on this split-sample technique, see David G. Kleinbaum et al., *Applied Regression Analysis and Other Multivariate Models,* 2nd ed. (Boston: PWS-Kent, 1988), pp. 328–31.

FIGURE 14–12
Interactive Model Building Procedure

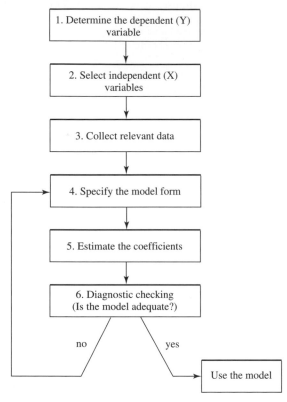

quarter, or year? Maybe we should look at change in sales. By sales, do we mean shipments, orders, or demand?

In making the choice of dependent variables, three criteria should be considered. How *useful* is the dependent variable to the purposes for which the model is being built? A forecast of sales for next quarter may be more useful than a forecast of sales for next year if we update our production schedule quarterly. Second, how *attainable* is the dependent variable that is needed? Some dependent variables are easier to collect than others. Number of shipments is probably much easier to measure and obtain than total number of units demanded, which is almost impossible to measure because it is meant to include lost sales. The last criterion is how *modelable* the variable is. This consideration ties in with the considerations of step 4, determining the functional form of the model. The dependent variable is but one side of the model equation, and as such it must be chosen to make sense when coupled with the independent variables. For example, whether to use sales or change in sales depends on which makes better sense in light of the available independent variables.

2. Choose the Potential Independent Variables   The primary concern in choosing the list of potential independent (X) variables is that they make sense. The model builder should consider only those variables for which there is reason to believe (from prior experience or theory) that they have an effect on the dependent variable. It should be kept in mind, however, that even as a blind hog sometimes finds an acorn, a long list of nonsensical X-variables will be sure to include one or more that show a strong historical relationship to Y. For such a finding to have meaning (i.e., to be due to an actual relationship rather than chance), the list of X-variables must be limited to those that have been preselected as reasonable.

In addition to making sense, the attainability and usefulness of a variable should also be considered. If the model is to be used for forecasting, the independent variables must be known (or at least more predictable than the dependent variable) in order to be functional. Similarly, the decision maker must be able to manipulate the independent variable if it is to be used to control the dependent variable.

3. Collect Relevant Data   The key to this step is to collect data that are from similar situations. Each observation must be similar to all others in the sense that the underlying relationship between the Xs and Y must be the same in each case. It is expected that the Xs change from observation to observation, but the relationship (i.e., the coefficients of the underlying model) must remain constant. Thus, the data must come from situations that are indistinguishable from each other in the sense that the expectation of Y is a function only of the Xs, and not on some other factor. If another factor exists that can be used to distinguish the data, that factor is a candidate for an independent variable. A second way to handle distinguishable data is to separate the data into smaller sets that can reasonably be considered to represent similarly indistinguishable situations.

4. Hypothesize the Model Form   This step is probably the most important and requires the most judgment. The model builder must attempt to incorporate his or her knowledge of the situation (based on experiences and available theory) into a single algebraic equation. The equation should be as simple as possible, yet remain consistent with the modeler's knowledge of the important complexities of the situation.

Simpler models are generally better models for two reasons. First, the simpler the model, the less it depends on the peculiarities and uncertainties of the limited data set to which it was fit. The more complicated the model, the better it will fit the data, but the more likely it will be to go wrong sometime in the future. A second reason for preferring a simple model is that it will be easier to use.

The desire for a simple model, however, conflicts with the importance of building a model that is entirely consistent with the manager's knowledge of the situation. Each model form implicitly makes certain assumptions about the way things work. The modeler must scrutinize a candidate model to be sure she understands its implications and assumptions and agrees with them.

For example, if Q is the quantity demanded of a given product and P its price, three reasonable functional forms for the relationship between Q and P are

$$Q = a + bP \tag{14–4}$$

$$Q = a + b(1/P) \tag{14–5}$$

$$\ln(Q) = a + b\ln(P) \tag{14–6}$$

All three of these models are relatively simple, although an argument can be made that (14–4) is the simplest.

A careful look at these models clarifies the differences in the assumptions behind each. Model (14–4) says that an increase in P of one unit will change Q by b units at every level of P. Therefore, we probably expect b to be negative, but wonder if the effect of price on quantity can be the same no matter what the absolute level of price. In addition, the model says that when P = 0, Q will equal a. Also, for a P large enough, Q will be negative. Obviously, this model can only be good over a limited range of prices. Model (14–5) says that a unit increase in price will change Q by an amount that decreases with the level of price, perhaps something that makes a little more sense. In addition, because b will be positive if Q decreases as P increases, model (14–5) says that as P decreases to zero, Q becomes extremely large. Likewise, as P becomes very large, Q approaches the value a. Thus, we would expect a to be about zero. Model (14–5) may make more sense than model (14–4) and it is definitely better if the range of prices used is large.

Finally, model (14–6) may appear to be weird, but it does have a very important property. It says that a percentage change in price produces the same percentage change in Q at all levels of price. This property is called constant elasticity. The elasticity, or ratio of the percentage change in Q to the percentage change in P, is measured by b in this equation.

In summary, each model makes a different statement about the relationship between P and Q. We stress the importance of recognizing the assumptions and implications behind a candidate model form and judging their appropriateness before fitting the model to the data.

5. Fitting the Model   This is perhaps the easiest of the steps. Ordinary least squares is used to select the values of the model coefficients that minimize the sum of squared errors between past actual Y values and model predictions. Details of least-squares estimation were given earlier.

6. Diagnostic Checking   There are two steps in checking the proposed model. The first is to make sure all the assumptions required for the use of a linear model (homoscedasticity, lack of autocorrelation, etc.) are met. An earlier section addresses these issues and suggests ways to change the model (in effect, a return to step 4) if inadequacies are found.

The second aspect of diagnostic checking is testing the significance of the model coefficients. Consistent with the desire to build the simplest possible model and to avoid overreacting to the peculiarities of the data is the importance of checking to make sure the estimated coefficients are significantly different from zero. If a coefficient is not very different from zero (as measured by the t-statistic and p-value associated with that coefficient), the model builder should seriously consider removing the associated X-variable from the model. The new model will be simpler and will fit the data almost as well.

Because we know that adding any independent variable to the model will improve the fit and show some measure of significance, it is important to be conservative when choosing those variables to remain. The final model should include only those variables that we are convinced are actually related to the dependent variables. This conviction comes from both our knowledge of the situation and the observed relationship in the data. Dropping an insignificant variable from the model is a return to step 4.

Some caution must be exercised as variables are added and deleted from a model. Always keep in mind that if a single variable is added to or deleted from a model, the relative importance of all other variables changes. Thus, if two coefficients in a candidate model are not significant, it is a good idea to remove them one at a time. It can happen that once the first variable is dropped, the other may then appear significant. This often happens if the two X-variables in question are correlated with each other. The low significance of both t-statistics means that both Xs do not need to be in the model together. It does not necessarily mean that neither one belongs in the model.

Common Mistakes

In contrast to all that has been said about how to build a model, we close with a list of things *not* to do. By no means an exhaustive list, what follows are the most commonly made mistakes in building and using linear models.

The Fishing Expedition   The modeling effort begins with a brainstormed list of all the independent variables that could conceivably be related to the dependent variable. Data are gathered on as many of these as possible, and the modeler spends the rest of the time weeding through the mass of numbers. Just as it is no surprise that a diligent fisherman eventually catches something, it is also quite clear that such a procedure will probably produce a model that fits the data quite well. The important question, however, is whether the resulting model fits well because it is an accurate representation of some underlying relationship or because it happened by chance to be the best-fitting model of the many tried.

More Is Better   If a simple one- or two-variable model works well, will not a four- or five-variable model work even better? Although it is true that making a model more complicated will always improve the fit, it is another matter to assume that the better the fit, the more useful the model. An incredibly complicated model will certainly conform to the peculiarities of the available data and fit the past quite well, but it will also probably go wrong when used to predict the future.

Forecasting with a Forecast   No matter how strong the relationship between X and Y, the ability to use X to forecast Y is predicated on knowing X at the time the forecast is needed. It does no good to build a model to help forecast automobile sales as a function of gasoline prices if gasoline prices are just as hard to forecast as automobile sales.

Correlation as Causation   A strong linear relationship between X and Y does not necessarily mean that if you change X, you can cause a corresponding change in Y. Don't kill storks as a means of birth control.

What Was the R^2?   The percentage of variance explained (R^2) is often used as a single measure of the quality of a linear model. There are two good reasons you should not always be impressed with a high R^2: (1) complicated models and small data sets make it easy to get a high R^2, and (2) if both Y and X exhibit a trend across time (as do almost all business and economic variables), then a high R^2 is to be expected, irrespective of any real relationship between the two variables. In addition, R^2 attempts to check only the quality of fit of the regression, and we all know that a host of other things must be considered (residual plots, t-statistics, etc.) when judging a model.

Extrapolation—A Leap of Faith   Users often forget the assumptions that must be made in order to apply the model when forecasting a new situation. Foremost among them is the assumption that the underlying relationship specified by the model holds for the new situation. The new situation can be different only in that it involves a new set of X-values (that's the whole point of regression), but everything else (i.e., the relationship between the Y and Xs) must remain the same.

Summary

This section has briefly described the various uses of a linear model (description, forecasting, and control) and the types of relationships between variables (causal, correlative, and chance). A table summarizes the kinds of relationships necessary to each of these three uses.

The remainder of this section discussed how to build a good model. The main idea was that model building is much more than fitting curves to data. The procedure put forth called for a majority of effort to be spent in analyzing the situation, selecting variables, and specifying a form for the model—all before using a computer to calculate coefficients and fit curves. The iterative procedure then called for a judicious use of the data to estimate coefficients, check assumptions, test the significance of proposed variables, and refine ideas about how things work.

Forecasting Using the Linear Regression Model

In the previous section, we presented a procedure for building a model that will provide reliable forecasts of the relevant uncertain quantity (the Y-variable), given knowledge of one or more influential factors (X-variables). For a model to be useful in this forecasting role, it must (1) make sense (i.e, be consistent with the model builder's beliefs about the way things work); (2) be simple (i.e., not contain extraneous, insignificant terms); and (3) meet the assumptions underlying the model. Given that such a model has been built, exactly how do you use the model to forecast?

Point Forecast

The first step in using the chosen model to forecast is an easy one. Simply substitute the relevant X-value(s)[20] into the fitted equation

$$\hat{Y} = \hat{a} + \hat{b}(X)$$

to calculate $\hat{Y}$, the point forecast of Y for the given value of X.

As an example, recall that earlier in this chapter we used the construction cost (Y) and the square footage (X) of the 30 most recent homes built by Lawrence Construction to fit the model

$$\hat{Y} = \$56,104 + 63.11X.$$

To forecast the cost of a new home with 2,500 square feet, we substituted X = 2,500 into the least squares equation given above to calculate $\hat{Y}$ = $213,879. Thus, the best guess for the construction cost of a Lawrence new home containing 2,500 square feet, based on the fitted model and all the accompanying assumptions,[21] is $213,879.

For many purposes, this single point forecast will suffice. Early in conversations with prospective buyers, Baugher may be content to provide a single number in response to inquiries about the "typical" cost of a 2,500 square-foot home. Very quickly, however, Baugher would do well to point out that not every 2,500 square foot home costs exactly $213,879. Quite obviously, some will cost more and some will cost less depending on a host of factors. There is uncertainty in how much a new 2,500 sqare foot home will end up costing. As the conversation progresses, Baugher may want to provide some information about this range of possible costs. Offering a range of possible costs represents moving beyond a single point forecast to an interval forecast. The ultimate interval forecast is a complete probability distribution of costs. We turn now to the general question of how to construct a probability distribution for the uncertain Y-variable at a given value of X.

---

[20]Throughout this section, we refer to the simple (one-variable) linear model. The ideas presented, however, generalize to the multiple linear model.

[21]These assumptions (linearity, independence, homoskedasticity, and normality) are discussed in section 14.5.

Interval Forecast

The first step in obtaining the probability distribution for a new Y is to determine what shape this distribution will have. If we are willing to assume that the distribution of Y for a given value of X is normal, then the distribution of a new Y will also be normal.[22] Recall that a histogram of the residuals is a good way to check this assumption.

Once we decide to use the normal distribution, two quantities must be determined: the mean and the standard deviation. It makes sense that $\hat{Y}$, the point forecast, should be the mean of this distribution. Determining the standard deviation—the measure of how far Y is likely to be from $\hat{Y}$—is a little tricky.

At first you might think that the standard error of estimate should be used. After all, the standard error of estimate is the estimate of the unexplainable, random error in Y for a given X. As such, it measures how far Y is likely to be from a + bX, the unknown mean of Y. If we did know the mean of Y (i.e., if we knew a and b and did not have to estimate them using our small sample of n observations), then the standard error of estimate could be used. But because we do not know the actual mean of Y and must rely on the imperfect estimate ($\hat{Y}$), we face more uncertainty than is measured by the standard error of estimate.

When $\hat{Y}$ is used to forecast Y, there are two components of error that must be faced:

$$\text{Forecast error} = \text{random error} + \text{fitted error}$$
$$(Y - \hat{Y}) = (Y - \text{mean of Y}) + (\text{mean of Y} - \hat{Y})$$

The error in the forecast is composed of the random, unavoidable error in the process and the fitted error we make because our fitted regression line only estimates the true regression line.

Fortunately, theory provides a measure—the **standard error of fitted**—of the amount of fitted error faced. This standard error of fitted measures how far the actual mean of Y is likely to be from $\hat{Y}$. Memorizing the exact expression[23] for this standard deviation is usually not necessary because this measure is included in many commercially available regression-software packages. It might be useful, however, to note that the standard error of fitted depends on three things: (1) the standard error or estimate (the amount of underlying uncertainty in the process dictates the amount of uncertainty in every estimate associated with the model); (2) the sample size (as expected, the standard error of fitted decreases with the square root of the sample size); and (3) the relative size of the known X used to forecast Y (the standard error of fitted is smallest for X-values close to the average of the Xs and largest for extreme X-values).

---

[22]If n, the number of data points, is small, the t-distribution should be used instead of the normal distribution.

[23]Standard error of fitted = Standard error of estimate $[1/n + (X - \overline{X})^2/\Sigma(X - \overline{X})^2]^{1/2}$, where X is the current X used to forecast Y, $\overline{X}$ is the sample average of the n observed Xs, and $\Sigma(X - \overline{X})^2$ is the sum of squares of the n observed Xs about $\overline{X}$.

FIGURE 14–13

Confidence Intervals for the Mean of Y|X

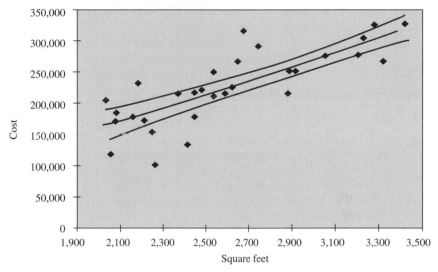

The standard error of fitted may be used to construct a confidence limit for the unknown, actual regression line. Figure 14–13 graphs these confidence limits ($\hat{Y}$ plus and minus two standard error of fitted) for Lawrence's mean cost as a function of the new home's square footage. Notice that the confidence limits are smallest near the sample average of the Xs and largest at the extremes. These curved confidence bounds should be intuitively appealing; they show the fitted model to be a better predictor at typical X-values than at extreme X-values.

Keep in mind, however, that these confidence limits account only for the sampling uncertainty in the fitted equation. They are curved because the effect of the uncertainty in b, the slope, is magnified at the extremes. A completely separate reason for a decrease in predictive ability at extreme X-values is that the model assumptions might hold only for a limited range of X-values. The possibility that the model assumptions are more tenuous at extreme X-values is not accounted for in these confidence intervals. The limits are drawn assuming that the mean of Y|X = a + bX for all X.

Because the forecast error, or prediction error, is the sum of the random error and the fitted error, the uncertainty surrounding the forecast should be a combination of these two components. The measure of the uncertainty surrounding the prediction is called the **standard error of prediction**. The standard error of prediction is the appropriate standard deviation to use in the probability distribution for a new Y. Because the random error and the fitted error are independent and add together to form the prediction error, the standard error of prediction is the square root of the sum of the squares of the standard deviations of the components:

$$\text{Standard error of prediction} = [(\text{Standard error of estimate})^2 + (\text{Standard error of fitted})^2]^{1/2}$$

Many commercially available regression packages will also provide the standard error of prediction.

We have now completed the forecasting task. The distribution of a new Y will be normal, with mean $\hat{Y}$ and standard deviation equal to the standard error of prediction. Because the standard error of fitted is a component in the standard error of prediction, the standard error of prediction will be a function of all the things that affect standard error of fitted. In particular, as the sample size increases, the uncertainty in the fitted value decreases (standard error of fitted goes to zero), and the standard error of prediction will approach the standard error of estimate.

For the Lawrence Construction example, the standard error of prediction is calculated to be $37,810, a value only slightly higher than the standard error of estimate of $36,879. The distribution of the construction cost of a 2,500 square-foot home is normal with a mean of $213,879 and a standard deviation equal to $37,810. Jerry Baugher of Lawrence Construction is now very prepared to discuss the range of possible costs of a new 2,500 square-foot home. Although this probability distribution is the ultimate answer to his forecasting question, it is not an answer many audiences are prepared to hear. Baugher's next task is to decide how much of this information to communicate to his audience.

Analogy to Simple Random Sampling

This section has addressed several issues surrounding the use of a fitted simple linear model to forecast an uncertain Y given knowledge of a predictor X-variable. The concepts and terminology presented can be directly compared with simple random sampling, wherein a random sample of n observations from a normal population is used to forecast a new uncertain observations.

In simple random sampling, there is no predictor X-variable. The mean of Y is assumed to be a constant, and $\overline{Y}$, the sample average of the n observed Ys, is used as the point forecast of a new uncertain Y. The sample standard deviation, s, measures the uncertainty in Y about the mean of Y and is directly analogous to the standard error of estimate. The standard deviation $s/\sqrt{n}$ measures how close the unknown mean of Y is likely to be to $\overline{Y}$. The standard error of fitted associated with the linear model is analogous to $s/\sqrt{n}$.

Finally, in Chapter 12 we learned that $\sqrt{(s/\sqrt{n})^2 + (s/\sqrt{m})^2}$ is the standard deviation to use when $\overline{Y}$ is used to forecast a new sample average of size m. Because forecasting a new Y is equivalent to forecasting a new sample average of size $m=1$, the forecast of a new Y will have a standard deviation equal to $\sqrt{(s/\sqrt{n})^2 + (s/\sqrt{1})^2}$ which can be rewritten as $s\sqrt{1/n + 1}$. Notice that this standard deviation accounts for the two sources of uncertainty faced

FIGURE 14–14

Forecasting an Uncertain Y-Variable

Using the Simple Linear Model	*Using Simple Random Sampling from a Normal Population*

Assumes:
  Mean of $Y|X = a + bX$
  Independence
  Homoscedasticity
  Normality
	Assumes random sampling from a normal population

Samples n (X, Y) pairs	Samples n Ys
Point forecast is $\hat{Y} = \hat{a} + \hat{b}(X)$.	Point forecast is $\overline{Y}$.
The standard error of estimate measures the uncertainty in Y about the mean of Y.	The sample standard deviation, s, measures the uncertainty in Y about the mean of Y.
The standard error of fitted measures the uncertainty in the mean of Y about $\hat{Y}$.	The standard deviation $s/\sqrt{n}$ measures the uncertainty in the mean of Y about $\overline{Y}$.
The standard error of prediction measures the uncertainty in Y about $\hat{Y}$.	The standard deviation, $s\sqrt{1/n + 1}$, measures the uncertainty in Y about $\overline{Y}$.

when $\overline{Y}$ is used to forecast a new Y: the sampling error association with $\overline{Y}$ $(s/\sqrt{n})$ and the underiling uncertainty in Y (s). Notice also that this standard deviation is analogous to the standard deviation of prediction associated with the linear regression model.

Figure 14–14 summarizes the comparisons between forecasting using the simple linear model and simple random sampling.

Using Dummy Variables to Represent Categorical Variables

In a number of practical business situations, an important explanatory variable is categorical rather than numerical. For instance, an MBA's starting salary may be related to his or her undergraduate degree program (liberal arts, business, science, or engineering). The sales of a consumer packaged good may be related to its position in the store (checkout register versus regular store rack). Or the price-to-earnings ratio of a stock may be related to the presence (absence) of a dividend (irrespective of the size of the dividend). In each of these examples, the potential explanatory variable is not numerically scaled and thus not directly usable as an independent X-variable in a linear model. This section describes and illustrates a technique (called dummy variables) for transforming categorical information into numerically scaled variables suitable for use in a linear model.

Example

An extensive questionnaire was administered to several autoworkers in four U.S. assembly plants. The variable of interest, Y, was a weighted combination

TABLE 14–5   Reported Levels of Job Satisfaction for Two Plants

	Plant A	Plant B
	59	67
	55	57
	61	57
	57	54
	55	56
	45	59
	64	38
	58	43
	48	52
	57	51
Average	55.9	53.4
Standard deviation	5.7	8.2

of responses to several questions measuring job satisfaction. Management wanted to compare the levels of reported job satisfaction at the four plants. A small subsample of the data from two plants is given in Table 14–5.

To use a linear model to describe the relationship between job satisfaction and plant, we must first convert the plant information into a form suitable for use with a linear model. We do this by creating a new variable, D, defined to equal 1 if the reporting employee is from plant B and 0 if the employee is from plant A. Variable D is called a dummy or 0-1 variable. As we shall see, the assignment of 0 to plant A and 1 to plant B is arbitrary. The model would work just as well if $D = 1$ referred to A and $D = 0$ referred to B. The data and a plot of Y (job satisfaction score) versus D (the dummy variable used to designate plant) are given in Figure 14–15.

Let us now consider the linear model

$$\text{Mean}(Y) = a + bD.$$

At $D = 0$ (corresponding to plant A), the model says that the mean of Y is equal to a, a constant. At $D = 1$ (corresponding to plant B), the model says the mean of Y is equal to a different constant, $a + b$. This model assumes only that the mean of Y is different for the two plants. When we fit the model to the data, coefficient a is the estimate of the mean of Y for plant A and coefficient b measures the difference between the mean of Y for plant B and the mean of Y for plant A. The model is capable of providing only two point forecasts, one corresponding to $D = 0$ (plant A) and the other corresponding to $D = 1$ (plant B). Not surprisingly, the fitted model turns out to be

$$Y = 55.9 - 2.5(D).$$

FIGURE 14–15

Y versus D

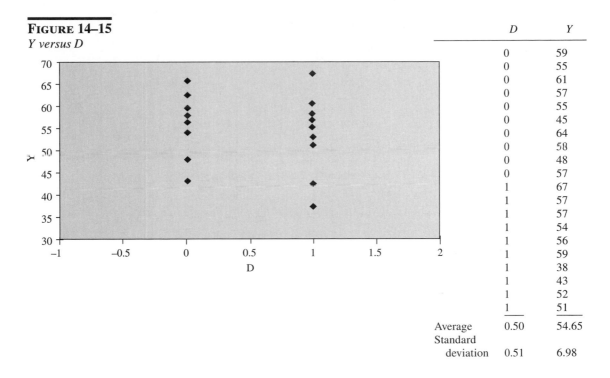

D	Y
0	59
0	55
0	61
0	57
0	55
0	45
0	64
0	58
0	48
0	57
1	67
1	57
1	57
1	54
1	56
1	59
1	38
1	43
1	52
1	51

	D	Y
Average	0.50	54.65
Standard deviation	0.51	6.98

This least-squares fitted line goes through the sample averages of the two groups of data.

Dummy Variables for More than Two Groups

How would we use this dummy-variable technique if there were more than two groups? Suppose we had data from workers in all four plants. Could we define D as

> D = 0 if plant A
> D = 1 if plant B
> D = 2 if plant C
> D = 3 if plant D

and use the linear model mean $(Y) = a + b(D)$?

In general, the answer is no. This model, with only one X-variable, assumes that the mean of Y changes linearly as we move from plant A to B to C to D. It assumes that the means of the four plants fall on a straight line, and we usually have no reason to expect the group means to line up in such a manner. A less restrictive assumption is that the means of Y for the four plants can each be different, with no constraints on the ordering or relative size of the group means.

To incorporate this assumption into a linear model, we must define more than one dummy variable. Let D_B, D_C, D_D, be defined as

$$D_B = \begin{cases} 1 & \text{if plant B} \\ 0 & \text{if not} \end{cases}$$

$$D_C = \begin{cases} 1 & \text{if plant C} \\ 0 & \text{if not} \end{cases}$$

$$D_D = \begin{cases} 1 & \text{if plant D} \\ 0 & \text{if not} \end{cases}$$

and consider the multiple linear model

$$\text{Mean}(Y) = a + b1(D_B) + b2(D_C) + b3(D_D).$$

Substituting, in turn, the dummy-variable values associated with each of the four plants shows that this model specifies a separate mean of Y for each of the four plants:

Plant	D_B	D_C	D_D	Mean(Y)
A	0	0	0	a
B	1	0	0	a + b1
C	0	1	0	a + b2
D	0	0	1	a + b3

The constant term in the model is interpreted as the mean of the baseline group designated if all dummies are set equal to 0 (plant A). Each of the b-coefficients are interpreted as the difference between the mean of the designated group and the mean of the baseline group.

In general, p-1 dummy variables are used to represent p groups or categories. Any of the p groups may be chosen to be the baseline group (designated if all dummies equal zero), and the remaining p-1 groups each correspond to a single 0-1 dummy. The linear model constructed in this manner assumes a separate and distinct mean for each group, with no restrictions on the ordering or relative size of the group means. Given the flexibility of a separate constant coefficient for each of the p groups, the least-squares fitted model will always go through the sample averages of all the groups.

Useful Data Transformations

One of the important assumptions behind the linear model is that the mean of Y is linearly related to X:

$$\text{Mean of } Y|X = a + bX.$$

An implication of this assumption is that the change in the mean of Y for a unit increase in X is equal to b, a constant, regardless of the magnitude of X. For example, the point forecast of Y is b units higher at $X = 11$ than at

X = 10, and it is also b units higher at X = 91 than at X = 90, even though on a percentage basis the change from 90 to 91 is much smaller than the change from 10 to 11. Although this linearity assumption is often reasonable, especially over a limited range of X and Y values, situations will arise where it is not tenable.

In some cases, the change in Y for a unit increase in X will decrease with the size of X. Think of the relationship between sales (measured in dollars) and the level of sales force effort (measured in number of salespeople). As the number of salespeople assigned to a region increases, the resulting sales should increase, but at a rate that eventually decreases. Because customers will be serviced in decreasing order of their sales potential, assigning a larger sales force means going after increasingly smaller customers and thus decreasing the average sales per salesperson. A plot of sales versus sales force would show a nonlinear, **decelerating** relationship as in Figure 14–16.

In still other situations, the relationship between Y and X may be nonlinear and **accelerating**. Think of the relationship between the accumulated value of an investment and the number of periods it is held. If the investment earns a fairly constant per-period rate of return over its life, its accumulated value will increase by an ever-increasing amount. A plot of accumulated value versus number of periods held (see Figure 14–17) shows this nonlinear, accelerating relationship.

This section addresses what can be done in those situations where it is not reasonable to assume that the relationship between Y and X is linear. The technique proposed is called transformation of variables, and the main idea is to create carefully a new variable from one of the old variables in such a way that the new, transformed variable can then be used in a linear model.

FIGURE 14–16

Decelerating Relationship

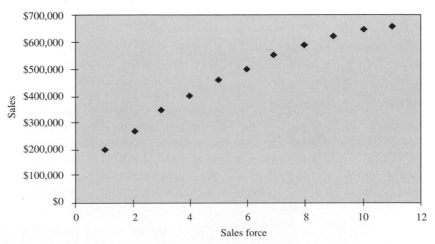

FIGURE 14–17

Accelerating Relationship

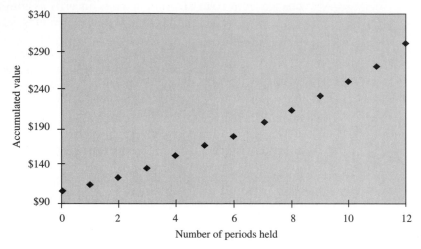

Example

For the last several months, a spare-parts manufacturing company has been conducting an experiment on the effect of batch size on productivity. It tried several different batch sizes and carefully kept track of the total direct labor hours required to produce the monthly production quota of 100,000 units. The results showed that total labor hours decreased with batch size:

Hours	Batch Size (number of units)
72.0	1,000
47.0	2,000
42.0	2,500
38.0	3,125
34.5	4,000
32.0	5,000
30.0	6,250

A plot of hours versus batch size in Figure 14–18 shows the relationship to be decidedly nonlinear and decelerating. The change in hours for a change in batch size from 1,000 to 2,000 (a decrease of 25 hours) is much larger than the change in number of hours for the same size change in batch size from 4,000 to 5,000 (a decrease of 2.5 hours).

If we ignored this decelerating nonlinearity and fit the simple linear model

$$\text{Hours} = a + b \text{ (batch size)}$$

FIGURE 14–18

Total Labor Hours versus Batch Size

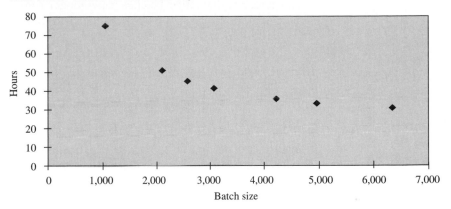

FIGURE 14–19   *Residual Scatter Plot*

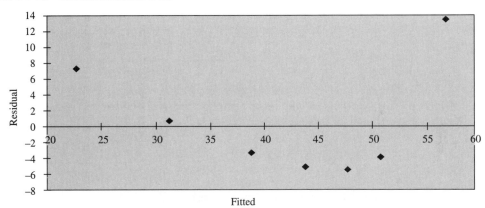

to these data, we might get a large R^2 and significant t-statistic. But a plot of the data or the model residuals (see Figure 14–19) would clearly show that this model does not fit. The model underforecasts at both high and low batch sizes and overforecasts at intermediate values. This systematic pattern in the residuals indicates that the model does not fit and should not be used.

We now need some way to model this nonlinear, decelerating relationship between hours and batch size. One approach is to use a carefully chosen function of the batch-size variable as the independent variable in a new, simple linear model. The creation of a new variable from an old one is called a **transformation**, and several ways are available to do it. The conversion of degrees Fahrenheit to degrees Celsius is one common example of the transformation of a variable. In the spare-parts manufacturer's case, we need to choose a transformation such that the relationship between hours and the transformed batch-size variable is linear.

The search for a useful transformation begins with an examination of the situation being modeled. If we ask ourselves why hours decrease with batch size, we realize that larger batches mean longer runs and fewer setups. Since a fixed number of parts (100,000) were made each month, the actual run time to produce the parts was fairly constant. Batch size will affect only the amount of time spent in setup activities, and this setup time is probably proportional to the number of batches produced. The number of batches can be calculated as 100,000 times the reciprocal of batch size, or

$$\text{Number of batches} = 100,000 \ (1/\text{batch size}).$$

This conversion from batch size to number of batches is an example of a transformation of variables. Because it makes sense that hours should be linearly related to number of batches, the simple linear model

$$\text{Hours} = a + b \ (\text{number of batches})$$

will be tried. The coefficient a in this model represents the run time for the 100,000 parts, and the coefficient b represents the setup time for each batch.

Converting the available batch-size data to number of batches and plotting hours versus number of batches (see Figure 14–20) shows just how well this transformation works (and how carefully this example was constructed):

Hours	Batch Size	Number of Batches
72.0	1,000	100
47.0	2,000	50
42.0	2,500	40
38.0	3,125	32
34.5	4,000	25
32.0	5,000	20
30.0	6,250	16

This transformation works because it changes the scale of the independent variable in just the right way. Notice that the change in number of batches for a change in batch size from 1,000 to 2,000 (a decrease of 50 batches) is much larger than the change in number of batches for the same size change in batch size from 4,000 to 5,000 (a decrease of only five batches).

The fitted model

$$\text{Hours} = 22.0 + 0.5 \ (\text{Number of batches})$$

fits the data perfectly and shows that it takes 22 hours to make the 100,000 units and 0.5 hours to set up each batch.

This simple example has illustrated the use of the transformation of variables to model a nonlinear relationship between two variables. First, it was noted that the relationship between hours and batch size was not linear, but rather decelerating. A plot of hours versus batch size confirmed this non-linearity and suggested that the linear model would not fit. As an alternative,

FIGURE 14–20
Hours versus Number of Batches

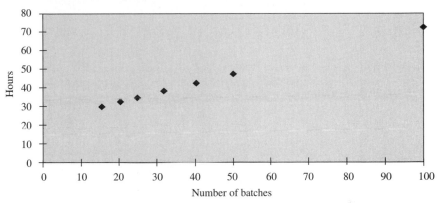

the model, Hours = a + b (Number of batches), was proposed. In one sense, this model is linear; number of hours is expressed as a linear function of number of batches. The simple linear model and least squares can now be used with number of batches as the independent variable. In a separate sense, however, this model is nonlinear. If we rewrite it as

$$\text{Hours} = a + b \,(100{,}000/\text{Batch size}),$$

hours are expressed as a nonlinear function of batch size. The particular transformation chosen (100,000 times the reciprocal of batch size) was one that converts the nonlinear, decelerating relationship between hours and batch size to one that is linear.

Choosing a Transformation

The criteria for choosing a transformation are identical to the criteria for building a model. Above all, the transformation should make sense (i.e., it must be consistent with the model builder's belief about the underlying relationship between the variables). And second, the transformation should fit the available data.

To make an intelligent choice, then, it will be necessary to understand the implications of several candidate transformations and the relationships they represent. For example, to know that the reciprocal (1/X) is the appropriate transformation to use in a situation, you must know what a graph of Y versus X looks like if Y is actually a linear function of 1/X,

$$Y = a + b(1/X).$$

The remainder of this section presents and describes several useful transformations. Included in each section is a graph of what Y versus X can look like if that transformation is the appropriate one to use.

Reciprocal   The reciprocal of X, written as either 1/X or X^{-1}, is defined as 1 divided by X. The hours/batch size example has already shown us that the reciprocal transformation can be useful when the relationship between Y and X is decelerating (see Figure 14–21).

FIGURE 14–21
$Y = a + b(1/X)$

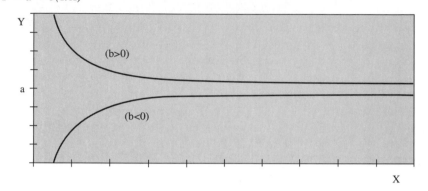

Notice that because $1/X$ approaches 0 as X approaches infinity, coefficient a represents the limiting value of Y as X gets large. Because $1/X$ approaches infinity as X approaches 0, this transformation is not appropriate if $X = 0$ is a possible value. This transformation is sometimes used to represent the relationship between sales and price. At a price $= 0$, we expect a large value for sales, and as price increases, sales might decrease to some minimum level a.

Square Root   The square root of X, written as $\sqrt{X}$ or $X^{1/2}$, is defined as the number that, when multiplied by itself, gives X. For example, the square root of 9 is 3, the square root of 4 is 2, and the square root of 0.25 is 0.5. (The square root is not defined for negative numbers and thus should not be used if X can be negative.) Figure 14–22 graphs $Y = a + bX^{1/2}$ for both a positive and negative value of b.

FIGURE 14–22
$Y = a + b(X^{1/2})$

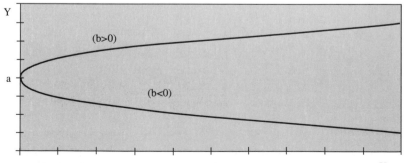

Notice that this relationship between Y and X is also decelerating, but at a slower rate of deceleration than that of the reciprocal. The square root is thus a less drastic transformation than the reciprocal and might be used if the relationship between Y and X exhibits only a small degree of nonlinearity.

Natural Logarithm   The natural logarithm of X, written as ln(X), is defined as the number that, when used as an exponent of e, gives the value X. The value e is a carefully chosen constant equal to 2.718. Thus, the natural logarithm of 2.718 is 1, the natural logarithm of 1 is 0, and the natural logarithm approaches negative infinity as X approaches 0. (Like the square-root transformation, the natural logarithm is not defined for negative values of X.) Figure 14–23 graphs Y = a + b[ln(X)] for both a positive and negative value of b.

FIGURE 14–23
Y = a + b[ln(X)]

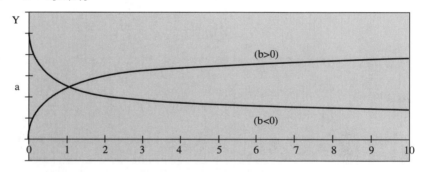

The ln(X) transformation also represents a decelerating, nonlinear relationship. It decelerates faster than the square root but not as fast as the reciprocal and is useful if the degree of nonlinearity is greater than that of the square root but less than that of the reciprocal. Because the natural logarithm of 1 is 0, the coefficient a represents the Y value at X = 1. As X approaches 0, ln(X), and therefore Y will approach either plus or minus infinity (depending on the sign of b).

Square   A simple transformation that might be used to represent an accelerating relationship is the square. The square of X is defined as the product of X times itself: Figure 14–24 graphs Y = a + bX^2 for both a positive and negative value of b.

The square of X is defined for all values of X (positive and negative), and a graph of Y = a + bX^2 versus X is that of a parabola. The relationship graphed is called accelerating because the magnitude of change in Y for a unit increase in X *increases* with the magnitude of X (if X is positive). Raising

FIGURE 14–24

$Y = a + b(X^2)$

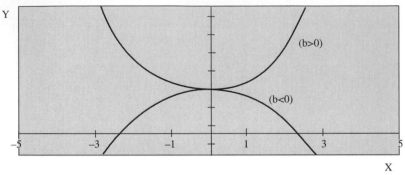

X to powers greater than 2 also represents accelerating relationships, where the rate of acceleration is proportional to the size of the exponent used.

Transforming the Y-Variable

So far we have discussed several possible transformations of the independent variable. It is also possible to use these transformations on the Y-variable. (Again, these transformations should be used if they help capture the underlying relationship between X and Y.) Transforming the Y, however, creates several complications.

Because the linear model is often used to forecast the dependent variable, transforming the Y-variable will change the nature of the quantity being forecast. Transformations of the Y-variable also affect the distribution of the model residuals, the interpretation of the measures of fit, and the pattern of scatter in the residuals (hetero- or homoscedasticity). These changes are sometimes desirable; one way to handle heteroscedasticity is to transform the Y-variable using the square root or natural logarithm. Keep in mind, however, that using a transformation on the Y-variable changes the forecasting problem; instead of forecasting Y and explaining a certain percentage of the variance of Y, you will now be forecasting the square root of Y, for example, and explaining a *different* percentage of the variance of the square root of Y.

Exponential Model—the Learning Curve   Two important model forms can be converted to a linear model with a transformation of the Y-variable. The first will be called the exponential model,

$$Y = ae^{bx},$$

in which e is the constant equal to 2.718. This model is used in business contexts (particularly in the field of operations), where it is called the learning curve (see Figure 14–25).

FIGURE 14–25

$Y = a(e^{bX})$

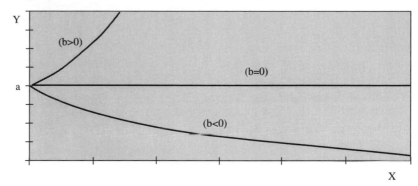

The model can represent either an accelerating (b > 0), decelerating (b < 0), or constant (b = 0) relationship between X and Y. To transform this model to a linear form, we take the natural logarithm of both sides. Because the natural logarithm of e^{bx} is, by definition, bX, we obtain[24]

$$\ln(Y) = \ln(a) + bX,$$

which is just the simple linear model with dependent variable ln(Y) and independent variable X. The constant in this linear model, ln(a), is just the natural logarithm of a, the multiplicative constant in the exponential model.

Multiplicative Model—Constant Elasticity   The second important model form that can be transformed into a linear model is

$$Y = aX^b.$$

This model has the important property that the percentage change in Y for a given percentage change in X is a constant for all values of X. The ratio of the percentage decrease in Y for an incremental percentage increase in X is sometimes called the elasticity of Y with respect to X. In the model, elasticity is a constant equal to −b. Figure 14–26 graphs $Y = aX^b$ for three negative values of b.

To transform this model to a linear form, we again take the natural logarithm of both sides to get

$$\ln(Y) = \ln(a) + b \ln(X).$$

Thus, if $Y = aX^b$, the relationship between ln(Y) and ln(X) will be linear with intercept ln(a) and slope b. The simple linear model can be used if both X and Y are transformed using the natural logarithm.

---

[24]We also use the property that ln(UV) = ln(U) + ln(V).

FIGURE 14–26

$Y = a(X^b)$

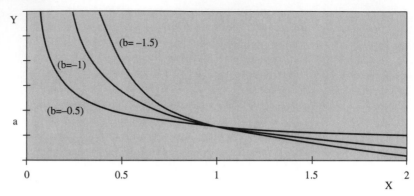

This model is called the multiplicative model because the combined effects of several independent variables *multiply* together to determine the mean of Y:

$$\text{Mean}(Y) = a(X1^{b1})(X2^{b2})(X3^{b3})$$

This model is often used to represent the relationship between a product's share of market and marketing-mix variables such as price, advertising, and promotion. The multiplicative model is used if the effects of each of the marketing variables are assumed to depend on the levels of all the others. Taking the natural logarithm of this model,

$$\ln(Y) = \ln(a) + b1\ln(X1) + b2\ln(X2) + b3\ln(X3)$$

converts it to a multiple linear model.

15   DISCRETE-EVENT SIMULATION

In this chapter, we will consider a slight variation on the general concept of simulation as it has been used in this text. Until now, the relationship between input assumptions and performance measures has been easily captured by a spreadsheet model, via a series of intermediate calculations, each capable of being captured within a single cell. In some problems, however, these intermediate calculations are difficult to determine directly. *Discrete-event simulation* offers one possibility for deriving an appropriate set of intermediate calculations. It is appropriate for problems in which the relationships between the input assumptions and performance measures are most easily determined by modeling the actual process by which inputs are transformed into outputs, and then observing and analyzing the operation of that model over a period of simulated time. Included in this class of problems are many involving operations—even relatively simple ones—where there is uncertainty in precisely when inputs become available to be processed by the system and/or in the time required to process them through the system once they become available.

The term *discrete event* refers to something happening at a particular point in time. For example, an input arriving to the system—ready to be processed—at a specific point is a discrete event, as is the completion of the processing of a particular input by some component of the system at a specific instant. The input assumptions of a discrete-event simulation model, coupled with the model of how the system operates (one set of intermediate calculations), determine when precisely the discrete events occur. The model is then "run," which means the system's clock is advanced, stopping temporarily whenever a discrete event is encountered for the system to react to that event. Data for calculating the performance of the system is collected while the model is being run, and at the end of the run, the performance measures are calculated.

For example, if the objective is to investigate the length of the line of cars waiting at a particular intersection if the stop-go cycle is one minute for "stop" and 30 seconds for "go," we would build a model that has cars approach the intersection according to the rate at which they typically arrive, stop when appropriate (thus becoming part of the line), and go when appropriate, at typical speeds. Any of the following would be considered discrete events: the arrival of a car to the intersection, the changing of the light from stop to go, and the changing of the light from go to stop. Running the model would mean having the model process the arrival of cars over a period of simulated clock time and directly observing how the length of the line fluctuates. One measure of interest might be the maximum length of the line, particularly if too long a line causes other traffic problems. Another might be how long in minutes on average cars wait in line at the intersection. Still another might be the percentage of cars having to wait more than one stop–go cycle before passing through the intersection.

In this case, the "intermediate calculations" are those that cause the system to run and track the data necessary to calculate the value of the performance measures. Unfortunately, these types of calculations are not easily performed within a spreadsheet. For this reason, discrete-event simulation is seldom implemented within a spreadsheet; instead, specially designed software is used to facilitate building the models and tracking the performance measures.

In this chapter, we will illustrate discrete-event simulation through a "pencil-and-paper" example. We will then discuss some of the important issues in using discrete-event simulation to analyze a business problem.

An Example Application of Discrete-Event Simulation

Consider the customer service department of a large packaged goods company. The customer service director is trying to determine how many telephone operators—and consequently, telephone lines—to have standing by to respond to calls to the company's 800 number. She also must determine how long the waiting list is allowed to be (i.e., how many callers will be placed on hold for the next available operator before additional callers will be instructed to try again later).

This is a typical example of the type of situation for which discrete-event simulation is appropriate. To analyze the situation, we need two pieces of information: how frequently we expect prospective customers to call, and how long it takes to process each call. If we expect 40 calls per hour, and on average it takes 4 minutes to process each call, an initial analysis might indicate that three operators are sufficient: each operator can process $60/4 = 15$ callers per hour, and hence the three of them can handle 45 calls per hour, greater than the 40 calls we expect. However, this initial analysis fails to consider three important uncertainties: the number of calls in a given hour may be more or less than 40, the calls may arrive bunched up rather than spread out evenly over the hour, and the amount of time it takes to process a call might be more or less than 4 minutes. A more thorough analysis should take into account these uncertainties.

One way to do this is through a branch of applied math called *queuing theory*. If we are willing to make certain assumptions about how calls arrive—assumptions affecting both the actual number of calls that arrive within a given hour and when during that hour they arrive—and certain assumptions about how the amount of time it takes to process a call varies, we can use a set of intermediate calculations to determine some important operating characteristics of the system, such as how long on average customers will have to wait before reaching an operator, what percentage of time operators will be busy on average, and how many customers on average will be waiting in the queue at any given time. These calculations can be found in many basic textbooks and can be easily carried out in a spreadsheet.

The limitations of queuing theory are twofold. First, the validity of the results of the intermediate calculations depends on the validity of the assumptions: if calls do not arrive in the prescribed manner, or if processing time does not vary in the prescribed fashion, the results from actually operating the system might differ significantly from those suggested by the queuing theory calculations.[1] Second, queuing theory calculations may not produce values for all performance measures of interest, such as what percentage of callers are turned away because the queue is full.

Discrete-event simulation overcomes both these limitations. It enables us to include whatever input assumptions we deem appropriate about the arrival pattern, and it enables us to track anything of interest to us. We will now discuss precisely how we would apply discrete-event simulation to analyze this situation.

The Model

As recently as the early 1980s, building a discrete-event simulation required much technical programming expertise. Since then, the field has seen a dramatic increase in the number and quality of user-friendly interfaces for discrete-event simulation software packages. With these interfaces, it is relatively simple to model basic operating systems. The better packages retain the ability to construct more complicated models, although at the expense of requiring more technical expertise. Rather than go into the details of any particular package, we will outline how a discrete-event simulation model

---

[1]In practice, the results often are not all that dissimilar, even if the input assumptions are not satisfied; queuing theory results are, therefore, relatively *robust*. However, for important decisions, a decision maker should be careful about relying on queuing theory results when the input assumptions are not satisfied, as it can produce significantly misleading results.

for the decision facing our customer service department would be built using pencil and paper.

First, we need a way to *simulate* the arrival of calls to the system. To do this, we must describe an underlying arrival pattern. This pattern could, of course, be deterministic: a call arrives every 1.33 minutes (40 calls per hour). However, this pattern fails to capture the variability in calling patterns that exists in real situations.

To capture this variability, we need a probability distribution that describes the number of calls that can arrive in an hour and another that somehow captures how calls tend to bunch up or be spread out. One way to do this is to create a probability distribution describing the amount of time *between* calls. This is often referred to as the *interarrival time*. Queuing theory assumes that the interarrival time is an *exponential distribution*. If we were willing to accept this assumption for our example, we could set the mean of the distribution to 1.33 and use it to generate interarrival times, expressed in minutes.

Figure 15–1 contains an example sequence of interarrival times generated by such an exponential distribution. The interarrival times are contained in the second column. The third column transforms the interarrival times into *clock time*; that is, the time at which the call actually arrives. This is a very important feature of discrete-event simulation models: clock time describes when the discrete events captured in the model actually occur. The clock is assumed to start at 0. Hence, the first call (discrete event) arrives at minute 0.28, the second arrives at minute 0.83, etc. Notice how the use of a distribution of interarrival times captures variability in both the number of calls received in any particular hour and the bunching of calls. The variability in the former is captured because we do not know precisely how many calls will be received between clock time 0 and 60 (or any other hour we care to consider). That the variability of the latter is being captured is illustrated in the sequence in Figure 15–1: three calls are received in the first 1.06 minutes of clock time, but 3.68 minutes elapse after call 3 before call 4 is received.

Each individual interarrival time in Figure 15–1 is generated in exactly the same way as the value of one input uncertainty in a single trial in the risk-analysis simulation models described elsewhere in this book. The difference between those risk-analysis simulation models and discrete-event simulation is in the intermediate calculations used to calculate the resulting values of the performance measures.[2] The first set of intermediate calculations we need for our discrete-event simulation model is one that describes how these calls will be handled.

Figure 15–2 contains a log that can be used to track the activity of Operator 1. The first column contains the number of the call routed to Operators 1.

---

[2] A related difference is that while in risk-analysis simulation we run many trials and get a value of the performance measures for each trial, in discrete-event simulation we essentially run only one trial. We control for the uncertainty in our results by making that one trial very large—it can contain as many calls, for example, as we want.

FIGURE 15–1

Sequence of Calls Arriving to the System
(Generated by an Exponential Distribution with Mean 1.33 Minutes)

Call Number	Interarrival Time (in minutes)	Arrival Time (in clock time)
1	0.28	0.28
2	0.55	0.83
3	0.23	1.06
4	3.68	4.74
5	1.73	6.48
6	0.21	6.69
7	1.35	8.04
8	1.41	9.45
9	0.29	9.73
10	1.17	10.90

FIGURE 15–2

Log to Track Activity of Operator 1

Operator 1 Call Number	Start Service (clock time)	Service Time (in minutes)	End Service (clock time)
1	0.28		

The second column contains the time at which the call is routed to Operator 1. Notice that since Operator 1 was unoccupied when the call arrived, the clock time at which Operator 1 received the call and began service is the same as the clock time at which the call arrived (Figure 15–1). The importance of this observation will become clear once calls begin arriving to the system when all operators are busy.

Before moving to the final two columns of the log in Figure 15–2, we should observe that we arbitrarily chose to route the first call to Operator 1; we could have just as easily chosen to route it to either one of the other operators. One of the decisions we must make and include in our model is how calls will be routed to individual operators when a call is received and more than one operator is unoccupied. We have decided at the outset to

FIGURE 15–3

Log to Track Activity of Operator 1 (First Call Recorded)

Operator 1 Call Number	Start Service (clock time)	Service Time (in minutes)	End Service (clock time)
1	0.28	0.27	0.55

simply route calls to Operators 1, 2, and 3 in that order. However, if we maintain that decision rule throughout, Operator 1 is apt to be much busier than Operator 2, who in turn is apt to be much busier than Operator 3. An alternative, frequently used in practice, is to route the call to the operator who has been waiting the longest since completing service on her or his previous call. We will adopt this rule for our simulation and will shortly see how it works.

The third column requires knowing how long it will take to service each call. Recall that we assumed it takes 4 minutes on average to service each call. We could, therefore, simply assume it takes 4 minutes to service the first call. However, this assumption fails to capture the variability we know exists in the actual time required to service a call.

The alternative is to assume a probability distribution on how long it takes to service a call. Queuing theory assumes that the amount of time required to service a call is also exponentially distributed. Thus, if we are willing to make this assumption for our example, we generate service times according to an exponential distribution with mean of 4, the average number of minutes it takes to process one call.[3] To illustrate this, we now generate a service time for the first call and record it in the log for Operator 1 (Figure 15–3). Column four is then calculated from the starting time (column two) and required service time (column three). Thus, the log in Figure 15–3 tells

_____

[3]Making this assumption implies no difference in the processing ability of the three operators that would affect the required processing time. If there is a difference—one is significantly slower than the other two—we could represent that difference by using different distributions (or parameters) for each operator.

us that Operator 1 began processing the first call at the 0.28-minute mark, required 0.27 minutes to process the call, and hung up at the 0.55-minute mark.

We proceed in this manner to dispose of the first three calls. Consider what happens when the fourth call arrives at the 4.74-minute mark. All three operators are available, as depicted by their logs in Figure 15–4, having completed service on their first call. Using the rule we discussed previously, we would assign the fourth call to the operator who has been idle the longest, in this case, Operator 1 (idle since the 0.55-minute mark, as compared to the 1.93-minute mark for Operator 2 and the 4.23-minute mark for Operator 3).

Figure 15–5 depicts the logs of the three operators after the first six calls have been received and routed to the appropriate operator. Consider what happens when the seventh call arrives at the 8.04-minute mark. Notice that Operator 1 is not free from processing the current call until the 13.30-minute mark, Operator 2 is not available until the 8.74-minute mark, and Operator 3 is not available until the 8.54-minute mark. Hence, no one is available to process the seventh call when it arrives. The seventh caller is then put on hold and placed in the queue awaiting the availability of the next operator (and no doubt forced to listen to music not to the caller's liking, interrupted periodically by reassurances of how important this call is to the firm). The next discrete event to occur will then be Operator 3 becoming available at the 8.54-minute mark to take the seventh call. The seventh caller will then have had to wait .50 minutes (8.54 − 8.04) to receive service.

Figure 15–6 contains the logs of the three operators with all 10 calls included. Figure 15–7 contains the log of incoming calls with an additional column added in which the amount of time the caller had to wait on hold before receiving service is recorded. From these data, a number of potentially important statistics relative to how the system is operating can be calculated. For example, the total amount of waiting time for the 10 calls is 1.18 minutes (0.50 for caller 7 and 0.68 for caller 10), or an average of .118 minutes per call. Twenty percent of all callers are put on hold, for an average of 0.59 minutes apiece (the average of 0.50 and 0.68). Operator 1 is busy for a total of 8.83 of the first 13.30 minutes of the simulation, or 66 percent of the time. Out of the first 16.79 minutes of the simulation, the three operators are busy a combined total of 29.32 minutes of the 50.37 minutes available (16.79 × 3), a utilization rate of 58 percent.[4] The final step in building a discrete-event simulation model is deciding what data you want to collect in order to measure the performance of the system.

The discrete-event simulation model is now complete. All that remains is to allow the model to run for a period of simulated time and observe what

---

[4]Of course, this final statistic does not include any additional calls that might arrive before the 16.79-minute mark, were we to continue the simulation. This is one of the key issues to consider when using a discrete-event simulation model to analyze a business problem and will be discussed more fully in the next section.

FIGURE 15–4

Logs to Track Activity of Each of the Three Operators (First Three Calls Recorded)

Operator 1 Call Number	Start Service (clock time)	Service Time (in minutes)	End Service (clock time)
1	0.28	0.27	0.55

Operator 2 Call Number	Start Service (clock time)	Service Time (in minutes)	End Service (clock time)
2	0.83	1.10	1.93

Operator 3 Call Number	Start Service (clock time)	Service Time (in minutes)	End Service (clock time)
3	1.06	3.17	4.23

FIGURE 15–5

Logs to Track Activity of Each of the Three Operators (First Six Calls Recorded)

Operator 1	Start Service	Service Time	End Service
Call Number	(clock time)	(in minutes)	(clock time)
1	0.28	0.27	0.55
4	4.74	8.56	13.30

Operator 2	Start Service	Service Time	End Service
Call Number	(clock time)	(in minutes)	(clock time)
2	0.83	1.10	1.93
5	6.48	2.26	8.74

Operator 3	Start Service	Service Time	End Service
Call Number	(clock time)	(in minutes)	(clock time)
3	1.06	3.17	4.23
6	6.69	1.85	8.54

FIGURE 15–6

Logs to Track Activity of Each of the Three Operators (All 10 Calls Recorded)

Operator 1 Call Number	Start Service (clock time)	Service Time (in minutes)	End Service (clock time)
1	0.28	0.27	0.55
4	4.74	8.56	13.30

Operator 2 Call Number	Start Service (clock time)	Service Time (in minutes)	End Service (clock time)
2	0.83	1.10	1.93
5	6.48	2.26	8.74
8	9.45	2.13	11.58
10	11.58	5.21	16.79

Operator 3 Call Number	Start Service (clock time)	Service Time (in minutes)	End Service (clock time)
3	1.06	3.17	4.23
6	6.69	1.85	8.54
7	8.54	0.88	9.42
9	9.73	3.90	13.63

FIGURE 15–7

Log of Incoming Calls Recorded (Column for Waiting Time Included)

Call Number	Interarrival Time (in minutes)	Arrival Time (in clock time)	Service Time (in minutes)	Waiting Time (in minutes)
1	0.28	0.28	0.27	
2	0.55	0.83	1.10	
3	0.23	1.06	3.17	
4	3.68	4.74	8.56	
5	1.73	6.48	2.26	
6	0.21	6.69	1.85	
7	1.35	8.04	0.88	0.50
8	1.41	9.45	2.13	
9	0.29	9.73	3.90	
10	1.17	10.90	5.21	0.68

happens to the performance measures of interest. Notice that the intermediate calculations in the model are those that take care of the disposition of individual calls and the work activity of the operators, as well as those that collect the data needed to track the performance measures. It is these intermediate calculations that are difficult to model in a spreadsheet.[5] Because we chose to use the assumptions of queuing theory to build our model, the performance results we get from running the simulation will equal those we would get from applying queuing theory directly—at least for those performance measures queuing theory is able to generate—except that simulation can track some performance measures not calculable from queuing theory, and simulation produces only sample estimates of the performance measures, not their true mean values.

Important Issues in Discrete-Event Simulation

The following are some important issues to consider when building or using a discrete-event simulation model.

Calibrating the Uncertainties

In our example, we borrowed the standard assumptions of queuing theory for how interarrival and service times are distributed. These assumptions are attractive because they enable us to derive some performance measures mathematically without having to resort to simulation (this is what queuing theory is all about); they are also frequently good approximations of what really happens.

However, there are many situations in which either the assumptions clearly do not apply, or it is not clear that they are appropriate. In these

---

[5]It can be done, but typically requires the use of more complicated programming, such as macros, than the typical spreadsheet user is capable of or interested in doing.

situations, the modeler is faced with precisely the same challenge and options as in Chapter 4: Do I subjectively assess the probability distribution? Are data available to help me assess that distribution? Do I need to collect data to use to calibrate the distribution? The techniques discussed in that chapter can be used here to construct the distributions of the relevant uncertainties.

Validating the Model

Obviously, if a discrete-event simulation model fails to accurately represent the real functioning of the process it is meant to model, the performance measures it yields for any possible alternative are potentially inaccurate and hence virtually useless. It is therefore important to *validate* that the model is accurately reflecting reality. There is a relatively simple first pass at this validation process if the system under investigation already exists and you are simply exploring the impact of making changes to the system. In this case, you can first construct a discrete-event simulation model of the existing system and compare the results of the model to actual results.

Validating models of systems that do not already exist, or validating specific changes to existing systems, is more difficult. One approach is to duplicate the paper-and-pencil approach we used in the preceding section, to make sure you understand all the subtleties of the system you are trying to model. For example, in the customer service department telephone-answering process, the need to have a decision rule regarding how to route calls when more than one operator is available is an easy one to overlook. Many software packages will have default decision rules; in this instance, the default might be to assign the call to the operator with the lowest index number—1, 2, or 3. This would lead to Operator 1 being utilized more than Operator 2, who in turn would be utilized more than Operator 3. Presumably, on running the model, you would get performance measures indicating these disparities, which would lead you to search for an explanation of why the disparities exist and to discover the need for the decision rule in question.

This latter process is yet another approach to validation. Specifically, run the model, look at the values of the resulting performance measures, and see if they match your intuition. If not, you have either discovered an important, counterintuitive insight into the operation of your system, or your model is invalid. Clearly, you would want to investigate the model's details until you have figured out which of these two conclusions is correct.

How do you search for the invalidity? One approach is to go back and walk through the process with pencil and paper, as discussed previously, attempting to replicate what the model is doing. If you cannot reproduce the results you are getting from running the model, then the problem probably is that the model is not doing what you think it is doing. You need to spend your time figuring out why. Another approach is to change the input distributions—possibly using extreme distributions—to see if the results change in the direction you would expect. If not, this often provides helpful clues as to where the problem might lie. Yet another approach, more or less difficult to implement depending on the software you are using, is to segment the process and run those parts of the model associated with the individual segments separately, making sure you are getting the results you would expect from each segment.

Model validation is a critical part of model development. As a consumer of discrete-event simulation models (i.e., someone else builds them and you use them), you should be particularly demanding with respect to model validation, requiring evidence that the model is in fact doing what it is supposed to be.

Avoiding Peculiarities Associated with Start-up

At the beginning of our pencil-and-paper simulation for the customer service department, all the operators were free because no calls had arrived. This means that the early part of the simulation will be distinguishable because the simulation began with three free operators. Thus, we expect performance measures from this early part of the simulation to be systematically different from what they will be later in the simulation. This part of a specific simulation run in which the values of the performance measures differ from what they will be later is called the *start-up* period.

The results gleaned from the simulation once any residual effects associated with the start-up of the system have disappeared is called the *steady-state performance* of the system. Often, start-up effects can have a significant impact on the performance measures well into the simulation. For this reason, we often do not begin collecting data for the performance measures during a particular run until after the system reaches steady state. How long this takes can vary widely. One way to determine whether the system has reached steady state is to track how much the values of the performance measures fluctuate as the simulation proceeds. At some point, these values will appear to stabilize, and the system can be safely assumed to have reached steady state.

Start-up issues related to the simulation should not be confused with start-up issues inherent to the system. For example, it may be true that the telephone operators in our example start work every day at 8 A.M., so the start-up period in our simulation model is a real characteristic of the system and is not simply an artifact of our model. If this is the case, then we would want to measure the performance of our system over the start-up period as well as during steady state.

Terminating the Model Run

The issue of when to halt a particular simulation is a function of how accurate you want the results to be. Just as with the risk-analysis simulation results with which we dealt in Chapter 5, the performance-measure results we obtain from a single run are sample statistics, subject to all the vagaries of sample results. The longer the simulation, the more we reduce the uncertainty surrounding the value of the true population statistic.

Summary

Discrete-event simulation is a potentially valuable tool when the intermediate calculations linking input assumptions and performance measures are difficult to construct. It is particularly appropriate when the managerial decision revolves around a system that takes uncertain inputs and processes them in an uncertain way. In the example considered in this chapter, the model we built could be easily modified to analyze alternative configurations, such as having more or fewer operators, or allowing a longer or shorter queue of callers on hold. Also, the sensitivity of the system to changes in the uncertainties—such as the arrival pattern or the speed and/or variability with which calls are processed—could be easily investigated.

16 INTRODUCTION TO OPTIMIZATION MODELS

As we saw in Chapter 2, the primary source of difficulty in some decisions is the sheer number of available alternatives from which to choose. This is most frequently the case when the decision to be made is the specification of a *quantity*, such as how large to make a production batch size, what percentage of a portfolio to put into each available investment alternative, or how to allocate an advertising budget among possible vehicles. For these types of decisions, a model that simply *evaluates* the performance of a given alternative can be useful in facilitating a search over the possible alternatives. However, such a model is limited in its value: The search it requires can be time-consuming, with no guarantee of ever finding the exact optimal quantity.

Frequently, in situations like this, it is possible to identify the optimal quantity without resorting to such a search, using a technique known as *mathematical programming*. We refer to a model that uses mathematical programming to find an optimal quantity as an *optimization model*. Thus, an *optimization* model differs from an *evaluation* model in that it goes beyond simply evaluating the consequences of proposed alternatives: It actually identifies the "optimal" alternative.

How does an optimization model accomplish this impressive task? In this age of readily available computing power and ever more user-friendly software, it is possible to build and use optimization models without a detailed understanding of the mathematics that underlie the answer to this question. However, to truly take advantage of this capability, it *is* necessary to have a basic understanding of some core concepts. The primary objective of this chapter is to introduce these concepts. The chapter is highly pragmatic; the next chapter explores more deeply the mathematical foundations of the concepts and is designed for the user with the motivation and mathematical background to explore the topic more deeply.

In this chapter, we will first provide a framework for building an optimization model *given* that you have a good evaluation model. A good evaluation model is a crucial component of an optimization model. The optimization model *uses* the evaluation model to direct its automated search and to determine when it has found the optimal solution. Thus, a necessary first step in building an optimization model is to have a working evaluation model. We will use three examples of business situations for which optimization models have proved useful. The three examples were chosen to illustrate the three main categories of optimization models, distinguished by the specifics of their shared structure and the mathematical programming technique required to "solve" the model (i.e., find the optimal alternative) given those specifics. Understanding these categories of optimization models—and the basic concepts underlying their associated solution techniques—is essential to being an effective user. In this chapter, we address each category and outline its solution technique; in the next chapter, we go into more detail on the mathematics of the different solution techniques.

One limitation of an optimization model is that it generally ignores uncertainty in the decision-making environment. However, the procedures used to solve *some* optimization models also generate information regarding how the solution will or will not change as specific inputs change. Because we can use this information to assess how *sensitive* the solution is to uncertainty in the inputs, this information is referred to in mathematical programming as *sensitivity analysis* and is the subject of the next section in the chapter.

Finally, we address the issue of how to build an optimization model from scratch. Specifically, we present tips on how to build the foundational evaluation model knowing that you are eventually going to transform it into an optimization model.

Transforming an Evaluation Model into an Optimization Model

Consider the following frequently encountered business decision first encountered in Chapter 2:

Example 1: Optimal Order Quantity

The XYZ Company assembles a product for which an important component, subassembly A, is purchased from an outside vendor. Annual demand for the component is 10,000 units and is distributed evenly throughout the year (i.e., there is no significant seasonality). Each subassembly A unit costs $325, delivered. There is a fixed cost of approximately $500 to place an order for subassembly A, irrespective of how many units are included in the order. The company estimates a cost of 12 percent of the unit cost per year to carry a unit in inventory (this includes the cost of capital). To minimize production costs, how many units of subassembly A should be ordered at a time, and how many orders should be placed per year?

The knowledgeable reader may recognize this as a classic inventory problem for which the economic order quantity (EOQ) is appropriate. However, this problem can also be addressed by building a simple optimization model, which might be desirable for a variety of reasons that will be discussed shortly. First, however, let's consider how we can build such a model.

Observe that, associated with how many units of subassembly A to order at a time, there are two primary components of the total annual costs that vary with respect to order size—*ordering* cost and *carrying* cost. The more units ordered at a time—and hence the fewer orders placed during the year, at $500 per order—the lower our total annual *ordering* costs. However, the more units ordered at a time, the greater the average inventory level, and hence the higher our annual *carrying* costs. For example, at the extreme, if we order only one unit at a time, our average inventory level will be between 0 and 1, whereas if we order all 10,000 items at the beginning of the year, our average inventory level will be 5,000: 10,000 units at the beginning of the year, 0 at the end, and 5,000 on average assuming evenly distributed demand. (Notice that we are assuming that the actual per-unit cost of subassembly A remains the same irrespective of how many units we order at a time or how many orders we place per year. Hence, we do not need to include this cost in our analysis.)

We can construct an evaluation model to calculate the annual relevant costs associated with ordering subassembly A for any particular order quantity (Figure 16–1). In the case of Figure 16–1, an order quantity of 1,000 is used, and a total cost of $3,274,500 results. As illustrated in the figure, this total cost includes $5,000 in ordering costs and $19,500 in carrying costs.

This evaluation model could be used, in a trial-and-error fashion, to explore the cost of various order quantities. However, since the number of possible order quantities is very large, using this approach to find the single best (i.e., cost-minimizing) order quantity would quickly become tiresome.

To turn this evaluation model into an optimization model, we have to do three things: (1) specify which cells contain quantities that can be changed—i.e., contain the *decision quantities* that are our alternatives; (2) indicate the cell that contains the quantity to be optimized, which we will call the *objective quantity*; and (3) identify any restrictions—direct or indirect—on the values the decision quantities can assume. These restrictions are generally referred to as *constraints*, because they constrain the values of the decision quantities.

Step 1 is easily accomplished: the decision quantity—or cell that can be altered—is the cell containing the order quantity. It is this quantity we are required to specify as our decision. Notice that this cell contains a *value*; more to the point, it does not contain a *formula*. This is always true in an optimization model.

PRACTICAL HINT: Only a cell that contains a *value*—not a formula—can be designated as a decision quantity, or changing cell.

Step 2 is also easily accomplished: The cell to be optimized is the cell containing the total annual cost. Notice that this cell contains a formula.

FIGURE 16–1

Evaluation Model for Example 1

Alternative	
Order quantity	1,000
Input Assumptions	
Annual demand	10,000
Purchase cost per unit	$ 325
Cost per order	$ 500
Annual inventory carrying cost	12%
Intermediate Calculations	
Number of orders per year	10
Average inventory	500
Annual purchase cost	$3,250,000
Annual ordering cost	$ 5,000
Annual carrying cost	$ 19,500
Performance Measure	
Total annual cost	$3,274,500

Number of orders per year = Annual demand/Order quantity
Average inventory   = Order quantity/2

Annual purchase cost = Annual demand × Purchase cost per unit
Annual ordering cost   = Number of orders per year × Cost per order
Annual carrying cost   = Average inventory
                                        × Annual inventory carrying cost
                                        × Purchase cost per unit

Total annual cost   = Annual purchase cost
                                        + Annual ordering cost
                                        + Annual carrying cost

Furthermore, it contains a formula that depends—albeit indirectly—on the cell containing the order quantity, the decision to be specified. This is always true in an optimization model.

FIGURE 16–2
Relationship between Order Quantity and Total Annual Cost

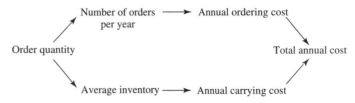

PRACTICAL HINT: The cell containing the objective quantity will always contain a *formula*—not a value—that is related directly or indirectly to the cells containing the decision quantities.

The relationship between order quantity and total annual cost exists along two paths, represented pictorially in Figure 16–2. Also notice that we want to *minimize* the objective quantity (the alternative choice would have been to *maximize* the objective quantity).

Step 3 requires answering the question: Are there any restrictions we wish to place on the value the order quantity can assume? At first, the answer to this question may appear to be no. However, on further reflection, there are some constraints. First, the order quantity cannot be a negative number. Second, the order quantity should be an integer (or whole number) (i.e., we cannot order a fraction of a unit). In fact, it may be true that the order quantity has to be a multiple of 5, 10, or some greater number.

For reasons that will be made apparent later, we will accept this first constraint—that the quantity must be nonnegative—but not the second—that the quantity must be an integer. If we fail to specify the first condition, the solution approach may think it can drive costs down by ordering a *negative* number of units of subassembly A and thereby incur a *negative* cost, or contribution. There is nothing in the evaluation model itself that precludes this interpretation. There is a pragmatic rationale for ignoring this second apparent constraint: The optimal order quantity is apt to be so large that simply dropping whatever fractional component it contains—or rounding the optimal solution to the nearest integer—is likely to either be the optimal integer order quantity or very close to it. (However, this is not *why* we choose to ignore the second constraint. Including it creates an optimization model that is much more difficult to solve, as we shall see later.)

We can now invoke a mathematical programming algorithm[1] to identify the optimal order quantity; we refer to this as *optimizing the model*. The

---

[1]In mathematical programming parlance, an *algorithm* is a sequence of steps, or recipe, that accomplishes a specific task, in this case finding the optimal solution to an optimization model.

FIGURE 16–3
Optimized Model for Example 1

Alternative	
Order quantity	506
Input Assumptions	
Annual demand	10,000
Purchase cost per unit	$ 325
Cost per order	$ 500
Annual inventory carrying cost	12%
Intermediate Calculations	
Number of orders per year	20
Average inventory	253
Annual purchase cost	$3,250,000
Annual ordering cost	$ 9,874
Annual carrying cost	$ 9,874
Performance Measure	
Total annual cost	$3,269,748

optimized model (i.e., the model with the optimal order quantity identified) is contained in Figure 16–3. The optimal solution is to order 506 units (rounded off) per order, which will result in 19.75 orders per year, and a total annual cost of $19,748.[2] This is the minimum total annual cost that can be incurred while satisfying demand for subassembly A. Any deviation from this order quantity will result in a higher total annual cost, as the student can readily verify.

_____

[2]We are not concerned with placing a noninteger number of orders per year. There is no rule that says our order cycles have to correspond neatly to a calendar year.

Notice first that this is precisely the order quantity that applying the EOQ formula would identify:

EOQ = SQRT(2 × Annual demand × Cost of ordering/Cost of
      carrying)
    = SQRT(2 × 10,000 × $500/$39)
    = 506

We can thus take some comfort in the validity of either the EOQ or our newfound optimization model methodology, whichever is in greater need of comfort.

But why do we need an optimization model methodology if the EOQ formula gives us the right answer? The simple answer is: you don't, *if* you are familiar with the EOQ approach, that is, and unless you happen to prefer working with a spreadsheet model you understand than a formula that you don't! However, there is another reason to prefer an optimization model. The EOQ formula is appropriate only under some fairly stringent conditions, ones that happen to be satisfied in this particular example. In the absence of these conditions, applying the EOQ formula can lead to very misleading results. Furthermore, there is no easy way to modify the EOQ formula to use it in many of the situations for which it is not strictly applicable.[3]

An optimization model, on the other hand, can be readily adapted to handle situations in which the EOQ is not appropriate. Consider the following commonly encountered variations on the situation facing the XYZ Company.

Example 1a: Multiple Products, Limited Storage Space

In addition to subassembly A, XYZ also requires subassemblies B, C, and D for its product. Figure 16–4 contains pertinent information regarding each of the subassemblies, as well as the EOQ for each, and the total annual cost that results from ordering the EOQ for each subassembly. The XYZ Company has only 15,000 cubic feet of space available for storing subassemblies. Historically, the company has never needed more storage space than what has been required to store the sum of 75 percent of the order quantities of all four subassemblies. Thus, the company has decided to require as policy that this sum not exceed the amount of storage space available. How does this limited storage space affect the optimal order quantities for each subassembly?

From the evaluation model in Figure 16–4, it is clear that ordering the EOQ of each subassembly is not feasible, since it requires a maximum of over 48,000 cubic feet of storage space. It is unclear how to adjust the EOQs to account for this limited availability.

However, it is relatively simple to transform the evaluation model in Figure 16–4 into an optimization model that will determine the optimal order

---

[3]On the other hand, as proponents of EOQ analysis are—and should be—quick to point out, the EOQ formula *is* frequently a good estimate of optimal order quantity, certainly an improvement on much existing practice!

FIGURE 16–4 *Evaluation Model for Example 1a Using Economic Order Quantities*

Alternative		A	B	C	D	Total
Order quantity		506	540	603	577	
Input Assumptions						
Annual demand		10,000	10,000	10,000	10,000	
Purchase cost per unit		$ 325	$ 200	$ 275	$ 150	
Cost per order		$ 500	$ 350	$ 600	$ 300	
Annual inventory carrying cost		$ 39	$ 24	$ 33	$ 18	
Unit volume (cubic feet)		30	25	45	15	
Intermediate Calculations						
Number of orders per year		20	19	17	17	
Average inventory		253	270	302	289	
Maximum volume required		11,385	10,125	20,351	6,491	48,353
Annual purchase cost		$3,250,000	$2,000,000	$2,750,000	$1,500,000	$9,500,000
Annual ordering cost		$ 9,881	$ 6,481	$ 9,950	$ 5,199	$ 31,512
Annual carrying cost		$ 9,867	$ 6,480	$ 9,950	$ 5,193	$ 31,490
Performance Measure						
Total annual cost		$3,269,748	$2,012,961	$2,769,900	$1,510,392	$9,563,002

Maximum volume required = .75 × Unit volume × Order quantity

quantities for each subassembly. To do so, we must replicate the three tasks we performed for the original model. The cells (more than one, in this case) that contain decision quantities are again easy to specify—they are the cells containing the order quantities of each subassembly. The objective quantity is also again relatively straightforward—we wish to minimize total annual cost. Now, however, this total is the sum of the total annual costs of each of

FIGURE 16–5

Relationship between Decision Quantities and Objective Quantity

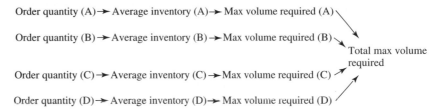

the four subassemblies, and it is the cell containing this sum that we wish to minimize.

Specifying constraints on the values the decision quantities can assume is now a little more involved. First, similar to our earlier optimization model, we must specify that the values in these cells be nonnegative. (We will again ignore the need for integers, for the same reasons as before.) There is now, however, an additional consideration—the volume of space available to store the units of subassemblies is limited. For example, as mentioned previously, ordering the EOQ of each subassembly is now *not* possible; it would require far more storage space than the 15,000 cubic feet available. Somehow we have to build into our model the constraint that the combination of order quantities cannot violate our storage space availability.

The company has chosen to handle this constraint by observing that the maximum storage space required has never exceeded the sum of 75 percent of each of the individual order quantities. We can thus ensure that the storage-space constraint is satisfied by constraining this sum—of 75 percent of each of the individual order quantities—to be no greater than 15,000. In terms of the spreadsheet, the row labeled *Max volume required* contains the cubic feet required to store 75 percent of each individual order quantity; the *Total* column contains the sum of these. Hence, the constraint in our model is that the value in this total cell must be less than or equal to 15,000.

Notice that, as with the objective quantity, the cell whose value is being constrained is indirectly related to the decision quantities (see Figure 16–5). This leads to the following potentially helpful hint when searching for what needs to be constrained in an optimization model.

PRACTICAL HINT: Constraints will always be on the values of cells that contain either the decision quantities themselves or formulas directly or indirectly related to the decision quantities. One systematic approach to checking for what cells you might want to constrain is to check through the progression of cells related to the cells containing the decision quantities, using for example the Trace command in Excel. For each cell, ask if there are any values this cell is not allowed to assume and express the constraint accordingly.

FIGURE 16–6 *Optimized Model for Example 1a with Volume Constraint*

Alternative		A	B	C	D	Total
Order quantity		180	168	165	198	
Input Assumptions						
Annual demand		10,000	10,000	10,000	10,000	
Purchase cost per unit		$ 325	$ 200	$ 275	$ 150	
Cost per order		$ 500	$ 350	$ 600	$ 300	
Annual inventory carrying cost		$ 39	$ 24	$ 33	$ 18	
Unit volume (cubic feet)		30	25	45	15	
Intermediate Calculations						
Number of orders per year		56	60	60	51	
Average inventory		90	84	83	99	
Maximum volume required		4,046	3,143	5,584	2,227	15,000
Annual purchase cost		$3,250,000	$2,000,000	$2,750,000	$1,500,000	$9,500,000
Annual ordering cost		$ 27,804	$ 20,883	$ 36,263	$ 15,155	$ 100,104
Annual carrying cost		$ 3,507	$ 2,011	$ 2,730	$ 1,782	$ 10,030
Performance Measure						
Total annual cost		$3,281,310	$2,022,894	$2,788,993	$1,516,937	$9,610,134

We can now again invoke a mathematical programming algorithm to optimize the model. The result is contained in Figure 16–6, in which we are instructed to order far fewer than the EOQ of each subassembly, resulting in a total annual cost of $9,610,134. Notice that not only did the absolute order quantity of each subassembly change, but the relative magnitude of these order quantities changed as well. For example, while the EOQ of subassembly C is considerably larger than the others, the optimal order quantity for subassembly C given the storage space constraint is roughly the same as for subassemblies A and B and less than that of subassembly D. From a managerial perspective, it is also useful to observe that the annual cost of ordering and carrying the subassemblies is $47,132 ($9,610,134 − $9,563,002) greater with the storage space limitation than without. Hence, management may wish to consider whether or not to increase the amount of storage space available, using this annual cost figure as a guide. Notice that the optimization model can be used to explore the costs associated with different amounts of storage space by simply changing the constraining value of the cell containing the total maximum volume required.

Here is another variation.

Example 1b: Volume Discounts

Returning to the situation involving the single component subassembly A, the vendor that supplies subassembly A offers the XYZ Company the following discounts based on size of order:

Order Quantity	Per-Unit Price
Less than 750	$325
From 750 to less than 1,000	$320
1,000 or more	$315

Now how many units of subassembly A should XYZ order at a time?

The EOQ requires a fixed carrying cost, which in XYZ's case is a function of the unit cost (12% × Unit cost). If the unit cost changes, the carrying cost changes; hence, we cannot use EOQ directly. However, we can easily modify our basic spreadsheet (Figure 16–1) to incorporate volume discounts, and then transform it into an optimization model to determine the optimal order quantity.

Figure 16–7 contains the modified spreadsheet with volume discounts included. Notice that, in addition to annual ordering and carrying costs, total annual *purchasing* cost is also now relevant to our decision, since total purchasing cost now depends on our choice of order quantity (even though annual demand is still fixed). In the previous situations, with no volume discounts, the total annual purchasing cost was unaffected by our choice of order quantity and could have been ignored. Currently, the spreadsheet is set to calculate the cost of ordering 506 units, the EOQ.

The only "tricky" part of this spreadsheet is the use of a table lookup or IF statement to make sure the correct unit cost—a function of the number of units ordered—is used.

The form of the optimization model for this new situation is precisely the same as that of the original situation. We are still trying to minimize total

FIGURE 16–7

Evaluation Model for Example 1b Using Economic Order Quantity

Alternative		
Order quantity	506	
Input Assumptions		
Annual demand	10,000	
Purchase cost per unit	$ 325	
Cost per order	$ 500	
Annual inventory carrying cost	12%	
Intermediate Calculations		
Number of orders per year	20	
Average inventory	253	
Annual purchase cost	$3,250,000	
Annual ordering cost	$ 9,874	
Annual carrying cost	$ 9,874	
Performance Measure		
Total annual cost	$3,269,748	
Smallest Quantity to Obtain This Price		
	Quantity	*Price*
Base	—	$ 325
Break 1	750	$ 320
Break 2	1,000	$ 315

Unit cost = IF (Order quantity < Break 1 quantity, Base price, IF (Order quantity < Break 2 quantity, Break 1 price, Break 2 price))

annual cost by changing order quantity, with the single constraint that the order quantity cannot be negative. The new situation is captured entirely by the modifications we have made to the spreadsheet; specifically, the inclusion of total purchasing cost, and the use of an IF statement to determine the appropriate per-unit cost. The resulting optimized model is contained in Figure 16–8. Notice that it recommends an order quantity of 1,000 units.

We now consider the use of an optimization model in a very different situation.

Example 2: Product Mix Planning

Consider a firm that manufactures two products, PROD1 and PROD2. Each product is made from the same three raw materials, RM1, RM2, and RM3. The products differ, however, in selling price and the amount of each raw material needed to produce one unit of product. The table below contains the specifics of each product:

		Units of Raw Material Required to Produce 1 Unit of Product		
Product	*Price per unit*	*RM1*	*RM2*	*RM3*
PROD1	$120	1	3	2
PROD2	$140	3	2	3
Raw material price per unit		$10	$20	$15
Raw material units available		1,200	2,000	1,500

To keep our illustration simple, we will assume that the only cost involved in preparing a unit of either PROD1 or PROD2 for sale is the cost of the component raw materials, making both products profitable, as the following table confirms:

	PROD1	*PROD2*
Per-unit revenue	$120	$140
Less: COGS		
RM1	$10 × 1 = $10	$10 × 3 = $30
RM2	$20 × 3 = $60	$20 × 2 = $40
RM3	$15 × 2 = $30	$15 × 3 = $45
Per-unit contribution	$120 − ($10 + $60 + $30) = $20	$140 − ($30 + $40 + $45) = $25

Given that we can sell as many units of each product as we can produce, how many units of PROD1 and PROD2 should we produce to maximize contribution?

FIGURE 16–8
Optimized Model for Example 1b

Alternative		
Order quantity	1,000	
Input Assumptions		
Annual demand	10,000	
Purchase cost per unit	$ 315	
Cost per order	$ 500	
Annual inventory carrying cost	12%	
Intermediate Calculations		
Number of orders per year	10	
Average inventory	500	
Annual purchase cost	$3,150,000	
Annual ordering cost	$ 5,000	
Annual carrying cost	$ 18,900	
Performance Measure		
Total annual cost	$3,173,900	

Smallest Quantity to Obtain This Price		
	Quantity	*Price*
Base	—	$ 325
Break 1	750	$ 320
Break 2	1,000	$ 315

Our challenge in this example is to find the product combination, or mix, that maximizes contribution but does not use more of any raw material than what is available. We can construct an evaluation model to help us do this (Figure 16–9). This model permits us to select production quantities for each of the two products, and then calculates total contribution and raw material usage. In Figure 16–9, we have selected to produce 400 units of PROD1 and 200 units of PROD2. The model informs us first that this product mix is feasible with respect to raw material usage: It requires 1,000 units of RM1 (1,200 units available), 1,600 units of RM2 (2,000 available), and 1,400 units of RM3 (1,500 available). The model also calculates the total contribution of this product mix—$13,000.

To transform this evaluation model into an optimization model, we follow the same three steps we did in the first example.

1. The decision quantities are how many units of each product to produce. Thus, the cells to be altered are those containing the number of units of PROD1 and PROD2 to produce.

2. We wish to maximize contribution. Hence, the cell for total contribution—the sum of the contributions from each product—is the objective quantity, in this case, to be maximized.

3. As before, the production quantities must be nonnegative, and we will again ignore requiring the number of units be integer. In addition, the amount of each raw material required in the production mix must not exceed the amount available. This restriction is analogous to the one in the previous section in which the XYZ Company had a limited amount of storage space for its four subassemblies. But whereas in that example we specified that the cell containing the total storage space consumed by the set of order quantities could not exceed a certain number (15,000), we now specify that the total usage of each raw material must not exceed the available amounts.

We can now use mathematical programming to find the optimal product mix; the optimized model is in Figure 16–10.

As with Example 1, we could conceive of many variations on this situation, many of which could be addressed through minor modifications to the optimization model. Instead, however, we turn our attention to yet another situation for which an optimization model is useful.

Example 3: Facility Location

The ABC Company has eight major customers for whom it needs to establish a system of warehouses from which to supply them. The company has decided to establish three warehouses and has explored five possible locations. The following table contains the per-unit cost of supplying each customer from each possible location, along with each location's capacity and each customer's demand

FIGURE 16–9
Evaluation Model for Example 2

Alternative	PROD1	PROD2	
Number produced	400	200	
Input Assumptions			
Per-unit revenue	$ 120	$ 140	
Per-unit RM1 usage	1	3	
Per-unit RM2 usage	3	2	
Per-unit RM3 usage	2	3	
Cost per unit RM1	$ 10	$ 10	
Cost per unit RM2	$ 20	$ 20	
Cost per unit RM3	$ 15	$ 15	
Intermediate Calculations			**Total**
Revenue	$48,000	$28,000	$76,000
RM1 usage	400	600	1,000
RM2 usage	1,200	400	1,600
RM3 usage	800	600	1,400
RM1 cost	$ 4,000	$ 6,000	$10,000
RM2 cost	$24,000	$ 8,000	$32,000
RM3 cost	$12,000	$ 9,000	$21,000
Performance Measure			
Contribution	$ 8,000	$ 5,000	$13,000

FIGURE 16–10
Optimized Model for Example 2

Alternative	PROD1	PROD2	
Number produced	600	100	
Input Assumptions			
Per-unit revenue	$ 120	$ 140	
Per-unit RM1 usage	1	3	
Per-unit RM2 usage	3	2	
Per-unit RM3 usage	2	3	
Cost per unit RM1	$ 10	$ 10	
Cost per unit RM2	$ 20	$ 20	
Cost per unit RM3	$ 15	$ 15	
Intermediate Calculations			**Total**
Revenue	$72,000	$14,000	$86,000
RM1 usage	600	300	900
RM2 usage	1,800	200	2,000
RM3 usage	1,200	300	1,500
RM1 cost	$ 6,000	$ 3,000	$ 9,000
RM2 cost	$36,000	$ 4,000	$40,000
RM3 cost	$18,000	$ 4,500	$22,500
Performance Measure			
Contribution	$12,000	$ 2,500	$14,500

(both in units). At which three locations should the ABC Company establish warehouses in order to minimize the cost of supplying its customers?

	Facility (Per-unit sourcing cost)					
Customer	A	B	C	D	E	Demand
1	$13	$15	$15	$5	$3	30
2	3	2	5	3	13	45
3	8	13	12	14	1	20
4	6	8	4	3	13	25
5	10	7	3	6	4	15
6	6	12	12	10	3	35
7	12	2	4	1	7	30
8	15	1	11	6	11	40
Capacity	140	125	95	130	110	

A model to help evaluate the various location and sourcing alternatives can be found in Figure 16–11. This model takes advantage of the structure for keeping track of demand for each customer and capacity required at each facility, and hence deviates from the general model format we have been using. The current plan contained in the model calls for establishing warehouses at locations A, B, and C, and sourcing customers as described: customers 1–5 from A, 6 and 7 from B, and 8 from C. The total distribution cost of this sourcing plan is $1,905.

To transform this into an optimization model, we return to our three steps:

1. There are now two types of decisions to make: where to locate the warehouses, and how much of each customer's demand to source from each warehouse site selected. Thus, there are two cell ranges we wish to designate as decision quantities: the range B4:F11—where each cell contains how much of the customer's (row) demand to source from the facility (column)—and the range B14:F14—whether or not a location is selected for a warehouse.

This latter range of cells is different from the decision quantities with which we have dealt thus far. In fact, they do not appear to be "quantities" at all; rather, they simply need to indicate either "yes—establish a warehouse here" or "no—do not establish a warehouse here." We can accomplish this by constraining these cells to take on one of two possible values, where one by definition means yes and the other no. Perhaps the simplest way to do this is to constrain each cell to take on a value of either 1 or 0, where we define 1 as yes and 0 as no. In this way, we are able to represent a yes/no decision as a decision quantity, for which mathematical programming can find the optimal solution. This significantly increases the number of situations for which optimization models can be used.

FIGURE 16–11   *Evaluation Model for Example 3*

	A	B	C	D	E	F	G	H	I
1	**Sourcing Plan**								
2				**Facility**					
3	*Customer*	*A*	*B*	*C*	*D*	*E*	*Total*	*Demand*	*Cost*
4	1	30	—	—	—	—	30	30	$ 390
5	2	45	—	—	—	—	45	45	$ 135
6	3	20	—	—	—	—	20	20	$ 160
7	4	25	—	—	—	—	25	25	$ 150
8	5	15	—	—	—	—	15	15	$ 150
9	6	—	35	—	—	—	35	35	$ 420
10	7	—	30	—	—	—	30	30	$ 60
11	8	—	—	40	—	—	40	40	$ 440
12	Capacity required	135	65	40	—	—			$1,905
13	Capacity if open	140	125	95	130	110	**Total facilities**		
14	Facility open?	1	1	1	—	—	3		
15	Capacity available	140	125	95	—	—			
16									
17									
18	**Per-Unit Sourcing Cost**								
19					**Facility**				
20	*Customer*	*A*	*B*	*C*	*D*	*E*			
21	1	$13	$15	$15	$ 5	$ 3			
22	2	$ 3	$ 2	$ 5	$ 3	$13			
23	3	$ 8	$13	$12	$14	$ 1			
24	4	$ 6	$ 8	$ 4	$ 3	$13			
25	5	$10	$ 7	$ 3	$ 6	$ 4			
26	6	$ 6	$12	$12	$10	$ 3			
27	7	$12	$ 2	$ 4	$ 1	$ 7			
28	8	$15	$ 1	$11	$ 6	$11			

For Facility A:

Capacity required = Sum of column
Capacity if open = 140
Facility open? = 1
Capacity available = Capacity if open $\times$ Facility open?

We implement this representation by first constraining—for the first time in this chapter—the cells to be *integer*. (If it appears we are skipping ahead to step 3 here, we are: In this kind of situation, the constraints are an integral—no pun intended—part of the definition of the decision quantities.) Next, we further constrain the cells to be greater than or equal to 0 and less than or equal to 1. This effectively forces them to take on a value of either 0 or 1. (Some software packages may let you define 0/1 decision quantities directly, without having to do these two steps explicitly.)

2. We wish to minimize distribution cost. The objective quantity is thus contained in cell I12—the sum of the costs to supply each customer's demand.

3. We have a much richer set of constraints now than we have had in our earlier examples. First, we still have the constraint that the decision quantities must be nonnegative. Also, we still will not worry about whether or not the actual quantity sourced from a particular facility to a particular customer is integer. However, as discussed in step 1, we *will* require the cells corresponding to whether or not a facility is established at a particular location be integer.

We have a number of other constraints as well. First, since we have established *Minimize cost* as our objective, we must make sure the solution satisfies customer demand (or else we can minimize cost by not shipping *anything* to *anybody*!). We do this by requiring each entry in the *Total* column to be equal to its corresponding entry in the *Demand* column. (We could instead have required the *Total* entries be "greater than or equal to" the *Demand* entries. Since we are minimizing cost, the model would have no incentive to exceed the minimum required demand—which would increase cost—and hence equality would result.)

As a second set of constraints, we cannot source more from one facility location than its capacity. This is absurdly true if there is no facility at that location! Thus, we must require the entries in the row *Capacity required* (by the solution) be no greater than the corresponding entries in the row *Capacity available* (at the facility). Notice how the entries in the *Capacity available* row are developed: each is the product of the corresponding entry in the *Capacity if open* and the *Facility open?* rows. Thus, if the entry in the *Facility open?* row is 0—which we defined in step 1 as meaning there is no facility at that location—then the corresponding entry in the *Capacity available* row is forced to be 0 (because it is the product of two factors, one of which is 0). Since the *Capacity required* of the solution is constrained to be no greater than the *Capacity available* at the location, this prevents any demand from being sourced from that location.

A final constraint is that the number of facilities must be three. We can invoke this constraint by requiring that the sum of the cells in the *Facility open?* row be 3. This is facilitated by having the cell G14 contain the sum of the cells in the range B14:F14.

The optimized model is contained in Figure 16–12. It specifies that facilities should be established at locations B, D, and E, and that the overall cost of satisfying customer demand will then be $510.

Summary of Examples

Transforming an evaluation model into an optimization model always requires three steps: (1) specifying the cells that contain the decision quantities—those whose value can be changed by the decision maker; (2) indicating the cell that contains the objective quantity—the formula to be optimized; and (3) identifying any constraints—restrictions on the values the decision quantities can assume. The latter is typically the most involved of the three steps, as the number and types of constraints can be large. There are also situations in which you want to restrict decision quantities to assume one of two possible values, typically 0 or 1.

We now turn our attention to the issue of how mathematical programming actually finds the optimal solution to a properly specified optimization model. We will discover that there are basically three types of optimization models, each with its own unique—albeit interrelated—solution approach. We will also see why it is important to know with which category you are dealing.

FIGURE 16–12

Optimized Model for Example 3

Sourcing Plan								
	Facility							
Customer	*A*	*B*	*C*	*D*	*E*	*Total*	*Demand*	*Cost*
1	—	—	—	—	30	30	30	$ 90
2	—	45	—	—	—	45	45	$ 90
3	—	—	—	—	20	20	20	$ 20
4	—	—	—	25	—	25	25	$ 75
5	—	—	—	—	15	15	15	$ 60
6	—	—	—	—	35	35	35	$105
7	—	—	—	30	—	30	30	$ 30
8	—	40	—	—	—	40	40	$ 40
Capacity required	—	85	—	55	100			$510
Capacity if open	140	125	95	130	110			
Facility open?	—	1	—	1	1	3		
Capacity available	—	125	—	130	110			

Categorizing and Solving Optimization Models

Example 1: Nonlinear Programming

Example 1 belongs to the category of optimization models known as *nonlinear*; hence the term *nonlinear programming* for the construction and solution of such models. In all three variations of Example 1, a primary characteristic of the situation is that the relationship between the *decision quantity(ies)*—the order quantity—and the objective quantity—the *total annual cost*—is nonlinear. This means that a one-unit change in the order quantity results in a change in the total annual cost that is not the same across all order quantities. For example, consider the following relationships that were calculated from the spreadsheet in Figure 16–1:

	Old	New	Change	Old	New	Change
Order quantity	500	1,000	500	1,500	2,000	500
Total annual cost	$19,750	$24,500	$4,750	$32,583	$41,500	$8,917

Notice that in each of the two pairs of order quantities listed above, there is a 500-unit difference in the order quantity. However, for one pair, the difference in the corresponding total annual cost is $4,750, while for the other it is $8,917. If the relationship between order quantity and total annual cost had been linear, the change in total annual cost would have been the same for all 500-unit changes in order quantity, including the two above.

The nonlinearity of the relationship between order quantity and total annual cost is driven by the nature of the relationships represented by the arrows in Figure 16–2. If any of these relationships is nonlinear, then the overall relationship between order quantity and total annual cost is nonlinear. In this case, the relationship between order quantity and number of orders per year is nonlinear. This is because the number of orders per year is proportional to the *inverse* of order size; that is, number of orders per year is a *decelerating* function of order quantity (see Figure 16–13). This is caused by the way annual ordering cost—a component of total annual cost—is calculated. Specifically, as can be seen from Figure 16–2, order quantity relates to total annual ordering cost via its relationship first to number of orders per year as one of its factors, and number of orders per year is determined by taking the annual demand and *dividing* it by the order quantity. It is this division in the sequence of calculations leading from order quantity to total annual cost that renders the relationship between the two nonlinear.

What is the significance on solution methodology of the fact that the relationship between order quantity and total annual cost is nonlinear? The first thing a user should know about solving nonlinear optimization models is that it is not easy mathematically. The software to solve nonlinear optimi-

FIGURE 16–13

Relationship between Order Quantity and Number of Orders

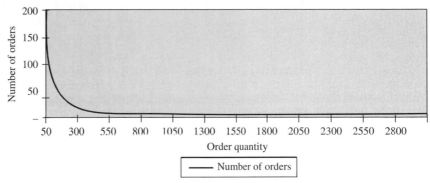

zation models within spreadsheets has only become widely and affordably available during the 1990s, and it is still relatively slow compared to other spreadsheet functions, due to the computational effort required.

Most mathematical programming approaches to solving nonlinear optimization models involve some type of calculus-derived technique to determine, for any particular solution (i.e., specific value for each decision quantity), how the objective quantity would change if small changes were made in the values of the individual decision quantities. If the approach identifies a set of changes that improve the objective quantity, a new solution is generated based on this information, and the approach repeats itself. When the approach is unable to identify a set of changes that improves the objective quantity, the search ends, and it is assumed that the optimal solution has been identified. Each new solution generated is referred to as an *iteration* within the solution approach. In nonlinear optimization, each iteration takes a relatively long time to perform (this will be contrasted with a later category—linear programming—where iterations are much easier to perform).

In addition to time, there is another potential difficulty with solving a nonlinear optimization model in this fashion. Figure 16–14 contains a graph of the relationship between order quantity and total annual cost for the volume-discount version of our example. From the graph, it is easy to see that an order quantity of 1,000 produces the lowest total annual cost. However, there are two abrupt changes in price, at the two break points for volume discounts—order quantities of 750 and 1,000. These break points divide the graph into three segments: ordering less than 750, ordering at least 750 but fewer than 1,000, and ordering 1,000 or more. It is the existence of these segments that can pose a problem for nonlinear solution methodologies.

A key word in our description of the solution methodology for nonlinear optimization is *small*, as in what happens to the objective quantity if *small* changes are made in the values of the individual decision quantities. In our

FIGURE 16–14

Relationship between Order Quantity and Total Annual Cost

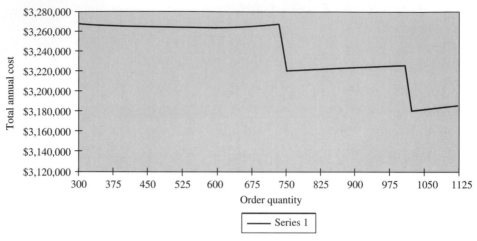

example, consider what happens if the approach starts with an order quantity less than 750, say 600. From the graph in Figure 16–14, notice that the line in the segment below 750 is a slight curve, with a low point at an order quantity of 506. From any point on this segment, the total annual cost can be decreased by moving toward a value of 506. Hence, at 600, decreasing the order quantity is an improvement, while increasing it makes the objective quantity worsen slightly, at least for a *small* change. Thus, if we start the approach at an order quantity less than 750, it will inevitably settle at an "optimal" order quantity of 506, never recognizing that by making a *large* increase in the order quantity it could significantly improve the total order cost.

What if we start the approach at an order quantity close to 750, say 749? Unfortunately, the mathematics of the approach are such that *small* means very, *very* small, as in "calculus small." Hence, there is no quantity less than 750 from which the approach would recognize 750 as being a small change. Hence, once locked into the range of order quantities less than 750, the approach cannot escape. It will inevitably lock in on a value of 506 and assume it to be optimal.

The same reasoning holds if the approach is started at an order quantity in either of the other two segments. If started at an order quantity of 750 or higher but less than 1,000, 750—the cost-minimizing quantity in this segment (see the graph in Figure 16–14)—will eventually be identified as the optimal solution. If started at an order quantity of 1,000 or higher, 1,000—the cost-minimizing quantity in this segment—will eventually be recognized as the optimal solution. (Notice that for both of these latter two segments, *small* changes from the optimal order quantity—for example, a slight decrease from 750—will throw the approach into another segment. However, in this particular example, those changes do not improve the total order cost, and hence the solution algorithm rejects them.)

Each of these three solutions—506, 750, 1,000—are called *local* optimal solutions, because they satisfy the property that each is optimal relative to *small* changes in the order quantity (i.e., each is optimal in its own *locality*). However, we wish to find the *global*, or overall, optimal solution, and thus we need to find a way to overcome the possibility that the approach will settle on a local—but not global—optimum.

How do we do this? First, if it is possible to identify "segments" of solutions, such as is often the case with price breaks based on volume discounts, you could choose an order quantity within each of the segments and start the approach from each one. You would then compare the resulting local optimal solutions to determine which one is best overall. (If you try such an approach, do not be alarmed if the particular software you are using appears to jump segments; remember, it would have done so in our example if it had started in the middle segment and discovered that decreasing the order quantity from 750 improved the quantity to be optimized.)

However, it is frequently impossible with nonlinear models to easily identify even the existence of such segments. For these more complex problems, the best strategy is simply to start the approach from various starting points (allowable solutions), and see if it converges to the same or different optimal solutions. If different, record each one, and when you are finished, choose the one with the best overall value. How do you know when to stop trying different starting points? The answer, unfortunately, is that you don't. The more you try, the better the chance that you will find the true, global optimal solution. And even if you don't find the global optimal solution, the more you try, the better the local optimal solution you end up with.

The nonlinearity of the model is not always created by the relationship between the decision quantities and the objective quantity. Sometimes it is caused by the nature of the relationship between the decision quantities and a quantity that is being tracked because it imposes a constraint on the values the decision quantities can assume. In Example 1, the storage space required for the subassemblies is an example of a quantity being tracked because it constrains the decision quantity values. However, in the example, the relationship between the decision quantities and required storage space is linear: Each additional unit ordered increases the required space by .75, irrespective of how many units are ordered. If the nature of this relationship had been nonlinear, then the model would have been classified as nonlinear, *even* if the relationship between decision quantities and the objective quantity had been linear. Most nonlinear algorithms are sufficiently general to handle nonlinearity in either or both places.

There are efforts within the mathematical programming community to find ways to speed up nonlinear programming solution approaches and to overcome their inability to distinguish local from global optimal solutions. In time, improved approaches will undoubtedly become available. In the meantime, however, the builder and user of a nonlinear optimization model must be aware of its potential limitations.

Example 2: Linear Programming

Despite the appearance of the model for Example 2, which looks as complex if not more so than that of Example 1, this optimization model is actually easier to solve. It belongs to a category of models referred to as *linear programming*. As you might suspect, a primary characteristic of Example 2 is that the relationship between the decision quantities—the number of units of each product to produce—and the objective quantity—total contribution—is *linear,* as opposed to nonlinear. This means that a one unit change in either of the production quantities results in a change in the total contribution that is the *same* across all production quantities. In Example 2, increasing the production of PROD1 by one unit will increase total contribution by $20—assuming the production level of PROD2 does not also change—irrespective of the absolute number of units of PROD1 being produced. The table below, calculated from the spreadsheet in Figure 16–8, illustrates this (we assume the production of 200 units of PROD2 in each of the calculations below):

	Old	*New*	*Change*	*Old*	*New*	*Change*
Quantity of PROD1 to produce	100	200	100	300	400	100
Total contribution	$7,000	$9,000	$2,000	$11,000	$13,000	$2,000

Notice that in both pairs of production quantities, a 100-unit difference in production quantity generates a $2,000 difference in total contribution. This holds for any 100-unit difference in PROD1 production quantity; it will always generate a $2,000 increase in total contribution.

The linearity of the relationship between PROD1 production quantity and total contribution is caused by the way total contribution is calculated based on PROD1 production quantity. Each produced unit of PROD1 generates a contribution of $20, as calculated in the *Contribution* row of Figure 16–9 of the column labeled *PROD1,* irrespective of how many units of PROD1 are produced. This value is then added in the *Total contribution* cell to the contribution from PROD2 to determine the total contribution. The only arithmetic operations that are ever performed on the production quantity of PROD1 as it feeds into total contribution are *multiplication by a constant* and *addition* (or subtraction). Unlike the example in the previous section, it is never *divided* into another quantity. It is also never *multiplied by an expression containing another decision quantity, raised to a power,* nor is its *square root* taken, other common sources of nonlinearity. In general, anything that prevents this consistent relationship between changes in the two quantities causes nonlinearity.

In addition, for a model to be linear, the relationships between the decision quantities and a quantity that is being tracked because it imposes a constraint on the values the decision quantities can assume, must be linear as well. In Example 2, increasing the production of PROD1 by one unit will increase the number of units of RM2 required by 3 units, again irrespective of the absolute number of units of PROD1 being produced. The relationship between decision quantities and RM1 and RM3 usage are similarly linear.

It is possible to solve a linear programming model using a nonlinear solution algorithm. However, there is a more efficient way to solve linear models. This specifically linear solution methodology is called the *simplex algorithm*. Two of the primary advantages of solving a linear model with the simplex rather than a nonlinear algorithm are *speed* and *size* of the model you can build and solve. The simplex algorithm finds an optimal solution much more quickly and—in part because of this increased speed—can be used to solve much larger models than nonlinear algorithms.

The simplex algorithm operates similarly to the nonlinear algorithm described above in that it progresses through a series of iterations involving solutions that are increasingly more optimal with respect to the objective quantity. However, because of the linearity of the model, calculus is not required to explore the impact on the objective of changes in the decision quantities; simple algebra is sufficient. Furthermore, once a direction of improvement is identified, the same algebra can be used to determine the next solution to be considered. The net effect is that iterations are executed much faster in the simplex algorithm than in a nonlinear algorithm, and even though a nonlinear algorithm typically requires fewer iterations, this does not offset the within-iteration advantage of the simplex method.

Whether solved as a linear or nonlinear model, a linear programming model has an additional advantage over a nonlinear programming model: Local optimal solutions are not a problem. If you refer back to the example from the previous section (Figure 16–14), it was precisely the nonlinear characteristic of the relationship between order size and total annual cost that created the possibility of ending up with a local, but not global, optimal solution. If the graph in Figure 16–14 had been a straight line—which it would have been had the relationship been linear—the issue of getting stuck in a particular segment of the line would not have arisen. This leads to the following practical insight.

PRACTICAL HINT: A linear model can be solved as either a linear or nonlinear model; that is, nonlinear solution algorithms are sufficiently general that they can solve linear models as well. However, the simplex algorithm, a solution approach that works only for linear models, is a much more efficient way to solve linear models in terms of the time it takes to solve the model and the size of the model that can be solved.

The majority of mathematical programming models built and used in practice are linear. This may appear surprising, given that the world is more often than not nonlinear. However, this is primarily because the simplex algorithm for solving linear models has been around much longer than nonlinear algorithms, due to its less demanding computational requirements. In addition, in a real decision environment, nonlinear relationships often can be approximated by linear relationships in such a way that the usefulness of the model is not compromised.

Example 3: Integer Programming

Example 3 belongs to the category of models known as *integer programming*.[4] In Example 3, this designation is due to the nature of the decision quantities used to specify whether a facility is established in a given location. The flexibility of being able to use decision quantities that are restricted to take on a value of either 0 or 1 as an "on-off" switch significantly enhances our ability to accurately represent real-world decisions. However, this additional flexibility comes at a price.

On first consideration, it might appear that a model with decision quantities restricted to 0 or 1 should be easier to solve than one with continuous decision quantities. After all, with a 0/1 decision quantity, there are only two possible choices, while for a continuous decision quantity, there are an infinite number of possible choices. However, this is not the case. Both the simplex and nonlinear algorithms depend precisely on the *continuity* of the decision quantities to identify how to improve on the solution being considered in the current iteration. That is, for any given solution (iteration), both methods depend on investigating the impact of *small* changes in the decision quantities. With a 0/1 decision quantity (or, more generally, a decision quantity restricted to assume an integer value), small changes are by definition not possible—the decision quantity is either 0 or 1. Thus, what happens to the objective quantity if the decision quantity is increased slightly from 0 is not only irrelevant, but potentially misleading as well.

Thus, solving integer programming models requires a different approach. The most commonly encountered (and generally applicable) of these approaches is called *branch and bound*. Perhaps the best way to conceptualize branch and bound is to visualize a decision diagram for Example 3 such as the one depicted in Figure 16–15. In this diagram, the 0/1 decision quantities of whether or not to establish the warehouse at each location are listed first, followed by the continuous decision quantities of how much of each customer's demand to supply from each warehouse. For any given path through the 0/1 decision quantities (i.e., a specification of where to locate warehouses) finding the optimal solution associated with that particular path involves solv-

---

[4]More specifically, it is a *mixed integer programming* model because some of the decision quantities are required to be integers and some are not.

FIGURE 16–15
Decision Diagram for Example 3

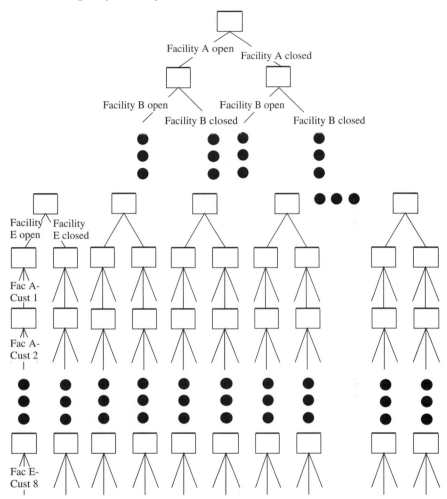

ing for the optimal values of the remaining continuous decision quantities, given that particular set of warehouse locations. In general, this "subproblem" of finding the optimal solution for a set of continuous decision quantities given values for the 0/1 decision quantities is either a nonlinear or linear programming model—as defined above—depending on the nature of the relationships in the model. As such, it can be solved by either a nonlinear or the simplex algorithm.

Thus, one possible approach to finding the optimal solution to a 0/1 integer programming model would be to find the optimal solution associated with each sequence of "branches" through the 0/1 decision quantities and then to simply choose the sequence with the best optimal solution over the remaining continuous decision quantities. However, for even small models, the number of such sequences gets large quickly as the number of 0/1 decision quantities grows. Just enumerating—much less evaluating—all possible sequences is impractical for all but the smallest problems. For example, in Example 3, there are $2^5 = 32$ such sequences, of which 6 are not feasible because they involve having more than three warehouses, for a total of 26 possible combinations.

Branch and bound was developed to mitigate the need to *directly* check all possible sequences through the 0/1 decision quantities of the diagram. To see how this is accomplished, suppose you were at the top of the decision diagram in Figure 16–15, and you solved the associated optimization model *ignoring* the fact that the values of the first five decision quantities had to be integer, but still requiring that they be between 0 and 1, inclusive. The resulting optimal solution can be found in Figure 16–16. Observe that the optimal solution now contains values other than 0 or 1 for the 0/1 decision quantities, which of course is not a *real* solution since a *real* solution must have values of 0 or 1 for those quantities. However, the value of the objective quantity—$495—associated with this nonreal optimal solution must be at least as good as the value of the objective quantity associated with any *real* solution to the model, or else a *real* solution would have been identified as optimal. Hence,

---

FIGURE 16–16

Optimal Solution to Example 3 without 0/1 Restriction on Facility Open?

Sourcing Plan								
	Facility							
Customer	A	B	C	D	E	Total	Demand	Cost
1	—	—	—	—	30	30	30	$ 90
2	—	45	—	—	—	45	45	$ 90
3	—	—	—	—	20	20	20	$ 20
4	—	—	—	25	—	25	25	$ 75
5	—	—	15	—	—	15	15	$ 45
6	—	—	—	—	35	35	35	$105
7	—	—	—	30	—	30	30	$ 30
8	—	40	—	—	—	40	40	$ 40
Capacity required	—	85	15	55	85			$495
Capacity if open	140	125	95	130	110			
Facility open?	0.00	0.68	0.16	0.42	0.77	2.03		
Capacity available	0	85	15	55	85			

the value of the objective quantity associated with this nonreal optimal solution is a *bound* on the best possible objective quantity we could achieve with a *real* solution to the model.

The key to branch and bound is the recognition that this technique can be applied at any node of the decision diagram to generate a *bound* on the best possible *real* solution for the rest of the decision quantities in the model. The *branching* part of branch and bound simply refers to starting at the top of the diagram and *branching* down the tree one node at a time. Notice that moving from the top node of the decision diagram to its two immediate successor nodes is equivalent to evaluating what happens in our model if the first decision quantity is set to 0 and 1, corresponding to whether or not we locate a facility at location A. We then calculate bounds at each one of those nodes; from Exhibit 16–17 we see that the bound on the best we can do if we *do not* locate a facility as A is still $495, while the best we can do if we *do* locate a facility at A is $499. Hence, we next explore the two options of what to do with location B, given that we decided *not* to locate a warehouse at A. Observe, however, that we cannot rule out the possibility that the optimal solution *will* involve having a warehouse at A, because we are not sure at this point whether or not we will be able to find a *real* solution without a facility at A that is better than the *possible* $499 we might get from having a facility at A. Thus, we can continue down the path of "no facility at A," but if we do not find a *real* solution with cost less than $499, we will have to eventually come back and explore the options stemming from having a facility at A. If, however, we *do* find a *real* solution down the path of "no facility at A" with cost less than $499, we will not have to go back and explore *any* of the options stemming from having a facility at A, since they cannot be better than the bound of $499, and we already have a solution that beats that bound. It is in this manner that branch and bound precludes our having to *directly* check all possible sequences through the 0/1 decision quantities of the diagram. (For the complete branch and bound solution to this example, see Chapter 17.)

It may now be apparent why solving an integer program takes much more time than solving a model without integer restrictions. Implementing branch and bound requires solving a *sequence* of linear or nonlinear programming models. As the number of 0/1 decision quantities increases, the number of linear or nonlinear models that may potentially have to be solved increases *exponentially*. Furthermore, if the basic underlying model *is* nonlinear, branch and bound requires solving a sequence of nonlinear optimization models, which can really increase the computation time (yet another reason for modeling a situation as linear if at all possible).

This, then, is the price one pays for the ability to use 0/1 decision quantities in a model. The variety of situations you can model increases significantly, but the computational effort required to solve those models also increases significantly. For small problems, this is generally not an issue, and even some large problems can be solved in a relatively short time, particularly if you already know of a relatively good *real* solution to the problem and are

FIGURE 16–17

Bounds on Best Possible Solutions with and without Facility A

Sourcing Plan								
	Facility							
Customer	*A*	*B*	*C*	*D*	*E*	*Total*	*Demand*	*Cost*
1	—	—	—	—	30	30	30	$ 90
2	—	45	—	—	—	45	45	$ 90
3	—	—	—	—	20	20	20	$ 20
4	—	—	—	25	—	25	25	$ 75
5	—	—	15	—	—	15	15	$ 45
6	—	—	—	—	35	35	35	$105
7	—	—	—	30	—	30	30	$ 30
8	—	40	—	—	—	40	40	<u>$ 40</u>
Capacity required	—	85	15	55	85			$495
Capacity if open	140	125	95	130	110			
Facility open?	—	0.68	0.16	0.42	0.77	2.03		
Capacity available	—	85	15	55	85			

Sourcing Plan								
	Facility							
Customer	*A*	*B*	*C*	*D*	*E*	*Total*	*Demand*	*Cost*
1	—	—	—	—	30	30	30	$ 90
2	4	41	—	—	—	45	45	$ 94
3	—	—	—	—	20	20	20	$ 20
4	—	—	—	25	—	25	25	$ 75
5	—	—	15	—	—	15	15	$ 45
6	—	—	—	—	35	35	35	$105
7	—	—	—	30	—	30	30	$ 30
8	—	40	—	—	—	40	40	<u>$ 40</u>
Capacity required	4	81	15	55	85			$499
Capacity if open	140	125	95	130	110			
Facility open?	1	0.65	0.16	0.42	0.77	3.00		
Capacity available	140	81	15	55	85			

using software that permits you to specify that solution at the outset. However, it is impossible to tell just by looking at an integer programming model whether or not it will solve quickly.

Thus far, we have assumed that all the numerical inputs to our model are known. Suppose there is uncertainty in the value of these inputs? This is the topic of the next section.

Uncertainty in Optimization Models: Sensitivity Analysis

The mathematical approaches used to solve optimization models are both a blessing and a curse—a blessing because they implicitly make the difficult economic trade-offs inherent in the numbers in the model in order to squeeze every last ounce of optimality from the decision, a curse because this automatic "squeezing" is driven by the exact values of the numbers in the model—there is no "fudging" done to allow for possible uncertainty in the inputs. Once the mathematical solution approach is invoked, any uncertainty in the numbers is ignored, and the resulting optimal solution is truly only as good as the accuracy of the inputs.

On the other hand, in the case of linear and nonlinear programming, the nature of the mathematics of the solution approaches generates information that provides insight into how much the optimal value of the objective quantity would (or might) change if certain inputs to the model were changed and the model reoptimized. This allows us to get at least some feel for the impact of uncertainty on our model results.

Lagrange Multipliers

The one set of inputs for which both linear and nonlinear solution approaches provide information is related to the constraints on the values the decision quantities are allowed to assume. For each such constraint, as a by-product of the optimal solution, a number is generated that measures how the value of the optimal objective quantity would change if the constraint were relaxed; that is, made less restrictive. For example, in Example 1a, what if we had more than 15,000 cubic feet of storage? It turns out that for each additional cubic foot of storage, we could reduce our annual costs by $6. It is this number—$6—that the nonlinear solution approach produces as a by-product of its main task of finding the optimal solution. It can be used to help us determine the value of procuring additional storage space.

In the language of mathematical programming, this number is called a *Lagrange multiplier*. The term itself is derived from economics; it would take us too far afield to explain how it came to be used. However, there are several points we need to make about Lagrange multipliers in general. First, the Lagrange multiplier applies equally to *tightening*—making a constraint *more* restrictive—as to relaxing a constraint. Hence, the number $6 also represents the amount our annual costs would *increase* if we lost one cubic foot of storage (from 15,000). Thus, we can also use the Lagrange multiplier to help us determine the cost of losing existing storage space.

Second, the Lagrange multiplier is only guaranteed to describe the impact of making small changes in the amount of storage space available relative to the existing 15,000 cubic feet. Remember: nonlinear solution algorithms use calculus. Hence, small changes mean *calculus-small* changes. Thus, while we interpreted $6 as the value associated with a one-foot increase or decrease in the amount of storage space available, in reality, this value might change as soon as we move away from 15,000 cubic feet. In fact, a more precise statement of the Lagrange multiplier at 15,000 is $6.0049; at 15,000.5 cubic feet, the Lagrange multiplier is $6.0043. Thus, our interpretation of the Lagrange multiplier as being associated with a one-unit increase or decrease is not precisely accurate; it is the rate of change in the optimal objective quantity at exactly 15,000 cubic feet, expressed in terms of one-unit (cubic feet) changes in the storage space.

Another important characteristic of Lagrange multipliers has to do with when they assume a value of 0. Every constraint has a Lagrange multiplier associated with it. For any constraint that is not *binding* on the optimal solution (i.e., the "constraint" turns out to not actually "constrain" the values the decision quantities assume in pursuit of the optimal objective quantity) the Lagrange multiplier for that constraint will be 0. This should make sense based on our interpretation of the Lagrange multipliers: if a constraint does not restrict our ability to do what we want to do, then relaxing (or tightening) the constraint a small amount will similarly not restrict what we are trying to do. Consider, for example, the constraint in Example 1 that the order quantity be nonnegative—greater than or equal to 0. This constraint turned out *not* to be binding: our optimal order quantity was 506. Relaxing this constraint would have meant allowing the decision quantity to be nonnegative *or slightly negative* (say, greater than or equal to -1, for example). Admittedly, this is nonsensical, but the point is that this new, relaxed restriction would have had no impact on what we wanted to do—namely, order 506 units at a time—and hence no impact on the minimal annual ordering cost. The Lagrange multiplier for this constraint was hence $0.00. Alternatively, we could have more sensically asked the impact of tightening the constraint: forcing the decision quantity to be greater than or equal to 1. Again, this would have had no impact on our optimal order quantity or ordering cost, and the multiplier would have been seen to be $0.00.[5] Thus, one of the following statements will

---

[5]For the nonnegativity constraints, the Lagrange multiplier will be other than 0 only if the value of the associated decision quantity is 0 in the optimal solution. In this case, the Lagrange multiplier is generally best interpreted as the cost associated with forcing a decision quantity to assume a value greater than 0. Because of its somewhat unique status, the Lagrange multiplier associated with the nonnegativity constraints is often given its own name, generally the *reduced cost* of the decision quantity. The derivation of this term is also too obscure to warrant our spending time on it.

be true about each constraint and the optimal solution to the model: the constraint will be binding and the Lagrange multiplier will have a nonzero value, or the constraint will not be binding, in which case the value of the Lagrange multiplier will be zero.[6]

A final important fact about Lagrange multipliers: they hold under the assumption that everything else in the model stays the same. Thus, the Lagrange multiplier of $6.00 is predicated on the fact that only the amount of storage space available changes and nothing else. Any change in the value of the other numbers in the model, or in the restrictiveness of any other binding constraints (moot in this example, since there are no other binding constraints), could cause the Lagrange multiplier to be different. Hence, the Lagrange multiplier is useful for determining the *relative* sensitivity of the optimal solution to the constraints, but care must be taken when investigating the impact of several constraints changing simultaneously.

Lagrange multipliers can also be obtained from solving integer programs. However, in the case of integer programs, the existence of integer decision quantities renders the multipliers meaningless. In calculating a Lagrange multiplier, the solution procedure traces the ripple effect of making a small change in the constraint, which in turn makes *a (generally) small change in the values of the optimal decision quantities*, which in turn makes a (relatively) small change in the optimal value of the objective quantity. (It is this last change that is reported as the Lagrange multiplier.) It is the italicized part of this connection that creates the difficulty: Integer decision quantities cannot be changed a *small* amount and remain *real* solutions. Unfortunately, the same math that generates the Lagrange multipliers does not accommodate decision quantities restricted to be integers, and hence treats them as though they were continuous. Thus, the Lagrange multiplier generally assumes that integer decision quantities *can* be changed by small amounts, and hence no longer be integer. This can lead to such serious mistaken estimates of the true impact of changes in the constraint so as to render Lagrange multipliers meaningless for integer programs.

PRACTICAL HINT: Lagrange multipliers are essentially meaningless for integer programming models.

---

[6]It is possible for the constraint to be binding and have a Lagrange multiplier of 0. This happens if relaxing the constraint does not lead to an improved optimal objective criterion value, which can happen if the existence of other constraints precludes being able to take advantage of the additional flexibility. An important implication of the occurrence of this phenomenon is that there is more than one value of the decision quantities that yields the optimal objective criterion value. In terms of the economics captured in the model, none of these solutions is to be preferred to any others. However, there may be reasons unrelated to the economics in the model to prefer one. Ascertaining that *multiple optimal solutions* exist can encourage you to consider the impact of these noneconomic factors on the choice of which of the optimal solutions is "best."

Linear Programming Models

Lagrange multipliers exist for both linear and nonlinear programming models. However, when dealing with linear programming, additional sensitivity analysis is available. One type has to do with the "smallness" of changes over which a Lagrange multiplier holds. A second type has to do with the sensitivity of the optimal decision quantities to their per-unit impact on the objective quantity. We will consider each in turn.

Shadow Prices and Ranges   In a linear (as opposed to nonlinear) programming model, a Lagrange multiplier is more frequently referred to as a *shadow price*. The use of this term stems from the earliest applications of linear programming, in which the constraints were scarce resources (such as Raw Materials 1–3 in Example 2). The *price* component of the term derives from a logical implication of the definition of Lagrange multiplier: if *relaxing* a constraint refers to having more of a scarce resource, and the Lagrange multiplier measures the value of having an additional unit of resource, then it also represents a bound on the price you would be willing to pay to acquire an additional unit of that resource. The term *shadow* reflects the fact that this is not a real market price for RM2, but rather the *value* of additional units of RM2 to the firm.

Because of the linear nature of the relationships in a linear programming model, the Lagrange multiplier does not necessarily change over small relaxations (or tightenings) of the constraint, as it does for nonlinear programming (see the example in the previous section). For example, consider the constraint on the availability of RM2 in Example 2. In the optimal solution of 600 units of PROD1 and 100 units of PROD2, all 2,000 units of RM2 are consumed. The shadow price (or Lagrange multiplier) of this constraint is $2.00, meaning (as before) that with one additional unit of RM2 we could generate an additional $2.00 of contribution. However, if we now change the amount of RM2 available to 2,100 units and rerun the model, we get a new optimal contribution of $14,700, which is exactly $200 more than our contribution with 2,000 units of RM2 (see Figure 16–18). Thus, it would seem that each additional unit of RM2 generated $2.00 of additional contribution. Similarly, if we now change the amount of RM2 available to 1,900 units and rerun the model, we get a new optimal contribution of $14,300, which is exactly $200 less than our contribution with 2,000 units of RM2 (see Figure 16–19). Again, the $2.00 shadow price appears to hold over the entire range of decrease down to 1,900 units.

This example is not anomalous. In every linear program, shadow prices hold—without changing—over ranges of relaxations and tightenings of constraints. The simplex algorithm produces these ranges as well as the shadow prices as part of its solution process. In the example above, the shadow price of $2.00 holds for an additional 250 units of RM2—up to 2,250 units total—and for a loss of 500 units—down to 1,500 units total. Outside the range, the

FIGURE 16–18

Optimal Solution for Example 2 with 2,100 Units of RM2

Alternative	PROD1	PROD2	
Number produced	660	60	
Input Assumptions			
Per-unit revenue	$ 120	$ 140	
Per-unit RM1 usage	1	3	
Per-unit RM2 usage	3	2	
Per-unit RM3 usage	2	3	
Cost per unit RM1	$ 10	$ 10	
Cost per unit RM2	$ 20	$ 20	
Cost per unit RM3	$ 15	$ 15	
Intermediate Calculations			**Total**
Revenue	$79,200	$ 8,400	$87,600
RM1 usage	660	180	840
RM2 usage	1,980	120	2,100
RM3 usage	1,320	180	1,500
RM1 cost	$ 6,600	$ 1,800	$ 8,400
RM2 cost	$39,600	$ 2,400	$42,000
RM3 cost	$19,800	$ 2,700	$22,500
Performance Measure			
Contribution	$13,200	$ 1,500	$14,700

shadow price—the value of additional or fewer units of RM2—will be different from $2.00. For units above 2,250, the shadow price will be lower. For the 2,251st unit, we have to drop down to a less profitable way of taking advantage of RM2, as we have exhausted the way we are using RM2 when its

FIGURE 16–19

Optimal Solution for Example 2 with 1,900 Units of RM2

Alternative	PROD1	PROD2	
Number produced	540	140	
Input Assumptions			
Per-unit revenue	$ 120	$ 140	
Per-unit RM1 usage	1	3	
Per-unit RM2 usage	3	2	
Per-unit RM3 usage	2	3	
Cost per unit RM1	$ 10	$ 10	
Cost per unit RM2	$ 20	$ 20	
Cost per unit RM3	$ 15	$ 15	
Intermediate Calculations			**Total**
Revenue	$64,800	$19,600	$84,400
RM1 usage	540	420	960
RM2 usage	1,620	280	1,900
RM3 usage	1,080	420	1,500
RM1 cost	$ 5,400	$ 4,200	$ 9,600
RM2 cost	$32,400	$ 5,600	$38,000
RM3 cost	$16,200	$ 6,300	$22,500
Performance Measure			
Contribution	$10,800	$ 3,500	$14,300

availability is between 1,500 and 2,250 units. For units below 1,500, the shadow price will be higher. We have a more profitable way of taking advantage of units up to 1,500 (maybe several different ways, depending on how many shadow-price ranges exist between 0 and 1,500), and at the 1,500th unit we have to drop down to the less profitable way that holds for the 1,500 to

2,250 range.[7] It is impossible to determine the new shadow price in either direction without explicitly changing the restrictiveness of the constraint (to a value outside the range) and reoptimizing the model (i.e., the value of the new shadow prices is not a by-product of the solution process).

The advantage of having (and knowing) a range over which shadow prices hold should be clear. As long as the uncertainty surrounding the precise restrictiveness of the constraint is within the range, we can use the shadow price to determine the exact impact of the uncertainty. Hence, if we are not sure we will have precisely 2,000 units of RM2, but know we will have somewhere between 1,700 and 2,200, we can use the $2.00 shadow price to determine the maximum contribution for any specific amount without having to modify and reoptimize the model. (For a probability distribution on the amount of RM2 available within the range, it would be relatively simple to generate a risk profile and expected contribution.) This cannot be done for Lagrange multipliers in nonlinear programming models.

Finally, just like a shadow price (Lagrange multiplier), a shadow-price range holds only under the condition that everything else in the model remains unchanged. Changes in the restrictiveness of more than one constraint simultaneously may change the ranges over which the shadow prices hold.[8]

Relationship between Decision Quantities and the Objective Quantity
In Example 2, each produced unit of PROD1 generates a $20 contribution, while each produced unit of PROD2 generates $25. Inherent in the nature of a linear program is that there is a per-unit relationship between decision quantities and the objective quantity that holds for all feasible values of the decision quantities, in this case $20 for PROD1 and $25 for PROD2. This combination of contribution margins—coupled with how much of each raw material the two products require on a relative basis—is what drives the optimal solution—600 units of PROD1 and 100 units of PROD2. A logical question to ask is how sensitive this solution is to changes in these contribution levels. For example, suppose we are concerned that we will not be able to sell PROD1 for $120 but may have to cut the price to $118. Would we still want to produce 600 units of PROD1 given a contribution margin of $18 instead of $20? The answer to this question would help us determine how much we need to worry about the actual price we will be able to charge for PROD1.

---

[7]It is possible that a shadow price will remain the same outside the associated range. This would be the result of having *redundant* constraints (i.e., constraints that impose essentially the same restrictions on the decision quantities) which is somewhat of an anomaly. There is no easy way of determining whether or not this is the case, so it is reasonable to assume the shadow price will change until you find out differently.

[8]If the changes in restrictiveness are small relative to the sizes of the respective ranges (in the direction of the changes), it is likely that the optimal solution will not change. In fact, if the sum of the percentage changes is less than 100 percent, you can be sure the solution will not change.

The simplex algorithm generates this information as a by-product of finding the optimal solution. Specifically, for the present example, we would learn that as long as everything else in the model remains the same, the contribution margin for PROD1 could be anywhere from $16.67 to $37.50, and the optimal solution would still call for producing 600 units of PROD1 and 100 units of PROD2. Thus, the possibility that we might be able to charge only $118 rather than $120 has no effect on how many units we would choose to produce, and we can therefore proceed with production without worrying about it. On the other hand, if we thought it possible we would be able to charge only $115 for PROD1, this sensitivity analysis tells us that we might make more total contribution by producing some number other than 600 units of PROD1 (undoubtedly fewer). The only way to determine this new optimal product mix is to change the *Revenue* cell in the model to reflect a new sales price of $115 and reoptimize; the resulting new solution may be found in Figure 16–20. As you can see, the optimal solution did change, to producing 300 units each of PROD1 and PROD2. The analogous information for PROD2 is that its contribution can range from $13.33 to $30 without the optimal solution changing.

There is one important caveat to the interpretation of these ranges. As with shadow prices and their ranges, each range on the per-unit impact of the decision quantities on the objective quantity assumes that everything else in the model remains the same, *including the per-unit impacts of the other decision quantities*. Hence, the range around PROD1 is based on an assumed contribution margin of $25 for PROD2, and the range around PROD2 is based on an assumed contribution margin of $20 for PROD1. To investigate substantial, simultaneous changes in both, you would have to actually change the model and reoptimize (see footnote 6).

In summary, being able to recognize and specify an optimization model as being linear offers advantages in the amount of information that is available above and beyond the optimal solution. However, this additional information is available only if the linear model is solved *as a linear model* (i.e., using the simplex algorithm). Remember: it is possible to solve a linear model with a nonlinear algorithm (this is typically what happens if you use a software package that solves both linear and nonlinear models, and you do not specify—or the software cannot ascertain—that your model is linear). However, solving a linear model with a nonlinear approach will preclude you from receiving the additional sensitivity analysis available from the simplex algorithm.

Building an Optimization Model from Scratch

Obviously, it is not always the case that you have a good evaluation model and simply wish to transform it into an optimization model. Sometimes you know an optimization model is going to be appropriate, but you first need to

FIGURE 16–20
Optimal Solution for Example 2 with PROD1 Price of $115

Alternative	PROD1	PROD2	
Number produced	300	300	
Input Assumptions			
Pcr-unit revenue	$ 115	$ 140	
Per-unit RM1 usage	1	3	
Per-unit RM2 usage	3	2	
Per-unit RM3 usage	2	3	
Cost per unit RM1	$ 10	$ 10	
Cost per unit RM2	$ 20	$ 20	
Cost per unit RM3	$ 15	$ 15	
Intermediate Calculations			**Total**
Revenue	$34,500	$42,000	$76,500
RM1 usage	300	900	1,200
RM2 usage	900	600	1,500
RM3 usage	600	900	1,500
RM1 cost	$ 3,000	$ 9,000	$12,000
RM2 cost	$18,000	$12,000	$30,000
RM3 cost	$ 9,000	$13,500	$22,500
Performance Measure			
Contribution	$ 4,500	$ 7,500	$12,000

build the evaluation model to have something to optimize. You have had a great deal of practice building evaluation models throughout this book, and the techniques you have learned to facilitate that process are all applicable here as well. However, building a good evaluation model is at least in part art. For this reason, understanding the important elements of the optimization model you are going to eventually want to transform your evaluation model into can be helpful in guiding the construction of the evaluation model.

To accomplish this, it is a good idea to first think through these important elements before starting to build the evaluation model. You can follow the same three steps used to transform an evaluation model into an optimization model, only now using words rather than spreadsheet cell locations. You can then use this list as you build the evaluation model, to make sure that you include all the necessary elements of the optimization model.

1. What are the decision quantities that constitute the decision you need to make? This step is often relatively straightforward if there are clearly identifiable numerical quantities required. However, it can get trickier if yes/no decisions are involved.

Frequently, in either case, there is more than one way to express the decisions you need to make. In Example 2, we could have expressed the decision we were required to make as, How much of each resource should I allocate to the production of each product? This might have led to an evaluation model like the one in Figure 16–21. Is this model better or worse than the one in Figure 16–9? As an evaluation model, the answer to this question is subjective. Does the decision maker find it easier to specify a production quantity and observe the impact on raw material usage, or to specify raw material usage and observe the impact on production levels? Although the answer is probably the former in this case, there is no reason it could not be the latter, in which case Figure 16–21 would contain the preferred evaluation model.

As an optimization model, the one in Figure 16–21 is equivalent to the one in Figure 16–9 in terms of accurately capturing the essence of the decision we need to make; in concept, both should yield the same optimal solution. However, the model in Figure 16–21 is *nonlinear*, due to the use of the MIN function. Observe in Figure 16–22 what can happen if we optimize it using a nonlinear solution algorithm and the initial inputs given in Figure 16–21. We get a different solution—and one not as good—as the optimal solution we got using the model in Figure 16–9. This is an example of obtaining a *local* optimal solution. By starting with a different set of inputs, the nonlinear optimizer may be able to find the true global optimum, but as we discussed earlier, this can be a hit-or-miss proposition. This, then, is why you should generally prefer a linear to a nonlinear model and should prefer a statement of the decision quantities that enables you to build a linear model. However, it is not always possible to foresee how to do this; this is part of the *art* of building an optimization model that can be developed only through practice.

2. What is the objective quantity? As with the decision quantities, this can sometimes be stated in different ways, although it is not in the two models we have now presented for Example 2. In general, the challenge here will not be at the conceptual level, but rather at the implementation level.

FIGURE 16–21

Alternative Model for Example 2

Alternative	PROD1	PROD2	TOTAL
RM1 usage	600	600	1,200
RM2 usage	1,000	1,000	2,000
RM3 usage	750	750	1,500
Input Assumptions			
Per-unit revenue	$ 120	$ 140	
Per-unit RM1 usage	1	3	
Per-unit RM2 usage	3	2	
Per-unit RM3 usage	2	3	
Cost per unit RM1	$ 10	$ 10	
Cost per unit RM2	$ 20	$ 20	
Cost per unit RM3	$ 15	$ 15	
Intermediate Calculations			
Units produced	333	200	
Revenue	$40,000	$28,000	
RM1 cost	$ 6,000	$ 6,000	
RM2 cost	$20,000	$20,000	
RM3 cost	$11,250	$11,250	
Performance Measure			
Contribution	$ 2,750	$(9,250)	$(6,500)

Units produced of PROD? = MIN(RM1 usage/Per unit RM1 usage,RM2 usage/Per unit
RM2 usage,RM3 usage/Per unit RM3 usage)

Units produced of PROD1 = MIN(600/1,1000/3,750/2)

Units produced of PROD2 = MIN(600/3,1000/2,750/3)

FIGURE 16–22

Locally Optimal Solution to Alternative Model for Example 2

Alternative	PROD1	PROD2	TOTAL
RM1 usage	362	769	1,131
RM2 usage	1,086	513	1,599
RM3 usage	724	769	1,492
Input Assumptions			
Per-unit revenue	$ 120	$ 140	
Per-unit RM1 usage	1	3	
Per-unit RM2 usage	3	2	
Per-unit RM3 usage	2	3	
Cost per unit RM1	$ 10	$ 10	
Cost per unit RM2	$ 20	$ 20	
Cost per unit RM3	$ 15	$ 15	
Intermediate Calculations			
Units produced	362	256	
Revenue	$43,417	$35,869	
RM1 cost	$ 3,618	$ 7,688	
RM2 cost	$21,715	$10,255	
RM3 cost	$10,854	$11,529	
Performance Measure			
Contribution	$ 7,229	$ 6,397	$13,626

For example, it is fairly clear in Example 1 that we wish to minimize annual costs associated with purchasing subassembly A. However, we initially could ignore the per-unit purchase price of subassembly A, as it did not vary with order quantity; when volume discounts were available (Example 1b), we could no longer ignore this price but had to include it in our model. Thus, the major challenge in this step is to accurately include in our evaluation model all costs (or contributions) that vary with the specified decision quantities. (An influence diagram is particularly well suited to help identify these costs.)

3. One of the most difficult aspects of constructing an optimization model is making sure the underlying evaluation model enables you to account for all the relevant constraints on the decision quantities. Here, having a list (in words) of the different constraints of which you arc aware *before* constructing your evaluation model is particularly useful. Your evaluation model is then not complete until all the constraints on your list are being "measured" somewhere in your model.

Sometimes, constraints that are not explicitly a part of the decision environment can be artfully employed to achieve a more mechanical modeling objective, such as transforming a nonlinear into a linear model. Consider again the model in Figure 16–21 for Example 2. Rather than specify that the production quantity of each product can be no greater than the *minimum* of what can be produced with the allocated amount of any of the three raw materials, we could have allowed the production quantities of the two products to be decision quantities and constrained these quantities to be less than or equal to what could be produced with the allocated amount of each of the three raw materials taken one at a time. Thus, instead of a formula, the "units produced row" would have contained values, and three new constraints would have been added for each product. This would have allowed us to avoid a nonlinear program—and the potential for a local optimal solution—but at the expense of requiring additional decision quantities, constraints, and perhaps a less intuitive model.

In summary, a good optimization model requires an accurate evaluation model. Knowing what you are trying to achieve with your optimization model can help guide the construction of your evaluation model. However, building a good optimization model is as much art as building a good evaluation model. Both require practice and experience to become skilled.

17 The Mathematics of Optimization

In Chapter 16, we explored the basics of using optimization models, or mathematical programming. In this chapter, we turn our attention to the mathematics underlying optimization. While not essential, a deeper understanding of the math can help you become a significantly more effective and efficient user of optimization models. It is well worth the investment if you anticipate using optimization on a regular basis. Among other things, a deeper understanding of the math enables you to use the more advanced options that are generally available in most optimization software packages. (These options enable you, for example, to solve large models more quickly than you otherwise might.)

In Chapter 16, we used the language of the spreadsheet to describe, build, and solve optimization models. This was useful, since the spreadsheet is clearly the preferred medium for implementing quantitative business analysis of all kinds, including math programming. However, in this chapter, we will draw heavily on the language of *algebra*, particularly graphs. This was the original language of optimization models and will help us deal with some of the more technical issues.

We begin by considering the algebraic statement of optimization models. Using algebra, it is easy to distinguish between the three different categories of optimization models explored in Chapter 16—nonlinear, linear, and integer. We then devote a section apiece to the most commonly encountered "solution" techniques for each category of program (remember: "solving" an optimization model means finding an optimal solution). Most advanced options in optimization software packages are levers that allow you to direct and control the solution procedures for the various categories of problems. Understanding the solution techniques enables you to control the levers.

Algebraic Framework for Optimization Models

Functions

The algebraic term *function* is defined as a relationship between *outputs* and *inputs*; that is, for each input (or inputs), a function specifies an output. Inputs and outputs are generally numbers, although from a purely theoretical view, they do not have to be. Examples of functions in business might include the net present value (output) of a stream of cash flows (inputs); the total amount of raw material consumed (output) by a production plan specifying how many units of each of the firm's different products to produce (inputs); the total shipping cost (output) of a distribution plan that specifies how many units of product to ship between each source-destination pair (inputs).

Functions that possess similar *behaviors* can be grouped in categories. By behaviors, we mean the way in which outputs vary with inputs. Two common categories of functions correspond precisely to two of our major categories of optimization models—nonlinear and linear. In distinguishing between these two types of functions, it is useful to consider linear functions first.

A *linear* function is one for which changes in the output level are *proportional* to changes in the inputs. Furthermore, if there is more than one input, an output can be calculated for each individual input and the resulting outputs *added* together to determine the overall output. For example, consider the following linear functions:

$$f(x) = 2x + 3$$
$$g(x,y) = 4x - 3y - 1$$

The symbol $f(x)$ is read *the value* (output) *of the function f at x* (the input), while the decision rule $2x + 3$ specifies the output value the function f assigns to the input value x. The output is proportional to x because for each increase of 1 in x, the output increases by 2, irrespective of the starting value of x. Notice that there are two inputs in the function g—x and y. The overall output is determined by first calculating the output from x (4x), then the output from y (3y), and then subtracting the one from the other.

The term *linear* is derived from the geometrical representations of these algebraic functions. For example, the function f above can be represented graphically as depicted in Figure 17–1. Notice that the outputs of the function f for all possible inputs form a straight line on the graph; hence the term *linear* for these types of functions. To graph the function g, we need three dimensions: one for the input x, one for input y, and one for the output $g(x,y)$. The resulting graph (Figure 17–1) of outputs forms a *plane*, which in a specific mathematical sense is the three-dimensional equivalent of a line on a two-dimensional graph.[1]

---

[1]For two or more dimensions, a line is defined mathematically as a function of one less dimension than the space, possessing the characteristics of proportionality and additivity discussed above.

FIGURE 17–1
Graph of Linear Functions

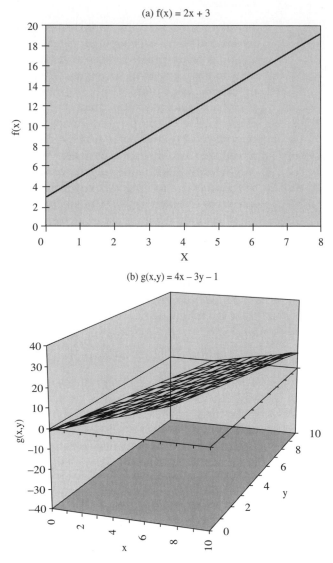

A *nonlinear* function is one in which changes in the output level are *not* proportional to changes in one or more of the inputs. For example, the following functions are all nonlinear:

$$f(x) = 3x^2 + 1$$
$$g(x) = \max\{x,20\}$$
$$h(x,y) = (x + 1)/y$$

The function f is nonlinear because the decision rule contains the input x raised to a power other than 1. Increasing x from 1 to 2 increases the output level by 9 [from $f(1) = 3(1)^2 + 1 = 4$ to $f(2) = 3(2)^2 + 1 = 13$], while increasing x from 2 to 3—an identical increase of 1 unit—increases the output level by 15 [to $f(3) = 3(3)^2 + 1 = 28$]. Hence, changes in the output level are not proportional to changes in the input x. The function g is nonlinear because of the use of the "max" operator, which specifies that we choose the greater of the two values within the braces. Increasing x from 1 to 2 does not change the output level [$g(1) = \max\{1,20\} = 20$ and $g(2) = \max\{2,20\} = 20$] while increasing x from 21 to 22 does [$g(21) = \max\{21,20\} = 21$ and $g(22) = \max\{22,20\} = 22$], another violation of proportionality. The function h is nonlinear because the input x is divided by the input y (multiplying the two together would have similarly resulted in a nonlinear function). If x is fixed at 1, increasing y from 1 to 2 decreases the output level by 1 [$h(1,1) = (1 + 1)/1 = 2$ and $h(1,2) = (1 + 1)/2 = 1$] while increasing y from 2 to 3 decreases the output level by .33 [$h(1,3) = (1 + 1)/3 = .67$]. As with linear functions, the term *nonlinear* refers to the appearance of the associated graphs (see Figure 17–2).

With the use of functions, we can now provide the algebraic representation of an optimization model.

General Structure of an Optimization Model

In Chapter 16, we discussed the three main components of an optimization model: decision quantities, the objective quantity, and constraints. In its most general form, an optimization model has the following structure:

$$\text{Max} \quad f(x_1, \ldots, x_n)$$
$$\text{subject to} \quad g_1(x_1, \ldots, x_n) \leq b_1$$
$$g_2(x_1, \ldots, x_n) \leq b_2$$
$$\vdots$$
$$g_m(x_1, \cdots, x_n) \leq b_m$$

In this model, there are n decision quantities, represented by the symbols $x_1, \ldots, x_n$. The objective quantity is the function f. Notice that f takes as inputs the decision quantities $x_1, \ldots, x_n$ and from them returns the output $f(x_1, \ldots, x_n)$, the value of the objective quantity for that particular set of inputs. Notice also that the objective in this model is to maximize this quantity. Finally, there are m constraints on the values the decision quantities can assume, given by the m functions $g_1, \ldots, g_m$ and their associated limiting values $b_1, \ldots, b_m$. Thus, the output $g_1(x_1, \ldots, x_n)$ of the n input quantities $x_1, \ldots, x_n$ must not exceed the value b_1.[2]

---

[2]In traditional optimization parlance, decision quantities are called *decision variables* and the objective quantity the *objective function*. Also, optimization modeling is traditionally called *mathematical programming*.

FIGURE 17–2
Graph of Nonlinear Functions

(a) $f(x) = 3x^2 + 1$

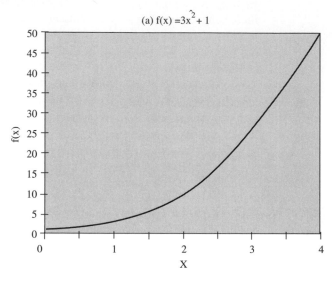

(b) $g(x) = \max\{x, 20\}$

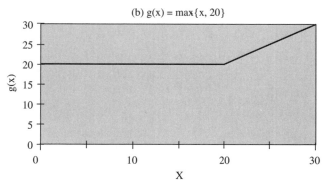

(c) $h(x,y) = (x + 1)/y$

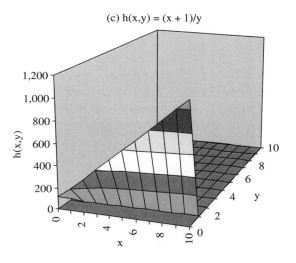

Some variations are allowed on this basic form. First, it is possible to want to *minimize*, rather than maximize, the objective quantity. Second, it is possible for the constraints to assume either of the following forms:

$$g_i(x_1, \ldots, x_n) \geq b_i$$

or

$$g_i(x_1, \ldots, x_n) = b_i.$$

Finally, the reader should simply note that we have not specified the nature of any of the functions—linear or nonlinear. It is the nature of these functions that determines the categorization of the optimization model:

Linear: *If all the functions in an optimization model are linear, then the model is **linear** and the analysis and solution of the model is called linear programming (LP).*

Nonlinear: *If any of the functions—f or any of the g_i—in an optimization model are nonlinear, then the model is **nonlinear** and the analysis and solution of the model is called nonlinear programming (NLP).*

Integer Programming

The term *integer* in integer programming refers to the values the decision quantities can assume. In general, all decision quantities are assumed to be continuous (can take on fractional values as well as integers). In some cases, however, we want to use decision quantities that can take on only integer values, such as was done in Example 3 from Chapter 16. Furthermore, by far the most common situation in which we want decision quantities to assume integer values is when we want to further restrict them to take on only two possible values—0 or 1 (again as illustrated by Example 3).

If the value of any decision quantity—whether in an LP or NLP—is restricted to integer values only, the entire model is called an *integer programming* (IP) model. Notice that we could further subclassify models as *linear integer* or *nonlinear integer*; the relevant distinction between the two is whether you embed a linear or nonlinear solution algorithm within the general branch-and-bound solution approach to IP outlined in Chapter 16.

Recall that the significance of the different categories of optimization models—linear, nonlinear, integer—is that the process by which the optimal solution (set of inputs that optimizes the objective quantity) is identified varies for each. We are now ready to consider these solution methodologies and their implications for the sophisticated user of optimization models.

Linear Programming (LP)

By far the most used solution methodology for LP models is the *simplex algorithm*.[3] Developed in the early 1950s during the early stages of the

---

[3] An *algorithm* is a set of steps to accomplish a specific task; that is, a recipe.

computer era, the simplex algorithm has proved to be remarkably robust in its ability to quickly solve linear programs.

Although the details of the simplex algorithm are best communicated using the language of algebra, the algorithm can be best understood at the conceptual level through the language of geometry. Hence, we return to Example 2 from Chapter 16 and consider the graphical description of that problem. First, however, we redescribe the problem in algebraic terms using the general form for an optimization model defined above:

$$\text{Max} \quad 20x_1 + 25x_2$$
$$\text{subject to} \quad 1x_1 + 3x_2 \leq 1{,}200$$
$$3x_1 + 2x_2 \leq 2{,}000$$
$$2x_1 + 3x_2 \leq 1{,}500$$
$$x_1, x_2 \geq 0$$

where x_1 and x_2 are the number of units of PROD1 and PROD2, respectively, to produce. The last line of constraints reflects the fact that we cannot produce a negative number of units of either product.

Graphical Representation of Example 2

To describe this problem geometrically, we can use a two-dimensional graph (Figure 17–3). The dimensions of the graph are how many units of each product to produce: along the horizontal axis we measure how many units of PROD1 to produce, while along the vertical axis we measure how many units of PROD2 to produce. Each point on the graph corresponds to a production plan for PROD1 and PROD2. For example, point A corresponds to producing 100 units of PROD1 and 200 units of PROD2.

Some of the points on the graph represent production plans that consume more than the available amount of one or more raw materials. For example, point B in Figure 17–3 corresponds to producing 500 units of PROD1 and 600 units of PROD2, requiring $1 \cdot 500 + 3 \cdot 600 = 2{,}300$ units of RM1. This exceeds the 1,200 available units of RM1. A plan that requires more than the available supply of any resource is *infeasible*. Conversely, a plan for which we have a sufficient supply of each resource to satisfy its requirements is called *feasible*.

To identify which points on the graph are feasible (i.e., correspond to feasible production plans), we superimpose lines corresponding to the availability of each raw material. For example, consider RM1. If we allocate all 1,200 units of RM1 to the production of PROD1, we can produce $1{,}200/1 = 1{,}200$ units of PROD1 (point C in Figure 17–4). Similarly, if we allocate all 1,200 units of RM1 to the production of PROD2, we can produce $1{,}200/3 = 400$ units of PROD2 (point D in Figure 17–4). Because each unit of PROD1 (or PROD2) produced requires the same number of units of RM1, every production plan that consumes exactly 1,200 units of RM1 falls on the straight line connecting points C and D. For example, point E corresponds to

FIGURE 17–3

Two Possible Production Plans for Example 2

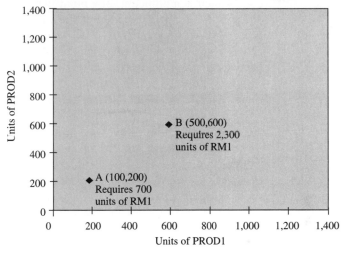

FIGURE 17–4

Set of Production Plans that Consume all of RM1

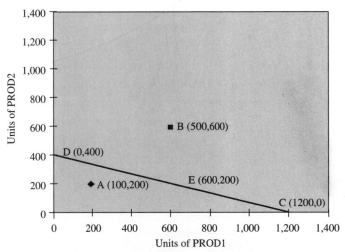

producing 600 units of PROD1 and 200 units of PROD2, thereby consuming $1 \cdot 600 + 3 \cdot 200 = 1,200$ units of RM1, as expected.

We now reconsider point B in Figure 17–4 (500 units of PROD1 and 600 units of PROD2). As noted previously, the plan associated with this point consumes 2,300 units of RM1, more than the 1,200 units available. On the other hand, point A, corresponding to 100 units of PROD1 and 200 units of

PROD2, consumes only 700 units of RM1; this makes it feasible with respect to RM1. The fact that these points lie on opposite sides of the line we just constructed is significant: any point that lies on the same side of the line as point B corresponds to a production plan that consumes more than 1,200 units of RM1, while any point falling on the same side of the line as point A corresponds to a production plan that consumes less than 1,200 units of RM1. Hence, all plans represented by points on or below the line in Figure 17–4 (the same side of the line as point A) are feasible with respect to RM1, while those that fall above the line (the same side of the line as point B) are not.

This procedure can be repeated to identify the set of points on the graph that are feasible with respect to RM2 and RM3 as well. By superimposing all three lines and their associated regions of feasibility on the same graph, we can determine the set of points that are feasible with respect to all three raw materials. This is represented as the cross hatched area in Figure 17–5. This set of points is called the *feasible region*. In our search for an optimal production plan, we can ignore any point not in the feasible region because it corresponds to a plan that would require consuming too much of one or more raw materials. (You may wish to experiment with several points on the graph to convince yourself that this is true.)

The corner points of the feasible region—(0,0), (0,400), (300,300), (600,100), and (666 2/3,0)—will turn out to be of particular interest. They are called the *extreme points* of the feasible region. We will see shortly why they are important.

Before describing how the simplex algorithm works graphically, we first illustrate a more intuitive graphical approach to identifying the best (in terms of contribution) feasible production plan. Consider a series of parallel lines

---

FIGURE 17–5

Lines Corresponding to Production Plans that Consume All of Each Raw Material

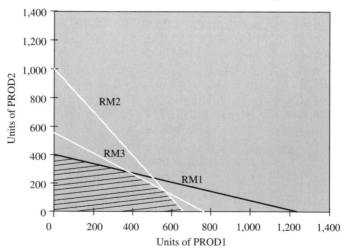

superimposed on the feasible region (Figure 17–6). Each line represents the set of all production plans generating the same contribution. For example, every point on the $10,000 contribution line corresponds to a production plan that generates $10,000 in contribution, as illustrated by points F ($20 · 100 + $25 · 320 = $10,000) and G ($20 · 400 + $25 · 80 = $10,000). Thus, finding a feasible contribution-maximizing production plan corresponds to finding a point in the feasible region that lies on the contribution line with the greatest contribution.

Because the contribution lines increase in value from the lower left (southwest) to the upper right (northeast) of the graph, finding this point is conceptually analogous to placing a pencil on the origin of the graph (the point where the axes intersect) parallel to the contribution lines and moving the pencil as far to the upper right as possible without losing contact with the feasible region. The last point of contact with the feasible region corresponds to a contribution-maximizing production plan (Figure 17–7). In this case, it is the plan to produce 600 units of PROD1 and 100 units of PROD2, which generates a contribution of $14,500. No other feasible production plan generates more contribution than this one, and hence it is the optimal solution to the example, which supports our finding from Chapter 16.

The Simplex Algorithm

While the "pencil approach" makes sense intuitively, it is impossible to implement algebraically. The simplex algorithm hence takes a different approach to identifying the optimal solution. It is based first on the observation

---

FIGURE 17–6

Lines Representing the Set of All Production Plans Generating Contributions of $5,000, $10,000, $15,000, and $20,000

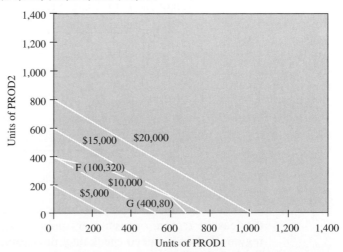

FIGURE 17–7

The Optimal Solution to Example 2

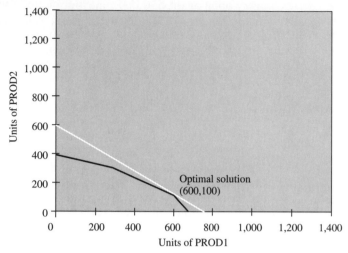

that all of the lines in our model are straight (which is consistent with the notion that this is an LP model). This linearity ensures that at least one of the extreme points of the feasible region is optimal. (If you don't believe this, try sliding your pencil out in such a way that the optimal solution is something other than an extreme point. The only way you can do this is to make the pencil parallel to one of the constraints, in which case there are an infinite number of optimal solutions—all the points on the portion of the boundary of the feasible region formed by that constraint—including two extreme points. Hence, at least one extreme point is still optimal.) Thus, in the case of Example 2, we could have found an optimal solution by simply calculating the contribution of each of the extreme points:

Extreme Points	Contribution
(0,0)	$ 0
(0,400)	$10,000
(300,300)	$13,500
(600,100)	$14,500
(666⅔,0)	$13,333.33

Thus, (600,100) is an optimal solution, which replicates the conclusion we reached by observing Figure 17–7.

Thus, to find an optimal solution, we need not consider every point in the feasible region, or even every point along the boundary of the feasible region. Rather, we need check only the extreme points, which are relatively easy to generate algebraically. However, for a realistic sized problem—unlike the present example—the number of extreme points may still be quite large. Calculating the value of each one would still represent a formidable task.

The simplex algorithm is essentially a clever way to generate and check a small number of extreme points in such a manner that guarantees generating and identifying the optimal solution. Each time the algorithm generates and checks a new extreme point is called an *iteration*. For Example 2, the algorithm would work roughly as follows:

Iteration 0: The algorithm would start with the easily identified extreme point (0,0).

Iteration 1: The algorithm would essentially consider the two extreme points *adjacent* to the current solution—in this case, the current solution is (0,0) and the two adjacent extreme points are (0,400) and (666⅔,0). Adjacent extreme points are defined as those along the boundaries forming the current solution—in this case, the horizontal (which corresponds to the constraint $x_1 \geq 0$) and vertical ($x_2 \geq 0$) axes. Actually, the algorithm does not consider both extreme points per se, but rather how the objective quantity changes as one moves along the boundaries leading to the two adjacent extreme points. Moving in the direction of (666⅔,0) results in the following rate of change: for each 1-unit move along the horizontal axis, x_1 increases by 1 unit, and the objective quantity increases by $20 \times 1 = \$20$. Moving in the direction of (0,400) results in the following rate of change: for each 1-unit move along the vertical axis, x_2 increases by 1 unit, and the objective quantity increases by $25 \times 1 = \$25$. Hence, a move in the direction of (0,400) increases the objective quantity faster than a move in the direction of (666⅔,0), and the simplex algorithm would replace the old current solution (0,0) with the new current solution (0,400).

Iteration 2: From the current solution (0,400), we know a move (back) in the direction of the adjacent point (0,0) would lead to a worse solution, so we need only consider a possible move in the direction of the adjacent point (300,300). Here, calculating the impact on the objective quantity is a little trickier, since a 1-unit move along the line determined by the RM1 constraint, $1x_1 + 3x_2 \leq 1,200$, results in a change in both decision quantities. Algebraically, it is easy to determine that a 1-unit move along this boundary results in an approximately .95 increase in x_1 and a .32 decrease in x_2.[4] The net effect on the objective quantity is then $20 \times .95 + \$25 \times (-.32) = \$11$. Thus, a 1-unit move in the direction of the extreme point (300,300) increases the objective quantity by $11. Hence, the simplex algorithm would replace the old current solution (0,400) with the new current solution (300,300).

Iteration 3: Repeating the above step, a 1-unit move from (300,300) along the RM3 boundary $2x_1 + 3x_2 \leq 1,500$ toward the adjacent extreme point (600,100) results in an approximately .83 increase in x_1 and a .55

---

[4]This can be calculated from the equation for the boundary line and the Pythagorean theorem (the square of the hypotenuse of a right triangle is equal to the sum of the squares of the other two sides).

decrease in x_2. The net effect on the objective quantity is then $20 \times .83 + $25 \times (-.55) = 3. Thus, a 1-unit move in the direction of the extreme point (600,100) increases the objective quantity by $3. Hence, the simplex algorithm would replace the old current solution (300,300) with the new current solution (600,100).

Iteration 4: Again repeating the above step, a 1-unit move from (600,100) along the RM2 boundary $3x_1 + 2x_2 \leq 2,000$ toward the adjacent extreme point (666⅔,0) results in an approximately .55 increase in x_1 and a .83 decrease in x_2. The net effect on the objective quantity is then $20 \times .55 + $25 \times (-.83) = -$10$. Thus, a 1-unit move in the direction of the extreme point (666⅔,0) *decreases* the objective quantity by $10. The simplex algorithm would thus determine that it could not improve on the current solution by moving to an adjacent solution. Hence, the algorithm terminates, and the current solution (600,100) is correctly declared optimal.

Several points about the simplex algorithm need to be emphasized. First, in a realistic example (i.e., one with more than two decision quantities) an extreme point would have far more than two adjacent extreme points, and the challenge of in which direction to go would be much richer. Even though we cannot visualize the process graphically with more than two (or certainly three) decision quantities, it remains analogously the same. Second, observe that in this model, the algorithm would have found the optimal solution more quickly had it initially (iteration 1) chosen the adjacent extreme point (666⅔,0) rather than (0,400). However, in general, it is not worth the effort required to determine that, although the rate of improvement in the objective quantity is greater in the direction of (0,400), one can go farther in the direction of (666⅔,0). Third and finally, although in this instance we ended up considering every extreme point, in general the number of extreme points that are considered is a tiny fraction of the total number of extreme points.

Some Final Comments on the Simplex Algorithm and LP

Notice that it is possible for more than one extreme point to be optimal. This happens if the lines of equal contribution are parallel to one of the boundaries of the feasible region (in the desired direction). In this instance, not only are both extreme points of the corresponding boundary optimal, but *every* point on the boundary is optimal as well, since all of the points on the boundary lie on the same maximum-contribution line. When this anomaly occurs, we say that there are *multiple optimal solutions*.

An additional assumption of LP is that the level at which any activity can be undertaken is continuous (i.e., in the XYZ Company example, the production level of either product does not have to be integer, but may include a fractional amount as well). That the optimal production plan for Example 2 calls for integer amounts of both products is fortuitous—extreme points can involve fractions, as for example the point (666⅔,0). If the contributions-per-unit of PROD1 and PROD2 were such that (666⅔,0) was the extreme point on the line of greatest contribution, then LP would have identified it as the optimal solution under the assumption that it was possible to produce two-thirds of a unit of PROD1 and receive the resulting contribution (this could be viewed, for example, as work in process). If, in reality, producing two-thirds of a unit of PROD1 was not possible, then we could have simply rounded down and produced 666 units of PROD1. This would not necessarily have been the best possible *integer* solution, however (although given the magnitude of the numbers, it would have undoubtedly been close). If finding the best possible integer solution were truly important, then we would go to integer programming.

For large LP models the simplex algorithm can require a large number of iterations—and, as a result, computing time—to find the optimal solution. (How "large" is large is a question for which there is not a definite answer, since two LP models of the same "size" can require dramatically different numbers of iterations and time, due to the particular structure of the problem—structure that cannot be easily recognized a priori.) As a result, to guard against a situation in which the simplex algorithm gets bogged down, you can control its operation by limiting the number of iterations or amount of computer time allowed.

Another potential problem with the simplex algorithm occurs when the magnitude of quantities included in the model are vastly different; for example, when maximizing the percentage of profit based on million-dollar investments. The problem is created by the algebraic technique the simplex algorithm employs in moving from one extreme point to another. To avoid this problem, it is desirable in these instances to make the offending quantities less different, by for example, expressing investments in millions of dollars and/or percentages as whole numbers ($\times$ 100). This is generally not a big problem and can generally be ignored; if it occurs, you will easily recognize it because the simplex algorithm will simply fail without returning an optimal solution. (Many commercially available software packages include a feature that will automatically adjust the magnitudes of numbers if they are way out of line.)

Karmarkar's Algorithm: An Alternative Approach to Solving LP Models

As mentioned, the simplex algorithm was developed in the early 1950s. For over 30 years, experts were unable to find a better (i.e., more efficient) way to solve LP models. Then, in the mid-1980s, a researcher developed a legitimate competitor to the simplex algorithm. It was based on the deceptively simple notion that it might be easier to find the optimum by going directly toward it, through the feasible region, rather than by skirting around the boundary, a la the simplex algorithm. This notion had been around for some time, but it was not until *Karmarkar's algorithm*—named after its developer—that it was transformed into a workable approach.

On the surface, it appears obvious that Karmarkar's algorithm should be more efficient than the simplex algorithm. It requires two inputs: in what direction does the optimal solution lie, and how far. The first input turns out to be relatively simple, thanks to calculus. From any point (possible solution) and for any objective quantity, calculus can be used to determine in which feasible direction (i.e., direction into the feasible region) one must move to maximize (or minimize) the rate of change in the objective quantity. The second input turns out to be far more difficult. Conceptually, one should travel in this direction until the boundary of the feasible region is reached, and then along the boundary until the optimal extreme point is reached. However, it is very difficult to determine mathematically "when" this boundary is reached. Karmarkar's contribution was in discovering a mathematically elegant way of doing this.[5]

In application, Karmarkar's algorithm has proved to outperform the simplex algorithm on very large LP models, ones involving thousands of variables and constraints. It has enabled us to solve LP models that we would not even have tried to solve with the simplex algorithm. However, for small and medium-sized LP models, the simplex algorithm has proved to still be more efficient, due to the rapidity with which it races around the boundary of the feasible region. Thus, virtually all commercially available LP solution packages use the simplex algorithm.

Nonlinear Programming (NLP)

There are two primary ways in which an optimization model can be nonlinear: either the objective quantity is nonlinear, or one or more of the constraints is nonlinear. Figure 17–8 contains graphical representations of a possible instance of both these conditions. Example 1 of Chapter 16 is nonlinear because of the objective function. Its statement algebraically reveals how simple an NLP model it actually is:

$$\text{Min} \quad 10{,}000 \times (\$325) + (10{,}000/x) \times (\$500) + (x/2) \times (\$325) \times (12\%)$$

$$\text{subject to} \quad x \geq 0$$

where x is the order quantity. The nonlinearity lies in the second term of the objective quantity, where we are calculating the annual ordering cost, and dividing by the decision quantity to do so.

The first important concept to recognize is that it is no longer true that the optimal solution must fall on an extreme point, as illustrated in Figure

---

[5]Though far beyond the scope of this text, Karmarkar's approach to this involves fitting a series of ellipses into progressively smaller regions until a sufficiently small region (including one extreme point—the optimal solution) is identified.

FIGURE 17–8

Two-Decision Quantity NLP Model

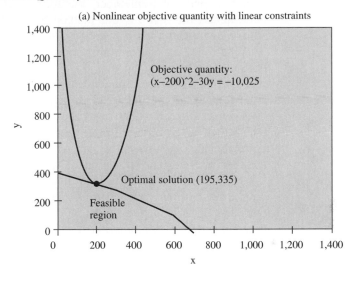

(a) Nonlinear objective quantity with linear constraints

Objective quantity:
$(x-200)^2-30y = -10,025$

Optimal solution (195,335)

Feasible region

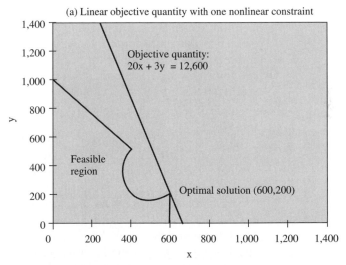

(a) Linear objective quantity with one nonlinear constraint

Objective quantity:
$20x + 3y = 12,600$

Feasible region

Optimal solution (600,200)

17–8. Thus, the simplex method is useless, since it examines only extreme points. How, then, do we find the optimal solution to a nonlinear program?

The answer lies in the basic approach of Karmarkar's algorithm.[6] Specifically, rather than wind our way around the outside of the feasible region,

---

[6]This approach for solving NLP models was being used long before Karmarkar found a way to make it practical for LP models.

hopping from extreme point to extreme point, we cut straight through the feasible region in the direction that offers the maximum improvement in the objective quantity. Remember: the simplex algorithm is *not* an alternative here; hence, the fact that this method turns out to be not as efficient as the simplex algorithm for LP models is irrelevant.

The direction of maximum improvement is identified, as with Karmarkar's algorithm, using calculus. However, an advantage of Karmarkar's algorithm is that it is being applied to a *linear* objective quantity. You might recall from your calculus that the direction of optimal change for a linear function does not change irrespective of the particular point (i.e., set of inputs) at which you are considering that function. Hence, in an LP, the direction of optimal change is always the same: Karmarkar need calculate it only once, and then just continue to head in that direction.

If the objective quantity is *non*linear, however, this is no longer true: the direction of optimal change varies depending on the point at which the objective function is being considered. The formula that gives the optimal direction of change—now a function of the point at which it is evaluated—is called the *gradient*. Thus, with a nonlinear objective quantity, the optimal direction from the initial starting point can—and generally does—change as you move away from that point. Technically, then, the gradient should be monitored continuously as you move away from the starting point and the optimal direction updated. As you might expect, however, continuous monitoring is impractical due to the large amount of computing time and resources it would require. In its stead, we monitor periodically by calculating the optimal direction, moving in that direction as far as we can and still improve the objective quantity (without becoming infeasible) and then recalculating the optimal direction. The process is repeated until we eventually converge on the optimal solution.

A key issue is how far to go in the direction of optimal improvement before recalculating a new optimal direction. Here, we encounter the other problem related to applying a Karmarkar-type approach to an NLP model. Recall that the true accomplishment of Karmarkar's algorithm versus previous attempted approaches was in determining how far to move in the optimal direction to arrive at the optimal solution. His approach to this—as his approach to finding the optimal direction—relied heavily on the linearity of the model—in this case, of the linearity of the boundaries of the feasible region as determined by the constraints. His approach is no longer valid if the boundaries of the feasible region (i.e., one or more of the constraints) are not linear. Thus, even if the objective quantity is linear, the question of how far to go in the optimal direction is more difficult with an NLP.

The common solution for handling this issue for NLP—irrespective of whether or not the objective quantity is nonlinear—is to take a predetermined sized step in the currently assessed optimal direction, find the optimal point between your starting point and your "stepped" point, and then to gradually reduce this step size as the algorithm proceeds (and as you presumably get closer and closer to the optimal solution). Each step can be thought of as an iteration, although this term is not often used to avoid confusing this approach with that of the simplex algorithm.

This approach to solving NLP models is called the *gradient search (GS)* approach and is the most widely used general approach to solving such models. This approach can be applied to *any* NLP model, irrespective of the nature of the nonlinearities, in contrast to other, specialized solution algorithms designed to exploit specific types of nonlinearities in NLP models. In general, these specialized approaches solve their specific class of models much more efficiently than GS, but (*a*) they are less readily available than GS software, and (*b*) they require recognizing the special structure of the model, which is not easy.

The primary drawback to the GS is the same one that plagued our attempt to solve Example 1b in Chapter 16: the presence of solutions that are locally, but not globally, optimal. In Example 1b, the local optimal solutions were caused by the volume discount, which created an objective quantity that was nonlinear due to "jumps" in the cost structure. Almost any nonlinearity—whether in the objective quantity or one of the constraints—can cause a locally optimal solution.[7] One can generalize our definition of the term *locally optimal* used in Chapter 16 to the GS approach: at a locally optimal solution, there is no feasible direction that improves the value of the objective quantity. Figure 17–9 contains examples of local optimal solutions for two NLP models, one where the nonlinearity is in the set of constraints, the other where it is in the objective quantity.

Unfortunately, as discussed in Chapter 16, there is no easy way to recognize that you have a locally but not globally optimal solution. The most common approach to overcoming this potential difficulty, again discussed in Chapter 16, is to start the GS algorithm from several different starting points and then to simply select the best of the locally optimal solutions found. (If each starting point produces the same optimal solution, it may be that you have one of those NLP models for which there is only one locally optimal solution, which must by default then be the global optimal solution.) In general, the more different starting points you try, the better the likelihood that you will find the global optimal solution. However, it cannot be guaranteed that this approach will find the global optimal solution.

Levers to Control the GS Solution Approach

The most direct lever you have available to control the GS solution approach is in the precision you require. This applies to both finding the optimal objective quantity and satisfying all constraints. With continuous decision

---

[7]There are certain NLP models for which it can be guaranteed that any solution that is locally optimal is also globally optimal. However, in practice, the characteristics necessary to ensure this guarantee are not easy to recognize.

FIGURE 17–9
Example of Locally Optimal Solution in NLP

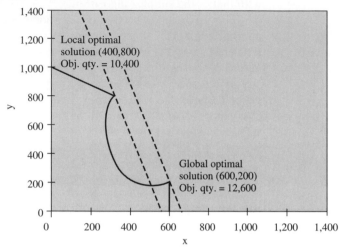

quantities and using calculation to approximate calculus-based solution approaches, it is very difficult to achieve precise optimization, or to precisely satisfy all constraints. We can mitigate this difficulty by specifying how precise we require our calculations to be. Requiring greater precision will cause your algorithm to take longer to solve the model; requiring less precision increases the chance that there might be a better solution than the one the algorithm identified (although setting the level of precision enables you to control how much better this better solution could be). In practice, it is generally not necessary to satisfy the mathematical statement of a constraint as precisely as mathematics requires.

There are several additional ways in which you can control the GS approach to make it work more efficiently on your particular problem. All of them relate to how the algorithm iterates from point to point en route to the optimum. Three of the more commonly available methods are discussed below.

As discussed above, the optimal direction in which to move for a nonlinear objective quantity varies depending on the starting point of the move. The first step in the GS procedure is to calculate the *partial derivatives* of the objective quantity; partial derivatives quantify how the objective quantity changes as small changes are made in the individual decision quantities. The collection of these partial derivatives—one for each decision quantity—is then used to determine the *gradient* (from which the name of this approach is taken), which is the direction of steepest ascent from the current point. We then search in the direction of the gradient until we find the point of maximum improvement in the objective quantity. At this new point, we recalculate the partial derivatives, find the new direction of maximum improvement, and search again in this new direction. The procedure terminates when an examination of the partial derivatives reveals that we cannot move in any direction that would improve the objective quantity.

Finding the optimal solution to an NLP model can be compared to finding the highest point in a hilly terrain. At any given point, the collection of partial derivatives describes how the area in the immediate vicinity of the point is *graded*: for any direction from this point, the partial derivatives can be used to tell you how quickly you ascend or descend if you head in that direction. The gradient is then the direction of steepest ascent in the immediate vicinity of the point. The GS approach is to locate the direction of steepest ascent from the present location, move in that direction as long as we are still ascending, then—once we stop ascending—recalibrate our direction of steepest ascent from this new location and continue. We stop when we reach a point where no matter which direction we go, we descend.

There are three basic steps in each iteration of the GS approach: calculate the partial derivatives; determine the gradient; find the point in the direction of the gradient that optimizes the objective quantity. Each step has levers that can be manipulated to affect the solution procedure.

Calculating the Partial Derivatives.   The easiest way to estimate a partial derivative with a computer is to simply change the value of the decision quantity slightly and observe the change in the objective quantity. (This avoids our having to use calculus.) The general way of doing this is to increase the value of the decision quantity, observe the new objective quantity, and calculate the difference. This is known as *forward differencing*, because it involves simply looking forward in all directions from the present location. An alternative would be to both increase *and* decrease the value of the decision quantity, observe the two objective quantity values, and calculate the difference. This *centers* the partial derivative around the present point and is thus known as *central differencing*. This approach obviously takes more effort (computing time), but it can be worthwhile if the objective quantity is highly nonlinear—such as if it has dramatic increases or decreases in value—because it takes a broader look at the surrounding area. Trying the latter approach is sometimes useful if the software package you are using is having trouble finding a direction to improve the objective quantity from the present location.

Determining the Gradient.   This step involves searching over the set of all possible directions, using the partial derivatives (which enable you to calculate the steepness in any direction), to find the direction of steepest ascent (the gradient). There are many ways in which this search can be conducted. Two commonly encountered ones are the *Newton* and *conjugate* search techniques. The Newton technique is the more sophisticated of the two. It involves carefully selecting new directions to try, in a manner that requires a lot of effort (relatively speaking). The payoff is that the gradient is discovered after considering only a (relatively) small number of directions. The conjugate method, on the other hand, is less careful of how it chooses each new direction to try. As a result, it requires considering more directions before the gradient is identified. However, it requires (relatively) less effort to identify each new direction. The determining factor for which approach to use is the size of the model you are analyzing. The Newton method, because of its sophistication, requires a great deal of computer memory to calculate each new direction, and this usage increases as the model gets larger. Typically, using the Newton method on a large model will not cause the algorithm to crash, but it may cause it to run very slowly. For this reason, the conjugate method is often better for large NLP models. A tip that this may be a problem is if the GS algorithm with the Newton method is running very slowly.

Finding the Step Size.   A number of search techniques can be used to find the point along a line segment that optimizes a function defined on the points of that line. This is essentially the problem we have once we identify the gradient, which determines the line of search (the objective quantity is the function we are trying to optimize). The present point is one end of the line segment; the challenge is how far along the line (i.e., in the direction of the gradient) to place the other end of the line segment, from whence to begin the search of points in between. This point is sometimes referred to as the *initial estimate*. The trade-off is rather straightforward: the further out we go (the longer the initial line segment), the more time it will take to find the optimal point along the line (the step size); on the other hand, the further out we go, the better our chances of not missing a better point because we did not search far enough from the starting point. The default of most GS algorithms is to simply use a constant k that determines how far to go to establish the other end of the segment; this value then decreases as the algorithm proceeds. This is often called a *linear*, or *tangent*, estimate of how far to go. An alternative is to square this value k at each iteration. Hence, instead of k, the algorithm goes out k^2 for its initial estimate. This latter approach is particularly useful when you have a highly nonlinear problem, in which it is relatively easier to get caught on locally optimal solutions. It is, however, more time-consuming.

Integer Programming (IP)

An IP model looks like either an LP or NLP model, with the extra condition that some decision quantities must take on integer values only (in our case, 0 or 1). We can thus state Example 3 from Chapter 16 as an IP as follows:

x_{ij} = Number of units to ship from potential warehouse
location i (i=1, . . . ,5) to customer j (j=1, . . . ,8)
y_i = 1 if warehouse located at i, 0 if not

$$\text{Min} \quad 13x_{11} + 3x_{12} + \cdots + 11x_{58}$$

$$\text{subject to} \quad \left.\begin{matrix} x_{11} + x_{21} + \cdots + x_{51} \geq 30 \\ \vdots \\ x_{81} + x_{82} + \cdots + x_{85} \geq 40 \end{matrix}\right\} \begin{matrix} \text{Customer demand} \\ \text{must be satisfied} \end{matrix}$$

$$\left.\begin{matrix} x_{11} + x_{12} + \cdots + x_{18} \leq 140y_i \\ \vdots \\ x_{51} + x_{52} + \cdots + x_{58} \leq 110y_5 \end{matrix}\right\} \begin{matrix} \text{Capacity at any location} \\ \text{cannot be exceeded} \end{matrix}$$

$$y_i + y_2 + y_3 + y_4 + y_5 \leq 3$$

$$x_{11}, \ldots, x_{58} \geq 0$$

$$y_1, \ldots, y_5 \geq 0$$

$$y_1, \ldots, y_5 \leq 1$$

$$y_1, \ldots, y_5 \text{ integer}$$

Since all the functions in the model are linear, this is an LP. However, the restriction that some decision quantities must take on integer values makes it an IP.

We discussed the branch-and-bound solution approach at some length in Chapter 16. In this chapter, we wish to highlight some of the more technical issues related to its implementation and discuss what you can do to manage the solution process more efficiently. We will restrict our attention in this chapter to IP models where the integer decision quantities are restricted to 0 or 1. However, the branch-and-bound solution approach can be applied with only slight modification to problems with decision quantities that can take integer quantities other than 0 and 1.

Since the underlying model for Example 3 is linear, the program we solve at each node of a branch-and-bound algorithm is an LP, and we can therefore use the simplex algorithm. In practice, each new LP does not have to be solved from scratch but can draw on the solution to the LP of its parent node. Hence, the fact that we have to solve a series of LPs is not as onerous as it could be. Unfortunately, there is not as well-developed a methodology to deal with the series of NLPs we have to solve if the underlying model is nonlinear.

Figure 17–10 contains the complete, step-by-step implementation of the branch-and-bound algorithm to Example 3 of Chapter 16.

There are two primary levers that you can use to control the branch-and-bound solution of an IP model. The first is to specify initially as good a solution as you can come up with, and provide that as the starting point for the branch-and-bound algorithm. The objective quantity value of this solution becomes the target against which all bounds are compared. The better the target, the more nodes will be eliminated without branching. This can significantly speed up the solution process.

FIGURE 17–10 *Expanded Branch-and-Bound Solution to Example 3 of Chapter 16*

BASE CASE LP (no integer restrictions)   Min $13x_{11} + 3x_{12} + \cdots + 11x_{58}$

$$\text{subject to} \quad x_{11} + x_{21} + \cdots + x_{51} \geq 30$$
$$\vdots$$
$$x_{81} + x_{82} + \cdots + x_{85} \geq 40$$
$$x_{11} + x_{12} + \cdots + x_{18} \leq 140y_i$$
$$\vdots$$
$$x_{51} + x_{52} + \cdots + x_{58} \leq 110y_5$$
$$A + B + C + D + E \leq 3$$
$$x_{11}, \ldots, x_{58} \geq 0$$
$$A, \ldots, E \geq 0$$
$$A, \ldots, E \leq 1$$

Initial LP Solution. B&B first solves the above LP, ignoring all integer restrictions. Notice that although A through E are not required to be integer, they are bounded to be between 0 and 1.

> Optimal objective quantity = $495
> A =   —
> B =   1.000
> C =   0.158
> D =   0.423
> E =   1.000

Branches 1 and 2. One of the primary ways different implementations of B&B vary is in how the integer variable on which to branch is chosen. In general, there is not a "best" way to select this variable; i.e., there is no rule that is guaranteed to always identify the branching variable that will lead to finding the optimal solution in the shortest time. Thus, most B&B algorithms choose the branching variable somewhat arbitrarily. In this instance, B is selected as the first branching variable. The base case LP is then modified in the following manner: along one branch, the constraint B = 0 is added, while along the other the constraint B = 1 is added. The two new LPs are then solved, producing the following.

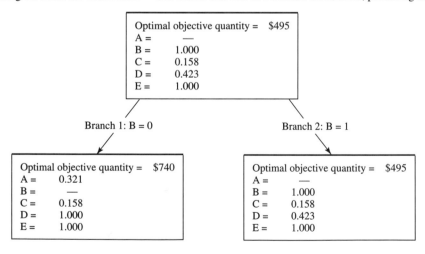

FIGURE 17–10   *(continued)*

Branches 3 and 4. Notice that neither the solution to the LP for Branch 1 nor Branch 2 is feasible, because some of the variables A–E are still not integer. Thus, we have yet to find a feasible solution and must continue to branch. Since the optimal objective quantity for the node on Branch 2 is better (less) than that of Branch 1, we choose to branch on the node at the end of Branch 2 next. While a better feasible solution is not guaranteed to exist along the part of the tree associated with Branch 2, it does seem to make sense to investigate the more attractive options first. The algorithm arbitrarily chooses to branch on D next.

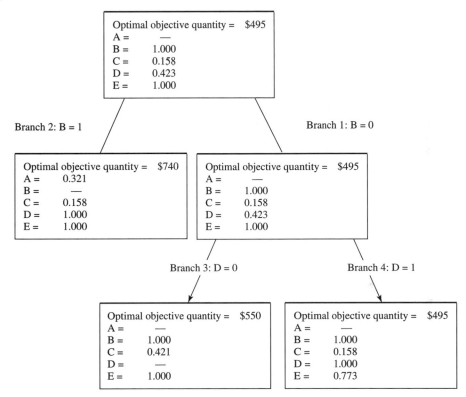

FIGURE 17–10 *(continued)*

Branches 5 and 6. Again, neither the solution to the LP for Branch 3 nor Branch 4 is feasible, because some of the variables A–E are still not integer. Thus, we must continue to branch. Since the optimal objective quantity for the node on Branch 4 is better (less) than that of either Branch 1 or Branch 3, we choose to branch on the node at the end of Branch 4 next. The algorithm arbitrarily chooses to branch on E next.

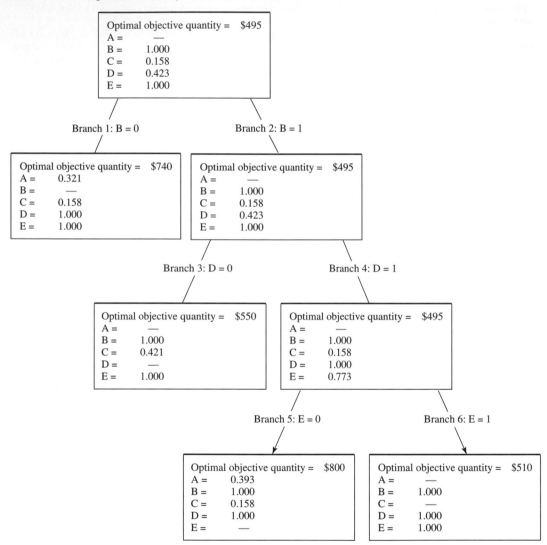

FIGURE 17–10   *(concluded)*

A feasible solution and pruning. Finally, a feasible solution has been identified, with Branch 6. The challenge now remains to see if branching on any of the remaining nodes—Branches 1, 3, or 5—could possibly lead to a better feasible solution. Here is where the power of the bounding process comes into play. The optimal objective quantity for any feasible solution we might eventually find by branching on the node at the end of Branch 1 can be no better (less) than the $740 optimal quantity associated with the Branch 1 solution. (The set of feasible solutions to the LP model at Branch 1 includes all feasible solutions that might subsequently surface were we to branch on the node at the end of Branch 1. Hence, none could generate an objective quantity less than $740 or it would have been identified when the Branch 1 LP was solved.) Since we already have a feasible solution (Branch 6) better than this $740 bound, we do not need to branch on the node at the end of Branch 1; in math programming terminology, Branch 1 can be *pruned*. Using the exact same reasoning, Branches 3 and 5 can be pruned as well. Hence, B&B has identified the optimal solution.

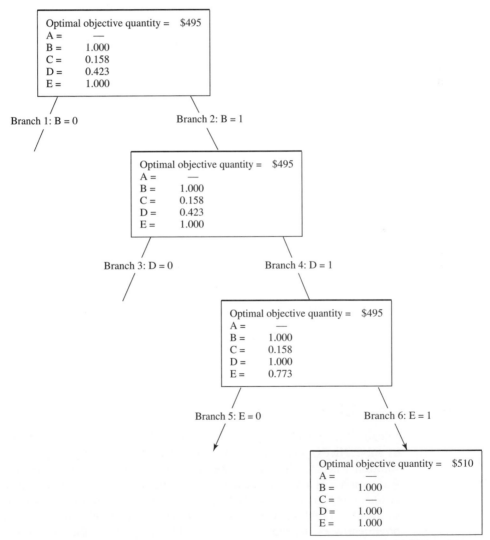

The second lever is to specify how "good" your solution has to be. Ideally, of course, you would always like to identify the optimal solution. However, you may be able to solve your model much more quickly if you are willing to settle for the *chance* that you may not have the absolute optimal solution. Mitigating this possibility of suboptimality somewhat is the fact that you can be guaranteed that the objective quantity value of the solution you end up with is within some percentage of the objective function value of the absolute optimal solution, if it is different. You accomplish this by specifying a *tolerance* level, such as 5 percent. This tolerance level is then used whenever a bound is compared to the current trial solution: if the bound is not at least 5 percent better than the value of the current trial solution, the node is pruned. The positive result of this is that the algorithm runs more quickly, since the bounds are now being required to clear a higher hurdle. The negative result is that we may miss a better solution, albeit not a lot better.

It is virtually impossible to look at a model and determine a priori how quickly branch-and-bound will identify the optimal solution and thus whether or not you should establish a tolerance level, and if so, how much. In practice, you may want to let the algorithm try to solve the model without a tolerance level (or, from a practical standpoint, with whatever default tolerance level your software uses). If the algorithm gets bogged down, you can halt it, raise the tolerance level, and reinvoke the algorithm. An advantage of this approach is that the algorithm can proceed with the best solution found in the first attempted branch-and-bound solution, and hence with a fairly good bound from the outset.

We should reiterate that even though our example involves integer decision quantities that are restricted to 0 or 1, branch-and-bound can also be used to solve models where decision quantities can take on integer values other than 0 or 1. In this case, if a decision quantity x had a value of 2.139 at the end of a particular branch, you could branch on that decision quantity by adding the constraints $x \leq 2$ to one branch and $x \geq 3$ to the other. Continue as before until a feasible and then optimal solution is identified.

Final Observations: LP, NLP, and IP

Because the methodology to solve LPs is more efficient than the methodology to solve NLPs, and because we are always guaranteed to get the optimal solution when solving an LP, we prefer to solve an LP whenever possible. But, you might ask, isn't the decision of whether or not the underlying model is linear or nonlinear beyond our control? The model that accurately describes the situation is either linear or nonlinear, right? Isn't the linearity or nonlinearity of the model a reflection of the reality of the situation and not something we have control over?

The answer to these questions is yes and no. When the simplex algorithm was developed, skeptics claimed it would have little impact because *all* business problems of practical interest were inherently nonlinear. Their concern was ill-founded, and not only because there turned out to be many important business problems that were intrinsically linear: many *non*linear models can be approximated by linear models without losing their essence. For example, some nonlinear functions can be easily approximated by a series of linear functions, analogous to replacing a smooth curve with a series of short line segments. A nonlinear constraint can thus be transformed into a set of linear constraints, and the model solved as an LP with no adverse consequences.

When building models in a spreadsheet, the message is to make your models linear whenever possible and solve them as linear rather than nonlinear models. An example of a frequently encountered situation where this can be done is one in which percentages are involved. Suppose two materials, A and B, are to be combined to form a new material, and the new material can consist of no more than 40 percent of A. If x_A and x_B represent the amount of A and B to combine, and $x_A + x_B$ is the total amount of new material, then this constraint can be written algebraically as

$$x_A/(x_A + x_B) \le .40.$$

However, this expression is nonlinear, since we are dividing by decision quantities, and hence we would have to solve the model in which it is used as an NLP. However, we can make a simple algebraic transformation of the constraint to

$$x_A \le .40(x_A + x_B),$$

which is linear, and hence (assuming all other relationships are linear as well) solve the model as an LP. In this case, the model was not *intrinsically* nonlinear and hence could be represented and solved as an LP. If you are trying to solve in a spreadsheet a model that you think is linear, but are being told that your formulation is not linear, this is precisely the kind of situation you might look for.

For novice users of optimization models, the ability to use 0–1 decision quantities is frequently naively viewed as a panacea with which to build models of all sorts of situations. The reality is that IPs can take a very long time to solve with even a modest number of integer decision quantities. While there may be ways to speed up the solution process (as discussed above), required computation time is still a big issue. Just as many researchers have constructed special algorithms to solve particular classes of NLP models, so they have developed special algorithms to solve particular classes of IP models. Often these classes of IP models can be represented as networks, where the integer decision quantities correspond to arcs in the network. As with special-case NLP algorithms, whether or not you have a model for which a special-case IP algorithm is appropriate as well as how to get access to such an algorithm generally requires the assistance of an expert.

Summary

In this chapter, we have explored the mathematics behind the optimization models first presented in Chapter 16. Understanding the math enables you to use the models more effectively, both in selecting what type of model to build, and in controlling the solution of the model once it is built. LP models are far and away the easiest models to solve, which means that you can build large models with confidence that whatever LP software is at your disposal will be able to solve it in a reasonable amount of time (depending, of course, on the computer hardware you are using). NLP models can also be solved relatively quickly, but with the potential danger of ending up with a solution that is locally, but not globally, optimal. To mitigate this possibility, you can start the model solution procedure from several different initial solutions, and simply choose the best solution so derived. IP models are by far the most difficult models to solve; i.e., they require the most computing time. Adding a single 0/1 integer decision quantity doubles the number of possible solutions; models with as few as 20 integer decision quantities can require a significant amount of computing time to solve.

The task of deciding how much realism to build into your model often becomes a trade-off between the computing effort required to solve the model and the value of the resulting solution. An NLP model might be a more technically accurate representation of reality than an LP model, but an LP model will be more easily solvable. The question becomes how much more valuable the NLP solution is than the LP solution.

Finally, there are a number of levers you can manipulate to control the solution of each class of optimization models. The levers enable you to control the solution procedures themselves, speeding them up or directing them in a manner that makes them more effective—i.e., able to find the optimal solution. The specific levers available to you depends on the particular software you are using.

CASE 1
AMERICAN LAWBOOK CORPORATION (A)

Ed Troy glanced briefly out the window of his downtown office toward the busy street below, then returned his gaze to the three Publication Proposals on his desk (Exhibit 1). He had just finished filling in his assessment of the first year's sales potential for these titles (Exhibit 2). As director of educational and professional publishing for the American Lawbook Publishing Company (AL), he was ultimately responsible for choosing which of these titles the company would offer for use in American law schools in the fall of 1982.

Law school professors were normally offered a complimentary examination copy of every book published for classroom use in their fields. When deciding whether or not to "adopt" any of these books, a professor might consider the reputation and background of the author; the breadth and organization of topics covered; the length of individual chapters and of the book itself; whether an innovative pedagogical approach was used; the availability of auxiliary teacher's notes; the style and readability of the prose; whether cases and examples were up to date; the aesthetics of the typeface, layout, and binding; the retail price that their students would have to pay (usually in the range of $25 to $35); and similar considerations.

As a graduate of the Duke University Law School, and a veteran of the law school publishing business, Troy had a strong intuitive understanding for the many factors that influenced the performance of a new book. Indeed, everyone at AL recognized that Troy was the person most qualified to synthesize the available information on a new title into a subjective forecast of first-year sales. Troy, however, was never entirely comfortable with the task. He maintained that AL needed a more systematic approach for evaluating and weighing the critical factors affecting sales, assessing the risks, and ranking different proposals. He was therefore concerned not just with the disposition of these three proposals but with the more fundamental questions of what marketing information should be collected and how it should be analyzed to guide future publishing activities. Since law school publishing would always retain a substantial element of risk, he believed it was essential to know the odds against which one was playing.

Law and Law School Publishing

The American Lawbook Corporation was founded in Boston, Massachusetts, in 1897 and had grown to employ over 350 people, including approximately 70 lawyer-editors. The company specialized in the editing, annotation, and printing of the statutory output of state legislatures. Having submitted a winning bid to

---

EXHIBIT 1   Three Publication Proposals

Proposal One: Casebook in Admiralty Maritime Law

Authors:	Thomas Schoenbaum, J. D. Michigan 1965, Professor of Law, Tulane University
	A. N. Yiannapoulos, J. S. D. Berkeley 1956, Professor of Law, Tulane University
Pages:	800

Enrollment:*		
	Percentage of students with opportunity	0.5816
	Percentage of students enrolling	0.0317
	Estimated national enrollment	2,139

Books in field:[†]	2 case, 1 text

Proposal Two: Casebook in Administrative Law

Authors:	Donald P. Rothschild, LL.M. Harvard 1965, Professor of Law, George Washington University
	Charles H. Koch, LL.M. Chicago 1975, Professor of Law, College of William and Mary
Pages:	950

Enrollment:*		
	Percentage of students with opportunity	0.9269
	Percentage of students enrolling	0.1202
	Estimated national enrollment	12,929

Books in field:[†]	10 case, 3 text

Proposal Three: Casebook in Criminal Law

Authors:	Robert Misner, J.D. Chicago 1971, Professor of Law, Arizona State University
Pages:	450

Enrollment:*		
	Percentage of students with opportunity	0.9407
	Percentage of students enrolling	0.2798
	Estimated national enrollment	30,544

Books in field:[†]	14 case, 6 text

---

*First percentage is the percentage of all law students attending those schools that offer a course for which the book is suited.

Second percentage is the average percentage of those students with the opportunity who actually enroll in the course.

Estimated national enrollment is the total enrollment at all American Bar Association–approved law schools (116,047) multiplied by the two percentages.

[†]Number of comparable books, including this one, competing for adoption in this subject area.

perform this service for a state, a law publisher generally became the only source from which attorneys in that state could obtain an up-to-date copy of the state code—a necessity for general legal practice. As there was relatively little turnover among code publishers, the business tended to be characterized by consistent and predictable profitability.

EXHIBIT 2 **Ed Troy's Assessment of First-Year Sales**

		Fractiles				
Proposal	*Proposed Retail Price*	*0.05*	*0.25*	*0.50*	*0.75*	*0.95*
1. Schoenbaum & Yiannapoulos $35		10	400	600	1,000	2,000
2. Rothschild and Koch $30		200	800	1,000	2,000	6,000
3. Misner $25		10	200	500	1,100	4,000

In 1968, AL merged with the Tinline-Geary Publishing Company of Cincinnati, Ohio, and shortly thereafter the activities of both companies were consolidated in Boston. Among the Tinline-Geary properties were an existing line of casebooks and treatises for the law school market, including several titles under contract but not yet published.

In contrast to code publishing, law school publishing proved to be a strikingly unpredictable business. It was quite possible for the large prepublication investment in a new title (frequently in the range of $30,000 to $50,000) to be lost through an indifferent sales response. Moreover, whereas AL was a major publisher of state codes and a monopoly supplier in most of its markets, the law school course markets were commonly saturated with many published offerings of a number of much larger companies.

West Publishing Company of St. Paul, Minnesota, and Foundation Press of Mineola, New York, dominated the law school publishing business. West owned Foundation, and together they held an estimated 60-65 percent of the total law school market. Little, Brown of Boston accounted for another 15 percent and was the publisher of choice for many Harvard Law School professors. The third largest firm, The Michie Company of Charlottesville, Virginia, held about 5 percent of the market. AL was the largest of several small firms that made up the remainder of the estimated $15 million annual law school market.

In addition to code and law school books, AL also published what were referred to as author books. These books were written on law-related subjects and were sold primarily to practicing lawyers. AL found author books an attractive way to smooth the demand on its production facilities. Whereas code and law school books required rigid time schedules, author books could be published at any time.

Genesis of a Law School Publication

Law school curricula offered publishers an astonishing variety of publishing options. While only six to eight courses (such as contracts or torts) were required at all schools, many others (e.g., evidence or future interests) were tested on most state bar examinations and were therefore widely attended. Enrollment in the hundreds of other subject areas could range from dozens in an admiralty course to a handful studying Zairan tribal legal systems.

Courses might be taught with one or more teaching approaches, including traditional lecture methods. The "case" approach was the study of court cases with their judicial decisions and opinions. The "problem" approach was akin to the case method used in graduate business schools. In the Socratic method, professors attempted to stimulate intellectual curiosity and tenacity among students by directing repeated and probing questions toward individual class members.

Reliance on a particular teaching method strongly influenced a professor's choice of type of book. Most prevalent in law schools was the "casebook" or "coursebook" containing edited cases and opinions linked by the author's commentary and questions. "Problem" books were used less commonly and primarily in courses with a practical bent, such as tax or estate planning. Textbooks, "treatises," "hornbooks," and "handbooks," the distinctions among which were not rigorous, were most often used as supplemental materials.

The initial inspiration to write—for example, a casebook in environmental law—most frequently arose with a professor who was dissatisfied with existing teaching materials in that field. His or her proposal, which ranged from single paragraphs to 1,000-page typed manuscripts, could reach the publisher's office in several ways. First, "law school travelers" visited campuses to promote good will and solicit new manuscripts. At AL, Donald Layton, the administrative editor for law school publications, performed this function.

Second, AL employed an advisory board of prominent legal academicians who reviewed proposals, suggested authors, and occasionally submitted proposals. Finally, and most often, professors who had assembled sets of teaching materials for their own courses mailed proposals to one or more publishers. Such unsolicited proposals were received at AL several times each week.

Many proposals could be rejected immediately. To illustrate, a book might be proposed for an arcane field not currently studied in American law schools (e.g., French administrative law). Alternatively, the subject area might be already dominated by one or more universally acclaimed works. Occasionally, sample chapters would exhibit a dismaying lack of clarity or grammatical accuracy.

Proposals that offered initial promise were subjected to review by advisory board members, by their colleagues, and by the AL staff. Since this process could last several months, it was not unusual for many proposals to be "under consideration" at any given time.

Production of a Law School Publication

Unlike many publishing houses, but in common with West/Foundation, AL maintained its own in-house composition, pressroom, and bindery facilities. This total production capacity was believed to provide AL advantages in cost and quality control, as well as considerable scheduling flexibility.

Once a proposal was approved and contracted for publication, AL waited for the submission of a completed manuscript. The manuscript copy was then edited, arranged into pages and chapters, and sent to the manufacturing plant. Edited materials were electronically typeset, and the resulting "camera copy" was photographed and made into printing plates. High-speed printing on a web offset press and hard- or soft-cover binding yielded a finished book.

Several weeks before a book was printed and bound, prepublication announcements, which included an offer of a complimentary copy, were mailed to all professors teaching an appropriate course. Every attempt was made to provide potential adopters with a review copy before professors informed law school bookstores of their text selections, which normally occurred in mid to late spring.

Performance Measurement for New Publications

Specific objectives for the performance of published law school titles were derived from corporate return on sales (ROS) and return on investment (ROI) goals. The custom at AL was to pursue these ROS/ROI goals through the intermediate objective of a 40 percent gross margin on individual products. (Troy had also adopted a goal of a 10 percent annual growth rate in sales dollars for law school publications and usually required a one-year payback on investments in new products.)

Most AL products (code books) were sold through competitive bidding to markets with well-defined sizes and purchase rates. To achieve a 40 percent gross margin, costs were estimated, prices set to yield the desired margin, and a skillful selling job performed to justify what might be a premium price on the basis that publishing the code books was an irreplaceable service. Because academic titles faced a highly uncertain market, however, the standard AL "profit planning" formulas were not easily applicable to law school publications titles. Since assuming responsibility for this product line, Troy had evaluated the profit potential of new titles in the following manner:

1. Proposals were reviewed for quality and timeliness by the advisory board.
2. Total costs for an approved proposal were estimated by using a formula supplied by the manufacturing department:

Editorial . . . . 120 hrs/500 pages @ $12.80/hr
Prepress $17.50/page
Print/bind $4.25/copy

---

3. Sales revenues were estimated by multiplying the likely manufacturer's selling price by an estimated sales volume. This estimate was derived from a subjective assessment of the size of the market in question and the relative strengths of competitors' titles.
4. Total costs were compared with sales revenues to estimate total profits.

Troy worried about the reliability of this approach. Among recently published titles, many were doing significantly better or worse than had originally been predicted. While their aggregate performance was respectable, he was sure that those results could be improved dramatically if the potential for individual titles could be identified more accurately. To do so, Troy felt that the procedures used for estimating both costs and sales should be scrutinized.

Cost Estimation

Troy had several reservations about the cost formula supplied by manufacturing, all of which were related to the unusual cost structure of law school titles. The production process through plate-making was very labor intensive, and prepress costs were unaffected by the number of copies ultimately produced. The variable

EXHIBIT 3   Labor Hours and Material Costs (1981 dollars) for Recent AL Titles

	Copies	Pages	Edit (hours)	Composition (hours)	Press (hours)	Bindery (hours)	Paper (dollars)	Bindery (dollars)
1	2,525	1,400	1,002.0	1,931.1	61.2	296.5	$4,465.2	$813.4
2	1,552	328	159.7	537.1	13.9	108.6	863.5	379.9
3	1,539	734	480.1	790.1	22.4	127.5	2,347.5	612.5
4	1,967	1,328	680.4	1,827.1	46.7	227.7	3,408.3	671.7
5	3,043	1,352	620.6	1,852.9	87.6	394.0	7,169.6	1,102.6
6	2,081	656	456.3	876.3	25.6	134.7	1,969.6	615.7
7	3,034	1,176	737.1	2,079.5	62.0	417.6	2,391.7	1,002.2
8	3,075	944	312.1	983.4	51.4	290.0	4,154.5	1,211.0
9	3,010	960	453.9	1,032.2	51.7	242.3	5,711.7	1,087.8
10	3,025	1,156	701.5	1,710.6	47.8	264.5	5,545.4	1,114.4
11	2,046	520	223.7	686.5	22.5	134.0	1,924.3	780.6
12	3,048	872	844.1	1,163.6	44.1	239.0	4,597.5	1,046.7
13	2,025	440	326.4	672.2	23.1	109.5	1,944.7	785.9
14	1,015	1,218	1,017.3	1,671.5	28.1	141.5	1,802.7	525.1
15	9,009	262	193.1	304.9	52.5	231.1	4,146.5	3,672.5
16	2,042	704	499.8	1,015.2	27.4	130.5	3,854.2	797.2
17	2,067	752	510.7	1,100.1	36.9	138.3	5,043.7	859.7
18	3,654	368	202.1	772.1	28.4	206.8	3,081.0	1,386.4
19	1,091	344	231.1	736.1	10.4	67.5	504.7	349.5
20	2,083	532	337.8	969.0	20.2	128.0	1,999.9	841.8
21	1,583	1,236	915.8	1,424.4	32.0	194.8	4,948.2	705.3
22	1,080	376	266.4	665.3	23.5	83.5	892.5	442.2
23	2,046	998	507.2	1,457.3	44.5	204.8	4,197.3	876.1
24	2,105	672	559.4	863.5	19.0	121.9	2,278.0	849.8
25	1,031	960	842.2	1,971.2	30.9	107.4	2,437.2	571.6

printing and binding expenses were quite small and resulted mainly from paper costs. Because law school course enrollments were relatively small, press runs were short. Prepress costs thus became by far the largest component of the total investment required to publish a new title.

Troy had found law school professors, as authors, to be somewhat capricious in their dealings with publishers. It was not unusual for a professor's late delivery of manuscript copy to cause AL to miss the late-spring coursebook review period. Moreover, the professor might then insist on costly revisions to accommodate late statutory and judicial developments in the book's field. Troy was concerned that the manufacturing formula might not acknowledge how expensive and how variable the prepress investment in a new law school title might really be.

In addition, the manufacturing formula did not provide for costs associated with wholesale discounts, which averaged 20 percent off suggested list price; authors' royalties, which averaged 20 percent of sales net of wholesale discounts; or promotion costs, which ranged from $1,000 to $5,000 per new title. Troy wondered how best to incorporate all these costs into the publication decision.

Toward that end, he had requested that accounting prepare some data on the costs of past AL law school publications. Those data, including labor hours accumulated by those titles in editorial, prepress, pressroom, and bindery categories, plus average 1981 dollar rates charged each category of labor hour, are presented in Exhibits 3 and 4.

EXHIBIT 4   1981 Average Hourly Labor and Overhead Rates

Rate Category	1981 Direct Labor $ Rates	1981 Budgeted Hours	1981 Overhead $ Rates*	1981 Total Dollar Rates
Editorial	$5.20	157,500	$ 5.67	$10.87
Composition	5.76	150,550	8.75	14.51
Total pressroom	7.52	15,700	10.96	18.48
Total bindery	5.55	75,750	11.21	16.76

*A detailed study had not been undertaken to determine what percentage of AL overhead rates represented "direct" costs. However, if the portion of overhead expenses representing overtime premiums and supplies is considered "direct" and the portion including depreciation, taxes, and the like is considered "nondirect," the breakdown of overhead costs was as follows:

	Direct (%)	Nondirect (%)
Editorial	59	41
Composition	51	49
Pressroom	31	69
Bindery	42	58

Moreover, the performance of law school publications was measured on the basis of profit after allocation of full costs, not divisional cash flow.

Sales Estimation

Predicting sales for individual titles posed considerably greater difficulty than did estimating costs, for a far less deterministic process was involved. Not merely the number of students enrolled in a course, the number of competing texts, and the month of publication, but a host of less-quantifiable factors influenced the sales potential of a particular volume. The effective sales life of a law school book had been estimated at an average of three years, however, and, as a general rule, Troy assumed that total sales would be double those achieved in the first year.

To investigate these questions, and to develop the best approach for evaluating current and future publication proposals, Troy had commissioned a survey of course enrollments at American Bar Association–approved U.S. law schools. He hoped to use data from this survey along with other information regarding sales of existing AL law school titles (consolidated in Exhibit 5) to search for patterns in sales.

Marketing Research

Although AL had never undertaken a market survey for a new law school book, the company had conducted surveys for author books. Quite recently, as a matter of fact, Troy had received the results of a mail survey of Kentucky law offices (Exhibit 6), in which 47 percent of those responding indicated they would buy *Kentucky Contract Law* if AL went ahead with publication. Considering the conclusions of the study, Troy was fairly confident that this percentage could be applied to the 3,840 known "law-practice units" in Kentucky to forecast approximate sales of 1,805 for this new title.

He wondered whether a similar survey could be justified for a textbook. Certainly $340, the cost of this recent survey, did not seem a large amount to pay for the additional information on potential sales. Perhaps an even more thorough survey might be justified, with a personal interview of each and every law school professor who taught a course for which the proposed text could be used. Although such a survey would be considerably more expensive than the Kentucky example, it would tell Troy almost exactly what the first year's sales would be.

EXHIBIT 5   Sales Data for Recent AL Titles

	Estimated Market[a]	Percent Opportunity[b]	Percent Enroll[c]	Number Books[d]	Months[e]	Sales[f]
1	4,909	74.85%	5.65%	3	16	1,324
2	13,222	97.44	11.69	8	14	946
3	1,510	26.90	4.84	2	12	667
4	2,172	64.47	2.90	5	21	741
5	4,945	78.17	5.45	8	18	2,509
6	192	7.16	2.31	1	17	531
7	750	11.72	5.51	1	16	409
8	25,525	97.89	22.47	15	12	1,547
9	21,259	89.83	20.39	15	11	1,451
10	3,333	38.32	7.49	2	11	1,151
11	6,294	73.88	7.34	5	10	310
12	19,774	99.08	17.20	11	20	3,436
13	41,405	100.00	35.68	16	16	421
14	5,378	59.18	7.83	6	16	628
15	26,510	100.00	22.84	5	15	7,198
16	2,696	74.17	3.11	5	15	977
17	37,460	100.00	32.28	11	15	497
18	1,059	7.90	11.55	1	14	2,027
19	3,938	65.65	5.17	3	12	507
20	4,020	62.97	5.50	6	11	273
21	2,628	67.01	3.38	12	11	692
22	8,337	95.52	7.52	5	20	1,612
23	21,505	96.52	19.20	4	18	1,418
24	5,257	83.57	5.42	8	18	1,401
25	39,892	98.74	34.81	11	17	1,317

[a] *Estimated Market* is total law school enrollments times Percent Opportunity times Percent Enroll.

[b] *Percent Opportunity* is the percentage of all law school students with the opportunity to take the course for which the book was written.

[c] *Percent Enroll* is the average percentage of students who, given the opportunity, take the course for which the book was written.

[d] *Number of Books* is the number of competing texts, including this one.

[e] *Months* is the number of months for which the title was available for sale towards use in its first July-through-June academic year.

[f] *Sales* is total copies sold in the first year.

Exhibit 6   Mail Survey Report, March 31, 1982

Proposed book: *Kentucky Contract Law,* by Samuel K. Kline, Jr.
Market: Kentucky lawyers

No. of attorneys 6,618		Sole practitioners 3,110	
Law firms 2–9 730		Total law-practice units (LPUs) 3,840	

Survey:
Total no. mailed 400
Responses 115
Percent responses 28.8%

	Number	*Percent*
Respondents indicating would buy 54		47%
Respondents indicating book useful but		
would not buy (or not sure) 36		21
Respondents indicating not buy 25		22

Statistical Analysis

If n samples are drawn (independently and without replacement) from a population of size N, the standard error (SE) of the resulting sample proportion ($\overline{P}$) is given by the following formula:

$$SE = [\overline{P}(1-\overline{P})/n]^{1/2} [(N-n)/N]^{1/2}$$

The minimum number of samples (n) required to obtain a desired standard error (SE) is given as

$$n = N/[4(N)(SE^2) + 1]$$

Conclusions

In this example, $N = 3,840$. If we desire a standard error (SE) less than 0.05, we require

$$n = 3,840/[4(3,840)(0.05^2) + 1]$$
$$= 97.5$$

Since the realized sample size was 115, the standard error will be less than 0.05 for all estimated proportions.

There are two caveats to the use of these survey results. First, the 400 attorneys and firms surveyed were randomly selected from our computer file of American Lawbook customers, not the practicing bar at large. This could cause a bias in favor of sales. However, the American Lawbook Corporation list of 2,056 customers should be representative of the bar generally.

Secondly, the survey was made in early 1982. If conditions should change significantly (e.g., by the publication of a competing book), the survey results would be invalid.

Upon the assumptions and caveats stated and results analyzed, we can conclude that 47 percent plus or minus 5 percent, or 1,805 plus or minus 90, LPUs would buy *Kentucky Contract Law.*

We can further conclude that 68 percent plus or minus 5 percent, or 2,611 plus or minus 130, LPUs believe this book would be useful to the Kentucky bar. These potential sales do not include other customers who would be likely to purchase this book, including libraries, state agencies, small and large corporations in the energy industry, public utilities, and the like. The survey also makes no allowance for the additional sales that would be made by personal contact and selling by our market representatives.

EXHIBIT 6   *Continued*

Kentucky Contract Law Survey

1. Total of population being surveyed (LPUs) (estimated) 3,840
2. Total responses required for 5 percent standard error 97
3. Total surveys mailed to achieve responses:

	Sent	Received
1st mailing, Dec. 1, 1981 400		60
2nd mailing, Feb. 22, 1982 340		55

4. Costs of survey:

	Cost
a. Secretarial time*: 2 days at $6.00/hr.	$ 96
b. Postage, 740 mailings at $0.20	148
c. Return postage, 115 at $0.25	29
d. Photocopying, 740 × 3 pages at $0.03	67
Total	$340

---

*Secretarial time and costs on future comparable surveys can be reduced to one day and $48.

CASE 2
AMERICAN LAWBOOK CORPORATION (B)

Ed Troy hired an MBA student for the summer to help him tackle the general problem of selecting law school books to be published by the American Lawbook Corporation. After hearing the basic components of the problem, the student became very excited about the possibility of using regression analysis to estimate the cost of a new title. Given permission to pursue this idea, the student returned in two weeks with a report on his results.

"As you can see in the table in Exhibit 1, I put together the total direct cost of each of the 25 recent AL titles," began the student. "And then I ran a regression to explain these costs using the number of copies printed and the number of pages per copy. The regression results were fantastic. I've summarized them in Exhibit 2. We obtained an adjusted R-square of 90.5 percent, and the t-statistics for both coefficients were significant at the 95 percent level.

"Next I tried to forecast first year's sales using the data we compiled from our survey of law schools. The results here are not as fantastic, but I don't think you can expect to predict sales as well as you can predict costs. The explanatory variable is market-per-book, defined as the estimated market divided by the total number of competing books. The resulting model shown in Exhibit 3 has an adjusted R-square of 23.3 percent and a t-statistic significant at the 95 percent level. The coefficient tells me that on average each new book gets 52 percent of its share of the market."

Troy did not know quite how to react to these new cost and sales equations and the student's enthusiastic reporting. There was quite a difference between this regression equation and the manufacturing formula AL had been using to estimate the cost of a new title. Troy wondered if these new equations would indeed give a more accurate indication of the costs and profit potential of new law school titles.

EXHIBIT 1   **Total Direct Costs (1981 dollars) for Recent AL Titles**

Titles	Copies	Pages	Total Cost (dollars)
1 2,525	1,400	$37,289.0*
2 1,552	328	9,362.9
3 1,539	734	16,691.2
4 1,967	1,328	31,414.3
5 3,043	1,352	37,510.1
6 2,081	656	17,099.8
7 3,034	1,176	35,906.0
8 3,075	944	21,618.1
9 3,010	960	24,277.6
10 3,025	1,156	33,373.1
11 2,046	520	13,252.8
12 3,048	872	27,684.6
13 2,025	440	13,815.8
14 1,015	1,218	29,865.7
15 9,009	262	15,528.2
16 2,042	704	20,936.9
17 2,067	752	23,333.4
18 3,654	368	16,516.0
19 1,091	344	11,158.5
20 2,083	532	17,165.7
21 1,583	1,236	30,387.1
22 1,080	376	11,524.3
23 2,046	998	26,887.7
24 2,105	672	18,192.6
25 1,031	960	31,793.6

*Calculated as follows:

	Hours	Direct Labor $ Rates	Direct OH $ Rate	Total Dollars
Edit 1,002.0		$5.20	$3.35	$ 8,567.1
Composition 1,931.1		5.76	4.46	19,735.8
Press 61.2		7.52	3.40	668.3
Bindery 296.5		5.55	4.70	3,039.1
Paper				4,465.2
Bindery				813.4
Total				$37,288.9

EXHIBIT 2 Regression Results for Total Direct Costs

Variable	Coefficient	Std. Error	T
Copies	0.94	0.36	2.62
Pages	23.68	1.56	15.21
Constant	1,394.90	1,744.00	0.80

Adjusted R-square 0.9053
Std. dev. of residuals 2,702.27
Sample size 25

Prediction equation:

$$TDC = 1,394.90 + 0.94 \text{ (Copies)} + 23.68 \text{ (Pages)}$$

Correlation matrix:

	TDC	Copies	Pages
TDC	1.000		
Copies	−0.003	1.000	
Pages	0.941	-0.175	1.000

EXHIBIT 3 Regression Results for First Year's Sales

Variable	Coefficient	Std. Error	T
Market-per-book	0.52	0.18	2.88
Constant	503.40	38.80	1.30

Adjusted R-square 0.233
Std. dev. of residuals 1,247
Sample size 25

Prediction equation:

$$FYS = 503.40 + 0.52 \text{ (Market-per-book)}$$

Correlation matrix:

	FYS	MPB	Market	Books
FYS	1.000			
MPB	0.515	1.000		
Market	0.243	0.734	1.000	
Books	0.027	0.164	0.698	1.000

AMORE FROZEN FOODS

Macaroni and Cheese Fill Targets

Tom Jenkins, manager of quality services at Amore's frozen foods plant in Cortland, New York, thought the summer of 1984 might be the time to return the fill target for Amore's 8-ounce frozen macaroni and cheese pie to 8.22 ounces. Amore had been filling each aluminum tin to an uncharacteristically high target of 8.44 ounces ever since problems with underweight macaroni and cheese appeared in New York City in 1978. The higher target had protected Amore from fines levied against several producers for underweight product, but at the expense of an extra 0.22 ounces of macaroni and cheese in each pie.

Cortland Production Facility

The production facility in Cortland, New York, was originally a cold storage warehouse for locally grown apples and peaches. When these forms of agriculture dwindled, a former Cortland State University student associated with the Duncan Packing Company of Louisville, Kentucky, suggested that the company purchase and convert the warehouse for use as a frozen foods production and storage facility. The Duncan Packing Company had been founded in 1940 and prospered as a supplier of canned goods to the United States military. With the end of World War II, the company decided to expand into frozen foods and chose the Cortland apple and peach storage facility as part of that expansion.

By 1954, Duncan Packing Company sales of frozen meat and fruit pies reached $11 million. The company employed 925 people in its facilities in Cortland (126,000 square feet) and Webster City, Iowa (116,000 square feet). Duncan was acquired a year later, 1955, by the American Baking Company, which changed the name to Duncan Frozen Foods. The International Communications Corporation acquired American Baking in 1968 and in 1981 sold Duncan to the Amore Corporation (a subsidiary of K. J. Kyburg Industries, Inc.). At that time, Duncan's annual sales of $187 million represented a significant expansion by the Amore Corporation (primarily involved in canned foods) into the higher-margined areas of processed and frozen foods.

By 1984, the Cortland facility had grown to 500,000 square feet and employed 1,250 people. It produced 30,000 cases a day of finished products that carried the names Amore, Duncan, and Won Ton. Exhibit 1 lists the products made in the Cortland facility.

EXHIBIT 1   Cortland Products

— Beef, chicken, and turkey pot pies
— Full line of frozen dinners (13 varieties)
— Two-pound entrees (10 varieties)
— Casseroles (macaroni and cheese, and spaghetti and meat)
— Boil-in-Bag (10 varieties)
— Donuts (4 varieties)
— Full line of Food Service meals—primarily in-flight service for airlines

---

EXHIBIT 2   Standard Cost Breakdown

Item	Dollars per Dozen
Ingredients:*	$1.82
Cheese	
Macaroni	
Packaging:	0.62
Tins	
Cartons	
Case	
Direct labor	0.07
Indirect labor	0.13
Overhead	0.36
Total	$3.00

---

*At the 8.44-ounce target.

Macaroni and Cheese Production

The Cortland facility produced 60,000 dozen 8-ounce frozen macaroni and cheese pies each month on a line staffed with 25 workers making about $6 an hour. When this line was not making macaroni and cheese, it produced any number of other similar products.

Raw materials entered the preparation area where the cheese sauce was made and the macaroni cooked and cooled. The two were then blended in horizontal mixers and pumped to the filling line. At the filling line the aluminum trays were placed on a conveyor, mechanically filled with the macaroni and cheese, and then placed in cartons. The product was then cased (24 pies to the case), frozen, and placed in storage for distribution. The line operated at a speed of 1,000 dozen pies every 20 minutes. It took nine minutes for the mixed macaroni and cheese to end up packaged, cartoned, and cased, and another 40 minutes to freeze the cased product.

Exhibit 2 gives the standard cost breakdown for a dozen 8-ounce macaroni and cheese pies as estimated by the accounting department. Pies sold at a whole-sale price of $4.50 per dozen, $1.50 above the $3.00 standard cost per dozen.

Fill Targets

The practice in the food and beverage industry was to set a target weight or volume to which each container or package was filled. Because of the variability associated with the physical mechanisms that actually filled each package, fill targets were always set above the amount stated on the package. Industry practice was to set targets at one standard deviation above the package amount so about 85 percent of all packages would be in compliance. Exhibit 3 gives a detailed table of normal probabilities used to determine the percentage of underweight packages. The filling device for macaroni and cheese at Amore's Cortland plant could fill amounts that were normally distributed around the target value with a standard deviation of 0.22 ounces. Industry practice would then dictate a fill target for an 8-ounce macaroni and cheese pie of 8.22 ounces.

During the energy crisis of the late 70s, Amore (then Duncan Frozen Foods) discovered that cost-conscious supermarkets were turning off their freezers when they went home for the evening. The effect on frozen macaroni and cheese was to cause a softening of the product and a subsequent weight loss due to dehydration. Local government inspectors discovered several examples of underweight macaroni and cheese for which some producers were fined several thousand dollars. In particular, inspectors from the Bureau of Weights and Measures of New York City levied fines of up to $15 for each 8-ounce package of frozen macaroni and cheese found to be substantially underweight.[1] Despite the industry's presentation of evidence that improper storage of the product led to dehydration that caused the underweight product, the fines were not rescinded. In response to these problems, Amore quickly raised the target to 8.44 ounces in 1978, a full two standard deviations above the package weight. This unusually high target protected Amore from most of the problems brought on by the energy crisis. In 1984, with energy costs at normal levels, fines for substantially underweight frozen macaroni and cheese were virtually nonexistent in the industry.

Weight Control System

The United States Food and Drug Administration (FDA) was the arm of the federal government responsible for monitoring the practices of the food and beverage industry. One part of the FDA's activities required each food packager to submit a program designed to ensure that packages contained the stated amounts (weights) of product.

For Amore's macaroni and cheese pies, the FDA had approved a weight control system that required a sample of five pies be taken every 20 minutes. The five pies were selected consecutively at the beginning of a 20-minute run by a quality control technician, who then spent almost the entire 20 minutes weighing and checking various attributes of the sample. The technician cost the company close

---

[1]The guidelines for levying fines varied with locality. In general, fines were imposed if an average of some number of pies fell under the package amount. It was possible, however, for one significantly underweight pie (e.g., one weighing less than 7.5 ounces) to warrant a fine.

EXHIBIT 3 Normal Probabilities

	0.00	0.01	0.02	0.03	0.04	0.05	0.06	0.07	0.08	0.09
	0.	0.	0.	0.	0.	0.	0.	0.	0.	0.
-3.2	00069*	00066	00064	00062	00060	00058	00056	00054	00052	00050
-3.1	00097	00094	00090	00087	00084	00082	00079	00076	00074	00071
-3.0	00135	00131	00126	00122	00118	00114	00111	00107	00104	00100
-2.9	00187	00181	00175	00169	00164	00159	00154	00149	00144	00139
-2.8	00256	00248	00240	00233	00226	00219	00212	00205	00199	00193
-2.7	00347	00336	00326	00317	00307	00298	00289	00280	00272	00264
-2.6	00466	00453	00440	00427	00415	00402	00391	00379	00368	00357
-2.5	00621	00604	00587	00570	00554	00539	00523	00508	00494	00480
-2.4	00820	00798	00776	00755	00734	00714	00695	00676	00657	00639
-2.3	01072	01044	01017	00990	00964	00939	00914	00889	00866	00842
-2.2	01390	01355	01321	01287	01255	01222	01191	01160	01130	01101
-2.1	01786	01743	01700	01659	01618	01578	01539	01500	01463	01426
-2.0	02275	02222	02169	02118	02068	02018	01970	01923	01876	01831
-1.9	02872	02807	02743	02680	02619	02559	02500	02442	02385	02330
-1.8	03593	03515	03438	03362	03288	03216	03144	03074	03005	02938
-1.7	04457	04363	04272	04182	04093	04006	03920	03836	03754	03673
-1.6	05480	05370	05262	05155	05050	04947	04846	04746	04648	04551
-1.5	06681	06552	06426	06301	06178	06057	05938	05821	05705	05592
-1.4	08076	07927	07780	07636	07493	07353	07215	07078	06944	06811
-1.3	09680	09510	09342	09176	09012	08851	08691	08534	08379	08226
-1.2	11507	11314	11123	10935	10749	10565	10383	10204	10027	09853
-1.1	13567	13350	13136	12924	12714	12507	12302	12100	11900	11702
-1.0	15866	15625	15386	15151	14917	14686	14457	14231	14007	13786

Note: Row and column headings give number of standard deviations from mean, and table entry gives the probability that a normally distributed uncertain quantity will be less than the specified number of standard deviations from the mean.

*Read: There is a 0.00069 probability that a normally distributed uncertain quantity is more than 3.200 standard deviations below the mean.

to $12 an hour with fringe benefits. The pies were taken from the line after being cartoned and just prior to being cased and frozen. To weigh a macaroni and cheese pie, the technician placed the completed pie (complete with tin and carton) on one side of a balance scale and a tin, a carton, and a "tare" bottle (a standard weight constructed to weigh exactly the target weight of 8.44 ounces) on the other. The scale then read in units of 50ths of an ounce above or below the target. A reading of +28 thus meant the pie weighed 9 ounces (28/50 of an ounce above the target of 8.44 ounces).

Light samples, those that averaged less than −11 (8.22 ounces), were reported immediately to the line supervisor for corrective action. The workers had enough experience to easily respond to any unusual situation, so the worst that could happen was that the line ran below target for 20 minutes before it was noticed and corrected. Exhibit 4 shows an example of a weight control reporting sheet for the macaroni and cheese line, with reaction lines drawn at plus and minus 11.

Although it was Amore's company policy to react to samples averaging less than 8.22 ounces, the FDA-approved system required formal action only if the sample average weight was less than 8 ounces. In such cases, the entire 20-minute production had to be either fixed (weighed individually with extra ingredient added to all those found underweight, carton destroyed), reworked (ingredient reused, tins and cartons destroyed), or sold as underweight. To avoid the costs of fixing or reworking, Amore usually chose to send the entire 20-minute production to the company-operated Thrift Store on those rare occasions that the sample average weight fell below 8 ounces. In the first six months of 1984, only one such run was sent to the Thrift Store.

EXHIBIT 4   Example Weight Control Report

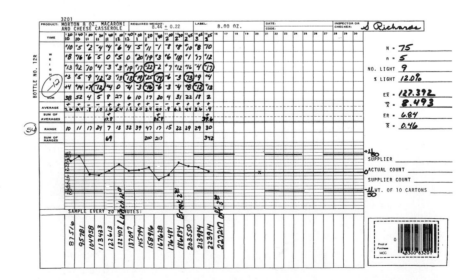

Thrift Store

The company-operated Thrift Store, located across the road from the main plant, sold a variety of underweight and second-quality frozen food merchandise to the general public. The selection of products available for sale was dictated by the "mistakes" made in the plant. However, any product that presented a potential health hazard, no matter how remote, was destroyed immediately.

Underweight macaroni and cheese was stamped with a 7-ounce label and sold fairly briskly at $3.60 per dozen. The local demand was such that approximately 60 dozen were sold each week when macaroni and cheese pies were available. This limited local demand and relatively high energy costs of storage led to an inventory policy that limited the amount of stored macaroni and cheese pies to 1,000 dozen pies. If more became available, the oldest cases in inventory were donated to charity.

CASE 4
ATHENS GLASS WORKS

In early August 1993, Christina Matthews, the product manager for nonglare glass at the Athens Glass Works (AGW), met with Robert Alexander, the controller of the Specialty Glass Division, to review the product's performance and prepare a pricing recommendation for the coming quarter. Once approved by the division president, the price would be announced and, as was customary in this segment of the glass industry, adhered to for at least 90 days.

The flat-glass industry was a $10.0 billion industry worldwide, of which $2.7 billion was generated in the United States. Approximately 57 percent of domestic production was for the construction industry, 25 percent for the automotive industry, and the remaining 18 percent for specialty products ranging from the mundane, like mirrors, to a wide variety of high-tech applications. Among the many technical applications of specialty glasses were solar panels, laminated and tempered safety glasses, heat- and bullet-resistant glasses, electrical and insulating glasses, phototechnical and photosensitive glasses, aerospace glass, and cookware. Nonglare glass was a fairly simple specialty product designed to reduce the glare of reflected light. It was used primarily to frame and protect artwork.

With 1992 sales of $195 million, Athens Glass Works was a midsized, regional glass company serving several niche markets in the southeastern United States. For a number of reasons, AGW enjoyed a dominant market position for nonglare glass in its region: (1) AGW was known for its fast, reliable service; it was willing to deliver glass on short notice at no extra charge in any of a variety of cut-to-order sizes, including the industry-standard delivery size (48-by-96-inch sheets) and all of the standard picture-frame sizes. (2) AGW provided an exceptionally high-quality nonglare glass with little light loss and virtually no blemishes. (3) AGW operated its own fleet of delivery vehicles so delivery times were well managed and shipping charges were kept low. And (4) AGW's salaried sales staff was widely acknowledged for its helpful, courteous service and customer orientation.

The production of nonglare glass, like many other coated-glass products, began with flat glass, the output of one of Specialty Glass's sister divisions. The flat glass was treated by the Specialty Glass Division with a patented coating that provided the desired optical characteristics. This process required specialized equipment that was usable only in the production of nonglare glass. The finished, treated glass was then cut to order and shipped.

The business outlook for nonglare glass, like that for flat-glass products in general, had been flat for the past several years. As a result, last September, in response to increased corporate pressure to improve margins, Christina and Rob-

This case was prepared in conjunction with Professor Dana Clyman (Darden). Copyright © by the University of Virginia Darden School Foundation, Charlottesville, Virginia. All rights reserved.

EXHIBIT 1   Sales Volume and Price History of Nonglare Glass

Year	Quarter	Sales Volume (000 square feet)		Price ($ per square foot)	
		AGW	Competitors	AGW	Competitors
1991	3	241	443	$2.05	$2.05
1991	4	313	592	2.05	2.05
1992	1	204	381	2.15	2.15
1992	2	269	513	2.15	2.15
1992	3	251	456	2.15	2.15
1992	4	238	672	2.36	2.15
1993	1	139	474	2.36	2.15
1993	2	162	642	2.36	2.15

ert increased the price of nonglare glass by slightly less than 10 percent, from $2.15 to $2.36 per square foot. This pricing decision was one of many made during the past year in anticipation of the company's considerable capital requirements to fund a recently approved long-term expansion and modernization program. At the time of the price increase, Christina and Robert hoped that competitors would follow AGW's lead and increase their prices as well.

Unfortunately, AGW's competitors held the line on the price of nonglare glass, and Christina believed that AGW's significant loss of market share in the last nine months was due solely to AGW's price change, as little else had changed in the industry during that period. To document the decline, Christina prepared Exhibit 1, which presents the sales-volume and price-history data for nonglare glass in AGW's market region for the past eight quarters. Looking ahead, Christina believed that a reasonable forecast of total regional volume for the fourth quarter of 1993 (usually the best quarter of the year) was 920,000 square feet. Christina believed that if AGW were to return to the $2.15 price, it could regain a major portion of its original market share with sales of 275,000 square feet. On the other hand, if competitive prices were not met, she feared a further decline. Nonetheless, because of AGW's outstanding reputation in the crafts marketplace, she reasoned that a sufficient number of customers would stay with AGW and prevent sales from falling below 150,000 square feet, even at the current price of $2.36 per square foot.

While reflecting on the upcoming meeting with Christina, Robert realized that price would be the major topic of discussion, so he had his staff prepare a schedule of expected costs to produce nonglare glass over a wide range of production levels. This schedule is presented in Exhibit 2.

During their discussion, Christina and Robert together reviewed the historical sales levels and pricing data as well as the anticipated-cost schedule. They began by discussing the cost schedule. Christina noticed that unit costs grew with in-

EXHIBIT 2   **Nonglare Glass**
Estimated Cost per Square Foot at Various Production Volumes

	Production Volume (000 sq. ft.)							
	150	*175*	*200*	*225*	*250*	*275*	*300*	*325*
Material	$0.45	$0.45	$0.45	$0.45	$0.45	$0.45	$0.45	$0.45
Energy	0.38	0.36	0.36	0.35	0.35	0.37	0.37	0.38
Labor	0.32	0.31	0.30	0.31	0.33	0.35	0.36	0.38
Shipping	0.11	0.11	0.11	0.11	0.11	0.11	0.11	0.11
General overhead*	0.08	0.08	0.08	0.08	0.08	0.09	0.09	0.09
Depreciation	0.27	0.23	0.20	.18	0.16	0.15	0.14	0.13
Manufacturing cost	1.61	1.54	1.50	1.48	1.48	1.52	1.52	1.54
Selling and admin. costs†	0.72	0.69	0.67	0.66	0.67	0.68	0.68	0.69
Total cost	$2.33	$2.23	$2.17	$2.14	$2.15	$2.20	$2.20	$2.23

*General overhead includes a variety of corporate expenditures. It is allocated as 25 percent of labor.

†Selling and administrative costs include the costs of the sales and administrative support staff. It is allocated as 45 percent of manufacturing cost.

creasing volumes, but Robert said that the increasing unit costs were simply the result of the company's cost allocation system. Next, Robert asked whether there was any possibility that competitors might reduce their prices below $2.15 per square foot if AGW returned to that price. Christina replied that she was confident no competitor would do so, because all were facing the same general economic conditions resulting from the long recession and several were in particularly tight financial straits. They then discussed whether the pricing decision for nonglare glass would have any repercussions on other Specialty Glass products; both were convinced it would not. Finally, they explored the implications of AGW's returning to the industry price of $2.15 per square foot. Christina believed recapturing lost market share was essential for AGW to maintain its dominant role in the nonglare-glass niche. Robert, however, was concerned that, at $2.15, the product would show a loss, an outcome that would not be welcomed by senior management.

CASE 5
BUCKEYE POWER & LIGHT COMPANY

Don Peters was manager of the Production Fuels Department of Buckeye Power & Light Company (BP&L), a small utility in southeastern Ohio. BP&L had three steam electric power plants—located in Athens, Zanesville, and Steubenville—whose primary energy source was coal. Each month, coal for these plants was purchased from a heterogeneous collection of vendors in Ohio, Pennsylvania, and West Virginia, ranging in size from small father-and-son operations to large mining companies. Peters was responsible for the monthly coal-procurement process, including how much to purchase from each vendor and which specific plant (or plants) each vendor should supply.

In October 1986, Peters' immediate task was to determine November's coal-procurement schedule. BP&L had recently retained the services of a consulting firm to analyze aspects of its operations, including the coal-procurement process. Peters hoped to use the opportunity of the consultants' analysis to rethink the entire procurement process. He also hoped the report would shed some light on two related issues that had been a source of controversy within the department.

Coal

Compared with oil, natural gas, and nuclear energy, coal was a relatively cheap source of fuel during the 1980s. Coal is a combustible rock formed by the underground compression of partially decomposed plant matter over millions of years. There are four major types of coal, classified according to energy content: lignite (lowest energy content), subbituminous, bituminous (most widely used as a fuel source), and anthracite (highest energy content). Coal's energy content (or thermal value) is measured in British thermal units (Btus). (One Btu is the amount of heat needed to raise a pound of water one degree Fahrenheit.) Pure bituminous coal typically contains on the order of 15,000 Btu per pound (Btu/lb).

There are three major determinants of the quality of coal. One is *total moisture content*. There are two distinct types of moisture associated with coal. *Free* moisture lies on the surface of the coal. Its presence, which depends primarily on conditions in the mine and in transit, is an important parameter in the design of coal-handling and -preparation equipment. *Inherent* moisture is trapped within the pores of the coal itself, and is present even when the surface of the coal appears dry. Both types of moisture reduce energy content.

A second determinant of coal quality is *ash content*. Ash is the incombustible residue that remains after coal is burned. Like moisture, a high ash content increases shipping, handling, and preparation costs while reducing thermal value.

Additional equipment and expense is required periodically to remove ash from a coal-fired furnace. Failure to do so adequately has a long-term impact on the life of a furnace.

The third major determinant of quality is *sulfur content*. When coal is burned, sulfur oxides are released, causing pollution and contributing to the corrosion of vital plant parts. Some sulfur can be removed prior to burning by "washing" the coal. To further control pollution, "scrubbers" can be attached to smokestacks to filter out a substantial number of sulfur oxide particles. During the 1980s, the maximum level of sulfur oxide pollution was regulated by law. Each coal-fired plant was thus forced to restrict the amount of sulfur in the coal it burned on the basis of the specific pollution-control equipment it was using.

BP&L's Coal-Procurement Process

Each month, vendors interested in supplying one or more of BP&L's coal-fired power plants completed an offer sheet specifying the amount of coal they had to sell, along with its quality and price. Quality was expressed in terms of Btu/lb and moisture, ash, and sulfur content. Vendors were asked to quote a per-ton price, transportation included, for each power plant they were willing and able to supply. The Production Fuels Department took all offers, adjusted them for past performance (particularly the amount of coal available for purchase, which was often overstated and had to be adjusted downward), and summarized the results in a document called the Offers Edit Report (see Exhibit 1).

At the same time, each of the three coal-fired power plants submitted its requirements for the upcoming month. Corporate policy dictated that a plant have sufficient Btus on hand each month to satisfy 120 percent of expected demand. Exactly how many Btus to order for the upcoming month thus depended on both the estimated ending inventory of coal in the current month (stated in terms of Btus) and expected demand during the upcoming month.

Each plant also provided minimum acceptable quality standards for moisture, ash, and sulfur content. Each of these was stated in terms of a weighted average of all coal delivered to the plant in the month. For example, 1,000 tons of coal with 2 percent sulfur content and 500 tons of coal with 1 percent sulfur content would produce an overall 1.67 percent sulfur-content level; this number was not allowed to exceed the sulfur standard. The sulfur standards were set by law; moisture and ash standards were left to the discretion of the individual plant managers, who were familiar with the costs associated with handling increased levels of moisture and ash at their respective plants.

The Production Fuels Department was responsible for taking the Offers Edit Report and the plant requirements, summarized in a Plant Requirements Edit Report (Exhibit 2), and arriving at an overall coal-procurement plan. Peters, as manager of the department, had the flexibility to negotiate with both vendors and plant managers to strike a better overall deal for the company. For example, he

EXHIBIT 1   Offers Edit Report for November

Vendor	Quantity Available (tons)	Btu/Lb	Moisture (%)	Ash (%)	Sulfur (%)	Plant	$/Ton
Willis Bros.	2,500	10,980	6.2%	21%	1.2%	Ath	$30.80
MacMillan	9,000	11,590	6.0	20	0.9	Ath	36.80
K. Barnes	3,000	11,550	6.4	18	1.1	Ath	34.00
Foster &	27,000	12,065	6.1	12	1.0	Stb	42.00
Hughes						Zan	41.60
						Ath	45.60
Western	22,500	12,210	6.2	14	0.9	Stb	43.92
						Zan	42.70
						Ath	41.48
Pellham	6,000	11,240	6.8	18	1.8	Stb	33.15
McIntyre	3,000	11,000	6.3	17	2.2	Stb	32.00
Monongahela	30,000	12,640	5.8	10	0.8	Stb	44.10
Consolidated						Zan	45.36
Pope	3,600	12,570	6.4	10	1.0	Zan	35.00
Lyon Valley	2,700	11,950	6.8	12	0.9	Zan	33.12
Crescent Rock	2,300	12,080	6.6	13	1.1	Zan	32.40

Long-term contracts:
  MacMillan (minimum of 8,000 tons)
  Foster & Hughes (minimum of 20,000 tons)
  Western (minimum of 16,000 tons)
  Monongahela Consol. (minimum of 18,000 tons)

EXHIBIT 2   Plant Requirements Edit Report for November

		Maximum Allowable Weighted Average Percent		
Plant	Btus (billions)	Moisture	Ash	Sulfur
Steubenville	800*	6.0%	15%	1.0%
Zanesville	500	7.0	11	2.0
Athens	600	7.0	18	1.0

*Number of Btus that, when added to October's expected ending inventory, would equal 120 percent of November's expected demand.

could negotiate price reductions or quantity increases with vendors, or both. Similarly, he could make plant managers aware of particularly restrictive quality requirements and negotiate to have them relaxed. Ultimately, Peters was responsible for approving the overall coal-procurement plan.

Recently, the Production Fuels Department had been struggling with two issues relating to the coal-procurement process: long-term contracts and safety-stock levels.

Long-Term Contracts

Because of a utility's need to have a guaranteed source of fuel, long-term contracts with coal vendors were a long-standing industry practice. A long-term contract with a vendor obligated the utility to buy a minimum amount of coal each month from that vendor at the contract-specified price. The balance of the utility's needs was met by purchasing additional coal on the spot market.

Prior to 1973, BP&L had purchased approximately 65 percent of its coal on long-term contract. The energy crisis of the 1970s and resulting surge in demand for coal and coal prices had precipitated an upward trend in this figure. By 1986, BP&L was purchasing 80 percent of its coal on long-term contract (vendors in late 1986 with whom BP&L had long-term contracts and the contract amounts are indicated in Exhibit 1).

As the energy crisis eased, however, the availability of coal became less of a concern. Moreover, by 1986, prices on the spot market were running about $6 per ton less than long-term contract prices. Many people in the Production Fuels Department thought that the percentage of coal purchased on long-term contract should be reduced, perhaps back to the 65 percent level.

Peters estimated that returning to the 65 percent figure would allow BP&L to reduce the amount of coal purchased on long-term contract by 12,000 tons. If such a reduction were to be made, it was not clear to Peters which of the current long-term contracts should be reduced or eliminated.

20 Percent Safety Stock

Running out of coal forced a utility to purchase energy from a neighboring utility at a premium price. In August, for example, BP&L had sold 10 billion surplus Btus on an emergency basis to a utility in western Pennsylvania for $20,000. A rash of such purchases by BP&L in the 1970s had driven the company to raise its required safety-stock level from 15 to 20 percent.

Since the safety stock had been increased, however, none of BP&L's plants had ever been forced to purchase outside energy. In fact, over the past three years, actual monthly energy demand had rarely exceeded 110 percent of expected demand. Some BP&L officials attributed this situation to improved forecasting techniques, while others thought it represented a leveling off of demand.

Whatever the reason, many at BP&L were now pushing to reduce the safety-stock level back to 15 percent. Peters recognized that such a reduction would save BP&L carrying costs on the coal needed to supply 5 percent of overall Btu demand. From October's coal-procurement numbers, Peters estimated that the average cost of a billion Btus at each plant were as follows:

Plant	Average Cost of 1 Billion Btus
Steubenville	$1,740
Zanesville	$1,610
Athens	$1,625

He wondered if these were the appropriate costs to use, and, if so, how to balance the cost savings against the increased possibility of running out of coal.

CASE 6
BUCKEYE POWER & LIGHT COMPANY SUPPLEMENT

Early in October 1986, Don Peters, manager of the Production Fuels Department of Buckeye Power & Light Company (BP&L), received a preliminary report from a consultancy commissioned to analyze various aspects of its operations, including the coal-procurement process. The consultants had been given, among other items, the Offers Edit Report and the Plant Requirements Edit Report for the November coal-procurement decision. The section of the report dealing with the coal-procurement process, reproduced below, contains the consultants' recommendations with respect to the November purchase, as well as an explanation of their methodology. Peters was anxious to understand how this approach might help him more aggressively manage the procurement process and resolve the internal debates on long-term contracts and safety-stock levels.

Section of the Consultants' Report Dealing with the Coal-Procurement Process

Attached is a spreadsheet model (Exhibit 1) of the November coal-procurement decision. The model is constructed to facilitate the use of *What'sBest!*, a linear programming (LP) software package for spreadsheets. Based on the information contained in the model, LP can be used to identify the optimal (i.e., minimum cost) procurement and shipping plan. In addition, LP provides valuable ancillary information on related questions of interest, such as how much you would be willing to pay for additional coal from certain vendors, how much your long-term contracts are costing you, and how much the quality restrictions imposed by the various plants are costing the company.

Below is a summary of LP and a guide to interpreting the spreadsheet model.

In LP, a decision is viewed as an allocation of *resources* to potential *uses* of those resources. The allocation is made with a specific *objective* in mind—such as to maximize profit or minimize cost—and is subject to *constraints*, or restrictions, on how the resources can and should be allocated. These constraints may be either environmental in nature (outside the control of the decision maker) or policy (within the control of the decision maker). Within the limitations imposed by these constraints, LP identifies the allocation of resources to uses that achieve the best, or optimal, result in terms of the objective.

In the coal-procurement decision, the resources are the supplies of coal from the various vendors. There are three potential uses of these resources: the Btu requirements of each of BP&L's three coal-fired plants. The objective is to minimize the cost of satisfying these requirements.

EXHIBIT 1

	A	B	C	D	E	F	G	H	I	J	K	L
1	Buckeye Power & Light Company											
2												
3	Total cost											
4	—											
5	$3,165,119[1]											
6												
7	Vendor	Steubenville	Zanesville	Athens	Total purchased		Maximum available	Slack	Shadow price	Range Decrease	Increase	
8	—	—	—	—	—		—	—	—	—	—	
9	Willis			2,500	2,500[2]	<	2,500	0	$1.52	2,500	239	
10	MacMillan			8,000	8,000	<	9,000	1,000	$0.00	1,000	**********	
11	Barnes			227	227	<	3,000	2,773	$0.00	2,773	**********	
12	F & H	16,036	3,964	0	20,000	<	27,000	7,000	$0.00	7,000	**********	
13	Western	1,487	0	14,513	16,000	<	22,500	6,500	$0.00	6,500	**********	
14	Pellham	0			0	<	6,000	6,000	$0.00	6,000	**********	
15	McIntyre	2,277			2,277	<	3,000	723	$0.00	723	**********	
16	Monongahela	12,921	7,664		20,585	<	30,000	9,415	$0.00	9,415	**********	
17	Pope		3,600		3,600	<	3,600	0	$10.12	3,600	2,594	
18	Lyon Valley		2,700		2,700	<	2,700	0	$4.94	2,700	346	
19	Crescent		2,300		2,300	<	2,300	0	$3.62	2,300	228	
20	—	—	—	—								
21	Total	32,721[3]	20,228	25,240								
22	Total cost	$1,381,502[4]	$802,487	$981,131								
23												

[1] @SUM(B22..D22) [2] @SUM(B9..D9)
[3] @SUM(B9..B19) [4] $42.00*B12 + $43.92*B13 + $33.15*B14 + $32.00*B15 + $44.10*B16

EXHIBIT 1 (CONTINUED)

	A	B	C	D	E	F	G	H	I	J	K	L
24			**Contract Requirements**									
25												
26					Total		Minimum		Shadow		Range	
27			Vendor		purchased		contract	Surplus	price	Decrease	Increase	
28			—		—		—	—	—	—	—	
29			Willis		2,500[5]							
30			MacMillan		8,000	>	8,000	0	$2.68	2.763	226	
31			Barnes		227							
32			F & H		20,000	>	20,000	0	$3.15	4.208	345	
33			Western		16,000	>	16,000	0	$5.54	2.623	215	
34			Pellham		0							
35			McIntyre		2,277							
36			Monongahela		20,585	>	18,000	2,585	$0.00	*********	2,585	
37			Pope		3,600							
38			Lyon Valley		2,700							
39			Crescent		2,300							
40												
41							**Minimum Plant Btu Requirements**					
42									Shadow		Range	
43			Plant		Actual		Required	Surplus	price	Decrease	Increase	
44			—		—		—	—	—	—	—	
45			Steubenville		800[6]	>	800	0	$1,653	15	151	
46			Zanesville		500	>	500	0	$1,696	17	208	
47			Athens		600	>	600	0	$1,472	5	64	
48												

[5] +E9

[6] $((12{,}065*B12 + 12{,}210*B13 + 11{,}240*B14 + 11{,}000*B15 + 12{,}640*B16)*(2{,}000/1{,}000{,}000{,}000))$

391

EXHIBIT 1 *Concluded*

	A	B	C	D	E	F	G	H	I	J	K	L
49												
50					Minimum Quality Requirements				Shadow	Range		
51			Steubenville		Actual		Allowed	Slack	price	Decrease	Increase	
52			——		——			——				
53			Moisture		$1,963^7$	<	$1,963^8$	0	$1,048	1	9	
54			Ash		3,812	<	4,908	1,096	$0	1,096	*********	
55			Sulfur		327	<	327	0	$103	27	2	
56												
57			Zanesville									
58			——		——							
59			Moisture		$1,252^9$	<	$1,416^{10}$	164	$0	164	*********	
60			Ash		2,225	<	2,225	0	$248	7	74	
61			Sulfur		187	<	405	218	$0	218	*********	
62			Athens									
63			——									
64												
65			Moisture		$1,549^{11}$	<	$1,767^{12}$	217	$0	217	*********	
66			Ash		4,198	<	4,543	346	$0	346	*********	
67			Sulfur		235	<	252	17	$0	17	*********	
68												

[7] .061*B12 + .062*B13 + .068*B14 + .063*B15 + .058*B16
[8] .06*B21
[9] .12*B12 + .14*B13 + .18*B14 + .17*B15 + .10*B16
[10] .15*B21
[11] .010*B12 + .009*B13 + .018*B14 + .022*B15 + .008*B16
[12] .010*B21

There are several constraints on the allocation:

Resource Availability.   Each vendor is offering a limited supply of coal. We cannot buy more coal than a vendor has available.

Btu Requirement.   Each plant has a required number of Btus. The coal we ship to each plant must have sufficient thermal value to satisfy that plant's Btu needs.

Contracts.   From certain vendors, we are obligated to purchase a minimum amount of coal.

Quality Restrictions.   Each plant has restrictions on the weighted-average moisture, ash, and sulfur content of incoming coal. We must make sure that the average of all coal we ship to each plant satisfies these requirements.

To apply LP, we must first model the relationship between resources and uses. This is accomplished by first defining a set of spreadsheet cells that represents the allocation of resources to uses. There needs to be one cell for each potential resource-use combination. In the coal-procurement model, there is a cell for each vendor/plant combination (cells B9-E19). For all vendor/plant combinations that are not feasible, the corresponding cell is left blank. The remainder of the cells are allowed to vary in search of a minimum cost allocation. (Because these adjustable cells form the core of the decision, they are referred to as *decision variables* in traditional LP terminology.)

We next must specify the relationship between uses and the objective. Associated with allocating some or all of a particular resource to a specific use is the impact of that allocation on the objective. In the coal-procurement model, purchasing one ton of coal from a particular vendor and shipping it to a specific plant costs us the per-ton offering price for that vendor/plant combination. For a given allocation plan, the total cost of the plan is calculated by multiplying the number of tons assigned to each vendor/plant combination by the associated per-ton cost, and summing these totals across all vendor/plant combinations. In the coal-procurement model, this total is in cell A5 (the sum of cells B22-D22). It is precisely this figure that we are trying to minimize.

The final step in setting up our LP model is to make sure that the optimal allocation does not violate any of the constraints. In the coal-procurement plan, this is accomplished as follows:

Resource Availability.   Cells E9-E19 contain the total number of tons purchased from each vendor, irrespective of plant destination. These totals cannot exceed the vendors' corresponding supplies of coal, contained in cells G9-G19. The "<" symbol between the two is *What'sBest!*'s way of stating that, for example, cell E9 must be "less than or equal to" cell G9. Cells H9-H19 contain the number of tons of coal offered by each vendor but not purchased. (In LP terminology, this is referred to as *slack*.)

Btu Requirement. To see how this constraint is modeled, consider the Steubenville plant. This plant requires 800 billion Btus; this number is entered in cell G45. Given a particular allocation scheme, cell E45 contains the total number of Btus in the coal shipped to the Steubenville plant. It is calculated by first multiplying each vendor's average Btu/lb by the number of lbs shipped from that vendor to Steubenville and then summing across vendors. The ">" symbol specifies that cell E45 must be greater than or equal to cell G45. The number in cell H45 specifies how many billions of Btus above the required 800 are being sent to Steubenville. (This is often referred to as the *surplus.*)

Contracts. Cells E29-E39 duplicate the total number of tons ordered from each vendor (also contained in cells E9-E19). The minimum order quantities for each of BP&L's long-term contracts are in cells G30 (MacMillan), G32 (Foster & Hughes), G33 (Western), and G36 (Monongahela). As with the Btu requirements, actual tonnage must exceed the minimum order quantities; hence, the ">" symbols and the surplus column.

Quality Restrictions. To see how these 9 constraints (3 plants times 3 quality considerations) are modeled, consider the moisture constraint for the Steubenville plant. For a given allocation scheme, the actual number of tons of moisture sent to the Steubenville plant is contained in cell E55. It is found by multiplying the moisture percentage of each vendor's coal by the number of tons shipped by that vendor to Steubenville and then summing these totals across vendors. The total number of tons of moisture allowed in Steubenville is found by multiplying Steubenville's maximum allowable weighted-average moisture percentage (6 percent, from Exhibit 2) by the total number of tons shipped to the plant (cell B21). The use of "<" and the slack cells parallel the resource-availability constraints above.

Using *What'sBest!*, we arrive at the procurement plan outlined in the attached hard copy. Notice that all constraints are satisfied. The algebra underlying the LP solution approach used by *What'sBest!* guarantees that we have found a plan that minimizes total cost (cell A5).

Shadow Prices. There is one additional bit of valuable information that is provided. For a variety of reasons, it is often useful to know the *value* of resources and the *cost* of restrictions placed on how we are allowed to allocate them. One assessment of value is the amount by which our economic position would be improved if we had one additional unit of resource. For a restriction, an assessment of value is the amount by which our economic position would be improved if we could "relax" the restriction (make it less restrictive). In both cases, the amount by which our position would be improved represents an upper bound on how much we would pay to receive the benefit. *Shadow prices* provide this information.

For example, how valuable is coal supplied by Willis? Notice that, in the optimal procurement schedule, we purchase all of the Willis coal offered. The shadow price for Willis coal (cell I9) is $1.52. The proper interpretation of this number is as follows: If we had one additional ton of Willis coal available (i.e., 2,501 instead of 2,500) at the current price, we could improve our economic position by $1.52. Purchasing an additional ton from Willis would allow us to purchase less from another vendor; the net effect would be an overall cost reduction of $1.52. Analogously, if we had one less ton available from Willis (2,499 instead of 2,500), the net effect of having to purchase additional coal elsewhere would drive up our overall procurement cost (thereby worsening our economic position) by $1.52.

Alternatively, consider the ash restriction at the Zanesville plant. The shadow price is $248 (cell I62). The correct interpretation is as follows: If we could allow one additional ton of ash (over and above the 15 percent of the total currently allowed) to be handled at the Zanesville plant, we could improve our economic position by $248. Relaxing this constraint (allowing more ash to be sent to Zanesville) would allow us to allocate a less-expensive mix of coal to Zanesville, with repercussions echoing throughout the procurement plan. The net effect would be a cost reduction of $248. Analogously, if our ability to handle ash at Zanesville were decreased by one ton (below the 15 percent of the total currently allowed), our cost would increase (thereby worsening our economic position) by $248. Tightening this constraint (allowing less ash to be sent to Zanesville) would force us to send a more expensive mix of coal to the plant.

For each ">" constraint, the interpretation of shadow prices is analogous to the above, adjusting for the fact that *relax* now carries a different meaning. For example, consider the minimum order quantity due to the long-term contract with Foster & Hughes. We are currently purchasing precisely the minimum amount, and the shadow price is $3.15 (cell I32). The proper interpretation: If we could purchase one less ton from Foster & Hughes (i.e., 19,999 instead of 20,000), we could improve our economic position by $3.15 (alternatively, having to purchase an additional ton would worsen our economic position by $3.15). Again, this represents the net effect of purchasing one less ton from Foster & Hughes and some additional coal elsewhere. Relaxing a ">" constraint means reducing the quantity on the right-hand side of the inequality (lowering the hurdle we have to clear), while relaxing a "<" constraint means increasing the right-hand side (raising the bar we have to get under).

Three additional points should be made. First, notice that the shadow price is $0 for any constraint where there is a slack or surplus. The rationale for this is simple: If we are not currently using up all the available quantity of a particular resource, having more of that resource available does not affect our optimal procurement plan and, hence, has no effect on total cost. Analogously, if the weighted average of the coal we are shipping to a particular plant is of better than required quality along any of the relevant dimensions, then relaxing the allowable quality along that dimension will not change the optimal procurement plan and, hence, does not reduce overall cost.

Second, a shadow price tells us the marginal value of relaxing a constraint by *one* unit only (e.g., the cost savings of being allowed to buy one less ton of coal on contract from MacMillan or, conversely, the additional cost of having to buy one additional ton on contract from MacMillan). This per-unit cost only holds over a limited range. At some point, the per-ton cost savings of being allowed to buy less coal from MacMillan is bound to decrease and, conversely, the per-ton additional cost of having to buy additional coal from MacMillan is bound to increase. *What'sBest!* reports the amount by which the current right-hand side value of any constraint can be increased or decreased and the reported per-unit shadow price still be guaranteed to apply. For example, the $2.68 (cell I30) per-ton cost savings of being allowed to buy less MacMillan coal applies for a reduction of at least 2,763 (cell J30) tons. Once the contract amount is reduced to less than $8,000 - 2,763 = 5,237$ tons, the per-ton shadow price associated with an additional reduction may drop. Conversely, the same $2.68 per-ton additional cost of having to buy additional coal from MacMillan holds for at least an additional 226 (cell K30) tons. Once the contract amount is increased to more than $8,000 + 226 = 8,226$ tons, the per-ton shadow price of having to buy an additional ton may go up. Hence, the marginal cost of $2.68 of a ton of MacMillan coal purchased on contract is guaranteed to hold over the range of 5,237 to 8,226 tons. To find the new shadow prices (if they do in fact change) outside of this range, the right-hand side of the constraint must be changed to a value outside the range, and the LP reoptimized.

Third and finally, each shadow price can, strictly speaking, be interpreted only within the context of everything else in the model remaining unchanged. For example, the shadow price of $1.52 for Willis coal is based on the assumption that the available quantities from all other vendors and the quality restrictions imposed by the plants do not change. To investigate changes in more than one constraint simultaneously, the model should be rerun. Practically speaking, however, using shadow prices to gauge the net effect of multiple changes is often acceptable as long as the changes are relatively small. For example, shadow prices can be used to investigate the marginal impact of an event that would change several quantities simultaneously.

The model is set up to allow you to make changes and reoptimize using *What'sBest!* Be careful when doing so to change only those cells that have numbers—not formulas—in them. Do not replace cell formulas with numbers, as this might destroy some of the important LP relationships built into the model. To reoptimize, make whatever changes you wish to make to the model itself, then reoptimize with *What'sBest!*

CASE 7
CALIFORNIA OIL COMPANY

Carl Shimer, research and development director for California Oil Company (COC), had been studying the proposed construction of a supertanker port and pipeline. The new facility would supply COC's Richmond refinery in the San Francisco Bay area. The port would consist of a single-point mooring two or three miles from shore to unload supertankers. Submarine pipelines would take the oil into a shore-based pumping station, where it would enter the pipeline to the Richmond refinery. After a preliminary screening, four sites had been selected for more detailed evaluation: Moss Landing, Estero Bay, Port Hueneme, and Oso Flaco Dunes. Shimer had to recommend a site to COC's research and development committee.

The major considerations in evaluating the sites were economic, political, and environmental. These were then refined and expanded into 10 criteria (see Table 1). The importance of each criterion was discussed at length at a committee meeting, after which Shimer received the following memo from his assistant:

TO: Mr. C. Shimer, Research and Development Director
FROM: Mr. D. Klopp, Assistant Director of Research and Development
SUBJECT: Tanker Port Selection

At Friday's meeting (April 2), it was decided that 10 criteria be used for evaluating promising sites. The 10 criteria were ranked in order of importance. The list developed on Friday places the "attitude of local politicians" as the *most* important factor and "environmental impact from placement of

---

TABLE 1 California Oil Company 10 Criteria Selected for Proposed Supertanker Port Evaluation

Economic	Facilities
	Port characteristics
	Location
	Initial cost
	Annual cost
	Possibilities for future development
Political	Attitude of local populace
	Attitude of local politicians
Environmental	Environmental impact from operation and accidents
	Environmental impact from placement of facilities

Note: Adapted from Elwood S. Buffa and James S. Dyer, *Management Science Operations Research* (New York: John Wiley & Sons, 1977).

Source: Unpublished report by G. Hill, A. Kokin, and S. Nukes. Reproduced with permission.

facilities" as the *least* important factor. I have enclosed the ranked criteria with comparative site descriptions for your information.

DATE: April 5, 1978   SIGNED: D. Klopp
                       _____

With this information, Shimer pulled out his notes from the committee meeting, which held evaluations of each of the sites broken down by the 10 criteria. He placed the criteria in the order suggested by the committee (see Table 2). Shimer examined each criterion and decided the "best" and "worst" situation possible under the circumstances. For example, the "best" outcome for the criterion "attitude of local politicians" would be a favorable vote assured, and the "worst" outcome would be an unlikely favorable vote (see Table 3).

For each criterion, Shimer assigned the "worst" situation a value of 0 and the "best" situation a value of 1. He then hoped to assign values between 0 and 1 for each site characteristic, weighing them by the relative importance of each of the 10 criteria to achieve an overall evaluation of each site (see Figure 1). He anticipated this method would help differentiate between sites rated favorably on high-priority criteria from those with good ratings on low-priority items. At

---

FIGURE 1   California Oil Company Work Sheet

		Alternatives			
Criterion	*Weight*	*Moss Landing*	*Estero Bay*	*Port Hueneme*	*Oso Flaco Dunes*
Attitude of local politicians					
Initial cost					
Annual cost					
Location					
Possibilities for future development					
Port characteristics					
Attitude of local populace					
Environmental impact from operation and accidents					
Facilities					
Environmental impact from placement of facilities					

TABLE 2 California Oil Company Assessment of Port Sites

Criterion	Moss Landing	Estero Bay	Port Hueneme	Oso Flaco Dunes
		Alternatives		
Attitude of local politicians	Possibly opposed	Possibly favorable	Favorable	Possibly favorable
Initial cost	$40 million less than Estero Bay	The cost-base location	$60 million more than Estero Bay	$5 million more than Estero Bay (estimate)
Annual cost	$2 million per year less than Estero Bay	Base location	$5 million more than Estero Bay	Near cost of base location
Location	Close to Richmond, farther from Elk Hills than base location	Base location	90 miles farther from Richmond than base location	Central location
Possibilities for future development	Area already populated	Rolling terrain will hamper large expansion	Navy interference	Area available, subject to local politicians
Port characteristics	Fair	Good	Excellent	Good
Attitude of local populace	Possible opposition	Vocal opposition	Little effect on population	Little effect on population
Environmental impact from operation/accidents	High impact: area is sandy to marshy, possibly difficult to clean up; possible long-term effects	High impact: tourism and fishing industry will be seriously affected; marshy area and rocky coastline extremely difficult to clean up; possible long-term damage to bird sanctuary and oyster beds	Minimal impact: area sandy; easy cleanup; area already industrialized	Minimal impact: area sandy; easy cleanup
Facilities	No	Some	No	No
Environmental impact from placement of facilities	Tank farm highly visible	Tank farm hidden; major restructure of existing creek	Tank farm visible (no nearby population)	Tank farm visible (no nearby population)

TABLE 3   California Oil Company Reference Port Descriptions

Criterion	"Worst" Value for Each Criterion	"Best" Value for Each Criterion
Attitude of local politicians	Favorable vote unlikely	Favorable vote assured
Initial cost (Estero Bay cost as base)	$60 million above base	$60 million below base
Annual cost (Estero Bay cost as base)	$5 million above base	$5 million below base
Location (Estero Bay as base)	Near Los Angeles with poor access to the San Joaquin Valley and Richmond	Between the Elk Hills oil field and San Francisco, but closer to Elk Hills with easy pipeline access to San Joaquin Valley
Possibilities for future development	No future development or expansion possible after initial part is completed	No limit on future growth or expansion of facilities
Port characteristics	Very rough seas and more than four miles from shore	Calm seas and one mile from shore
Attitude of local populace	Large, strong, vocal, and effective opposition	Small, weak, and ineffective opposition
Environmental impact from operation/accidents	Oil spill would seriously disrupt the community and harm wildlife; extreme danger due to proximity to military operations or other industry	Oil spill could be cleaned up relatively swiftly with no serious effect
Facilities	No facilities to support supertanker operations	All facilities completed for supertanker port operations
Environmental impact from placement of facilities	Extreme blight on the area and interference with the natural environment	No major adverse effects from placement of facilities

the moment, he favored Moss Landing because it was superior for the criteria ranked second, third, and fourth. Specifically, Moss Landing was

1. The cheapest to build.
2. The cheapest to operate.
3. The closest to Richmond.

On a Sunday in mid-September 1993, Christine Schilling was in the office of Ralph Purcell, president of C. K. Coolidge, Inc. (CKC). Schilling, recently hired as Purcell's analyst, was presenting the details of an analysis she had prepared on Saturday. Purcell hoped that by the end of the afternoon, aided by Schilling's insights, he would be able to establish a course of action that might hasten the final settlement of a patent suit brought against CKC three years earlier by the Tolemite Corporation and its licensee, Barton Research and Development (BARD).

The Contenders

CKC was founded in Milwaukee, Wisconsin, in 1932 as a commercial outlet for the inventive genius of Dr. Charles K. Coolidge, an astute organic chemist. The company had weathered the Great Depression and then participated in the prosperity associated with World War II and the postwar years. By 1970, annual sales were in the neighborhood of $3 million.

Dr. Coolidge owned and managed the company until 1980, when, desiring to retire, he sold it along with all its patents and products to Arrow Industries, a small Chicago-based conglomerate. CKC continued to prosper as an Arrow subsidiary and by 1993 had annual sales of $10.5 million,[1] 14 percent of the Arrow total. About 10 percent of CKC's sales in 1993 were derived from a chemical component called Varacil, whose manufacturing process was the subject of the patent suit. The remainder of its sales included a wide range of specialty organic chemical products, sold in relatively small volume, primarily to the pharmaceutical industry.

Tolemite, also headquartered in Chicago, was a large chemical and pharmaceutical manufacturer with estimated 1993 sales in excess of $300 million. In 1984, Tolemite had been awarded a patent covering various aspects of a new, low-cost method for synthesizing Varacil. The techniques covered by the patent had been discovered at Tolemite's research facility in 1979 as an offshoot of another project. Because Tolemite was neither a user nor a producer of Varacil, it had decided to offer the use of the patent, under license, to BARD, the principal Varacil producer in the United States.

---

[1]Based on actual sales for January–August and an estimate for September–December.

BARD, located in Evanston, Illinois, had begun as a small research company. By 1984, however, it had dropped all research and was involved solely in the production of Varacil. To maintain its position as industry leader, BARD had accepted Tolemite's licensing offer and had converted all Varacil production to the new process. In return for the use of the patent, BARD had agreed to pay Tolemite a 4 percent royalty on all sales of synthetic Varacil. In addition, BARD had received rights to sublicense any other Varacil producers who became interested in the process and to work out individual royalty agreements with producing firms. Under these sublicensing agreements, royalties of 4 percent would go to Tolemite, and any excess would accrue to BARD.

In 1989, five years after Tolemite had received its patent, a research chemist at CKC had, quite independently, discovered a very similar process for synthesizing Varacil. The CKC researchers, however, had not felt that the new processing techniques could be patented. Thus, no patent search had been initiated and production facilities had simply been converted to the new process. At the time, no one at CKC had suspected the degree to which its new process was similar to the one originated by Tolemite and covered by Tolemite's patent. It was with some surprise then that CKC management learned that it was being sued by Tolemite and BARD for patent infringement.

Varacil

Varacil was a chemical substance sold almost exclusively to pharmaceutical manufacturers. Although it appeared in a variety of drug preparations, it represented only a minor fraction of any one drug. The economics of its manufacturing (high fixed and low variable costs plus economies of scale), however, suggested that it be made in relatively long runs involving substantial volume. Thus the major drug companies themselves were not involved in its preparation.

Before 1984, Varacil had been processed from naturally occurring organic chemicals found in animal tissue. As a result of the high cost of these natural chemicals, the cost of Varacil itself had been relatively high. With the advent of synthetic Varacil, this situation was dramatically changed. Variable costs in the manufacture of synthetic Varacil represented only about 15 percent of sales, so the synthetic soon drove the natural product virtually out of the market. (A few Varacil users still specified the natural product in the belief that it had certain superior properties.)

In 1993, the national market for synthetic Varacil amounted to some $9 million in sales. On a unit basis (pounds sold) this market had been relatively stable for several years. As drugs requiring Varacil had been phased out, new ones requiring similar amounts of the compound had always seemed to appear. There was, furthermore, no reason to believe that this stability would be lost over the next several years. Industry unit sales projected thus tended to be quite flat as far as 5 and 10 years out.

On the dollar value side, however, the story was quite different. Prices for Varacil, and industry dollar sales as well, had been in decline for several years.

EXHIBIT 1   **Unit and Dollar Sales of Synthetic Varacil by Company**

	Bard		Coolidge		All Others	
Year	*Lbs.*	*$*	*Lbs.*	*$*	*Lbs.*	*$*
1984	1,000	153,000	0	0	0	0
1985	5,000	738,000	0	0	0	0
1986	20,000	2,676,000	0	0	0	0
1987	60,000	6,569,000	0	0	0	0
1988	68,000	8,022,000	0	0	0	0
1989	76,000	9,045,000	0	0	0	0
1990	83,000	9,624,000	1,000	111,000	0	0
1991	89,000	9,546,000	6,000	576,000	2,000	213,000
1992	94,000	7,899,000	11,000	936,000	19,000	1,608,000
1993*	100,000	6,000,000	17,000	1,050,000	35,000	2,100,000
1994	100,000	6,000,000	17,000	1,020,000	35,000	2,100,000
1995	100,000	5,700,000	17,000	969,000	35,000	1,995,000
1996	100,000	5,400,000	17,000	918,000	35,000	1,890,000
1997	100,000	4,800,000	17,000	816,000	35,000	1,680,000
1998	100,000	4,500,000	17,000	765,000	35,000	1,575,000
1999	100,000	4,500,000	17,000	765,000	35,000	1,575,000
2000	100,000	4,500,000	17,000	765,000	35,000	1,575,000
2001	100,000	4,500,000	17,000	765,000	35,000	1,575,000
2002	100,000	4,500,000	17,000	765,000	35,000	1,575,000
2003	100,000	4,500,000	17,000	765,000	35,000	1,575,000
2004	100,000	4,500,000	17,000	765,000	35,000	1,575,000

*Estimated.

Note: Total unit sales of Varacil (including the natural product) were roughly 150,000 lbs. annually for the period 1984–93. Sales for 1984–93 were actual; sales for 1994-2004 were projected.

Source: C. K. Coolidge, Inc.

When converting to the synthetic process, each competitor in the industry had tooled up to supply an optimistic share of the market. Then, when market share objectives were not met, prices were slashed in an attempt to keep manufacturing facilities operating at efficient levels and to bring in as much contribution as possible toward fixed costs. This situation was expected to continue for at least five years. Exhibit 1 shows industry unit and dollar sales of synthetic Varacil for the period 1984–93, as well as projections for 1994–2004.

In 1993, there were seven principal competitors in the synthetic Varacil market. BARD, with $6 million in sales, took 67 percent of the market. CKC, with $1,050,000 in sales, was the second largest operator and held a 12 percent share. The remaining five competitors, none of whose Varacil sales exceeded $570,000, then constituted the remaining 21 percent of the market. By 1990, all seven of the principal competitors were manufacturing synthetic Varacil by nearly identical processes. Only BARD, however, was paying royalties to Tolemite.

Background on the Litigation

On June 12, 1990, Tolemite and BARD had jointly filed suit in the Superior Court of the Fifth District of Wisconsin charging CKC with having infringed on Tolemite's patent. To remedy the infringement, Tolemite and BARD were seeking a royalty payment of 20 percent of all of Coolidge's future sales of synthetic Varacil over what remained on the 17-year life of the patent, as well as a lump-sum indemnity to cover past sales.

When confronted with the suit, Purcell had immediately discussed the matter with Aaron Mantiris, general counsel for Arrow Industries. Both men had felt there was considerable evidence indicating that Tolemite's process might not be patentable. At Mantiris's suggestion, CKC had obtained the services of Evans and Blaylock, a well-known and highly reputable firm of patent attorneys in New York. These attorneys agreed with Mantiris on the potential weakness of the Tolemite suit. Thus, in 1990, Evans and Blaylock had begun to prepare a case for CKC's defense.

Tolemite's patent contained 12 claims of originality. To obtain it, Tolemite, like all successful patent applicants, had had to demonstrate to the patent examiners that there was no "prior art," and that there was invention. Prior art could consist of previous patents, applied-for patents, or processes in the public domain—unpatentable but generally known—that were similar. To show invention, it was necessary to demonstrate that the applied-for process was not obvious to a person reasonably knowledgeable about related chemical processes.

Any patent was always subject to later challenge in the courts. All or part of a patent could be overturned on the basis of prior art or absence of invention. As a practical matter, it was sometimes possible to argue the absence of invention years later. Ideas that had seemed novel at the time of the invention often seemed far more obvious at a later date. The patent holder, in defense, attempted to re-emphasize the novelty of the ideas at the time of the invention. Nevertheless, there were many instances of patents being successfully challenged. In the matter of synthetic Varacil, Mantiris argued that Tolemite had not, in fact, introduced any novelty. It had merely observed and harnessed a naturally occurring process which, in itself, was not patentable.

A patent holder whose patent was infringed was entitled to sue the infringer for sales and profit wrongfully gotten. In determining the amount to be demanded in a lawsuit, the plaintiff usually calculated these damages in a way most favorable to itself. However, if the plaintiff prevailed in court, the actual damages awarded were often considerably less. In the Varacil matter it was the opinion of both the Evans and Blaylock lawyers and Mantiris that the royalty amount awarded, if CKC lost the suit, would be approximately 10 percent, or about half of the amount demanded.

From 1990 to 1993, a partner in Evans and Blaylock worked intermittently in liaison with Mantiris researching and preparing the case. CKC considered the suit to be little more than a nuisance and was content to drag its feet in hope that Tolemite's case might simply collapse from inertia. Late in 1992, however, a tentative trial date was set for January 1993. Before a firm date could be set, Purcell and Mantiris decided, with the concurrence of the patent attorneys, to make at least a token effort at a pretrial settlement. Their offer amounted to the payment of all future liabilities at a royalty rate of 2.5 percent of sales. This offer was rejected out of hand by Tolemite and BARD. Eventually, the case reached the court docket and a trial date in October 1993 was set.

By September, Purcell was becoming uneasy over the high—and increasing—level of attorneys' fees. These fees had already reached a total of $300,000 and, if the trial were to take place as scheduled, they would surely loom large in comparison with the total value of any successful defense. Furthermore, these legal fees and any future ones would not be recoverable, even if CKC won its case.

In response to this uneasiness about both the progress of the suit and the alarming accumulation of the attorneys' fees, Purcell decided on two immediate actions. First he arranged, through Mantiris, for a meeting in New York City to review the case thoroughly with the patent attorneys. Second, he asked his new analyst, Schilling, to review the case and, he hoped, to bring a fresh viewpoint to bear.

Schilling's Analysis and the Meeting with the Patent Attorneys

Christine Schilling was a recent graduate of the Harvard Business School, who was quite interested in the quantitative analysis of decision problems. Thus her approach to this problem took the form of a decision tree. It recognized two options open to CKC:

1. Go to court and contest the patent, which would cost an additional $150,000 in legal fees and lead to winning the suit with probability X or losing it with probability $1-X$; or
2. Settle out of court for an amount $Y\%$ of past and future sales. She summarized these options in the decision diagram shown in Figure A.

Her analysis sought to determine for any given out-of-court settlement offer Y, how large the probability X of winning the suit would have to be to justify rejecting the offer. To do this break-even analysis she solved the following equation for X, given various values of Y:

$$[\text{Cost of winning}] \ (X) + [\text{Cost of losing}] \ (1-X) = [\text{Cost of settlement at } Y\%]$$

This resulted in the break-even curve shown in Figure B. For all offers above the curve it was preferable to go to court. Offers below the line were worthy of consideration. For example, if CKC personnel felt that the probability of winning was 0.6, then settling up to a 7.5 percent royalty rate (shown by the dotted line in Figure B) could be justified.

Schilling's principal conclusion from this analysis was that, unless the odds on winning the suit were extremely good, any reasonable pretrial settlement was

FIGURE A Decision Diagram

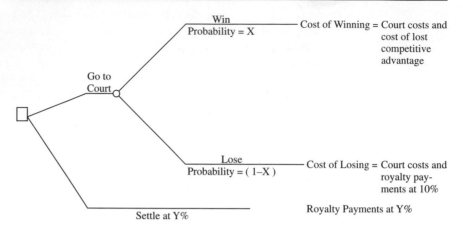

Note: If CKC wins the suit, BARD would no longer have to pay 4% royalty to Tolemite. Because of the highly competitive nature of the industry, Schilling believed that BARD would pass this savings along to customers, forcing CKC to retaliate. Thus CKC's revenues would be reduced from the status quo by 4% if the suit is won.

FIGURE B Break-even Curve

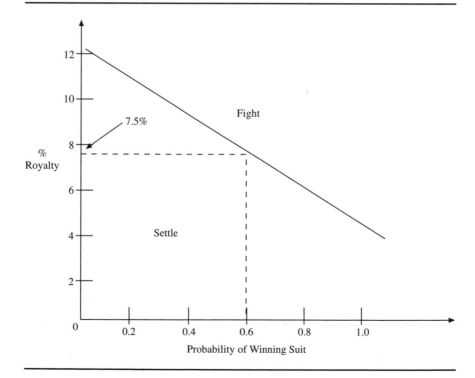

preferable to paying the additional costs and taking a chance on going to court. Purcell, a chemical engineer, was himself well attuned to quantitative analysis and, in fact, liked to support his own arguments with numerical data whenever possible. He was intrigued by Schilling's presentation and invited her to join him and Mantiris on the trip to New York City to meet with the patent attorneys. At that meeting Purcell intended to confront the attorneys with Schilling's analysis and then to obtain their opinion on the benefits of pursuing the case to trial.

In New York the patent attorneys began the meeting by presenting an outline of their case. Everyone attending agreed that the case was indeed a strong one with a high probability of success in the trial phase. The attorneys demurred, however, when asked to give a precise figure for their probability of success in court. At that point, Purcell sketched out Schilling's analysis. He then asked the patent attorneys if they still felt that their probability of success was high enough to merit going to trial. The attorneys were visibly uncomfortable with Schilling's approach. Although they remained convinced of the merits of their case, they agreed that some rethinking was probably necessary before proceeding to trial.

On the flight back to Milwaukee, Purcell discussed with his general counsel and his analyst what had happened at the meeting. As a result of that conversation he decided that Schilling should pursue her analysis further and take into account such things as potential appeals and to appraise the sensitivity of the analysis to the underlying assumptions. All three agreed that settlements well in excess of 2.5 percent would, in all probability, be preferable to a court fight.

Final Analysis

The next day, Saturday, Schilling broadened her analysis as Purcell had requested. The expanded analysis took into account the possibility of appeals by Tolemite or CKC and the additional legal expenses in the event of appeals. The result was the revised break-even curve shown in Figure C, which strengthened the conclusion that any reasonable settlement would be preferable to going to court. (The complete analysis is presented in the Appendix.) On Sunday afternoon Schilling presented her findings to Purcell in an informal meeting and they began to map a strategy for resolving the suit.

APPENDIX
CHRISTINE SCHILLING'S ANALYSIS

Objective: To determine the range of payment Arrow Industries can offer to pay in pretrial settlement relative to future costs and the probability of success in court.

Conclusion: If the likelihood of winning the trial is between 75% and 100% Arrow can pay a pretrial settlement royalty rate of up to 8.5% and save money. In fact, Arrow can afford to pay a royalty rate of 7% even if the probability of winning the trial is 100%, because of the magnitude of future attorneys' fees and subsequent appeals. (See Figure C for the break-even probability curve.)

FIGURE C   **Revised Break-even Curve**

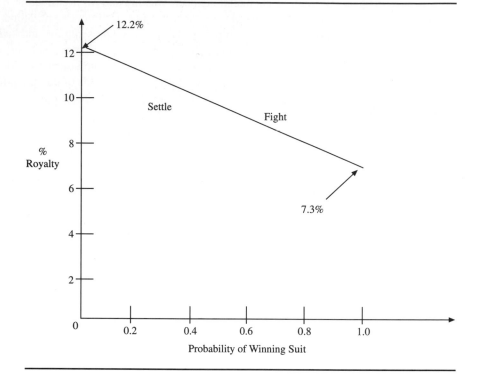

Assumptions:

    I. Expected Proceedings:
       A. If Arrow wins the trial, there is a 90% chance that Tolemite will appeal.
       B. If Tolemite wins the trial, there is a 10% chance that Arrow will appeal.
       C. If Arrow wins the trial, there is a 75% chance that Arrow will win the appeal.
       D. If Tolemite wins the trial, there is a 75% chance that Tolemite will win the appeal.

   II. Future Attorneys' Fees and Court Costs Will Be:
       A. For the trial—$150,000
       B. For the appeal:
          1. If Arrow wins the trial—$75,000.
          2. If Tolemite wins the trial—$150,000.

  III. Exposure to Liability:
       A. Past liabilities:
          1. If Tolemite wins the trial, it will be awarded 10% of sales 1990–1993—total liability of $267,300.
          2. Tolemite will settle past liabilities prior to the trial at the same royalty rate applied in future sales. (See III.B.2.)

B. Future royalties:
  1. If Tolemite wins the trial, it will receive 10% of future sales.
  2. The Tolemite pretrial settlement royalty requirement is unknown but will be approached in this analysis as that rate at which Arrow Industries would break even in the alternative of facing the costs and risks of trial. (See Figure C.)

IV. Actual Royalty Costs Involved:
  A. C. K. Coolidge will continue to produce 17,000 pounds of Varacil per year for the next seven years (remaining life of the patent).
  B. The price/pound for Varacil will erode as expected and produce the total sales shown in Table A–1.
  C. In this industry of high fixed and low variable costs, resulting in severe pressure upon price, BARD will have a competitive advantage directly proportional to the royalty differential between itself and CKC. The assumption is that it will lower the price, rather than simply absorb extra profit. The extent of BARD's use of this advantage and its significance on CKC's profitability will be illustrated in the analysis.
  D. The "value of money" to the corporation is approximately 10%.

Analysis: The objective of this analysis is to define, in general terms, the relationship between the future expenses and risks faced in the Tolemite suit with the cost of an immediate settlement. An attempt has been made to break the overall problem into a

---

TABLE A-1   Present Value of Royalties and Lost Competitive Advantage ($ in thousands)

			Cost of 10% Royalty Payments and Past Liability Claims		Cost of 4% Lost Competitive Advantage		Cost of Settlement at 8% Royalty	
Year	*Discount Factor**	*Sales*	*Royalty (10%)*	*NPV†*	*Lost Competitive Advantage (4%)*	*NPV*	*Royalty (8%)*	*NPV*
0 .... 1.000		$2,673‡	$267.3	$267.3	—	—	$213.9	$213.9
1 .... 0.909		1,020	102.0	92.7	$40.8	$37.2	81.6	74.1
2 .... 0.826		969	96.9	80.1	38.7	31.8	77.4	63.9
3 .... 0.751		918	60.9	69.0	36.6	27.6	73.5	55.2
4 .... 0.683		816	81.6	55.8	32.7	22.2	65.4	44.4
5 .... 0.621		765	76.5	47.4	30.6	18.9	61.2	38.1
6 .... 0.564		765	76.5	43.2	30.6	17.4	61.2	34.5
7 .... 0.513		765	76.5	39.3	30.6	15.6	61.2	31.2
				$694.8		$170.7		$555.3

* Rate = 10%.
† Net present value.
‡ Past sales (1990–93).

410

FIGURE A-1 Decision Diagram

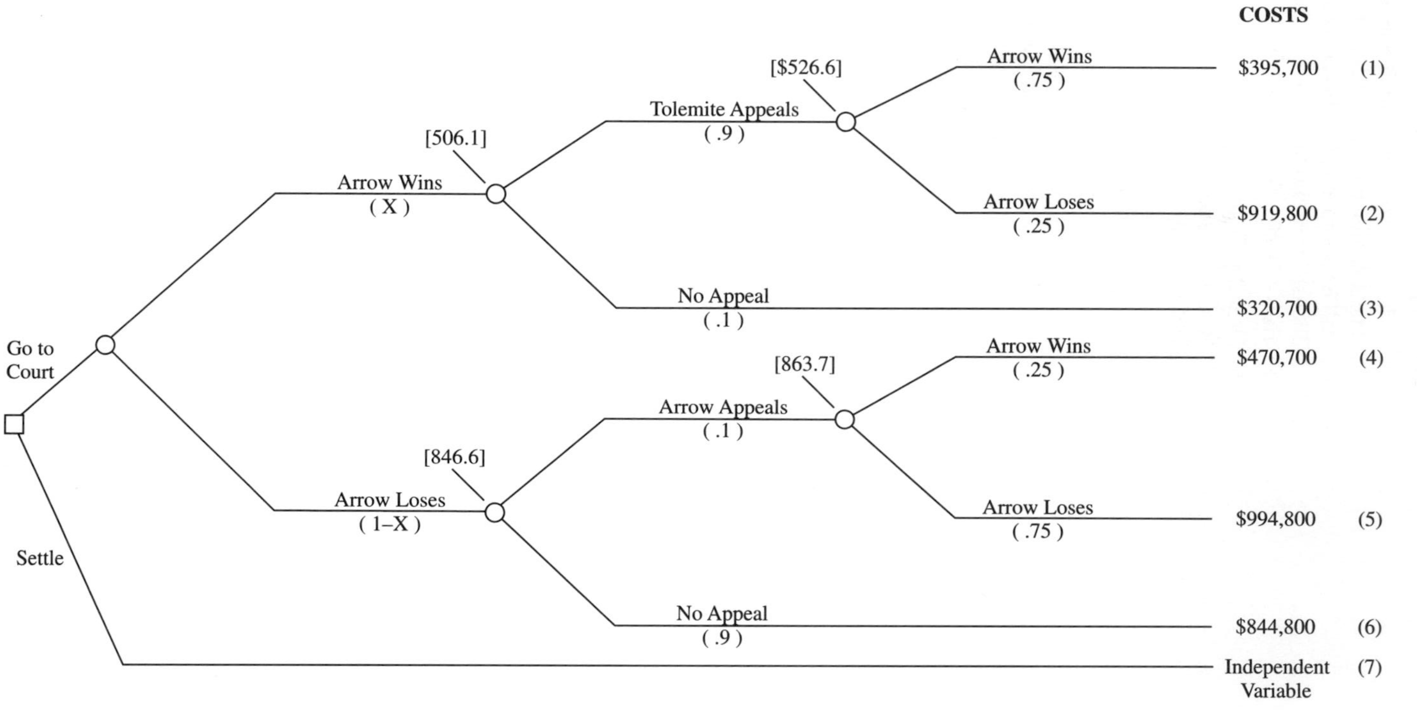

COSTS

$395,700	(1)
$919,800	(2)
$320,700	(3)
$470,700	(4)
$994,800	(5)
$844,800	(6)
Independent Variable	(7)

Arrow Wins (.75)

Arrow Loses (.25)

[$526.6]

Tolemite Appeals (.9)

No Appeal (.1)

Arrow Wins (.25)

Arrow Loses (.75)

[863.7]

Arrow Appeals (.1)

No Appeal (.9)

[506.1]

Arrow Wins (X)

[846.6]

Arrow Loses (1–X)

Go to Court

Settle

number of smaller events and action alternatives and to assess reasonable ranges of event probability and consequence; these elements are then related mathematically to obtain a solution.

There can be a substantial advantage in this approach in illuminating the basic issues, which generally remained submerged in a single assessment of the entire situation. There is a potential danger in quantification and simplification of complex problems—the result is apparently so precise and straightforward that it can be very easily overlooked that this result is no better than the assumptions on which it is based.

Based on the above assumptions and the decision diagram shown in Figure A–1, the following costs were calculated:

1. Cost associated with Endpoint (1)   (Arrow wins trial, Tolemite appeals, Arrow wins appeal)

Present value of 4% lost competitive advantage (See Table A–1)	=	$170,700
Appeal costs	=	75,000
Trial costs	=	150,000
Total		$395,700

2. Cost associated with Endpoint (2)   (Arrow wins trial, Tolemite appeals, Arrow loses appeal)

Present value of royalty payments and past liability claims at 10% (Table A–1)	=	$694,800
Appeal costs	=	75,000
Trial costs	=	150,000
Total		$919,800

3. Cost associated with Endpoint (3)   (Arrow wins trial, no appeal)

Present value of 4% lost competitive advantage	=	$170,700
Trial costs	=	150,000
Total		$320,700

4. Cost associated with Endpoint (4)   (Arrow loses trial, Arrow appeals, Arrow wins appeal)

Present value of 4% lost competitive advantage	=	$170,700
Appeal costs	=	150,000
Trial costs	=	150,000
Total		$470,700

5. Cost associated with Endpoint (5)   (Arrow loses trial, Arrow appeals, Arrow loses appeal)

Present value of royalty payments and past liability claims at 10%	=	$694,800
Appeal costs	=	150,000
Trial costs	=	150,000
Total		$994,800

6. Cost associated with Endpoint (6)   (Arrow loses trial, Arrow
                                                          does not appeal)

Present value of royalty payments and
   past liability claims at 10%   = $694,800
Trial costs   =   150,000
              Total $844,800

The next step is to find, for a given settlement rate of $Y\%$ royalty, the probability of winning the trial that will make the expected cost of going to court equal to the cost of the settlement. For example, assuming a settlement rate of 8% royalty payments, the present value of the cost of settlement is $555,300 as shown in Table A–1. The break-even probability of winning, X, could be calculated from the following equation:

$$\text{Expected cost of going to court} = \text{Cost of settlement}$$

$$\$506,100X + 846,600\,(1-X) = \$555,300$$

$$\text{To get: } X = 0.85$$

Solving this equation for different settlement rates resulted in the break-even probability curve shown in Figure C.

CASE 9
THE COMMERCE TAVERN

H. Franklin Nilson sipped on a tankard of ale and surveyed the guests in the lounge of The Commerce Tavern. As usual, the room was filled, and Nilson was pleased to see that everything was running smoothly. His staff had no particular problems in handling the full house—an empty table at The Commerce was a rarity Ever since its opening in 1982, Nilson's establishment had enjoyed all the business it could handle. Even though it was mid-October, Nilson was content in the knowledge that The Commerce was booked solid, straight through the holiday season. The first available reservation was for mid-January.

Nilson's thoughts this particular evening drifted to his recent conversation with Anne Hamlet of the Virginia Merchants Bank (VMB). Over the past several weeks, Hamlet had been providing Nilson with information regarding the potential acceptance of credit cards at the tavern. The Commerce Tavern had never accepted credit cards, personal checks, or house charges. Nilson often wondered if this cash-only policy hurt his business. He had been pleasantly surprised to learn that Hamlet and VMB were quite willing to authorize The Commerce to honor MasterCard and Visa cards. He also realized that, if this change in credit policy were to be attractive, the fees levied by VMB would have to be made up by increased business. Nilson always struggled with decisions like this one, and, as he returned to his ale, he decided to think about it later.

The Tavern

For over a decade, The Commerce Tavern had enjoyed the reputation of being one of the finest colonial-cuisine restaurants in Colonial Williamsburg. Located in Merchants Square, a business-and-shopping district at the west end of Duke of Gloucester Street, the tavern was adjacent to the Historic Area but technically outside it. Even so, Merchants Square was a stop on the free bus route through Colonial Williamsburg.

The Commerce Tavern, like all other buildings in Merchants Square, was designed in a late-18th-century style. It was patterned after the typical alehouse of that era: a center entrance with a large room on either side (the public bar to the left and the lounge to the right). The traditional division of rowdiness in the public bar and gentility in the lounge was not maintained at The Commerce. Both rooms provided the guests of the tavern the opportunity for elegant dining in a quiet and intimate atmosphere. The rooms were illuminated only by candlelight, were paneled in hand-rubbed walnut, and were decorated simply with "alehouse artifacts" of colonial times and with flowers of the season. To complete the colonial effect, the service staff dressed in period attire. The Commerce was proud of the colonial charm and ambience it had created in a modern building.

413

EXHIBIT 1   **Typical Menu**

Commerce Tavern

~ Bill of Fare ~
Choice of entrée denotes price of entire meal

~ Relish Tray ~

Spiced Cantaloupe	Pickled Onions
Moist Quinces	English Chop Pickle

~ Choice of Soups ~

Peanut Soup	Terrapin Stew
Cat Fish Chowder	Mulligatawny Soup

~ Choice of Flesh or Fowl ~

English Steak and Kidney Pie $13.95	Oxford John $14.95
The Kings Roast Beef $15.95	Buttered Shrimp $14.95
Williamsburg Veal Partridges $15.95	Baked Stuffed Sturgeon $13.95

~ Selection of Fresh Vegetables, of the Season ~

~ Green Salad ~

~ Bread Tray, served with creamery butter ~

Williamsburg Buns	Coach Wheels
Sally Lunn	Sweet Potato Buns

~ Choice of Dessert ~

Blanc Mange	Indian Pudding
Regency Trifle	Pumpkin Pye
Plum Ice Cream	Deep Dish Apple Pye

~ Your choice of fine Coffees and Teas ~

Many believed that the dining experience provided by The Commerce was on a par with that of the Kings Arms Tavern and Christiana Campbell's Tavern in the Historic Area. The Commerce had been featured in several gourmet magazines and had received three stars from a popular guidebook. The tavern offered a limited menu of well-prepared, authentic Colonial dishes. The price of an entrée ranged from $13.95 to $15.95 and included relishes, a choice of soups, vegetables

---

EXHIBIT 2   Budget for 1993 (revised 10/5/93)*

Revenues:
Food	$560,000
Wine/liquor	180,000
Total	$740,000

Expenses:
Food	$168,000
Wine/liquor	44,000
Service staff	68,800
Administrative staff	40,000
Utilities	20,000
Trash	2,000
Supplies	10,000
Fringe	13,000
Interest	64,000
Laundry	26,500
Total	$456,300

* Reflects actual revenues and expenses for the first three quarters of 1993 and projections for the final quarter.

---

of the season, a green salad, breads of the house, and a choice of dessert with a selection of coffees and teas. The bill of fare is shown in Exhibit 1. The tavern offered full bar service emphasizing specialty drinks of imported ales, grogs, and punches priced from $1.75 to $3.50. In addition, The Commerce maintained an extensive wine cellar of domestic and European wines ranging in price from $12 to $36 a bottle.

The Commerce's reputation was so renowned that virtually every table was occupied for each of its two sittings on both Friday and Saturday nights. As a result, approximately 400 guests were served each night. Even though Nilson had experienced considerable public pressure to open the tavern for weekday dining, he had resisted the temptation. Weekday service would interfere with his personal involvement with the tavern, and he believed that operating at full capacity provided very attractive efficiencies. Exhibit 2 presents the tavern's budget for 1993.

Nilson believed that a substantial portion of his patrons came from the Williamsburg area—townspeople as well as faculty and students of the College of William and Mary. Because of the lead time on reservations, less than one-third of his guests were visitors to Williamsburg and most of those diners were returning for another visit. As a result of the strong base of local customers, The Commerce had barely noticed the periodic tourist crises that had virtually crippled most other establishments in the area.

Visa and MasterCard

Virginia Merchants Bank had sent Nilson the standard bank credit-card-participation agreement. This agreement specified in great detail the responsibilities of

The Commerce with respect to credit-card transactions. In particular, for each transaction, it was the restaurant's responsibility to (1) check the expiration date of the card, (2) check that the card number did not appear on any restricted- or revoked-card bulletin, (3) check that the card was signed on the back and that the cardholder's signature on the sales slip was similar, and (4) fill out correctly the sales slip furnished by the bank with the required information. On delivery of a sales slip to the bank within three bank-business days of the sales slip's completion, the bank agreed to credit the restaurant immediately for the face amount of the sales slip less a fee computed at the rate that was in effect at that time. The agreement required the bank to give written notice within 30 days of any change in the fee.

Hamlet had informed Nilson during an earlier telephone conversation that the initial rate charged The Commerce would be 4 percent—the rate charged all new participants in the Virginia Merchants Bank Credit Card Agreement. She mentioned that this rate would remain in effect for a year, at the end of which the bank would review the account. The rate would probably be lowered at that time based on the total yearly credit-card sales of The Commerce. If the total credit-card sales for the year were greater than $500,000, the rate would be lowered to 2 percent. If, however, total yearly credit-card sales were less than $200,000, the rate would remain at 4 percent. For totals between $200,000 and $500,000, the rate would be set at 3 percent. Hamlet said that there was no set period for subsequent reviews, but she hinted that this new rate would remain in effect for at least a couple of years.

Hamlet had also sent Nilson credit-card-usage information (see Exhibit 3) that she said might help give a rough idea about which of the three rates (2 percent, 3 percent, or 4 percent) The Commerce would end up paying. Unfortunately, the bank did not have information on total-sales dollars or increases in total sales after credit cards had been accepted at similar restaurants. In Hamlet's words:

> Oh yes, I'm sure that most businesses see an increase in sales after honoring Visa and MasterCard cards, sometimes up to 50 percent. But, as I'm sure you appreciate, our participants hold their total-sales data in confidence and don't share them with me, let alone allow me to distribute them to potential clients. It's tough enough getting cooperation on usage data, let alone total sales. I do remember, however, hearing about a recent article in a restaurant journal that concluded that credit cards were economically attractive if only 1 additional customer in 10 comes to your restaurant because you honor credit cards.

Nilson reviewed the chart provided by Hamlet. He was familiar with all the establishments listed on it. With the exception of the family restaurants, The Laughing Lobster and Bill and Ellen's Family Steak House, each restaurant had a price range comparable to that of The Commerce and distinctive cuisine or decor that would attract patrons similar to those of The Commerce. As a result, credit-card usage at The Commerce could well be like the usage at any of the eight restaurants. Unfortunately, when Nilson focused his attention on the previous year's data, no consistent pattern emerged. The usage ranged from 25 percent to 69 percent. He observed that a usage rate of 43 percent was the median of the

---

Exhibit 3   Credit-Card Usage

	Bills Paid by Credit Card (%)		
Restaurant	*1990*	*1991*	*1992*
Madison Inn	40%	39%	39%
Italian-American menu, partly à la carte, $3.95–$16.95			
Specialties: spare ribs, seafood, fresh-fruit rum cake			
Candlelit			
Lordsmill	38	35	38
Continental-American menu, partly à la carte, $6.25–$12.75			
Specialties: *esculopes de veau,* fresh seafood, veal Oscar			
Contemporary decor, facing the James River			
The Laughing Lobster	19	20	19
Seafood menu, partly à la carte, $4.95–$9.95			
Specialties: fresh seafood, all-you-can-eat specials			
Family restaurant			
Grecian Urn	51	51	52
Continental-American menu, partly à la carte, $6.50–$15.95			
Specialties: shrimp à la Grecque, moussaka			
Owned by chef			
Black Beard's Hold	70	70	69
American menu, partly à la carte, $6.95–$16.95			
Specialties: seafood, steak			
Nautical decor			
Settlement Dining Room	29	29	25
Varied menu, partly à la carte, $6.95–$9.75			
Specialties: veal Oscar, Virginia ham, seafood kabob			
Colonial decor			
Bill and Ellen's Family Steak House	10	12	12
American menu, partly à la carte, $3.95–$7.95			
Specialties: charbroiled steaks			
Family restaurant			
The Salty Dog Inn	43	41	42
Continental-American menu, partly à la carte, $3.95–$12.95			
Specialties: broiled seafood, crab rolled in Smithfield ham			
Owned by chef, waterfront			
Neptune's Seafood Pavilion	44	47	44
Continental-American menu, partly à la carte, $8–$16			
Specialties: lobster Bien Dien rice, seafood shish kabob			
Grecian atmosphere, art collection			
Peyton's Ordinary	60	62	61
Varied menu, partly à la carte, $4.95–$14.95			
Specialties: fresh seafood, Virginia ham			
Colonial-tavern decor, built in 1732			

---

data and that 38 percent and 57 percent seemed to divide the data in half again. These figures certainly left the issue of the extent of credit-card usage at The Commerce rather ambiguous.

Further Investigations

Nilson devoted the next day, Sunday, to obtaining more information about credit cards. He first stopped at the College of William and Mary Business Library to find the article to which Hamlet had referred. He looked up everything he could find on credit cards. The only relevant article appeared in *Food Service Marketing* and did report Hamlet's figure of 1-in-10. As he had feared, the article focused on increases in the number of customers, a phenomenon from which The Commerce would not benefit. The article did point out, however, that the honoring of credit cards might be justified by increased customer spending: The credit-card user need not worry about having sufficient cash to cover the bill or about the impact that the restaurant check might have on a monthly budget.

He then decided to contact several acquaintances in the restaurant business. The information he received was mixed. One friend, Marcia Fitzgerald of The Barnacle, stated that The Barnacle had always honored credit cards and had never considered dropping them. Fitzgerald said, "We have found that credit-card customers almost always spend more than cash customers, and almost half my customers use credit cards." Nilson found this comment rather encouraging.

A second call, to Paul Pickering of The Wayside Inn, brought up an area that Nilson had not considered—the errors that could be made in filling out the sales slip.

> Didn't you read paragraph 3 of the VMB Agreement? If you mess up, you lose. After my hostess accepted three or four expired cards, I had to tell her that the next one was coming out of her pay. Also, you do realize that the bank takes its cut off of the grand total, a total that includes the 4 percent sales tax and tips?

This perspective was rather disconcerting, but Nilson decided that his host and hostess would not make these kinds of mistakes and, regardless, he would institute Paul Pickering's policy from the start. In addition, for those tips charged on credit cards, he would reimburse his staff for the tips less the bank's charge on them. Although he believed they might object to the idea initially, he could argue that the customers would not only spend more when using credit cards but also tip at a higher percentage. Finally, regarding the bank's attaching its fee to the sales tax, Nilson asked himself, "What's 4 percent of 4 percent, anyway?"

A crucial factor in the decision would be the increase in the amount spent on food and drink by someone using a credit card over what he or she might have spent if cash were required. There was no easy way to figure out what this percentage might be: The experience of other restaurants was irrelevant, because of differences in clientele and menu; questionnaires would not measure actual behavior, just expectations; and a trial period was ruled out, because of its disruptive effects. Nilson decided that his only option was to draw on his experience in running The Commerce. Over the years, he had overheard many of his customers' conversations concerning their food and wine decisions and had gained some insight, albeit loosely structured, into how the cash-only policy influenced those choices.

After thinking about those experiences and reviewing his menu and wine list, Nilson believed that the increase in the dollar amount of bills paid by credit card was just as likely to be more than 5 percent as less than 5 percent when compared with bills paid by cash. Nilson also decided that the increase in a year's credit-card sales over what those same customers might have spent using cash would have to amount to something—say, 1 percent at a minimum—but it was inconceivable that the increase could ever reach 15 percent. Approaching a finer estimate, Nilson believed it was three times as likely that the yearly increase would be less than 8 percent as more than 8 percent, and three times as likely to be over 3 percent as under. Having seen the year-to-year consistency in credit-card usage in Hamlet's data, Nilson thought that the increased spending experienced in the first year would hold for several years.

As Nilson reviewed the results of his inquiries of the past few days, he saw clearly that the decision hinged on the trade-off between the increase in sales and the discount taken by the bank. He decided to evaluate this opportunity—just as he evaluated projects in his other businesses—by using a 20 percent hurdle rate and by considering the next three years only.

It then occurred to Nilson that he might want to back out of the arrangement—say, after a year—if it did not turn out to be profitable. On Monday, he called Hamlet to see if there was any penalty for such an action. She replied,

Well, the bank will not reimburse you for unused sales slips, but we will buy back, for $15, the credit-slip imprinter you originally purchased for $25. Other than that, there is really no other penalty, except perhaps a few confused and angry customers.

CYBERLAB: A NEW BUSINESS OPPORTUNITY FOR PRICO (A)

The Precision Instrument Corporation (PRICO) was a major manufacturer of equipment used in the research laboratory. CyberLab, a new venture in the field of lab robotics, had just offered 30 percent of CyberLab equity to PRICO in exchange for $1 million in capital and a marketing agreement. Under the plan, PRICO would market all of CyberLab products through its existing international distribution system. CyberLab had a patent pending on its robot system and had just finished construction of a small manufacturing facility in New Milford, Connecticut. It also had operational prototypes for all its products, but now needed a capital infusion to develop a major manufacturing facility and to provide working capital for expanded operations. Some aspects of the CyberLab proposal were attractive to James Campbell, president of PRICO, but others were downright frightening. A significant new market could be harvested by his company, or the million dollar investment could vanish down a rat hole. Campbell needed to understand the financial soundness of PRICO's opportunity.

The Inception of CyberLab

Cyberlab had started in 1985 as a result of the frustration of Dr. H. Meltzer, a biochemist working at the New York Psychiatric Institute. Dr. Meltzer was preparing and testing human enzymes[1] in bioassays.[2] Preparing samples was taking an inordinate amount of time and expense; human enzymes were extremely expensive, and manual sample preparation tended to waste enzymes. Dr. Meltzer was looking for an automated system that could prepare his samples, but none existed with the accuracy and reliability he needed for his tests. When he outlined his needs to his son, Walter Meltzer thought a system could be developed and the project began.

Two years later, the CyberLab system prototype was complete. Walter had designed the prototype with the idea that, eventually, all the components that needed machining could be subcontracted, and the remaining parts could be purchased from readily available sources.

---

[1] Enzymes are complex protein substances that are essential to life. They act as catalysts in promoting reactions at cell temperatures without undergoing destruction in the process.

[2] A bioassay is the determination of the relative effective strength of a new substance by comparing its effect on a test organism with that of a standard substance.

This case was prepared in conjunction with Research Assistant Larry Weatherford (Darden). It was based on a Supervised Business Study by Thomas E. Johnstone (Darden Class of 1988). Some numbers and the name of the interested party have been disguised.

Laboratory Robotics

Francis Zenie, president of a major lab-robot developer and manufacturer (Zymark Corporation), summed up the need for laboratory automation: "You've got 10 or 20 years of advancements in instrumental data measurements and data reduction, but our interviews revealed that people are still preparing samples like they did in the Dark Ages." Zymark personnel spent six months interviewing laboratory chemists and chemical-industry personnel by asking "What is your biggest problem?" The most common answer: sample preparation prior to analysis. Zymark correctly identified a need for new technology and introduced the first laboratory robot in 1982.

Laboratory technicians worked in the 2-D environment: *d*ull and *d*emanding. Preparing lab samples was tedious and required a high level of concentration. Humans could work as quickly as robots, but robots could maintain their work pace indefinitely (excluding maintenance and downtime) and were not prone to such errors as mixing up samples. The advantage of robotics lay in the increased output, enhanced consistency of preparations, and lower labor costs. Most robots currently on the market operated on a work-station principle, with the station arranged in a circle about an arm fixed in the center. The arm moved the sample to the stations for various preparations and tests. The CyberLab 800, however, worked in three dimensions and the arm was controlled by a computer, such as the IBM PC. Programming involved numerous commands to control each movement. Starting and stopping the arm in the same place was the critical factor. It allowed the arm to "find" the sample and move it to the next station. Programming was essentially specific to each application and, therefore, took time to implement and verify.

CyberLab Products

The CyberLab 800 System was a robot, although it certainly did not have the futuristic appearance of the more publicized of its kind (see Exhibit 1). Simply put, the CyberLab 800 was a liquid transfer or pipetting device. It was capable of performing any repetitive laboratory liquid-preparation procedure currently done by hand. The system consisted of three separate components and a computer to execute the functions.

The main component was a pipette transport device that worked in three dimensions using eight independent probes for transferring liquid into or out of the test tubes. It was extremely accurate, operating within 1 percent with volumes as low as 10 microliters (a microliter is one millionth of a liter).

The second component was a precision syringe pump with three channels that delivered the liquid to the pipetting system. A typical setup had two of these units.

The third component was a reversible pump. It could draw out samples that were complete from the test tubes and transfer them to other analytical equipment for further testing.

EXHIBIT 1   The CyberLab 800

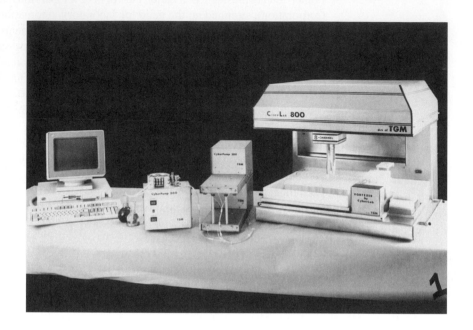

At the end of the summer of 1987, one complete CyberLab system was at work in the New York Psychiatric Institute. Dr. Meltzer used federal grant money to pay for the machine. It replaced two lab technicians who were doing sample preparation, saving over $70,000 the first year. Dr. Meltzer's review of the new system's performance showed that less enzyme was being wasted and that the samples being prepared were more accurate.

News of the system spread within the psychiatric community, as well as without, because of the system's accuracy, associated savings in wasted material, and relatively low cost. By the end of July 1988, CyberLab had sold 4 units, and had interested buyers for 25 more.

Competition in the Laboratory Robotics Industry

An estimated 18,000 sites in the United States could use the CyberLab system. In addition, Zymark had indicated that the worldwide market was around 30,000 to 50,000 units. At the end of the second quarter of 1988, only 3,050 of those potential sites had lab robots installed. Zymark, the first entrant in the lab robot industry in 1982, had 42 percent of the installations to date. Two other competitors, Cetus and Micromedic, entered in 1983 and had 15 percent and 17 percent of installations, respectively. Cetus was acquired in 1986 by Perkin-Elmer, a large corporation in the analytical instruments field with $1.3 billion in sales for fiscal year 1987. Three more players entered in 1985, one of which was Beckman Instruments, a subsidiary of SmithKline Beckman, a very large corporation in the health care and life-sciences industry with $4.3 billion in sales in fiscal year 1987. In 1987, Hewlett-Packard and Dynatech entered the market. See Exhibit 2 for a more complete description of the major competitors.

In spite of the eight other companies manufacturing lab robots, CyberLab believed its presence was needed because none of the existing players offered a machine similar to the "800" system for a similar cost. A CyberLab system cost $32,470 and would replace one chemist (average salary of $41,800 in 1987). Thus CyberLab had a payback of 0.78 years.

The Current Negotiations

To obtain necessary financing, Tom Friedlander, CEO of CyberLab, had hired a full-time consultant from a large venture-capital firm. This consultant had brought the CyberLab proposal to PRICO. Earlier this consultant had helped in a deal for PRICO, and so James Campbell was interested in studying the proposal. In presenting CyberLab's proposal, the consultant acknowledged reluctantly that he had already approached Dean Witter and Salomon Brothers for financing, but with no success. CyberLab's proposal to PRICO was to give them 30 percent of their equity and the rights to market CyberLab products through PRICO's distribution system in exchange for $1 million in capital. Under this agreement, PRICO would become the sole wholesale purchaser and marketer of the CyberLab systems produced. CyberLab would manufacture the machines and sell them at a prearranged transfer price to PRICO. Exhibit 3 shows the pro forma spreadsheet provided by CyberLab of the manufacturing-only venture. Campbell was concerned about the value this business would have, given PRICO would own 30 percent of it if he took the current offer. He saw a number of potential measures of performance in the spreadsheet that could be useful to him and assumptions that he would need to evaluate. This would be part of considering whether the entire package of the marketing opportunity and the equity investment was attractive. If not, he might think about a counteroffer to CyberLab with different terms for the equity percentage, transfer price, or amount of investment. Unfortunately, it appeared that CyberLab did need the entire $1 million to make a viable start, and, of course, a different transfer price would both help and hurt CyberLab, given their participation on both the marketing and manufacturing sides of the business.

As to the marketing issue, PRICO would provide its established name, sales force, and advertising in exchange for a 23 percent margin. The company had been in the laboratory-equipment business for over 50 years and currently had 100 sales and service offices in the United States and 220 such offices in 60 countries throughout the world. Campbell was effectively paying $700,000 for the PRICO patent and the business idea as it stood, since he would retain 30 percent ownership of anything purchased with the $1 million investment. It certainly seemed reasonable to Campbell that if CyberLab's patent and

EXHIBIT 2 Major Competitors

Company Name	Yrs. in Bsns.	No. Instld. to Date	Percent Instld. to Date	Genl. Description of Company	Sales of Company ($MM)	Sales of Lab Instr. Div. ($MM)	Competing Product Description
Zymark	6	1,000	42.0%	First one to market, privately held	$ 15	$ 15	Slow, cost 50K to 70K
Micromedic	5	400	17.0	Subsidiary of ICN Biomedicals, govt. contract, intl. sales	43	17	Only dilutes and dispenses, cost 5K
Perkin-Elmer/Cetus	5	350	15.0	Design and mfg. of hi-tech analytic equip., intl. sales	1,334	416	No computer, robot arm, cost 50K
Tecan	3	300	13.0	Subsidiary of Swiss corp., been in US 4 yrs	?	?	Limited use and warranty, cost 20K
Beckman	2.5	175	7.0	Technology intensive health care/life science company, intl. sales	4,329	693	Moves sample to probe, cost 26K
Hamilton	3	100	4.0	Been in lab equip. bsns. 30 yrs, intl. sales	25	25	One probe w/ steel tip, cost 20K
HP/GenenChem	1	50	2.0	Established force in computers, starting in scientific equipment	8,090	405	Slow w/ genl. purpose, only works w/HP computers, cost 40-55K
Dynatech	1	4	0.2	Plan to go national	305	13	Cost 6K

Sources: Annual reports, S&P OTC reports, *Million Dollar Directory.*

EXHIBIT 3   CyberLab's Pro Forma Income Statement: Manufacturing Only

Year	1	2	3
Selling price/unit	$25,000	$25,000	$25,000
Matrl. & labor/unit	$8,651	$8,651	$8,651
Units sold	29	47	51
Sales revenue	$725,000	$1,175,000	$1,275,000
Material, dir. labor	250,879	406,597	441,201
Overhead	138,000	196,430	207,641
Cost of goods sold	$388,879	$603,027	$648,842
Gross margin	$336,121	$571,973	$626,158
Selling, gen. & adm.	$258,044	$343,047	$344,908
Depreciation	16,000	9,600	5,760
Profit before tax	$62,077	$219,326	$275,490
Taxes	$24,831	$87,730	$110,196
Profit after tax	$37,246	$131,596	$165,294
Return on sales	5.14%	11.20%	12.96%
Equity at beginning of year ...	$1,000,000	$1,037,246	$1,168,842
Return on equity	3.72%	12.69%	14.14%

Year	1	2	3	Term Value
Pat	37,246	131,596	165,294	
Dep'n add-back	16,000	9,600	5,760	
Change in work cap.	(47,176)	(58,841)	(72,912)	
Cash flow fr. opns	6,070	82,355	98,142	1,750,199
Cash flow (1,000,000)	6,070	82,355	1,848,341	
NPV opns	$1,350,861			
IRR	25.17%			

Assumptions:

Total market size—yr. 1	595
CyberLab mkt. share—yr. 1	5.00%
Total mkt. growth—yr. 2+	7.00%
Cyber mkt. share—yr. 2+	7.50%
Discount rate	13.00%
Tax rate	40.00%
Material and labor/unit	$8,651

EXHIBIT 4   PRICO's Pro Forma Income Statement: Marketing Only

Year	1	2	3
Selling price/unit	$32,470	$32,470	$32,470
Transfer price/unit	$25,000	$25,000	$25,000
Margin/unit	$7,470	$7,470	$7,470
PRICO margin (%)	23.0%	23.0%	23.0%
Units sold	29	47	51
Sales revenue	$941,630	$1,526,090	$1,655,970
Cost of goods sold	725,000	1,175,000	1,275,000
Gross margin	$216,630	$351,090	$380,970
Advertising	$51,000	$60,000	$60,000
Sales expense	$137,400	$208,200	$210,600
Total sell., gen. & admin	$188,400	$268,200	$270,600
Profit before tax	$28,230	$82,890	$110,370
Taxes	$11,292	$33,156	$44,148
Profit after tax	$16,938	$49,734	$66,222
Return on sales	1.80%	3.26%	4.00%
Return on investment	11.29%	33.16%	44.15%

Year	1	2	3	Term Value
Pat	16,938	49,734	66,222	
Change in work cap.	(28,249)	(45,783)	(49,679)	
Cash flow fr. opns.	(11,311)	3,951	16,543	295,015
Cash flow .... (150,000)	(11,311)	3,951	311,558	
NPV	$59,010			
IRR	25.80%			

Assumptions:

Total market size—yr. 1	595
CyberLab mkt. share—yr. 1	5.00%
Total mkt. growth—yr. 2+	7.00%
Cyber mkt. share—yr. 2+	7.50%
Discount rate	13.00%
Tax rate	40.00%
Initial investment $150,000	

manufacturing business as it stood was worth the $700,000 up front, then his company's marketing clout should be worth at least the $59,010 he had calculated as the net present value (NPV) of the marketing agreement (see Exhibit 4).

To establish the marketing of CyberLab products, PRICO would actually incur initial expenses of $150,000, for a one-time seminar and new brochures to train all the sales force on the new product, as well as ongoing expenses of $51,000 the first year and approximately $60,000 per year for the second and third years for advertising. Additional expenses included a commission of $600 per CyberLab system sold.

Another possible expense was the sales force. Frank Adams, the vice president of sales, argued there was an "opportunity" cost associated with using the sales force. He estimated the new product would take about 1.0 percent of each salesperson's schedule the first year and 1.5 percent for years two and three. The total sales expense the previous year for PRICO was $12 million, which made the opportunity cost equal to $120,000 (0.01 × 12,000,000). Because the average salary for one salesperson was $24,000 a year in addition to expenses of $36,000 a year, this "cost" was the equivalent of two full-time salespeople the first year and three in years two and three.

PRICO would not actually have to hire any new salespeople, but adding CyberLab products would take away some of the sales force's time spent on existing products. In a "typical" sales call to a lab director, part of the time was spent ordering routine supplies (beakers, cylinders, test tubes, pipettes, and the like), while the remainder was spent talking about new and existing nonroutine products. Campbell believed there would be some erosion of the standard-supply selling, and Adams and his staff concurred. Even if there were some erosion, it would probably be made up by the increase in disposable pipette tip sales that would certainly accompany sales of the CyberLab system. Vince Pauli, the financial analyst for new ventures at PRICO, had argued that competing effects were a wash and that the sales force's time should not be included as an expense in the analysis.

The projected cash flows from PRICO's perspective, for the marketing aspect only, are shown in Exhibit 4 (*Note:* this exhibit includes the opportunity cost for the sales force's time in the "sales expense" line). The lab-instrument manufacturing industry average for return on sales (based on profit after tax) was 3.1 percent. Other major corporations in this industry had values for return on equity of 12 to 13 percent. Overall, for the million dollar investment, PRICO would get 30 percent of the value of CyberLab or $405,258 (0.3 × $1,350,861) plus the value of the marketing agreement, $59,010 for a net of −$535,732.

Campbell thought he had some negotiating room, even though CyberLab had made it clear that it wanted both the marketing arrangement and an investment. Friedlander had just called to say that he had received an offer from a privately held company, Sperling Equipment Company, to buy a fixed number of units per year for the first three years and market them in exchange for a 30 percent discount from retail price. This raised questions about the desirability of the exclusive marketing proposal. However, the immediate task was to evaluate the offer on the table.

CASE 11
CYBERLAB: SUPPLEMENT

Lab-Robot Market Growth

Lab robots were highly suited for any area that required repetitive testing and sample preparation on a large scale. These areas included such biotechnology industries as pharmaceuticals, agricultural products, genetic engineering, and medical technology, in addition to the research and development division of almost any company. The biotechnology market anticipated sales of $1.2 billion in 1988 and was expecting to grow to $25 billion by 2000, which would represent 28.8 percent annual growth. R&D expenditures were forecast by *Predicasts* to grow at 7 to 9 percent annually in the near future. Lab and analytical equipment sales were forecast to grow from $1.65 billion in 1985 to $2.35 billion in 1990—an annual growth rate of 7.3 percent. In the past two years, sales had grown 5 to 9 percent. Experts believed that the annual growth would be between 5 and 9 percent more often than not, but growth rates as high as 10 percent and as low as 0 were possible over several years. The rates generally centered around 7 percent. Retention of the 20 percent R&D tax credit would provide continued investment incentives.

Market Size for Current Year

Based on Zymark's actual 1987 sales of $15 million and the cost of its systems of $50,000 to $70,000, Zymark sold approximately 250 units (15,000,000/$60,000) in 1987. When CyberLab combined this estimate with Zymark's estimated 42 percent share of installations to date, the result was an estimate of the annual market of 595 units (250/0.42).

A high-side estimate of the market was made using Zymark's average cost as $50,000 and assuming that its market share had dropped to about 35 percent in 1987 from the 42 percent share of total installations from 1982 to 1987. This approach gave an estimated market size of 809 units. Similarly, a low-side estimate was calculated of 510 units using an average cost of $70,000 and assuming that current-year market share equaled cumulative market share.

CyberLab Market Share

Tom Friedlander estimated that first-year market share could be as low as 0 if the product completely bombed and as high as 7 percent, with a median value of 5 percent. In his mind, he believed that market share was more likely to fall near the 5 percent level than near the 0 percent extreme based on observations of other new product situations. He gauged that it would be equally likely to fall in the

This case was prepared in conjunction with Research Assistant Larry Weatherford (Darden).

0 to 4 percent market share interval as to fall between 4 and 5 percent. His impressions were similar about the side above the median: The 6 percent level would split the 5 to 7 percent interval into equally likely intervals. He had thus defined four quartile intervals. Rather than push further, he was willing to assume that the likelihood was spread evenly over each of those intervals. In the second and successive years, he figured CyberLab would achieve an extra 2.5 percent of the market over the first-year share.

Cost of Materials and Labor

Walter Meltzer, the CyberLab-system inventor, had kept track of how long it took him to machine the 80 parts he bought and then machined, as well as what it cost to buy the other 75 parts he used unchanged in creating the system. To estimate the total cost, he added up the cost of the 75 purchased parts and his estimate of the labor and material cost for the 80 machined parts. The labor portion of the machined parts' cost was calculated by multiplying the time he took by the labor rate charged by local machine shops in New England ($100/hour). His conservative estimate of the total cost came out to be $8,651.

Both the time to do the machining and the rate charged for machined parts could vary from previous estimates. Because Meltzer was conservative when assigning the overall costs, he expected that they might tend to be a little high already. After reviewing the components of cost, he could not see how they could vary by more than 9 percent below his estimate. They might, on the other hand, be as much as 5 percent higher than his estimate.

Tax Rate

A 40 percent tax rate was used as an estimate (the top federal rate was 38 percent; the top Connecticut rate 10 percent), but if the company did not do well, the tax rate would be much lower. Another factor that could change the tax rate was the presidential election coming in November of 1988.

CASE 12
CYBERLAB: A NEW BUSINESS OPPORTUNITY FOR PRICO (B)

James Campbell, president of Precision Instrument Corporation (PRICO), had come to work early to finish up his evaluation of the CyberLab proposal. Vince Pauli, financial analyst for new ventures, had just worked out the numbers for what he thought represented the best estimate of CyberLab's future. Pauli had taken his estimate from a combination of the business plan he'd received from Tom Friedlander, chief executive officer of CyberLab, and a separate estimate from a consultant for the venture-capital firm with which PRICO worked.

Pauli found that Friedlander and the consultant had made different estimates for just about every variable from total market size to the cost of the CyberLab 800 system. He thus decided to sketch out the major uncertainties for each variable and identify the range of possible values along with their appropriate probabilities. Of all the variables that had to be estimated, he selected the three that he believed would have the most impact on the bottom line and spent the remainder of his time with them.

The first quantity Pauli wrestled with was CyberLab's *first-year market share*. Friedlander's best guess was that CyberLab could achieve 5 percent; whereas the consultant's estimate was 4 percent. Pauli decided the market share could be as low as 0 percent and as high as 7 percent, with it being equally likely to be greater than or less than 5 percent. He further felt that it was as likely as not that the actual market share would be within 1 percent of Tom's estimate. For a graph of the cumulative probability distribution function, see Exhibit 1.

The next quantity Vince looked at was the *cost of materials and direct labor for the system*. He figured the total cost could vary as much as 9 percent below the engineer's prediction of $8,651 to 5 percent above the prediction and that any percentage in this interval was possible. The following risk table was developed:

Cost Variance (percent)	Probability of Value or Less
−9%	0.00
−4	0.25
−2	0.50
0	0.75
+5	1.00

The last quantity was *total market growth*. Pauli figured that the fastest the lab-robot market would grow was 10 percent and the slowest it would grow was

This case was prepared in conjunction with Research Assistant Larry Weatherford (Darden).

Exhibit 1

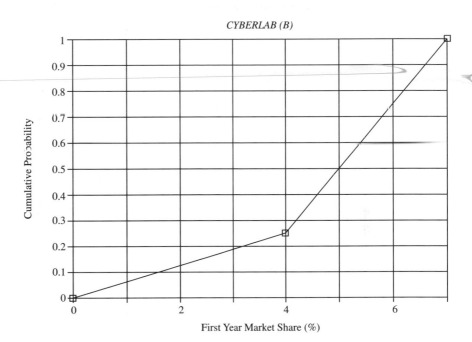

CYBERLAB (B)

(Vertical axis: Cumulative Probability; Horizontal axis: First Year Market Share (%))

0 percent. His best guess was that market growth would be 7 percent. In fact, it seemed to him that the chances were about the same that actual growth would be above or below 7 percent. It also seemed to him that the growth wouldn't be too far away from the 7 percent. Half the time it should come out between 6 and 8 percent, he thought.

Now that his financial analyst had hammered out these new ranges for each quantity and the associated probabilities, Campbell wanted to see what they implied for the evaluation of CyberLab. Pauli had offered to run for him worst- and best-case scenarios to complement the existing "most likely" scenario. Campbell told him it was fine to look at these scenarios, but "Who's to say these extreme scenarios will ever happen?"

Campbell asked Pauli to choose realistic scenarios based on the assessments of what really could happen with each of the three uncertain quantities. For each scenario Pauli was to calculate the financial impact on PRICO using the spreadsheet. "Then create a detailed picture of the financial risk from these scenarios," Campbell directed.

"And what about all the other scenarios that could happen? No matter how many we do, there are still other scenarios possible," Pauli responded.

"Just run enough to get a complete picture so we can decide if we want to take this opportunity."

CASE 13
DHAHRAN ROADS (A)

Hassan Malik, the financial manager of SADE, a Bahrain-based civil engineering company, reread the recently received fax. He was delighted that the nearly endless conversations with the Transportation Ministry of the municipality of Dhahran in eastern Saudi Arabia were finally coming to a close.

SADE had been selected as the prime contractor for a 168 million Saudi riyal (SR) project that involved the reconstruction and upgrading of the highway network linking the several terminals of the Dhahran airport and connecting the entire complex with the city. The Dhahran Roads project was indicative of projects on which SADE had established its international reputation for being a leading construction contractor. The total cost of the project was estimated to be SR 146 million, so the SR 168 million value provided only a 15 percent return, which was, unfortunately, below the 18 percent hurdle rate required by SADE for projects of this nature. On the other hand, the slightly less-than-desired return seemed a small cost to pay to maintain a steady flow of new projects during these slow economic times.

The fax requested that Malik respond to the project proposal within a week. The wording of the contract would then be finalized in the subsequent weeks and the contract signed by mid-January 1993.

The Project

The terms of the proposed contract contained several provisions:

- At the signing of the contract, the ministry would advance to SADE 15 percent of the contract's total value.
- If work progressed on schedule, SADE could bill the ministry as milestones were reached in accordance with the following schedule:

1993	SR 11,000,000
1994	SR 36,000,000
1995	SR 45,000,000
1996	SR 43,000,000
1997	SR 33,000,000

- The ministry would pay 80 percent of each bill received. Payment would, of course, be subject to a satisfactory inspection of the site by

This case was prepared in conjunction with Professor Michel Schlosser (the Swedish Management Institute, IFL).

the ministry. The 20 percent deduction would be withheld for (1) the recovery of the advance payment (15 percent) and (2) the accumulation of a retention fund (5 percent).

- Half of the retention would be reimbursed at the time of completion (end of 1997). The second half would be repaid at the end of 1998, provided the roads did not show any flaws in their first year of use.

During the past several months, the SADE engineering department had inspected the site, confirmed the surveys, and reviewed the drawings that had been provided by the ministry. In the opinion of the vice president of engineering, the project presented "no unusual challenges." It was similar to several SADE projects in other countries that were now nearly complete and that had moved ahead without difficulty.

For SADE to proceed, equipment would have to be ordered immediately so it would be available in the fourth quarter of 1993 when earth moving would commence. The cost of the equipment would be SR 38 million. Seventy-five percent of the cost would have to be paid upon placement of the order; the balance was due on delivery. At the end of the project, the equipment would have no salvage value. The engineering department estimated that the cost of completing the project (not including the equipment) would be SR 108 million. SR 7 million would be expended in 1993 for preliminary site work. The project would then proceed with estimated costs of SR 25 million, SR 29 million, SR 27 million, and SR 20 million for the subsequent years.

Preliminary discussions with several banks indicated that SADE would be able to raise SR 4 million in loans to help finance the project. The loans would carry a 12 percent annual interest (2 percent above prime, 5 percent above government securities) and would have to be repaid in full at the end of 1997.

The project would be managed by one of SADE's experienced project managers, Harold Smithers. Smithers had just completed a major waterworks project in East Africa and was noted for strong engineering skills and tight fiscal control.

Although the contract would be denominated in Saudi riyals, the foreign exchange exposure would be minimal since the Bahraini dinar was pegged to the Saudi riyal. In addition, Saudi Arabian and Bahraini tax laws would not require SADE to pay taxes on the profits of this contract.

CASE 14
DHAHRAN ROADS (B)

Although the base-case analysis indicated that the Dhahran Roads contract would generate substantial value to SADE, Hassan Malik recognized that such a favorable result would require all facets of the project to proceed smoothly. Even though the task was unpleasant, he turned his thoughts to those aspects of the project that could go wrong.

As he thought about the risks associated with the Dhahran Roads project, he decided that there were two key areas in which former projects of a similar nature had run into trouble.

Delayed Payments by the Client

SADE had occasionally experienced problems with a client failing to pay in accordance with an agreed billing schedule. SADE was not the only contractor that faced these problems; in fact, several informal discussions had taken place among contractors to share their experiences in this area. During these conversations, a pattern of customer behavior seemed to emerge. If problems in honoring the billing schedule occurred, the delay usually appeared in the third year of long-term contracts, but occasionally in the second year. A delay usually lasted a year and pushed back all subsequent payments by a year. Many contractors believed that clients purposely delayed payments at a point when the project had gone so far that the contractor could not afford to abandon it. Delays had occurred in about 30 percent of the recent projects, and they were often justified by the client on the basis of the slightest of deviations from the performance specifications or the invoicing procedures of the contract. About 80 percent of the delays began in the third year of the project and 20 percent in the second year.

Cost Overruns

Even though SADE prided itself on its ability to control costs, it occasionally experienced overruns—sometimes substantial ones. Malik reviewed the files of the following 10 completed projects, each of which was the size of the Dhahran Roads project (see Exhibit 1).

Malik was not surprised with these results, because the numbers were consistent with his informal assessment of SADE's cost-control performance. A subsequent examination of the progress of each of the projects showed that there was no pattern in when the cost deviations began to arise, and he concluded that the deviations were spread rather evenly over the lives of the contracts.

This case was prepared in conjunction with Professor Michel Schlosser (the Swedish Management Institute, IFL).

EXHIBIT 1   Historical Accuracy of Estimated Costs

Project	Estimated Cost (in millions)	Actual Cost (in millions)	Actual as Percent of Estimated
India-2	620 rupees	633 rupees	102.1
India-13B	790 rupees	789 rupees	99.9
India-15	640 rupees	650 rupees	101.6
Kuwait-4	11.3 dinars	12.6 dinars	111.5
Kuwait-5A	5.9 dinars	5.65 dinars	95.8
UAE-1	117 dirhams	118 dirhams	100.9
UAE-3	106 dirhams	129 dirhams	121.7
UAE-4C	128 dirhams	128 dirhams	100.0
UAE-5	143 dirhams	142 dirhams	99.3
Pakistan-3	780 rupees	832 rupees	106.7

CASE 15
DISCOUNTED CASH FLOW EXERCISES

1. In each of the following situations, which alternative is the better, assuming that you would put whatever money you receive in a secure investment that returns 10 percent annually?
   a. $100 now, or $130 three years from now.
   b. $250 now, or $350 five years from now.
   c. $500 two years from now, or $675 five years from now.

2. The Financially Astute Company (FAC) is considering two different options for repayment of a loan. The first option requires payments of $40,000 at the end of each of the next four years. The second option requires $20,000 at the end of the first year, $30,000 at the end of the second, $50,000 at the end of the third, and $70,000 at the end of the fourth. Thus the second option requires the payment of an extra $10,000 in all, but it allows FAC to make smaller payments in the first two years. Which option should the company choose if its hurdle rate is 12 percent? 16 percent?

3. The Quick Response Company is considering the purchase of a piece of labor-saving machinery. The machine has a useful life of five years. It would result in a net cash outflow (after consideration of tax effects) of $100,000, immediately followed by net cash inflows (after tax) from increased sales of $28,000 in each of the next five years. Is the equipment attractive if the company has adopted a hurdle rate of 10 percent? 12 percent? 14 percent? What is the internal rate of return?

4. In advertising its five-year guaranteed certificate of deposit, the Neighbor's Bank states: 12.50 percent per annum compounded quarterly (13.10 percent effective annual yield).
   a. What does this mean and how are these numbers related?
   b. To strengthen the appeal of their certificates, the bank is considering a change to compounding monthly. How much would it cost them? How much would it cost them to change to daily compounding?

5. The Information Technology Company (ITC) is considering the purchase of a new minicomputer for data processing. The purchase price is $150,000 delivered and installed. It has been estimated that the new computer will produce annual savings of $50,000 in enhanced productivity as compared with the current computer. ITC assumes the new computer will have an economic life of five years, at which time it will be essentially obsolete and have zero salvage value over the costs of removal. The present computer, which is fully depreciated, is in good

working order and could conceivably be used for at least five more years, but its present salvage value is zero, net of all costs of removal. The company has adopted a hurdle rate of 12 percent. For ease in calculation, assume that the marginal tax rate is 50 percent, that the new computer will be straight-line depreciated over no less than five years, and that the cash flows occur in a lump sum at year's end.

a. Show that the company cannot justify the computer on purely economic grounds. What happens if the flows are assumed to occur quarterly?

b. What would the salvage value of the present computer have to be to make the new computer attractive? Assume that the salvage income is subject to the 50 percent tax rate. Why does the old computer's salvage value influence the new computer's attractiveness?

c. Suppose again that the present computer has zero salvage value. What would the salvage value of the new computer at the end of its five-year life have to be to make the new computer attractive? Assume that the book value of the computer at the end of year five is zero.

CASE 16
EDGCOMB METALS (A)

The Troy Plant

Alex Tereszcuk, plant manager of Edgcomb Metals' Troy, Virginia, facility, had a problem. Frank Spencer, considered to be the best and most conscientious of the seven Troy truck drivers, had complained at the July 1983 drivers' meeting that some drivers were not working as hard as others. Spencer went on to point out that a driver who took 10 hours to complete a run that could actually be done in 8 was rewarded with "time-and-a-half" for the 2 overtime hours. To investigate these claims, Alex had compiled data on total hours, total miles, and number of delivery stops for each of several delivery runs made from his facility in recent months. He was now faced with the tasks of analyzing these data and preparing an appropriate response. Alex wanted to respond to the issue as soon as possible—perhaps at the August meeting.

Company Background

Founded in Philadelphia in 1923, Edgcomb Metals had expanded to 21 service centers serving 37 eastern, midwestern, and southern states, with total sales of over $500 million a year by 1983. These service centers acted as middlemen between the large metal manufacturers, such as U.S. Steel, and the myriad of diverse companies using metal products in their operations.

The service centers stored and distributed thousands of standard metal products (steel bars, sheets, and rods) and also provided specialized cutting and shaping services to customer specification. In total, Edgcomb offered some 15,000 products to 35,000 different customers. The company had a reputation for providing a high-quality product coupled with excellent service and delivery standards.

The Troy plant, constructed in 1976, was Edgcomb's most modern facility. It covered 72,000 square feet and housed a full line of metal processing equipment. The Troy plant serviced the entire state of Virginia with the exception of a small area bordering Washington, D.C.

The Distribution System

The state was divided into seven distribution sectors, as shown in Exhibit 1. Deliveries were made five days a week, with the busier sectors receiving one or more deliveries daily. Each afternoon the plant scheduler determined which

This case was based on the Supervised Business Study of Glenn A. Ferguson (Darden Class of 1985).
Copyright © by the University of Virginia Darden School Foundation, Charlottesville, Virginia. All rights reserved.

EXHIBIT 1   Distribution Sectors

Sector Number	General Location	Days Delivered per Week
1	Virginia Beach/Norfolk	5
2	Richmond	5
3	Charlottesville	5
4	Harrisonburg	3
5	Roanoke	5
6	Lynchburg	5
7	Southwest Virginia	2

---

orders would be delivered the following day, grouped the orders into runs within each sector, and carefully sequenced the orders within each run. This sequencing attempted to minimize the amount of time and distance for the run, while at the same time accommodating special customer delivery requests. Trailers were loaded during the night according to this schedule (the last order to be delivered was loaded first into the trailer). The customers took responsibility for unloading their particular orders. The scheduler also assigned drivers to runs, trying to achieve an equitable pattern of assignments so each driver had the same percentage of long (or short) runs.

Because Edgcomb's drivers and tractor/trailers were the primary representatives of Edgcomb Metals (few customers had ever seen the Troy facility), the company took special pride in their image and appearance. The drivers wore customized uniforms, complete with epaulets and an American flag. The tractor/trailers were brightly painted with the Edgcomb logo and were replaced every four years. Traffic violations were rare, and the drivers paid their own traffic fines.

Drivers were paid well ($9.50 an hour with a 50 percent premium for overtime) with an extensive benefit package. The standard day was eight hours with a half-hour for lunch (unpaid) and two paid 10-minute breaks. The eight-hour day was guaranteed, so a driver finishing early had the option of working in the plant or taking the time off without pay. Approximately one half-hour per day was allocated for paperwork, consisting primarily of a daily log listing customers delivered, miles driven, and hours spent. Overtime was accumulated any time more than eight hours were worked in a given day. The nonunion Troy drivers accumulated 1,950 overtime hours in the first half of 1983. Exhibit 2 gives recent monthly data for total driver hours, overtime, miles, and number of deliveries.

Edgcomb leased seven trucks and eight trailers at a cost of $1,600 per month for a tractor/trailer combination. The company estimated variable costs (excluding driver wages) to be 27 cents per mile. The fleet covered 207,293 miles during the first six months of 1983, delivering a total of 15,806 tons of metal and making 4,227 stops.

EXHIBIT 2   Monthly Data for the Troy Facility

Month	Tons	Miles	Stops	Regular Hours	Overtime
1983:					
June 3,043	34,907	719	1,182	362
May 2,889	38,799	728	1,259	360
Apr. 2,384	33,367	695	1,230	382
Mar. 2,500	35,288	763	1,345	283
Feb. 2,312	29,876	613	1,205	257
Jan. 2,678	35,056	709	1,253	306
1982:					
Dec. 1,678	27,171	568	962	187
Nov. 2,209	29,917	624	915	276
Oct. 2,382	30,143	713	962	239
Sept. 2,315	34,771	617	1,091	272
Aug. 2,624	36,523	724	1,108	283
Jul. 1,745	34,693	640	1,030	249

Drivers' Meeting, August 1983

Shortly after assuming the job of plant manager in July of 1982, Alex Tereszcuk initiated a regularly scheduled series of drivers' meetings. He hoped these meetings would facilitate communication between him and the drivers and give the drivers an opportunity to air their gripes and make suggestions.

The first few meetings produced a small number of minor complaints and suggestions, and Alex made several small changes in response. It was not until the July meeting, however, that the first significant problem was brought up. Frank Spencer, one of the more experienced drivers, stood up during that meeting to speak his mind:

> First, I'd like to say that I think these drivers' meetings are a real good thing. It's always nice to know that management is willing to listen.
>
> I want to bring up something that bothers me and I know bothers some of the rest of you. Quite simply, I don't think we're all pulling our weight. I work hard and conscientiously and get done in 8 hours what takes others 10. We all enjoy our freedom out there on the road, and we also know that the harder we work, the more we deliver, and the faster we finish. And we also know that this freedom brings plenty of opportunity to goof off.
>
> What's doubly bad about the situation is that the best drivers, those who finish in 8 hours, don't get paid as well as those who take 10 and get overtime. It's discouraging to see that I'm penalized for doing a good job.
>
> I enjoy my work and I think we've got real good jobs, but I think there's something wrong and unfair with this system that pays you more if you're not doing your job.

Frank's comments were seconded by a couple of other drivers, and Alex got the sense that it was one newer driver in particular, John Williams, who was the target of these criticisms. The meeting ended with a promise from Alex that he would look into the matter.

Alex believed that Spencer was probably the best and most conscientious driver in the plant, and he also believed that Williams was as poor as Spencer was good. But Alex did not believe that Williams was intentionally goofing off. He thought it was more a matter of Williams' being less energetic and skillful than the others—and just plain slower in general. He could see that Williams was being paid slightly more; Williams had made close to $30,000 a year in 1982 because of overtime. Exhibit 3 gives the 1983 overtime accumulations of the seven full-time delivery drivers.

Data Analysis

Alex decided to see what he could learn from the daily logs of the two drivers, Spencer and Williams. The total accumulated overtime had to be judged relative to the number of days worked, the number of miles traveled, and the number of stops made. To do this, Alex compiled data on hours worked outside the plant (excluding any explainable nonproductive hours, such as tire changes, breakdowns, and so on) versus miles driven and stops made over a four-month period (April to July of 1983) for both Spencer and Williams. These data are in Exhibit 4. Several days' were found to be unusable because of the presence of extenuating circumstances (poor weather, malfunctioning truck, and the like) and were not included.

In the period covered by the daily log data, Spencer averaged 10.6 hours per run while Williams averaged only 9.72, which conflicted with the contention that Williams tended to be slower than Spencer. Alex wondered whether the four-month period considered might not be representative or whether Spencer's higher time per run might be explained by his larger average number of miles and stops.

To check his belief that sectors made a difference in the number of hours to expect for a given run, Alex compiled daily data on two sectors. The Virginia Beach/Norfolk sector and the local Charlottesville sectors were picked to represent extremes. A delivery run to the Charlottesville sector was one of the

EXHIBIT 3   Overtime by Driver in First Six Months of 1983

Driver	Regular Hours	Overtime Hours
1	960	320
2	924	291
3	969	325
4	896	199
5	928	277
Williams	907	215
Spencer	931	284
Total*	6,515	1,911

* The hours of one other back-up driver are not included in this total.

EXHIBIT 4   Daily Data for Williams and Spencer

Williams Data

Miles	Stops	Hours		Miles	Stops	Hours
331	3	10.17		176	5	7.75
206	2	8.00		147	7	9.10
221	4	8.25		536	2	13.32
193	4	10.00		55	4	7.50
129	4	7.50		191	6	11.00
208	5	9.33		237	7	10.33
368	3	11.50		258	6	12.17
163	6	8.50		276	1	9.67
264	1	8.00		130	3	9.25
238	3	9.00		241	5	10.00
193	5	9.00		364	8	13.00
145	6	8.00		207	3	7.25
331	5	12.50		251	8	9.75
427	5	14.00		157	5	7.83
204	6	9.00		179	3	7.75
298	4	7.75		335	12	10.67
225	12	13.17		179	2	8.67
203	8	13.08		398	1	10.33
253	6	10.67		147	3	5.42
279	9	12.00		132	4	9.00
193	4	8.00		378	2	10.50
182	8	10.00		218	4	10.00
279	6	10.50		401	4	13.25
177	5	7.50		275	1	9.33
195	5	9.75		123	5	7.67
171	4	9.17		174	8	9.50
223	5	10.00		119	3	8.00
320	4	11.33		261	7	11.40
226	4	8.00		292	3	10.75
193	4	7.75		200	7	10.50
				292	4	11.33

	Miles	Stops	Hours
Average	235.52	4.80	9.72
St. dev.	87.48	2.34	1.84
Count	61	61	61

EXHIBIT 4   *(Continued)*

Spencer Data

Miles	Stops	Hours		Miles	Stops	Hours
182	3	8.25		189	8	8.25
364	9	12.50		326	6	11.00
227	9	10.50		176	7	8.00
188	4	6.50		352	7	11.50
275	6	9.50		197	5	8.00
440	4	11.50		312	10	12.00
214	6	8.50		110	6	6.00
265	4	8.00		334	5	10.50
352	6	10.50		339	9	12.00
321	4	9.00		201	11	9.50
174	8	9.75		340	7	12.00
372	11	13.50		382	4	9.83
188	6	8.00		189	8	8.50
249	2	9.00		262	6	9.50
386	5	14.00		290	2	7.75
112	3	6.00		350	6	10.50
164	6	7.67		286	6	10.00
338	2	10.50		178	3	7.10
522	8	15.75		286	2	9.50
262	6	10.00		292	5	10.00
333	3	9.25		392	5	12.85
321	6	10.50		379	5	11.50
240	3	8.67		199	8	9.50
345	2	8.75		226	9	10.00
262	8	9.25		176	6	8.50
254	3	9.00		379	8	11.00
310	6	10.83		225	4	8.00
203	11	11.50		311	8	11.75
540	11	16.00		186	9	9.00
216	9	9.50		228	10	9.00
415	3	11.75		205	2	8.42
375	2	10.00		346	9	10.00
306	11	11.75		320	9	11.50
341	10	11.50		181	9	9.50
311	9	13.25		369	7	11.75

	Miles	Stops	Hours
Average . . .	284.00	6.29	10.06
St. dev.	88.63	2.69	1.99
Count	70	70	70

shortest, while a delivery run to the Virginia Beach sector was one of the longest and most difficult. A comparison of the averages for these two sectors (shown in Exhibit 5) confirmed that Virginia Beach runs were indeed longer (both in miles and hours) and required more stops.

If the analysis of these data confirmed Frank Spencer's contentions, Alex had several options.

- One of the more extreme alternatives was to remove John Williams from his position as driver. Alex wondered whether the data provided enough evidence to support such a decision.

- A second, and less drastic, alternative was to set up some sort of monitoring system that would track the drivers' performances. Alex envisioned a system that would periodically compare the performance of each driver with a standard. The standard would be based on the miles driven and stops made and might also consider the particular sectors in which the driver's runs were made.

- A third alternative was to equip the trucks with tachographs, machines that kept a record of miles per hour over the course of a run. Such a record would provide almost complete information about the speed and activities of the drivers; but several other plants in the Edgcomb Metals Company had used tachographs with mixed success. After several phone calls to these plants, Alex learned that drivers universally disliked the little machines. The idea of being "watched" and recorded did not sit well with the drivers, individuals who generally enjoyed the freedom of being alone on the road. There was also some question about whether overall performance would improve because of the tachographs. From a purely economic standpoint, Alex wondered if the $75-per-month lease cost of a tachograph could be justified by improved performance. If the installation of tachographs changed Williams' performance to, for example, a level equal to that of Spencer's, would the tachograph be attractive?

- One final alternative that had several attractive features was to change the basis on which drivers were paid. Rather than pay by the hour and reward the poorer performers, Edgcomb might pay instead by the mile and number of deliveries. Paying drivers only for the amount of work accomplished would remove any incentive to stretch out a run to incur overtime.

EXHIBIT 5   Daily Data by Sector

Sector 1—Virginia Beach/Norfolk

Miles	Stops	Hours		Miles	Stops	Hours
331 3		10.17		366	11	12.50
364 9		12.50		329	4	11.42
304 4		10.00		348	9	11.75
419 7		12.25		368	10	13.00
341 5		9.92		372	9	12.67
349 6		12.25		373	11	13.00
340 7		11.00		416	3	11.75
334 2		9.50		320	4	11.33
368 3		11.50		367	5	12.00
280 3		9.25		399	12	13.83
352 6		10.50		328	1	8.75
339 7		12.00		341	10	11.50
264 1		8.00		353	7	12.00
326 5		11.00		366	9	12.25
420 3		11.67		337	5	12.25
372 11		13.50		288	4	10.00
335 4		9.50		352	7	11.50
273 2		8.00		363	9	11.25
331 6		10.50		373	8	12.75
328 9		13.00		278	4	10.00
331 5		12.50		339	3	11.25
311 4		10.00		312	5	10.75
322 4		9.25		327	5	10.42
338 2		10.50		334	5	10.50
368 4		10.75		360	8	11.75
347 7		12.50		272	4	10.00
347 4		10.00		310	3	11.50
333 3		9.25		276	1	9.67
321 6		10.50		340	7	12.00
335 5		12.00		354	11	15.00
370 10		12.80		276	2	8.25
343 7		12.00		364	8	13.00
353 9		11.75		354	7	13.00
279 9		12.00		343	6	11.00
333 7		12.00		350	6	10.50

	Miles	Stops	Hours
Average . . .	339.27	5.89	11.26
St. dev.	33.62	2.80	1.41
Count	70	70	70

EXHIBIT 5   *(Continued)*

Sector 3—Charlottesville

Miles	Stops	Hours		Miles	Stops	Hours
182	3	8.25		179	4	7.50
131	4	6.75		125	6	6.00
136	4	8.00		149	5	6.50
193	4	10.00		108	5	6.00
129	4	7.50		152	3	6.00
214	6	8.50		55	4	7.50
162	6	8.50		165	4	8.75
227	4	8.75		197	5	8.00
226	5	8.00		131	4	8.50
215	4	8.50		110	6	6.00
197	2	7.50		191	5	8.25
112	3	6.00		105	7	8.00
156	5	7.50		240	3	8.00
204	6	9.00		130	3	9.25
298	4	7.75		265	4	10.60
109	6	7.50		207	3	7.25
231	8	11.08		88	3	5.00
127	5	7.25		178	3	7.08
184	3	7.50		158	5	9.67
89	5	8.00		188	6	8.25
93	3	6.67		151	6	8.75
176	4	7.33		132	4	9.00
131	6	8.50		142	2	6.67
177	5	7.50		204	5	8.50
171	4	9.17		205	6	8.50
223	5	10.00		123	5	7.67
193	4	7.75		180	7	8.25
				62	4	8.00

	Miles	Stops	Hours
Average	163.75	4.53	7.93
St. dev.	50.11	1.29	1.10
Count	55	55	55

CASE 17
FLORIDA GLASS COMPANY (A)

As Oscar Paik, materials manager of the Florida Glass Company, reviewed his day planner, he noted that the monthly run of the Energy Planning Model was scheduled for today. This model calculated the optimal mix of products for the coming month, October 1982, and the quantities of energy (electricity and distillate-fuel oil) required. In the past, when Paik received the results of the model, he simply placed an order for the recommended quantity of distillate-fuel oil. On this particular occasion, however, he decided to take the time to question his perfunctory monthly ordering of distillate.

The model made calculations on a monthly basis, and, as a result, it ignored the opportunity to purchase more than one month's supply of distillate, even though ample storage capacity was available. During the past few years of oil price volatility, Paik had never taken advantage of a relatively low price, even when he firmly believed that prices would rise in the subsequent month. The current situation was another of these opportunities. Paik was convinced that the price he now faced at the end of September (93.66 cents per gallon) marked a temporary low in distillate prices. He believed that the price at the end of October (the next time he would normally purchase distillate) would be 94.5 or even 98.0 cents. This seemed an ideal time to address the policy of single-month purchases.

The Flat-Glass Industry

The major products of the flat-glass industry (Standard Industrial Classification [SIC] 3211) included float, plate, tempered, and laminated glass. Float glass was formed by cooling a layer of molten glass on a bed of molten tin. Plate glass was formed by a rolling process and then ground and polished on both sides. Tempered glass was flat glass that had been toughened by being heated above its strain point, then quickly cooled. Laminated glass consisted of plates of glass bonded to a sheet of plastic that provided protection against shattering.

In 1981, the industry shipped only $1.657 billion of product, approximately the same level at which it had been stagnating for the past four years. Forecasts for 1982 were no brighter, still at the $1.6 billion level. In fact, ever since World War II, depressed growth had plagued the industry. During this period, the industry had grown more slowly than the economy as a whole and more slowly than the two major industries that it supplied, building construction and automobile production. This performance reflected the loss of market to two types of competitors: foreign producers of glass and domestic producers of substitute materials. The outlook for the next five years was closely tied to the expansion of the economy. Forecasts were hopeful. It was anticipated that 1983 would present a welcome upturn. Shipments to the automobile industry would lead the way as a result of lower interest rates, increased consumer confidence, and pent-up demand. The construction industry was expected to rebound in 1984 as the current vacancy rates were reduced.

The flat-glass industry was dominated by four major corporations, Libby-Owens-Ford, PPG Industries, Corning Glass Works, and Guardian Industries. These firms accounted for 90 percent of the industry shipments. According to the *1977 Census of Manufacturers*, the remaining 10 percent was shared by 58 firms.

The glass industry was a major energy consumer. Among industries with two-digit SIC codes, Stone, Clay, and Glass (SIC 32) had the fourth-largest gross energy consumption (1,864 trillion Btus,[1] or 8 percent of the total manufacturing consumption), and glass accounted for 20 percent of this amount. The sources of the glass industry's energy had been shifting over the past decade. There had been a sharp increase in the relative use of oil (from 6.1 percent in 1971 to 29.7 percent in 1980), a sharp drop in the relative consumption of gas (from 72.4 percent to 40.2 percent), and a moderate rise in the use of electricity (from 20.4 percent to 27.0 percent).

Over the last two decades, however, aggregate energy use by the glass industry had increased more slowly than output, despite increases in energy consumption by pollution-control equipment. A number of technological developments were credited for these gains in efficiency, including the use of larger furnaces, the reuse of waste heat, the introduction of an auxiliary heating unit inside the body of the molten glass in the furnace, and the widespread adoption of the "float" process of making plate glass, which eliminated grinding and polishing of the flat surfaces.

Glass Manufacturing

The hard, brittle substance that is known as glass is actually a liquid. It is one of a number of substances that are formed from chemical compositions that have the property of cooling below their freezing point without crystallizing, thus becoming liquids of increasingly high viscosity until eventually they are so stiff that, to all ordinary appearances, they are solids. Scientifically, glass is classified as a "supercooled" liquid. Toffee is another such substance—a supercooled sugar solution.

Glass is made from three primary raw materials: sand (silicon dioxide), limestone (calcium carbonate), and soda ash (sodium carbonate). The ideal composition is approximately 75 percent silica, 10 percent lime, and 15 percent soda. In the actual manufacturing of glass, crushed waste glass (cullet) is added to the

---

[1]One Btu (British thermal unit) is the amount of heat required to raise one pound of water by one degree Fahrenheit. One gallon of fuel-oil distillate produces on average 105,000 Btus, one kilowatt-hour (kWh) of electricity 3,400 Btus, and one cubic foot of natural gas 1,000 Btus.

batch of materials in an effort to speed the melting process, because glass melts at a lower temperature than any of its separate ingredients.

The production of glass involves (1) mixing the ingredients; (2) heating the mixture in a furnace to 850 degrees Celsius until the ingredients combine and melt; (3) forming the product by one or more means, such as drawing, molding, pressing, and floating; (4) annealing, or reheating and slowly cooling the products to relieve stresses caused by the uncontrolled and unavoidable cooling that takes place during the forming process; (5) cutting, inspecting, and packaging. (See the flowchart in Exhibit 1.) Flat glass is made in such volumes that manufacturing is a continuous process from melting to packing. The melting operation accounts for more than half of the process's energy requirements.

In the past decade, considerable attention had been devoted to energy conservation in the melting operation. Improved refractory materials had lengthened furnace campaign lives and thus reduced the number of energy-consuming start-ups. Electric "boosters" had been added to the fuel-fired furnaces. By passing current between electrodes placed near the bottom of the furnace, these boosters had introduced more heat and created a stirring action that had improved furnace output by more than the relative amount of additional energy.

The widespread adoption during the late 1960s and early 1970s of the "float" process of making plate glass had been an important energy-conservation development in the flat-glass industry. Previously, the production of flat, distortion-free glass had involved extensive grinding and polishing, which consumed 10 to 20 percent of the glass. In the float process, the molten glass left the furnace in a continuous strip and floated directly on the surface of an enclosed pool of molten

EXHIBIT 1   Process Flowchart

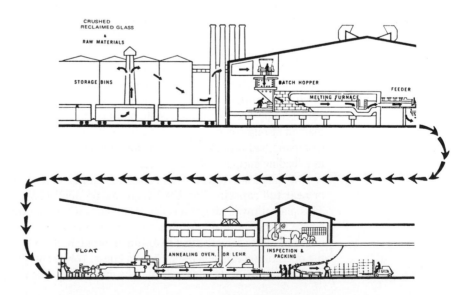

tin. By surrounding the glass with a controlled atmosphere and sufficient heat, irregularities on both surfaces of the glass flowed out, yielding flat, smooth, and parallel surfaces. Elimination of the grinding and polishing of the flat surfaces saved both the direct energy of grinding and the indirect energy of making the glass that had been ground into waste.

Finished flat glass could be processed further to improve its safety characteristics. There were two principal methods. The first consisted of laminating a sheet of plastic between two sheets of glass; the second of heat-treating a single layer of glass. In laminated glass, splinters firmly adhered to the plastic layer when a fracture occurred. In heat-treated (or tempered) glass, a fracture resulted in cracks throughout the entire body of the glass, and the glass broke into a large number of comparatively small, harmless pieces. This unusual property was the result of heating finished glass sheets to just below their softening point, then uniformly and rapidly cooling them with a blast of air. This rapid cooling placed the outside surfaces of the glass under compressional strain. If the glass fractured, this strain was catastrophically relieved throughout the piece of glass.

Florida Glass Company

The Florida Glass Company, located in Seffner, Florida, produced float, laminated, and tempered glass in its 37,500 square feet per month plant. It employed the float process for manufacturing its glass and fueled its furnaces by oil with electric boosters.

Even though it was not located in the primary glass-producing states of Ohio, Tennessee, Illinois, and Pennsylvania, where raw materials were readily accessible and less expensive, Florida Glass was more profitable than the rest of the industry. In 1981, it posted over a 4 percent return on sales, compared with a 2 percent return for the rest of the industry. Exhibit 2 was the 1981 operating statement. This performance was attributed to Florida Glass's having developed a strong position in an attractive market niche as well as having paid careful attention to manufacturing efficiencies, particularly with regard to energy.

Although the flat-glass industry as a whole had been weak for the past five years, the Florida market had been moderately strong. The architectural designs in Florida continued to be heavily glass oriented, and residential and commercial construction had persisted despite national economic conditions, so demand remained strong for glass products. Since its founding in 1951, the Florida Glass Company had promoted itself in this regional market and had established itself as a leading supplier to the market.

For the past five years, sales had been sufficient to keep the plant operating at or near full capacity. The 1982 aggregate production plan is shown in Exhibit 3. This plan allowed ranges on certain products when market conditions permitted. These ranges in turn gave flexibility in production planning so the product mix could be altered in an effort to optimize profitability. This flexibility was a key to the operational efficiencies at Florida Glass. When energy costs severely affected the industry, Florida Glass adjusted its mix to control energy expense.

EXHIBIT 2   1981 Operating Statement (in thousands of dollars)

	Float	*Tempered*	*Laminated*	*Total*
Shipments ('000 sq. ft.)	217.8	78.6	85.2	211.1
Revenue	$272.2	$255.4	$238.6	$766.2
CGS (excluding energy)	63.1	48.7	96.3	208.1
Energy—electricity*	88.5	98.9	69.0	256.4
Energy—distillate†	62.7	93.5	38.9	195.1
Selling, admin., R&D	32.2	16.6	12.6	61.4
Total cost	246.5	257.7	216.8	721.0
Income before taxes	25.7	(2.3)	21.8	45.2
Income after taxes				33.3

*At an average cost of $0.0351 per kWh.

†At an average cost of $0.9926 per gallon.

EXHIBIT 3   1982 Aggregate Market Plan (square feet of finished output)

	Float		**Tempered**		**Laminated**	
	Min.	*Max.*	*Min.*	*Max.*	*Min.*	*Max.*
January	—	14,000	6,500	12,000	—	14,000
February	—	14,000	6,500	12,000	—	14,000
March	10,500	15,500	5,000	12,000	—	15,000
April	12,000	16,500	5,000	12,000	4,000	16,500
May	12,000	18,500	—	9,000	4,000	16,500
June	12,000	19,500	—	9,000	7,000	17,500
July	14,500	20,000	—	9,000	7,000	17,500
August	14,500	20,000	—	9,000	7,000	17,500
September	16,000	21,000	—	8,500	—	15,000
October	16,000	21,000	—	8,500	—	15,000
November	16,000	21,000	—	8,500	—	15,000
December	—	17,000	4,500	7,500	—	16,500

Note: All figures are for nominal ¼-inch product. Because laminated glass requires two sheets of ⅛-inch float, a planning factor of 1.75 must be applied to the output when computing capacity requirements. This factor is less than two because the process time is slightly reduced for the thinner glass.

Energy Planning

For the past several years, the strong market position of Florida Glass had helped to keep its cost per square foot of finished product significantly below the industry average. Because the plant operated at full capacity, costs were spread over as wide a base as possible. More important, Florida Glass was able to address its energy expense through adjustments in its product mix. At the end of each month,

EXHIBIT 4 **Distillate Fuel Price History (end-of-month prices in cents per gallon)**

Month	1980	1981	1982
January	75.02	94.86	99.11
February	77.77	102.51	94.68
March	78.84	102.83	87.42
April	78.85	100.86	86.00
May	79.38	100.69	91.16
June	80.28	99.30	95.45
July	79.14	98.51	93.81
August	79.28	98.16	92.51
September	79.25	97.84	93.66
October	80.74	98.00	
November	83.99	100.02	
December	88.60	100.56	

on the basis of the current price for distillate fuel and the contract price for electricity, the product mix was set for next month's manufacturing.

Electricity and distillate fuel were the two sources of energy in the Florida Glass manufacturing process. The distillate fired the melting furnaces, the annealing kilns, and the tempering furnaces. Electricity powered the process flow, the boosters in the melting furnaces, and the cutting and grinding wheels in the finishing area.

Distillate was purchased at the end of each month in sufficient quantity to fuel just the next month's operations, even though there was sufficient storage capacity (32,000 gallons) for two months of normal operations. The one-month purchase policy was adopted for a variety of reasons: (1) there had never been a disruption in operations due to fuel shortages; (2) working-capital needs were reduced and short-term money, which currently cost 18 percent, was kept to a minimum; and (3) the savings due to avoiding the delivery charge of $150 were minimal. The end-of-month prices that Florida Glass paid for distillate fuel over the past three years are shown in Exhibit 4.

Electricity was supplied by the local utility and was billed on the basis of both peak demand and usage. Demand was measured in terms of the peak kilowatts demanded in any 30-minute interval during the billing month. This charge was directly related to the amount of production capacity brought on line. Because Florida Glass had operated at capacity for some time, the peak demand was virtually unchanged from month to month and the charge was treated as a fixed cost.[2] The usage charge was based on the kilowatt-hours consumed and was billed at a progressive rate, according to the following schedule:

---

[2]Approximately $6,500 per month, which was allocated one-sixth to float, one-half to tempered, and one-third to laminated.

- First 72,000 kWh at $0.0331 per kWh.
- Next 462,000 kWh at $0.0348 per kWh.
- Additional kWh at $0.0396 per kWh.

The usage charge varied from month to month depending on the production mix.

For several years, Florida Glass had been using its Energy Planning Model on a monthly basis to establish the monthly production schedule. The model was a linear program that determined the product mix that maximized total contribution for a given distillate price and appropriate aggregate market planning ranges.

CASE 18
FLORIDA GLASS COMPANY (A) SUPPLEMENT

The results of the monthly run of the Energy Planning Model had just been received by Oscar Paik, materials manager of the Florida Glass Company. Exhibit 1 presents those results. The model's relationships with the October 1982 inputs are shown in Exhibit 2.

Paik noted that for the current market price of 93.66 cents per gallon, the optimal October production schedule called for 13,425 gallons of distillate-fuel oil. Before placing the order, however, Paik decided to explore the possibility of ordering at this time a two-month supply that would last through both October and November. He reasoned that the current 93.66 cents per gallon price was too good an opportunity to miss, that the company's storage capacity was large enough to handle delivery of a double order, and that next month's ordering and delivery charges ($150) would be avoided.

To see exactly how much distillate would be needed in November, Paik knew he would have to rerun the Energy Planning Model using November's data. This run required a price for distillate, and Paik thought that 94.5 was a reasonable guess for the distillate price at the end of October. Alternatively, Paik thought a higher price of 98 cents was quite possible (especially in light of the recent history of volatile distillate prices) and would serve as a best case for the "savings" associated with the option of buying a two-month supply now.

EXHIBIT 1   Model Results for October

Total Contribution $10,290

Production	Square feet	Price per square ft. ($)	Contribution (excl. energy) ($)	Oil Required (gallons)	Electricity Required (kWh)
Float	21,000	$0.96	$20,160	6,090	243,180
Tempered . . .	3,234	2.63	8,505	3,848	115,935
Laminated . . .	7,581	1.67	12,660	3,487	174,885
Total			$41,325	13,425	534,000

Production Capacity	Used		Avail.	Slack	Shadow Price ($)	Allowable Decrease	Allowable Increase
	37,500	<	37,500	0	$0.24	8,388	5,560

Market Constraints	Actual		Limit	Slack or Surplus	Shadow Price ($)	Allowable Decrease	Allowable Increase
Float:							
Minimum	21,000	>	16,000	5,000	$0.00	—	5,000
Maximum	21,000	<	21,000	0	0.04	5,000	12,390
Tempered:							
Maximum	3,234	<	8,500	5,266	0.00	5,266	—
Laminated:							
Maximum	7,581	<	15,000	7,419	0.00	7,419	—

Energy Requirements	Used		Required	Slack or Surplus	Shadow Price ($)	Allowable Decrease	Allowable Increase
Oil	13,425	>	13,425	0	$0.9366	13,425	—
Electricity:							
Step 1	72,000	<	72,000	0	0.0025	72,000	119,369
Step 2	462,000	<	462,000	0	0.0008	73,303	119,368
Step 3	0						
Total electricity	534,000	>	534,000	0	0.0356	119,369	73,303

Energy Costs	Cost per Unit ($)	Use	Total Cost ($)
Oil	$0.9366	13,425	$12,574
Electricity:			
Step 1	0.0331	72,000	2,383
Step 2	0.0348	462,000	16,078
Step 3	0.0396	0	0
Total			$31,035

EXHIBIT 2   Energy Planning Model—October 1982 Inputs

Variables

FLOAT . . . . .   production of float glass (square feet)
TEMPD . . . .   production of tempered glass (square feet)
LAMIN. . . . .   production of laminated glass (square feet)
OIL . . . .   amount of oil purchased (gallons)
E1 . . . .   amount of electricity purchased-step 1 (kilowatt-hours)
E2 . . . .   amount of electricity purchased-step 2 (kilowatt-hours)
E3 . . . .   amount of electricity purchased-step 3 (kilowatt-hours)
ETOTAL . . . .   total amount of electricity purchased (kilowatt-hours)

Objective

$$\text{Maximum contribution} = 0.96 \times \text{FLOAT} + 2.63 \times \text{TEMPD} + 1.67 \times \text{LAMIN} -$$
$$0.9366 \times \text{OIL} - 0.0331 \times \text{E1} - 0.0348 \times \text{E2} - 0.0396 \times \text{E3}$$

Constraints

Energy:

Capacity: $\text{FLOAT} + \text{TEMPD} + 1.75 \times \text{LAMIN} \leq 37{,}500$

Oil purchase: $0.29 \times \text{FLOAT} + 1.19 \times \text{TEMPD} + 0.46 \times \text{LAMIN} - \text{OIL} = 0$

Electricity requirement: $11.58 \times \text{FLOAT} + 35.85 \times \text{TEMPD} + 23.07 \times \text{LAMIN} -$
                         $\text{ETOTAL} = 0$

Electricity purchase: $-\text{E1} - \text{E2} - \text{E3} + \text{ETOTAL} = 0$

Electricity 1st step: $\text{E1} \leq 72{,}000$

Electricity 2nd step: $\text{E2} \leq 462{,}000$

Market:

Float minimum: $\text{FLOAT} \geq 16{,}000$
Float maximum: $\text{FLOAT} \leq 21{,}000$
Tempered maximum: $\text{TEMPD} \leq 8{,}500$
Laminated maximum: $\text{LAMIN} \leq 15{,}000$

CASE 19
FOULKE CONSUMER PRODUCTS, INC.

The Southeast Region

In 1977 Foulke Consumer Products, Inc., was a small manufacturer and distributor of Brand A of a durable consumer product, with $42 million in sales and less than 5 percent of the market. Ten years later, Foulke had almost $600 million in sales and over 25 percent of the market. This tremendous growth, achieved primarily through acquisitions, caused a strain on the organization, particularly the manufacturing side. The company had grown from 4 plants serving five states to over 40 plants serving the entire country. Many of the acquired plants had formerly competed within the same regions; hence, some redundancies existed. Foulke faced the task of dealing with these regional capacity/profitability problems.

The Industry

The industry in 1987 was composed of a diverse group of manufacturers serving a $1.9 billion wholesale market. Over 800 firms, ranging from small local producers to industry giants, each typically aligned with a particular brand, competed in this brand-sensitive market. Nine brands controlled 67 percent of the market; the four top brands and their respective market shares were:

Brand A	25%
Brand B	11%
Brand C	10%
Brand D	7%

The business was highly competitive at the retail and wholesale levels. Industry growth was low and not expected to pick up in the near future. The product was sold primarily through manufacturers' sales forces directly to retailers.

The Company

Foulke Consumer Products, Inc., founded in 1907, became one of eight Brand A licensees in 1924, with exclusive manufacturing and distribution rights in Massachusetts. Foulke began acquiring other Brand A licensees in 1956, and, by the time the company went public in 1970, it had four plants from which it distributed Brand A in five states and Puerto Rico.

This case was based on a Supervised Business Study prepared by William Hosler (Darden, Class of 1989).
Copyright © by the University of Virginia Darden School Foundation, Charlottesville, Virginia. All rights reserved.

EXHIBIT 1   The Southeast Region

Average Plant Income Statement

Net sales	100.0%
Material	45.8
Labor	7.0
Overhead:	
Variable	7.5
Fixed	4.0
Cost of sales	64.3
Gross margin	35.7%
Delivery:	
Variable	2.7%
Fixed	1.0
Selling and advertising:	
Variable	12.0
Fixed	4.0
Plant administration	3.9
Operating expense	23.6
Operating margin	12.1
Corporate charge	5.8
Income before tax	6.3
Taxes	2.8
Net income	3.5%

Brand A and the other licensees, not pleased with Foulke's success, tried to stall further expansion by the company. In response, Foulke filed an antitrust suit against Brand A in 1971. While the suit stalled in court, Foulke continued to expand by acquiring Brand A's Dallas licensee in 1976 and Brand E, a competitor, in 1983. The company began to market and sell aggressively nationwide—in the process competing directly with other Brand A licensees in their own backyards. Prices and margins in the industry fell, and product historically shipped no farther than 200 miles was routinely transported over 1,000 miles.

In 1986, a jury ruled in favor of Foulke over Brand A and its main licensees. As settlement of the $77 million judgment, Foulke acquired Brand A and all but one of its licensees, thereby doubling its sales and assets and increasing its number of manufacturing facilities to 42.

Although the company now had nationwide rights to Brand A, the earlier competition meant that some markets were being served by as many as four different Foulke plants. These plants operated completely autonomously, with responsibility for both sales and production in their territories. As profit centers, plants were provided with all the functions of small companies (see Exhibit 1 for an average plant income statement). Although sales territories had been redrawn after the acquisition to improve delivery efficiency, problems remained. Some

---

EXHIBIT 2   The Southeast Region
Brand A Product Demand (pieces/year)

Brand A	
Markets	*Demand*
Atlanta	89,179
Birmingham	17,750
Charleston	8,093
Columbia	24,604
Columbus	5,339
Greensboro/W.S.	77,640
Knoxville	19,316
Miami	109,902
Orlando	29,173
Raleigh/Durham	37,900
Savannah	6,493
Tampa	86,799

plants lacked capacity, while others had excess. Not all plants had the same profitability, and some suffered from severe operating problems. Traditionally, these types of problems had been addressed plant by plant; no effort was made to examine them on a national, or even regional, basis.

The Southeast Region

The Southeast region was one of Foulke's most profitable, with operating margins of 12.5 percent (Exhibit 2 presents annual Brand A demand in the Southeast region by market). The company had three plants in the region (see Exhibit 3). Exhibit 4 gives profit-and-loss statements for the first seven months of 1988 for each plant. Prior to the acquisition, these plants had competed for sales in the region. Sales territories within the region had been reorganized to minimize delivery expense, but no attempt had been made to balance capacity and service with long-term profitability.

Following is a brief description of each plant.

Orlando, Florida, Plant (225,000 units capacity). The Orlando plant was the largest in the region but the least profitable in terms of operating margin. Little could be done to improve margins. Delivery costs were high because most of Orlando's product was shipped south to the Miami area. The plant had a worsening workforce situation because of the area's recent urbanization and rapid growth of high-paying service industries. On the other hand, Orlando's growth also had caused the value of the plant and land on which it was located to skyrocket, to approximately $3.25 million. The plant could be expanded by an additional 75,000 units at a cost of $900,000. With an expansion, however, would

EXHIBIT 3   The Southeast Region

The Southeast Region

○   Existing plant site

●   Potential plant site

□   Center of market area

come an estimated increase in variable manufacturing costs of approximately $2 per unit for all units, and fixed costs would increase by about $400,000 per year.

Atlanta, Georgia, Plant (175,000 units capacity).   In contrast to Orlando, the Atlanta plant had a good work force with high stability. Also unlike Orlando, the facility was short on space and had no room to expand. Like Orlando, however, the market value of the plant and the land on which it was situated had increased rapidly, to about $4 million.

Lexington, North Carolina, Plant (187,500 units capacity).   The Lexington plant, the most profitable brand-label plant in the entire company, was ideal in almost every way. It had an excellent work force and was close to its suppliers.

EXHIBIT 4   The Southeast Region

Southeast Region Income Statements (7 months ending June 30, 1988)

	Orlando	Atlanta	Lexington
Net sales ($000)	$ 11,788	$ 8,075	$ 7,444
Total pieces	125,952	84,177	78,677
Net sales	100.0%	100.0%	100.0%
Material	46.5	45.4	43.9
Labor	7.1	6.2	6.1
Overhead	9.1	10.2	7.4
Cost of goods	62.7%	61.8%	57.4%
Gross margin	37.3%	38.2%	42.6%
Delivery	4.6	4.1	3.2
Sell. & adv.	18.6	17.8	15.4
Administration	3.5	3.4	3.8
Operating expense	26.7%	25.3%	22.3%
Operating margin	10.6%	13.0%	20.3%

The plant and property itself was not as valuable as the other plants (market price of around $2 million). The plant could be expanded by an additional 50,000 units at a cost of $600,000. The estimate was that expansion would increase variable manufacturing costs by $1 per unit for all units and fixed costs by $250,000 per year.

In addition to these three plants, the company was considering two potential new plant sites: Lake City and Ft. Myers, Florida. The Lake City site was attractive primarily because of its rural location, which was similar to that of the Lexington plant. A recent study of Foulke's plants had shown that rural locations tended to be more efficient and profitable than urban ones. The hope was that a plant in Lake City could emulate the production performance of the Lexington plant.

Ft. Myers, on the other hand, was attractive because of its proximity to the Miami-area market. Such a location would significantly reduce the company's overall delivery costs (see Exhibit 5 for per-unit delivery costs from each plant to each major market area). Unfortunately, the company was not optimistic about the possibility of achieving a Lexington-like production record at Ft. Myers, because of the surrounding demographics. More likely, a plant in the Ft. Myers area would resemble Orlando's less-efficient operation. In addition, building a plant of any size in Ft. Myers would cost a base amount of $4.0 million plus $4 per unit of capacity, compared with a $3.5 million base with the same $4 per unit of capacity at Lake City. At either location, the capacity of the new plant would have to be between 62,500 and 250,000 units.

EXHIBIT 5 **The Southeast Region**
Per-Unit Transportation Cost

	Plants				
Markets	*Orlando*	*Atlanta*	*Lexington*	*Ft. Myers*	*Lake City*
Atlanta	$ 5.72	$ 0.66	$ 4.61	$ 8.62	$ 3.36
Birmingham	6.45	1.97	6.58	9.34	4.08
Charleston	5.53	3.80	3.62	8.42	3.16
Columbia	6.18	2.63	2.63	9.08	3.82
Columbus	56.85	14.62	74.71	92.58	27.61
Greens./W.S.	7.89	4.61	0.66	10.79	5.53
Knoxville	8.29	2.54	2.89	11.18	5.92
Miami	4.34	8.62	12.24	1.97	6.71
Orlando	0.66	5.72	7.89	2.89	2.37
Ral./Durham	8.82	4.89	1.97	11.71	6.45
Savannah	20.21	15.16	28.87	36.09	7.22
Tampa	1.38	5.92	9.47	1.58	3.09

CASE 20

FOULKE CONSUMER PRODUCTS, INC., SUPPLEMENT

Memorandum

To: Leander Green, VP–Operations, Southeast Region
From: Paul Jenkins, Senior Analyst
Re: Distribution Issues in the Southeast Region

As per your request, I have analyzed the impact on sourcing of the proposed new plant in Lake City, assuming the closing of the Atlanta plant.

First, it was necessary to estimate the variable production costs of each of our existing plants. These data, along with each plant's annual fixed operating expenses, can be found in Exhibit S1. I derived these figures from the information in case Exhibits 1 and 4 (see Case 19).

I then constructed a linear programming (LP) model using the variable production costs and the per-unit transportation costs provided in case 19 Exhibit 5. The LP model is designed to minimize the Southeast region's total annual transportation and variable production costs; Exhibit S2 contains an annotated version of the spreadsheet. The resulting sourcing plan for the base case (existing plants and capacities) can be found in Exhibit S3. These results seem to suggest that Lake City is indeed a more promising site than Ft. Myers for a new plant. Exhibit S4 shows the new sourcing plan given a large new plant in Lake City (capacity of 250,000), assuming that we close down the Atlanta facility and that the new plant emulates the cost performance of the Lexington facility. As you can see, the annual savings are dramatic.

I am sending you this report today because you indicated time was of the essence. Though generally pleased with the model and convinced that the Lake City plant does in fact reduce our annual distribution costs, I must qualify my recommendation for the following reason. After building the original model, it occurred to me that, for the sake of presentation and to accentuate the positive, maybe we should be *maximizing* contribution, rather than *minimizing* cost. I thought the two approaches would yield the same result and was surprised when—in the case of the new Lake City plant—they did not (see Exhibits S5 and S6). Admittedly, the difference is not great, but it is still somewhat disconcerting. I will get back to you as soon as I have resolved the matter.

EXHIBIT S1   Per-Unit Variable Cost of Production

	Orlando	Atlanta	Lexington
Net sales (000)	$11,788	$8,075	$7,444
Total pieces	125,952	84,177	78,677
Price per unit	$93.59	$95.93	$94.61
Variable costs per unit:			
Material	$43.52	$43.55	$41.54
Labor	6.64	5.95	5.77
Variable overhead*	5.55	6.38	4.57
Variable selling/admin.[†]	13.06	12.81	10.93
Total variable cost per unit	$68.78	$68.69	$62.80

*Variable overhead calculated as 7.5%/(7.5% + 4.0%) of total.

[†]Variable selling/admin. calculated as 12.0%/(12.0% + 4.0%) of total.

EXHIBIT S2 Annotated *What's Best!* Linear Programming Spreadsheet

	A	B	C	D	E	F
3	COST SUMMARY					
4						
5			Per-Unit			
6			Variable	Variable		
7		Production	Production	Production	Distribution	
8	Plant	Volume	Cost	Cost	Cost	Total
9						
10	Orlando	+C37	$68.78	+B10*C10	+C39	+D10+E10
11	Atlanta	+D37	$68.69	+B11*C11	+D39	+D11+E11
12	Lexington	+E37	$62.80	+B12*C12	+E39	+D12+E12
13	Ft. Myers	+F37	$0.00	+B13*C13	+F39	+D13+E13
14	Lake City	+G37	$0.00	+B14*C14	+G39	+D14+E14
15						
16	TOTAL ANNUAL VARIABLE OPERATING COST			=	@SUM(COL) (MINIMIZE)	

19 DISTRIBUTION SCHEDULE AND COST

			--------Plants--------						Brand		Shadow	-----Range-----	
22	Markets	Orlando	Atlanta	Lexington	Ft. Myers	Lake City	Total		Demand	Surplus	Price	Decrease	Increase
23													
24	Atlanta	0	0	0	0	0	@SUM(ROW)	>	89,179	+H24-I24	$0.00	0	0
25	Birmingham	0	0	0	0	0	@SUM(ROW)	>	17,750	+H25-I25	$0.00	0	0
26	Charleston	0	0	0	0	0	@SUM(ROW)	>	8,093	+H26-I26	$0.00	0	0
27	Columbia	0	0	0	0	0	@SUM(ROW)	>	24,604	+H27-I27	$0.00	0	0
28	Columbus	0	0	0	0	0	@SUM(ROW)	>	5,339	+H28-I28	$0.00	0	0
29	Greens./W.S.	0	0	0	0	0	@SUM(ROW)	>	19,316	+H29-I29	$0.00	0	0
30	Knoxville	0	0	0	0	0	@SUM(ROW)	>	77,640	+H30-I30	$0.00	0	0
31	Miami	0	0	0	0	0	@SUM(ROW)	>	109,902	+H31-I31	$0.00	0	0
32	Orlando	0	0	0	0	0	@SUM(ROW)	>	29,173	+H32-I32	$0.00	0	0
33	Ral./Durham	0	0	0	0	0	@SUM(ROW)	>	37,900	+H33-I33	$0.00	0	0
34	Savannah	0	0	0	0	0	@SUM(ROW)	>	6,493	+H34-I34	$0.00	0	0
35	Tampa	0	0	0	0	0	@SUM(ROW)	>	86,799	+H35-I35	$0.00	0	0
36													
37	Production volume	@SUM(COL)	@SUM(COL)	@SUM(COL)	@SUM(COL)	@SUM(COL)							
38													
39	Distribution cost	TOTAL*	TOTAL	TOTAL	TOTAL	TOTAL							
40													

* +C24*C60+C25*C61+C26*C62+C27*C63+C28*C64+C29*C65+C30*C66+C31*C67+C32*C68+C33*C69+C34*C70+C35*C71

EXHIBIT S2 *Concluded*

	A	B	C	D	E	F	G	H	I	J	K	L	M	N

43 PRODUCTION SCHEDULE/COST

	Produced		Capacity	Slack	Shadow Price	Range Decrease	Increase
48 Orlando	+C37	v	225,000	+D48-B48	$0.00	0	0
49 Atlanta	+D37	v	175,000	+D49-B49	$0.00	0	0
50 Lexington	+E37	v	187,500	+D50-B50	$0.00	0	0
51 Ft. Myers	+F37	v	0	+D51-B51	$0.00	0	0
52 Lake City	+G37	v	0	+D52-B52	$0.00	0	0

55 PER-UNIT DISTRIBUTION COSTS

58 MARKETS	----Plants----				
	Orlando	Atlanta	Lexington	Ft. Myers	Lake City
60 Atlanta	$5.72	$0.66	$4.61	$8.62	$3.36
61 Birmingham	$6.45	$1.97	$6.58	$9.34	$4.08
62 Charleston	$5.53	$3.80	$3.62	$8.42	$3.16
63 Columbia	$6.18	$2.63	$2.63	$9.08	$3.82
64 Columbus	$56.85	$14.62	$74.71	$92.58	$27.61
65 Greensboro/W.S.	$7.89	$4.61	$0.66	$10.79	$5.53
66 Knoxville	$8.29	$2.54	$2.89	$11.18	$5.92
67 Miami	$4.34	$8.62	$12.24	$1.97	$6.71
68 Orlando	$0.66	$5.72	$7.89	$2.89	$2.37
69 Raleigh/Durham	$8.82	$4.89	$1.97	$11.71	$6.45
70 Savannah	$20.21	$15.16	$28.87	$36.09	$7.22
71 Tampa	$1.38	$5.92	$9.47	$1.58	$3.09

EXHIBIT S3 Cost-Minimization Solution for Base Case

COST SUMMARY

Plant	Production Volume	Per-Unit Variable Production Cost	Variable Production Cost	Distribution Cost	Total
Orlando	225,000	$68.78	$15,475,500	$615,435	$16,090,935
Atlanta	99,688	$68.69	$6,847,569	$257,728	$7,105,296
Lexington	187,500	$62.80	$11,775,000	$370,556	$12,145,556
Ft. Myers	0	$68.78	$0	$0	$0
Lake City	0	$62.80	$0	$0	$0

TOTAL ANNUAL VARIABLE OPERATING COST = $35,341,787

DISTRIBUTION SCHEDULE AND COST

Markets	Orlando	Atlanta	Lexington	Ft. Myers	Lake City	Total		Brand Demand	Surplus	Shadow Price	Range Decrease	Range Increase
Atlanta	0	70,106	19,073	0	0	89,179	>	89,179	0	$65.35	70,106	75,312
Birmingham	0	17,750	0	0	0	17,750	>	17,750	0	$70.66	17,750	75,312
Charleston	0	0	8,093	0	0	8,093	>	8,093	0	$66.36	8,093	19,073
Columbia	0	0	24,604	0	0	24,604	>	24,604	0	$67.37	24,604	19,703
Columbus	0	5,339	0	0	0	5,339	>	5,339	0	$83.31	5,339	75,312
Greens./W.S.	0	0	77,640	0	0	77,640	>	77,640	0	$65.40	70,106	19,073
Knoxville	0	0	19,316	0	0	19,316	>	19,316	0	$67.63	19,316	19,073
Miami	109,902	0	0	0	0	109,902	>	109,902	0	$76.31	874	19,073
Orlando	28,299	0	874	0	0	29,173	>	29,173	0	$72.63	874	19,073
Ral./Durham	0	0	37,900	0	0	37,900	>	37,900	0	$66.71	37,900	19,073
Savannah	0	6,493	0	0	0	6,493	>	6,493	0	$83.85	6,493	75,312
Tampa	86,799	0	0	0	0	86,799	>	86,799	0	$73.35	874	19,073
Total production volume	225,000	99,688	187,500	0	0							
Distribution cost	$615,435	$257,728	$370,556	$0	$0							

EXHIBIT S3 *Concluded*

PRODUCTION SCHEDULE/COST

	Produced		Capacity	Slack	Shadow Price	Range Decrease	Increase
Orlando	225,000	<	225,000	0	$3.19	19,073	874
Atlanta	99,688	<	175,000	75,312	$0.00	75,312	*********
Lexington	187,500	<	187,500	0	$1.94	19,073	70,106
Ft. Myers	0	<	0	0	$5.56	0	874
Lake City	0	<	0	0	$13.83	0	6,493

EXHIBIT S4 Cost-Minimization Solution for Case of 250,000-Volume Plant in Lake City; No Plant in Atlanta

COST SUMMARY

Plant	Production Volume	Per-Unit Variable Production Cost	Variable Production Cost	Distribution Cost	Total
Orlando	74,688	$68.78	$5,137,041	$324,146	$5,461,187
Atlanta	0	$68.69	$0	$0	$0
Lexington	187,500	$62.80	$11,775,000	$367,689	$12,142,689
Ft. Myers	0	$68.78	$0	$0	$0
Lake City	250,000	$62.80	$15,700,000	$1,072,964	$16,772,964

TOTAL ANNUAL VARIABLE OPERATING COST   = $34,376,840

DISTRIBUTION SCHEDULE AND COST

Markets	Plants					Total	Brand Demand	Surplus	Shacow Price	Range	
	Orlando	Atlanta	Lexington	Ft. Myers	Lake City					Decrease	Increase
Atlanta	0	0	19,974	0	69,232	89,179	89,179 >	0	$69.77	69,232	35,214
Birmingham	0	0	0	0	17,750	17,750	17,750 >	0	$70.49	17,750	35,214
Charleston	0	0	8,093	0	0	8,093	8,093 >	0	$68.78	8,093	19,947
Columbia	0	0	24,604	0	0	24,604	24,604 >	0	$67.79	24,604	19,947
Columbus	0	0	0	0	5,339	5,339	5,339 >	0	$94.02	5,339	35,214
Greens./W.S.	0	0	77,640	0	0	77,640	77,640 >	0	$65.82	69,232	19,947
Knoxville	0	0	19,316	0	0	19,316	19,316 >	0	$68.05	19,316	19,947
Miami	74,688	0	0	0	35,214	109,902	109,902 >	0	$73.12	74,688	150,312
Orlando	0	0	0	0	29,173	29,173	29,173 >	0	$68.78	29,173	35,214
Ral./Durham	0	0	37,900	0	0	37,900	37,900 >	0	$67.13	37,900	19,947
Savannah	0	0	0	0	6,493	6,493	6,493 >	0	$73.63	6,493	35,214
Tampa	0	0	0	0	86,799	86,799	86,799 >	0	$69.50	74,688	35,214
Total production volume	74,688	0	187,500	0	250,000	250,000					
Distribution cost	$324,146	$0	$367,689	$0	$1,072,964	$0 $1,072,964					

EXHIBIT S4 *Concluded*

PRODUCTION SCHEDULE/COST

	Produced		Capacity	Slack	Shadow Price	Range Decrease	Range Increase
Orlando	74,688	<	225,000	150,312	$0.00	150,312	*********
Atlanta	0	<	0	0	$10.71	0	5,339
Lexington	187,500	<	187,500	0	$2.36	19,974	69,232
Ft. Myers	0	<	0	0	$3.89	0	0
Lake City	250,000	<	250,000	0	$3.61	35,214	74,688

EXHIBIT S5   Annotated *What's Best!* Linear Programming Spreadsheet with Maximize Contribution Objective

	A	B	C	D	E	F	G	H
				Per-Unit				
			Per-Unit	Variable				
		Production	Selling	Production	Per-Unit	Total	Distrib.	
8	Plant	Volume	Price	Cost	Contrib.	Contrib.	Cost	Total
		-------	-------	-------	-------	-------	-------	-------
10	Orlando	+C37	$93.59	$68.78	+C10-D10	+B10*E10	+C39	+F10-G10
11	Atlanta	+D37	$95.93	$68.69	+C11-D11	+B11*E11	+D39	+F11-G11
12	Lexington	+E37	$94.61	$62.80	+C12-D12	+B12*E12	+E39	+F12-G12
13	Ft. Myers	+F37	$94.71	$68.78	+C13-D13	+B13*E13	+F39	+F13-G13
14	Lake City	+G37	$94.71	$62.80	+C14-D14	+B14*E14	+G39	+F14-G14

TOTAL ANNUAL CONTRIBUTION = @SUM(COL)

DISTRIBUTION SCHEDULE AND COST

Markets	Orlando	Atlanta	Lexington	Ft. Myers	Lake City	Total		Brand Demand	Surplus	Shadow Price	Decrease	Increase
Atlanta	0	0	0	0	0	@SUM(ROW)	<	89,179	+J24-H24	$0.00	0	0
Birmingham	0	0	0	0	0	@SUM(ROW)	<	17,750	+J25-H25	$0.00	0	0
Charleston	0	0	0	0	0	@SUM(ROW)	<	8,093	+J26-H26	$0.00	0	0
Columbia	0	0	0	0	0	@SUM(ROW)	<	24,604	+J27-H27	$0.00	0	0
Columbus	0	0	0	0	0	@SUM(ROW)	<	5,339	+J28-H28	$0.00	0	0
Greens./W.S.	0	0	0	0	0	@SUM(ROW)	<	77,640	+J29-H29	$0.00	0	0
Knoxville	0	0	0	0	0	@SUM(ROW)	<	19,316	+J30-H30	$0.00	0	0
Miami	0	0	0	0	0	@SUM(ROW)	<	109,902	+J31-H31	$0.00	0	0
Orlando	0	0	0	0	0	@SUM(ROW)	<	29,173	+J32-H32	$0.00	0	0
Ral./Durham	0	0	0	0	0	@SUM(ROW)	<	37,900	+J33-H33	$0.00	0	0
Savannah	0	0	0	0	0	@SUM(ROW)	<	6,493	+J34-H34	$0.00	0	0
Tampa	0	0	0	0	0	@SUM(ROW)	<	86,799	+J35-H35	$0.00	0	0
Production volume	@SUM(COL)	@SUM(COL)	@SUM(COL)	@SUM(COL)	@SUM(COL)	@SUM(COL)						
Distribution cost	TOTAL*	TOTAL	TOTAL	TOTAL	TOTAL	TOTAL						

Range is indicated by the header "Shadow ------Range------ Price Decrease Increase".

* +C24*C60+C25*C61+C26*C62+C27*C63+C28*C64+C29*C65+C30*C66+C31*C67+C32*C68+C33*C69+C34*C70+C35*C71

Exhibit S5 *Concluded*

	A	B	C	D	E	F	G	H
							Range	
		Produced		Capacity	Slack	Shadow Price	Decrease	Increase
43	PRODUCTION SCHEDULE/COST							
47								
48	Orlando	+C37	v	225,000	+D48-B48	$0.00	0	0
49	Atlanta	+D37	v	0	+D49-B49	$0.00	0	0
50	Lexington	+E37	v	187,500	+D50-B50	$0.00	0	0
51	Ft. Myers	+F37	v	0	+D51-B51	$0.00	0	0
52	Lake City	+G37	v	250,000	+D52-B52	$0.00	0	0

PER-UNIT DISTRIBUTION COSTS

MARKETS	Orlando	Atlanta	-----Plants----- Lexington	Ft. Myers	Lake City
Atlanta	$5.72	$0.66	$4.61	$8.62	$3.36
Birmingham	$6.45	$1.97	$6.58	$9.34	$4.08
Charleston	$5.53	$3.80	$3.62	$8.42	$3.16
Columbia	$6.18	$2.63	$2.63	$9.08	$3.82
Columbus	$56.85	$14.62	$74.71	$92.58	$27.61
Greensboro/W.S.	$7.89	$4.61	$0.66	$10.79	$5.53
Knoxville	$8.29	$2.54	$2.89	$11.18	$5.92
Miami	$4.34	$8.62	$12.24	$1.97	$6.71
Orlando	$0.66	$5.72	$7.89	$2.89	$2.37
Raleigh/Durham	$8.82	$4.89	$1.97	$11.71	$6.45
Savannah	$20.21	$15.16	$28.87	$36.09	$7.22
Tampa	$1.38	$5.92	$9.47	$1.58	$3.09

COST SUMMARY

Plant	Production Volume	Per-Unit Selling Price	Per-Unit Variable Production Cost	Per-Unit Contrib.	Total Contrib.	Distrib. Cost	Total
Orlando	69,349	$93.59	$68.78	$24.81	$1,720,549	$300,975	$1,419,574
Atlanta	0	$95.93	$68.69	$27.24	$0	$0	$0
Lexington	187,500	$94.61	$62.80	$31.81	$5,964,375	$367,689	$5,596,686
Ft. Myers	0	$94.71	$68.78	$25.93	$0	$0	$0
Lake City	250,000	$94.71	$62.80	$31.91	$7,977,500	$961,379	$7,016,121

TOTAL ANNUAL CONTRIBUTION = $14,032,381

DISTRIBUTION SCHEDULE AND COST

			-----Plants-----							-----Range-----	
Markets	Orlando	Atlanta	Lexington	Ft. Myers	Lake City	Total		Brand Demand	Surplus	Shadow Price	Decrease	Increase
Atlanta	0	0	19,974	0	69,232	89,179	<	89,179	0	$23.82	69,232	40,553
Birmingham	0	0	0	0	17,750	17,750	<	17,750	0	$23.10	17,750	40,553
Charleston	0	0	8,093	0	0	8,093	<	8,093	0	$24.81	8,093	19,947
Columbia	0	0	24,604	0	0	24,604	<	24,604	0	$25.80	24,604	19,947
Columbus	0	0	0	0	5,339	5,339	<	5,339	5,339	$0.00	5,339	*********
Greens./W.S.	0	0	77,640	0	0	77,640	<	77,640	0	$27.77	69,232	19,947
Knoxville	0	0	19,316	0	0	19,316	<	19,316	0	$25.54	19,316	19,947
Miami	69,349	0	0	0	40,553	109,902	<	109,902	0	$20.47	64,349	155,651
Orlando	0	0	0	0	29,173	29,173	<	29,173	0	$24.81	29,173	40,553
Ral./Durham	0	0	37,900	0	0	37,900	<	37,900	0	$26.46	37,900	19,947
Savannah	0	0	0	0	6,493	6,493	<	6,493	0	$19.96	6,493	40,553
Tampa	0	0	0	0	86,799	86,799	<	86,799	0	$24.09	69,349	40,553
Total production volume	69,349	0	187,500	0	250,000							
Distribution cost	$300,975	$0	$367,689	$0	$961,379							

EXHIBIT S6 *Concluded*

PRODUCTION SCHEDULE/COST

	Produced		Capacity	Slack	Shadow Price	Range Decrease	Increase
Orlando	69,349	<	225,000	155,651	$0.00	155,651	*********
Atlanta	0	<	0	0	$21.53	0	0
Lexington	187,500	<	187,500	0	$3.38	19,947	69,232
Ft. Myers	0	<	0	0	$5.01	0	0
Lake City	250,000	<	250,000	0	$4.73	40,553	69,349

In September 1976, William Jaeger, a member of the partnership that owned Freemark Abbey Winery, had to make a decision: should he harvest the Riesling grapes immediately or leave them on the vines despite the approaching storm? A storm just before the harvest is usually detrimental, often ruining the crop. A warm, light rain, however, will sometimes cause a beneficial mold, *botrytis cinerea*, to form on the grape skins. The result is a luscious, complex sweet wine, highly valued by connoisseurs.

The Winery

Freemark Abbey was located in St. Helena, California, in the northern Napa Valley. The winery produced only premium wines from the best grape varieties. Of the 25,000 cases of wine bottled each year (about the same as Chateau Lafite-Rothschild), most were Cabernet Sauvignon and Chardonnay. About 1,000 cases of Riesling and 500 cases of Petite Syrah were also bottled. (A case contains 12 bottles of wine.)

The Napa Valley extends for 30 miles, from Calistoga in the north to Napa in the south. The average temperature decreases as one moves south, closer to San Francisco Bay and the cold ocean waters. Freemark Abbey's grapes came from an ideal climate in the central and southern parts of the valley.

Winemaking

Wine is produced when the fruit sugar, which is naturally present in the juice of grapes, is converted by yeast, through fermentation, into approximately equal molecular quantities of alcohol and carbon dioxide. Sparkling wines excepted, the carbon dioxide is allowed to bubble up and dissipate. The wine then ages in barrels for one or more years until it is ready for bottling.

By various decisions during vinification—for example, the type of wooden barrel used for aging—the winemaker influences the style of wine produced. The style adopted by a particular winery depends mainly on the owners' preferences, though it is influenced by marketing considerations. Usually, as the grapes ripen, the sugar levels increase and the acidity levels decrease. The winemaker tries to harvest the grapes when they have achieved the proper balance of sugar and acidity for the style of wine sought. The ripening process is variable, however, and, if the weather is not favorable, the proper balance might never occur.

Several different styles of Riesling (more accurately, Johannisberg Riesling) are on the market. If the grapes are harvested at 20 percent sugar, the wine is fermented "dry" (all the sugar is converted to alcohol and carbon dioxide) or "near dry." The resulting wine, at about 10 percent alcohol, is light bodied. If the grapes are harvested at 25 percent sugar, the winemaker can produce a wine with the same 10 percent alcohol but with 5 percent residual sugar; this wine is sweet and relatively full bodied.

A third and rare style results when almost-ripe Riesling grapes are attacked by the *botrytis* mold. The skins of the grapes become porous, allowing water to evaporate while the sugar remains. Thus, the sugar concentration increases greatly, sometimes to 35 percent or more. The resulting wine, with about 11 percent alcohol and 13 percent residual sugar, has extraordinary concentration, and the *botrytis* itself adds to the wine's complexity. Freemark Abbey had already produced a *botrytised* Riesling from its 1973 vintage.

Jaeger's Decision Problem

From the weather reports, Jaeger concluded that there was a 50-50 chance that the rainstorm would hit the Napa Valley. Since the storm had originated over the warm waters off Mexico, he thought there was a 40 percent chance that, if the storm did strike, it would lead to the development of the *botrytis* mold. If the *botrytis* did not form, however, the rainwater, which would be absorbed into the grapes through the roots of the vines, would merely swell the berries by 5–10 percent, decreasing their concentration. This would yield a thin wine that would sell wholesale for only about $2.00 per bottle, about $0.85 less than Jaeger could obtain by harvesting the not-quite-ripe grapes immediately and eliminating the risk. Freemark Abbey always had the option of not bottling a wine that was not up to standards. It could sell the wine in bulk, or it could sell the grapes directly. These options would bring only half as much revenue, but would at least avoid damaging the winery's reputation, which would be risked by bottling an inferior product.

If Jaeger decided not to harvest the grapes immediately in anticipation of the storm, and the storm did not strike, Jaeger would probably leave the grapes to ripen more fully. With luck, the grapes would reach 25 percent sugar, resulting in a wine selling for around $3.50 wholesale. Even with less-favorable weather, the sugar levels would probably top 20 percent, yielding a lighter wine selling at around $3. Jaeger thought these possibilities were equally likely. In the past, sugar levels occasionally failed to rise above 19 percent. Moreover, while waiting for sugar levels to rise, the acidity levels must also be monitored. When the acidity drops below about 0.7 percent, the grapes must be harvested whatever the sugar level. If this happened, the wine would be priced at only about $2.50. Jaeger felt that this event had only about 0.2 probability.

EXHIBIT 1

Winery label.

The wholesale price for a *botrytised* Riesling would be about $8 per bottle. Unfortunately, the same process that resulted in increased sugar concentration also caused a 30 percent reduction in the total juice. The higher price was, therefore, partly offset by a reduction in quantity. Although fewer bottles would be produced, there would be essentially no savings in vinification costs. The costs to the winery were about the same for each of the possible styles of wine and were small relative to the wholesale price.

CASE 22
GALAXY MICRO SYSTEMS

For the past three months, Taylor Jansen of Galaxy Micro Systems had been discussing with a national computer sales-and-service franchiser the subcontracting of the warranty contract for the new Galaxy work station, the GMS-II. In addition to featuring an advanced technology chip and a state-of-the-art processor, the GMS-II would be sold with a three-year warranty that included parts and labor. Galaxy had decided to subcontract the service support for the warranty, rather than expand its regional offices to include a technical support staff. As the GMS-II project manager, Jansen had moved contract discussions to a point where the specification of the terms and conditions of the warranty contract were acceptable to both parties, but the pricing of the contract was undecided.

At a recent meeting, the franchiser's negotiating team had proposed to Jansen the choice of two pricing schemes for the warranty of those units installed during the introductory year. The first approach was a fixed-price contract with a lump-sum payment of $770,000 due on May 1, 1993, the planned date for the introduction of the GMS-II. Alternatively, the price could be a function of the number of units installed during the introductory year, and payments would be spread over three years. The specific terms would be $70,000 payable on May 1, 1993, plus three annual installments of $80 per unit for those units installed during the introductory year, May 1, 1993, to April 30, 1994. The annual installments were subject to a minimum of $250,000 and were payable on the first of May of 1994, 1995, and 1996. For either alternative, a new contract would be negotiated for sales occurring after the introductory year.

For the services to be rendered by the franchiser, both proposals seemed reasonable to Jansen and compatible with the negotiating limits specified by Galaxy senior management. The choice between the alternatives, however, was difficult. The deferred-payment schedule of the installment contract was a real advantage in light of Galaxy's hurdle rate of 18 percent. Offsetting that advantage, however, was the sense that the installment contract was riskier than the fixed-price contract, because first-year sales of the GMS-II were very uncertain.

During the introductory year, GMS-II sales would come from two sources: (1) the successful closure by senior management of an extraordinarily large purchase by a single customer and (2) the efforts of the Galaxy regional offices. Unfortunately, Jansen was uncertain about the final results of both sources.

The potentially large purchase would be from a long-standing customer that had been provided, as part of the development effort, a prototype version of the GMS-II. The initial feedback from this firm had been quite positive, and a purchase of 1,500 units was mentioned. Galaxy senior management had aggressively pursued this opportunity. They had confirmed the size of the potential order but believed that the firm was still months away from a final commitment, even though the prototype had already been under evaluation for six months. The delay in the decision made the Galaxy management nervous; current sentiment put the chances of closing the deal at about 60 percent. This major purchase was pivotal to the successful launch of GMS-II. Not only was it a significant order, but it could also be used by the sales force in discussions with smaller clients as testimony to the "recognized advantages of the GMS-II work station."

In addition to the potential 1,500-unit purchase by the long-standing client, Jansen estimated that first-year sales of the GMS-II from the efforts of the regional offices would be 3,000 units. She recognized that this figure was only a "best guess" and that actual sales would be in a range around this figure. If the major purchase were landed, she believed that the range would be skewed to the high side. She feared that, without the big purchase, not only would the range be skewed to the low side, but also her best guess would also have to be revised downward. In a rough-cut fashion, the following outcomes and their respective probabilities captured Jansen's assessment of sales from the regional offices during the introductory year of the GMS-II.

Sales by Regional Offices			
If Major Purchase		**If No Major Purchase**	
Sales	*Probability*	*Sales*	*Probability*
2,000	0.2	1,000	0.4
3,000	0.4	2,500	0.4
4,500	0.4	4,000	0.2

The pricing issue had to be resolved expeditiously, because deadlines were approaching. The final text of the promotional literature was due at the printers in a week, and the public introduction of the GMS-II was only two months away.

CASE 23
GALAXY MICRO SYSTEMS SUPPLEMENT

Taylor Jansen, after reviewing her assessment of GMS-II sales from the regional offices, felt uneasy about the forecast's simplicity. Focusing on three possible outcomes did not seem to capture adequately the possibility that sales could be anywhere within a range of values and that the extremes of the range could be beyond the high and low figures of her forecasts. In addition, the three outcomes were given extraordinary weight in the decision, even though they were just a few among many possible outcomes.

The Galaxy planning system required that sales forecasts be made in the form of cumulative distribution functions, using the terminology below to describe the 0.05, 0.25, 0.50, 0.75, and 0.95 fractiles. Jansen saw this forecasting format as a means to address her concerns with her rough-cut forecast. The resulting forecasts were:

Sales by Regional Offices

	If Major Purchase	*If No Major Purchase*
1 in 20 low	1,900	500
1 in 4 low	2,500	1,500
Midrange	3,000	2,300
1 in 4 high	4,000	3,000
1 in 20 high	5,500	4,000

CASE 24
GEORGE'S T-SHIRTS

For the last six years, George Lassiter, a project engineer for a major defense contractor, had enjoyed an interesting and lucrative side business—designing, manufacturing, and hawking "special event" T-shirts. He had created shirts for a variety of rock concerts, major sporting events, and special fund-raising events. Although his T-shirts were not endorsed by the event sponsors and were not allowed to be sold within the arenas at which the events were held, they were cleverly designed, well produced, and reasonably priced (relative to the official shirts). They were sold in the streets surrounding the arenas and in the nearby parking lots, always with the appropriate licenses from the local authorities. Lassiter had a regular crew of vendors to whom he sold the shirts on consignment for $100 per dozen. These vendors then offered the shirts to the public at $10 apiece.

A steady stream of T-shirt business came to Lassiter, and he was generally working on several designs in various stages of development. His current problem centered around the number of shirts he should have stenciled for a rock concert that was scheduled to be staged in two months.

This concert was almost certain to be a huge success. Lassiter had no doubt that the 20,000 tickets for the standing area around the stage would be instantly bought by the group's devoted fans. The major unknown was the number of grandstand seats that would be sold. It could be anywhere from a few thousand to more than double the number of standing tickets. Given the popularity of the performing group and the intensity of the advance hype, Lassiter believed the grandstand sales were more likely to be at the high, rather than the low, end of the spectrum. He decided to think in terms of three possibilities (a high, a medium, and a low value), specifically, 80,000, 50,000, and 20,000 grandstand seats. Despite his optimism, he believed that 50,000 was as likely as either of the other two possibilities combined. The two extreme numbers were about equally likely; maybe 80,000 was a little more likely than 20,000.

A second unknown was the percentage of the attendees who would buy one of his shirts. To the credit of his designs and the quality of the shirts, the number generally (about 6 times out of 10) ran about 10 percent of the attendance, but sometimes it was in the range of 5 percent. On a rare occasion, sales would be in the vicinity of 15 percent (maybe 1 time out of 10, if Lassiter's memory served him right).

Several weeks ago, Lassiter had requested a cost estimate for this concert's design from the silk screener/shirt supply house with which he had been working for several years. He used this particular firm almost exclusively because he had found it to be reliable in both quality and schedule and to have reasonable prices. The estimate had arrived yesterday. It was presented in the usual batches of 2,500 shirts with the usual volume discounts:

Order Size	Cost
10,000	$32,125
7,500	$25,250
5,000	$17,750

The order had to be one of the quoted multiples of 2,500 shirts.

On the basis of his volume estimates, Lassiter was prepared to place an order for 5,000 shirts. With his sales generally about 10 percent of attendance, he didn't believe he could justify an order for 7,500 shirts. Such an order would require the concert's attendance to be 75,000, and while he was optimistic about the popularity of the event, he wasn't quite that optimistic. Also, in the past, he had taken the conservative route and it had served him well. He had never had an appreciable number of shirts left over, but those that were left were sold to a discount clothing chain for $1.50 per shirt.

CASE 25
HARIMANN INTERNATIONAL

My first impression was that the Pioneer order would be a very attractive opportunity so late in the season. Not only would I be supporting an old and established customer, but the order would be profitable and the unexpected business would permit me to keep some of my workers on the payroll during the early portion of the off-season. These small gestures often pay handsome rewards in future years. But that April 6 deadline to ship the goods seems terribly close. If I accept the order and miss the date, I could be left with a substantial amount of finished goods that would be impossible to move at this time of the year. I have squeezed the production schedule as far as possible, and I don't know what else I can do. Do you think I should turn down the order?

> Vikram Dhawan
> President, Harimann International
> March 2, 1992

Harimann International was a Delhi-based manufacturer and exporter of finished textiles (primarily table linens and women's clothing) with sales in excess of 10 million Indian new rupees (INR). The company was launched in May 1990 by Vikram Dhawan after his graduation with a bachelor of arts degree in mathematics from St. Stephen's College. In addition to providing a livelihood in the short term, the business was to be a stepping-stone to an MBA in the United States. Dhawan believed that the experience of managing a small company would be of invaluable assistance during the MBA program and hoped that the profits from a successful business would provide the necessary funds to finance the education.

Dhawan's decision to be an exporter of finished goods was influenced by the variety of incentives the Indian government offered in an effort to reduce the country's international trade deficit. Whenever goods were exported to one of several targeted countries, any profits from the sale were accorded tax-exempt status. In addition, if the order resulted in payments in excess of 150,000 INR, several other attractive incentives applied, including a partial rebate of duties paid for imported raw materials used in the manufacture of exported goods (duty drawback), a cash incentive designed to improve the competitiveness of Indian products in world markets (cash compensatory support), and the granting of licenses to replenish domestic raw materials used in the production of exported goods (replenishment licenses).

During the first year of operations, Dhawan limited his business to brokering linen household goods. He bought finished linens from a supplier, labeled and packaged them according to customer specifications, and shipped the packaged

This case was prepared in conjunction with Professor Dana R. Clyman (Darden) and Research Assistant Hasmeeth S. Uppal (Darden).

goods to the customer. The first nine months were slow: Customers were few and orders were small. Toward the end of the year, however, a particular style of hand-embroidered table linen became very popular and sales were excellent. On the strength of this product, it appeared that the goal for first-year sales would be achieved. Unfortunately, Dhawan's sources could not keep up with demand, and sales were lost. The frustration of being unable to satisfy customer demand led Dhawan to enlarge the scope of his business and to become directly involved in manufacturing.

In May 1991, Dhawan added women's blouses and skirts to his product line in response to requests by satisfied customers. Thereafter, the business grew quickly. Over the remaining months of 1991, shipments were made to Canada, France, Great Britain, Italy, Japan, and the United States. Over the final few months of the year—Harimann's peak season—internal production had averaged 1,000 garments per day. The company had recently acquired a second manufacturing facility and now employed over 100 people.

Pioneer Trading Company, Ltd.

The Pioneer Trading Company was one of Dhawan's first customers and had been a regular customer ever since. Pioneer was a large importer with over 20 retail outlets in Japan. It sourced many of its goods from India and Hong Kong to spread political risks and to encourage competitive pricing.

Over the years, Mori Fuji, the founder and president of Pioneer, had emphasized that his interests were "quality goods delivered on time at reasonable prices." Dhawan believed that Fuji had been fair in all of their previous transactions. Although Fuji looked after himself, he never did so at the expense of his suppliers, and he made special efforts to help his suppliers meet his expectations. For example, instructions for the labels and hang tags that were to be attached to the garments were not only detailed, they were pictographic. This practice greatly reduced the chance of error in printing the labels in Japanese and in meeting the specifications of the applicable laws. This attention to detail not only benefited Pioneer and its suppliers but was appreciated as well.

The Pioneer Order

Discussions regarding the most recent order from Pioneer began at the end of January 1992, when Dhawan received Pioneer's request for samples of six styles of garments along with a preliminary order should the samples and prices prove satisfactory. The samples were prepared within a week and sent by courier, with their respective prices. Because the cloth vendors were moving into their off-season, to be sure of the availability of material, Dhawan ordered all of the necessary fabric, lining, and zippers for Pioneer's order at this time. He reasoned that the investment of 188,400 INR was not really significant because, even though embroidered cloth could only be sold for about 65 percent of cost, unembroidered cloth and the other materials could always be resold for 90 percent of their respective costs.

EXHIBIT 1 Pioneer Profit Analysis (figures in INR)

	Style E 1756	Style E 1757	Style E 1758	Style E 1759	Style E 1760	Style E 1761	Total
Unit costs							
Materials:							
Grey cloth	18.75	22.50	14.25	36.00	17.00	21.00	
Lining cloth	6.75			11.25			
Zipper	7.00			7.00			
Processing:							
Bleaching	4.75	5.00	4.50	5.75	4.00	5.00	
Embroidery	19.50			50.00	22.00		
Cutting/sewing	9.00	5.25	5.50	13.00	8.00	7.50	
Washing/packing	5.00	5.00	5.00	5.00	5.00	5.00	
Other direct costs	7.00	5.00	5.00	12.00	5.00	6.00	
Total unit cost	77.75	42.75	34.25	140.00	61.00	44.50	
Contract							
Quantity	1,000	1,400	1,400	1,000	1,100	1,500	
Selling price (per unit) . . .	82.75	47.75	38.25	146.00	65.00	48.50	
Revenue	82,750	66,850	53,550	146,000	71,500	72,750	493,400
Materials cost	32,500	31,500	19,950	54,250	18,700	31,500	188,400
Processing cost	38,250	21,350	21,000	73,750	42,900	26,250	223,500
Other direct costs	7,000	7,000	7,000	12,000	5,500	9,000	47,500
Total cost	77,750	59,850	47,950	140,000	67,100	66,750	459,400
Contribution*	5,000	7,000	5,600	6,000	4,400	6,000	34,000
Government Incentives†							281,238
Total value							315,238

* Because Japan was one of the qualifying countries, no taxes were assessed.

† Because Japan was one of the qualifying countries and because the revenues received would exceed 150,000 INR, the order qualified for the government incentives (duty drawback 10 percent, cash compensatory support 15 percent, and replenishment licenses with a 40 percent face value, which Dhawan valued at 80 percent of face value). In total, these incentives were valued at 57 percent of revenues received.

Several weeks later, Dhawan received the order from Pioneer for all six styles, conditional on Harimann's ability to make minor changes to three of the styles and to meet a shipping date of April 6.

Although he was somewhat concerned about meeting the April 6 shipping date, Dhawan thought that the order was an attractive opportunity. The Indian government was encouraging exports to Japan, and, as a result, the profits from the Pioneer contract would be tax-free. (See Exhibit 1 for Dhawan's profit analysis of the contract.) More important, however, because receipts would exceed the qualifying minimum of 150,000 INR, the contract would also qualify for the other government incentives. Thus, Dhawan would be able to claim 10 percent of the actual receipts in duty drawback and 15 percent in cash compensatory support. Each of these incentives would be paid in cash by the Indian government. In addition, Dhawan would also qualify for a replenishment license with a face value of 40 percent of actual receipts. Although replenishment licenses were not cash instruments, they were very liquid assets due to an informal yet well-established market. Prices for these licenses were relatively stable at 80 percent of face value. Because Dhawan had no direct need for the licenses, he routinely sold any he received in this market. As a result, Dhawan valued the total package of government incentives at 57 percent of revenue, which in this case amounted to 281,238 INR, as shown in Exhibit 1.

Dhawan was inclined to accept the order, not only because it was profitable but also because it would allow him to keep many of his employees on the payroll longer than he had anticipated. Since the Pioneer order was being placed late in the manufacturing season, Dhawan would be able to delay the planned furlough of many of his manufacturing-plant workers. An extra week or two of work would be greatly appreciated by most of them.

The Schedule

Dhawan was nervous about the production schedule, however, particularly because the first step of the process—embroidery—would be contracted out to a third-party vendor. (The rest of the production process would be carried out in-house.) If production began on the morning of March 3, the date on which the embroiderer said that he could begin work, Harimann would have to complete the order within 35 days to meet Pioneer's April 6 shipment deadline. Dhawan estimated that, with considerable personal attention, the order could be completed and shipped within 27 days (by the end of the day, March 29). This estimate allowed the eight days required by the embroider, two days for cutting, eight days for sewing, eight days for washing and packing, and one day for final shipping activities. Although the cloth that was not to be embroidered would have to be bleached, this process would not influence the schedule, because bleaching (which would take five days) would be done in parallel with embroidery. Exhibit 2 presents Dhawan's proposed schedule pictorially.

In all, the benefits of accepting the order seemed to outweigh the difficulties of meeting the schedule. Nevertheless, Dhawan, hoping to arrange for extra time in case any unanticipated problems arose, faxed Pioneer a confirmation of the order on the condition that the shipment date be postponed to April 17. Pioneer's response was immediate: April 6 was preferred, and would Dhawan please confirm that it would indeed be possible for him to meet that date.

Pioneer's response prompted Dhawan to look again at the schedule. Although he was fairly confident that he would be able to ship the order by April 6, he admitted to himself that there was a possibility of missing that date. In fact, he knew that unanticipated problems arose fairly regularly in this business, and in this case he estimated there was a 20 percent chance some problem would arise that caused him to miss the date. In the event that the shipping date was missed, Pioneer would probably still accept the order but—in keeping with industry

---
EXHIBIT 2   Proposed Schedule

	March															April		
	3	5	7	9	11	13	15	17	19	21	23	25	27	29	31	2	4	6
Activity																		
Embroidery	▬	▬	▬	▬														
Bleaching	▬	▬	▬															
Cutting				▬														
Sewing						▬	▬	▬	▬	▬								
Washing & packing											▬	▬	▬	▬	▬			
Shipping															▬			

---

practice—only at a greatly reduced price. Generally, a buyer would pay 30 to 50 percent of the contract price for a late shipment, though in some circumstances payment had been as little as 20 percent. Even though the relationship with Pioneer was a good one, it was late in Pioneer's season and, as a result, a 20 percent payment was a definite possibility. In this particular case, Dhawan believed there was a 40 percent chance that Pioneer would pay 50 percent of the contracted price, a 40 percent chance it would pay only 30 percent, and a 20 percent chance it would pay as little as 20 percent. What's more, Dhawan knew that once he accepted the order, he would have to deliver the goods to protect his future business relationship with Pioneer, even if that meant incurring a loss.

Before deciding whether to accept the order, Dhawan explicitly considered the possibility of a late delivery and each of the possible percentages that might be applied to the contracted price to reduce the payment should the order be late. After weighing all of these possibilities and their chances of occurring, Dhawan concluded that the order would still be profitable, on average. On the basis of this analysis, which is presented in Exhibit 3, Dhawan was inclined to accept the order.

The Embroiderer

Prior to faxing back his confirmation of the order, Dhawan called the embroiderer to confirm the schedule. To his dismay, the embroiderer was no longer willing to confirm the schedule he had originally proposed. The original commitment had been made on the basis of starting the Harimann job on March 3, just as soon as the embroiderer's current job was completed; this start date would have permitted completion of embroidery on March 10. Unfortunately, since they had last spoken, the embroiderer had accepted several other important jobs, and the Harimann order would have to take its place behind them. The embroiderer was apologetic, but he would only commit to completing the order by March 27.

EXHIBIT 3   Dhawan's Analysis (figures in INR)

On-Time Delivery
(chance of occurring, 80%)

Receipts	493,400
Costs	459,400
Contribution	34,000
Government incentives*	281,238
Total value	315,238

Late Delivery
(chance of occurring, 20%)

Average percent payment†	36%
Average receipts‡	177,624
Costs	459,400
Contribution	(281,776)
Government incentives*	101,246
Total value	(180,530)

Average Value

$$315,238 \times 0.80 + (180,530) \times 0.20 = 216,084$$

---

* When receipts exceed 150,000 INR, government incentives apply and Dhawan values them at 57 percent of receipts.

† Average percent payment: 50 percent $\times$ 0.40 + 30 percent $\times$ 0.40 + 20 percent $\times$ 0.20 = 36 percent.

‡ Average receipts: 493,000 $\times$ 36 percent = 177,624.

Dhawan was outraged by the change and argued strongly for the original timetable. Because the embroiderer agreed that he would reexamine his schedule, Dhawan believed that he had made some progress, but he remained pessimistic. By the end of the conversation, Dhawan believed there was about a one in eight chance that the embroiderer would adjust his schedule and complete the Harimann order by the original date of March 10. The discussions, however, had also enabled Dhawan to piece together the vendor's production schedule and discover that it would be possible for the embroiderer to complete the Harimann job on March 20. When Dhawan raised this possibility, the vendor agreed that this was possible and that he would try to make it happen, but he did not commit. Based on this part of the conversation, Dhawan believed that he was four times as likely to receive the goods on March 20 as on March 10.

Although Dhawan made clear to the embroidery vendor that he was infuriated by the vendor's behavior, he had no other choices. Only 8 to 10 firms in all of India embroidered cloth. This oligopolistic condition encouraged exploitation by vendors, who made production decisions on the basis of the profitability of the order and the extent to which the customer could be delayed before the order would be canceled. The current situation was even worse than usual because it was near the end of the season and all of the other embroiderers' schedules were

EXHIBIT 4   **Revised Schedule (assuming a March 20 embroidery delivery date)**

	March													April		
	3	5	7	9	11	13	15	17	19	21	23	25	27	29	31	2	4	6

Activity
Embroidery
Bleaching
Cutting
Sewing
Washing & packing
Shipping

full. Dhawan would have to live with the possibility of a March 27 completion date.

The Schedule Revisited

The potential delay in embroidery prompted Dhawan to look even more closely at his own operations for ways to reduce his production schedule. His initial thinking had been very sequential—cut, then sew, then wash and pack, and finally ship. This sequence allowed the batches to remain intact and, as a result, required far less management attention to control than a schedule that broke up the batches. In light of the schedule demands, however, the Pioneer order would have to be treated differently. Even though two days would be needed to complete the cutting, sewing could begin after the first day's cutting. Similarly, washing and packing could begin before all of the sewing was completed, thereby saving an additional three, or possibly even five, days.

Dhawan was encouraged. At no extra cost, the parallel processing of the Pioneer order could reduce production time from 19 days to 15 or maybe even 13 days, if everything went smoothly. These time savings would allow him to ship the order just before the April 6 deadline, even if he did not receive the embroidered cloth until the evening of March 20, as shown by the revised schedule in Exhibit 4.

If a problem arose during parallel processing, however, the usual control systems might not identify it. Dhawan believed that, if such a problem arose, by the time it was all sorted out, his in-house production time for cutting, sewing, washing and packing, and shipping could take anywhere from 20 to 22 days to complete. Furthermore, because he had never before attempted to control such a complicated operating process, Dhawan believed that the chance of such a problem arising had to be about 40 percent, twice the rate at which problems normally arose when processing was sequential.

CASE 26
HIGHTOWER DEPARTMENT STORES: IMPORTED STUFFED ANIMALS

On the morning of January 17, 1993, Julia Brown gathered together the past sales data on stuffed animals. As toy buyer for the chain of Hightower Department Stores, she knew that a careful review of the performance of the various models of stuffed animals sold during 1992 was necessary prior to her annual round-the-world buying trip in late January.

During this trip she would be buying all the imported toys that the Hightower chain would carry during the 1993 Christmas season. In particular, she would choose approximately 15 different types of bears, raccoons, elephants, and so on from the stuffed animals offered by various manufacturers in West Germany. These choices would be made after viewing what each manufacturer had to offer and then considering the overall attractiveness of this menagerie. She often made the decisions fairly quickly, using the sound judgment she had gained through her many years of buying experience.

Julia knew that her major purchase would be Steiff stuffed teddy bears, which Hightower had carried almost every year since they were first manufactured in Germany in 1903. She also had had experience with other stuffed-animal manufacturers and planned to reorder with them. But in choosing the last few animals for her assortment, Julia sometimes hedged her bets by ordering a minimum quantity of new models to test their sales potential. These test models were sold in only one store within the chain, and the results of the sales were then used to decide the fate of each animal for the succeeding year.

Julia was preparing to go over the test sales data for the three models tested in 1992: a bear, a pig, and a raccoon. A description of these models and the sales results are given in Exhibit 1. At first glance, the raccoon results looked very promising. Julia tentatively decided she would go with it for 1993 but knew she still needed to determine what quantity to order. In contrast, the pig had turned out to be a real "dog," and Julia was ready to admit that her attraction to this model on last year's trip may have been a mistake. Last, deciding whether to order the bear was one of those tough choices Julia had to make quite often. Although the test market had indeed succeeded in separating the raccoon from the pig, it had done nothing to help determine the future success of the bear.

Hightower Department Stores

The Hightower chain was a small but profitable company operating 16 full-line department stores in six major metropolitan areas in the eastern United States. The Hightower name was associated with quality, large selection, and good

---

EXHIBIT 1   1992 Test Animals

Animal	Description	Landed Cost*	Retail Price	Sales Proj.[†]	Purchases	Sales	Closeout Inventory
Bear	Dark brown, long nose, 12 inches, handmade, plush	$5.43	$12.95	150	50	10	40
Pig	Cartoon-like, pink, 10 inches, soft plastic handmade	$6.23	$13.95	180	50	4	46
Raccoon	Grey/black, 14 inches, plush, realistic, handmade	$6.42	$13.95	170	50	32	18

* Total cost per unit; includes manufacturer's cost, shipping, import duties, and insurance.

[†] During her January 1992 buying trip, Julia Brown projected these holiday-season unit sales volumes based on all stores.

value. The company envisioned itself as a fashion leader; it took special pride in its ability to respond quickly to changes in fashion and style. Management also emphasized that TV and newspaper advertising, point-of-sale presentations, and knowledgeable and friendly sales personnel had been important to the success of the chain.

For the fiscal year ending January 31, 1992, the Hightower chain had reported $371 million in sales and $17.5 million net profit after taxes (see Exhibit 2). The expectations for the 1993 fiscal year were for small increases over 1992, but, as in previous years, these increases would not keep up with the general inflation rate.

Toy Department

Buying toys that could be sold at a profit had been an increasingly difficult challenge for Julia Brown and department stores in general. Toy departments were typically not so profitable as other store departments. Competition from general merchandise chains, mass merchandisers, variety stores, toy supermarkets, and toy specialty stores had lowered conventional department store toy sales to about 9 percent of the total market. The department stores' need for high margins made it difficult for them to compete in the toy business. Whereas the Hightower chain looked for margins of 40 to 50 percent, specialty toy chains such as Toys R Us operated with only 30 percent margins for most merchandise.

EXHIBIT 2 **Store Sizes and Sales Volume (year ending January 31, 1992)**

Store	Size (thousand square feet)	Sales Volume ($ millions)
Washington, D.C.		
Downtown	370	$36.7
Prince George's Plaza, Md.	182	22.2
Columbia, Md.	150	19.7
Tysons Corner, Va.	205	26.8
Boston		
Downtown	361	34.0
Burlington Mall	104	14.4
South Side Plaza	139	18.3
Philadelphia		
Downtown	369	32.8
King of Prussia	145	17.7
Cherry Hill, N.J.	105	12.3
Baltimore		
Downtown	320	27.4
Towson	139	17.0
Golden Ring	107	12.4
Pittsburgh		
Downtown	420	39.2
Monroeville	150	18.3
Westmoreland Mall	171	21.6
Total	3,437	$370.8

Julia Brown had developed the following strategies to help cope with the increasing competition:

1. Deemphasizing TV-promoted toys—the high-demand, lower-margin toy category.
2. Excelling in areas that mass merchants could not, such as special events, displays, and demonstrations.
3. Emphasizing imported items and exclusive items not available elsewhere.
4. Varying the amount of floor space devoted to toys; in many department stores, toy floor space tripled during the Christmas season.
5. Developing the "grandmother" business—that is, stocking toys often purchased by grandmothers, who tended to shop in department stores and usually were not as concerned about price as other toy buyers.

As a consequence of these strategies, about one-half of Hightower's toy business was imports, compared with probably less than 20 percent for the mass merchandisers and toy supermarkets.

EXHIBIT 3 Stuffed-Animal Performance History: Christmas-Season Sales

Year	1988	1989	1990	1991	1992*
Unit sales	5,932	5,837	5,879	6,025	5,983
Dollar sales (thousands)	52.7	58.0	63.9	66.8	68.5
Gross margin† (thousands)	25.0	26.2	26.8	31.0	31.5

*Preliminary figures.

†Retail sales plus end-of-year closeout minus landed cost.

EXHIBIT 4 Performance Statistics (year ending January 31, 1992)

	Toy Departments	Total Stores
Net sales percentage change from last year	2.8%	4.7%
Cumulative mark-on	41.3%	47.5%
Mark-downs (total price reductions from original retail—as a percentage of net overall sales)	13.3%	11.6%
Stock shortage (lost merchandise from theft, unrecorded mark-downs, and so on—as a percentage of sales)	2.2%	2.6%
Gross margin	30.8%	43.4%
Gross margin return on inventory cost (gross margin/ average inventory)	$1.40	$2.60
Stock turns	3.2×	3.4×
Sales per square foot	$86.00	$108.00

In almost all types of stores, nearly 50 percent of the toy sales occurred in November and December each year. Data on sales and gross margins for November and December of the last five years for Hightower's stuffed animals are given in Exhibit 3. Although the margin figures appeared considerably higher than those for the toy department in general, Julia knew that, when the total year was considered, stuffed animals performed only slightly better than average.

Figures for 1991 (see Exhibit 4) showed that the Hightower toy department's performance was like other department stores. The two figures Brown paid particular attention to were gross margin return on investment (inventory) and sales per square foot. Gross margin return on investment was calculated as the ratio of gross margin (sales minus cost of goods sold) to average inventory at cost. Sales per square foot was relevant, because it specifically considered the amount of selling space consumed to produce a given dollar of sales volume.

Stuffed animals occupied about 20 square feet of display space in each store during the Christmas season, compared with 5 square feet at all other times. The nature of the display varied somewhat from one year to the next, but the animals were always exhibited together in a single display. Anywhere from 15 to 20 different animals were available in a given year.

Imported stuffed animals were items consistent with Brown's merchandising strategy. They carried relatively high margins, responded well to creative display efforts and to advertising, and appealed to the grandmother business. If carefully chosen, they could be distinctive Hightower department store items; in most cases a particular imported animal would be exclusive to the Hightower chain.

Imported stuffed animals were carried only through the Christmas season. In January unsold inventory was unloaded at 80 cents on the dollar[1] to Fernstone's, a job-lot retailer. This policy had been instituted to clear out year-end inventories in preparation for the cut-back in display space allocated to toys. Brown felt this alternative was preferable either to marking the merchandise down for the year-end sale or storing unsold animals until the next season. Marking down items hurt the Hightower image, and carrying inventory until the next year was costly and greatly interfered with the selection of new animals for the succeeding year. The higher-valued imports were thus always sold before fiscal year-end, and the small selection carried in the off-season consisted entirely of domestic products.

Imported Toy Buying

Each January a number of buyers from the Hightower Department Stores chain went on round-the-world buying trips to select and order merchandise Hightower would offer during the fall and Christmas seasons. Since most foreign manufacturers operated on a make-to-order basis, lead times ranged from six to eight months. Hence, a January trip was necessary to ensure deliveries in time for the next Christmas selling season.

Julia Brown had bought toys for 15 years and had been on 10 previous Hightower foreign buying trips. This large base of experience served her well when evaluating new items. Her usual procedure was to decide a retail price and project a sales volume for each item of interest. If these projections were particularly encouraging, Julia would then place an order on the spot, using a very rough rule of thumb to determine exactly how many to order.

For the riskier items, she would try to buy test models for possible inclusion in the succeeding year's line of toys. Specific offerings changed greatly from one year to the next; but Julia was often able to persuade some of the smaller manufacturers to provide a small lot in one year, with a promise that the same item would be manufactured the next.

---

[1]Sold at 80 percent of the landed cost. *Landed cost* included all costs associated with buying an imported item: manufacturer's cost, freight, import duties, and so on.

Terms for the purchase of European-manufactured toys were delivery net 30. Payment was due within 30 days of delivery, and the purchaser was responsible for import duties, freight, insurance, and so forth.

The buying procedure for stuffed animals differed slightly from that used with other toy merchandise. Because the stuffed-animal manufacturers were concentrated in West Germany, Julia was able to visit each in turn before placing any orders. At the end of these visits, Julia determined her desired stuffed-animal merchandise assortment for the following season. In this manner she was able to judge each item relative to the others available that year.

This buying strategy necessitated a careful system of note-taking and evaluation. For each animal of interest, Julia filled out a form she had personally developed. The completed form contained a description of the animal, information on the manufacturer, the manufacturer's price (in U.S. dollars), and estimated landed costs. In addition, Julia usually jotted down her evaluation of the salability of the animal, the features that differentiated this item, and any other information that might make her order-writing easier.

Two quantitative judgments also included were the retail price Julia thought the animal should carry and a projected sales potential at that price. Mark-ups on stuffed animals were customarily at least 50 percent over landed cost, and Julia set the retail price based on her feel for the appeal and price sensitivity of a particular animal. To round out her notes, Julia would then estimate the unit sales to expect if this animal was placed in the Hightower chain for the Christmas season.

Test Market

Each year Julia selected up to three imported animals as test models, which she bought in small lots of 50 units, the customary minimum order accepted by the German manufacturers. They were then sold exclusively in the Tysons Corner, Virginia, store (chosen as a representative Hightower store because of its size, sales volume, and consumer profile).

Once purchased, the test animals were treated like the other imported items. To avoid complications associated with the test, each test animal replaced a similar nontest animal. Thus the total number of animals was the same at the test store as at all other stores. Likewise, the display space per animal was not affected by the test.

Over the past 10 years, 20 different animals had been tested. Eighteen of these had been adopted for the succeeding year, and data were available on resulting total sales. The two animals not chosen were a rabbit in 1984 and a skunk in 1988, because both had very poor sales during their test years. Exhibit 5 contains the relevant information on these 20 test animals, including the projected sales volume Julia had estimated on her first exposure to each item. When a test animal was adopted as a regular the next year, it was offered at all 16 stores (the Tysons Corner store included) at the same retail price used in the test.

EXHIBIT 5 Past Test Results

Test Year	Animal	Landed Cost (dollars)	Retail Price (dollars)	Sales* Projection (units)	Test Sales (units)	Realized Sales (units)
1981. . . .	Ape	$2.33	$4.95	260	27	304
1982. . . .	Bear	3.15	5.95	280	19	374
1982. . . .	Dragon	2.52	4.95	230	14	234
1983. . . .	Bird	2.63	5.95	170	7	144
1984. . . .	Rabbit	2.85	5.95	180	6	ANA[+]
1984. . . .	Bear	3.18	6.95	140	8	133
1985. . . .	Dog	2.99	5.95	260	12	209
1986. . . .	Elephant	2.74	6.95	250	11	140
1986. . . .	Cat	3.20	6.95	270	30	458
1987. . . .	Bear	3.91	8.95	160	13	245
1987. . . .	Monkey	4.39	9.95	210	10	208
1987. . . .	Dinosaur	2.70	5.95	150	14	308
1988. . . .	Skunk	3.14	5.95	190	4	ANA[+]
1988. . . .	Mouse	4.91	10.95	150	7	47
1989. . . .	Raccoon	4.29	8.95	200	16	244
1990. . . .	Bear	4.34	9.95	220	23	385
1990. . . .	Alligator	5.88	11.95	250	8	269
1990. . . .	Dog	5.04	10.95	270	15	243
1991. . . .	Monkey	5.88	12.95	270	8	146
1991. . . .	Bear	5.19	11.95	170	10	259

*Made prior to the test market.

[+]ANA means animal not adopted.

Brown's Analysis

Julia Brown called up her Lotus spreadsheet file that contained historical test sale data. Her first step in analyzing test animals was to update her plot of the first full year's unit sales versus the previous year's test sales. This year she had two points to add, one for a monkey that sold 8 during its 1991 test and 146 when adopted for 1992 and the other for a bear that tested at 10 units and sold 259 last year. This scatter plot is given in Exhibit 6.

The general shape of this cloud of points convinced Julia that test results were a good indicator of eventual sales volume. It appeared to her that the better the animal did during the test market, the better it would generally do when offered in all stores the succeeding year.

Turning to the three items tested in 1992, Julia made some mental notes about the sales potential of each. The pig, tested at four units, was in uncharted territory. Julia guessed that, if she did adopt it for 1993, sales would run about 100 units. Julia figured that the bear, with a test of 10 units, ought to sell about

---

EXHIBIT 6   Scatter Plot of Realized versus Test Sales

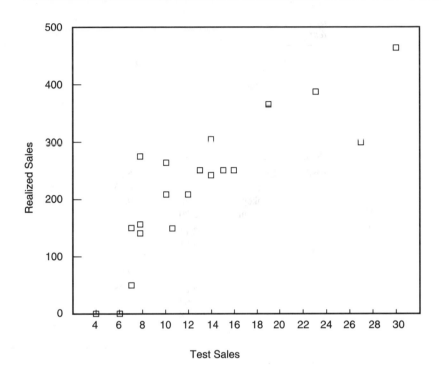

Test Sales

200 units. Last, the raccoon looked like the leading seller of the season. Test sales of 32 projected to a total sales volume of 500 for the coming year.

Next, Julia ran some numbers to decide the fate of the three animals. Exhibit 7 shows the calculated gross margin of each animal at its projected sales volume. The figures for the raccoon and bear looked promising, but Julia felt the pig was not worthy of adoption. She reasoned that Hightower was better off using the display space for another animal. She could certainly find a domestic animal that would still bring in at least $1,150 contribution during the Christmas season. In addition, the domestic animals could be ordered as needed, avoiding the inevitable mark-down and closeout to Fernstone's.

Julia then turned to work out order quantities for the two adopted animals. Her 150 percent rule of thumb implied ordering 300 bears and 750 raccoons. This rule had worked well in the past—she had almost never stocked-out of an imported stuffed animal. She had always felt that the only way to turn a profit was to make sure her inventories lasted through the Christmas season. In her mind a stock-out would be deadly to profits. Not only would Hightower lose the foregone contribution of the stocked-out item, but it might also lose some amount

EXHIBIT 7   Calculated Gross Margins of Each Animal

Animal	Projected Unit Sales	Gross Margin per Unit	Estimated Total Gross Margin
Bear 200		$7.52	$1,504
Pig 100		7.72	772
Raccoon 500		7.53	3,765

of future sales to those customers upset because a particular item was not available. On the other hand, Julia could also see that, since stock-outs would probably occur at the very end of the year, panicky last-minute buyers might easily switch to another animal. In this situation, the consequences of stocking-out of any one item were not that damaging. Julia figured that upset customers and switchable customers might cancel each other out, so the net effect of a stock-out was probably just the lost contribution of that item. Julia promised herself she would think more about lowering the order quantities.

INTERNATIONAL GUIDANCE AND CONTROLS

Time was running out on the $20 million CARV (Confined Aquatic Recovery Vehicle) project, and project manager Thomas Stearns was concerned about meeting the schedule. With 10 months left, considerable portions of the software remained to be developed, and he was by no means certain that all necessary development work would be completed on time.

Software Development

Stearns had had his project team working all out in recent months on the software development for CARV's command and guidance system. His headcount (the number of full-time-equivalent workers assigned to the project) had been increased recently, so total development costs were running at $300,000 per month, 25 percent over budget. Stearns believed there was but an 80 percent chance that the necessary software would be completed in the remaining 10 months. Despite this risk of not meeting the schedule, he could not increase the headcount on the project or increase the rate of software development in any way.

If the software were not completed on time, Stearns was fairly certain that one or two extra months of work would suffice to complete the project. Unfortunately, each month's delay in project completion meant a 2.5 percent ($500,000) reduction in the price of the contract. In addition to this precisely defined cost of not meeting the schedule, a hard-to-quantify but no less significant cost of lost reputation was associated with not completing a project as scheduled.

Hardware Expansion

Part of the difficulty in developing the software for CARV was a result of the original design for the hardware. This somewhat underdesigned hardware was making the software development much more difficult and time-consuming than originally planned.

One remedy that would virtually eliminate schedule risk would be to immediately begin an expansion of the hardware portion of the system. This expansion would require five months of effort at a total cost to the project of $1.5 million. In addition, this action would significantly reduce the software-development effort, to a point where software-development costs would decrease to $200,000 per month for the remaining 10 months of the project.

Delaying the Hardware Expansion

Because the hardware expansion could be completed in five months, Stearns thought continuing with the all-out development of the software for the next five months would be prudent before committing to the hardware expansion. The software progress of the next five months would certainly give him a better idea of the chances of completing the project on schedule. If the five-month progress were favorable, then Stearns reasoned that the chances of completing the project on time would rise to 90 percent. If the progress were unfavorable, the chances would decrease to something like 40 percent. However, the distinct possibility also existed that the progress over the next five months would leave him in the same position in which he now found himself, with an 80 percent probability of completing the project as scheduled. Stearns believed that this latter event (not learning anything new in the next five months) had a probability of about 30 percent. He thought carefully about how to distribute the remaining 70 percent probability between the "favorable progress" and "unfavorable progress" events and soon realized that, in order to remain consistent with all of his earlier assessments, the probability of "favorable progress" had to be 56 percent and the probability of "unfavorable progress" had to be 14 percent.

If he decided to expand the hardware at the end of five months, he would again eliminate all the risk of not meeting the schedule and would also alleviate much of the software-development burden. He reasoned that the remaining five months of software development would cost only $150,000 per month because much of the previous five months of developed software would be usable.

CASE 28
JADE SHAMPOO (A)

Debbie Kennedy, assistant product manager for Jade Shampoo, was delighted with the results of the just-completed test market of her proposed change to the Jade bottle cap. From the beginning of the 18-month project, she had been convinced that replacing Jade's traditional twist-off cap with a more convenient flip-top-dispenser cap would more than pay for itself in increased sales and profits. The test results confirmed her position—sales in the test market exceeded the break-even level.

The only remaining hurdle was to convince the product manager to endorse the national introduction of the change.

Shampoo Market

The shampoo market was one of the most competitive, highly fragmented markets in the health-and-beauty-aids (HBA) business. With retail sales exceeding $1.8 billion in 1986, it was the largest HBA category after analgesics. The category was very profitable, with high margins and simple technology, and it was fashion driven, with different additives and scents appealing to different consumers. As a result, there were over 200 national shampoo brands, most of them commanding less than 1 percent of the market.

Jade Shampoo was a relatively large, stable player in this volatile market. It was positioned as a basic, all-family shampoo and avoided the frequent formulation and fragrance changes of its more trendy competitors. The strategy had been successful: Jade commanded a steady 5 percent share of the market and was usually in the top five shampoo brands in sales.

Kennedy was forecasting 1987 sales to be $91,500,000 retail, $58,560,000 factory. At Jade's average factory price of $1.28 per unit, the sales forecast translated into a projected volume of 45,750,000 units. The current contribution of 36 cents per unit was not expected to change in the coming year.

The Dispenser-Cap Project

The dispenser-cap project had special significance for Kennedy; it was the first project that she had begun as a recently hired MBA, almost 18 months ago. She had come up with the idea while reviewing the results of the brand's biannual usage and attitude survey, in which consumers had been questioned as to their likes and dislikes about various shampoo brands. Kennedy noticed that several brands had improved their overall preference ratings since the previous study,

This case was based on a Supervised Business Study prepared by Donna M. Packard (Darden, Class of 1987).

with the strongest gains in the area of convenience. When she investigated any changes that these brands may have made in the past two years, she discovered that all of them had introduced flip-top-dispenser caps to replace their old-fashioned twist-off caps.

Although management had historically been reluctant to change Jade in response to market trends, Kennedy believed that this was one trend she could not afford to overlook. The study showed that convenient dispensing was especially important to Jade's primary target markets, children and over-40 adults. A dispenser cap might help attract consumers in these groups who were now using another family shampoo. The product manager of Jade Shampoo, Marion Hoffman, to whom Kennedy reported, agreed with the assessment and suggested that Kennedy form a Dispenser-Cap-Project team. In addition to Kennedy, this task force included representatives of the departments in the company that would be involved in developing, testing, producing, and selling the new dispenser cap. After several meetings, the group agreed on a plan for testing and implementing the proposed Jade dispenser cap.

The cap would be the same color as the current Jade cap and, to minimize costs, would be of a standard flip-top design, rather than a custom design. It would require the purchase of a new molding machine and a set of molds at a cost of $1 million. The new cap would use a different kind of plastic and would cost 1.5 cents more than the old cap. The team did not expect any other costs to increase with the new cap, nor did the team expect the price to change in response to this product improvement.

There was general enthusiasm among the members of the project team for the new cap. The "product news" would help obtain better advertising and display support from retailers. The brand's advertising agency was looking forward to incorporating the dispenser cap into a new "all-family-convenience" campaign. Both the sales department and the ad agency expressed confidence that the dispenser cap would increase sales for Jade. The only notes of caution came from the brand's research and development technician, who suggested that the smaller aperture in the dispenser cap might lead to the use of less product on each application as well as a reduction in spillage, an often overlooked source of sales. Kennedy noted both points but was not overly disturbed by them. She believed that users would continue to dispense the amount of product they felt appropriate, regardless of the size of the opening, and that spillage could not be a significant portion of sales.

In a memorandum to Hoffman (Exhibit 1), Kennedy expressed her confidence that the dispenser cap would result in a sales increase substantially above her calculated break-even increase of 7.8 percent. She also argued that the downside risk of moving ahead with the new cap was outweighed by the upside potential.

The Test Plan

The first step in testing the new cap was a product-use test, which was intended to determine if current Jade users would like the new dispenser at least as well as the current cap. It was a blind, paired comparison in which 100 current Jade users were given two bottles of Jade, one with the dispenser cap and one with the current cap. The bottles were not labeled, and the subjects were not told what product they had or if there were any differences between the actual products (there were not). The subjects were instructed to use one bottle for one week and the other bottle for the next week. At the end of the second week they were telephoned and asked which of the shampoos they preferred overall and how the shampoos compared on specific attributes such as convenience, cleaning, and manageability.

The results (Exhibit 2) were very encouraging to Kennedy. Consumers preferred the dispenser cap product over the current-cap product for convenience. They also preferred the dispenser-cap product overall, even though there was no other difference between the two products than the cap.

With these successful results in hand, Kennedy obtained permission to proceed to a full-market test of the dispenser cap—a much more comprehensive test

---

EXHIBIT 1   Break-Even Volume for Dispenser Cap

To: Marion Hoffman, Product Manager, Jade Shampoo
From: Debbie Kennedy, Asst. Product Manager, Jade Shampoo
Subject: Jade Dispenser-Cap Economics

The following calculations are based on the recently promulgated guidelines for capital-expenditure analysis: three-year horizon, 18 percent hurdle rate, straight-line depreciation, and a 40 percent tax rate.

On the basis of our detailed cost estimates for the special tooling investment associated with the proposed dispenser cap ($1.0 million) and the incremental cost of the new caps themselves ($0.015 per unit), the break-even volume is 49.316 million units per year. See the attachment for the spreadsheets that detail this calculation.

A volume of 49.316 million units represents a 7.8 percent increase over current volume. This increase is well within my most likely estimate of a 10 to 12 percent increase.

On the downside exposure, let us take a pessimistic view of the cap's success and suppose that volume in the first year increases by only half of the amount required for break-even (3.9 percent): Profitability with the dispenser cap ($9.640) would then be below the forecasted level with the current cap ($9.882). Under these conditions, company policy would require that we drop the dispenser cap and return to the old cap. The net present value of this scenario is $20.755 million, $0.731 million less than staying with the current cap. See attached spreadsheet for details.

On the other hand, if the volume were to be double the break-even increase (15.6 percent—less than 4 percentage points above my most likely range), the net present value would be $23.093 million. See the attachment for details. This is $1.607 million more than staying with the current cap. The downside exposure seems small relative to this potential!

Attachment

(Continued)

EXHIBIT 1   *Concluded*

Calculation of the break-even-sales level

NPV without the dispenser cap

Unit volume		45.750	45.750	45.750
BT contribution		16.470	16.470	16.470
AT profits		9.882	9.882	9.882
Cash flow		9.882	9.882	9.882
NPV @ 18%	21.486			

NPV with the dispenser cap

Initial investment	1.000			
Unit volume		49.316	49.316	49.316
BT contribution		17.014	17.014	17.014
Depreciation		0.333	0.333	0.333
AT profit		10.008	10.008	10.008
Cash flow	(1.000)	10.342	10.342	10.342
NPV @ 18%	21.486			

Pessimistic scenario (3.9% increase—50% of break-even increase)

Initial investment	1.000			
Unit volume		47.534	45.750	45.750
BT contribution		16.399	16.470	16.470
Depreciation		0.333	0.667	0.000
AT profit		9.640	9.482	9.882
Cash flow	(1.000)	9.973	10.149	9.882
NPV @ 18%	20.755			

Optimistic scenario (15.6% increase—200% of break-even increase)

Initial investment	1.000			
Unit volume		52.887	52.887	52.887
BT contribution		18.246	18.246	18.246
Depreciation		0.333	0.333	0.333
AT profit		10.748	10.748	10.748
Cash flow	(1.000)	11.081	11.081	11.081
NPV @ 18%	23.093			

---

than the product-use test. The national plan for introducing the new cap would be replicated in a small portion of the country to measure the new cap's effect on volume. The market research department recommended that the test be conducted in Phoenix, Arizona, and offered a long list of reasons. Phoenix contained almost exactly 1 percent of the U.S. population and represented about 1 percent of Jade sales. The size was large enough to yield statistically significant results but small enough to minimize test costs and the risk of disrupting brand sales should the cap prove to have problems. Phoenix was indicative of the U.S. market

EXHIBIT 2   Results of Product-Use Test

	Percentage of Respondents Preferring		
Attribute	*Dispenser Cap*	*Current Cap*	*No Preference*
Overall	55%	37%	8%
Convenience	76	19	5
Cleaning	21	19	60
Manageability	23	25	52

Note: results based on 100 respondents.

for Jade in both demographics and share trends. The managers of the 94 grocery stores were accustomed to test markets and were known to be cooperative. From an advertising point of view, the Phoenix market was well contained, in that advertisements for the dispenser cap would not be picked up on TVs in other areas where the new cap was not available. The market test began on June 1, 1986, at a budgeted cost of $500,000.

Thirteen months later, Kennedy received a phone call from a friend in the market research department. The test results had just come in and average volume was 5,341 units per store with a standard deviation of 2,131 units. Kennedy was delighted with the news—the test-market performance would amount to 50,205,400 units (5,341 × 94 × 100) on a national basis. This was almost a million units above the break-even volume of 49,316,000 units. She could now push ahead with the national introduction of the change.

Hoffman, however, was less enthusiastic. In a brief hallway conversation, Hoffman had focused more on the standard deviation than on the average and had expressed concern that, with such a large standard deviation, the introduction could in fact result in a loss.

CASE 29
JADE SHAMPOO (B)

The good news of the morning was shattered in the afternoon when Warren Jenkins, the director of market research, walked into Debbie Kennedy's office and glumly announced:

> You heard, the test results are in. Unfortunately, they aren't what we had hoped for. Even though average store sales for the year were 5,341 units and this is above our break-even, the individual-store data had a standard deviation of 2,132 units. Our standard hypothesis test cannot reject at the 0.05 level the null hypothesis that the new cap generates sales at or below break-even. In fact, there is a 33 percent chance that we could have a test result of at least 5,341 even if the true sales were at the break-even. Here's a copy of the memo [Exhibit 1] that I just received from my staff statistician. I'm sorry, Debbie, but the way we look at things, these results don't support the national introduction of the dispenser cap.

It had been a long time since Kennedy had thought about hypothesis tests, and the language seemed rather remote. That evening, she reviewed her notes from a statistics course (Exhibit 2) and began to think about why the hypothesis-test approach did not seem right.

She knew that she would have to get her thoughts straightened out quickly. The next morning there was to be a meeting with Marion Hoffman, the Jade product manager, and Carol Williams, the director of marketing. At that meeting, she would have to take a position on the future of the dispenser cap. On the one hand, the easy position would be to go along with company procedure and let the hypothesis test make the decision. On the other hand, she was committed to the project. The cap had been her idea, and she had directed the study team since its inception. If it increased sales as she expected, the new cap would generate additional profits for her brand. But then again, she was not anxious to be the one responsible for reducing profits if sales proved to be below the break-even level, particularly if she had gone against company guidelines to continue the product. Regardless, it just did not seem right that a simple statistical test could so easily kill an 18-month project to which she was firmly committed.

This case was based on a Supervised Business Study prepared by Donna M. Packard (Darden, Class of 1987).

EXHIBIT 1   Analysis of the Test-Market Results

To: Warren Jenkins, Director of Market Research
From: Susan Hauser, Statistician
Subject: Jade Dispenser Cap Test Market—Final Results

The year-long (June 1, 1986–May 31, 1987) market test of the proposed Jade dispenser cap in our 94 retail markets in Phoenix has resulted in an average volume of 5,341 units per store with a standard deviation of 2,132 units.

The 49.316 million break-even volume that was provided by Product Management translates into 5,246 (49.316 × 0.01 / 94) units per store.

With this figure in mind, I performed our usual hypothesis test by taking as the null hypothesis the statement that the "average annual sales of Jade with the dispenser cap will be less than or equal to the break-even level of 5,246 units per store." Assuming that this hypothesis is true, and making the conservative assumption that the average annual sales will be equal to the break-even figure, there is a 33 percent probability that we could have observed a test result at least as large as the one we did. More specifically, the t-statistic is

$$0.432 = [5341 - 5246] / [2132 / \sqrt{94}]$$

with 93 degrees of freedom. The chances of an outcome being greater than 0.432 are 33 percent. As a result, there is a high probability that our test result could have occurred with an average annual sales equal to break-even. Consequently, this test result does not provide sufficient evidence to change our assumption that the average annual sales will be at or below break-even.

In traditional statistical parlance, we cannot reject the null hypothesis at the 0.05 level of significance.

EXHIBIT 2   Class Notes on Hypothesis Testing

Hypothesis testing

- Decision-making tool.
- Assesses evidence provided by data in an effort to select between two hypotheses (claims) concerning an unknown population parameter.
- Each hypothesis has a different action associated with it.

The two hypotheses

- The null hypothesis (H_0, H-nought)—a claim of disbelief, of no change, of no effect. "Despite what you say, I don't believe your claim." Generally, the associated action is to do nothing.
- The alternative hypothesis (H_1)—the claim that there is a difference and that action is warranted.
- Both hypotheses make claims about an unknown population parameter; hypotheses must be mutually exclusive and exhaustive.

(Continued)

EXHIBIT 2   *Concluded*

- Generally the null hypothesis refers to parameter values on one side of a cut-off value (CO); the alternative hypothesis refers to values on the other side of CO.

Types of errors

- Because you must choose either H_0 or H_1, two types of errors are possible:
    - —Type 1 error: accept the alternative hypothesis when the null hypothesis is correct.
    - —Type 2 error: accept the null hypothesis when the alternative hypothesis is correct.
- Generally we want to have the chances of making a Type 1 error to be no more than 0.05 (0.01, if more conservative); don't want to make a change when it is unjustified; the 0.05 (or 0.01) is called the "level of significance" of the test.

Interpreting sample data

- The n observations, sample average (x-bar), sample standard deviation (s).
- Assume the null hypothesis to be true, but be as generous for H_1 as possible by assuming that the mean of the distribution of sample averages is CO, the cut-off value between H_0 and H_1 (closest value to H_1 range that is still in H_0).
- The standard deviation of the distribution of sample averages is $s/\sqrt{n}$.
- The distribution of sample averages is the normal distribution (t if s is based on less than 30 observations—not a big difference, though, between normal and t).
- Find the region of rejection—the tail of the distribution that has probability 0.05, equal to $CO + 1.645 \times s/\sqrt{n}$.
- If x-bar falls in the region of rejection, then either H_0 is true and we got an unusual result (probability is at most 0.05), or the null hypothesis is false; the second explanation is the more reasonable.
- If x-bar is not in the region of rejection, we cannot reject H_0 without increasing the probability of making a Type 1 error.

CASE 30
JAIKUMAR TEXTILES, LTD.: THE NYLON DIVISION (A)

In early April, N. S. Kadiyala, deputy general manager of the Nylon Division of Jaikumar Textiles, Ltd. (JTL), had two days in which to make a decision that would have a major impact on May's production schedule. A proposal from one of JTL's major customers for the purchase of 5,000 kilograms (kgs) of denier 15/1g nylon (see Nylon Production section) had just crossed Kadiyala's desk. The offering price was 182 rupees (Rs) per kg. Kadiyala knew that, if he accepted the order, it would have to be filled entirely from May's production of that denier, which would require a major commitment of production resources.

Prior to the mid-1980s, such considerations as future business potential and goodwill had dwarfed the immediate economic impact of decisions of this type, but intense competition, much of it stemming from the introduction of new fiber technology by competitors, had changed all that. Kadiyala was sure that JTL now needed to squeeze every potential rupee of contribution from its production facilities.

Nylon Production at JTL

The production of nylon yarn in JTL's main nylon-production facility took place in four basic areas: polymerization, spinning, drawtwisting, and packing and testing.

In the polymerization area, the raw material *caprolactum powder* was first washed in large vats and reshaped into small pellets. These pellets were then channeled into heating tanks, where they were transformed, through the addition of various acids and chemicals, into three basic types of nylon—glittering, semi-dull, and full dull. The resulting chips were melted down and sent to the spinning area.

In spinning, nylon yarn was formed by forcing the melted caprolactum chips (now about the consistency of honey) through the tiny holes of a device called a *spinneret*. Unlike natural fibers, nylon yarn could be extruded into different thicknesses. The spinneret, used in the production of all man-made fibers, was similar in design to a shower head, with anywhere from one to literally thousands of tiny holes. Melted chips were forced through these holes, the size and number of which determined the weight and thickness of the resulting nylon. The thickness and weight of a particular yarn was called its *denier*. The 15/1g denier was a monofilament (single strand) of glittering nylon weighing 15 kgs per 9,000 meters, for example, while a 84/21fd denier was a multifilament (in this case, 21 strands) of full dull nylon weighing 84 kgs per 9,000 meters.

As the filaments, still in a semiliquid state, emerged from the holes in the spinneret, cold air was forced across them, causing them to solidify. The filaments were spun onto spools using one of two types of spinning machine groups: an old grid system or a more modern and efficient extruder system. After the filaments hardened, the spools were taken to the drawtwisting area.

In drawtwisting, the spools were stretched on special machines, causing a reduction in the diameter of the filaments. This reduction was accomplished by a rearrangement of the molecules in the fiber into a more orderly pattern. This new pattern strengthened the filaments, making the fiber more resistant to breaking.

After drawtwisting, spools were systematically tested to assure quality. Once a batch of spools was approved, it was moved to the packing area, where each type of denier was packed by hand into a special container. The packing process was expected to be automated in the near future. Currently, there was ample, albeit expensive, capacity in the packing and testing area to handle all denier production.

Production Planning

Kadiyala and his staff were responsible for the monthly decision of how much of each denier to produce during the upcoming month. The resulting production plan was required to conform to the broad guidelines of an annual master plan, the purpose of which was to ensure the efficient use of production facilities and to smooth the production of individual deniers throughout the year, thus controlling inventory cost. For example, the master plan for this year specified that deniers 15/1g and 84/21fd be produced exclusively on extruder spinning machine group #5. A maximum of 300 hours of spinning time on this machine group was allocated each month, to be divided between production of these two deniers. Furthermore, it was specified that deniers 15/1g and 84/21fd require no more than 1,600 hours of drawtwisting time between them each month. (See Exhibit 1 for spinning-machine and drawtwisting utilization rates for deniers 15/1g and 84/21fd.) In addition, the annual plan specified that no fewer than 3,000 nor more than 10,000 kgs of denier 15/1g, and no fewer than 6,000 nor more than 15,000 kgs of denier 84/21fd, could be produced in a given month. (Because both polymerization and packing and testing capacities were plentiful, no constraints were placed on use of either area.)

Kadiyala met with his staff on the first of each month to determine the production plan for that month. Thus, the final production plan for May would be determined on May 1. By waiting until the first of the month to make this decision, Kadiyala and his staff retained maximum flexibility to respond to changes in the market price of each denier. Based on the prevailing prices at that time, the production plan would be set and the month's planned output would be presold to vendors at the current market prices for delivery at the end of the month.

While Kadiyala was quite comfortable using the prevailing market prices on the first of the month to set and presell the month's production, he had some concerns about the ad hoc way he and his staff used the prevailing prices to arrive

----

EXHIBIT 1   Resource Use by Deniers 15/1g and 84/21fd

Extruder Spinning Group #5

	Denier	
	15/1g	*84/21fd*
Average number of kgs that could be processed in an hour of machine time	30 kgs	60 kgs

Drawtwisting

	Denier	
	15/1g	*84/21fd*
Average number of kgs that could be processed in an hour of drawtwisting time	15 kgs	12 kgs

Raw material cost

	Denier	
	15/1g	*84/21fd*
Variable cost of producing 1 kg	Rs 88	Rs 74

----

at production levels. In April, for example, the decision had been made to produce 4,200 kgs of denier 15/1g and 9,600 kgs of denier 84/21fd. At market prices of Rs 178 and Rs 124 per kg, respectively, this plan had resulted in a contribution of Rs 858,000 from April's production. Kadiyala wondered if a more profitable production plan might not have existed.

The Proposal

At first glance, the proposed purchase of 5,000 kgs of May's production of denier 15/1g appeared to be attractive. The Rs 182 per kg offer was not only above the current market price of Rs 178 but also above the marketing department's May 1 forecasted price of Rs 179. (Each month, for planning purposes, the marketing department made a forecast of the price of each denier on the first of the following month; see Exhibit 2 for a recent history of marketing department forecasts for 15/1g.) Yet, the price of denier 15/1g (also in Exhibit 2) had fluctuated widely over the past couple of years. If prices were to rise unexpectedly, Kadiyala might regret being locked into the contract. On the other hand, the 5,000 kgs specified by the contract would count toward the required minimum May production level of 3,000 kgs of denier 15/1g. Hence, if prices were to drop, Kadiyala would avoid having to sell 3,000 kgs at the reduced price. Whether or not to accept the proposal thus appeared to depend on the expected market price in May for denier 15/1g.

EXHIBIT 2 **Recent History of Actual Market Prices of Deniers 15/1g and 84/21fd and Marketing Department Forecasts of 15/1g (in rupees)**

Month	Actual 15/1g	Actual 84/21 fd	Forecast 15/1g
Jan	158	123	146
Feb	171	123	161
Mar	231	124	165
Apr	223	125	210
May	237	124	225
Jun	203	123	215
Jul	180	123	190
Aug	192	124	175
Sep	174	124	185
Oct	162	124	165
Nov	162	126	170
Dec	155	125	165
Jan	154	124	156
Feb	158	123	160
Mar	157	124	158
Apr	178	124	160
May	—	—	179

Case 31
Jaikumar Textiles, Ltd.: The Nylon Division (B)

On May 1, N. S. Kadiyala and his staff met to determine the production plan for May. The market price for denier 15/1g was Rs 168, making Kadiyala wish he had accepted the contract to produce 5,000 kgs of 15/1g at Rs 182 back in April. Now he was left with having to decide how much of deniers 15/1g and 84/21fd to produce during May at the prices Rs 168 and Rs 124, respectively. Also for his attention were a set of related memoranda (Exhibits 1–4).

Exhibit 1   Memorandum 1

TO:	N. S. Kadiyala, Deputy General Manager
FROM:	———, Production Head, Drawtwisting
DATE:	April 30
RE:	Available drawtwisting hours for the May production of deniers 15/1g and 84/21fd

We have had an unfortunate mechanical breakdown in the drawtwisting area. The effect of this breakdown is that total drawtwisting capacity for May will be significantly reduced (by about a third). As a result, we can allocate no more than 1,000 hours of drawtwisting time in May to the production of deniers 15/1g and 84/21fd.

Exhibit 2   Memorandum 2

TO:	N. S. Kadiyala, Deputy General Manager
FROM:	———, Production Head, Spinning
DATE:	April 27
RE:	Renting additional spinning hours

Last month, you complained that we should be allocating additional spinning machine hours to deniers 15/1g and 84/21fd. We now have the opportunity to rent additional spinning time from a competitor. We have yet to discuss price or amount, pending your input. In order to rent the additional capacity for May, we need to let them know something as soon as possible.

EXHIBIT 3   Memorandum 3

TO: N. S. Kadiyala, Deputy General Manager

FROM: ———, Special Assistant to the General Manager

DATE: April 29

RE: Denier 44/10sd

We need additional spinning capacity for denier 44/10sd due to a recent surge in demand. 15/1g and 84/21fd are among those deniers that have been identified as prime candidates to lose allocated capacity. To help us in making our final decision, would you estimate the impact of such a move on deniers 15/1g and 84/21fd?

EXHIBIT 4   Memorandum 4

TO: N. S. Kadiyala, Deputy General Manager

FROM: ———, Marketing Department

DATE: April 30

RE: Price of denier 84/21fd

There appears to be a possibility that the price of denier 84/21fd, relatively stable for some time now, may experience a significant jump in the upcoming month, possibly by as much as 25 percent. Perhaps you should consider boosting your production of denier 84/21fd in response to this very real possibility.

James Vaughan looked over the balcony railing to the sea beyond. As he settled comfortably into the rattan chair, he watched the sweat roll down the side of his glass. He sniffled repeatedly. After three months in the Caribbean, James had become somewhat acclimatized, but the effects of a summer cold lingered. With a sigh, he thought of his imminent return to the United States for the second year of his MBA program. San Huberto was his last assignment for the summer.

The evening's sea breeze blew across the balcony of the Gran Hotel San Huberto, and James thought about the recommendations he would make about pricing strategy to his summer employer, Lesser Antilles Lines (LAL). LAL was a very successful containerized shipping firm moving cargo between Ft. Lauderdale, Florida, and about 15 Caribbean islands. Vaughan was hired to investigate eight potential new markets in the Caribbean and Central America. On his way back to Ft. Lauderdale, he received a call asking him to stop in San Huberto. Because LAL was embroiled in a particularly vicious price war, San Huberto was the only market in which LAL was not producing impressive earnings. Vaughan was asked to survey the scene and evaluate LAL's pricing strategy for the island.

Lesser Antilles Lines

LAL was born in the early 1960s when a Florida construction firm successfully bid on a contract to build sidewalks on a Caribbean island. Much to the manager's disgust, transporting equipment and materials to the particular location was virtually impossible. Although the occasional vessel might call at the port, voyages were infrequent and unreliable. In true West Indian style, vessel operators' attitudes toward scheduling were relaxed and unhurried. The construction firm was unwilling to tolerate the vagaries of local shipping, so it purchased an old barge and began regular "sailings" between Ft. Lauderdale and the island. In a short time, grocery wholesalers, hardware stores, and other businesses on the island requested that their goods be transported on the barge for a fee. They claimed that such a service was better than any other available at that time. LAL "came of age" when revenues from the shipping service began to approach those from the construction end of the business.

In 20 years, LAL's service network grew from 1 island to 15. Revenues in 1985 were almost $50 million. LAL specialized in serving the small islands that historically received little attention from established shipping lines. By offering reliable and frequent transportation in previously neglected regions, LAL garnered impressive market shares and, by providing the highest levels of service to

This case was prepared in conjunction with James V. Gelly (Darden, Class of 1987).

even the smallest customers, the firm defended its market share in spite of intense competition. LAL became something of a legend in the region for its punctuality—it was said that you could set your watch by LAL's vessels.

Maritime Trade

Ocean shipping always played a central role in the world economy, with virtually all internationally traded goods transported by sea. Maritime trade was divided into two categories, bulk and general cargo. The bulk category accounted for roughly 75 percent of total world tonnage shipped in 1985 and was principally made up of petroleum, mineral ores, coal, and grain. General cargo, which comprised the remaining 25 percent of total world tonnage shipped, referred to manufactured goods and consumer products. Because general cargo represented relatively high-value goods, fast and efficient transportation was required to move them. LAL competed in this higher-value general cargo industry, commonly known as the liner trade.

Containerized Transportation.　　Before the 1950s, general cargo was moved by the "break-bulk" method. Individual boxes, drums, crates, and sacks were loaded on and off ship by crane and by hand; stevedores and longshoremen supplied labor at the ports of origination and destination. This system was not an efficient one, however. Ocean transportation was a labor-intensive industry—in the early 1960s, a modern liner spent approximately half the year in port being loaded and unloaded.

Although a simple concept, "containerization" did not begin until the mid-1950s when Malcolm McLean, the owner of a Virginia-based trucking firm, began shipping entire trailer-loads of goods. After removing the wheels from 35-foot trailers commonly seen on U.S. highways, McLean shipped full, sealed trailers, rather than individual parcels that were formerly the unit of transportation. Containerization quickly transformed the liner industry. By the mid-1980s, the industry was almost completely standardized, with the Trailer Equivalent Unit (TEU) the unit of measure. A TEU could be moved "intermodally" (by road, rail, and sea) with a minimum of labor and without disturbing the contents (see Exhibit 1).

Competitive Environment in the Mid-1980s.　　The liner industry traditionally operated within conferences, which were international groups of private liner companies that collectively agreed on routes, schedules, and rates. Some have observed that conferences resembled institutionalized price-fixing. The conference shipping system became increasingly unstable in the late 1970s and early 1980s. Having once controlled 80 to 90 percent of traffic volume in certain trades, the conferences' control dropped to less than 50 percent by the mid-1980s. As containerization spread, productivity increased, and prices adjusted downward. Furthermore, adaptable firms withdrew from the conferences to take advantage of new trade patterns.

EXHIBIT 1   A Liner Loaded with Containers

By 1985, the world shipping industry was in a severe slump. Subsidized ship-yards in most industrialized countries caused new-vessel prices to drop, and the supply of vessels outstripped demand. The contraction in world petroleum consumption caused tremendous under-utilization of bulk vessels, and tanker ships were laid up or scrapped at unprecedented rates. Overcapacity struck the liner industry, also, as the growth in vessel capacity outpaced the growth in demand. Because the industry was one of high fixed costs, freight rates were cut to keep cargoes, and revenues—in real terms—dropped well below 1970s levels.

The market value of all types of vessels fell to a fraction of their replacement cost. Shipyards began offering liberal financing for new construction contracts. As both market value and replacement costs fell, the liner industry became easy to enter. Even as large shipping firms filed for bankruptcy, new firms announced their entry into already overcrowded routes.

Caribbean Environment

The small island-states in the Caribbean were among the last to convert to containerization. Because they were developing countries with near-subsistence economies, they could not afford the cost of modernizing port infrastructures, and many were forced to borrow heavily from developmental agencies to support a shift to containerization.

LAL successfully anticipated the move toward containerization in the Caribbean and was one of the first firms there to convert completely to containerized operations. LAL was also the first to introduce a regular, reliable container service in many markets, and the firm dredged harbors and installed cranes in ports where such improvements were not forthcoming.

Demand Characteristics.   Imports of Caribbean islands reflected the structure and development of the underlying economies. Because many countries were underdeveloped, imports consisted mainly of corrugated tin roofing, lumber, foodstuffs, tools, clothing, and vehicles. The small islands were almost totally dependent on imports for manufactured goods. Countries with tourist industries imported goods to which American and European vacationers were accustomed. In this region, the local importer of goods bore the entire cost of transportation, which was often included on invoices as a surcharge. Exports consisted of agricultural products, such as copra and tropical fruit, as well as hand-crafted items. Balance of payments constraints were chronic.

Because many Caribbean economies claimed tourism as their only industry, increased demand for shipping depended on natural population growth and the size of the tourist sector. Demand could not drop below a critical level of importation, however, because these less-developed economies had no alternative but to import essential commodities.

One of the most important aspects of the Caribbean liner industry was the almost perfect price inelasticity of demand—the price of shipping services could change dramatically in either direction and have almost no effect on the amount of services demanded. Transportation costs played such a small part in the retail price of most imported goods that even a 50 percent reduction or rise in freight charges had little impact on demand. For example, assume a grocery wholesaler paid $2,000 per TEU in freight charges to import frozen chicken parts. A TEU could hold as much as 40,000 pounds of chicken, so the transportation cost per pound was $0.05. Assume a cut in freight rates per TEU of $1,000; the $0.025 savings per pound would have little effect on sales of frozen chicken. Also, Caribbean importers were notorious for absorbing any such savings. Thus, necessity, as well as pricing practices, caused Caribbean demand for shipping services to be almost perfectly price inelastic.

San Huberto.   Discovered in the 16th century, San Huberto (see Exhibit 2 for a map of the Caribbean) was colonized by the English in the 1630s. In 1788, St. Hubert's, as it was then called, was ceded to Spain. After a century of neglect, the island was claimed by a Latin American country and its name changed to its Spanish form, San Huberto. Since World War II, Spanish had been the official language on San Huberto, although Caribbean-English or patois was the language for over three centuries.

In 1985, the majority of San Huberto's 34,000 inhabitants were English-speaking blacks, the descendants of plantation slaves brought from Jamaica. Unemployment among them was over 35 percent. By the mid-1980s, a substantial

---

EXHIBIT 2   Map of the Caribbean

tourist industry evolved in response to the island's duty-free status, and San Huberto had two industries, subsistence farming and modern, international resort-class tourism. An estimated 100,000 tourists visited the island each year, and the volume of consumer durables moving in and out of San Huberto was considerable. Catering to wealthy Colombians, Salvadoreans, Costa Ricans, Guatemalans, and Hondurans in search of duty-free bargains and white-sand beaches, San Huberto offered numerous hotels, restaurants, and stores selling such luxuries as perfume, appliances, and jewelry.

Virtually all goods imported to San Huberto originated in the United States. Dominant users of the container service between the United States and San Huberto were the local importers of food, pharmaceuticals, consumer durables, clothes, alcohol, and hotel supplies. Importers wishing to arrange transportation typically contacted the shipping agent representing a given liner firm. The shipping agent was knowledgeable about sailing schedules, prices, and capacity, and, in a small market such as San Huberto, he or she might also serve as salesman, marketing manager, and even the dock-side supervisor.

The most important facet of the San Huberto market was the island's shallow-draft port. (Draft refers to the depth to which a ship extended under water.) Because the maximum draft of San Huberto's port was only 16 feet, the number and size of vessels able to call there were quite limited. Of firms operating in those waters, only LAL and Kronos Lines (KL) were equipped with the shallow-draft class of vessel required to call on San Huberto. In effect, the San Huberto shipping market was an oligopoly simply because of its remote location and physical limitations.

LAL entered the San Huberto market in 1980, at which time KL had a monopoly on service to the United States. LAL chose Stanley Montagu, one of the island's best-known agents, to help it gain a share of the market serving the United States. Montagu operated a small agency begun by his grandfather in the 1880s and had historically acted as agent for the yachters who called at San Huberto. Although he was a first-rate agent, Montagu had to work hard to gain share for LAL. As a member of the island's black community, he was only slowly gaining the business of the predominantly Spanish-speaking hoteliers, retailers, and restaurateurs.

Although they were the only two firms offering a U.S.–San Huberto connection, LAL and KL became bitter rivals. Begun in the 1960s, KL was owned and operated by Anatoly Rapport, a flamboyant southern European of uncertain origin with a reputation for being cheap, tough, and ruthless. KL operated 4 vessels (versus LAL's 11) and competed in several of the same markets as LAL. KL was a good example of the tough "niche" player that offered service to only a few markets, but was renowned for the tenacity with which it clung to those markets. KL met with some bad luck when one of its vessels was seized by the Venezuelan government for alleged smuggling operations and two others were detained by the Colombian government. These problems did not limit KL's ability to service the islands, however. TransCaribe, which had strong ties with many of the major importers, was the agent KL used in San Huberto for the past 15 years.

San Huberto Market Data

Vaughan's first initiative after arriving in San Huberto was to determine the exact size of the market. This task entailed eight hours of studying shipping manifests (the records of each vessel's cargo), which he found in a cardboard box in a disordered "file-room." After poring over the last three months' shipping manifests in the hot, airless room, Vaughan estimated a total of 3,900 TEUs per year imported into San Huberto. While his total ignorance of Spanish worried him a little, he believed the number to be accurate. On the basis of these same manifests, Vaughan was able to calculate that LAL had a 40 percent unit share of the market.

He then began the extensive series of interviews that served as market research. His custom during the summer was to identify himself as a consultant for an unidentified shipping firm and attempt to interview importers, exporters, and shipping agents to get a feel for the more subjective dimensions of the market. The task in San Huberto was difficult, because he could not communicate with many of the businesspeople to whom he spoke, and he was forced to hire an employee at his hotel to translate for him at considerable expense. Vaughan learned first that LAL's choice of Montagu, based on Montagu's abilities, was a wise one, but that the racial and language barrier on San Huberto might work against the agent. Many of the importers stated that they preferred to work with KL's agent, TransCaribe, but could not offer any economic reason for the preference. Montagu, however, was respected by the entire San Huberto market and had made real inroads during the six years that LAL served San Huberto.

Based on his interviews, Vaughan believed that KL had built up a certain loyalty among the major importers during its long period of monopoly in San Huberto. He learned, however, that the usual practice in San Huberto was for importers to divide their orders between both shipping lines in varying proportions. This double-sourcing was considered a legacy from the not-too-distant past of infrequent and unreliable transportation.

Vaughan wanted to know which shipping firm importers would prefer if LAL's and KL's rates were identical, so in his interviews he collected subjective estimates of LAL's market share on that basis. He was surprised to learn that, at equal freight rates, KL was likely to retain a 60 percent market share. The more experienced shipping agents seemed to feel that each difference of $100 per TEU in freight rates would equal about a 10 percent loss of share for the more expensive firm. Exhibit 3 shows a graph of the relationship between LAL market share and the difference in price that these assumptions implied.

EXHIBIT 3   LAL Share as a Function of Price Differential

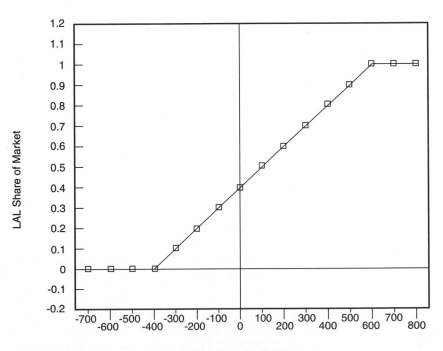

Price (KL) - Price (LAL)

Vaughan was surprised at these results, but the pattern recurred throughout his interviews. LAL, at equal freight rates, would still enjoy only a 40 percent market share; to gain share, LAL would have to set its price below KL's. This conclusion apparently explained LAL's poor profit performance in San Huberto. In trying to gain share, Montagu seemed to touch off the vicious price war of the last year. Because lower freight rates would not stimulate more volume (due to the severe price inelasticity of demand), cutting prices led to shrinking contributions for both firms. Vaughan wondered if Montagu's strategy was either appropriate or wise. His stated objective was to dominate KL and to "run them out of the market," but KL did not seem capable of being pushed around. Indeed, KL had met every one of LAL's price changes shortly after Montagu announced them.

After some work with LAL's controller, Vaughan worked out the various costs associated with shipping one TEU. The costs were for rental on containers, handling expenses in Ft. Lauderdale, vessel costs, and handling costs at LAL's "hub" port of San Juan, Puerto Rico. The firm's TEUs originated in Ft. Lauderdale, were shipped to Puerto Rico on LAL's large "line haul" vessels, were off-loaded in San Juan, and were then reloaded onto smaller "feeder" vessels that sailed to small islands throughout the Caribbean.

LAL's variable cost per TEU in 1986 was:

	Cost per TEU
Trailer rental	$246
Ft. Lauderdale variable handling	308
San Juan variable handling	287
Total	$841

The firm's marketing managers in San Juan believed that KL's cost per TEU was about 5 percent greater than LAL's ($883) because of inefficiencies and KL's smaller-scale operation. The two firms called at the port of San Huberto with the same frequency (i.e., bi-monthly).

James constructed a matrix showing both LAL's and KL's contribution, given the different pricing combinations covered in his market-share analysis. His assumptions for the matrix (shown in Exhibit 4) were as follows:

$$\text{Market size} = 3,900 \text{ TEU per year}$$
$$\text{Market share}_{\text{LAL}} = 0.40 + (P_{\text{KL}} - P_{\text{LAL}})(1/1,000)$$
$$\text{Market share}_{\text{KL}} = 0.60 + (P_{\text{LAL}} - P_{\text{KL}})(1/1,000)$$
$$\text{Contribution}_{\text{LAL}} = (P_{\text{LAL}} - \$841)(3,900)(\text{Market share}_{\text{LAL}})$$
$$\text{Contribution}_{\text{KL}} = (P_{\text{KL}} - \$883)(3,900)(\text{Market share}_{\text{KL}})$$

After completing the matrix, Vaughan learned that KL had just announced that it would match LAL's most recently posted freight rate of $800 per TEU to San Huberto. Studying his findings, he wondered what strategy recommendations he could make to Montagu regarding future LAL prices.

EXHIBIT 4 Contribution Matrix

KL Price

KL Price	800	900	1000	1100	1200	1300	1400	1500	1600	1700	1800	1900
1900	0 / -160	0 / 230	0 / 620	0 / 1010	0 / 1400	0 / 1790	397 / 1962	793 / 2056	1190 / 2072	1587 / 2010	1983 / 1870	2380 / 1652
1800	0 / -160	0 / 230	0 / 620	0 / 1010	0 / 1400	358 / 1611	715 / 1744	1073 / 1799	1431 / 1776	1788 / 1675	2146 / 1496	2503 / 1239
1700	0 / -160	0 / 230	0 / 620	0 / 1010	319 / 1260	637 / 1432	956 / 1526	1275 / 1542	1593 / 1480	1912 / 1340	2230 / 1122	2549 / 826
1600	0 / -160	0 / 230	0 / 620	280 / 909	559 / 1120	839 / 1253	1119 / 1308	1398 / 1285	1678 / 1184	1957 / 1005	2237 / 748	2517 / 413
1500	0 / -160	0 / 230	241 / 558	481 / 808	722 / 980	963 / 1074	1203 / 1090	1444 / 1028	1684 / 888	1925 / 670	2166 / 374	2406 / 0
1400	0 / -160	202 / 207	403 / 496	605 / 707	807 / 840	1008 / 895	1210 / 872	1411 / 771	1613 / 592	1815 / 335	2016 / 0	2016 / 0
1300	163 / -144	325 / 184	488 / 434	651 / 606	813 / 700	976 / 716	1138 / 654	1301 / 514	1464 / 296	1626 / 0	1626 / 0	1626 / 0
1200	247 / -128	371 / 161	495 / 372	618 / 505	742 / 560	865 / 537	989 / 436	1113 / 257	1236 / 0	1236 / 0	1236 / 0	1236 / 0
1100	254 / -112	339 / 138	423 / 310	508 / 404	592 / 420	677 / 358	762 / 218	846 / 0	846 / 0	846 / 0	846 / 0	846 / 0
1000	183 / -96	228 / 115	274 / 248	319 / 303	365 / 280	411 / 179	456 / 0	456 / 0	456 / 0	456 / 0	456 / 0	456 / 0
900	33 / -80	40 / 92	46 / 186	53 / 202	60 / 140	66 / 0	66 / 0	66 / 0	66 / 0	66 / 0	66 / 0	66 / 0
800	-194 / -64	-227 / 69	-259 / 124	-291 / 101	-324 / 0	-324 / 0	-324 / 0	-324 / 0	-324 / 0	-324 / 0	-324 / 0	-324 / 0
	800	900	1000	1100	1200	1300	1400	1500	1600	1700	1800	1900

LAL Price

Note: -194 is KL contribution.
       -64 is LAL contribution.

CASE 33
LIGHTWEIGHT ALUMINUM COMPANY: THE LEBANON PLANT

Paul Smith, manager of the Lebanon, Indiana, alloy production plant of Lightweight Aluminum Company, was the last to reach the conference room for the November monthly production planning meeting. The others, including Lonny Gorban, operations research specialist and primary developer of the scrap blending/purchasing linear programming (LP) model the plant was considering for adoption, were already present. In preparation for the meeting, Smith had asked Gorban to use his LP model to determine how best to accomplish December's planned production of two key alloys, and to circulate the results. Smith could tell from the disgruntled looks on the faces of those present that the meeting was not apt to be a smooth one.

Alloy Production

An *alloy* is a mixture of two or more metals, or metals and other substances. Aluminum alloys consist primarily of aluminum, with smaller quantities of other metals, such as manganese and zinc, and/or substances, such as silicon. The proportions of the component materials determine the alloy's physical properties and characteristics.

At Lightweight, aluminum alloys were produced by melting down component materials in large furnaces. In their molten states, the materials combined, and, when cooled, became the desired alloys. It was possible to produce alloys of a specific composition by combining component materials in their pure forms. For example, a sufficient amount of pure zinc could be added to a furnace load to produce an alloy containing 2 percent zinc. At the time of the case, however, metals (and other substances) in their pure form tended to be quite expensive. An alternative, more economical approach was to use scrap alloys. For example, scrap containing 2 percent zinc could be combined with an equal amount of scrap containing 4 percent zinc to produce an alloy containing 3 percent zinc.

In deciding which scrap alloys to combine, and in what quantities, to produce an alloy of specified composition, several factors had to be considered. Most obviously, the proportion of each component material in the finished product had to fall within the required specifications. These specifications were typically stated in the form of ranges on the allowable proportions of each material. For example, it might be specified that zinc comprise no less than 2 percent nor more than 4 percent of a particular alloy. Another factor that had to be considered was the proportion of each type of scrap lost during the melting process, typically expressed as the percentage retained after melting. Still another factor was the

---

EXHIBIT 1   Specification of Alloys AL311 and AL262—December 1985

Alloy	Silicon Percent	Specifications Manganese Percent	Zinc Percent	Required	Allotted Furnace Production Hours*
AL311	8.0–9.0	0.1–0.3	2.0–3.0	2,000	400
AL262	4.0–6.0	1.0–1.2	1.5–2.5	3,000	500

---

*Expressed in thousands of pounds.

charge rate, the rate at which each type of scrap melted, typically expressed as lbs./hr. (pounds per hour).

Production Planning at the Lebanon Plant

Each month, the first step in the production planning process was to determine how many pounds of each alloy to produce in the upcoming month. Next, a set number of furnace hours was allocated to each alloy. From the scrap currently in inventory and what was available for purchase, it was then decided (at the monthly production planning meeting) which scraps should be used to produce which alloys and in what quantities. The cast house (or production) superintendent knew what was in inventory; the scrap buyer had a good feel for what was available on the market and at what price. With the aid of the plant manager, the production plan and its associated purchasing schedule were developed.

The scrap blending/purchasing LP model had been built over the course of the previous year to facilitate determining the best production and purchasing plan, given the number of furnace hours allocated to each product. Formulating a production plan for December was to be the model's first test, although it was generally felt that the model would probably require some additional fine tuning, and hence its recommendation for December would probably not be implemented.

Early in November, it had been decided to produce two important alloys in December: AL311 was allocated 400 hours of furnace time, and AL262 was allocated 500 hours. Gorban had taken the specs for these two products (Exhibit 1), along with the scrap availability data (Exhibit 2, gleaned from discussions with the cast house superintendent, John Forrester, and the scrap buyer, Melissa Johnson), and run them through the LP model. The results (Exhibit 3) had been circulated to Smith, Forrester, Johnson, and chief accountant Arthur Miller prior to the November production meeting.

The Meeting

"I presume that you have all received and had a chance to look at the December production and purchasing plan determined by the LP model," Smith began. "Let's start by getting your reactions. John?"

EXHIBIT 2 **Scrap Availability—December 1985**

Scrap	Percent Si	Percent Man	Percent Zi	Metal Available[1]	Cost[2] ($)	Melt Cost[3] ($)	Percent Retained	Charge Rate[4]
Scrap 1	0.0	0.0	0.0	4,000[5]	$360	$41	95%	8.0
Scrap 2	10.0	0.4	2.5	1,750[5]	330	35	85	7.5
Scrap 3	0.2	1.0	0.3	800[5]	310	40	85	7.5
Scrap 4	0.3	4.0	3.0	600[6]	290	67	87	6.5
Scrap 5	4.0	1.5	0.4	200[6]	260	41	75	2.5
Scrap 6	3.0	0.8	5.0	1,000[6]	300	22	93	7.0
Silicon	100.0	0.0	0.0	—	600	43	90	3.0
Manganese	0.0	100.0	0.0	—	525	36	92	6.0
Zinc	0.0	0.0	100.0	—	450	31	90	4.0

[1]Expressed in thousands of pounds.

[2]Expressed in dollars per thousand pounds at the current market price.

[3]Expressed in dollars per thousand pounds at the current market price.

[4]Expressed in thousands of pounds per hour.

[5]Currently in inventory.

[6]None currently in inventory; listed amount is pounds available at the market price.

John Forrester, cast house superintendent

"I wish I could be more positive, Paul, but I have a number of problems with the solution proposed by the LP model. First of all, it has us buying and using Scrap 5. The throughput on that stuff is terrible. The workers end up spending most of the day standing around. If you're interested in improving productivity, that's one way *not* to do it. Furthermore, as you all know, using dirty scrap makes it that much sooner that we have to shut the furnace down and clean the whole thing out.

"Secondly, do we really want to use up all of Scraps 2 and 3 in December? Suppose we come along in January and decide to produce an alloy for which one or both of them is perfect? It strikes me as irresponsible and shortsighted to get rid of our entire inventory of versatile scraps.

"But thirdly, and most importantly, I don't think the solution being proposed by the model is optimal, and I think I can prove it. According to my calculations, the LP solution plan has us producing AL311 at a cost of about $850,000. I think we can produce it for less by doing the following: use 1,200,000 lbs. of Scrap 1; 800,000 lbs. of Scrap 6; and throw in 150,000 lbs. or so of silicon and 3,000 lbs. of zinc. I think you will find that this plan produces more than enough AL311 for less money. The rationale is simple: Scraps 1 and 6 are perfect for AL311, except for the lack of silicon. While silicon is expensive, the additional cost is more than offset by the savings that accrue from using Scraps 1 and 6, which are relatively cheap. I don't know if there is an error in the model, or a bug in the software, but something isn't right. I sent these numbers to Lonny yesterday; maybe he can shed some light on them."

Smith spoke before Gorban had a chance to respond. "Perhaps we should let everybody have their say before giving Lonny a chance to respond. Melissa?"

Melissa Johnson, scrap buyer

"The model results look fine to me, Paul, but I do have a couple of nagging concerns. The most important is the precision with which LP treats some of the inputs. For example, I told Lonny that I could get a million pounds of Scrap 6 at $300 per thousand pounds, but that was a loose approximation, both in terms of quantity and price. In actuality, I might be able to get a lot more, and, since the LP solution has us using all one million pounds, is it safe to assume that we would like to get our hands on more? At the same time, the $0.30 per pound is not firm; it's an estimate based on talking with several vendors. Once word gets around that we're buying, the price might easily go up. At what point does it become prohibitively expensive?"

Arthur Miller, accountant

At this point, Miller interrupted. "While we are on the subject of prices, this is probably as good a point as any to question the use of market replacement cost versus actual purchase price to value the scraps in inventory. While I am fully aware of the danger of applying standard costing in decision making, there are times where it is an accurate estimate of the value of raw materials, specifically when we are not going to sell them on the open market. Pretending that we are by assuming market replacement cost is only deceiving ourselves."

"Art, on that very point," Forrester interrupted. "I don't understand why we're assigning any cost at all to the stuff in inventory. The money has already been spent, the stuff is just sitting there waiting to be used. It sure seems like a sunk cost to me."

"Hold on a minute," Smith interrupted. "This seems to be getting out of hand. Maybe we should slow down a bit and give Lonny a chance to respond."

Lonny Gorban, operations research specialist

For a moment, Gorban was silent, trying to decide where to begin. He had, in fact, received Forrester's "better" plan the day before and had rerun his model to check it out (see Exhibit 4). He could address Forrester's plan and then proceed to each of the other issues raised. Alternatively, there was an issue he himself wanted to raise, namely the arbitrary tightening of the allowable maximum proportions of key elements in the production of alloys.

For example, the maximum allowable proportion of manganese in AL311 was actually 0.5 percent, not the 0.3 percent used to determine the production plan. The tightening of the upper bound was done to minimize the chance that the finished product would not meet specs. This could happen if, for example, the stated proportion of a particular material in a component scrap was incorrect. Minimum allowable amounts were of less concern, since a shortfall could always be corrected by adding material in its pure form to the furnace load. However, if a maximum limit was exceeded, the furnace (which was considered "off-analysis") had to be drained and the process of making the alloy restarted. The

EXHIBIT 3   Results

Memorandum
To: Forrester, Johnson, Miller, Smith
From: Gorban
Date: November 10
Re: LP model for production planning

Below and attached is a spreadsheet model for December's production schedule. The model is a linear program and has been optimized using an LP software package called What's Best! Formulas for selected cells are included in footnotes.

	A	B	C	D	E	F	G	H	I
2									
3	I. INPUT								
4									
5	Exhibit 1: Specification of Alloys AL311 and AL262–December								
6									
7		Silicon		Manganese		Zinc			
8	Product	Min	Max	Min	Max	Min	Max	Required	Hours
9		—	—	—	—	—	—	—	—
10	AL311	8.0%	9.0%	0.1%	0.3%	2.0%	3.0%	2,000	400
11	AL262	4.0%	6.0%	1.0%	1.2%	1.5%	2.5%	3,000	500
12									
13	Exhibit 2: Scrap Availability–December								
14								Charge	
15		Percentage of				Total	Percent	rate	
16	Scrap	Silicon	Manganese	Zinc	Available	cost	retained	per 1,000	
17	—	—	—	—	—	—	—	tons	
18	SCRAP1	0.0%	0.0%	0.0%	4,000	$401	95%	0.125	
19	SCRAP2	10.0%	0.4%	2.5%	1,750	$365	85%	0.133	
20	SCRAP3	0.2%	1.0%	0.3%	800	$350	85%	0.133	
21	SCRAP4	0.3%	4.0%	3.0%	600	$357	87%	0.154	
22	SCRAP5	4.0%	1.5%	0.4%	200	$301	75%	0.400	

EXHIBIT 3 *Continued*

	A	B	C	D	E	F	G	H	I
23	SCRAP6	3.0%	0.8%	5.0%	1,000	$322	93%	0.143	
24	Silicon	100.0%	0.0%	0.0%	—	$643	90%	0.333	
25	Manganese	0.0%	100.0%	0.0%	—	$481	90%	0.250	
26	Zinc	0.0%	0.0%	100.0%	—	$561	92%	0.167	
27									
28	II. LINEAR PROGRAMMING MODEL								
29									
30	A. Decision Variables								
31									
32		Input			Output				
33	Scrap	AL311	AL262		AL311	AL262			
34	—	—	—		—	—			
35	SCRAP1	1,005	216		955[1]	205[2]			
36	SCRAP2	613	1,137		521	967			
37	SCRAP3	0	800		0	680			
38	SCRAP4	0	562		0	489			
39	SCRAP5	105	95		79	71			
40	SCRAP6	367	633		342	588			
41	Silicon	105	0		95	0			
42	Manganese	0	0		0	0			

[1] +G18*B35
[2] +G18*C35

Exhibit 3 *Continued*

	A	B	C	D	E	F	G	H	I
43	Zinc	10	0		10	0			
44		—			—	—			
45	TOTAL	2,206[3]	3,442		2,000	3,000			
46									
47	B. Objective Function								
48									
49	TOTAL COST		$2,064,371[4]						
50									
51	C. Constraints								
52									
53	SCRAP AVAILABILITY								
54							Shadow	Range	
55		Required		Available	Slack	price	Decrease	Increase	
56		—		—	—	—	—	—	
57	SCRAP1	1,220[5]	<	4,000[6]	2,780	$0.00	2,780	********	
58	SCRAP2	1,750	<	1,750	0	$17.41	388	226	

[3] @SUM(B35..B43)

[4] @SUMPRODUCT(F18..F26,B35..B43)+@SUMPRODUCT(F18..F26,C35..C43)

[5] +B35+C35

[6] +E18

EXHIBIT 3 *Continued*

	A	B	C	D	E	F	G	H	I
59	SCRAP3	800	<	800	0	$6.06	155	312	
60	SCRAP4	562	<	600	38	$0.00	38	********	
61	SCRAP5	200	<	200	0	$7.64	101	68	
62	SCRAP6	1,000	<	1,000	0	$76.02	177	103	
63									
64									
65	SPECIFICATIONS, AL311								
66						Shadow		Range	
67					Slack	price	Decrease	Increase	
68	Production	2,000[7]	>	2,000[8]	0	$444.64	256	398	
69	Silicon								
70	Max	160[9]	<	180[10]	20	$0.00	20	********	
71	Min	160	>	160	0	$292.34	95	20	
72	Manganese								
73	Max	6	<	6	0	$1,535.56	1	1	
74	Min	6	>	2	4	$0.00	********	4	
75	Zinc								
76	Max	40	<	60	20	$0.00	20	********	
77	Min	40	>	40	0	$187.68	10	20	
78	Hours	339[11]	<	400[12]	61	$0.00	61	********	

[7] +E45
[8] +H10
[9] @SUMPRODUCT(B18..B26,E35..E43)
[10] +C10*E45
[11] @SUMPRODUCT(H18..H26,B35..B43)
[12] +I10

531

EXHIBIT 3 *Concluded*

	A	B	C	D	E	F	G	H	I
79									
80									
81	SPECIFICATIONS, AL262								
82					Slack	Shadow price	Range Decrease	Increase	
83					—	—	—	—	
84	Production	3,000	>	3,000	0	$437.04	189	110	
85	Silicon								
86	Max	120	<	180	60	$0.00	60	*********	
87	Min	120	>	120	0	$300.12	69	33	
88	Manganese								
89	Max	36	<	36	0	$264.05	6	1	
90	Min	36	>	30	6	$0.00	*********	6	
91	Zinc								
92	Max	71	<	75	4	$0.00	4	*********	
93	Min	71	>	45	26	$0.00	*********	26	
94	Hours	500	<	500	0	$46.38	18	29	

Exhibit 4 Optimized Spreadsheet with Forrester's Solution for AL311

	A	B	C	D	E	F	G	H
28	II. LINEAR PROGRAMMING MODEL							
29								
30	A. Decision Variables							
31			Input			Output		
32								
33	Scrap	AL311	AL262		AL311	AL262		
34								
35	SCRAP1	1,200	471		1,140	448		
36	SCRAP2	0	1,273		0	1,082		
37	SCRAP3	0	800		0	680		
38	SCRAP4	0	600		0	522		
39	SCRAP5	0	109		0	82		
40	SCRAP6	800	200		744	186		
41	Silicon	150	0		135	0		
42	Manganese	0	0		0	0		
43	Zinc	3	0		3	0		
44								
45	TOTAL	2,153	3,454		2,022	3,000		
46								
47	B. Objective Function							
48								
49	TOTAL COST		$2,082,167					
50								
51	C. Constraints							
52								
53	SCRAP AVAILABILITY							Range
54						Shadow		
55		Required		Available	Slack	price	Decrease	Increase
56								
57	SCRAP1	1,671	<	4,000	2,329	$0.00	2,329	*********
58	SCRAP2	1,273	<	1,750	477	$0.00	477	*********
59	SCRAP3	800	<	800	0	$7.64	613	165
60	SCRAP4	600	<	600	0	$8.08	142	38
61	SCRAP5	109	<	200	91	$0.00	91	*********
62	SCRAP6	1,000	<	1,000	0	$71.78	200	217

533

EXHIBIT 4 *Concluded*

	A	B	C	D	E	F	G	H
						Shadow	Range	
					Slack	price	Decrease	Increase
65	SPECIFICATIONS, AL311							
66								
67					—	—	—	—
68	Production	2,022	>	2,000	22			
69	Silicon							
70	Max	157	<	182	25			
71	Min	157	>	162	(4)			
72	Manganese							
73	Max	6	<	6	0			
74	Min	6	>	2	4			
75	Zinc							
76	Max	40	<	61	21			
77	Min	40	>	40	0			
78	Hours	315	<	400	85			
79								
80								
81	SPECIFICATIONS, AL262					Shadow	Range	
82					Slack	price	Decrease	Increase
83					—	—	—	—
84	Production	3,000	>	3,000	0	$433.60	83	227
85	Silicon							
86	Max	120	<	180	60	$0.00	60	*********
87	Min	120	>	120	0	$88.36	37	40
88	Manganese							
89	Max	35	<	36	1	$0.00	1	*********
90	Min	35	>	30	5	$0.00	*********	5
91	Zinc							
92	Max	54	<	75	21	$0.00	21	*********
93	Min	54	>	45	9	$0.00	*********	9
94	Hours	500	<	500	0	$60.50	32	27

cost of draining a furnace load was estimated at $2,000, regardless of the particular alloy being produced. Since almost all of the molten conglomerate drained from the furnace could be reused, the material loss of a furnace being off-analysis was considered negligible.

Gorban felt that the 0.3 percent figure was much too restrictive. Using it, the odds of any of the roughly 10 December furnace loads of AL311 going off-analysis were virtually negligible. By relaxing it, the alloy could be produced much more economically. Gorban had spent considerable time with the production engineering staff collecting information on alloys similar to AL311. From this, he had developed the following estimates of the probability of the actual manganese proportion exceeding 0.5 percent given where the target was set:

Maximum Manganese Target	Probability of Manganese Exceeding 0.5%
0.5%	40%
0.4	15
0.3	1

Now, however, did not seem the best time to raise this issue. Gorban wondered how he should proceed.

CASE 34
LOREX PHARMACEUTICALS

Carter Blakely, manager of quality assurance for the manufacturing division of Lorex Pharmaceuticals, was pleased with the progress made so far toward the production of the company's newest product, Linatol. Linatol was a highly promising medicine for the treatment of high blood pressure developed and patented by Lorex several years ago. After eight years of thorough product testing, including clinical studies of the drug's effectiveness on humans, the Food and Drug Administration (FDA) had approved Linatol only a week ago. The manufacturing division had been able to prepare a production line during the past week and now one-shift production was scheduled to begin on Monday. The marketing division at Lorex had decided that the initial offering of Linatol would be in sealed 10-ounce bottles, packaged in cases of 12 bottles each. The wholesale price had been set at $186 per case. The one task remaining for Blakely on this Friday afternoon was the selection of a target amount to which each of the 10-ounce bottles of Linatol would be filled.

The Manufacturing of Linatol

Linatol was blended in 5,000-liter batches using a process and formula that were kept confidential by the company. The product was then bottled on one of the company's semiautomatic filling lines. These lines consisted of an automatic filling mechanism for liquids, a capping and sealing component, and an electronic sensor capable of measuring the volume of liquid in each bottle. Bottles that were filled properly were conveyed to a packaging machine that would load and seal cartons of 12 bottles each. At top speed, the line chosen for Linatol could fill and package 1,000 bottles per hour. Because of unavoidable delays and setup requirements, the production rate was expected to average 500 cases over an eight-hour shift. These rates were slower than most of the other filling lines in use, but the relatively low production volumes of Linatol dictated that it be filled on one of the older, slower lines, which was not needed for any other product.

The entire line was operated by two employees who earned $12.80 per hour, including fringe benefits. Every product was charged an overhead burden to cover the huge expense of maintaining an antiseptic filling room. For the line on which Linatol would be bottled, the overhead was charged at a rate of $89.50 per hour.

The cost of the materials used by the filling line (bottles, caps, cap seals, labels, and packaging) was estimated to be $1.10 per bottle.

Those bottles not filled to the 10-ounce requirement were identified by the electronic eye and automatically directed for special handling. A team of filling-room attendants periodically labeled these underfilled bottles as seconds and

---

EXHIBIT 1   Linatol Projected Operating Profit (5,000 liters; i.e., 169,088 ounces)

Item	Cost
Revenue:	
Commercial*	$218,405
Seconds (15% rejects)	30,834
Total	$249,239
Costs:	
Active ingredients	$ 67,662
Blending direct labor	432
Blending indirect labor	170
Blending overhead	1,698
Filling materials	18,235
Filling direct labor	566
Filling overhead	1,978
Seconds packaging labor	147
Total	$ 90,888
Gross margin	$158,351

*At a 10.2-ounce target, one batch yields 1,381.44 cases. At an 85% acceptance rate, 1,174.22 of the cases are sold
in the commercial market, and 207.22 are sold as seconds. This fill target and acceptance rate are for planning
purposes only. The actual target and acceptance rate will be determined after the filling-line test.

---

hand-packaged them for sale to secondary markets (such as government hospitals) at 80 percent of the normal price of $186 per case. Although these attendants spent most of their time hand-packaging underfilled products, a variety of other activities kept them busy. Each attendant was capable of labeling and packaging about 12 cases per hour. Attendants made $8.50 per hour, including fringe benefits.

The initial production of Linatol had been scheduled for one 40-hour-per-week shift on the filling line for the foreseeable future. The actual batch blending of Linatol would be scheduled accordingly. An approximate operating profit statement for Linatol (prepared prior to the filling-line test) is given in Exhibit 1.

The Filling-Line Test

Prior to the start-up of production of a new product, the process capability of the filling line was tested—first with an inexpensive liquid with physical properties similar to the product and finally with the product itself. Once the filling process was "perfected," samples of the filled bottles were individually measured. The results of 144 bottles of Linatol filled during a test are given in Exhibit 2. This exhibit also shows which of the 144 bottles were selected by the electronic sensor as underfilled. For this test, the filling mechanism was adjusted to fill to a target of 10.2 fluid ounces. The consistency of amounts in the 144 test bottles left little doubt that the fill mechanism could be set to any desired target.

Setting the Fill Target

It now remained for Carter Blakely to determine the fill target. The 10.2-ounce target chosen for the test was arbitrary, and certainly no economic justification existed for keeping this target. A rule often used for setting fill targets was to pick a target that was one standard deviation above the required amount. The relevant standard deviation was, of course, the standard deviation of the amounts placed in individual bottles. However, a one-standard-deviation rule, although cloaked with a certain amount of statistical justification, also seemed to ignore the peculiar economics associated with each filling situation. In fact, a one-standard-deviation rule in the past had led to several occasions when the buffer storage area for underfilled bottles had become clogged with rejected bottles, which caused a temporary stoppage of the entire filling line.

Exhibit 2   Filling-Line Test Results

9.89*	10.41	10.53	10.20	10.23	10.15
10.17	10.17	10.32	10.04	10.48	10.11
10.29	10.35	10.16	10.16	10.17	10.19
10.00	10.06	10.21	10.22	9.76*	10.22
10.04	10.19	10.09	10.12	10.06	10.10
10.35	10.17	10.02	10.35	10.17	9.99*
10.05	10.07	10.32	10.24	10.04	10.40
10.19	10.27	10.14	10.07	10.41	10.76
10.21	10.13	10.11	10.40	10.27	10.20
9.79*	10.24	10.20	10.29	10.00	10.31
10.53	10.14	10.35	10.21	10.23	10.16
10.47	9.84*	9.96*	10.10	10.11	10.23
10.24	10.36	10.30	10.23	10.19	10.17
10.17	10.11	10.33	10.19	9.97*	10.00
10.15	10.42	10.36	10.19	10.05	10.11
10.06	10.16	10.17	10.29	10.12	10.30
10.13	10.21	10.15	10.25	10.33	10.64
10.04	10.01	10.14	10.18	10.18	10.10
10.20	10.25	10.07	10.42	10.54	10.23
10.37	10.44	10.37	9.85*	9.91*	10.45
10.24	10.44	10.40	10.45	10.28	10.17
10.03	10.44	10.25	10.37	10.23	10.19
10.01	10.13	10.24	10.22	9.98*	9.98*
10.20	10.29	10.03	10.19	9.99*	10.13
Average 10.16	10.22	10.22	10.22	10.15	10.22
Std. dev. 0.17	0.16	0.14	0.13	0.18	0.19
Grand avg. 10.20					
Std. dev. 0.16					

*Identified by the sensor as underfilled.

CASE 35
MAXCO, INC., AND THE GAMBIT COMPANY

Part I

Maxco, Inc., and the Gambit Company were fully integrated, major oil companies each with annual sales over $1 billion and exploration and development budgets over $100 million. Both firms were preparing sealed bids for an oil rights lease on block A-512 off the Louisiana Gulf coast. Although the deadline for the submission of bids was only three weeks away, neither firm was very close to a final determination of its bid. Indeed, management at Maxco had yet to decide whether to bid at all, let alone how much to bid. Although Gambit was virtually certain to submit a bid, the level of Gambit's bid was far from settled. This uncharacteristic hesitancy in the preparation of both firms' bids was a direct result of certain peculiarities in the situation surrounding the bidding for block A-512.

Block A-512 lay in the Alligator Reef area immediately to the south of a known oil-producing region (see Exhibit 1). Just to the north were blocks A-497 and A-498, both of which were already under lease to the Gambit Company. On its leasehold Gambit had two completed wells, which had been in production for some time. In addition, Gambit had an offset control well in progress near the boundary between its leasehold and block A-512. When this well was completed, Gambit would have access to direct information concerning the value of any oil reserves lying beneath block A-512. Maxco's nearest leasehold, on the other hand, was some seven miles to the southeast. Any bid submitted by Maxco, therefore, would necessarily be based solely on indirect information.

The Role of Information in Bidding for Oil Rights Leases. In a bidding situation, information concerning either the object of the bidding or the notions of competing bidders is highly prized. This is even more the case in bidding for the rights to oil reserves lying, perhaps, thousands of feet below the surface. There are, of course, various kinds of information available to bidders for oil rights. To summarize these various types of information briefly, two categories—direct and indirect—may be established.

Information obtained by drilling on a parcel of land is called "direct information." Obviously this is the most precise information obtainable concerning the subsurface structure. From core samples taken up during the drilling operation, and from careful laboratory analysis of these samples, considerable information

Copyright © 1993 by the President and Fellows of Harvard College.
Harvard Business School case 174-091
This case was prepared by Donald L. Wallace under the direction of Dr. John S. Hammond III as the basis for class discussion rather than to illustrate either effective or ineffective handling of an administrative situation. Reprinted by permission of the Harvard Business School.

Exhibit 1 Subsurface Map of the Alligator Reef Area

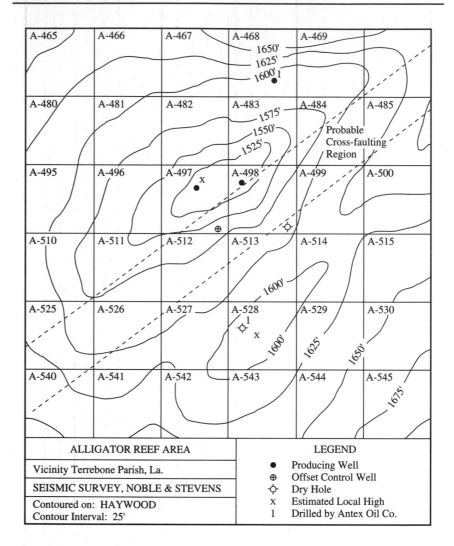

ALLIGATOR REEF AREA	LEGEND		
Vicinity Terrebone Parish, La.	●	Producing Well	
	⊕	Offset Control Well	
SEISMIC SURVEY, NOBLE & STEVENS	◇	Dry Hole	
	x	Estimated Local High	
Contoured on: HAYWOOD	1	Drilled by Antex Oil Co.	
Contour Interval: 25'			

may be accumulated not only about the presence or absence of oil but also about the type, thickness, composition, and physical properties of each of the various geological strata encountered. Such information then provides the driller with a relatively accurate estimate of the oil reserves lying beneath the parcel. Direct information concerning adjacent parcels may be obtained by drilling offset control wells. These wells are offset from the principal producing areas and are located near the boundaries of the leased parcel. Such wells may then provide a particular lessee with precise and valuable information about adjacent parcels.

Indirect information is obtained from sources other than drilling and may be roughly divided into two kinds: scouting and nonscouting. Scouting information is gained by observing the operations of other drillers. By counting the sections of drill pipe—each of known length—introduced into a hole, an observer may infer the depth of the hole. By observing the quantity of cement—required by law—used to plug the various porous strata that are encountered, the thicknesses of these strata may be determined. Normally, however, this type of scouting information will not yield nearly the precision available to the driller himself. It can help in the determination of whether or not oil reserves exist at a particular location, but it is much less useful in determining the size of the reserves.

More definite scouting information may sometimes be obtained by more clandestine means. Eavesdropping on information conversations in public places, subtle forms of bribery and interrogation, even forcible entry onto a competitor's drilling site may provide much more detailed—and more valuable—information. An extreme anecdote tells of two men caught while inspecting a competitor's drilling log—the source document of a driller's direct information. The men were reportedly held at gunpoint for several days in anticipation of the approaching deadline for the submission of bids. Managing to escape, the day before the deadline, the two men were able to report back what they had seen in the log. As a result, the operator whose log had been compromised was forced to raise his bid by $7 million.

Less melodramatic, but highly significant, sources of indirect information are available through means other than scouting. Nonscouting information is obtained, first, from published sources, such as government geological and geophysical surveys, and reports of previous explorations. Second, nonscouting information may be obtained from local seismic surveys conducted either by in-house personnel or private contractors. A third source of nonscouting information is found in the trading of dry hole information. The tradition among drilling operators is to reveal their dry hole experiences. The feeling seems to be that there is far more to be gained from the reciprocal exchange of dry hole information than could be gained from watching a competitor pour a considerable investment into a site that is known to be barren. Finally, nonscouting information may also be obtained from the independent prospectors, promoters, and traders who may have become familiar with certain tracts in the past and are willing to trade this information, again on a reciprocal basis.

As might be suspected in an environment where information has such a high and immediate value, internal security presents a clear and ever-present problem. Bank-type vaults, armed guards, and electrified fences are commonplace. On occasion, entire drilling rigs have been encased in canvas to thwart the efforts of prying eyes. Substantial slow-downs in operations, however, under almost unbearable working conditions have also resulted. Furthermore, a blanket of security must also be placed over the derivation and submission of bids. Information on the level of a particular bid can be even more valuable than information on the value of reserves. When bids were being prepared for the tracts surrounding Prudhoe Bay on Alaska's North Slope, one company packed its entire bidding organization onto a railroad train and ran it back and forth over the same stretch of track until bids had been prepared and submitted and the bidding deadline had passed.

Finally, with information such a prime concern, circulation of false information is often attempted. If an operator is successful in leaking false negative information about a particular parcel, he may be able to later "steal" the parcel with a relatively low bid. On the other hand, to divert attention from a particular parcel, an operator may feign interest in another one by seeming to conduct tests there.

Maxco's Bidding Problem.   Mr. E. P. Buchanan, vice president for exploration and development, had primary responsibility for preparing Maxco's bid. Mr. Buchanan's information on block A-512 was, as indicated previously, indirect in nature. Although some scouting information on Gambit's offset control well was available to him, the primary basis of his information was a private seismic survey, together with published government geological maps and reports. Maxco had acquired the survey data, in a jointly financed effort with Gambit, through the use of a private contractor. The contractor, Noble and Stevens, had prepared a detailed survey of the entire Alligator Reef area several years previously when blocks A-497 and A-498 were up for bid. Under the joint financing arrangement, identical copies of the completed report had then been submitted to both Maxco and Gambit. Such an arrangement, while unusual, was not without precedent in known oil-producing areas. Exhibit 1 represents an updated version of a subsurface map included in Noble and Stevens' report.

Based on all the information available to him, Mr. Buchanan's judgment concerning the monetary value of the oil reserves under block A-512 was essentially captured by the probability mass function given in Exhibit 2. Furthermore, Mr. Buchanan held that Maxco's bid should be based solely on this monetary value of the oil reserves. Since it was known that no nearby blocks were to be put up for bid for at least 10 years, Mr. Buchanan did not ascribe any informational value to owning a lease on block A-512.

Mr. Buchanan also felt—for the present at least—that Gambit's uncertainty was virtually identical to his own. He was sure, however, that Gambit's well would be completed by the deadline for the submission of bids. At that time Gambit would know the value of the reserves up to perhaps, ± 5 or ± 10 percent.

For the past several years, Mr. Buchanan had refused to bid on any parcels of land where he felt he was at a distinct disadvantage to a competing bidder. If a competitor had superior (direct) information about a parcel while Maxco had only indirect information, then Mr. Buchanan preferred not to bid at all.

Less than five months ago, however, in an area not far from Alligator Reef, Mr. Buchanan had *lost* a bid on a block adjacent to a Maxco leasehold. Maxco had gone to the expense of drilling an offset control well on its own block and had found a reasonably large oil reserve. Maxco had then lost the bid, however, to a competitor who was operating solely on the basis of indirect information. In

---

EXHIBIT 2   Probability Distribution of Monetary Values

Monetary Value of Oil Reserves* ($ millions)	Probability
$ 1.7	0.03
2.7	0.06
3.7	0.10
4.7	0.17
5.7	0.28
6.7	0.18
7.7	0.08
8.7	0.04
9.7	0.02
10.7	0.01
11.7	0.01
12.7	0.01
13.7	0.01
	1.00

Mean value = $5.83.

* Net present value at 10%.

addition, the competitor's winning bid had still been low enough to provide for a substantial profit on the venture.

Thus Mr. Buchanan was considering a change in his policy. While he very much doubted that anyone else would enter the bidding for block A-512, he was beginning to feel that he himself should do so. If he did decide to bid, he then wondered what sort of bid might be reasonable.

Part II

Gambit's Bidding Problem.   Mr. Buchanan's counterpart in the Gambit Company was a Mr. K. R. Mason; primary responsibility for preparing Gambit's bid thus rested with him.

Until Gambit's well on the Alligator Reef leasehold was completed, Mr. Mason's information concerning block A-512 would be indirect in nature. The primary basis of that information was still the private seismic survey, for which Gambit had contracted jointly with Maxco, together with published government geological maps and reports.

Although Mr. Mason also had detailed production logs on the two producing wells on Gambit's leasehold, he felt that this information was not relevant to the problem of assessing the potential value of block A-512. There was almost certainly some cross-faulting in the Alligator Reef area (see Exhibit 1). Since this cross-faulting would probably terminate the producing area, the principal uncertainty surrounding the value of block A-512 was the precise location of the northernmost cross-fault. Thus, Mr. Mason's judgment was also essentially captured by the probability mass function given in Exhibit 2. Although Mr. Mason's judgment certainly did not coincide precisely with Mr. Buchanan's, the facts available to the two men and the economics in the two companies were largely similar. Neither man's estimate of the situation, therefore, differed significantly from Exhibit 2.

This would, of course, change dramatically when Gambit's offset control well was completed. At that time Mr. Mason would be able to reevaluate the property with a much higher degree of precision.

Normally Mr. Mason would then be in a position to submit a bid relatively close to the true value of the block while still allowing a generous margin for profit. Other bidders, not knowing the true value of the block, would be unable to adopt such a strategy. If they bid at all, they would have to either bid relatively low or risk the possibility of "buying in high" to a disastrously unprofitable situation.

Over the past year, however, several operators in the Louisiana Gulf coast had narrowly lost out when bidding for blocks on which they had direct information. Granted that in no case were extremely large reserves lost; nevertheless, operators bidding with nothing but indirect information had been able to "steal away" substantial reserves from operators who were basing their bids on direct information.

With a view toward reassessing his approach to this kind of situation, Mr. Mason thought that it might be useful to prepare a whole schedule of bids. For each possible "true value" of the reserves, Mr. Mason felt that he should be able to establish an appropriate bid—given that value of the reserves. Thus, Mr. Mason felt that he ought to be able to complete a bid schedule similar to that given in Exhibit 3. He was wondering, however, what a reasonable schedule of bids might be like.

EXHIBIT 3   Gambit's Bid Schedule

If the True Value of the Reserves is:	*Then Gambit's Bid Should Be:*
$ 1.7 million	$_____ million
$ 2.7 million	$_____ million
$ 3.7 million	$_____ million
$ 4.7 million	$_____ million
$ 5.7 million	$_____ million
$ 6.7 million	$_____ million
$ 7.7 million	$_____ million
$ 8.7 million	$_____ million
$ 9.7 million	$_____ million
$10.7 million	$_____ million
$11.7 million	$_____ million
$12.7 million	$_____ million
$13.7 million	$_____ million

CASE 36
THE OAKLAND A'S (A)

Steward Roddey, general manager of the Oakland A's baseball team, stared at the attendance figures he had put together for the recently completed 1980 season (Exhibit 1). It was October 1980, and Roddey was in the middle of a difficult contract negotiation with the agent for Mark Nobel, one of the star players for the A's. Nobel and his agent had argued that, in addition to contributing to the recent success of the A's team, Nobel had also been an attraction at the box office. They claimed that people came to the game specifically to see Nobel pitch, and that Nobel should be compensated accordingly.

Roddey believed there could be some truth to Nobel's claims but wanted to look carefully at last year's figures, nonetheless. He put together the information in Exhibit 1 as a first step, recording everything he thought could possibly influence attendance. The next meeting with Nobel's agent was two weeks away, so Roddey had plenty of time to analyze the data.

Background—Professional Baseball

The Oakland Athletics Baseball Club was one of 28 professional teams that played baseball in the major leagues. Each team played 162 games a season within its league, half of which were played at home. (See Exhibit 2 for final 1980 standings.) At the conclusion of the regular season, the teams with the best won-lost percentages in each of the four separate divisions participated in a post-season single elimination tournament. The first round was a best-of-five game series between the division winners in each league. The two league championship teams then met in a best-of-seven game series called the World Series, the winner of which was designated World Champion.

Each team was owned and operated independently within a framework set forth in the 1921 document, "Major League Agreement." Although gross revenues from the sale of tickets to each game were shared (77 percent to the home team, 20 percent to the visiting team, and 3 percent to the league office), each team was responsible for its own expenses. The largest expense items for the A's were players' salaries, player development, travel, accommodations, and stadium rental. The major expenses associated with actually staging an Oakland home game in the 50,000-seat Oakland-Alameda County Coliseum were also incurred by the A's.

The 1980 Season

The Oakland A's finished second in their division in 1980 with a record of 83 wins and 79 losses, 14 games behind the division-winning Kansas City Royals. Many attributed this turnaround from their 1979 last-place finish (see Exhibit 3) to their

This case was based on a Supervised Business Study prepared by Ann C. Stephens (Darden, Class of 1982).

Exhibit 1 1980 Home Game Data

Date	No. of Tickets Sold	Opposing Team	Position	Games Behind	Day of Week	Average Temp.	Precipitation	Time of Game	Televised	Promotions	Nobel
4/10	24,415	2	5	1	4	57	0	2	0	0	0
4/11	5,729	2	3	1	5	66	0	2	0	0	0
4/12	5,783	2	7	1	6	64	0	1	0	0	0
4/13	6,300	2	5	1	7	62	0	1	0	0	1
4/14	5,260	1	7	2	1	60	0	2	0	1	0
4/15	2,140	1	6	1	2	60	0	2	0	0	0
4/16	2,418	1	4	1	3	61	0	1	0	0	0
4/18	6,570	3	3	1	5	58	0	2	0	0	1
4/19	5,239	3	2	1	6	59	0	1	1	0	1
4/20	9,014	3	1	0	7	57	1	1	1	0	0
(double header)											
5/2	8,636	5	1	0	5	57	0	2	0	0	0
5/3	7,062	5	1	0	6	59	0	1	1	0	0
5/4	18,217	5	1	0	7	58	0	1	0	0	1
(double header)											
5/5	12,605	11	1	0	1	60	0	2	0	0	0
5/6	24,272	11	1	0	2	60	0	2	0	1	0
5/7	4,731	11	1	0	3	60	0	1	0	0	0
5/10	4,929	7	1	0	6	55	1	1	0	0	1
5/11	7,839	7	1	0	7	57	0	1	0	0	0
5/23	4,141	12	4	2	5	56	0	2	0	0	0
5/24	5,061	12	3	2	6	55	0	1	1	0	0
5/25	10,549	12	5	3	7	57	0	1	0	0	1
5/26	21,882	13	4	2	1	58	0	1	1	0	0
5/27	4,488	13	4	3	2	58	0	2	0	0	0
5/28	4,094	13	3	2	3	59	0	1	0	0	1
6/6	15,947	9	3	6	5	59	0	2	0	0	0
6/7	12,990	9	3	6	6	61	0	1	0	0	0

EXHIBIT 1 Continued

Date	No. of Tickets Sold	Opposing Team	Position	Games Behind	Day of Week	Average Temp.	Precipitation	Time of Game	Televised	Promotions	Nobel
6/8	18,753	9	3	7	7	63	0	1	0	0	0
6/9	20,162	10	3	7	1	61	0	2	0	0	0
6/10	3,873	10	3	7	2	59	0	2	0	0	0
6/11	5,628	10	3	7	3	60	0	1	0	1	0
6/13	47,768	4	3	7	5	60	0	2	0	0	0
(double header)											
6/14	27,312	4	3	7	6	63	0	1	0	0	1
6/15	46,294	4	3	8	7	64	0	1	0	1	0
6/23	17,666	6	3	9	1	62	0	2	0	1	0
6/24	4,899	6	4	10	2	62	0	2	0	0	0
6/25	6,856	6	4	11	3	63	0	1	0	0	0
6/27	8,482	8	4	11	5	69	0	2	0	1	1
6/28	5,204	8	4	12	6	69	0	1	1	0	0
6/29	7,369	8	4	12	7	63	0	1	0	0	0
7/10	11,337	3	5	12	4	66	0	2	0	0	1
(double header)											
7/11	7,696	3	5	12	5	62	0	2	0	0	0
7/16	7,413	5	5	13	3	65	0	2	0	0	0
7/17	6,370	5	3	12	4	65	0	1	0	0	0
7/18	5,949	11	3	12	5	60	1	2	0	0	1
7/19	6,506	11	3	11	6	65	0	1	1	0	0
7/20	10,606	11	3	11	7	65	0	1	1	1	0
7/21	14,588	7	3	12	1	65	0	2	0	1	0
7/22	8,645	7	3	12	2	63	0	2	0	0	1
(double header)											
7/23	4,765	7	3	12	3	64	0	1	0	0	0
8/4	16,741	2	2	12	1	65	0	2	0	0	0
8/5	4,651	2	2	12	2	67	0	2	0	0	0
8/6	6,697	2	2	12	3	63	0	1	0	0	0
8/8	6,283	1	2	13	5	62	0	2	0	0	0

EXHIBIT 1 *Concluded*

Date	No. of Tickets Sold	Opposing Team	Position	Games Behind	Day of Week	Average Temp.	Precipitation	Time of Game	Televised	Promotions	Nobel
8/9	13,629	1	2	12	6	63	0	1	0	1	1
8/10	13,062	1	2	13	7	63	0	1	0	0	0
(double header)											
8/19	11,934	9	2	15	2	67	0	2	0	0	0
8/20	7,569	9	2	15	3	65	0	2	1	0	1
8/21	10,947	9	2	15	4	61	0	1	0	0	0
8/22	11,532	10	2	15	5	62	0	2	0	0	0
8/23	10,578	10	2	16	6	64	0	1	0	1	0
8/24	18,745	10	2	17	7	63	0	1	0	1	0
8/25	47,946	4	2	17	1	62	0	2	0	1	1
8/26	32,905	4	3	17	2	62	0	2	0	1	0
9/8	9,731	12	3	19	1	65	0	2	0	0	0
9/9	2,443	12	3	18	2	63	0	2	0	0	0
9/10	3,598	13	2	17	3	64	0	1	0	0	1
9/12	17,440	13	2	17	5	62	0	2	0	0	0
9/13	11,253	13	2	16	6	61	0	1	0	0	0
9/14	10,756	13	2	17	7	63	0	1	0	0	0
9/23	3,069	8	2	15	2	70	0	2	0	0	0
9/24	3,836	8	2	14	3	69	0	2	0	0	0
9/25	3,180	8	2	14	4	64	0	1	0	0	0
9/26	5,099	6	2	14	5	64	0	2	0	0	1
9/27	4,581	6	2	13	6	62	0	1	0	0	0
9/28	10,662	6	2	12	7	65	0	1	0	1	0

Position: A's Ranking in American League West.

Day of week: Monday = 1, Tuesday = 2, and so on.

Precipitation: 1 if precipitation; 0 if not.

Time of game: 1 if day game; 2 if night game.

Legend:

Opposing team:

1 Seattle	8 White Sox
2 Minnesota	9 Boston
3 California	10 Baltimore
4 Yankees	11 Cleveland
5 Detroit	12 Texas
6 Milwaukee	13 Kansas City
7 Toronto	

EXHIBIT 2   Final 1980 Standings

American League
Eastern Division

	W	L	Pct.	G.B.*
Yankees	103	59	.636	—
Baltimore	100	62	.617	3
Milwaukee	86	76	.531	17
Boston.	83	77	.519	19
Detroit.	84	78	.519	19
Cleveland	79	81	.494	23
Toronto	67	95	.414	36

Western Division

	W	L	Pct.	G.B.*
Kansas City	97	65	.589	—
Oakland.	83	79	.512	14
Minnesota	77	84	.478	19½
Texas.	76	84	.472	20½
Chicago	70	90	.438	26
California.	65	95	.406	31
Seattle	59	103	.364	38

National League
Eastern Division

	W	L	Pct.	G.B.*
Philadelphia.	91	71	.562	—
Montreal	90	72	.556	1
Pittsburgh	83	79	.512	8
St. Louis	74	86	.457	17
Mets.	67	95	.414	24
Chicago	64	96	.386	27

Western Division

	W	L	Pct.	G.B.*
Houston	92	70	.568	—
Los Angeles.	92	70	.568	—
Cincinnati	89	73	.548	3
Atlanta	81	80	.503	11½
San Francisco.	75	86	.466	17½
San Diego	73	89	.451	20

*G.B. refers to games behind. Because the Yankees won three more games (and lost three fewer) than did
  Baltimore, Baltimore was three games behind the Yankees.
Source: *New York Times,* October 6, 1980.

new manager, Billy Martin.[1] Perhaps the most colorful manager in baseball, Martin had managed six different teams in 12 years. In each instance, he had brought faltering teams to the top of the standings but was fired a short time later.

A second ingredient in the success of the 1980 A's was the remarkable performance of their young pitching staff.[2] Led by Mark Nobel, they had an earned run average[3] of 3.46 (best in the league), compared with 4.74 the year before. Many baseball people attributed this abrupt improvement to the fact that Martin had instructed his pitchers in the art of throwing "spitballs," an effective, but highly illegal, pitch.

---

[1]The manager of a major league team had the responsibility for directing all activities of the team associated with playing and preparing to play the game of baseball. A baseball manager was roughly equivalent to a head coach in other sports.

[2]The pitcher, one of nine players on one side in the game at any one time, started each play by throwing the baseball toward the opposing team's batter. The pitcher had perhaps more influence on the outcome of the game than any one other player. Because he often threw over 100 pitches a game, his arm could not endure more than one game every four or five days.

[3]An earned run average was a measure of the average number of runs per game the opposition scored against each pitcher during a game. It was considered by many to be the most important measure of a pitcher's performance.

EXHIBIT 3   Past Team Performance

Year	W	L	Pct.	Pos.
1968	82	80	.506	6
1969	88	74	.543	2
1970	89	73	.549	2
1971	101	60	.627	1
1972	93	62	.600	1
1973	94	68	.580	1
1974	90	72	.556	1
1975	98	64	.605	1
1976	87	74	.540	2
1977	63	98	.391	7
1978	69	93	.426	6
1979	54	108	.333	7
1980	83	79	.512	2

EXHIBIT 4   Yearly Oakland Attendance

Year	Home	Road	Total
1968	837,466	960,210	1,797,676
1969	778,232	992,124	1,770,356
1970	778,355	971,568	1,749,923
1971	914,993	1,222,741	2,137,734
1972	921,323	1,115,553	2,036,876
1973	1,000,763	1,382,250	2,383,013
1974	845,693	1,526,630	2,372,323
1975	1,075,518	1,436,383	2,511,901
1976	780,593	1,392,109	2,172,702
1977	495,412	1,195,138	1,690,550
1978	526,412	1,381,142	1,908,141
1979	306,763	1,393,196	1,699,959
1980	843,319	1,572,926	2,416,245
Total	10,105,429	16,541,964	26,647,393
Average	777,341	1,272,458	2,049,800

The successes of the A's on the field carried over to the box office. Home attendance in 1980 nearly doubled over the previous season, and road attendance was the highest it had been in the A's history (see Exhibit 4). Total gross revenues from the sale of tickets at home games amounted to $3.085 million, compared with $1.489 million the year before. Ticket prices, lowest in the league, ranged from $2 to $6 (see Exhibit 5) with various discounts (such as half-price night and group rates) offered throughout the year. An aggressive series of promotions numbered 13 in 1980, compared with 4 the previous year (see Exhibit 6).

EXHIBIT 5   Ticket Prices and Starting Times

First deck tickets $6	Single night games.	7:30 P.M.
Second deck tickets. $5	Single day games.	1:30 P.M.
Third deck tickets. $4	Day double headers	12:30 P.M.
Bleacher tickets $2	Twi-night double headers	5:00 P.M.

Special Group Plan: A group of 25 or more could receive $1 off the regular full price for each ticket purchased to A's games (Monday excluded).

Source: Company records.

EXHIBIT 6   1980 Promotions

Date	Promotion
4/14.	Half-price night
5/6	Drawings for gifts
6/11.	Bartenders' & Culinary Union Day—free admission
6/15.	T-Shirt Day—free Billy Martin T-shirt
6/23.	Bartenders', Beauticians', Cabbies' Night—free admission
6/27.	East Bay Merchants' Night—$7,000 merchandise giveaway
7/20.	Poster Day
7/21.	Family Night
8/9	Cap Day—free caps to those 14 and under
8/23.	Farmers' Day—free drawings for produce
8/24.	Billy Martin Day
8/26.	Old Timers' Day
9/28.	Poster Day

Source: American League Office.

Factors Affecting Attendance

Exhibit 1 gives data on the following factors Roddey believed could influence attendance at home games:

Day of the Week.   Roddey was confident that the day of the week on which the game was played influenced attendance. Generally, he thought, weekend games were better attended because more people (especially children when school was in session) had leisure time on weekends.

Team Performance.   Everyone loves a winner, and Roddey believed that the better the A's played, the more people would want to see them play. Especially important was the A's performance relative to the teams in its division. Two measures of this factor are included in Exhibit 1: the A's ranking compared with other divisional teams and the number of games the A's were behind the leading team.[4]

Weather.   The Oakland Coliseum was an open-air stadium, and weather conditions (especially rain) could influence attendance. Included in Exhibit 1 is the average temperature and a record of precipitation during each game.

Double Headers.   Six times during the 1980 home season, the Oakland A's played double headers; that is, two consecutive games on the same day between the same teams. Thus the 75 entries in Exhibit 1 represent 81 home games. One ticket at the same price as a single-game ticket provided admission to both games. Roddey believed this two-for-the-price-of-one bargain increased attendance but was unsure if double headers were actually more profitable than two single games on separate days.

Starting Times.   Baseball could be played in daylight or under artificial lighting at night. Thirty-nine of the A's home dates represented daytime single games or double headers, with the remainder being night games or double headers starting in the late afternoon (see Exhibit 5 for starting times). Roddey was quite familiar with the difference in the composition of day- versus night-game crowds but was not sure if there was any real difference in total attendance. Exhibit 1 contains information on which of the 75 dates were played under the lights.

Starting Pitcher.   Many baseball aficionados thought that the quality of the starting pitcher affected attendance. The starting pitchers for each baseball game were scheduled days in advance, and this information was published in local newspapers. Roddey thought that pitcher Mark Nobel, who might have been considered a star attraction, could conceivably have influenced people to attend those ball games in which he performed. Exhibit 1 gives those games in which Nobel was the starting pitcher.

Opponent.   Although most people came to the ball park to root for the home team, characteristics of the opposing team could also be important criteria in choosing to attend a baseball game. In particular, the New York Yankees—perhaps baseball's most famous team—were known to attract larger crowds than many teams. Roddey was certain that the Yankees had a big effect on the 1980 season attendance since the A's manager Billy Martin had been fired by the Yankees the previous year. Exhibit 1 identifies the opposing team in each contest.

---

[4]"Games behind" may be interpreted as the number of consecutive games the A's would have to win and the division leading team would have to lose before the two would be tied for first place. As an example, if the California Angels were in first place with a record of 42 wins and 34 losses and the A's had won 37 and lost 39, the A's would be 5 games behind the Angels. Comparing the number of games behind to the number of games remaining gave some indication of the chances a team had of eventually winning the division.

Television.   In the past it had been generally thought that televising a home game would dissuade people from attending the game in person, thus depriving the home team of ticket revenue. Recently, however, the amounts of money local stations offered for broadcast rights to home games had convinced many local teams to televise a portion of the home schedule. Exhibit 1 shows that nine home games were carried on local Oakland station KPIX.

Promotions.   Exhibit 6 lists the kinds of promotions, all designed to bring people into the ball park, run by the A's in 1980. Roddey was fairly confident that they did increase attendance; thus Exhibit 1 includes them as part of the attendance data.

Nobel's Pitch

Mark Nobel's record before 1980 had not been impressive. The 26-year-old had won a total of only 11 games for the A's, although Nobel had been in the major leagues since 1975. An arm injury early in that first year had contributed to his poor performance. He was making only $40,000 a year in 1980, when he turned in a spectacular season. As he entered salary negotiations, he was talking in terms of $600,000 a year.

The major evidence presented by Nobel and his agent in support of his salary demands was performance statistics from the 1980 season. Nobel started 33 games, winning 22 and losing 9. He was the second best pitcher in the American League in four important categories: earned run average (2.53), completed games (24), innings pitched (284⅓), and strikeouts (180). He was voted the Gold Glove Award as best fielding pitcher and finished second in the balloting for the Cy Young Award, given each year to the most outstanding pitcher in each league.

Nobel also argued that he had the ability to attract people to the ball park. He had been quoted in *Sports Illustrated*[5] as saying:

> I'm not saying anything against Rick Langford or Matt Keough [fellow A's pitchers] . . .
> but I filled the Coliseum last year against Tommy John [star pitcher for the Yankees].

The implication was that Nobel felt he did indeed personally attract people to the games.

The hard numbers behind this argument had been presented to Roddey in a previous negotiation session. The average home attendance for the 16 games that Nobel started was 12,663.6. When Nobel did not start, the average was only 10,859.4. Nobel's agent multiplied the difference in attendance, 1,804.2, by the average ticket price, $3.66, and then by 16; he put forth the resulting figure, $105,650, as a rough measure of the value of Nobel to the Oakland A's as a box-office attraction. The agent also made it clear that this value was above and beyond the value associated with Nobel's ability to help the A's win ball games.

---

[5]Ron Fimrite, "Winning Is Such a Bore," April 27, 1981.

CASE 37
THE OAKLAND A'S (A) SUPPLEMENT

The following variables were constructed from the data in Exhibit 1 of the "Oakland A's (A)" case (Case 36).

Variable Name	Definition
TIX	Number of tickets sold
OPP	Opposing team (1 through 13)
POS	Position in the division
GB	Games behind
DOW	Day of week (1 = Monday)
TEMP	Temperature (° F)
PREC	Precipitation: 1 if; 0 if not
TOG	Time of game: 1 if day; 2 if night
TV	Television: 1 if televised locally; 0 if not
PROMO	Promotion: 1 if; 0 if not
NOBEL	1 if Mark Nobel started; 0 if not
YANKS	1 if the opposing team was the Yankees; 0 if not
WKEND	1 if Fri., Sat., or Sun.; 0 if not
OD	Opening day: 1 if, 0 if not
DH	Double header: 1 if; 0 if not
O1	Opponent number 1: 1 if; 0 if not
.	
.	
.	
O13	Opponent number 13: 1 if; 0 if not

Exhibit 1 presents the average and standard deviations of these variables, Exhibit 2 presents the correlation coefficients between several pairs of variables, and Exhibit 3 presents the results of various regressive models to explain TIX as a function of various other variables.

This case is based on a Supervised Business Study prepared by Ann C. Stephens (Darden, Class of 1982).

EXHIBIT 1 Averages and Standard Deviations

Variable	Average	Standard Deviation
TIX	11,244.25	9,729.86
OPP	7.05	3.83
POS	2.85	1.34
GB	8.76	6.06
DOW	4.24	2.06
TEMP	62.03	3.32
PREC	0.040	0.20
TOG	1.48	0.50
TV	0.120	0.33
PROMO	0.173	0.38
NOBEL	0.213	0.41
YANKS	0.067	0.25
WKEND	0.520	0.50
OD	0.013	0.12
DH	0.080	0.27
01	0.080	0.27
02	0.093	0.29
03	0.067	0.25
04	0.067	0.25
05	0.067	0.25
06	0.080	0.27
07	0.067	0.25
08	0.080	0.27
09	0.080	0.27
010	0.080	0.27
011	0.080	0.27
012	0.080	0.27
013	0.080	0.27

EXHIBIT 2   Correlation Coefficients

	TIX	OPP	POS	GB	DOW
TIX	1.000				
OPP	−0.112	1.000			
POS	−0.115	−0.206	1.000		
GB	0.075	0.185	−0.152	1.000	
DOW	−0.007	−0.056	−0.104	−0.123	1.000
TEMP	−0.061	−0.106	0.052	0.657	−0.135
PREC	−0.097	−0.003	−0.182	−0.161	0.176
TOG	0.129	−0.112	0.126	0.091	−0.556
TV	0.098	0.124	−0.082	−0.169	0.197
PROMO	0.267	−0.025	−0.002	0.118	−0.002
NOBEL	0.076	−0.093	0.033	0.005	0.082
YANKS	0.807	−0.214	−0.051	0.108	−0.005
WKEND	0.058	−0.043	−0.106	−0.145	0.896
OD	0.158	−0.154	0.187	−0.150	−0.014
DH	0.206	−0.249	−0.078	−0.070	0.158

	TEMP	PREC	TOG	TV	PROMO
TEMP	1.000				
PREC	−0.290	1.000			
TOG	0.113	−0.060	1.000		
TV	−0.078	0.134	−0.273	1.000	
PROMO	0.167	−0.093	−0.017	−0.061	1.000
NOBEL	−0.034	0.060	0.086	0.008	0.019
YANKS	0.014	−0.055	0.064	−0.099	0.160
WKEND	−0.178	0.196	−0.306	0.191	0.017
OD	−0.177	−0.024	0.121	−0.043	−0.053
DH	−0.077	0.191	0.012	0.042	−0.135

	NOBEL	YANKS	WKEND	OD	DH
NOBEL	1.000				
YANKS	0.122	1.000			
WKEND	0.109	0.043	1.000		
OD	−0.061	−0.031	−0.121	1.000	
DH	0.206	0.118	0.087	−0.034	1.000

Exhibit 3

Model 1: TIX versus NOBEL

Variable	Coefficient	Std. Error	T-Stat.
NOBEL	1,804.207	2,753.164	0.655
CONSTANT	10.859.356	587.342	18.489

R-squared = 0.006
Adjusted R-squared = −0.008
Std. deviation of residuals = 9,767.6
Durbin Watson D = 1.196

Model 2: TIX versus 01 through 012, NOBEL

Variable	Coefficient	Std. Error	T-Stat.
NOBEL	323.388	1,755.292	0.184
01	−4,627.963	3,396.590	−1.363
02	−1,607.024	3,224.109	−0.498
03	−3,810.322	3,578.674	−1.065
04	28,663.478	3,578.674	8.010
05	−2,177.244	3,526.638	−0.617
06	−3,412.231	3,358.582	−1.016
07	−3,628.322	3,578.674	−1.014
08	−6,516.065	3,358.582	−1.940
09	1,263.371	3,396.590	0.372
010	100.833	3,345.816	0.030
011	−927.898	3,358.582	−0.276
012	−5,839.463	3,396.590	−1.719
CONSTANT	11,652.167	983.1261	11.852

R-squared = 0.708
Adjusted R-squared = 0.645
Std. deviation of residuals = 5,795.1
Durbin Watson D = 2.291

EXHIBIT 3   *Continued*

Model 3: TIX versus 01 through 012, PREC, TEMP, PROMO, NOBEL, OD, DH

Variable	Coefficient	Std. Error	T-Stat.
PREC	−3,772.043	3,383.418	−1.115
TEMP	−184.293	237.731	−0.775
PROMO	5,398.545	1,780.857	3.031
NOBEL	−403.502	1,518.000	−0.266
OD	15,382.632	5,652.397	2.721
DH	7,645.224	2,429.894	3.146
01	−7,213.660	2,999.437	−2.405
02	−3,203.395	3,046.540	−1.051
03	−5,780.245	3,242.464	−1.783
04	25,640.501	3,196.000	8.023
05	−3,444.192	3,056.500	−1.127
06	−4,568.433	2,988.677	−1.529
07	−5,075.192	3,190.707	−1.591
08	−5,973.904	3,329.604	−1.794
09	1,966.401	2,971.357	0.662
010	−2,352.715	3,002.119	−0.784
011	−1,701.151	3,023.445	−0.563
012	−5,627.881	2,911.665	−1.933
CONSTANT	22,740.489	14,777.323	1.539

R-squared = 0.803
Adjusted R-squared = 0.740
Std. deviation of residuals = 5,011.0
Durbin Watson D = 2.269

EXHIBIT 3   *Continued*

Model 4: TIX versus OPP, NOBEL

Variable	Coefficient	Std. Error	T-Stat.
OPP	−269.135	297.809	−0.904
NOBEL	1,572.135	2,768.562	0.568
CONSTANT	12,807.161	2,182.002	5.869

R-squared = 0.017
Adjusted R-squared = 0.010
Std. deviation of residuals = 9,779.9
Durbin Watson D = 1.146

Model 5: TIX versus PREC, TOG, TV, PROMO, NOBEL, YANKS, WKEND, OD, DH

Variable	Coefficient	Std. Error	T-Stat.
PREC	−3,660.109	3,251.502	−1.126
TOG	1,606.406	1,334.121	1.204
TV	223.421	1,982.301	0.113
PROMO	4,382.173	1,658.644	2.642
NOBEL	−1,244.411	1,546.545	−0.805
YANKS	29,493.164	2,532.314	11.647
WKEND	1,468.269	1,328.585	1.105
OD	16,119.831	5,388.174	2.992
DH	5,815.814	2,375.194	2.449
CONSTANT	5,082.356	2,170.419	2.342

R-squared = 0.742
Adjusted R-squared = 0.706
Std. deviation of residuals = 5,273.5
Durbin Watson D = 1.733

EXHIBIT 3   *Continued*

Model 6: TIX versus PROMO, NOBEL, YANKS, DH

Variable	Coefficient	Std. Error	T-Stat.
PROMO	4,195.743	1,737.742	2.414
NOBEL	−1,204.082	1,607.869	−0.749
YANKS	29,830.245	2,641.516	11.293
DH	5,274.262	2,457.377	2.146
CONSTANT	8,363.238	527.298	15.861

R-squared = 0.692
Adjusted R-squared = 0.675
Std. deviation of residuals = 5,551.0
Durbin Watson D = 1.96

Model 7: TIX versus PREC, PROMO, NOBEL, YANKS, OD

Variable	Coefficient	Std. Error	T-Stat.
PREC	−1,756.508	3,227.439	−0.544
PROMO	3,758.92	1,687.895	2.227
NOBEL	−209.484	1,549.192	−0.135
YANKS	30,568.223	2,570.535	11.892
OD	15,957.998	5,491.220	2.906
CONSTANT	8,457.002	496.203	17.043

R-squared = 0.709
Adjusted R-squared = 0.688
Std. deviation of residuals = 5,434.5
Durbin Watson D = 1.873

EXHIBIT 3   *Concluded*

Model 8: TIX versus GB, TEMP, PREC, TOG, TV, PROMO, NOBEL, YANKS, WKEND, OD, DH

Variable	Coefficient	Std. Error	T-Stat.
GB	156.240	136.632	1.144
TEMP	−440.363	258.493	−1.704
PREC	−5,021.658	3,348.736	−1.500
TOG	1,807.918	1,331.109	1.358
TV	572.777	1,991.314	0.288
PROMO	4,736.968	1,665.964	2.843
NOBEL	−1,353.056	1,537.185	−0.880
YANKS	29,038.808	2,536.088	11.450
WKEND	1,319.888	1,330.660	0.992
OD	14,928.553	5,484.738	2.722
DH	5,968.288	2,362.325	2.526
CONSTANT	30,815.082	16,223.465	1.899

R-squared = 0.753

Adjusted R-squared = 0.710

Std. deviation of residuals = 5,237.0

Durbin Watson D = 1.80

CASE 38
THE OAKLAND A'S (B)

Steward Roddey, general manager of the Oakland A's major-league professional baseball team, was in the midst of contract negotiations with Mark Nobel, a star pitcher for the A's. Nobel had had an excellent season in 1980, winning 22 games and losing only 7, and had finished second in the balloting for the Cy Young Award, given each year to the outstanding pitcher in the 14-team American League. His fine performance had been a pleasant surprise to the A's, because Nobel had won only 11 total games for the team since he started playing major-league baseball in 1975.

Roddey knew that such a dramatic improvement in a player's performance would make contract negotiations particularly difficult. Although Nobel had made only $40,000 for the 1980 season, he had begun salary negotiations with a $600,000-a-year request.

The Resurgent Oakland A's

Mark Nobel's surprise performance in 1980 contributed to a fairly successful year for the Oakland team. In contrast to their last-place finish in 1979, the A's finished second in the seven-team American League West Division with a record of 83 wins and 79 losses (see Exhibit 1). The team's performance had rekindled Oakland's interest in baseball, and home attendance was the highest it had been since 1975 (see Exhibit 2 for attendance figures).

EXHIBIT 1   Past Team Performance

Year	W	L	Pct.	Pos.
1968	82	80	.506	6
1969	88	74	.543	2
1970	89	73	.549	2
1971	101	60	.627	1
1972*	93	62	.600	1
1973	94	68	.580	1
1974	90	72	.556	1
1975	98	64	.605	1
1976	87	74	.540	2
1977	63	98	.391	7
1978	69	93	.426	6
1979	54	108	.333	7
1980	83	79	.512	2

*A two-week player strike shortened this season.

EXHIBIT 2   Yearly Attendance

Year	Home	Road	Total
1968	837,466	960,210	1,797,676
1969	778,232	992,124	1,770,356
1970	778,355	971,568	1,749,923
1971	914,993	1,222,741	2,137,734
1972	921,323	1,115,553	2,036,876
1973	1,000,763	1,382,250	2,383,013
1974	845,693	1,526,630	2,372,323
1975	1,075,518	1,436,383	2,511,901
1976	780,593	1,392,109	2,172,702
1977	495,412	1,195,138	1,690,550
1978	526,412	1,381,142	1,907,554
1979	306,763	1,393,196	1,699,959
1980	843,319	1,572,926	2,416,245
Total	10,104,842	16,541,970	26,646,812
Average	777,296	1,272,459	2,049,755

This success on the field translated into increased revenues at the box office. Total gross revenue from ticket sales was $3.1 million in 1980, compared with only $1.5 million the year before. The A's received 77 percent of this home revenue, with 20 percent going to the visiting team and 3 percent to the league office. Ticket prices at the 50,000-seat Oakland-Alameda County Coliseum were the lowest in the league at $2, $4, $5, and $6, with no changes expected for 1981. The actual cost to the A's of staging a game at the Coliseum did not vary significantly with attendance.

Roddey was confident the team would improve on its 1980 performance. Hopes were high that the experience gained in 1980 would enable the relatively young Oakland team to win its division in 1981. The team planned no major personnel changes and was content to give its manager, Billy Martin, full responsibility for guiding the A's. Martin was an experienced manager, with a history of turning losing teams into winners in a relatively short time. The 1981 season would be Martin's second as manager of the A's.

Roddey's enthusiasm for the coming season showed in his personal forecast of 95 wins for 1981. Each year for the last 13, he had recorded a predicted number of wins for the coming season. Although far from perfect (he was 11 games off in 1977), Roddey was nonetheless proud of his record as a forecaster (see Exhibit 3).

Mark Nobel's Contract

Contract talks between Roddey and Mark Nobel's agent had slowed considerably until Nobel's agent brought up the possibility of a bonus clause tied to yearly attendance. One of the negotiating points made by Nobel and his agent was that

---

EXHIBIT 3   Roddey's Predictions

Year	Predicted Number of Wins
1968	79
1969	90
1970	91
1971	106
1972	89
1973	84
1974	92
1975	91
1976	88
1977	70
1978	67
1979	65
1980	80

Nobel attracted people to the ballpark. In addition, they were confident that Nobel and the A's were about to have an above-average year both on the field and at the box office. Rather than argue the validity of these contentions, Nobel's agent had suggested that the A's simply pay Nobel a bonus if and when the contingencies occurred.

One plan put forth was for Nobel to receive 50 cents for every ticket purchased over 1 million. Thus, if total attendance at 1981 home games was less than 1 million, Nobel would not receive a bonus. But if attendance reached 1,100,000 in 1981, for example, Nobel would receive a $50,000 bonus in addition to his fixed yearly salary.

A second alternative was for Nobel to receive lump-sum bonuses if and when home attendance reached certain specified levels. One suggestion would have Nobel receiving $50,000 if attendance exceeded 1 million, another $50,000 if attendance reached 1.5 million, and a final $50,000 if attendance reached 2 million.

When contract talks resumed, Roddey wanted to be prepared to respond to the incentive clause suggested by Nobel and his agent. He had checked with the league office and found that such a clause was allowable under the bylaws of major-league baseball. As a result, Roddey believed he needed to bring to the contract talks a measure of the cost to the A's of the two proposed attendance clauses. He knew the negotiations might come down to a choice between a fixed salary and a somewhat lower salary with one of the proposed clauses.

Personally, he found the idea of an attendance-incentive clause rather appealing. He did not think there was much of a chance that the A's would have to pay under such a plan. After all, only twice in the last 13 years had home attendance reached a million, and those had been championship years. And even if the A's did have to pay, it would be in a year when the team could most afford it.

CASE 39
PIEDMONT AIRLINES: DISCOUNT SEAT ALLOCATION (A)

Marilyn Hoppe smiled as she set aside the most recent edition of the *Piedmonitor*, the company's monthly news magazine. The lead article for April 1985 (see Exhibit 1) had done an excellent job of describing the function of Marilyn's Revenue Enhancement Department, and, in general, she was pleased with it. The article was both accurate and informative, and had stressed the importance of revenue enhancement to the financial success of the company. Because of the article, Marilyn believed that it might now be a little easier to obtain the cooperation of other departments in providing the vast array of data and information needed to successfully carry out the revenue enhancement activities.

The major function of the department was to decide exactly how many discount fare seats were to be sold on each of Piedmont's flights. The financial importance of revenue enhancement meant that Marilyn and her department shouldered a considerable burden of responsibility. Although she had every reason to be pleased with her department's performance, she often wondered whether there might be room for improvement. Piedmont's new information system was as good as most in the industry, and the seven analysts were both knowledgeable and quite good at using the information to allocate discount seats. The nagging problem was that the process still relied quite heavily on the judgments of these seven. Although the analysts were indeed well-informed experts with access to huge amounts of data and information, they were still humans making numerous daily decisions in a manner that was not as "scientific" as the article might suggest.

Discount Seat Allocation

The recent practice in the airline industry was to offer a wide variety of discount fares to passengers who were willing to purchase tickets far in advance of a flight's departure. The number of discount seats was limited, however, in order that the remaining seats could be reserved for full-fare (primarily business) travelers who made plans nearer departure time.

Piedmont scheduled 836 daily departures—almost 30,000 flights a month, for which discount seats had to be allocated. The company had committed over $1 million to Marilyn's department for a sophisticated computer system tailored to provide the necessary information to make these decisions. In addition to up-to-the-minute bookings, the department's seven revenue enhancement analysts could find out fares, schedules, how each flight booked a year earlier, and what the competition was doing in each market. They could also obtain bookings trends for each flight for each day of the week. With this information, the analysts determined the number of seats to be sold at a discount.

EXHIBIT 1 **Revenue Enhancement**
These People Make Certain Piedmont Maximizes Its Revenue

Cathy Howe scans the screen of her reservations computer, studying Flight 364 from DCA to GSO.

To determine how the flight has done in the past, she turns to her MAPPER computer and, moments later, has data on the flight for the past 90 days. She then pulls up information from MAPPER for the flight's next 30 days.

Howe can tell you our fares, our schedules, how the flight traditionally booked a year earlier, and what the competition is doing in this market. And she knows the booking trends for this flight for each day of the week.

This historical report coupled with current and future demand data give her enough analytical material to make an important decision for Piedmont. She will allocate the number of seats that Piedmont will sell on this flight at a discount.

And Howe is responsible for making similar decisions on 109 other flights in 16 Piedmont markets.

"If I can produce just $100 additional revenue every day on each of the flights I monitor, Piedmont will realize over a $4 million annual revenue improvement," she said, "and that's why I'm here, to help maximize the revenue on each of these departures."

Major Responsibility

Howe is one of seven revenue enhancement analysts, at the department's new offices at Madison Park, who has become an expert in Piedmont's markets. Each analyst is responsible for monitoring over 100 flights a day in 15 to 20 markets. Not only do they know the history on each of their flights, they are aware of the schedules, the many fares, booking trends, and what the competition is doing in each of these markets.

The person who set up the new departure and is responsible for its day-to-day operation is Marilyn Hoppe, manager–revenue enhancement. She joined Piedmont last summer after 10 years with Republic Airlines.

Input from Others

To ensure a system of checks and balances, Hoppe monitors what the analysts are doing and reviews their regular monthly reports. In addition, input from other departments is vital to the effective operation of Revenue Enhancement, and there are frequent meetings with other areas of the Company.

"What we have is a perishable commodity," Hoppe said. "We are striving to give each individual flight in a given market a careful mixture of discount and full-fare seats and thus increase our revenue."

The department, part of our Marketing Division, works closely with the Pricing, Tariff, and Scheduling departments.

Note: Terms to Know

Capacity control—allocating seats so as to best meet demand while preventing loss of revenue.

Load factor—percentage of seats filled on our flights.

Revenue—money we receive for services.

Revenue passenger miles (RPMs)—one passenger carried one mile.

Yield—the amount of money we receive for carrying one passenger one mile.

Source: *Piedmonitor* 36, no. 3, April 1985.

EXHIBIT 1   *Continued*

"Our Pricing Department develops fare programs, sets our fares, and performs fare analysis," Swenson said. "Tariffs put the fare programs into operation, and Revenue Enhancement determines the appropriate mix of discount and full-fare seats on each flight."

Piedmont has committed over $1 million to the newly created department for a sophisticated computer system, which has been tailored to our needs. The system has been developed specifically for Piedmont with input from many areas of the company, in particular Data Processing, which continues to provide considerable support.

"Trying to manage 836 departures a day—almost 30,000 flights a month—requires a state-of-the-art system," Hoppe said. "The company has provided us with this system so we can scientifically approach our job. Since deregulation, the whole area of pricing has become extremely complicated and competitive. These tools are necessary in order to control our discount programs."

The philosophy of the department is exactly opposite from the way the industry operated prior to deregulation. The theory then was that, in the final days before a flight, airlines should sell all remaining seats at a discount in order to fill the plane.

"But since deregulation, airlines have discovered the opposite to be true. The number of discount seats should be limited, based on the individual market characteristics, and the remaining seats should be reserved for full-fare business travelers who make plans nearer departure time," she said.

Marilyn Hoppe (right) manager–revenue enhancement, Steve Nelson, an analyst, and Mary Cline, secretary for the department, go over future Piedmont flight schedules, which are being transmitted to the department from our reservations system.

EXHIBIT 1 *Continued*

"What we're doing is getting a good base with the lower fares and reserving the remaining seats for higher-yield traffic, people who make plans closer to departure. Our late-booking passengers, usually business travelers, are probably our most valued customers, our frequent fliers. They often must make plans on short notice and, by allocating fewer discount seats, we give them more flexibility," Hoppe said.

The department allocates seats for each class of service so as to best meet demand while preventing loss of revenue. In most cases, this involves providing discount seats to those passengers who book early, but systematically limiting discount seats at a specific period of time before departure.

Discount seats, in fact, are generally available for over 300 days prior to departure and will only be pulled back, if appropriate, 7 to 14 days before departure, Hoppe said. This process is capacity control and results in more revenue.

"We're offering the business person a full schedule from which to choose and the ability to change flights," Hoppe said. "If we didn't offer discounts, fewer people would travel and, in the end, the businessman or woman would have to pay more and would have fewer flights from which to choose."

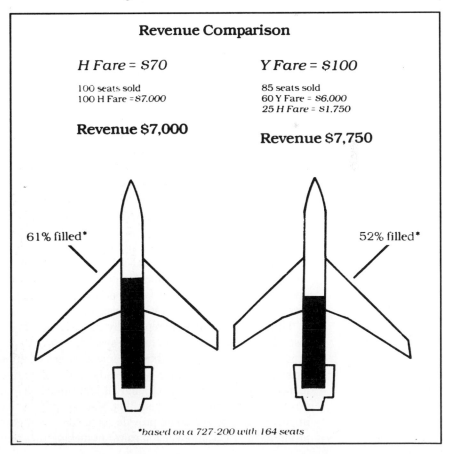

Revenue Comparison

H Fare = $70

100 seats sold
100 H Fare = $7.000

Revenue $7,000

Y Fare = $100

85 seats sold
60 Y Fare = $6.000
25 H Fare = $1.750

Revenue $7,750

61% filled*

52% filled*

*based on a 727-200 with 164 seats

EXHIBIT 1   *Concluded*

"The most successful airlines in the industry, by and large, are using similar techniques employing the same logic. During the last full-blown fare war three years ago, we all learned that we have to restrict discount fares to manage them. By allocating seats we hope to keep our yield up with little impact on load factor," she added.

Revenue Enhancement is already making an impact on Piedmont's financial picture. In 1984, our load factor was 52.42 percent, down 2.4 points from the year before. Yet our total operating revenues grew 36.1 percent to a record $1.3 billion. In 1984, our yield was 17.64 cents per revenue passenger mile, compared with 15.94 cents in 1983."

Monitoring Flights

"Everyone must realize how closely we monitor flights," she emphasized. "You can't determine the performance of a flight by looking only at the number of people who board that flight. Load factor is important, but you also must consider the revenue side. We may have fewer people on a flight but that flight may produce more revenue, because more passengers are paying full fare or another higher-yield fare."

This discount-seat-allocation decision involved a critical tradeoff: If too many seats were sold at a discount, the airline could lose the difference between the full fare and discount fare for every potential full-fare passenger lost—either because the plane sold out and full-fare customers were turned away, or because customers who might otherwise have paid the full fare "diverted" to the discount fare. The loss caused by diverting was the reason Piedmont often limited the sale of discount-fare seats even in those situations where there was no chance of selling out a flight. If, on the other hand, too few seats were sold at a discount, the airline lost the discount fare for every passenger who would have taken the flight had the discount fare been available but opted instead not to take the flight at all, rather than pay the full fare. This kind of customer was called a "stimulator," because the discount fare stimulated them to take the flight. If a discount fare was not available, potential sales to stimulators were lost. In contrast, a customer who would take the flight at either fare was called a "diverter." A diverter would pay the full fare if no discount seats were available but would divert to the discount fare if it was available.

The seven analysts were repeatedly called on to evaluate the tradeoffs between lost sales due to stimulators turned away and increased revenues from diverters kept at the full fare. Even though large amounts of information were available, striking the proper balance was mostly left to their judgments. Their performance was closely monitored, and all indications were that they were having a positive impact on the company, but Marilyn still wanted to search for ways to improve. Perhaps she could provide some additional guidance for them (maybe in the form of certain decision rules) in making these important decisions. She

---

EXHIBIT 2   Flight 224 Historical Bookings and Revenues

	Weekday	Weekend	Total
Number of flights	56	22	78
Number of sold-out flights	11	2	13
Number of passengers	7,683	2,075	9,758
H passengers	2,017	1,112	3,129
Y passengers	5,666	963	6,629
Segment* revenue	$707,790	$174,140	$ 881,930
H revenues	$141,190	$ 77,840	$ 219,030
Y revenues	$566,600	$ 96,300	$ 662,900
Total† revenue	$856,426	$210,710	$1,067,136
H revenues	$145,592	$ 94,820	$ 240,412
Y revenues	$710,834	$115,890	$ 826,724

---

* Segment revenue refers to the CLT-to-BOS flight only.

† Total revenue includes segment revenues and any additional revenues from Flight 224 passengers connecting to other Piedmont flights.

decided to start by examining the booking and seat-allocation history of Flight 224 from Charlotte (CLT) to Boston (BOS), a typical Piedmont flight.

Flight 224

Flight 224 was scheduled to leave CLT each day (seven days a week) at 8:30 A.M. and arrive at BOS at 10:20 A.M. Because the flight originated in CLT and terminated in BOS, any passengers with final destinations other than BOS changed planes there and made connections to a separate flight leaving BOS for their final destination. Approximately 25 percent of the flight's passengers had these connecting flights, one-half of which were with airlines other than Piedmont.

All 164 seats on the Boeing 727-200 used for this flight were sold as a single class; that is, there was no first class/coach distinction. All seats were not sold at the same fare, however. A limited number of discount seats, called "H-fares," were available for $70. In contrast, the regular fare, called a "Y-fare," was $100. These fares were for the CLT to BOS flight only. Passengers with other final destinations paid a total fare equal to the sum of the fares for each segment of their particular flight. This particular flight had been in existence for only about three months. Marilyn compiled the data given in Exhibit 2, describing the historical bookings and revenues for this flight, and Exhibit 3 shows the company's operating-cost estimates.

After compiling these data, Marilyn met with Cathy Howe, the analyst responsible for Flight 224, to review the decision process used in allocating H-fare seats. They agreed to focus on a particular allocation decision, and Cathy was happy to walk Marilyn through the decision she was about to make regarding Flight 224, which departed a few weeks later on May 8.

EXHIBIT 3   Flight 224 Cost Estimates*

	Cost per Flight
Fuel	$2,240
Maintenance	1,470
Flight crew	770
Ground crew	250
Landing fees	105
Overhead	2,230
Total	$7,065

*Single one-way flight.

EXHIBIT 4   Recent Wednesday Departures of Flight 224

Departure Date	H Bookings	Y Bookings	H Allocation	Total
4/24 42	97	42	139
4/17 44	88	44	132
4/10 45	92	45	137
4/03 52	112	52	164
3/27 35	111	35	146
3/20 46	56	46	102
3/13 52	89	52	141
3/06 57	107	57	164
2/27 26	114	26	140
2/20 28	90	28	118
2/13 50	114	50	164

"The first thing I'd do is check historical bookings for this flight. Since this is a Wednesday flight, I'd put together a relevant history of bookings for previous Wednesday departures of this flight. Here's where I have to be careful to consider all the other factors that can influence booking patterns. For example, the strike at National Airlines meant this flight saw an unusually large number of bookings during early March." A few seconds later, Cathy had a screen full of information on recent Wednesday departures of Flight 224 (Exhibit 4). "See there, our March 6 flight sold out because of that strike, and I seriously doubt that anyone's going to strike right before the departure of this May 8 flight.

"From looking at these data, I'd draw a couple of conclusions. First, you can see that demand for this flight is hard to predict. The flights departing on February 13 and April 3 both sold out, but the load factor [percentage of seats sold] for the March 20 departure was only 62 percent. You can see that, if I set any reasonable allocation, we'd almost certainly sell them all. That 62 percent load factor on March 20 was quite low for this flight, but it still meant we sold 102 seats—most of them at full fare. If I did not limit discount-fare seats for the upcoming May 8 flight, I would predict that total demand for seats would be about 180—much higher than the capacity of the plane. By 'total demand' I mean both stimulators and diverters, anyone willing to take the flight at the discount fare. If pressed to make a judgment on what total demand for discount seats might be, I'd think in terms of the bell-shaped curve and put a 68 percent chance that demand would be between 150 and 210. Looking at the other extreme, if I did not allocate any seats to be sold at the discount fare, I would have to think in terms of how many of our potential customers would pay the full fare or how many are stimulators. Because I think the diverter/stimulator mix for this flight is about 60/40, it follows that, if no seats were sold at a discount, 60 percent of the potential demand would remain. This would result in about 108 (180 × 0.6) full-fare sales. The uncertainty here is a little harder to judge, but I would say that there's a 68 percent chance we would sell between 90 and 126 seats if all seats were offered at the full fare.

"But, quite obviously, it is probably best to set the allocation somewhere between the two extremes of 164 (offer all seats at the H-fare of $70) and 0 (offer all seats at the Y-fare of $100). In reality, I always have the opportunity to reset this allocation at a later date if conditions change. But I still like to set a good initial allocation and then modify it only slightly as the time of departure draws near. One thing we never do, however, is raise the allocation once all discount-fare seats have been sold. This avoids the loss of goodwill associated with selling someone a full-fare seat, because we tell him or her no discount-fare seats are available, and then having that passenger discover that discount-fare seats were sold at a later date."

PIEDMONT AIRLINES: DISCOUNT SEAT ALLOCATION (B)

As Marilyn Hoppe thought about how to help Cathy Howe plan the number of discount seats to offer on Flight 224, she thought of the problem in terms of how many seats to reserve for the full-fare passengers. Past experience had been that Piedmont had virtually always been able to sell all the discount seats on Flight 224. If we reserve R seats, Hoppe reasoned, then the number of discount seats is simply $164 - R$. Suppose we decide R now, well in advance of the flight, and consider it fixed for the remainder of the time before departure?

She thought about what would happen if R were set too low: Suppose it were low by one seat? Then we would lose a full-fare passenger, but that seat would have been filled by a discount passenger. So the cost of R being low by one seat is the difference between full-fare revenue and discount fare, or $30 for Flight 224.

Suppose we set R too high, however, again by one unit only? She reasoned that the seat would go empty, because there would be no full-fare passenger to fly in it. Because the discount passengers would have been restricted, they couldn't fly in it. Thus, she proposed, the cost of being over is the revenue from one discount passenger, or $70.

Marilyn now thought about what to do with these costs. Had these costs been equal, she would have simply used an R that was the mean of the distribution of full-fare demand, or 108. Because it was less costly to reserve too few full-seat fares, however, she believed that she should make R less than 108. The question was: How much less? She seemed to recall a discussion of this somewhere in her past and thought that it was best to make the relative odds of being low match the relative cost of being low. She was not sure, so she looked through a few books to find the result.

In a text on quantitative methods for business, Hoppe found the so-called *news vendor* problem, which was the question of how many newspapers to buy in the face of uncertain demand. She read that, if she knew the cost of having one newspaper too few (cost of under) and the cost of having one newspaper too many (cost of over), and if the relevant costs were constant per unit, then she should order an amount that corresponded to the critical fractile of her demand distribution. This critical fractile is the ratio of the cost of under to the total of the cost of under plus the cost of over. If she could apply this approach to her problem, the critical fractile would be $30/(30+70) = 0.30$. The task was now a straightforward matter of finding the 30th percentile of Howe's assessed distribution for the number of full-fare passengers. Using a normal distribution with mean 108 and standard deviation 18, Hoppe calculated the result to be 99, to the nearest integer.

Based on this approach, the plan was to reserve 99 seats for full-fare passengers and allocate the other 65 seats to discount fares. Hoppe filed away this result for her next meeting with Howe and thought how impressed her boss would be when he learned about the new approach. She relaxed for a moment with *The Wall Street Journal*, but before 10 minutes had passed she had her notes out again on the table. Yield management made such a huge difference in bottom-line profits in her company that she had better not jump to any hasty conclusions; her reputation would be on the line.

Hoppe noted that this discount allocation of 65 was much larger than had been used before on Flight 224. Numbers don't lie, she thought; there had already been many times in her career when getting the numbers right had saved her. And she had found situations where her own analysis topped existing practice. Here, however, the use of the news vendor approach was new to her. Could it be directly applied to this situation? After all, the textbook example didn't talk about two types of customers.

She decided a Monte Carlo simulation would help her verify this new result—and allow her to test alternative plans as well. The Case 1 section of Exhibit 1

Exhibit 1   A Description of the Monte Carlo Simulation Model

Cell *C3*: Demand, the number of potential customers, drawn from a normal distribution with mean 180 and standard deviation 30, rounded off to the nearest integer.

Case 1

Cell *B6*: Choose R_1, the seats saved for full fare in Case 1 (59).

Cell *B7*: $Q_1 = 164 - R_1$ is the number of discount seats available (105).

Cell *B9*: If $C3 > Q_1$, then from the $C3 - Q_1$ customers that do not fit in the discount seats, determine the potential number of full-fare sales using a binomial distribution with p = 0.6.

    If $C3 \le Q_1$, then the number of full-fare sales is zero.

Cell *B10*: Minimum of *B6* and *B9*.

Cell *B16*: If $C3 > Q_1$, then Revenue = 70 * *B7* + 100 * *B10*.

    If $C3 \le Q_1$, then Revenue = 70 * *C3*.

Case 2

Cell *D6*: Choose $R_2 > R_1$, the seats saved for full fare in Case 2 (99).

Cell *D7*: $Q_2 = 164 - R_2$ is the number of discount seats available (65).

Cell *D9*: If $C3 > Q_1$, then from the *B7*−*D7* additional customers that do not fit in the discount seats for Case 2, determine the number of potential full-fare sales using a binomial distribution with p = 0.6 and add to *B9*.

    If $C3 \le Q_1$ and $C3 > Q_2$, then from the $C3 - D7$ additional customers that do not fit in the discount seats for Case 2, determine the potential full-fare sales using a binomial distribution with p = 0.6.

    If $C3 \le Q_2$, the number of full-fare sales is zero.

Cell *D10*: Minimum of *D6* and *D9*.

Cell *D16*: If $C3 > Q_2$, then Revenue = 70 * *D7* + 100 * *D10*.

    If $C3 \le Q_2$, then Revenue = 70 * *C3*.

Difference

Cell *C16*: *B16* − *D16*

explains the important cells in the electronic-spreadsheet model she developed. The simulation first generated the demand (i.e., the number of potential customers) and used this number, along with the number of seats allocated to full-fare customers, to determine the number of discount seats sold. Then the behavior of each remaining potential customer was simulated using a 60 percent probability of diverter to determine how many would buy a full-fare seat if no discount seat were available.

After Hoppe validated the model, she tried the simulation with several different values for R. To her surprise, the best revenues were not from setting R to 99, her critical fractile level. For example, the average revenue at R = 59 was higher than the average revenue at R = 99 (see Exhibit 2). She then expanded the model so that, each time it ran, it would calculate the revenue for an R = 59 strategy (cell *B16* of Exhibit 1), the revenue for an R = 99 strategy (cell *D16*), and the difference in revenue for the two strategies for each trial (cell *C16*). Exhibit 3 shows the distribution of this difference in revenue for the same 2,500 trials used in Exhibit 2. It looked pretty convincing, from this simulation at least, that R = 59 was better than R = 99, but she was not sure that this result might not be "the luck of the draw" resulting from not enough trials.

Next, she set up an experiment to search for the optimal level. She decided to look over the range of R = 30 to R = 80 and to compare the difference in revenues for strategies that varied by increments of five seats. In other words, first she tested R = 30 versus R = 35, then R = 35 versus R = 40, and so on, all the way to R = 75 versus R = 80. The results are contained in Exhibit 4. She puzzled over them for a while, then picked up the paper again. "I'll have to mull this over," she muttered to herself.

EXHIBIT 2   Graphs of Revenues Generated from R = 59 and R = 99 Strategies

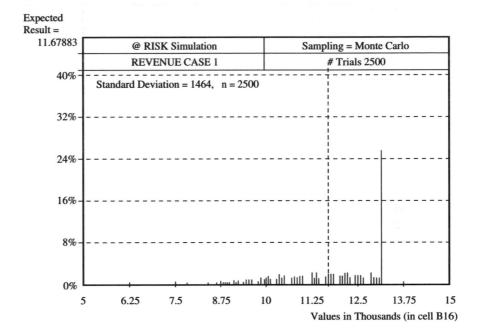

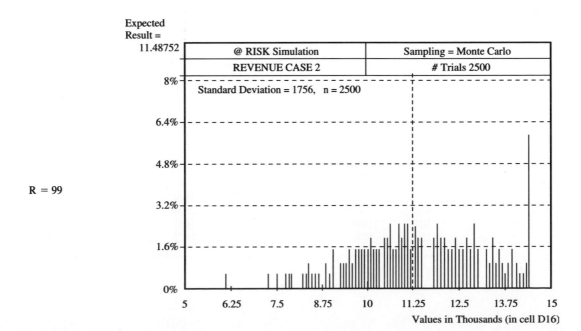

EXHIBIT 3   **Monte Carlo Results for Difference (Cell C16) in Revenue for the R = 59 and R = 99 Strategies**

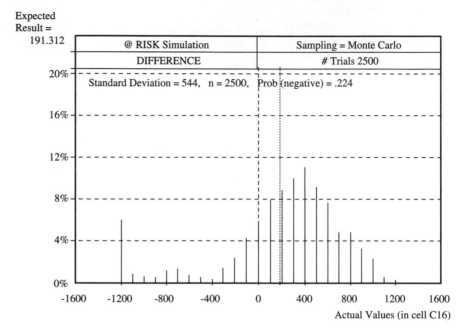

EXHIBIT 4   **Simulation Results for Different R-Values and for the Difference between R and R + 5**

R, Full-Fare Seats	Revenue for R		Revenue for R + 5		Difference: Revenue for R − Rev. for R + 5	
	Mean	*Std. Dev.*	*Mean*	*Std. Dev.*	*Mean*	*Std. Dev.*
30	11516	1156	11551	1215	−34.8	125
35	11550	1231	11577	1290	−27.5	126
40	11579	1289	11598	1348	−19.5	127
45	11601	1338	11611	1396	−10.3	128
50	11606	1389	11609	1442	−2.9	127
55	11584	1449	11578	1499	6.2	126
60	11617	1501	11607	1549	10.4	126
65	11609	1546	11593	1590	15.9	124
70	11583	1592	11561	1631	21.9	122
75	11553	1636	11528	1672	24.9	121

Number of trials = 16,000.

CASE 41
PROBABILITY ASSESSMENT EXERCISE

The purpose of this exercise is to explore how well you as an individual and your group as a team can assess cumulative probability distributions. As a result, the exercise consists of two parts:

1. Individual assessments, based on your private knowledge only.
2. Group assessment, in which your team pools its knowledge and develops a consensus forecast.

The 10 uncertain quantities, whose cumulative probability distributions are to be assessed, are described in Uncertain Quantities to Be Assessed. In the Individual Questionnaire (Exhibit 1), you are asked to assess five fractiles for each of the 10 probability distributions. When completing this questionnaire, *please do not consult* handbooks, statistical abstracts, or the like. We seek a faithful expression of your current imperfect state of knowledge, rather than the correct answer! After you and the other members of your group have made your individual assessments, please meet as a group, pool your knowledge, arrive at a consensus, and complete the Group Questionnaire (Exhibit 2). In your group, you will be assessing quantities 8, 9, and 10 only. Please do not alter your individual assessments as a result of the discussions in your group.

Be sure to bring the assessment sheet to class.

EXHIBIT 1   Individual Questionnaire

Your Assessments
Please assess the probability distributions of the 10 quantities described on page 580, and complete the table below.

	0.05 Fractile	0.25 Fractile	0.50 Fractile	0.75 Fractile	0.95 Fractile
1. First female driver	———	———	———	———	———
2. Japanese 500 companies	———	———	———	———	———
3. O'Hare departures	———	———	———	———	———
4. U.S. debt	———	———	———	———	———
5. 1987 MBAs	———	———	———	———	———
6. Airline deaths	———	———	———	———	———
7. NYC to Istanbul	———	———	———	———	———
8. Area of United States	———	———	———	———	———
9. German autos in Japan	———	———	———	———	———
10. U.S. trade deficit	———	———	———	———	———

Uncertain Quantities to Be Assessed

1. The year in which Mrs. John Howell Phillips of Chicago became the first female licensed driver in the United States.
2. The number of Japanese companies among *Fortune*'s 1990 "Global 500," the world's largest industrial corporations (in sales).
3. The number of passenger arrivals and departures at Chicago's O'Hare airport in 1989.
4. The U.S. national debt as of August 18, 1993.
5. The number of master's degrees in business or management conferred in the United States in 1987.
6. The number of passenger deaths that occurred worldwide in scheduled commercial airliner accidents in the 1980s.
7. The shortest navigable distance (in statute miles) between New York City and Istanbul.
8. The total area of the 48 contiguous states of the United States of America (in millions of square miles).
9. The number of German automobiles sold in Japan in 1989.
10. The total U.S. merchandise trade deficit with Japan (in billions of dollars) in the 1980s.

Source for some questions: "Managing Overconfidence" by J. Edward Russo and Paul J. H. Schoemaker, *Sloan Management Review* (Winter 1992).

EXHIBIT 2   Group Questionnaire

After the members of your group have entered their individual assessments, meet to complete the questionnaire below. The three assessments refer again to the quantities described in Uncertain Quantities, but this time pool the knowledge within the group. After you reach a consensus, each member of the group should enter the data in the table below.

	0.05 Fractile	0.25 Fractile	0.50 Fractile	0.75 Fractile	0.95 Fractile
8. Area of United States	_____	_____	_____	_____	_____
9. German autos in Japan	_____	_____	_____	_____	_____
10. U.S. trade deficit	_____	_____	_____	_____	_____

BRING THIS DATA TO CLASS.

CASE 42
PROBLEMS IN REGRESSION

1. Union Camp—Trenton

An important element in the scheduling procedure of the Union Camp Corporation's corrugated container plant in Trenton, New Jersey, involved forecasting the amount of processing time each job would require at each work center. One piece of information available was the number of thousand square feet (MSF) in the job. Data for 15 randomly selected jobs processed on a particular printing press follow:

MSF	Hours
26.0	2.00
34.2	4.17
29.0	4.42
34.3	4.75
85.9	4.83
143.2	6.67
85.5	7.00
140.6	7.08
140.6	7.17
40.4	7.17
101.0	10.00
239.7	12.00
179.3	12.50
126.5	13.67
140.8	15.08

Can regression be used to provide a forecast? Two jobs waiting to be processed contained 157.3 MSF and 64.7 MSF. What is the probability that the first, larger job will take less than eight hours to process? What is the probability that the second, smaller job will take less than eight hours?

2. South Wales Mining Company

The South Wales Mining Company often needs to make rapid and exact estimates of the weight of a pile of loose materials, such as coal. To help do this more accurately, the company has compiled information about 10 coal piles for which the actual weight was known. The information consists of the diameter of the base of the pile (D), the diameter of the top of the pile (d), and the height of the pile (h). These distances are all given in units of feet, and the weight (W) of the coal pile is given in metric tons.

W	D	h	d
56	20	10	15
93	25	10	20
161	30	12	24
31	15	12	10
70	20	14	13
76	20	14	13
375	40	16	32
34	15	14	8
45	20	8	16
58	20	10	15

How should South Wales Mining combine information in D, h, and d to predict the weight of a pile of coal?

EXHIBIT 1   Graphic for Problem 2

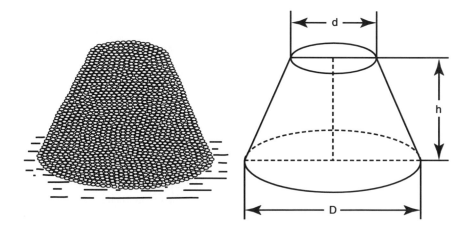

3. Longevity and Handedness

In the early 1990s, two psychologists surveyed the next of kin listed on public death certificate records in two counties in southern California. The survey asked the handedness of the recently deceased family member. Subjects were labeled right-handers if they wrote, drew, and threw a ball with their right hand. All other subjects were labeled as left-handers. Next of kin of young children and homicide victims were not surveyed.

The age of death (AOD) of the 867 right-handers averaged 75.00 years. The AOD of the 82 left-handers averaged 66.03. A dummy variable was created representing the handedness of the subjects:

$$DR = \begin{cases} 1 \text{ if subject was right-handed} \\ 0 \text{ if subject was mixed or left-handed} \end{cases}$$

and a regression analysis was performed relating AOD to DR. The results appear below:

Regression Statistics

Multiple R	0.1518763
R square	0.0230664
Adjusted R square	0.0220348
Standard error	16.418869
Observations	949

ANOVA

	df	SS	MS	F	Significance F
Regression	1	6027.699921	6027.7	22.35966	2.60415E-06
Residual	947	255291.5539	269.5793		
Total	948	261319.2538			

	Coef.	Std. Error	t Stat	P-value	Lower 95%	Upper 95%
Intercept	66.03	1.813160744	36.41707	2.9E-182	62.4717241	69.588276
X Variable 1	8.97	1.89696739	4.7286	2.6E-06	5.247255964	12.692744

What is your explanation for the rather surprising results?

4. Market Study

In a market-segmentation study, data on net income (*I*) in thousands, family size (*F*), and expenditures on consumer durable goods (*C*) were collected from 20 randomly selected households:

I	F	C
10	4	1960
10	3	2390
15	4	3060
15	5	3220
20	6	3570
20	5	4360
25	7	4970
25	6	5190
30	8	5390
30	7	5550

The company sponsoring the study was interested in isolating the effects of income and family size on the dollar amounts spent for consumer durable goods.

5. Class Participation

There is a popular notion that students sitting on the right side (right from a student's perspective) of the classroom are called on more often than students on the left. Ten students, randomly selected from each side of one of last year's classes, had the following numerical class-participation grades:

Right Side	Left Side
14	8
19	9
19	10
17	20
13	10
13	13
16	17
4	5
12	3
12	8

Use regression with a dummy variable to test the notion that the average class-participation grade is higher on the right side of the class.

CASE 43
ROADWAY CONSTRUCTION COMPANY

In late August, David Black, president of Roadway Construction Company, was preparing his capital-budgeting recommendation for the upcoming fiscal year. Paramount in his mind were the recently announced $9.25 billion Georgia highway program and the opportunities for growth that this program represented for Roadway. The most immediate need would be for another asphalt-manufacturing plant.

The New Highway Program

The August 3 issue of a contracting industry bulletin described the Georgia highway plans as follows:

> It's time to breathe a sigh of relief and celebrate! The state legislature approved on July 27 a funding plan to raise $9.25 billion for road construction over the next 13 1/2 years. . . . The legislation sets up a state highway trust fund to four-lane some 1,800 miles of the intrastate highway system. This will put 90 percent of the state's population within 10 miles of a four-lane highway. . . . Under the program all or portions of seven urban loops will be completed and 10,000 miles of unpaved secondary roads will be paved. . . . The new funding is in addition to the annual state highway construction program, which amounts to approximately $400 million.

Roadway

Roadway Construction Company, a division of Southern Highways, Inc., was a wholly owned subsidiary of a *Fortune* 500 conglomerate whose core business was the refining and marketing of petroleum products. Southern provided corporate management for 20 companies similar to Roadway located in the South from Virginia to California. These divisions were grouped geographically into six regions, each managed by a regional vice president who reported to the president of Southern Highways, Inc.

The Roadway division operated three branches, maintained six operating/marketing offices, and ran eight asphalt-manufacturing plants. It competed with 13 similar contractors, who operated a combined total of 26 asphalt plants. Roadway provided earth grading, drain-pipe installation, stone-base placement, asphalt paving, and curb gutter construction in a 20-county area of eastern Georgia. The work contributed to the completion of federal and state highways; city, county, subdivision, and military-base streets; airport runways; sites for manufacturing plants and commercial building; parking lots; and residential driveways.

This case was based on a Supervised Business Study prepared by Douglas L. Schwartz (Darden, Class of 1990).

Roadway was the primary provider of these services in the area (40 percent market share) and had annual revenues in excess of $40 million.

Roadway's main source of revenue was the manufacture and placement of asphaltic concrete (hot-mixed asphalt), the product that constitutes the traveling surface of asphalt streets and highways, and all other company functions operated to support this primary business. Asphaltic concrete is manufactured by mixing specifically sized and blended crushed stone and sand that have been dried and heated to approximately 300 degrees (F) in a rotating kiln with 4 to 6 percent of liquid asphalt (the residual of the manufacture of all other petroleum products). When placed on the roadway and properly compacted, this mixture produces a smooth and durable riding surface. Roadway manufactured and placed approximately 700,000 tons/year and sold approximately 40,000 tons/year to smaller competitors. This asphaltic concrete was produced from seven nonportable "batch" plants strategically located within the market area and one continuous-type, portable "drum-mix" plant. The basic raw materials of liquid asphalt and crushed stone were purchased; Roadway produced its own sand.

Strategic location was the key competitive consideration in the asphalt-paving business. All competitors could purchase raw materials, manufacture the product, and place the asphalt within the ranges of their manpower, equipment, and management efficiency. Competitive advantage lay in situating the asphalt plant in the optimum location relative to the sources of raw materials and the location of a project. The raw materials and the hot-mixed asphalt were transported by trucks, and because the mixed asphalt had to be placed and compacted before it cooled below 250 degrees, transportation time was limited to between two and six hours, depending on weather conditions.

The Decision Process

The divisions operated with a great deal of autonomy, and most management decisions were made independently by a division president. Through close communication over time with Charlie Meadows, his regional vice president, David Black knew the broad parameters within which he could operate independently. He consulted with Meadows only on decisions outside those established bounds. Generally, nonroutine purchases exceeding $100,000 received fairly close scrutiny and required a financial analysis to determine the net present value (NPV), payback, profitability index (the ratio of the present value of future cash flows divided by the initial investment), and internal rate of return (IRR). Once the available funds were approved, the specific purchases were prioritized, with considerable weight given to the division president's recommendations. On final approval, the actual purchase commitments were made by the division president.

Black was reviewing the asphalt-plant decision in preparation for his meeting with Meadows next month in Marietta, Georgia. At that time Black was expected to make and justify his recommendations.

The New Asphalt Plant

Two asphalt plants were available for expanding Roadway's capacity to meet the needs of the new highway program for the next 10 years: a new portable-drum plant and a used batch plant from one of the other divisions. Each plant would have 150,000 tons/year of asphalt-producing capacity with a mix value of $23/ton. The two options differed primarily in cost and service life.

The batch plant would cost $700,000 (plant, erection, and site preparation), have a five-year life, and have a $100,000 salvage value at the end of the five years. The raw materials for this plant were expected to cost $14.00/ton (sand, crushed stone, and liquid asphalt combined); the operating costs were expected to be $2.50/ton; and the maintenance and repair cost, $1.00/ton.

The drum plant would cost $1.5 million (plant, erection, and site preparation), have a 10-year life, and have a $300,000 salvage value at the end of the 10 years. This plant had a raw-material advantage over any batch plant, because it could utilize up to 30 percent RAP (*r*ecycled *a*sphalt *p*roduct) whereas a batch plant could use only 12–15 percent RAP. Thus raw-material costs for a drum plant were only $12.75/ton. Currently, competitors operated five drum-mix plants in the Roadway market area, which put Roadway at a cost disadvantage when bidding against these competitors. Additionally, because the drum plant was brand-new, maintenance costs would be only $.50/ton and operating costs were expected to be as little as $2.00/ton. The drum plant also had a nonquantifiable advantage as a "striking arm" for new markets because of its highly portable capabilities.

Wear and tear was expected to increase maintenance costs for the plants by 10 percent a year. Operating costs were expected to go up by 4 percent a year over the useful lives of the two plants. Roadway currently used a 12 percent hurdle rate for all capital investments, was taxed at an effective rate of 38 percent, and handled all depreciation on a straight-line basis for making investment decisions.

CASE 44
SHUMWAY, HORCH, AND SAGER (A)

Claire Christensen was involved in a new project in her second year with the management consulting firm of Shumway, Horch, and Sager (SHS). It appeared to be another situation in which she was expected to jump quickly out of the blocks with the project and make some clever money-saving recommendation, then find the follow-on project to produce next month's billable days.

The client was an organization of magazine publishers that had become aware of their inability to predict the circulation of their magazines in the future. The publishers wanted a good forecast for a variety of reasons; for example, to decide how many copies to print. The current concern to be resolved was the establishment of a contracted rate base. This was the number of copies that *Good House-keeping* guaranteed selling each month and was used to determine the advertising revenue. SHS was hired both to suggest a procedure for one-month-ahead forecasts and to make recommendations on the contracted rate base decision.

Christensen thought she could find a way to forecast each issue's sales. She started by picking the magazine *Good Housekeeping* and probing whether she could forecast January 1988 sales using previous data. She had obtained data on total circulation over the past nine years (July 1979-December 1987) from the Publisher's Statement to the Audit Bureau of Circulation. The 8 1/2 years of data are shown in Exhibit 1. She was aware that about 10 million copies of this magazine generally were printed each month, to ensure that no individual newsstand would run out of the magazine.

Christensen pondered how time patterns in past sales might help her predict the sales of a future issue. (See Exhibit 2 for a graph of the circulation data.) *Good Housekeeping* was not a magazine that she read, but she had seen it while waiting for the dentist, and her aunt had it in her house. She knew that the December issue greatly increased newsstand sales because of its holiday recipes and gift-giving ideas. The January issue always seemed to be low, because people evidently felt they had overspent and overeaten during the holidays and were trying to cut back. Changes in the interests of purchasers and in the content of the magazine were also important forces that could gradually move the sales up or down over time.

Just as Christensen was going to dive into the calculations, a representative from *Good Housekeeping* called to clarify the situation with the contracted rate base. The magazine would realize advertising revenue of $1 times the guaranteed rate base. There was a caveat, however. If they did not meet the base value, they would refund an amount to their advertisers equal to $1.25 times the shortfall in circulation. For example, if the contracted rate base was 5 million and only 4.5 million copies of the magazine were sold, the magazine would receive

EXHIBIT 1 *Good Housekeeping* Circulation Figures (July 1979–December 1987)

Date	Obs.#	Circulation		Date	Obs.#	Circulation
Jul79	1	5264165			52	5344570
	2	5313127			53	5334053
	3	5117969			54	5763516
	4	5098771		Jan84	55	5198585
	5	5187708			56	5501741
	6	5645295			57	5329592
Jan80	7	5023173			58	5322838
	8	5333352			59	5178815
	9	5224234			60	5247590
	10	5079207		Jul84	61	5194827
	11	5167277			62	5118408
	12	5006445			63	5291564
Jul80	13	5150974			64	5047946
	14	5180346			65	5105056
	15	5223467			66	5448542
	16	5153303		Jan85	67	5023818
	17	5247109			68	5099829
	18	5789798			69	5253739
Jan81	19	5350502			70	5138210
	20	5371371			71	5251664
	21	5327700			72	5450869
	22	5269993		Jul85	73	5022522
	23	5240438			74	5206132
	24	5273266			75	5042725
Jul81	25	5439920			76	5096277
	26	5378584			77	5067717
	27	5329516			78	5508198
	28	5292129		Jan86	79	5133963
	29	5378127			80	5180897
	30	5736465			81	5161222
Jan82	31	5073651			82	5174238
	32	5553245			83	5047775
	33	5439363			84	5152063
	34	5363948		Jul86	85	5001222
	35	5367404			86	5232314
	36	5316957			87	5235207
Jul82	37	5412745			88	5009584
	38	5387779			89	5352370
	39	5439224			90	5498755
	40	5341392		Jan87	91	5159840
	41	5396853			92	5274075
	42	5961612			93	5179002
Jan83	43	5335737			94	5269295
	44	5618540			95	5005048
	45	5604606			96	5166569
	46	5343116		Jul87	97	5068848
	47	5294990			98	5007388
	48	5327995			99	5265191
Jul83	49	5177176			100	5046595
	50	5290109			101	5300978
	51	5449099			102	5526153

EXHIBIT 2   Graph of *Good Housekeeping* **Total Sales over Time**

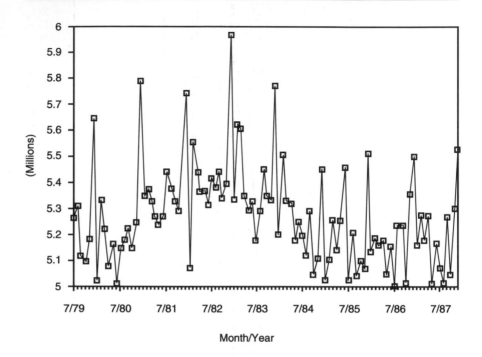

$5 million of advertising revenue, but have to refund $1.25 × (500,000) or $625,000. If they exceed the contracted rate base, however, they were not able to collect any revenues for the excess.

The representative said that *Good Housekeeping* had been planning to raise the advertising base rate from its current level of 4.78 million copies to 6.50 million, effective February 1. The magazine was wondering whether or not the date of the increase should be accelerated by one month, to take effect January 1. The representative was calling to ask if Christensen would, as part of her analysis, evaluate the impact of such an acceleration.

Christensen went back again to her forecasting task, realizing that no decision on the contracted rate base could be made without it.

CASE 45
SHUMWAY, HORCH, AND SAGER (B)

Christensen started to look at the circulation data of some of the other monthly magazines represented by the client organization (see Exhibits 1–3). The first set of data was for *Working Woman*, which was targeted at women who were in management careers in business. Contents included sections devoted to entrepreneurs, business news, economic trends, technology, politics, career fields, social and behavioral sciences, fashion, and health. It was sold almost entirely through subscriptions, as evidenced by the latest figures reported to the Audit Bureau of Circulation (823.6K subscriptions out of 887.8K total circulation).

The next graph represented circulation data for *Country Living*, a journal that focused on both the practical concerns and the intangible rewards of living on the land. It was sold to people who had a place in the country, whether that was a working farm, a gentleman's country place, or a weekend retreat.

The third set of data was for *Health*, which was a lifestyle magazine edited for women who were trying to look and feel better. The magazine provided information on fitness, beauty, nutrition, medicine, psychology, and fashions for the active woman.

A fourth graph was for *Better Homes and Gardens*, which competed with *Good Housekeeping* and was published for husbands and wives who had serious interests in home and family as the focal points of their lives. It covered these home-and-family subjects in depth: food and appliances, building and handyman, decorating, family money management, gardening, travel, health, cars in your family, home and family entertainment, new-product information and shopping. The magazine's circulation appeared to be experiencing increased volatility over time. Was this the beginning of a new pattern?

The last magazine was *True Story*. It was edited for young women and featured story editorials as well as recipes and food features, beauty and health articles, and home management and personal advice. This journal's circulation appeared to have a definite downward trend over the past nine years. Was the cause a general declining interest in the subject matter, or was this a cycle that would correct itself in the future (like the sine wave Christensen had studied in trigonometry)?

EXHIBIT 1   Graphs of *Working Woman* and *Country Living* Circulations

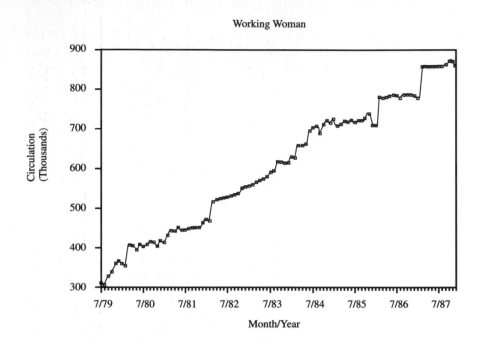

Working Woman

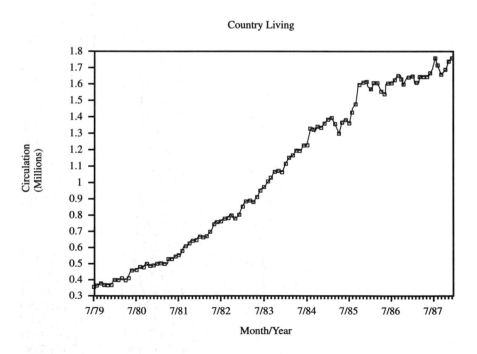

Country Living

EXHIBIT 2   Graphs of *Health* and *BH&G* Circulations

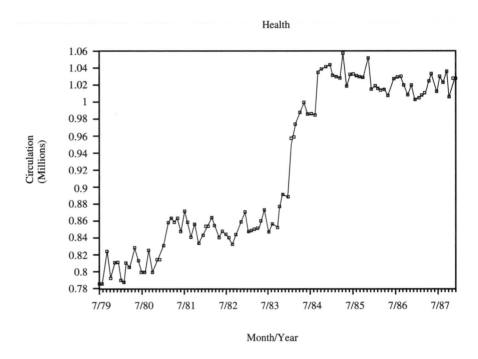

Health

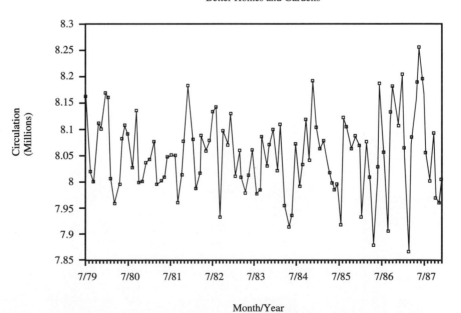

Better Homes and Gardens

EXHIBIT 3　Graph of *True Story* Circulation

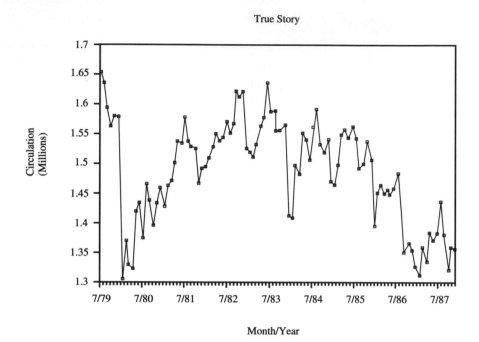

True Story

Month/Year

Case 46
Sleepmore Mattress Manufacturing: Plant Consolidation

W. Carl Lerhos, special assistant to the president of Sleepmore Mattress Manufacturing, had been asked to study the proposed consolidation of plants in three different locations. The company had just added several new facilities as a result of the acquisition of a competitor; some were in markets currently served by existing facilities. The president knew the dollar savings would be fairly easy to calculate for each location, but the qualitative factors and the tradeoffs among them were more difficult to judge. This was the area in which he wanted Carl to spend most of his time.

The major objectives in evaluating a consolidation plan for the sites were to maximize manufacturing benefits, maximize sales benefits, and maximize direct financial benefits. These objectives would be composed of exploiting 13 attributes (see Exhibit 1). After spending some time looking at each attribute individually, Carl and the other officers of Sleepmore ranked them in order of most

---

EXHIBIT 1   Hierarchy of Objectives

I.   Maximize Manufacturing Benefits
     a. Labor
     b. Management effectiveness
          1. Talent availability
          2. Plant size
     c. Operability
          1. Product-line complexity
          2. Training
          3. Production stability
     d. Facilities

          1. Layout
          2. Location
          3. Space availability
II. Maximize Sales Benefits
     a. Maximize service
     b. Maximize quality
III. Maximize Direct Financial Benefits
     a. Minimize initial cost
     b. Maximize ongoing benefit

EXHIBIT 2   **13 Attributes Selected for Evaluation of Consolidation**

Rank	Attribute	Worst Outcome	Best Outcome
1	Labor	Create hostile union	Eliminate hostile union
2	Quality	Drastically worsen quality	Strongly improve quality
3	Service	Lose business	Increase business
4	Annual savings	Lost $1 million/yr.	Save $1 million/yr.
5	Initial cost	Cost $5 million	Save $5 million
6	Management talent	Severely worsen management	Strongly improve management
7	Plant size (sales)	Create $35 million plant	Create $15 million plant
8	Plant location	Move from rural area to city	Move from city to rural area
9	Product-line complexity	Increase to full product line	Reduce product line
10	Space availability	Need a new facility (100,000 sq. ft.)	Save an expansion of 100,000 sq. ft.
11	Production stability	Increase demand variability	Decrease variability
12	Training	Train all new labor	Small layoff—no new training
13	Plant layout	Create poor layout	Eliminate poor layout

important to least important. They also added the best and worst possible outcomes for each attribute (see Exhibit 2).

Measurements

In each case, the attributes were assigned a number from 0 to 10, with 10 being the best possible outcome mentioned in Exhibit 2. Each location was in a different region, and each of the three locations involved a decision between two alternatives—consolidate the plants there or keep them separate. The plants produced different product lines. Exhibits 3 to 5 give brief descriptions and scores of the three potential consolidation opportunities. Only the "consolidate" alternatives are scored; in other words, each "keep separate" alternative has a default score of five for each attribute (except for the attribute plant size, which was undefined for the pair of plants prior to consolidation). Therefore, the attributes are really scored *relative* to the current situation, in which the plants are separate. The scores Carl assigned were based on subjective assessments after talking with the managers and visiting the sites.

Weights

After Carl had scored each attribute on his scale of 0–10, he faced the more difficult task of deciding how important one attribute was compared with another. The quantitative attributes would be fairly easy to weigh. He knew that the company's discount rate (15 percent), along with its planning horizon (10 years), might help in this regard, but he was not quite sure how.

EXHIBIT 3   Consolidation Evaluated at Site 1: Merge Plant 1A into Plant 1B

Attribute	Plant 1A	Plant 1B	Score for Combining
Labor	Poor	Excellent	9; large improvement
Quality	Poor	Good	9
Service	Poor	Good	8
Annual savings	High overhead	Efficient; merger saves $1 MM/yr.	——
Initial cost	Save $1MM if plant merged	N/A	——
Management talent	Poor	Excellent	9
Plant size (sales)	$3 million	$27 million	——
Plant location	Large city	Rural area	10
Product-line complexity	2 major product lines	2 separate lines	0; very complex
Space availability	N/A	Has extra space; needs 0 new sq. ft.	——
Production stability	Small demand/ high uncertainty	Large demand/low uncertainty	7; reduce variation
Training	N/A	Extra labor available	7.5
Plant layout	Congested plant	Well laid out	7.5

He had heard the president say, "The smaller a plant, the easier it is to manage. If we could improve from a $35 million plant size to a $15 million plant, the gain would be equivalent to a savings from the status quo of $1 million a year in operating costs." Carl made a quick mental calculation, which suggested the weight for plant size would be one-half the weight for annual savings—he'd check it later.

The mattress-manufacturing industry required a lot of space. If a consolidation required a new plant or a significant addition, the hassle of moving, as well as hidden expenses, would be additional negative factors. The cost would be $25/sq. ft. for each additional square foot of space.

To help him in assigning weights to the other, more qualitative attributes, Carl pulled out his notes from a meeting attended by the president, the vice president of operations, and the vice president of human resources. At this meeting, held at the time of the acquisition, the list shown in Exhibit 2 had been generated and the relative importance of each attribute had been discussed.

The vice president of human resources had said, "Labor is the most important because the quality of labor determines the major aspects of plant performance (like quality, profitability, and so on). Experience has shown that a good labor force can overcome many obstacles, but a poor labor force leads to trouble. In

EXHIBIT 4   Consolidation Evaluated at Site 2: Put Plant 2B into Plant 2A

Attribute	Plant 2A	Plant 2B	Score for Combining
Labor	Average	Poor	6
Quality	Average	Average	5
Service	Average	Good	7
Annual savings	Under capacity; merger saves $500K	Under capacity	——
Initial cost	N/A	Save $1MM if merge plant	——
Management talent	Average	Good	6
Plant size (sales)	$5 million	$10 million	——
Plant location	Industrial park	Large city	6
Product-line complexity	2 major product lines	2 different lines	0; very complex
Space availability	Need to add 50K sq.ft. if merge	No room	——
Production stability	Small demand/ high uncertainty	Counter-cyclical demand	9; reduce variation
Training	Underutilized labor	Underutilized labor	9; small layoff
Plant layout	Excellent	Poor	9

EXHIBIT 5   Consolidation Evaluated at Site 3: Put Plant 3B into Plant 3A

Attribute	Plant A	Plant B	Score for Combining
Labor	Below average	Good	3; may lose Plant 3A labor
Quality	Average	Average	5
Service	Average	Good	6
Annual savings	Under capacity; merger saves $200K/yr.	Efficient	——
Initial cost	N/A	Save $2MM if merge	——
Management talent	Average	Below average	6
Plant size (sales)	$9 million	$18 million	——
Plant location	Large city	Suburb	4
Product-line complexity	2 major product lines	2 different lines	0; very complex
Space availability	Need 30K sq. ft. if merge	No room	——
Production stability	Small demand/ high uncertainty	Uncertain demand	6; demand not counter-cyclical
Training	Underutilized labor	N/A	3; some labor quits
Plant layout	Good	Cramped	7

fact, I think labor is twice as important as the average of all 13 attributes." Carl wondered about the context for this statement. He verified that the vice president had the ranges of Exhibit 2 in mind: improving labor relations from "create hostile union" to "eliminate hostile union" was twice as valuable as improving the average attribute from worst to best.

The vice president of operations agreed with the comment about labor and said, "I think quality and service, although slightly less important than labor, are two other attributes that deserve more weight than average."

There seemed to be a consensus that management was the next most important qualitative attribute because, like labor, management would determine the fate of the plant. Unlike labor, however, management could be rather easily changed. Overall, this attribute was considered "average" in terms of importance.

The president then argued for consideration of plant location: "Plant location is as important as plant size. Our data show that plants in more congested areas [cities] tend to be less profitable than plants in rural areas."

The vice president of operations said, "Because Sleepmore produces a different product line in different plants, consolidations could drastically increase complexity and reduce long-term efficiency. I move that product-line complexity be considered the next most important qualitative attribute, albeit its importance is about two-thirds the importance of management talent, in my opinion."

The remaining three attributes—stability, training, and layout—were agreed to have individual effects that were relatively small; but their combined effect was considered about twice that of product-line complexity.

The hardest task was to evaluate the tradeoffs that management would be willing to make between quantitative and qualitative factors. In this regard, the president had expressed difficulty to Carl in choosing between a change in the labor from the status quo to eliminate a hostile union and a change in initial cost savings of $7 million.

Decision

Carl had to figure out an effective way to combine all this information about both quantitative and qualitative factors to make decisions whether to consolidate at *each* of the three sites. He wondered how sensitive his decisions would be to the weights he assigned each attribute.

CASE 47
SPRIGG LANE (A)

May 19, 1988, was a beautiful day in Charlottesville, Virginia. Tom Dingledine could see some cows grazing the pasture on the rolling hillside outside his window. He was grateful for the bucolic setting, which was made possible by his doing well with the projects he managed, one of which now required some concentration. Tom was the president of Sprigg Lane Natural Resources, a subsidiary of the Sprigg Lane Investment Corporation (SLIC). The decision at hand was whether to invest in the Bailey Prospect natural gas opportunity.

The Company

Sprigg Lane was a privately held investment corporation founded in 1961. It had become a diversified corporation composed of two major groups. The first was devoted to manufacturing high-quality home furnishings. Its masthead company was Virginia Metalcrafters, which produced handcrafted brass giftware. Other companies in the group included an outdoor lantern company in Maine and an antique reproduction furniture company in Maryland. With the establishment of National Legal Research Group in 1970, another major group—The Research Group—was started. Since then four other research companies had been added in the fields of consumer product marketing, computer software, tax research, and investment financial analysis.

The group's recent formation of Sprigg Lane Development Corporation, which was involved in the purchase and development of real estate, brought the total number of company subsidiaries to nine. SLIC sales for 1987 approximated $30 million and it employed over 525 people.

Drilling and Developing a Well[1]

The most common drilling rig in operation in 1988 was the rotary rig, composed of five major components—the drill string and bit, the fluid-circulating system, the hoisting system, the power plant, and the blowout-prevention system. To facilitate the drilling process, generally a fluid known as drilling mud (composed of water and special chemicals) was circulated around the hole being drilled. In some cases, such as the Bailey Prospect, air was used as the "drilling mud." The major purpose of the drilling mud was to lubricate the drill bit and to carry to the surface the cuttings that could otherwise remain in the hole and clog it.

---

[1]U.S. Department of Energy, *The Oil and Gas Drilling Industry,* 1981, pp. 13–16.

After the well was drilled, and if gas were found, the well had to be completed and prepared for production. A metal pipe of 8.625 inches diameter called "casing" was generally inserted about 1,300 feet into the ground. Then a pipe of 4.5 inches diameter called "production casing" was inserted into the cased hole all the way down through the production zone (about 5,400 feet) and cemented. After the cement set, the production casing was perforated so gas could flow to the surface through it.

The cost to drill an "average" well in Doddridge County, West Virginia, location of the Bailey Prospect, was $160,000. There was some uncertainty, however, in the cost from well to well because of such factors as differing depths of wells and different types of terrain that had to be drilled. Experts in the local area said that there was a 95 percent chance that the cost for any given well would be within $5,400 of the average cost, assuming a normal distribution.

SLIC's Entry into Natural Gas

In January 1987, Tom, who had been working as the CFO of a private oil and gas exploration and development company, met the president of SLIC and joined the company to find some investment opportunities for it. Tom became convinced that the company could enjoy higher potential returns (30-40 percent after tax) from natural resource exploration than from other investment opportunities, including real estate, which were yielding 15-20 percent. Although natural resource exploration was clearly riskier, Tom felt the risk could be managed by drilling only sites that were surrounded on three to four sides by existing wells. Through further research, he found two other factors that helped reduce the risk: first, contracts with the pipeline distributors typically locked in the natural gas selling prices for four years; and second, well operating expenses were covered by contracts that only allowed increases every three years, with the increase capped at 15 percent per three-year period. Tom thought that the annual increase in the total well cost would be equivalent to one-half the rate of inflation.

The president of SLIC was so impressed with Tom's presentation on the entire subject that he offered him the job as president of a new division to be called Sprigg Lane Natural Resources (SLNR). Tom took the offer, and in his first year on the job (1987), SLNR had drilled four wells. It had not been difficult operationally to drill the four wells, but it had been challenging to find enough high-quality investment opportunities. Tom considered wells to be "good" if they met all the following criteria: (1) payback of initial cash investment in 42 months or less, (2) at least 25 percent internal rate of return (IRR) on an after-tax basis, and (3) at least 15 percent IRR on a pretax basis.

In the first five months of production, one of the wells had already paid back 52 percent of its initial investment—well ahead of its target 28-month payout. The other wells were also doing well, and all of them were at least on schedule for meeting their targeted return on investment. Even though things had gone favorably for Tom so far, he knew the pressure was still on him to make good decisions because SLNR was planning to drill 20 more wells in 1988.

Investment Strategy

SLNR acted as the managing general partner in the gas-drilling ventures it formed, which gave it full responsibility for choosing sites and managing the well if gas were found. SLNR gathered information from the state of West Virginia and from other companies drilling in the vicinity of a well (if they were willing to engage in "information trading"). Tom would then put together a package of 10 wells that he considered good investments, based on all the information he had gathered. The total initial investment for a typical package would be around $1.6 million. SLNR would retain about 25 percent ownership and sell the rest to several other general partners.

As managing general partner, SLNR was responsible for hiring a general contractor who would actually hire a firm to do the drilling, and SLNR's geologist, Brad Thomas, would determine whether there really was enough gas to make it worth completing a well. If the decision was to go ahead, the general contractor would also be in charge of the day-to-day operations of a well. SLNR had entered into a joint venture with Excel Energy of Bridgeport, West Virginia, in which they agreed that Excel would act as the general contractor for all the wells on which SLNR acted as managing general partner.

The first-year production level varied significantly from well to well. Tom found the uncertainty could be described with a lognormal probability distribution with a mean of 33 million cubic feet and a standard deviation of 4.93 million cubic feet.

The Bailey Prospect

Exhibit 1 is a copy of the spreadsheet Tom had developed to analyze one well, called the Bailey Prospect, as a potential member of the package of 10 wells he was currently putting together. As Tom thought about the realization of this one well, he knew the Bailey Prospect was surrounded by producing wells from the target gas-producing formation. It was virtually certain, therefore, that SLNR would hit the formation and decide to complete the well; but there was a 10 percent chance that either an operational failure would cause zero production or that the gas formation would be depleted because of the surrounding wells, resulting in essentially zero production. In either of these cases, the pretax loss would be $160,000. In the more likely case, there would be gas produced and Tom would then find out how much the well would produce in the first and subsequent years. He would also learn what the Btu content (see Exhibit 2 for an explanation of the more commonly used abbreviations and terms in the well-drilling business) was for the gas, which would affect the total revenue generated by the well.

Revenues and Expenses. The spreadsheet was basically an income statement over the well's life. The price per mcf was calculated by multiplying the contracted price per MMBtu times the Btu content divided by 1,000. The production in mcf was then estimated for the first year and calculated for each succeeding year, based on the percentage decline values given in the assumptions. The gross

EXHIBIT 1 Bailey Prospect Base-Case Spreadsheet

WELL ASSUMPTIONS

TOTAL WELL COST	$160,000
INTANGIBLE COST (% OF TOTAL)	72.50%
MONTHLY OPERATING COSTS	$300
ANNUAL LEASE EXPENSE	$3,000
INFLATION FACTOR WELL EXP	1.75%
PRODUCTION DATA	
ENOUGH (0 = NO, 1 = YES)?	1
1st YEAR Mcf	33,000
PRODUCTION DECLINE AFTER . . .	
YEAR 1	22.50%
YEAR 2	17.50%
YEAR 3–5	12.50%
YEAR 6–14	10.00%
YEAR 15–24	5.00%

ENVIRONMENT

FEDERAL TAX RATE	34.00%
STATE TAX RATE	9.75%
SEVERANCE TAX RATE	3.40%
COUNTY TAX RATE	4.50%
SECTION 29 TAX CREDIT	$0.7600
% QUALIFIED	100.00%
GNP DEFLATOR	3.50%
ROYALTIES	15.2344%
GAS PRICE DATA	
CURRENT PRICE($/MMBTU)	$1.90
BTU CONTENT(BTU/FT3)	1,155
1ST YEAR OF PRICE INCREASE	5

RESULTS

EQUITY PAYOUT (AFTER-TAX) =	23.26 MO.
INTERNAL RATE OF RETURN (CF AFTER-TAX) =	41.07%
INTERNAL RATE OF RETURN (FBT) =	16.65%
NET PRESENT VALUE (CFAT) @ 15% =	$110,263
CUMULATIVE CASH FLOW AFTER-TAX =	$432,235

Years 0–12

	0	1	2	3	4	5	6	7	8	9	10	11	12
INITIAL INVESTMENT	($160,000)												
PRICE PER MCF		2.19	2.19	2.19	2.19	2.27	2.35	2.43	2.52	2.61	2.70	2.79	2.89
PRODUCTION(MCF)		33,000	25,575	21,099	18,462	16,154	14,135	12,721	11,449	10,304	9,274	8,347	7,512
GROSS REVENUE		$72,419	$56,124	$46,303	$40,515	$36,691	$33,228	$30,952	$28,832	$26,857	$25,017	$23,304	$21,707
LESS: ROYALTIES		11,033	8,550	7,054	6,172	5,590	5,062	4,715	4,392	4,092	3,811	3,550	3,307
NET REVENUE		$61,386	$47,574	$39,249	$34,343	$31,101	$28,166	$26,237	$24,440	$22,766	$21,206	$19,753	$18,400
OPERATING EXPENSES		6,600	6,716	6,833	6,953	7,074	7,198	7,324	7,452	7,583	7,715	7,850	7,988
SEVERANCE & COUNTY TAX		5,721	4,434	3,658	3,201	2,899	2,625	2,445	2,278	2,122	1,976	1,841	1,715
DEPRECIATION	116,000	6,286	6,286	6,286	6,286	6,286	6,286	6,286					
PROFIT BEFORE TAX	($116,000)	$42,779	$30,139	$22,472	$17,904	$14,843	$12,057	$10,182	$14,710	$13,061	$11,514	$10,062	$8,698
DEPLETION		9,208	7,136	5,887	5,151	4,665	4,225	3,936	3,666	3,415	3,181	2,963	2,760
STATE INC. TAX	(11,310)	2,042	1,289	830	555	369	199	83	587	484	387	296	210
FEDERAL INC. TAX	(35,595)	(18,247)	(15,853)	(14,484)	(13,821)	(12,937)	(12,141)	(11,631)	(9,231)	(8,796)	(8,393)	(8,022)	(7,679)
PROFIT AFTER TAX	($69,095)	$49,777	$37,567	$30,238	$26,018	$22,746	$19,775	$17,795	$19,688	$17,958	$16,339	$14,825	$13,407
AFTER TAX CASH FLOW	($113,095)	$65,270	$50,989	$42,411	$37,455	$33,697	$30,285	$28,016	$23,354	$21,373	$19,520	$17,788	$16,167
CUMUL. AFT TAX CASH FLOW	($113,095)	($47,825)	$3,164	$45,575	$83,030	$116,727	$147,013	$175,029	$198,383	$219,756	$239,276	$257,064	$273,232
NPV THROUGH YEAR N	($113,095)	($56,339)	($17,784)	$10,102	$31,518	$48,271	$61,364	$71,896	$79,531	$85,606	$90,432	$94,255	$97,277

Years 13–25

	13	14	15	16	17	18	19	20	21	22	23	24	25
INITIAL INVESTMENT													
PRICE PER MCF	2.99	3.10	3.20	3.32	3.43	3.55	3.68	3.81	3.94	4.08	4.22	4.37	4.52
PRODUCTION(MCF)	6,761	6,085	5,476	5,202	4,942	4,695	4,460	4,237	4,025	3,824	3,633	3,451	3,279
GROSS REVENUE	$20,220	$18,835	$17,545	$17,251	$16,962	$16,678	$16,399	$16,124	$15,854	$15,588	$15,327	$15,071	$14,818
LESS: ROYALTIES	3,080	2,869	2,673	2,628	2,584	2,541	2,498	2,456	2,415	2,375	2,335	2,296	2,257
NET REVENUE	$17,140	$15,966	$14,872	$14,623	$14,378	$14,137	$13,901	$13,668	$13,439	$13,214	$12,992	$12,775	$12,561
OPERATING EXPENSES	8,127	8,270	8,414	8,414	8,414	8,414	8,414	4,207	4,207	4,207	4,207	4,207	4,207
SEVERANCE & COUNTY TAX	1,597	1,488	1,386	1,363	1,340	1,318	1,296	1,274	1,252	1,231	1,211	1,191	1,171
DEPRECIATION													
PROFIT BEFORE TAX	$7,415	$6,208	$5,072	$4,846	$4,624	$4,405	$4,191	$8,187	$7,979	$7,775	$7,574	$7,377	$7,183
DEPLETION	2,571	2,395	2,231	2,193	2,157	2,121	2,085	2,050	2,016	1,982	1,949	1,916	1,884
STATE INC. TAX	129	52	(21)	(35)	(48)	(61)	(73)	324	312	300	288	276	265
FEDERAL INC. TAX	(7,364)	(7,074)	(6,808)	(6,737)	(6,668)	(6,599)	(6,532)	(5,175)	(5,110)	(5,046)	(4,983)	(4,921)	(4,860)
PROFIT AFTER TAX	$12,080	$10,836	$9,670	$9,424	$9,182	$8,945	$8,711	$10,987	$10,761	$10,539	$10,320	$10,105	$9,894
AFTER TAX CASH FLOW	$14,651	$13,231	$11,901	$11,618	$11,339	$11,065	$10,796	$13,037	$12,777	$12,521	$12,269	$12,022	$11,778
CUMUL. AFT TAX CASH FLOW	$287,882	$301,113	$313,014	$324,632	$335,971	$347,036	$357,832	$370,869	$383,646	$396,167	$408,436	$420,458	$432,235
NPV THROUGH YEAR N	$99,658	$101,528	$102,990	$104,232	$105,286	$106,180	$106,938	$107,735	$108,414	$108,992	$109,485	$109,905	$110,263

EXHIBIT 2   Explanation of Commonly Used Terms

Btu	British thermal unit—amount of heat required to raise the temperature of 1 pound of water by 1 degree Fahrenheit.
MMBtu	1 million Btus.
Decatherm	1 MMBtu.
FT³	1 cubic foot.
mcf	1,000 cubic feet.
Intangible well costs	Any expense for something that could not be used again (e.g., fees to the drilling crew, cement costs). A purchase of metal pipe, on the other hand, would represent a tangible cost.
Severance	Sales tax to state on gas or oil withdrawn and sold.
Depletion	Generally the concept is similar to depreciation. It compensated the company for the money spent to acquire the right to drill. Generally accepted accounting principles only recognized cost depletion, which amortized the cost on a unit of production basis (e.g., number of mcf produced this year divided by the total mcf in the ground times the cost). The IRS, however, allowed the company to calculate depletion under the more favorable of two methods. One of these being cost depletion, the other is called "percentage depletion." The latter was in the spreadsheet and was almost always more favorable.

---

revenue was just the product of the price per mcf times the mcf of gas produced in a given year. Out of the gross revenue came a 15.23 percent royalty payment to the owner of the mineral rights, leaving net revenue. Several expenses were deducted from net revenue to arrive at the profit before tax:

1. Monthly operating costs of $300 were paid to Excel Energy in addition to a budgeted amount of $3,000 for other operating expenses that might occur on an annual basis. These costs were increased annually by the well-expense inflation factor.

2. Local taxes of 4.5 percent times the gross revenue were paid to the county and a severance tax (see Exhibit 2) of 3.4 percent times the gross revenue was paid to the state of West Virginia.

3. Depreciation expense for year 0 equaled the intangible drilling cost, which was 72.5 percent of the total well cost. The remainder of the initial drilling cost was depreciated on a straight-line basis over seven years.

To compute profit after tax, the following equations applied:

$$\text{Profit after tax} = \text{Profit before tax} - \text{Depletion} - \text{State income tax} - \text{Federal income tax}$$

$$\textit{Where: Depletion} = \text{minimum of } 0.5 \times (\text{Profit before tax}) \textit{ or } 0.15 \times (\text{Net revenue})$$

EXHIBIT 3   Interest Rates and Yields

		Treasuries						Moody's*	
	Bills	Notes and Bonds							
	1-Yr	*3-Yr*	*5-Yr*	*7-Yr*	*10-Yr*	*30-Yr*	*Aaa*	*Baa*
1985		7.81	9.64	10.12	10.5	10.62	10.79	11.37	12.72
1986		6.08	7.06	7.30	7.54	7.68	7.78	9.02	10.39
1987		6.33	7.68	7.94	8.23	8.39	8.59	9.38	10.58
1988	Jan	6.52	7.87	8.18	8.48	8.67	8.83	9.88	11.07
	Feb	6.21	7.38	7.71	8.02	8.21	8.43	9.40	10.62
	Mar	6.28	7.50	7.83	8.19	8.37	8.63	9.39	10.57
	May 18	7.34	8.23	8.66	8.90	9.20	9.30	10.22	11.45

*Based on yields to maturity on selected long-term corporate bonds.

Sources: *Federal Reserve Bulletin*, June 1988, and *The Wall Street Journal*, May 19, 1988.

$$\text{State income tax} = \text{State tax rate} \times (\text{Profit before tax} - \text{Depletion})$$
$$- 1/2 \times (\text{Severance tax})$$

$$\text{Federal income tax} = \text{Federal tax rate} \times (\text{Profit before tax} - \text{Depletion}$$
$$- \text{State income tax}) - \text{Section 29 credit}$$

Section 29 of the federal tax code had been passed by Congress in 1978 to stimulate drilling for a particular kind of natural gas that was especially difficult to extract from the ground, namely, that found in rock called "devonian shale," which composed the Bailey Prospect. This rock consists of many very small pockets where the gas resides until it is ferreted out. It provided, in 1988, a tax credit of $0.76 per decatherm. This tax credit rate was increased each year with inflation, but its future value was in the hands of Congress and thus far from certain.

Initial Results and Investment Considerations.   To find the net present value (NPV), Tom added back the depreciation and depletion to the profit after tax to come up with the yearly cash flows. These flows were then discounted at the company's hurdle rate of 15 percent for projects of this risk (see Exhibit 3 for a table listing rates of return for investments of varying maturities and degrees of risk) to calculate the NPV through any given year of the well's life. His pro forma analysis indicated the project had an IRR of 41.1 percent and an NPV of $110,263.

Tom was feeling good about the Bailey Prospect, even though he knew he had made many assumptions. He'd used 1,155 Btu/FT^3 to estimate the heat content of the gas because it was the expected (mean) value, when in reality he knew it could be as low as 1,055 or as high as 1,250, with the most likely value (mode)

EXHIBIT 4   Historical and Forecast Data

Historical Natural Gas Prices

Year	Wellhead Price ($/MCF)	Year	Wellhead Price ($/MCF)
1987	1.78	1975	$0.44
1986	1.94	1974	0.30
1985	2.51	1973	0.22
1984	2.66	1972	0.19
1983	2.59	1971	0.18
1982	2.46	1970	0.17
1981	1.98	1969	0.17
1980	1.59	1968	0.16
1979	1.18	1967	0.16
1978	0.91	1966	0.16
1977	0.79	1965	0.16
1976	0.58	1964	0.15

ALL YEARS: MEAN = $0.976 STD DEV = $0.922
LAST 8 YEARS: MEAN = $2.189 STD DEV = $0.412

Source: *Basic Petroleum Data Book*, January 1988, Section VI, Table 2.

Percentage Change from Previous Period in GNP Deflator

Year	Percent Chg	Year	Percent Chg
1987	3.0%	1969	5.6%
1986	2.6	1968	5.0
1985	3.2	1967	2.6
1984	3.7	1966	3.6
1983	3.9	1965	2.7
1982	6.4	1964	1.5
1981	9.7	1963	1.6
1980	9.0	1962	2.2
1979	8.9	1961	1.0
1978	7.3	1960	1.6
1977	6.7	1959	2.4
1976	6.4	1958	2.1
1975	9.8	1957	3.6
1974	9.1	1956	3.4
1973	6.5	1955	3.2
1972	4.7	1954	1.6
1971	5.7	1953	1.6
1970	5.5		

LAST 16 YEARS: ARITHMETIC MEAN = 6.31%, STD DEV = 2.45%
LAST 25 YEARS: ARITHMETIC MEAN = 5.39%, STD DEV = 2.51%
LAST 35 YEARS: ARITHMETIC MEAN = 4.5%, STD DEV = 2.59%
25-YEAR MOVING AVERAGE: MEAN = 4.91%, STD DEV = 0.46%

Source: *Economic Report of the President*, 1988, p. 253

(Continued)

EXHIBIT 4   *Concluded*

Forecasts for Percentage Change in GNP Deflator

	1988	*1989*	*1990*	*Avg 1988–90*
Data Resources*	3.1	3.8	4.5	3.8
Wharton[†]	3.8	4.5	4.5	4.3
UCLA[‡]	2.7	2.8	3.9	3.1

*Data Resources, Inc., November 1987, p. 99.
[†]Wharton Econometrics, September 1987, p. 9.7–9.8.
[‡]UCLA National Business Forecast, December 1987, p. 47.

being 1,160. He also guessed that inflation, as measured by the gross national product (GNP) deflator (a measure similar to the consumer price index or CPI), would average 3.5 percent over the 25-year project life, but he thought he ought to check a couple of forecasts and look at the historical trends. See Exhibit 4 for both forecasts of GNP deflator values as well as historical GNP deflator values and historical natural gas prices. Tom's idea was to use the GNP deflator to forecast natural gas prices after the four-year contract expired and to increase the value of the natural gas tax credit on an annual basis.

Further Questions and Uncertainties.   When Tom showed the results to Henry Ostberg, a potential partner, Henry was impressed with the "expected" scenario but asked, "What is the downside on an investment such as this?" Tom had done his homework and produced Exhibits 5 and 6. Exhibit 5 showed the results if there was not enough gas to develop. Exhibit 6 showed what would happen if there was enough gas, but all other uncertain quantities were set at their 1 chance in 100 worst levels. Henry was somewhat disturbed by what he saw but said, "Hey, Tom, we're businessmen. We're here to take risks; that's how we make money. What we really want to know is the likelihood of this sort of outcome."

Tom realized he had not thought enough about the probabilities associated with potential risks that a project of this kind involved. He also put his mind to work thinking about whether he had considered all the things he had seen that could change significantly from one project to another. The only additional uncertainty he generated was the yearly production decline, which could vary significantly for a given well. He had used what he considered the expected values in this case, but now he realized he ought to multiply each one by some uncertain quantity, with a most likely value of 1.00, a low of 0.50, and a high of 1.75, to allow for the kind of fluctuation he had seen.

Tom wondered what would be the most effective way to incorporate all six of the uncertainties (total well cost, whether the well produced gas or not, first-year production of gas, the Btu content, rate of production decline, and the

Exhibit 5   Spreadsheet with No Gas Produced

WELL ASSUMPTIONS

TOTAL WELL COST	$160,000
INTANGIBLE COST (% OF TOTAL)	72.50%
MONTHLY OPERATING COSTS	$300
ANNUAL LEASE EXPENSE	$3,000
INFLATION FACTOR WELL EXP	1.75%
PRODUCTION DATA ENOUGH (0 = NO, 1 = YES)?	0
1st YEAR Mcf	33,000

PRODUCTION DECLINE AFTER . . .

YEAR 1	22.50%
YEAR 2	17.50%
YEAR 3-5	12.50%
YEAR 6-14	10.00%
YEAR 15-24	5.00%

ENVIRONMENT

FEDERAL TAX RATE	34.00%
STATE TAX RATE	9.75%
SEVERANCE TAX RATE	3.40%
COUNTY TAX RATE	4.50%
SECTION 29 TAX CREDIT	$0.7600
% QUALIFIED	100.00%
GNP DEFLATOR	3.50%
ROYALTIES	15.2344%

GAS PRICE DATA

CURRENT PRICE($/MMBTU)	$1.90
BTU CONTENT(BTU/FT3)	1,155
1ST YEAR OF PRICE INCREASE	5

RESULTS

		ERR MONTHS
EQUITY PAYOUT (AFTER-TAX) =		ERR
INTERNAL RATE OF RETURN (CF AFTER-TAX) =		ERR
INTERNAL RATE OF RETURN (PBT) =		
NET PRESENT VALUE (CFAT) @ 15%	($95,304)	
CUMULATIVE CASH FLOW AFTER-TAX	($95,304)	

YEARS 0–12

YEAR	0	1	2	3	4	5	6	7	8	9	10	11	12
INITIAL INVESTMENT	($160,000)												
PRICE PER MCF		2.19	2.19	2.19	2.19	2.27	2.35	2.43	2.52	2.61	2.70	2.79	2.89
PRODUCTION (MCF)		0	0	0	0	0	0	0	0	0	0	0	0
GROSS REVENUE		$0	$0	$0	$0	$0	$0	$0	$0	$0	$0	$0	$0
LESS: ROYALTIES		0	0	0	0	0	0	0	0	0	0	0	0
NET REVENUE		$0	$0	$0	$0	$0	$0	$0	$0	$0	$0	$0	$0
OPERATING EXPENSES		0	0	0	0	0	0	0	0	0	0	0	0
SEVERANCE & COUNTY TAX		0	0	0	0	0	0	0	0	0	0	0	0
DEPRECIATION	160,000	0	0	0	0	0	0	0	0	0	0	0	0
PROFIT BEFORE TAX	($160,000)	$0	$0	$0	$0	$0	$0	$0	$0	$0	$0	$0	$0
DEPLETION	0	0	0	0	0	0	0	0	0	0	0	0	0
STATE INC. TAX	(15,600)	0	0	0	0	0	0	0	0	0	0	0	0
FEDERAL INC. TAX	(49,096)	0	0	0	0	0	0	0	0	0	0	0	0
PROFIT AFTER TAX	($95,304)	$0	$0	$0	$0	$0	$0	$0	$0	$0	$0	$0	$0
AFTER-TAX CASH FLOW	($95,304)	($95,304)	($95,304)	($95,304)	($95,304)	($95,304)	($95,304)	($95,304)	($95,304)	($95,304)	($95,304)	($95,304)	($95,304)
CUMUL. AFT TAX CASH FLOW	($95,304)	($95,304)	($95,304)	($95,304)	($95,304)	($95,304)	($95,304)	($95,304)	($95,304)	($95,304)	($95,304)	($95,304)	($95,304)
NPV THROUGH YEAR N	($95,304)	($95,304)	($95,304)	($95,304)	($95,304)	($95,304)	($95,304)	($95,304)	($95,304)	($95,304)	($95,304)	($95,304)	($95,304)

YEARS 13–25

YEAR	13	14	15	16	17	18	19	20	21	22	23	24	25
INITIAL INVESTMENT													
PRICE PER MCF	2.99	3.10	3.20	3.32	3.43	3.55	3.68	3.81	3.94	4.08	4.22	4.37	4.52
PRODUCTION (MCF)	0	0	0	0	0	0	0	0	0	0	0	0	0
GROSS REVENUE	$0	$0	$0	$0	$0	$0	$0	$0	$0	$0	$0	$0	$0
LESS: ROYALTIES	0	0	0	0	0	0	0	0	0	0	0	0	0
NET REVENUE	$0	$0	$0	$0	$0	$0	$0	$0	$0	$0	$0	$0	$0
OPERATING EXPENSES	0	0	0	0	0	0	0	0	0	0	0	0	0
SEVERANCE & COUNTY TAX	0	0	0	0	0	0	0	0	0	0	0	0	0
DEPRECIATION	0	0	0	0	0	0	0	0	0	0	0	0	0
PROFIT BEFORE TAX	$0	$0	$0	$0	$0	$0	$0	$0	$0	$0	$0	$0	$0
DEPLETION	0	0	0	0	0	0	0	0	0	0	0	0	0
STATE INC. TAX	0	0	0	0	0	0	0	0	0	0	0	0	0
FEDERAL INC. TAX	0	0	0	0	0	0	0	0	0	0	0	0	0
PROFIT AFTER TAX	$0	$0	$0	$0	$0	$0	$0	$0	$0	$0	$0	$0	$0
AFTER-TAX CASH FLOW	($95,304)	($95,304)	($95,304)	($95,304)	($95,304)	($95,304)	($95,304)	($95,304)	($95,304)	($95,304)	($95,304)	($95,304)	($95,304)
CUMUL. AFT TAX CASH FLOW	($95,304)	($95,304)	($95,304)	($95,304)	($95,304)	($95,304)	($95,304)	($95,304)	($95,304)	($95,304)	($95,304)	($95,304)	($95,304)
NPV THROUGH YEAR N	($95,304)	($95,304)	($95,304)	($95,304)	($95,304)	($95,304)	($95,304)	($95,304)	($95,304)	($95,304)	($95,304)	($95,304)	($95,304)

EXHIBIT 6 Spreadsheet with Gas Found but All Other Uncertainties Set at 1 Chance in 100 Worst Level

WELL ASSUMPTIONS

TOTAL WELL COST	$166,237
INTANGIBLE COST (% OF TOTAL)	72.50%
MONTHLY OPERATING COSTS	$300
ANNUAL LEASE EXPENSE	$3,000
INFLATION FACTOR-WELL EXP	1.34%
PRODUCTION DATA ENOUGH (0 = NO, 1 = YES)?	1
1st YEAR Mcf	24,000
PRODUCTION DECLINE AFTER . . .	
YEAR 1 =	37.20%
YEAR 2 =	28.93%
YEAR 3–5 =	20.67%
YEAR 6–14 =	16.53%
YEAR 15–24 =	8.27%

ENVIRONMENT

FEDERAL TAX RATE	34.00%
STATE TAX RATE	9.75%
SEVERANCE TAX RATE	3.40%
COUNTY TAX RATE	4.50%
SECTION 29 TAX CRED	$0.7600
% QUALIFIED	100.00%
GNP DEFLATOR	2.67%
ROYALTIES	15.2344%
GAS PRICE DATA	
CURRENT PRICE ($/MMBT)	$1.90
BTU CONTENT(BTU/FT3)	1,060
1ST YEAR OF PRICE INCREASE	5

RESULTS

EQUITY PAYOUT (AFTER-TAX) =	65.08 MONTHS
INTERNAL RATE OF RETURN (OF AFTER-TAX)	-183.03%
INTERNAL RATE OF RETURN (PBT) =	-185.22%
NET PRESENT VALUE (CFAT) @ 15%	($30,191)
CUMULATIVE CASH FLOW AFTER-TAX	($18,096)

Years 0–12

	0	1	2	3	4	5	6	7	8	9	10	11	12
INITIAL INVESTMENT	($166,237)												
PRICE PER MCF		2.01	2.01	2.01	2.01	2.07	2.12	2.18	2.24	2.30	2.36	2.42	2.49
PRODUCTION (MCF)		24,000	15,073	10,712	8,498	6,742	5,349	4,465	3,727	3,110	2,596	2,167	1,809
GROSS REVENUE		$48,336	$30,356	$21,574	$17,116	$13,941	$11,356	$9,731	$8,340	$7,147	$6,124	$5,248	$4,498
LESS: ROYALTIES		7,364	4,625	3,287	2,607	2,124	1,730	1,483	1,270	1,089	933	800	685
NET REVENUE		$40,972	$25,732	$18,287	$14,508	$11,817	$9,626	$8,249	$7,069	$6,058	$5,191	$4,449	$3,813
OPERATING EXPENSES		6,600	6,688	6,777	6,868	6,960	7,052	7,147	7,242	7,339	7,437	7,536	7,637
SEVERANCE & COUNTY TAX		3,819	2,398	1,704	1,352	1,101	897	769	659	565	484	415	355
DEPRECIATION	120,522	6,531	6,531	6,531	6,531	6,531	6,531	6,531					
PROFIT BEFORE TAX	($120,522)	$24,023	$10,115	$3,275	($242)	($2,774)	($4,855)	($6,197)	($832)	($1,845)	($2,729)	($3,502)	($4,179)
DEPLETION		6,146	3,860	1,637	(121)	(1,387)	(2,427)	(3,099)	(416)	(923)	(1,365)	(1,751)	(2,090)
STATE INC. TAX	(11,751)	921	94	(207)	(303)	(372)	(430)	(468)	(182)	(211)	(237)	(260)	(280)
FEDERAL INC. TAX	(36,982)	(13,569)	(10,372)	(8,469)	(7,348)	(6,380)	(5,595)	(5,107)	(3,690)	(3,336)	(3,035)	(2,779)	(2,562)
PROFIT AFTER TAX	($71,789)	$30,525	$16,533	$10,314	$7,529	$5,365	$3,597	$2,476	$3,456	$2,624	$1,907	$1,288	$753
AFTER-TAX CASH FLOW	($117,504)	$43,202	$26,924	$18,482	$13,939	$10,509	$7,701	$5,908	$3,040	$1,702	$543	($463)	($1,337)
CUMUL. AFT TAX CASH FLOW	($117,504)	($74,302)	($47,378)	($28,896)	($14,957)	($4,448)	$3,253	$9,161	$12,201	$13,903	$14,445	$13,983	$12,646
NPV THROUGH YEAR N	($117,504)	($79,937)	($59,579)	($47,427)	($39,457)	($34,232)	($30,903)	($28,682)	($27,688)	($27,204)	($27,070)	($27,170)	($27,419)

Years 13–25

	13	14	15	16	17	18	19	20	21	22	23	24	25
INITIAL INVESTMENT													
PRICE PER MCF	2.55	2.62	2.69	2.76	2.84	2.91	2.99	3.07	3.15	3.24	3.32	3.41	3.50
PRODUCTION(MCF)	1,510	1,260	1,052	965	885	812	745	683	627	575	527	484	444
GROSS REVENUE	$3,854	$3,303	$2,831	$2,666	$2,511	$2,365	$2,227	$2,098	$1,976	$1,861	$1,753	$1,651	$1,555
LESS: ROYALTIES	587	503	431	406	383	360	339	320	301	283	267	251	237
NET REVENUE	$3,267	$2,800	$2,399	$2,260	$2,128	$2,005	$1,888	$1,778	$1,675	$1,577	$1,486	$1,399	$1,318
OPERATING EXPENSES	7,739	7,842	7,947	7,947	7,947	7,947	7,947	3,973	3,973	3,973	3,973	3,973	3,973
SEVERANCE & COUNTY TAX	304	261	224	211	198	187	176	166	156	147	138	130	123
DEPRECIATION													
PROFIT BEFORE TAX	($4,776)	($5,303)	($5,771)	($5,897)	($6,016)	($6,129)	($6,234)	($2,361)	($2,455)	($2,543)	($2,626)	($2,704)	($2,778)
DEPLETION	(2,388)	(2,651)	(2,885)	(2,949)	(3,008)	(3,064)	(3,117)	(1,180)	(1,227)	(1,271)	(1,313)	(1,352)	(1,389)
STATE INC. TAX	(298)	(315)	(329)	(333)	(336)	(339)	(342)	(151)	(153)	(156)	(158)	(160)	(162)
FEDERAL INC. TAX	(2,379)	(2,224)	(2,094)	(2,043)	(1,996)	(1,950)	(1,908)	(1,258)	(1,220)	(1,185)	(1,151)	(1,120)	(1,090)
PROFIT AFTER TAX	$289	($112)	($462)	($572)	($677)	($775)	($868)	$229	$146	$69	($4)	($72)	($137)
AFTER-TAX CASH FLOW	($2,098)	($2,764)	($3,347)	($3,521)	($3,685)	($3,839)	($3,985)	($952)	($1,081)	($1,202)	($1,317)	($1,425)	($1,526)
CUMUL. AFT TAX CASH FLOW	$10,547	$7,784	$4,437	$916	($2,769)	($6,609)	($10,593)	($11,545)	($12,626)	($13,829)	($15,145)	($16,570)	($18,096)
NPV THROUGH YEAR N	($27,760)	($28,151)	($28,562)	($28,939)	($29,281)	($29,591)	($29,871)	($29,929)	($29,987)	($30,042)	($30,095)	($30,145)	($30,191)

average inflation over the next 25 years) into his investment analysis. He remembered doing "what if" tables with Lotus™ back in business school, but he had never heard of a six-way table. As he skimmed back through his quantitative methods book, he saw a chapter on Monte Carlo simulation and read enough to be convinced that this method was ideally suited to his current situation.

When Tom told Henry about this new method of evaluation he was contemplating, his partner laughed and said, "Come on, Tom, it can't be that hard. What you're talking about sounds like something they'd teach brand-new MBAs. You and I have been doing this type of investing for years. Can't we just figure it out on the back of an envelope?" When Tom tried to estimate the probability of his worst-case scenario, it came out to 0.00000001 percent—not very likely! There was no way he was going to waste any more time trying to figure out the expected NPV by hand based on all the uncertainties, regardless of how intuitive his friend thought it should be. Consequently, Tom thought a little more about how Monte Carlo simulation would work with this decision.

In his current method of evaluating projects, he had used the three criteria mentioned earlier ($<$ 42-month payback of initial cash investment, $>$ 15 percent IRR on pretax basis, and $>$ 25 percent IRR on after-tax basis). He could see that calculating the average IRR after several Monte Carlo trials wouldn't be very meaningful, especially since there was a 10 percent chance that you would spend $160K on a pretax basis and get no return! It would be impossible to find an IRR on that particular scenario. He did feel he could calculate an average NPV after several trials and even find out how many years it would take until the NPV became positive. As he settled into his chair to finish reading the chapter, which looked vaguely familiar, he looked up briefly at the verdant hillside and wondered for a moment what resources were under the hill.

CASE 48
T. ROWE PRICE ASSOCIATES

Peter Gordon's day had begun as usual with *The Wall Street Journal*. As was his custom, he had started reading at the back, but he had not yet finished "Heard on the Street" when his direct lines to Salomon Brothers and Chemical Bank lit up almost simultaneously. It was 8:45 a.m. on Tuesday, June 21, 1983.

The trader at Salomon Brothers was offering to sell $50 million of a new issue of M-S-R Bond Anticipation Notes at 99.50. Salomon was co-manager of the deal, and Gordon had noticed the tombstone in the *Journal* that morning (Exhibit 1). Gordon put the Salomon call on hold, picked up the Chemical Bank line, and heard Chemical's trader offer him $52,780,000 of Montgomery County, Maryland, notes at 7.04 percent. Because he expected to receive $49,950,000 in cash on July 1 when several notes already in his portfolio matured, Gordon asked both traders if they would be willing to sell for delivery on that date. When they agreed, he said he would respond to their offers by 9:30 a.m. He had 45 minutes in which to choose the better investment.

The Municipal Bond Market

Although corporate bonds were more widely followed by the investing public, the municipal bond market was considerably larger. States, local governments, and municipal agencies offered $57.3 billion in new bonds in 1982, twice the amount of new corporate issues. "Munis" were distinguished from corporate bonds and U.S. Treasury instruments by the advantageous feature that interest income from municipal bonds was not subject to federal taxation. Consequently, the individual and corporate investor could frequently earn a better return by investing in municipal securities, which, although they earned lower rates of interest, produced a tax-free income stream. See Exhibit 2 for the yields of a selection of corporate, Treasury, and municipal bonds.

Municipal securities were of two major types—general obligation bonds (GOs) and revenue bonds. GOs were issued by state and local governments to raise funds for municipal capital improvements, such as school construction or renovation, street and highway development, or municipal building construction. Such bonds were backed by the "full faith and credit" as well as the taxing power of the state or municipality that issued them.

Revenue bonds, which composed more than three-quarters of the municipal market, were secured by the revenues of the projects to which they supplied capital. These projects included municipal utility projects (water, sewer, gas),

This case was prepared in conjunction with Edward R. Case (Darden, Class of 1984).

EXHIBIT 1 M-S-R Tombstone

This announcement appears as a matter of record only.

New Issue

$447,200,000
M-S-R Public Power Agency
(California)

$215,000,000 San Juan Project Bond Anticipation Notes, Series A
$232,200,000 San Juan Project Revenue Bonds, Series A

A Joint Exercise of Powers Agency consisting of the Modesto Irrigation District, the City of Santa Clara and the City of Redding

The Series A Notes and Series A Bonds are dated June 15, 1983 and due July 1, as shown below. The Series A Notes are not subject to redemption prior to maturity. The Series A Bonds are subject to redemption as described in the Official Statement.

In the opinion of Bond Counsel, under existing laws, regulations, rulings and court decisions, interest on the Series A Notes and Series A Bonds is exempt from present federal income taxes and State of California personal income taxes.

Neither the faith and credit nor the taxing power of the State of California or any political subdivision thereof or M-S-R or any member of M-S-R is pledged to the payment of the Series A Notes or Series A Bonds.

$215,000,000 6¾% Bond Anticipation Notes due July 1, 1986—Price 99.50%

Amount	Due	Coupon Rate	Price	Amount	Due	Coupon Rate	Price
$1,030,000	1988	7¼%	100%	$1,285,000	1991	8 %	100%
1,105,000	1989	7½	100	1,385,000	1992	8¼	100
1,190,000	1990	7¾	100	1,500,000	1993	8½	100
				1,625,000	1994	8¾	100

$ 3,700,000 9 % Term Bonds due July 1, 1996—N.R.*

$ 4,395,000 9¼% Term Bonds due July 1, 1998—Price 100%

$ 15,205,000 9⅝% Term Bonds due July 1, 2003—N.R.*

$ 159,210,000 9⅞% Term Bonds due July 1, 2020—Price 100%

$ 40,570,000 6 % Term Bonds due July 1, 2022—Price 64%

(Accrued interest to be added)

* Not Reoffered.

The Series A Notes and Series A Bonds are subject to the approval of legality by Orrick, Herrington & Sutcliffe, A Professional Corporation, San Francisco, California, Bond Counsel. Certain legal matters will be passed upon for M-S-R by McDonough, Holland & Allen, Sacramento, California, A Professional Corporation, Special Counsel to M-S-R. Certain legal matters will be passed upon for the Underwriters by their counsel, Brown, Wood, Ivey, Mitchell & Petty, San Francisco, California.

Smith Barney, Harris Upham & Co. Incorporated

E. F. Hutton & Company Inc. Merrill Lynch White Weld Capital Markets Group Merrill Lynch, Pierce, Fenner & Smith Incorporated

Salomon Brothers Inc

Bear, Stearns & Co. A. G. Becker Paribas Incorporated Blyth Eastman Paine Webber Incorporated Boettcher & Company Alex. Brown & Sons Clayton Brown & Associates, Inc.
Dillon, Read & Co. Inc. Donaldson, Lufkin & Jenrette Securities Corporation Drexel Burnham Lambert Incorporated A. G. Edwards & Sons, Inc. Ehrlich-Bober & Co., Inc. The First Boston Corporation
Goldman, Sachs & Co. Kidder, Peabody & Co. Incorporated Lazard Frères & Co. Lehman Brothers Kuhn Loeb Incorporated Miller & Schroeder Municipals, Inc. John Nuveen & Co. Incorporated
Oppenheimer & Co., Inc. Prudential-Bache Securities Refco Partners L. F. Rothschild, Unterberg, Towbin Shearson/American Express Inc. Thomson McKinnon Securities Inc.
Van Kampen Merritt Inc. Wertheim & Co., Inc. Dean Witter Reynolds Inc. Bateman Eichler, Hill Richards Incorporated William Blair & Company J. C. Bradford & Co.
Crowell, Weedon & Co. Glickenhaus & Co. Interstate Securities Corporation Matthews & Wright, Inc. McDonald & Company
Moseley, Hallgarten, Estabrook & Weeden Inc. MuniciCorp of California Wm. E. Pollock & Co., Inc. Prescott, Ball & Turben, Inc.
Rauscher Pierce Refsnes, Inc. M. L. Stern & Co., Inc. Sutro & Co. Incorporated Tucker, Anthony & R. L. Day, Inc. Underwood, Neuhaus & Co. Incorporated
Robert L. Adler & Co., Inc. Advest, Inc. American Securities Corporation Bancroft, O'Connor, Chilton & Lavell, Inc.
Barr Brothers & Co., Inc. Bevill, Bresler & Schulman Incorporated California Municipal Investors Inc. Craigie Incorporated Dain Bosworth Incorporated
Fahnestock & Co. First of Michigan Corporation Gabriele, Hueglin & Cashman, Inc. Gibralco, Inc. Hanifen, Imhoff Inc.
Herzfeld & Stern Howard, Weil, Labouisse, Friedrichs Incorporated Hutchinson, Shockey, Erley & Co. Johnson, Lane, Space, Smith & Co., Inc. Kirchner, Moore & Company
J. J. Lowrey & Co. Mabon, Nugent & Co. Moore & Schley Municipals, Inc. E. A. Moos & Co. Incorporated Morgan, Olmstead, Kennedy & Gardner Incorporated R. H. Moulton & Company
The Ohio Company Piper, Jaffray & Hopwood Incorporated Arch W. Roberts & Co. Roosevelt & Cross Incorporated Rotan Mosle Inc. Seattle-Northwest Securities Corporation
Spelman & Company, Inc. Stephens Inc. Stone & Youngberg Wedbush, Noble, Cooke, Inc. Westcap Securities Inc. Wheat, First Securities, Inc. Birr, Wilson & Co., Inc.
R. L. Crary & Co., Inc. Davis, Skaggs & Co., Inc. Diversified Securities, Inc. First Affiliated Securities Emmett A. Larkin Company, Inc.
Philip V. Mann & Co., Inc. J. A. Overton & Co. San Diego Securities Inc. Western Pacific Securities Inc. Thomas F. White & Co., Inc. Wulff Hansen & Co.

June 21, 1983

Source: *The Wall Street Journal,* June 21, 1983.

EXHIBIT 2   Relative Yields, June 21, 1983

Treasuries

3-month T-bill	8.76%
1-year T-bill	9.23
5-year T-note	10.74
30-year bond	11.11

Corporates

30-year AAA utility	12.30
30-year AAA corporate	11.65

Municipals

6-month project note	4.90
30-year prime GO.	9.10
30-year hospital revenue bond	10.00

---

transportation facilities (airports, seaports, toll roads), and hospitals. In addition, there were special tax revenue bonds secured by the income from taxes on alcoholic beverages or cigarettes. Revenue bonds had more risk than GOs, because, in the event of a default, the municipality that issued them had no responsibility for repayment.

Municipal bonds competed in the capital market for the same investors' funds as did corporate bonds. In fact, the structure of the municipal bond market was very similar to that of the corporate bond market. Most of the major investment banks underwrote and sold municipal as well as corporate securities. A secondary market also existed in which the bonds that were originally sold by underwriters were reoffered for sale by purchasers. The *Blue List* of current municipal offerings, which Standard & Poor's published daily, was the most complete source of information about bonds for sale in the secondary market. Exhibit 3 is a copy of a *Blue List* page.

The value of a bond is determined by price, the number of years to maturity, and coupon. A 10 percent coupon pays 10 percent per year of the par (face) value in two equal, semiannual payments. The owner of a 10 percent bond with $5,000 par value would receive $250, one-half of the annual coupon, every six months until the bond "matured." On the maturity date, the owner would receive the final coupon payment plus the par value of the bond for a total of $5,250.

Municipal bonds were traded either on the basis of price, which was stated as a percentage of par value, or on the basis of yield to maturity. A bond that traded at a price of 100, therefore, traded at par, while a discount bond that traded at 98.50 sold for 98.5 percent of its par value, or $985 per thousand of face value. Similarly, a premium bond that traded at 101 would cost $1,010 per thousand of face value. The yield to maturity of a bond was expressed as twice the six-month discount rate that set the bond's net present value to zero. For example, an eight-year bond whose coupon was 8.70 percent and was selling for 99 1/4 would have

Exhibit 3 Example of *Blue List* Information

50	VIRGINIA ED.LOAN AU.	7	6/ 1/86	100 SEARSBKI
250	VIRGINIA ED.LOAN AU.	8.10	6/ 1/89	8.00 FIRMERNB
5	VIRGINIA ED.LOAN AU.	8.40	6/ 1/90	99 1/2 CRAIGIE
40	VIRGINIA ED.LOAN AU.	8.40	6/ 1/90	100 FIRMERNB
90	VIRGINIA ED.LOAN AU.	8.40	6/ 1/90	100 HORNERBA
320	VIRGINIA ED.LOAN AU.	8.70	6/ 1/91	100 5/8 ABROWNBA
500	VIRGINIA ED.LOAN AU.	8.70	6/ 1/91	99 1/4 CRAIGIE
250	VIRGINIA ED.LOAN AU.	8.90	6/ 1/92	100 HORNERBA
60	VIRGINIA ED.LOAN AU.	9.10	6/ 1/94	9.00 ABROWNBA
100	VIRGINIA ED.LOAN AU.	9	3/ 1/95	99 AGEDARDS
10	VIRGINIA HSG.DEV.AUTH.	5	10/ 1/85	7.00 SCOTTSTR
10	VIRGINIA HSG.DEV.AUTH.	6.25	8/ 1/88	8.00 SCOTTSTR
10	VIRGINIA HSG.DEV.AUTH.	6-10	10/ 1/90	8.50 MERRILNY
45	VIRGINIA HSG.DEV.AUTH.	7.35	8/ 1/93	8.90 BBS
100	VIRGINIA HSG.DEV.AUTH.	7.70	8/ 1/94	8.90 KIDDERPH
10	VIRGINIA HSG.DEV.AUTH.	7.75	8/ 1/95	9.25 SHEARNYB
50	VIRGINIA HSG.DEV.AUTH.	7.60	10/ 1/95	9.25 HUTTONMD
5	VIRGINIA HSG.DEV.AUTH.	7.60	10/ 1/95	9.00 KIDDERPH
100	VIRGINIA HSG.DEV.AUTH. (SINGLE FAMILY)	6.40	10/ 1/96	9.25 THOMSON
5	VIRGINIA HSG.DEV.AUTH.	8.75	9/ 1/06	12.20 RODMANNY
635	VIRGINIA HSG.DEV.AUTH.	6.875	10/ 1/08	9.50 MATTHEWS
20	VIRGINIA HSG.DEV.AUTH. (SINGLE FAMILY MTGE)	6.20	10/ 1/09	10.00 DREXNYEX
100	VIRGINIA HSG.DEV.AUTH. (Y/M 10.75) (P/C @ 103)	12.375	11/ 1/13 C91	10.00 WHEATFST
25	VIRGINIA HSG.DEV.AUTH.FHA INS	5.75	6/ 1/14	9.50 ROGERSLB
1500	VIRGINIA HSG.DEV.AUTH.	0.000	9/ 1/14	3.65 BECKERMU
1000	VIRGINIA HSG.DEV.AUTH.	0.000	9/ 1/14	3 1/2 KIDDERNY
10	VIRGINIA HSG.DEV.AUTH.	6	9/ 1/14	9.50 CRAIGIE
15	VIRGINIA HSG.DEV.AUTH. REG	6	9/ 1/14	9.90 MERRILNY
100	VIRGINIA HSG.DEV.AUTH.	0.000	11/ 1/17	4 BEARSTER
3500	VIRGINIA HSG.DEV.AUTH.	0.000	11/ 1/17	4 1/4 HUTTONNY
500	VIRGINIA HSG.DEV.AUTH.	0.000	11/ 1/17	4 1/4 TRIPPCO
5	VIRGINIA HSG.DEV.AUTH.	6.40	11/ 1/18	9.50 MERRILNY
100	VIRGINIA HSG.DEV.AUTH.	6.20	11/ 1/20	9.30 MERRILNY
10	VIRGINIA HSG.DEV.AUTH.	6.40	11/ 1/20	9.40 MERRILNY
5	VIRGINIA HSG.DEV.AUTH.	6.70	11/ 1/21	9.50 CRAIGIE
5	VIRGINIA HSG.DEV.AUTH.	6.70	11/ 1/21	9.50 SCOTTSTR
10	VIRGINIA HSG.DEV.AUTH.	7.20	11/ 1/22	9.50 MERRILNY
25	VIRGINIA HSG.DEV.AUTH.	7.20	11/ 1/22	9.50 MERRILNY
50	VIRGINIA HWY.COMM.TOLL REV.	4	1/ 1/05	76 BEARSTER
150	VIRGINIA PUB.SCH.AU.	5.50	10/ 1/86	6.40 SOTRBALA
25	VIRGINIA PUB.SCH.AU.	5.50	1/ 1/88	7.00 ABROWNBA
5	VIRGINIA PUB.SCH.AU.	4.50	1/ 1/89	8.50 THOMSON
5	VIRGINIA PUB.SCH.AU.	5	1/ 1/94	8.50 DAVENPOR
20	VIRGINIA PUB.SCH.AU.	5.10	1/ 1/94	8.50 DAVENPOR
5	ALBEMARLE CO.	9.25	1/ 1/09	65 DERANDIN
40	ALBEMARLE CO.I.D.A. MBIA (FHA-INS) (MTGE/REV)	11.50	1/ 1/88	7.50 OPCOFTL
10	ALBEMARLE CO.I.D.A. CA @ 71 (HYDRALIC ROAD APT.)	0.000	7/ 1/97 C93	27.15 FISCHER
755	ALEXANDRIA SAN.AUTH. P/R @ 103	6	10/ 1/89 C86	6.00 CRAIGIE
15	AQUIA SAN.DIST.	6.25	9/ 1/99	9.50 CRAIGIE
25	ARLINGTON CO.HOSP.AU.	5.60	1/ 1/85	6.25 WHEATFST
770	ARLINGTON CO.H.F.A. FHA MBIA	0.000	12/ 1/05	12.50 OPCONY
5	BRISTOL I.D.A.	14.50	6/ 1/11	12.50 BUCHANAN

Source: *The Blue List of Current Municipal Offerings.*

EXHIBIT 4   Calculation of Yield to Maturity

On line 7 of Exhibit 3, Craigie Securities offered $500,000 of VELA 8.70s due on 6/1/91 at 99 1/4. The proceeds from the original sale of this issue provided funds for reduced-rate educational loans for Virginia residents. If these bonds had been offered at 99 1/4 on June 1, 1983, what would their yield to maturity have been?

No formula exists for computing yield to maturity. By trial and error, using a calculation similar to the one detailed below, the yield to maturity could be discovered to be slightly less than 8.84 percent. Maybe 8.834 percent is right? The only way to be sure is to discount the bond's cash flows at a six-month rate of 4.417 percent and determine the net present value (NPV).

Date	*Cash Flows for a $5,000 Bond*	*Discount Factor for a Six-Month Rate of 4.417 Percent*	*Discounted Cash Flow*
6/1/83	$(4,962.50)	1.00000	$(4,962.50)
12/1/83	217.50	0.95770	208.30
6/1/84	217.50	0.91719	199.49
12/1/84	217.50	0.87839	191.05
6/1/85	217.50	0.84123	182.97
12/1/85	217.50	0.80565	175.23
6/1/86	217.50	0.77157	167.82
12/1/86	217.50	0.73893	160.72
6/1/87	217.50	0.70767	153.92
12/1/87	217.50	0.67773	147.41
6/1/88	217.50	0.64906	141.17
12/1/88	217.50	0.62161	135.20
6/1/89	217.50	0.59531	129.48
12/1/89	217.50	0.57013	124.00
6/1/90	217.50	0.54601	118.76
12/1/90	217.50	0.52292	113.73
6/1/91	$5,217.50	0.50080	2,612.90
			$(0.35)

Because the NPV is approximately zero with a six-month discount rate of 4.417 percent, an investor would be indifferent between buying this bond or placing $4,962.50 in an alternative investment that paid 4.417 percent semiannually for eight years. The yield to maturity is, then, 8.834 percent (2 × 4.417 percent), the nominal annual rate.

---

a yield to maturity of 8.834 percent (see Exhibit 4 for the calculation of this figure). Buyers and sellers could quote the price of this bond as either "priced to yield 8.834 percent" or "priced at 99 1/4."

Peter Gordon

Peter Gordon, a vice president of T. Rowe Price Associates (TRPA), managed portfolios of municipal securities for a firm that provided investment research and counsel to individual and institutional investors. TRPA, with total net assets under supervision in excess of $16 billion, was among the largest independent investment advisory firms in the nation. A major portion of these assets was held in nine public, no-load, mutual funds that bore the Price Associates name. TRPA had a reputation for active but conservative investment policies that dated back to the "growth-stock theories" that Mr. T. Rowe Price, a Baltimore financier, developed in the 1930s. Now the firm employed investment analysts, marketing managers and researchers, note, bond, and stock traders, and portfolio managers to oversee its numerous public and private portfolios.

Peter Gordon was responsible for a $1.6 billion investment in municipal bonds and notes and was widely acknowledged to be one of the most successful portfolio managers in his field (see Exhibit 5 for a profile). He was also the first public member ever elected to the Municipal Securities Rulemaking Board, the regulatory agency for municipal bond issuers and dealers. The largest fund under his management, the Tax-Free Income Fund, invested primarily in municipal securities to produce for the fund's shareholders the highest income exempt from federal income taxes that was consistent with the preservation of principal. On June 21, 1983, the net assets of the fund were $982 million. For 1982, the fund had shown a yield of 10.4 percent, while net asset value per share had increased by a record 18.2 percent.

Doing a Deal

Salomon Brothers had offered $50 million worth (par value) of M-S-R Public Power Agency Bond Anticipation Notes. These notes were revenue bonds backed by the income of a power system owned jointly by three California municipalities: the Modesto Irrigation District, the City of Santa Clara, and the City of Redding. The capital raised by these bonds would be used to purchase a share in the ownership of a large coal-fired power plant in Arizona and to pay for power-transmission lines to the three municipalities.

Salomon's price was 99.50 percent, and Salomon offered to deliver the bonds on July 1, 1983, the "settlement date." The bonds would mature on July 1, 1986, and would make semiannual coupon payments on January 1 and July 1. The coupon rate was 6.75 percent.

Because the issue date (the "dated date") was June 15, 1983, if Gordon were to buy the bonds on July 1, he would have to pay 16 days of accrued coupon interest ($147,945.21) to the seller. Gordon would recover this accrued interest as part of the first coupon on January 1, 1984; the amount of the first coupon would thus be $147,945.21 greater than subsequent semiannual coupon payments.

Chemical Bank had offered $52,780,000 worth of Montgomery County Housing Loan Construction Notes, a specialized form of revenue bond, at a yield to maturity of 7.04 percent. These bonds, known in the trade as "monkeys," had a coupon rate of 4.50 percent, would pay interest on January 1 and July 1, and would mature on January 1, 1986. The bonds would raise inexpensive mortgage capital, which the county's housing agency would use to encourage the construction of new, moderately priced, single-family housing. Although Chemical Bank would have preferred to sell the bonds for next-day delivery, the trader was

EXHIBIT 5   Newspaper Article on Peter Gordon

Master trader holds own in bond market

By Michelle Osborn
USA TODAY

BALTIMORE — Meet Peter J.D. Gordon, 36, the tough, confident Scottish-born president of T. Rowe Price Associates Inc.'s fast-growing $1 billion Tax-Free Income Fund, the second-largest municipal bond mutual fund in the USA.

He trades in the bond market from his seventh-floor office in the IBM building here.

He is on the phone much of the day as he picks up information about the market: "The new three, it's at the buck, it's trading extremely well."

He and the brokers speak a shorthand language no outsider can understand: "What do you think of the Lutherans? Do you think they're worth the nine level?"

It's infectious, but Gordon takes care not to get lost in it.

"If you're totally involved in the chitchat of the marketplace, you lose the ability to think," he says.

An inability to think could be a costly proposition for Gordon.

He's a major player in the multibillion-dollar municipal bond market, routinely buying and selling millions of dollars worth of bonds a day for his fund.

The decisions Gordon makes affect the total return on your investment in the fund — both the interest income, or yield, and the fund's per-share net asset value, which is the price you pay to buy into the fund and the money you would get if you sold your shares. (Tuesday, Tax-Free shares closed at $8.96.)

Bond prices fall when interest rates rise and the converse. The share price of the Rowe Price fund follows those fluctuations.

Gordon, though, who's known as an aggressive manager of bond maturity risk, tries to cushion swings in the bond market by lengthening or shortening the maturities of

Tax-exempt bond funds: Here's how they work

Municipal or tax-exempt bond funds, like other mutual funds, pool your money with that of thousands of others who share your investment goals — in this case, tax-free income over a long period.

Like other mutual funds, a bond fund offers a diversified investment portfolio, professional management and liquidity. But with this kind of mutual fund, the share price reflects swings in interest rates: When interest rates go up, bond prices go down and the per-share price of a bond fund tends to follow that drop. When interest rates drop, the share price rises.

T. Rowe Price stresses the importance of total return — interest income or yield, plus appreciation in your original investment.

Reason: As the table at right shows, total return can be negative in a year in which share price falls so much that it offsets the yield. Or total return can soar when share prices rise and that gain is added to yield.

Whether a tax-exempt bond fund is for you depends primarily on your income tax bracket. You should be in at least a 30 percent marginal tax bracket, which means that if your taxable income increases $1, 30 cents would be paid in federal taxes.

If your *taxable* income is between $18,201 and $23,500, an 8 percent tax-free yield is equal to an 11.43 percent taxable yield; at $34,101 to $41,500, 8 percent tax-free is the equivalent of a 13.33 percent taxable yield; if your taxable income is $55,301 or more, 8 percent tax-free is equal to a 16 percent taxable yield.

Multimillion-dollar routine

By Bill Perry, UPI, Special for USA TODAY
GORDON: Misses the excitement when he's not at work

How Price fund performs

Here's the performance of the T. Rowe Price Tax-Free Income Fund compared with the total return on municipal bond funds ranked by Lipper Analytical Services Inc.

As of:	Price per share	Annual yield	12-month total return*	Lipper
Dec. 31, 1978	$9.54	5.30%	−2.1%	−3.4%
Dec. 31, 1979	9.20	5.56	+2.0	−1.5
Dec. 31, 1980	8.06	7.75	−5.3	−13.2
Dec. 31, 1981	7.26	9.52	−0.9	−8.4
Dec. 31, 1982	8.58	10.39	+31.0	+39.3
April 30, 1983	9.20	9.70	+35.3	+34.3

* percentage change in share price over a year plus yield
Source: T. Rowe Price Associates Inc.

the bonds in the portfolio.

On this day, he is lengthening the average maturity of the securities he holds to lock in high yields because he believes that another major drop in long-term interest rates — as much as 1 percentage point — is possible by the end of the year.

The fund's seven-day average yield on this trading day is 8.29 percent. By 10 a.m., Gordon already has invested about $28 million in new issues of Ohio housing revenue bonds and Hawaii airport revenue bonds at yields higher than 9 percent.

By tough negotiating in both cases he has purchased the bonds at, in effect, wholesale prices by refusing to pay brokers' commissions.

He doesn't hesitate to throw his weight around in the market. "We came to you first. We may consider buying bonds away from you," he tells one broker, disclosing that he has found other members of the syndicate underwriting the new bond issue who are willing to sell at a cut-rate price. This broker won't give up that commission, and Gordon picks up the bonds from other investment firms.

Some of Gordon's trades take all day to consummate. Some don't get beyond the snap of a finger.

A finger snap this day: Jeffrey J. Alexopulos, Gordon's chief credit analyst, warns him early that a $271 million bond issue by New York City's Metropolitan Transportation Authority has — in Alexopulos' opinion — credit problems.

The existence of in-house credit analysis means Gordon can both avoid overvalued bonds and buy those he thinks are undervalued by rating agencies such as Standard & Poor's Corp. and Moody's Investors Service Inc.

It also means Gordon can get out of issues before problems hit the market. He dumped troubled Washington Public Power Supply System bonds about three years before their credit ratings collapsed.

Gordon is cool, measured. He's a man of few words — and those few often are punctuated with long silences as he punches numbers on his calculator.

He has the guile of a master poker player. But he doesn't play poker. He says he has no need to gamble. The market is more exciting; he sometimes misses it on weekends.

By the time Gordon holds staff meeting at 3:30 p.m., the market's pace has picked up. Gordon already has decided to

put more money to work in Ohio housing bonds.

He has plenty of new money to invest: An average of $5 million to $6 million has flowed into the fund daily since the start of 1983.

When the working day ends around 5 p.m., Gordon figures the $51 million in bonds he bought this day will increase the net asset value of the fund by 4 cents a share — if interest rates decline by three-quarters of a percentage point, as he anticipates.

And if rates don't drop? Net asset value would fall 4 cents.

For a typical investor with about $20,000 in the fund, a 4 cent change means a gain or loss of $100.

Since that trading day recently, Gordon decided long-term interest rates were heading up, not down: He has sold about $300 million of bonds and used the proceeds to buy short-term securities to cushion the fund's share price against a decline.

Source: *USA Today,* June 1, 1983.

willing to accommodate Gordon's wishes and sell the bonds with a settlement date of July 1. Since July 1 was also a coupon date, no interest would accrue and the first coupon would be January 1, 1984.

The evaluation of these offers was complicated by the fact that there could be capital gains from the bonds and these gains would be taxable. The M-S-Rs, selling at a discount, would surely have a capital gain of $5 per thousand if the bonds were held to maturity. Gordon expected, however, that the Tax-Free Income Fund would show other, small, realized gains and losses before 1986; such gains and losses were common in successful "actively managed" portfolios. The tax laws allowed such gains to be carried forward or backward; thus, over time, they tended to net out. As a result, Gordon decided to ignore any tax effects in his investment decision.

Gordon also regarded the two securities as having approximately the same degree of credit risk. The M-S-Rs were secured by a "take-or-pay" contract, which required the California utility to repay the project's costs from its revenues even if the project produced no power. Although such contracts had been challenged the previous year in the courts of the state of Washington, the courts of other states such as Texas had upheld the legitimacy of take-or-pay contracts.

TRPA's municipal credit analysts regarded the M-S-R project as sound in spite of its large size. The Montgomery County notes had the advantage of security in the form of liens on the housing projects they financed. Consequently, Gordon believed that the market would not demand a premium for either bond; the M-S-Rs and the Montgomery County notes were equivalent investments from the standpoint of risk.

In the next 45 minutes, Gordon had to decide which bond purchase would be better for his shareholders; but to do so, several calculations would be necessary. First, he would have to find the dollar price of the Montgomery County bonds. Could he, on July 1, afford $52,780,000 in par value when he would only have $49,950,000 in available cash? Second, he would have to calculate the yield to maturity of the M-S-Rs. With these calculations behind him, he would then have to decide how to interpret the respective yields to maturity of the two bonds in light of the facts that (1) similar bonds of similar maturity were selling in the market at yields to maturity of 7 percent, (2) he expected interest rates to decline by year end to a level at which notes like the M-S-Rs and Montgomery County notes could yield 6 percent, and (3) the maturities of the bonds differed by six months.

CASE 49
WACHOVIA BANK AND TRUST COMPANY, N.A. (B):
Piedmont Operations Center Scheduling

A. Mebane Davis was reviewing the staffing needs for the Proof Department. He had recently become the manager of the Piedmont Operations Center of Wachovia Bank and Trust of North Carolina and was anxious to continue the work begun by his predecessor in evaluating a staffing and scheduling problem. As the bank continued to grow, it was necessary to make the staffing and scheduling process more formal to ensure continued cost-effective performance.

Company Background and Operations

Wachovia Bank conducted retail, corporate, and international banking activities and provided a full line of trust services to its customers. It also provided its domestic and international customers a full line of corporate banking services, including cash management, foreign exchange, and money market services. It had total assets of $3.5 billion and net income of $30.5 million.

Because of the statewide nature of Wachovia's business and its rapid growth in recent years, the paper-processing functions of the bank had been divided among five similar operations centers strategically located around the state to provide services to each geographic area. The Piedmont Operations Center in Winston-Salem, North Carolina, was the largest, servicing 58 branches in 10 cities in the surrounding area.

Proof Department

The Proof Department was the heart of the bank's check-clearing operations. The department received and processed checks and other documents to clear them in the shortest possible time to save on float, which averaged $220 million a day systemwide. The department was charged with the responsibility for sorting checks, proving the accuracy of deposits, distributing checks, and listing transactions arising from the daily operations of the bank.

The physical facility consisted of a large room filled with 35 proof machines and several tables. As the couriers arrived, they left their bags of paperwork on a table on one side of the room. The bags were emptied and the contents distributed to one of three tables on the other side of the room according to the type of work; tables were for commercial, personal, and "big-ticket" work. The big-ticket items were always processed first, followed by commercial and then personal items.

This case was based on a Supervised Business Study prepared by Charlotte R. Donnelly (Darden, Class of 1979).

The couriers made several pickups each day, including a visit to each branch shortly after 2:00 P.M. to pick up all the work that was to be included in that banking day. The proof operators were responsible for processing all this work by the end of their day. Work that was accepted at the branches after 2:00 P.M. and was picked up by the couriers at a later time could be left to be done on a subsequent shift. When the proof operators arrived at work in the morning, they finished any personal work left from the day before. The first courier was scheduled to arrive with new work from the branches at about 11:45 A.M., and most of the work arrived between noon and 2:00 P.M.

The department operated from 8:00 A.M. to 6:00 P.M. on Monday and 9:00 A.M. to 6:00 P.M. on Tuesday through Friday. Despite the practice by other banks of handling check processing almost entirely at night, Wachovia believed it was important to give its employees a normal workday.

The volume of items processed in the Proof Department had increased significantly in the last two years, from 38.01 million to 42.975 million. The scheduling problem in the department was magnified because of the uneven nature of the volume. Exhibit 1 contains weekly proof volumes (deseasonalized to take out the yearly seasonal pattern) going back to the beginning of the prior year. This volume pattern led management to use a large part-time staff to cover peak loads. Currently, 14 full-time and 22 part-time proof operators were working at the center. Each operator had an average processing rate of 1,000 items per hour.

Forecasting

The first thing Mr. Davis had to do was forecast demand for next week, week 67 (April 10–14), and then he would need to work out a schedule for the number of full- and part-time staff to meet the predicted demand. A couple of simple forecasting methods had been suggested to him. One was to use the previous week's actual deseasonalized demand for the next week's forecast of the deseasonalized number of checks. Another was to use his predecessor's long-run forecast of weekly volume of 730,000. This number represented the typical deseasonalized volume and was based on years of experience with the operations center. Davis wondered how accurate these simple methods were and whether there might be some other better approach.

He would use his forecast to determine how many hours of additional part-time workers to schedule for the next week. His base schedule, which includes full-time and some part-time workers, was enough to do 600,000 checks; he could add as many additional part-time hours as he wished to the schedule. If he scheduled either full- or part-time hours, he had to pay for them even if the workers completed the check processing early. On the other hand, if the volume of checks was so high that the checks couldn't be processed in the hours he scheduled for the week, he would need to pay overtime wages (which were 50 percent above regular wages) to complete the work for the week. There was no requirement to finish all checks on the day they arrived, but the checks that arrived during the entire week had to be done by Friday afternoon.

EXHIBIT 1   Deseasonalized Weekly Proof Volumes

Week	Volume (000)	Week	Volume (000)
1	633.7	34	809.7
2	628.8	35	778.6
3	725.6	36	818.9
4	670.8	37	789.5
5	718.1	38	791.2
6	752.0	39	842.5
7	714.2	40	875.9
8	740.5	41	847.3
9	817.2	42	894.7
10	721.8	43	855.5
11	710.3	44	836.5
12	741.7	45	763.9
13	827.0	46	820.3
14	824.9	47	780.2
15	726.2	48	828.7
16	813.4	49	838.2
17	780.7	50	910.7
18	828.2	51	921.0
19	804.6	52	711.5
20	816.2	53	694.7
21	836.9	54	811.4
22	735.2	55	733.1
23	800.6	56	749.9
24	814.7	57	733.8
25	757.2	58	849.4
26	849.2	59	846.5
27	696.5	60	802.9
28	796.0	61	823.9
29	802.7	62	814.6
30	833.5	63	777.4
31	807.8	64	797.3
32	785.8	65	781.5
33	760.7	66	931.4

His first task was to get a handle on the forecasting problem; then he could easily use it to find the number of part-time hours to schedule. He first planned to develop a forecast of deseasonalized checks. Then for the week of April 10–14, he could use the seasonal index of 0.975 to adjust the deseasonalized forecast. A seasonal index less than 1 meant that the week had an expected volume less than the average week.

CASE 50
WACHOVIA BANK AND TRUST COMPANY, N.A. (B): SUPPLEMENT

Three procedures were suggested for forecasting the weekly work-load requirements of the Piedmont Operations Center Proof Department.

Method 1.   This simple forecasting scheme uses the previous week's volume to forecast each succeeding week's volume. Based on the data in Exhibit 1, the forecast for week 13 would be 741.7 (the volume for week 12). This procedure would then use the volume of week 66 to forecast the volume during week 67.

Method 2.   This approach uses a forecast suggested by Mr. Mebanes' predecessor for each week in the future. This estimate of 730.0 reflects the prior experience during the entire time that the predecessor was on the job and would not need to be changed each week.

Method 3.   This method is something of a compromise between the previous two. With Method 1, each forecast is equal to the previous actual volume. With Method 2, the forecast is based on the long-run experience with the volume of checks and doesn't change from period to period. With this compromise method, each forecast is calculated by putting some weight (alpha) on the previous actual volume and some weight (with a total weight of one) on the previous long-run forecast:

Next forecast = Alpha * (Volume) + (1 - Alpha) * (Previous forecast)

where alpha is the weight given to the most recent actual volume. This method is called "exponential smoothing."

If equal weights are used, this forecasting method is described by the following equation:

$$F_{t+1} = 0.5 * (X_t) + 0.5 * (F_t)$$

where X_t is the volume in period t and F_t is the forecast in period t. Of course, to evaluate whether the forecast is working, we want to see whether F_{t+1} is close to X_{t+1}, not X_t.

Exhibit 1 shows a spreadsheet that calculates these forecasts. Notice that this forecasting method uses the forecast given by Mr. Mebanes' predecessor to start but updates the forecast each period using the new observation of volume.

This method calculates in week 12 a forecast of 735.4 for the volume of checks in week 13. Continuing the process for all of the data, the forecast for week 67 would be 860.4.

EXHIBIT 1   **Spreadsheet**

	A	B	C	D	
1		ALPHA =	0.5		
2					
3	WEEK #	VOLUME	AVERAGE	FORECAST	BACKGROUND
4	1	633.7	**730.0**←		
5	2	628.8	679.4	730.0	730.0
6	3	725.6	702.5	679.4	
7	4	670.8	686.6	702.5	
8	5	718.1	702.3	686.6	
9	6	752.0	727.2	702.3	
10	7	714.2	720.7	727.2	
11	8	740.5	730.6	720.7	
12	9	817.2	773.9	730.6	
13	10	721.8	747.9	773.9	
14	11	710.3	729.1	747.9	
15	12	741.7	**735.4**←	729.1	+$C$1*B15
16	13	827.0	781.2	735.4	+(1-$C$1)*C14
17	14	824.9	803.0	781.2	
18	15	726.2	764.6	803.0	
19	16	813.4	789.0	764.6	
20	17	780.7	784.9	789.0	
21	18	828.2	806.5	784.9	
22	19	804.6	805.6	806.5	
23	20	816.2	810.9	805.6	
24	21	836.9	823.9	810.9	
25	22	735.2	779.5	823.9	
26	23	800.6	790.0	779.5	
27	24	814.7	802.4	790.0	
28	25	757.2	779.8	802.4	
29	26	849.2	814.5	779.8	
30	27	696.5	755.5	814.5	
31	28	796.0	775.7	755.5	
32	29	802.7	789.2	775.7	
33	30	833.5	811.3	789.2	
34	31	807.8	809.6	**811.3**←	+C33
35	32	785.8	797.7	809.6	
36	33	760.7	779.2	797.7	
37	34	809.7	794.4	779.2	

(Continued)

EXHIBIT 1 *Concluded*

38	35	778.6	786.5	794.4
39	36	818.9	802.7	786.5
40	37	789.5	796.1	802.7
41	38	791.2	793.6	796.1
42	39	842.5	818.1	793.6
43	40	875.9	847.0	818.1
44	41	847.3	847.1	847.0
45	42	894.7	870.9	847.1
46	43	855.5	863.2	870.9
47	44	836.5	849.9	863.2
48	45	763.9	806.9	849.9
49	46	820.3	813.6	806.9
50	47	780.2	796.9	813.6
51	48	828.7	812.8	796.9
52	49	838.2	825.5	812.8
53	50	910.7	868.1	825.5
54	51	921.0	894.5	868.1
55	52	711.5	803.0	894.5
56	53	694.7	748.9	803.0
57	54	811.4	780.1	748.9
58	55	733.1	756.6	780.1
59	56	749.9	753.3	756.6
60	57	733.8	743.5	753.3
61	58	849.4	796.4	743.5
62	59	846.5	821.5	796.4
63	60	802.9	812.2	821.5
64	61	823.9	818.0	812.2
65	62	814.6	816.3	818.0
66	63	777.4	796.9	816.3
67	64	797.3	797.1	796.9
68	65	781.5	789.3	797.1
69	66	931.4	860.4	789.3
70				860.4

CASE 51
WAITE FIRST SECURITIES

Harold Gagnon, one of Waite First's most important customers, was on the line to Brenda Hagerty, a Waite First account representative. "Happy New Year, Brenda. Listen, good news this early in the year. Our firm did very well last year, and I just learned that my year-end bonus gives me $30,000. I want to use that money to buy a stock to add to my portfolio."

"Well, I believe there are still some good bargains in the market, Harold. I'm glad to hear you had a good year, but I think the good times for the market are still to come. I can recommend several promising stocks."

"You may want to suggest others later, but right now I need you to give me some advice about three stocks I have been following recently: Hilton, Texas Instruments, and Giant Food."

"Those are quite different companies, Harold. Hilton should be in a position to do well now that we are pulling out of the recession with some momentum. Texas Instruments may find a new resurgence in the electronics industry. As for Giant, you can't find anything more basic than selling groceries. I could find more information about these three companies for you and see whether our analysts are recommending them."

"Never mind that. I've already done a lot of research on my own and am convinced that the timing is good for any one of these companies. But I want to be careful to add something to my portfolio that has a lower amount of risk. As you know, I'm 10 years from retirement, and there are already a number of high-flying stocks in my portfolio. I only intend to buy one of these three stocks, and I don't want to see my retirement funds evaporate. Don't get me wrong, I'm bullish on the market but you and I both know that it's all but impossible to predict the market. The S&P can go up or down. I just think it makes sense for me right now to find a stock that does pretty well in both an up and a down market.

"Several of my associates here at the office have told me that the way to build a portfolio is to use beta analysis. Now I don't know the first thing about calculating a beta or any other Greek letter. But as I understand it, the beta of a stock indicates how risky it is, at least relative to the market as a whole. Can you find the beta value for these stocks?"

"Well, I think I can, Harold."

"I'm a little mistrustful of this beta business myself. My friends throw the term around as though any sophisticated investor wouldn't think of trading without examining the beta value. They think it's all you need to know to tell how risky a stock is. But the other day they were talking about two stocks with about the same beta value and one of the stocks seemed a lot more risky to me than the other. Can you do a little research for me and explain how I ought to interpret the beta and how much trust I ought to put into it as a risk measure?"

"Sure, Harold. I believe we have a recent memo on that. In fact, as I look at your account on my screen, I can see a beta calculation for your stock portfolio. We are experimenting with putting the beta calculation in the account information on a few of the larger accounts. I see that you are holding six stocks having roughly equal market value in your portfolio, which in total is worth $305,000 and has a beta of 1.4."

"I'm impressed! You seem to know a lot about me and about beta. Listen, I can't talk any longer now. I have some time tomorrow midmorning. Could I bring the money tomorrow, say around 10:00 A.M., and talk to you more about this beta business and which of the three stocks I should buy now?"

"That fits my schedule; our analyst briefing ends at 10. I can find the beta values for these stocks by then and prepare a little briefing for you on beta."

"Great, Brenda. See you tomorrow."

"Happy New Year, Harold."

As Brenda Hagerty hung up the phone, she had mixed feelings about the conversation. Gagnon was an important account, and there was a good broker's commission in this for her. With a considerable personal portfolio and a position as an influential board member of the local bank, Gagnon could steer considerable business Brenda's way. Hagerty had never calculated betas before, however, nor had she explained any statistical concepts to a customer as perceptive and knowledgeable as Gagnon.

Hagerty's first job was to find recent returns data for the three companies and for the Standard & Poor's 500, which she assumed would be the best surrogate for the market portfolio. She was able to get five years' worth of monthly data (Exhibit 1) by using the recently acquired data base of prices for the New York Stock Exchange. These data were total returns, including dividends.[1] While in the computer reference room, Hagerty ran into Doug Rogers from the research department. After she had explained her problem, Rogers offered to take the data and compute the betas for her.

"Please write down how you do the calculations, so I'll be able to do it myself," Hagerty requested.

An hour later, Rogers appeared at Hagerty's door. "I got tied up and didn't finish the calculations for you," he said. "I did find all the statistics you need for Hilton by hand, however, so you can see how the calculations are done (see Exhibit 2). The regression line provides a reasonably good fit, as you can see from this scatter diagram I made (Exhibit 3). I'm sorry, but I've got to get a memo out today and can't finish this for you. You can find the beta estimates in Value Line, rather than calculating them. Or you can let your electronic spreadsheet do the regression calculations."

"Thanks for your help, Doug. I'm sure I can take it from here."

Hagerty looked at the calculations and immediately searched her bookshelf for the notes from the statistics course she had taken the summer before in

---

[1]Total returns are defined as: (New price − Old price + Dividends)/Old price. In other words, it is the change in price plus the dividend yield.

preparation for returning to get her MBA. The statistical meaning of beta seemed a little fuzzy to her, and she never had really digested its financial meaning. While looking through her files for the Waite First memo on beta (Exhibit 4), she noticed her watch showed 5:00 P.M. Packing her laptop and calculator, the notes on regression, the beta memo, and the data into her briefcase, she set out for home. One way or the other, she knew she could prepare for Gagnon at home with all of these tools. She just hoped it would not take the whole evening.

EXHIBIT 1   Five Years of Monthly Total Returns

No.	Yr.	Mo.	S&P 500 (%)	HILTON (%)	TI (%)	GIANT (%)
1	1989	1	7.111%	−3.044%	7.012%	−0.619%
2	1989	2	−2.894	−5.340	−8.832	−5.729
3	1989	3	2.081	18.205	−0.800	8.840
4	1989	4	5.009	11.280	0.949	10.660
5	1989	5	3.039	33.138	11.599	4.608
6	1989	6	−0.335	16.006	−11.674	0.000
7	1989	7	8.837	6.345	0.639	28.194
8	1989	8	1.552	0.597	1.587	−13.793
9	1989	9	−0.654	0.474	−3.300	−2.400
10	1989	10	−2.518	−8.737	−17.208	−4.918
11	1989	11	1.654	−2.717	14.290	−3.896
12	1989	12	2.142	−12.000	−1.034	2.703
13	1990	1	−6.882	−25.606	−6.969	−5.702
14	1990	2	0.854	2.444	5.618	−5.607
15	1990	3	2.426	−13.174	3.348	4.455
16	1990	4	−2.689	−14.713	−6.207	2.464
17	1990	5	9.199	20.054	23.529	4.186
18	1990	6	−0.889	−1.354	−5.226	−0.446
19	1990	7	−0.522	−15.011	−19.243	3.498
20	1990	8	−9.431	−23.306	−13.281	−4.673
21	1990	9	−5.118	−15.901	2.000	−12.745
22	1990	10	−0.670	−2.941	−14.667	6.854
23	1990	11	5.993	13.160	32.521	6.878
24	1990	12	2.483	15.058	20.158	12.871
25	1991	1	4.152	−1.879	−1.645	5.351
26	1991	2	6.728	20.000	11.037	−2.092
27	1991	3	2.220	−6.322	−3.482	−0.427
28	1991	4	0.032	3.988	0.940	0.996
29	1991	5	3.860	16.342	−2.795	2.137
30	1991	6	−4.789	−14.541	−14.556	−1.674

(Continued)

EXHIBIT 1   *Concluded*

No.	Yr.	Mo.	S&P 500 (%)	HILTON (%)	TI (%)	GIANT (%)
31	1991	7	4.486	−0.776	−2.256	−3.268
32	1991	8	1.965	−1.515	−2.692	−18.584
33	1991	9	−1.914	−3.077	−10.103	0.543
34	1991	10	1.183	12.063	11.947	1.795
35	1991	11	−4.390	−10.652	−11.289	−5.882
36	1991	12	11.159	3.514	10.314	9.659
37	1992	1	−1.992	6.914	15.854	0.166
38	1992	2	0.959	2.035	5.263	4.688
39	1992	3	−2.183	6.268	−12.520	−6.965
40	1992	4	2.789	10.456	6.130	−8.364
41	1992	5	0.096	−5.728	8.664	−3.529
42	1992	6	−1.736	−4.922	−6.166	0.610
43	1992	7	3.940	1.471	19.217	−0.994
44	1992	8	−2.402	−1.622	−7.761	−1.852
45	1992	9	0.911	4.121	12.764	−10.692
46	1992	10	0.211	−7.124	13.256	0.958
47	1992	11	3.026	6.932	0.000	18.310
48	1992	12	1.011	−7.219	−4.723	6.548
49	1993	1	0.705	11.354	15.818	−2.034
50	1993	2	1.048	−4.167	4.630	−2.874
51	1993	3	1.870	5.163	3.416	15.976
52	1993	4	−2.542	−7.494	−2.146	4.286
53	1993	5	2.272	12.123	13.596	0.493
54	1993	6	0.076	−7.769	8.193	−2.941
55	1993	7	−0.533	−6.957	1.252	4.747
56	1993	8	3.443	7.353	13.958	−9.223
57	1993	9	−0.999	7.397	−6.133	−1.604
58	1993	10	1.939	−4.337	−13.079	5.652
59	1993	11	−1.291	−1.760	−2.095	−3.627
60	1993	12	1.009	32.787	−0.887	10.753

EXHIBIT 2   Doug Rogers' Calculations for the Regression Equation

$$\text{Hilton} = a + b \, (\text{S\&P } 500)$$

$$\Sigma y = 0.6534 \qquad \Sigma y^2 = 0.83473$$

$$\Sigma x = 0.5609 \qquad \Sigma x^2 = 0.08641$$

$$\Sigma xy = 0.15213$$

$$\hat{b} = \frac{\Sigma xy - \Sigma x \Sigma y/60}{\Sigma x^2 - (\Sigma x)^2/60}$$

$$= \frac{0.15213 - (0.5609)\,(0.6534)/60}{.08641 - (0.5609)^2/60}$$

$$= 1.80$$

$$\hat{a} = \bar{y} - \hat{b}\bar{x}$$

$$= \cdot \frac{6534}{60} - 1.80 \left\{ \cdot \frac{5609}{60} \right\}$$

$$= -0.006$$

$$\text{Hilton} = -0.006 + 1.80 \, (\text{S\&P } 500)$$

EXHIBIT 3   Scatter Diagram with Regression Line

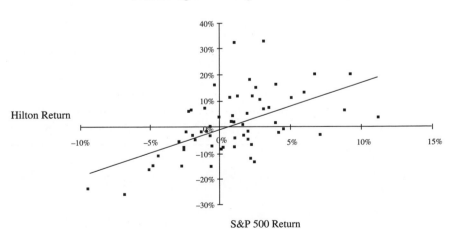

Scatter Diagram with Regression Line

Exhibit 4

TO:	Investment Advisors
FROM:	Research Department
DATE:	December 4, 1993
SUBJECT:	Risk Evaluation with Beta Coefficients

Due to numerous requests for a discussion of "beta" as a measure of market-associated risk, this short memo has been prepared for use by our staff.

The relationship between a security's return prospects and those of the market portfolio is often represented by a straight line. The chart below shows a scatter diagram of returns on an individual security plotted against the return on the S&P 500. A point in the diagram represents the stock return (% change in price) and the S&P 500 return in one time period (week, month, or quarter).

The line that provides the best fit to the data may be found by regression analysis. Mathematically, this is the line for which the sum of the squared vertical distances between the points and the line is smallest, hence it is called the "least squares estimate."

The beta coefficient is the slope of the regression line. It indicates the responsiveness of the security's return to that of the market portfolio. A beta of 1 means that, if the market portfolio return exceeds expectations by 1%, then the return of the security is estimated also to exceed expectations by 1%, and if the market portfolio return is lower than expected by 1%, then the return of the security is estimated to be 1% lower than expected. A beta of 2.0 indicates that the stock is "twice" as sensitive as the market portfolio to events that affect the market; if the market portfolio return is 1% above (or below) expectations, the return of this security is 2% above (or below) expectations. A beta less than 1.0, on the other hand, implies that the return of the security will rise (or fall) less, on average, than the return of the market portfolio.

The price of the stock is affected by events peculiar to the company as well as events that affect the market as a whole. Consequently, the actual returns do not all fall on the regression line, but are scattered around it. The standard deviation of the residuals (often called the standard error of the estimate) measures the dispersion of the points about the line. Residual standard deviation is important because it measures a security's nonmarket risk. The greater the residual standard deviation, the greater is the effect on price of company-specific events. Often standard errors are also reported for beta and alpha (the vertical intercept) as measures of the statistical accuracy of these estimates. The R^2 statistic represents the percentage of price fluctuations of a security that are explained by the comovement of the market price.

EXHIBIT 4   *Concluded*

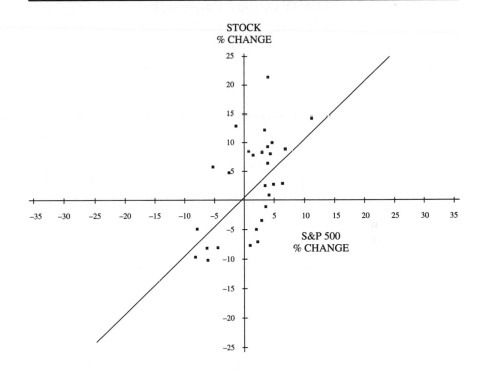

CASE 52
THE WALDORF PROPERTY

As Steve Miller, vice president of land development for Pflug Enterprises, turned his monthly desk calendar, he noted that only two weeks remained in the feasibility period of the Waldorf contract. Failure to terminate the agreement with the Acton Land Development Partnership by February 16, 1989, would, in effect, convert Pflug's refundable deposit of $150,000 into an irrevocable down payment of $150,000. While the Waldorf property was a desirable tract of undeveloped land in a particularly attractive area on the outskirts of suburban Washington, D.C., it did appear to be overpriced in light of potential limitations to the amount of usable acreage. Within the next several days, Miller would have to make a recommendation to Pflug's Management Committee about the continuation, cancelation, or renegotiation of the contract.

Pflug Enterprises

The origins of Pflug Enterprises could be traced to 1964 and the founding of a general contracting company in northern Virginia, which undertook a wide variety of projects from high-rise office buildings to warehouse/industrial facilities. With the launching of the BuildAmerica Condominiums concept in 1974, Pflug diversified into real estate development. In subsequent years, Pflug added Skyjet, a helicopter charter service, split the BuildAmerica activity into a development component and a property-management component, and engaged in a number of development partnerships.

BuildAmerica Condominiums addressed the largely neglected needs of the group of small-business owners who required industrial space of a size inefficient for a stand-alone structure. An industrial condominium was an ideal solution for such small- to medium-sized businesses. Since 1974, BuildAmerica had developed 900,000 square feet of condominium space with a total gross sales value of more than $50 million. Exhibit 1 details these projects.

Industrial firms were the primary targets of BuildAmerica Condominiums, but the Skyline project had broadened the target and mixed a number of retail users in with the traditional industrial base. This approach had proven to be very successful, and, if the Waldorf project were undertaken, it would adopt the mixed-use design.

Pflug Enterprises was still owned and managed by its 53-year-old founder, John R. Pflug. John Pflug was a self-made millionaire widely regarded as a street-smart, tough developer. He had earned his notoriety by surviving the serious downturns in the real estate markets in 1974 and 1981. Although he was a hard negotiator with an often volatile temper, he was considered to be fair in his dealings and to be someone who would stick to his word. His inclinations were

This case was based on a Supervised Business Study prepared by Steven R. Scorgie (Darden, Class of 1991).

Exhibit 1 BuildAmerica Condominiums

Project	Location	Type	Year	Units	Square Feet per Unit	Total Sq. Ft.	Units Sold	Gross Sales to Date
1.	Springfield	Industrial	1974	26	1,800	46,800	26	$ 1,274,000
2.	Springfield	Industrial	1976	26	1,800	46,800	26	1,482,000
3.	Tysons Corner	Industrial	1977	43	1,800	77,400	43	3,268,000
4.	Merrifield	Industrial	1978	21	1,800	37,800	21	1,827,000
5.	Alexandria	Industrial	1980	89	1,800	160,200	89	8,970,565
6.	Alexandria	Industrial	1981	42	1,800	75,600	42	4,978,686
@Skyline	Baileys Xroads	Mixed	1981	60	1,200	72,000	60	10,000,000
@64	Hampton	Industrial	1984	68	1,800	122,400	57	3,661,550
7.	Woodbridge	Industrial	1985	84	1,800	151,200	79	8,360,691
8.	Manassas	Industrial	1985	84	1,800	151,200	75	7,757,273

633

Exhibit 2   Pflug Management Team

Steve Miller, Vice President of Land Development
   Master's degree in Planning from the University of Virginia.
   Knowledgeable about northern Virginia land values.
   Quiet by nature, dislikes conflict.
   Although not trained in financial analysis, picked it up quickly and was able to explain it effectively.

Bob Pflug, Vice President of Marketing
   First-born son of John Pflug.
   Bachelor's degree in Commerce (Marketing and MIS) from the University of Virginia.
   Meticulously attentive to detail and systems.
   Cautious and conscientious in approaching new projects.

Steve Scorgie, Vice President of Finance
   Newest member of the management team.
   Former commercial banker.
   Bachelor's degree in Commerce (Finance) from the University of Virginia.
   Opinionated and prone to quick decisions.

---

to do without "fancy" analyses and to rely on his frequently repeated maxim: "If the deal doesn't make a 25 percent return, it isn't worth doing."

In addition to John Pflug, the management team was made up of Miller, Bob Pflug (vice president of marketing), and Steve Scorgie (vice president of finance). Exhibit 2 presents brief descriptions of these individuals.

The Waldorf Property

The Waldorf property was a 700,444-square-foot (16.080-acre) tract of retail land with excellent location and visibility in Waldorf, Maryland. During the fall of 1988, Waldorf was emerging as a hot area for retail development. The site was located between two major roads, Route 301 and Old Washington Boulevard. Moreover, the property was treeless and flat, which would reduce the cost of site work.

The property was owned by Acton Land Development Partnership (ALDP), which was associated with Sigal/Zuckerman, an experienced developer of retail shopping centers. When Niel Bien, a Sigal/Zuckerman partner, was asked why his firm was not interested in developing the property itself, he responded, "We have a lot on our plate right now and the property is further out [from residential centers] than our typical development." He went on to add that the property had been on the market for two years and that the two previous contracts on it, the most recent of which was with Hahn Development for the $3.5 million asking price, had been dropped.

Subsequent discussions between Miller and Bob Hahn, president of Hahn Development, revealed that Hahn was very bitter about his experience with the

Waldorf Property. He had the property under contract for one year and spent $250,000 on time extensions. The extensions were the result of Hahn Development's preliminary environmental study, which indicated a potential for up to seven acres of wetlands (land reserved for wildlife) that could not be used for development. In addition, the study suggested that benzine gas might be present on the site. Although the benzine issue was quickly cleared up and dismissed, the wetlands issue was more problematical and would require lengthy, bureaucratic investigations. When ALDP denied Hahn's request for a further contract extension to work on the wetlands problem, Hahn dropped the contract.

When asked by Miller about the wetlands, Bien insisted that there were no more than two acres on the site and that, in fact, there might be none.

The exact amount could be determined only by the Corps of Engineers, which had been charged with the preservation of wetlands since the mid 1970s. The Corps was also empowered to issue permits to developers that allowed wetlands to be filled in. The permits were freely granted until a 1987 suit filed by an environmental group in California. Since the suit, the Corps had been very protective in its wetlands policy. Recently, Congress had passed a bill mandating that any filling-in of wetlands required the creation of the same amount of wetlands reserve elsewhere on the property. Sarah White of the Corps of Engineers indicated to Miller in a phone conversation that a study of the property would take no more than 12 months and that, based on the specific property characteristics and the "results of similar studies in the area," there could be anywhere from zero to five acres of wetlands.

The Contract

In an effort to secure the property for detailed considerations without putting money at risk, Pflug Enterprises signed a purchase and sale agreement with ALDP that contained a provision for a three-month feasibility period. During this period, ALDP would hold in escrow a note from Pflug for $150,000. Prior to February 16, 1989 (the end of the feasibility period), Pflug could terminate the agreement without penalty. On February 16, 1989, the deposit would be converted to a down payment and forfeited if the contract were subsequently broken. As was customary in land transactions of this nature, the closing could be delayed a year (February 16, 1990, at the latest) if the property were indeed purchased.

The purchase price was $3.5 million, the initial asking price. Throughout the discussions leading to the contract, Bien had been firm on the price and had repeatedly emphasized that the $3.5 million was not negotiable. Frustrated by Bien's position on price, but anxious to move ahead with its investigation of the project, Pflug postponed further discussions of price until more was known about the details of the project.

The Development

As the project began to take shape during the early phases of the feasibility period, Pflug determined that 30,400 square feet (0.698 acres) would be needed for roads and buffer areas and that 194,144 square feet (4.457 acres) would

EXHIBIT 3   Waldorf Project Site Plan

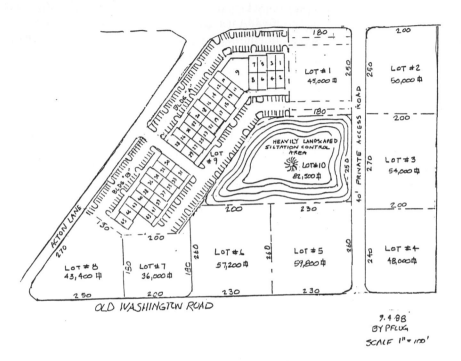

be reserved for a BuildAmerica condominium. The remaining 475,900 square feet (10.925 acres) would, after provision for wetlands acreage, be subdivided into commercial lots and sold off to end users. The area set aside for the wetlands would be landscaped into an aesthetically pleasing pool and fountain. Exhibit 3 presents a preliminary site plan with the assumption of 82,500 square feet (1.894 acres) of wetlands.

After a go-ahead decision was made, Pflug management anticipated that the project would extend over a 46-month period. The necessary wetlands study and approval of the site plan by appropriate governmental authorities would require the first 12 months. As the approval process came to a close, various architectural, legal, and building-permit expenses would be incurred. The estimate was that these costs would amount to $297,000 and could actually be paid during the first month of site preparation. Site preparation would then take four months at an estimated cost of $430,000. At the end of site work, the BuildAmerica parcel would be transferred to a partnership (within Pflug Enterprises) at $6 per square foot and the out-parcels marketed.

Pflug managers had considerable optimism regarding the sale of the out-parcels. Alan Levine, the commercial sales agent used by Pflug, was sure that he would have all of them sold and ready to close by the time site work was completed. His sales plan called for an average selling price of $10.28 per square foot. Levine generally met his plans, often within a dollar of his estimates, but in the course of a year, the market could shift dramatically and his estimate be substantially off, possibly by $2 per square foot. Sales commissions were 4 percent of the selling price with closing costs paid by the purchaser.

The BuildAmerica Condominiums would comprise 45 units, one 9,000-square-foot unit and 44 standard units with an average of 1,200 square feet per unit. Development was planned to begin immediately after completion of site development and continue for a period of 10 months. Pflug estimated that the architectural, legal, insurance, permit, and inspection costs would amount to $347,000 and that the buildings would cost $2,899,600. The estimates of these development costs were fairly accurate, but a 3 percent contingency was customarily set aside. The development costs would be expended evenly throughout the 10-month construction period.

BuildAmerica Condominiums were generally priced at 10 times the market rental rate. At this price, the mortgage amortization with the ownership advantages was comparable to the rental rate. Karen Palmer, the BuildAmerica sales manager, investigated market rental rates and determined that comparable new construction rentals were $12 per square foot. Her intention was to price the units at $120 per square foot, but she pointed out that the volume of new retail development within a five-mile radius could drive the average selling price $20 per square foot in either direction. More reasonably, the average selling price would be within $6 of the asking price. Palmer had a buyer committed to the 9,000-square-foot unit and expected that four of the standard units would be sold prior to completion of construction, but stated that the number could range between zero and eight units. After completion, she expected the units to sell at a rate of two per month, but acknowledged that the number for any given month could be between zero and four or five. Commissions would be 6.0 percent of gross sales, and closing costs would be 1.5 percent of gross sales. An advertising budget of $80,000 would be allocated and expended evenly over the anticipated 20 months of steady selling to follow completion of the construction.

The site development was expected to be fully financed with prime-plus-one debt (11 percent), and the condominium development with independent financing at prime-plus-two (12 percent). During construction periods, interest would be accrued as principal. Once construction was completed and sales began, the interest would be paid as incurred, and the outstanding principal at the completion of construction would be paid down in proportion to the square feet sold. Each project was evaluated on the basis of cash flow after financing, but before taxes. Taxes were treated on a corporatewide basis. The Pflug Enterprises' cost of capital was 15 percent. Exhibits 4 and 5 present Miller's analyses of the two phases of the project using Pflug's best estimates.

While these figures were positive, the question of the wetlands acreage cast a pall over the entire endeavor. If the Corps of Engineers determined that five acres had to be set aside for wetlands, the land-development project, at the $3.5 million land price, would be a loser.

EXHIBIT 4 Waldorf Land-Development Cash-Flow Projections

	Feb 89	Feb 90	Mar 90	Apr 90	May 90	Jun 90	Total
Land absorption:							
Roads, buffer, wetlands							
Feet sold—BuildAmerica		112,900				194,144	194,144
Feet sold—out-parcels						393,400	393,400
Feet remaining	700,444	587,544	587,544	587,544	587,544	0	0
Revenue:							
Gross sales revenue—BuildAmerica						$1,164,864	$1,164,864
Gross sales revenue—out-parcels						4,044,152	4,044,152
Commissions						208,361	208,361
Net sales revenue						5,000,655	5,000,655
Costs:							
Land	$150,000	$3,350,000					3,500,000
Soft costs		297,000					297,000
Hard costs			$107,500	$107,500	$107,500	$107,500	430,000
Total cost	$150,000	$3,647,000	$107,500	$107,500	$107,500	$107,500	$4,227,000
Loan balances:							
Opening balance		3,647,000	3,787,931	3,930,154	4,073,680	4,218,522	
Interest		33,431	34,723	36,026	37,342	38,670	180,192
Loan repayment						4,257,192	4,257,192
Ending balance		3,680,431	3,822,654	3,966,180	4,111,022	0	
Cash flow before taxes	($150,000)	$ 0	$ 0	$ 0	$ 0	$ 743,464	$ 593,464

EXHIBIT 5 Waldorf BuildAmerica-Development Cash-Flow Projections

	Jun 90	Jul 90	. . . .	Mar 91	Apr 91	May 91	. . . .	Dec 92	Total
Absorption:									
Feet sold					13,800	2,400	. . . .	2,400	61,800
Feet remaining			61,800		48,000	45,600	. . . .	0	
Revenue:									
Gross sales revenue					$1,656,000	$ 288,000	. . . .	$288,000	$7,416,000
Commissions					99,360	17,280	. . . .	17,280	444,960
Closing costs					24,840	4,320	. . . .	4,320	111,240
Net sales revenue					1,531,800	266,400	. . . .	266,400	6,859,800
Costs:									
Land	$1,164,864								1,164,864
Soft costs		$ 34,700	. . . .	$ 34,700	34,700				347,000
Hard costs		289,960	. . . .	289,960	289,960				2,899,600
Advertising						4,000	. . . .	4,000	80,000
Total cost	1,164,864	324,660	. . . .	324,660	324,660	4,000	. . . .	4,000	4,491,464
Loan balances:									
Opening balance	1,164,864	1,501,173	. . . .	4,315,581	4,358,736	3,385,426	. . . .	169,271	
Interest	11,649	15,012	. . . .	43,156	43,587	33,854	. . . .	1,693	
Loan repayment					1,016,897	203,126	. . . .	170,964	
Ending balance	1,176,513	1,516,184	. . . .	4,358,736	3,385,426	$3,216,155	. . . .	0	
Cash flow before taxes	$ 0	$ 0	. . . .	$ 0	$ 190,243	$ 59,274	. . . .	$ 91,436	$1,697,346